STRATEGIC BUSINESS PORTFOLIO MANAGEMENT

STRATEGIC BUSINESS PORTFOLIO MANAGEMENT

Make Better Asset and Project Decisions with Practical Portfolio Analysis

TONY KENCK

This book is intended to provide general information and insights regarding business practices, and should not be interpreted as financial advice. Readers should always consult with a qualified professional before making any business decisions based on the information presented herein. The author and publisher disclaim any liability for any losses or damages arising from the use of this book.

ISBN: 979-8-9884639-0-0
EPUB ISBN 979-8-9884639-1-7

LCCN on file at the Library of Congress

Published by:
Practical Portfolio Management LLC
Golden, Colorado, USA
Printed in the United States of America

ENDORSEMENTS

Marvelous. *Strategic Business Portfolio Management* is a masterclass in Portfolio Management."

Tom Grossman, Professor, University of San Francisco School of Management

A must-read for anyone who wants to help their business make more informed portfolio decisions."

Andrew Thrift, Director, Sustainability, Risk & Decision Quality, Teck Resources

Applicable to industries such as oil and gas, mining, pharmaceuticals, finance, and automobile manufacturing."

Linus Schrage, LINDO Systems and Professor Emeritus of Operations Management, University of Chicago Booth School of Business

These concepts and practices WORK."

Nicolas Cooper, Portfolio Strategy Senior Analyst, Chevron Environmental Management Company

CONTENTS

WHY THIS BOOK—WHY NOW?

Do you want to bring the performance of your business to the next level? Managing business assets requires intelligent planning and understanding of risk and how it changes over time. You'll learn about the principles involved, the construction of models, pitfalls in assessing the results of those models, and practical guidance for extracting essential insights and making decisions that stick. With the convergence of data, computer power, competitiveness, and interest from senior leadership, we have reached the point where this financial paradigm is ready for launch.

Business asset portfolio management differs from securities portfolio management because of the nature of the assets and the problems to solve. A set of buildings differs from stock holdings, a regional collection of oil fields with different operators differs from bonds, and a sprawling supply chain for gasoline going from field to refinery to consumer differs from a mutual fund.

Why Should You Do Portfolio Analysis and Management?

In a nutshell, good portfolio management will improve your firm's ability to achieve its goals and targets. Most companies use cash flow analysis to determine whether investments are good or bad. Leaders use a few simple metrics to make the go vs. no-go decision. They often overlook important attributes of how projects combine and act over time. As a result, companies may invest in projects that do not meet the implicit and explicit needs of the firm. Putting decisions into the most relevant organizational context is the goal of portfolio analysis.

Academic papers and practical experience demonstrate that the value of your investment program can increase by up to 30% or more using the methods shown in this book.

What makes this book unique?

You will learn the why, what, and how of portfolio analysis and management. Armed with this book's information, finance professionals will be able to create tools that will help them achieve their goals. Data and decision science professionals will be able to connect their tools with critical business imperatives. Engineers and scientists will be even more effective by tailoring their designs and plans to align with corporate goals.

This book connects the dots and is the missing link between the mean-variance techniques of Markowitz and strategic business management with modern data science.

You'll see practical guidance, tools, methods, and a structure to guide the decision-making frame for implementing a system and using it once it is built. In the first steps down this path, most analyses can be done in Excel with a few add-ons. You can avoid the expense of bringing in expensive consulting firms or spending millions on a system that soon falls into disuse.

Who Are You?

This information is useful for a broad audience. Here are some examples:

1. An engineer or economic analyst with solid technical skills has been asked to create a portfolio perspective for their firm, even though this is outside their area of expertise.
2. A planner or budgeter in a company who believes their process is missing something they cannot identify.
3. A strategic planner or executive struggling to develop a means to guide project teams into better alignment with corporate needs.
4. A project professional who doesn't understand why the portfolio people want them to create different development alternatives.
5. Perhaps you work in a large corporation's planning and strategy department, and the CEO has said, "I want to do portfolio management. Give me a tool."
6. Finally, if you work for a large corporate consulting firm, you may be interested in developing its portfolio management practice to help companies manage more effectively.

This book will benefit anyone who works with a company or other organization that needs to make tradeoffs between aspirations and limitations. By applying the lessons in this book, professionals around the world can become better analysts and strategists.

FOREWORD

I met Tony sometime right before the turn of the millennium. He was with Texaco's Brazil Country-Entry Team and finishing his MBA—completing his transition to "the dark side." I had recently left Conoco to form Decision Frameworks and gave a class to Texaco's Brazil team. Tony and I connected around the Decision Analysis (DA) body of knowledge, as well as both being Orediggers from the Colorado School of Mines.

When Chevron and Texaco merged, Tony moved to Chevron and went on a completely different tangent. Instead of DA, he was doing a lot of portfolio and planning work. Through the years, we kept up with each other—mostly at Decision Analysis conferences.

Now it comes full circle. While he wandered through the planning and portfolio wilderness, he continued to use and work with Decision Quality (DQ). As a result, he has created a book that does two things: provides information about the theory and practice of portfolio and integrates the tenets of Decision Quality.

Unlike many papers and books, *Strategic Business Portfolio Management* covers practical aspects of portfolio analysis and management with clear examples and interesting war stories. This book is a high-level handbook that weaves DQ into the practice of portfolio management. It is the only book I know of that puts together all the different methods that fall under the umbrella of portfolio analysis—from the principles of using standalone analysis for portfolio management all the way to stochastic optimization.

In addition to the framework, he conveys many "War Stories" covering insights gained through hard experience. It's clear that he made a significant impact at Chevron.

Although Tony's professional experience is in the upstream oil and gas industry, the principles are industry agnostic. His approach applies to any business that needs to coordinate choices on multiple opportunities that will drive enterprise success.

The book is full of tips and tricks and has a handy decision tree tool to guide your analytical frame (the selection of the tool to use for the problem you're trying to solve). It also includes an amazing bibliography that is pure gold.

The appendix is a great resource as well. It has a section on the fundamentals of finance that provides insight into the intricacies of the financial measures that companies use and that few seem to understand. It also includes two working papers that are fodder for new approaches to analysis.

As with Decision Analysis, bringing an analytical process into a corporation is an uphill climb. Getting the technical aspects right is a good start, but there is also significant change management that needs to happen. This is especially true if the practice is meant to endure beyond the exercise at hand. Although this book does not cover the details of how to do change management, it does include the two pitfall sections that have a lot of portfolio-specific insights.

Tony's experience with different sectors of the business and with leaders at the highest level of the industry, combined with his engaging style and stories, make this book a great addition to your analytics library.

Enjoy it!

Ellen Coopersmith
Founder, Decision Frameworks

PREFACE

> *As to methods there may be a million and then some, but principles are few. The man who grasps principles can successfully select his own methods. The man who tries methods, ignoring principles, is sure to have trouble."*
>
> **– Ralph Waldo Emerson**

This book focuses on the principles of portfolio analysis and management. While there are practical examples and plenty of dense information and jargon, the principles are the most important. While every portfolio problem or question is unique, portfolio analysis always focuses on company impact rather than project performance. The analyst can be creative and help decision-makers better envision the future by knowing portfolio principles.

The ongoing data science revolution will change many specifics about how portfolio work is done. In the near future, new algorithms, programming techniques, data storage, and statistical techniques that have yet to be invented will likely become available. However, the framework presented in this book will remain relevant despite any changes in methodology.

Why do we need another portfolio book? I have worked in portfolio management for over twenty years. Almost everything I learned has been through doing the work, attending seminars, exchanging personal communications, and reading technical papers. The books out there are either not focused on the type of work I was doing, are too theoretical, or simply talk about case studies. I have never found a single source that covers the background of portfolio work, why to do it, and the practical techniques for doing it. I believe this is the first book that covers the 'why,' 'what,' and some of the 'how' of business asset portfolio analysis and management.

While you can learn how to set up and run portfolio analyses in this book, there is no substitute for actually doing it. I must emphasize this: Be prepared to dive in and get your hands dirty. The power of portfolio analysis is best understood by applying and using it under various circumstances while being guided by theory and principles.

I have been involved in this field for so long that I have sometimes forgotten the source of various portfolio ideas. Despite not regularly linking specific ideas in the book to source documents, the book's Bibliography contains a comprehensive list of papers, books, and presentations that have helped shape my thinking. Many brilliant people have worked and still work in the field. I have listed some of the important ones in the book's Acknowledgments.

I hope that my experience, combined with the ideas and pioneering work of others, will serve as a concentrator of knowledge and wisdom, ultimately becoming something useful.

There are those who might argue that portfolio analysis is not necessary to understand. You can buy vendor programs that do this. Before making that decision, it is important to understand what portfolio analysis is, what you need, and how to use it. While off-the-shelf software may be a reasonable solution, it is important to be informed. You will need to build organizational capability if you view portfolio analysis and management as more than a one-time activity.

This book will teach you how to build and develop tools that are tailored to your needs and processes. Changing your internal processes can be difficult. Without the tools and capabilities to support the change, it is impossible.

I considered including a more thorough analysis of platforms, databases, and optimization systems but ultimately chose not to. To feed the beast, you *could* invest in server farms, artificial intelligence, machine learning, advanced data structures, and organizational capability. It would take years and cost millions of dollars. Few organizations have advanced enough in their portfolio journey to be ready for that. Walk before you run and all that. I have focused on the practical, not the perfect.

It is important to have all of that information in one place. I have added an additional aspect. I have integrated all of that into a decision quality (DQ) framework to ensure that the practice is not only mechanically sound, but also useful in making portfolio decisions.

Portfolio insights can be worth hundreds of millions or billions of dollars given the scale of today's corporations. So, buckle up, and let's start the journey.

INTRODUCTION

I can safely assume that you are reading this book for one of two reasons: (1) either your boss told you "We need to do portfolio,", and you needed a place to start, or (2) you have long believed that the way your company analyzed and decided on investments was not quite right. Perhaps it seemed overly simplistic or overly complicated, or maybe it was a black box full of correction factors that nobody understood. You have come to the right place, either way.

If you ask ten people what **portfolio analysis and management** means to them, you will likely receive eleven different answers. For some people, the process is about purchasing and selling assets. For others, it's about the right mix of securities. For many, it's some black box that the "quants" use. For an increasing number of people, it is '*something that we know we want to do more of*' — whatever it means.

Like the blind men and the elephant, the answers above are all right in some way. Portfolio analysis and management in this book refers to the art and science of examining a business from a high-level perspective, comprehending the impacts of decisions made across the company, and choosing actions based on that perspective.

I will use the following definitions for Portfolio, Portfolio Analysis, and Portfolio Management:

Portfolio - a collection of things (entities) for consideration and possible action of some sort. In the context of this book, assets, projects, oil or mining exploration prospects, or pharmaceutical compounds are generally considered as things.

Portfolio Analysis - helps decision-makers and project managers make better decisions by putting asset and project investment decisions into an organizational context. This is achieved by explicitly using tools, methods, and 'systems thinking' to guide them toward decisions that best align with well-formulated business goals and constraints. Done well, portfolio analysis creates a holistic view of the organization. This holistic view takes into consideration both synergies and the cost of lost opportunities.

Portfolio Management – involves making decisions about assets, projects, and strategies based on Portfolio Analysis, which "stick" and increase the probability of achieving your organization's objectives.

This book covers a wide range of methods that qualify as Portfolio Analysis. Portfolio Management will be lightly covered because it often requires change-management and concerns unique governance policies and specific company culture. Therefore, it is impossible to meaningfully address all the possible ways an organization can implement portfolio management in this book.

Managing a company by coordinating a set of asset alternatives may require buying and selling assets, implementing projects, and making decisions differently than you are used to. Some of the decisions will likely seem counterintuitive. Additionally, coordinating decisions across an organization conflicts with the decentralized governance model that many corporations choose. There are good reasons to decentralize, including better training for business unit managers and increased responsiveness to local situations. So why would a company change the way it has been making decisions? The short answer is that there is value in aligning those decisions from an enterprise-level perspective. Portfolio management, when done well, provides significant value to firms that use it. Additionally, if a company uses portfolio management to shape growth or performance, it can provide higher confidence in its leadership to Wall Street analysts, thus increasing the value of the stock. Large companies can see their market capitalization increase by billions of dollars.

This book aims to help you achieve excellent portfolio analysis and management by condensing twenty years of practice and trial and error into a digestible form. As you read and work through the concepts in the book, it is important to keep your mind at a high level and focus more on the 'why' and the 'what' rather than the 'how.' I have generally avoided being prescriptive, not because of indecision but because every situation is different.

The first section of the book discusses the "Why" of portfolio analysis and management, and the primary tools necessary to achieve excellence. The section provides the essential information to get started and is an entry point.

The second section of the book discusses the appropriate use of different analytic tools in portfolio analysis. The nature of the portfolio problem your organization is facing determines the tools needed to solve it.

The third section covers a range of issues that a portfolio team or practitioner may encounter when introducing these techniques and analyses into a process. This section includes some valuable information about what is effective.

Portfolio analysis and management can be applied to any organization or endeavor. These techniques can be used by any organization that needs to set priorities. This book describes methods that governments, non-profits, and corporations can use. Risk management uses many of the same portfolio techniques. Even the popular book and movie "*Moneyball*" describe managing an American baseball team by using 'portfolio management.'

The examples in this book use Excel, Crystal Ball (with OptQuest) for simulation and stochastic programming, *WhatsBest!* for linear programming, and Spotfire for visualization. These tools work well and are amenable to customization for your needs. This statement is not an endorsement beyond that. They are a great starting point. Developing your own tools can help you comprehend the logic behind them and gain expertise, as well as an appreciation for their limitations. Other platforms may be better suited to your needs and may be available on your organization's systems.

Throughout the book, when I speak of portfolio in general terms, I am usually referring to interaction techniques such as optimization. While Standalone and Comparison analysis may be sufficient, optimization and simulation are the sweet spot for most mid to large firms. I use "portfolio" as a shorthand for "portfolio analysis and management."

I have tried to limit jargon without introducing and defining the term in the book. Nonetheless, a certain level of knowledge of analysis, finance, and other topics is assumed. If you see a term that you do not understand, I have, with any luck, put it in the glossary in the appendix. If the glossary doesn't help, there is help available online.

The chapters in the book have multiple sections. The first section is an overview of the topic. This may be followed by short chapters that delve into foundational aspects of the chapter. There are also three types of other sections within chapter: Detail, Detour, and War Story. Detail is a topic directly related to the main topic that gives additional information. Detour may be a somewhat different but still related topic that may or may not be important to understanding but may be interesting to the reader. War Story is a lived story about the topic showing how things can go wrong, go well, or go sideways. For many organizations portfolio management is a new practice and change management and lessons learned are important to note.

When I refer to performance, I mean more than just financial results. Performance is a term that includes financial, operational, safety, greenhouse gas emissions, organizational effectiveness and anything else that leadership deems to be important. This frame is particularly important for government entities or non-profits that have a mission to accomplish, not just a financial bottom line.

There is redundancy in some of the points I make in this book for several reasons. First, I have no illusions that many will read the book from cover to cover, absorbing all of my accumulated wisdom in some linear fashion. Most of the redundancies are important across multiple concepts, so someone who is skipping around the book according to their needs will find the important points where they need them. Second, some important points need to be repeated. Repetition, whether it is a difficult or counter-intuitive concept, helps to reinforce the concept. I hope I have generally done the repetition in different contexts to provide additional clarity. Finally, people learn in different ways. One turn of phrase or a graphic may resonate better than another. So, I'll say, "Sorry—not sorry" for the redundancies!

My experience and training have been in the context of the upstream oil industry. The industry's defining challenge is the continuous depletion of its hydrocarbon reserve base. Starting with the first drop of oil produced from an oil field, the pressure drops, and the decline to empty begins. Therefore, a company must continually renew itself with new projects and ideas in new places with unique challenges. The common themes in many of the industries or organizations in which strategic portfolio management is most applicable include uncertainty in payoffs and large timeframes of concern. I have generalized the principles throughout the book so that they can be applied to challenges in other industries, and I believe this approach will work for readers across all industries.

A Caution

As you progress through this book, you will encounter powerful analytical techniques that will help you make the best asset decisions. Simply taking those answers and acting on them is "black box" thinking. Resist that temptation! Even the best models are not capable of capturing all the details that are contained in the projects, assets under your control, and the external environment. When making high-quality decisions, it is important to consider unmodeled circumstances. Good portfolio practice can get you 90% of the way to understanding the best decisions, but the "last mile" will require efforts to ensure that decisions are consistent with reality.

You should also abandon the idea that portfolio analysis will compute or forecast your business. It is not possible to do that because of the many variables involved. Rather, with portfolio analysis in a good decision framework, you can gain insight into the consequences of your decisions and find a path to making better ones.

Although linear programming and other tools used in portfolio analysis have other uses, they are not defined in this book as providing the one true answer.

Disclaimers and Conflicts of Interest

I have had business relationships with several companies that are mentioned in this book. I do not receive commissions or promises of benefits from any of them. In some cases, they have allowed me to use their software for free, to create examples for this book and for training and demos.

I am the sole proprietor of Practical Portfolio Management LLC, which offers consulting services to firms looking for portfolio solutions. This book should provide enough information for portfolio practitioners in a firm to start their own practices and use the tools to their advantage. I acknowledge that many people will find this challenging and may require support in establishing a portfolio practice, particularly for elements outside the scope of this book.

As a partner with TIBCO (Spotfire), I have the potential to earn money in the future by recommending Spotfire through my consulting business.

Mark Wiley of Lindo provided feedback early in the book's writing, and Lindo Systems has granted me a time-limited license for *What'sBest!* software. I have used *What'sBest!* to create portfolio optimization models and use the program for class demos. I use *What'sBest!* because it has many valuable features for the models I build for portfolio analysis, and it is software that I am familiar with. There are no other financial arrangements with Lindo.

As a Frontline Systems Partner, I have access to their training, support, and software, as well as demonstrated experience with their software platform. I can also provide consultation through Frontline's referral system.

Lumina granted an enterprise license for Analytica that was valid for a limited time. I have no other financial arrangement with Lumina.

I was a long-time employee of Chevron and Texaco. My personal portfolio contains Chevron securities.

Throughout the book, I have included quotes from friends, philosophers, celebrities, and businesspeople. I have done my best to attribute the quotes. Their quotes are used in this book, but their use does not imply their endorsement of anything within the book.

Many of the ideas and concepts in the book were developed during my tenure with Chevron. The book itself and all materials were developed independently after leaving Chevron in 2020.

Finally, throughout the book and in the bibliography, I have included affiliate links to books on Amazon.com. The typical commission is 3-5%, meaning a $10 book would give me about $0.40. If you want to avoid this, do not use the link. Instead, go directly to your preferred bookseller and search for the title or author.

A Note About the 'War Stories'

Throughout the book, I have included numerous 'war stories' that reflect my experience and stories from other practitioners. I have anonymized identifying details in the stories. The stories aim to convey that the work is difficult, particularly within large organizations with long histories and deep corporate cultures. They highlight potential pitfalls and reassure you that you are not alone on your portfolio journey.

Consider the war stories scattered throughout the book as either historical fiction or inspired by true events. The circumstances often arise from an amalgamation of different people and events. The dialogue has been fictionalized, just as my imagining of the thought processes of others has been. However, the 'war stories' reflect what many other portfolio practitioners and I have experienced doing this work.

A note about the examples in this book

The examples used throughout the book are not modeled after any particular real assets. These are only examples. For convenience, we have excluded abandonment costs from many of our calculations. Your corporate or accounting standards may treat some elements differently, and there are undoubtedly internal consistency errors.

In addition, some examples were created when the oil price was over $100. Costs, margins, and revenues may seem unrealistic. This changes nothing about the principles of portfolio analysis.

SECTION ONE

Background and Description of Key Enablers

CHAPTER 1

Portfolio Analysis and Management – What and Why?

"

The reasonable man adapts himself to the world; the unreasonable one persists in trying to adapt the world to himself. Therefore, all progress depends on the unreasonable man."

George Bernard Shaw

Businesses need to make investments to continue. A portfolio framework can add tremendous value when making investments, whether by a direct calculation using cash flow or by using proxies for value like revenue or market share. Your organization can make a significant leap forward by combining decision quality with portfolio management. A 30% increase in the value of an investment program is not uncommon when using portfolio techniques, as evidenced by both practice and literature.

Portfolio Management Connects Ideas with Execution

In the beginning, man created the project. And that project was good. It provided the basis of a company, and that company was fruitful and multiplied. That company begat more projects, and they too were good. Those projects bore fruit that contained the seeds of further projects, initiatives, and tests.

You get the point. Companies are composed of existing businesses, projects, and pilot experiments. Current cash is generated by existing businesses, near-term future cash is generated by projects, and longer-term positive cash flow may result from pilot tests. Projects and pilots are created to either improve existing businesses or to create new markets and products.

That is all good, but at some point, most companies must make difficult tradeoffs between long- and short-term results, growth rate, and efficiency. This book provides a framework for analyzing and making tradeoffs between those values.

Individual Asset Decisions

Most companies make investment decisions on a project-by-project basis using estimated future cash flow. The corporation typically provides standard input parameter assumptions about the external environment and some project target metrics, including internal rate of return (IRR) and net present value (NPV).

This approach assumes that IRR and NPV are proxies for the value added to the corporation. It is often a reasonable proxy and is the basis of the Capital Asset Pricing Model (CAPM), which is one of the main value frameworks used in the corporate finance field. In many cases, this approach does not lead to the best enterprise outcomes.

This individual lens may not place the opportunity in the specific context of your firm. It looks at cash out, cash in, timing, and risk. To find the value in the context of your firm, you need to apply the portfolio lens.

Many firms apply a qualitative strategic fit gate at the start, and that's the last time they think about portfolio fit. For most companies, there are more investment opportunities than resources to do them. For every positive investment decision, something else must be given up or delayed. That imposes a cost that offsets the investment value.

The concept is known as opportunity cost. In an organization, the opportunity cost of a new investment is a function of the investment, the existing inventory of opportunities, and organizational goals. It can be determined using portfolio methods and tools.

The portfolio lens brings in other considerations. It starts with the same numbers as an individual analysis, but then examines the investment from multiple perspectives. It puts the investment into a different context for more thorough tests of whether the investment makes sense for your firm specifically. The methods used can range from simple, indirect, and crude to sophisticated and direct. Portfolio analysis provides a holistic view to help a firm determine the best set of coordinated decisions, rather than a reductionist individual view to select individual projects.

What 'IS' Portfolio Management?

Asking this question in 1960 would have yielded an answer about the efficient frontier risk and reward tradeoff inherent in stocks or other financial instruments. When we go into the business asset realm and look at all the tradeoffs, we must expand the definition. Risk and reward are important, but external analysts use other characteristics of a company's performance to judge it. Tradeoffs between those characteristics must be considered.

Portfolio Analysis is the process of using portfolio techniques to understand the attributes of a portfolio and the best decisions for an enterprise. Portfolio Management is making decisions using the insights from portfolio analysis to help a firm achieve its goals and aspirations. Portfolio management lies at the intersection of portfolio analysis, decision quality, and economic and financial analysis. It allows us to allocate scarce resources towards the activities that will result in success.

The essence of investment opportunity analysis is comparison. How does the project look if we choose one decision over the other competing decisions? Portfolio analysis is at a higher level than standalone opportunity analysis; it puts individual opportunities into the frame of the enterprise. It asks, "What is the difference between the firm with this coherent set of decisions and the firm with a different coherent set of decisions?"

Strategy

There are many definitions of 'strategy.' As used here, it will mean a roadmap to achieve a platform or position from which to do business. A strategy statement can include goals, constraints, and position statements. It should not include specific actions. Actions are important, but tactical. Strategy is a broad, intermediate description of what you will focus on to achieve your goals.

In this context, a firm's goal may be to have the best total shareholder return in its competitive sector. A strategy statement to achieve that goal could be "To be #1 in the sales in the US market by the 4th quarter of this year." Tactics might include changing the advertising campaign and dropping the price.

Strategy Decisions

Portfolio thinking can be used to test the viability of a strategy. How reasonable is it to believe that some proposed action or positioning will achieve the hoped-for results? Someone always has an idea that pushes the concept of what a firm does. Sometimes they're good ideas. Portfolio techniques can provide insight into the consequences of outside-the-box investments. By looking at interactions driven by risk or budget, portfolio analysis puts these decisions into the context of the organization's aspirations. They can also be used in high-level capital allocation, such as between business sectors, or vastly different product lines within a firm.

Indeed, as the world moves towards a lower carbon future, companies will have to make consequential decisions about their future. Those decisions will affect investment levels, return on shareholder investment, and a firm's "license to operate." Sustainability and renewable energy investments may be profitable for some, while for others it will simply be a cost of doing business. Portfolio analysis can help a firm balance competing needs and manage the pace of investments.

Strategic Execution Framework

The book *Executing Your Strategy* (https://amzn.to/2DezIoV) provides a valuable view of business functions in the context of aligning decisions in a firm through the Strategic Execution Framework (SEF). The firm's leadership creates the vision, environment, and metrics that feed into the strategy. The project and operations groups ensure that everything goes well after leadership sets the direction. Companies without a portfolio process use metrics such as NPV and hurdle rates as a substitute for explicit portfolio models. We can do better.

Portfolio analysis and management link the leadership (thinking) side to an organization's project and operations (doing) sides. The thinking side figures out what is the right thing to do; the doing side does the thing right. In the SEF, the **thinking/do-the-right-thing** part is where leadership occurs; the **doing/do-the-thing-right** part is where management occurs. Portfolio management is the bridge that provides feedback to both sides to ensure alignment between leadership and management.

▸ **Strategic Execution Framework**

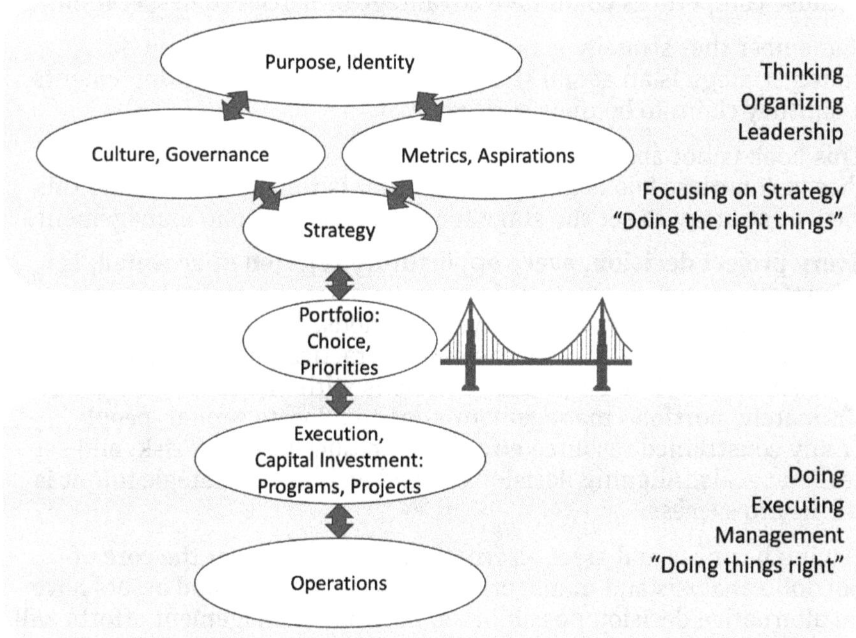

> *The Strategic Execution Framework shows the canonical relationship between leadership and management. Leadership focuses on Doing the Right Things, while management focuses on Doing Things Right. Portfolio Analysis provides the link between them to ensure that management actions support corporate goals.*

In this framework, note that strategy is the culmination of vision, nature, and portfolio. Hence, a well-formulated strategy includes goals and metrics, organizational structure and culture, and governance. It must ultimately contain the connection to management and on-the-ground reality. A well-formulated statement of strategy might look something like this, "Using competitive advantage from our engineering expertise [nature], we will achieve first quartile performance and 5% growth [vision and metrics] by enhancing our base production [management]." The leaders of the organization must fully comprehend and embrace all aspects of the strategy.

Strategy can and should also include other aspects, such as the role of business development, M&A, exploration, and enabling functions like HR and facilities management.

Strategy does not have to be widely publicized *in detail* to the external world or even internally. However, key leaders throughout the organization must be informed and able to communicate and drive their organizations' roles. As an example of why NOT to be transparent to the world, the 5% growth goal may best be kept under wraps because competitors could take advantage of perceived desperation.

Remember that strategy is not what you say—it's what you do. A stated strategy is an actual strategy only if management implements what they claim to be their strategy.

This book is not about strategy. Brilliant people have written about that in countless books and articles, but it is important to frame this view of strategy to set the stage for its role in portfolio management.

Every project decision, every opportunity rejected or accepted, is a portfolio decision. Our goal is to make better portfolio decisions using appropriate data and analysis methods. Our goal as portfolio analysts is to ensure that, to the extent practical, all decision-makers have a framework to align their decisions with organizational goals. Ultimately, portfolio management aims to allocate capital, people, or any constrained resource effectively, reduce business risk, and set realistic goals. Aligning decisions at all levels with strategic intent is the key to success.

Having business and asset alternatives or options is at the core of portfolio analysis and management. If your business and assets have no alternative decision possibilities, portfolio management efforts will be fruitless. If no significant business options exist, the only course of action is to focus on operational efficiencies. However, this is **never** the actual situation. There are always options. Potential options for a given asset or investment include divestiture, purchase, slower development, faster development, different scale of development, different development concept (e.g., automation versus labor tradeoffs), partial divestiture, different working interest on a purchase, corporate dividend rate, and timing on any of the above.

A business will usually have a base case or momentum case for each of its assets. It is essentially a roadmap, budget, or plan of what the firm plans to do with an asset over the next few years. Sometimes they will have a plan B option too, which lays out an alternative action that is possible but is considered less valuable. It is always good to have options. If you have only one option or course of action with no possible alternatives, then no matter what happens, you can't improve the outcome. Having even one option on an asset in addition to the base case can only add value. Think of it this way. If the world unfolds as envisioned in your base case, you can continue down that path. If the base case is suboptimal, you can choose the alternative, but only if it is better. If it's worse, you will continue with the base case.

▸ **Where Portfolio Lives**

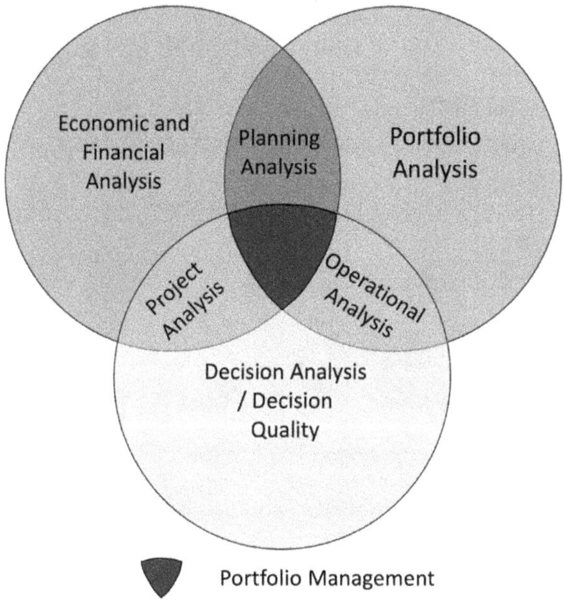

> *Portfolio Management is at the intersection of Economic, Portfolio, and Decision Analysis. It synthesizes all the information and develops an action plan that helps a firm achieve its aspirations.*

The options may not always be to your liking. If the manufacturing cost of a good exceeds its price, you can shut down the plant. While it may be an unpalatable and expensive choice, it is still better than producing at a loss, so it is the one you must make.

The decision to pursue some options may be subject to approval by another party, such as a partner or government entity. If we do not control the choice of action, it is not a decision but rather an outcome. *But we can treat it as a decision, understand the value of having control of the decision, and then act to maximize the likelihood of our preferred decision.* The point is to understand which decisions would be the best, then push to make those happen.

Creating and Selecting Alternatives – Example

To reiterate, if there are no alternatives, there is no decision to make, and we're done. You are operating your business, not managing it. However, options are needed to maximize performance when assets compete for scarce resources.

Consider the following scenario. You are the manager of Asset A. Your asset is performing well, and it is time to submit next year's budget.

You look at the asset and must decide how much capital to request for next year. You see three main distinct options:

1. Recommended case, normal production, and profitability. Input is at 100; output is at 100. Output to input ratio (O/I) is 100%, (units are arbitrary)
2. Lower growth, lower cost case. Input is 75; output is 80. O/I = 107%, and
3. Higher growth, higher cost case. Input is 125, and output is 105. O/I is 84%.

The alternatives are summarized below.

▸ Asset A Alternatives

Asset A Selection	Alternative Name	Cost	Output	Output/Cost
1	Asset A Recommended	100	100	100%
0	Asset A Low	75	80	107%
0	Asset A High	125	105	84%

The asset manager selects the Recommended Case for Asset A. Although the low case was more "efficient," it had lower output. The Recommended case was a happy compromise.

Imagine that under your corporate guidelines, any one of the alternatives is acceptable. How can the firm decide which alternative is best? In this context, the asset manager would typically speak with her boss, negotiate a bit, and request 125 while guaranteeing 80. Then they would agree on the recommended case of 100 input and 100 output. Everyone is happy.

Consider another scenario. You are the general manager of Asset A and Asset B. Asset A is as above; Asset B has the following characteristics.

1. Recommended case. Normal production and profitability. Input is at 100; output is at 100. Input to output ratio (O/I) is 100%,
2. Lower growth, lower cost case. Input is 75; output is 75. O/I = 100%, and
3. Higher growth, higher cost case. Input is 125, and output is 125. O/I is 100%.

This project has an even profitability profile. The early dollars have the same profitability as the later dollars.

The alternatives are summarized below:

▸ Asset B Alternatives

Asset B Selection	Alternative Name	Cost	Output	Output/Cost
1	Asset B Recommended	100	100	100%
0	Asset B Low	75	75	100%
0	Asset B High	125	125	100%

The Recommended Case for Asset B has the same investment efficiency as the other Asset B cases. It is a momentum case with the same budget as the previous year.

If you negotiate separately with the two asset managers, you will spend 200 and have an output of 200. This exemplifies a bottom-up approach to decision-making. Consider each asset as an independent, self-contained decision.

But perhaps you noticed that for that same input of 200, a higher output can be achieved by allocating inputs differently between the two assets. Can you spot an alternative investment approach to the two assets that would yield more than 200 as the output?

Before I reveal the answer, think about what is needed to get to this point. First, the two assets need managers who think through their business and generate meaningfully different alternatives. You need standards for data and inputs to ensure comparability. With two assets and three options each, this is a computationally simple problem that can be solved in your head or on the back of an envelope. More significant problems spanning multiple years, more assets, and additional metrics would require computer models that run specialized algorithms to solve.

All of the above is easy. However, you need one more critical element to be successful; an organizational culture that values the sharing of information and incentivizes the honest sharing of analyses without gaming. Leaders, managers, and executives must be trustworthy and committed.

You probably figured out that the solution is investing in Asset A at the low case and Asset B at the high case, where you can achieve an output of 205.

A top-down approach, which takes a higher-level perspective, adds value compared to a bottom-up approach, as demonstrated by this simple example of portfolio thinking. Without those high- and low-case alternatives, there would have been no way to make an informed decision to improve the outcome.

Project management and decision analysis literature are replete with the concepts of alternative generation. Some references can be found in the Bibliography.

How Do You Know If Portfolio Analysis and Management Would Help?

It is common for organizations to ignore new methods and technologies. This is especially true when their results have been good historically. If it's not broke, they believe there's no need to fix it. You can expend an enormous amount of time and energy unsuccessfully trying to convince someone who doesn't want to change. But even if results are generally good, there are sometimes symptoms that the wheels are beginning to fall off.

Some of the symptoms below indicate a lack of analytical capability, some are due to hubris, some are governance issues, and some suggest a lack of insight into better ways to inform tactical and strategic decisions.

1. Often, a leader in the organization believes that resource allocation can be done better than first in, first out that meets hurdle rates. In the best cases, the leader will endorse efforts to develop portfolio perspectives in decision-making.
2. Project delays due to the misallocation of people, attention, or cash.
3. Surprise when, despite everyone's best efforts, organizational results are not met.
4. Opportunistic decision-making. Approval of bright, shiny objects while ignoring stated strategies.
5. Lack of sharing information and coordination between different investment silos.
6. Lower-level, relatively uninformed people making strategic decisions. (Almost anyone can make a "No" decision.)
7. Lack of enforced standards for analysis and description of investment opportunities.
8. Underperformance relative to competitors with similar assets.

The will to effect change to portfolio methods may have to wait for a crisis, but you can prepare for the inevitable by knowing that another way exists.

Key Takeaways

All business decisions are portfolio decisions. Putting the decisions explicitly into a portfolio perspective helps drive high-quality decisions and enterprise value. The essence of good asset portfolio management is comparing possible futures based on different strategies. The art is in the creation of those strategies and comparisons. Asset portfolio analysis reframes typical project analysis by placing discrete decisions into a higher-level context (typically the enterprise). The cost to do portfolio analysis is quite low, while the benefit can be extraordinary.

Detail – A Plan is Not a Forecast

I will repeat throughout the book in some form that "A Plan is Not a Forecast." But why am I saying that in a portfolio book?

A sequence that includes portfolio analysis looks something like the following:

We start with the possible decisions on your inventory of assets, the assumptions about the external business environment, and guidance from leadership on the firm's aspirations.

Portfolio analysis then tries to find the set of decisions that will best meet enterprise aspirations. Leadership may consider modifying its aspirations and timing, if corporate aspirations are unrealistic given the inventory of possible decisions and the external environment, hence the double arrow between portfolio analysis and enterprise aspirations.

▸ **Idealized Portfolio Plan**

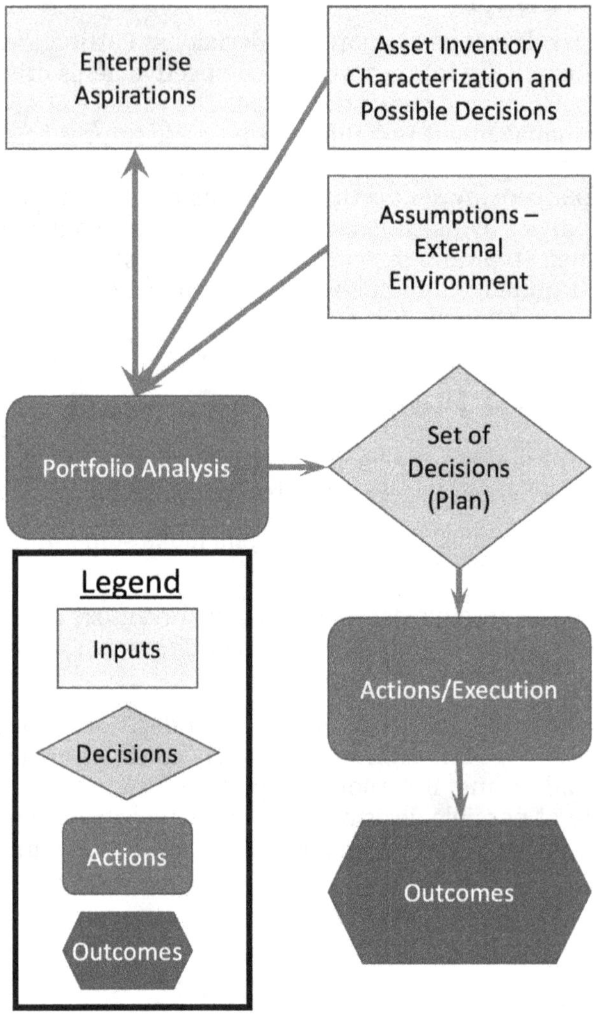

> *Combine your inventory and assumptions into a model, use it to inform your actions, and then roll it all together into a plan. When you perform the lookback test, the results will match your plan exactly. Right?... Right?... Bueller?...*

In the end, portfolio analysis and leadership discussions yield a set of coordinated decisions. This decision set includes sequencing, timing, cost, and revenue projections that result from the decisions. This is "The Plan."

The next step is to execute the plan and reap your just rewards, which, of course, align perfectly with the plan. Simple right? Not so fast. It's all a little messier than that.

Two important factors cause plans to be poor forecasts: the corporate culture, including cognitive biases and incentives, and the external environment. The culture affects all the inputs into the portfolio analysis and the teams' ability to execute. The results are driven by the external environment, which is entirely outside of corporate control.

Sometimes, these two giant elephants in the room cancel each other out and lead to good results. Other times, they reinforce each other and drive results into the toilet.

In the first decade of the 21st century, my colleagues and I coined what we called the project mantra. "The project was late, over budget, and underperformed, but it was saved by the oil price." In that environment, even though all of the inputs were wrong, they canceled out, and good results came. Sure, it didn't go as planned, but who really cared? Everyone was making money. Then came 2015.

Oil prices dropped precipitously. Suddenly, the poorly forecasted projects were no longer saved by oil prices. It was easy to point fingers at the people who generated project economics and execution failures, but those were driven by the previous inputs and failure to fix the root causes in the project mantra.

The characterization of timing, cost, performance, and assumptions about the external environment are all driven by an organization's culture, biases, and incentives. Culture also drives the ability to execute. Processes and checks have their place, but they also often induce delays. I am not aware of any companies that are able to completely eliminate biases, maintain an objective culture, and avoid blaming others. Even if all that were true, it would still need an analysis culture that realistically looks at the range of possible outcomes based on an assessment of the external world. The forecast would not be a single point; it would be a range of possible outcomes.

▸ **More Realistic Portfolio Plan**

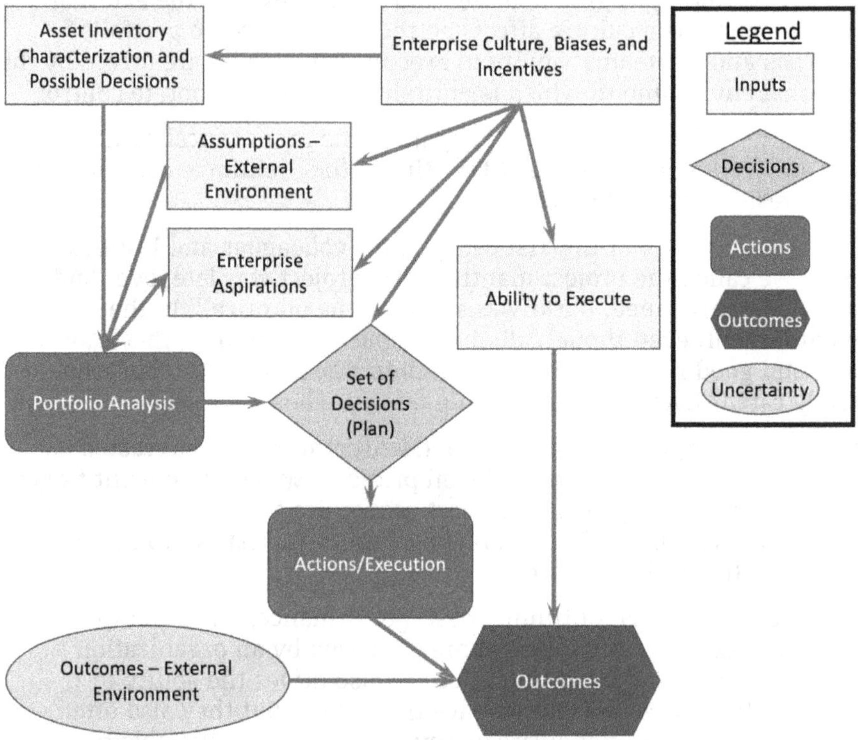

In reality, a firm's culture affects the characterization of plans, assumptions, and aspirations. It also affects the ability to execute those plans. Then, between the time the plans are finished, and we see results, the world changes. The updated world seldom matches our input assumptions about the external environment.

Most people are not trained to understand those types of results. They prefer "the number." Then if the number is met, everyone is happy; otherwise, blame is allocated.

I would love for firms to have a more objective and rigorous culture. Although it would be nice in theory, we must also recognize that it would impose costs. My preference is first to get people to stop thinking that plans are forecasts. Look at them as indicators and tools. For accountability, judge people on the aspects that are under their control.

Portfolio analysis and management is planning on steroids.

Detail – When is a Strategy Not a Strategy?

The word strategy, like the word portfolio, has many different meanings to different people.

This book blends two fields that use the word strategy differently (Decision Analysis and Portfolio), so I must clarify how I use it.

As a rule, my mental model is a hierarchy that consists of goals, strategies, and actions (or tactics). At a corporate level, the goal could be to achieve the highest total shareholder return (TSR) compared to competitors. The strategy to accomplish that goal defines a position—for example, having the highest margin and #2 in sales in a market (China). Then an action to achieve that goal could be to incorporate premium features in the Chinese market.

Simple Goal-Strategy-Tactic Hierarchy

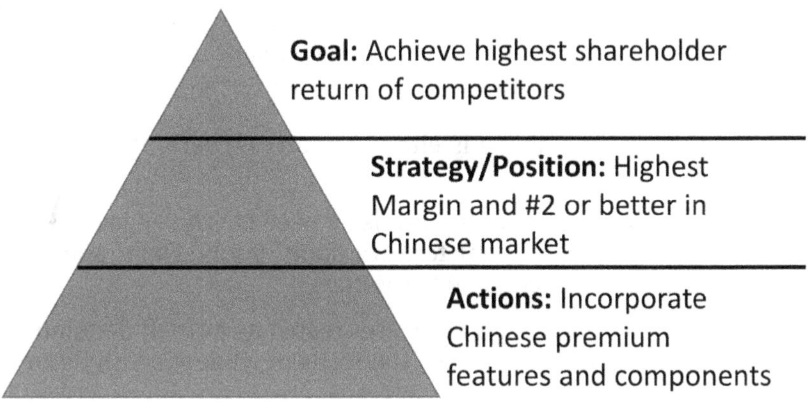

> *Think of this as a hierarchy. At the top of the hierarchy are your goals. They are set by the leadership to whom you report. They are a given. The next level contains what you have to achieve to reach that goal. The bottom level contains the actions that you will take to reach the strategic position.*

When you look at each of those three elements separately, they can each be goals (nouns) or actions (verbs). From the perspective of the highest level of the enterprise, it seems reasonable.

Let's go down to the next level in the organization, the one responsible for margins and market positioning. For them, the TSR goal is owned by the corporation. The lower-level organization's **goal** is the corporate **strategy**—Highest Margin and Market position in China. They will do this by incorporating Chinese premium features and components, and to make this happen, they will outsource manufacturing and design to Chinese firms.

▸ **Nested Goal-Strategy-Tactic Hierarchies**

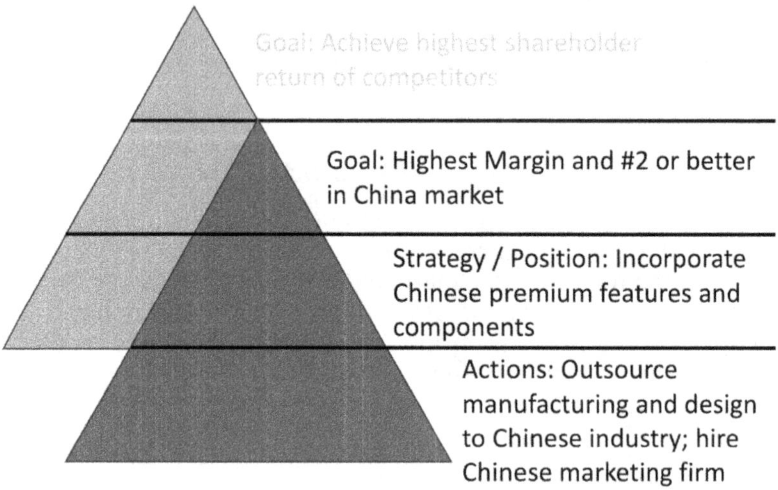

Goal hierarchies nest together. When setting objectives for your direct reports, they can take the strategic objective in the previous figure as their goal. They then attempt to achieve the position by taking action.

Again, each of those three items is either a noun or a verb. It depends on your perspective.

This can continue down to as many levels as needed. This objectives and strategy framework is similar to work done by John Doerr and documented in his book, *Measure What Matters*.

When developing a strategy, the goals are treated as a given decision or destination. The Strategy becomes the focus of what you will do to achieve the goal.

The Use of 'Strategies' in Decision Analysis

In the Decision Analysis field, Decision Analysts often create multiple strategies or strategic themes for consideration. In the above China case, they might have created a strategic theme that stressed volume over margin, so it was light on the premium features but came in at a much lower price point. Or perhaps they considered a global standardization approach that largely ignored geographic differences and focused on reducing costs through economies of scale. Each of those strategic themes could have design, marketing, and manufacturing dimensions.

Decision Analysts typically create three to six strategic themes with three to ten independent dimensions. The aim is to discover what tradeoffs exist between the different themes, then select the best theme or create one that steals from several others to create a hybrid strategic theme. Instead of goals, positions, and actions, a DA decision hierarchy has given decisions, focus decisions, and tactical decisions. The selected hybrid strategy (set of focus decisions) is similar conceptually to a corporate strategy. Even when working on a small project, the analysts and project teams consider the focus-level decisions to be their "strategic" decisions. They are strategic to that project but not to the overall firm.

This would all happen before the corporation or organization selects the strategy they will follow. Within the Strategic Execution Framework, the chosen combination of dimensional decisions becomes the strategy at that level. Portfolio analysis and management ensures that the selected actions align with the strategy.

When you create a strategy, it is best not to think of it as an unchanging set of positions or actions. It is more like a hypothesis to test—a well-constructed, logical, data-supported hypothesis capable of achieving the hoped-for goals. But executives are not clairvoyant—they don't have an infallible crystal ball. The world may change, and events may happen that render the strategy meaningless. In that case, they need to redirect their efforts. But in the meantime, employees in the organization have their 'North Star' to guide their actions and decisions.

The short answer to this section's title is that a strategy is not a strategy when it is a goal or action. Strategies define the 'what.' Goals define the 'why.' Actions define the 'how.' There are other ways to think about strategy. Indeed, there are volumes written about it. But this is how I think about strategy and use the word in this book.

Detail – How Does Innovation Fit In?

Like sharks, if companies stop moving, they die.

Operational efficiency is great, but you can squeeze only so much water out of a sponge. You can't grow by shrinking. At some point, revenue must also grow. There is often a need for a step change to continue growing and outperforming competitors.

Innovation may lead to that step change. But innovation is challenging. If it were easy, everyone would already be doing it. An organization must have a culture that allows for failure and is amenable to change.

Much simpler than step-change innovation is taking steps that shave a few cents off costs. They are more certain and have a tangible benefit. I am not here to criticize those actions. They are essential and they add up. But as you do those steps, do your best to ensure they are in service to a longer-term growth goal and do not lead you into a blind alley.

Incorporating portfolio perspectives in decision-making is itself an innovation. Portfolio tools can help manage innovation efforts. The tools won't drive innovation, but they can be helpful in better directing and scaling the efforts.

When I pushed for and developed a database to help manage long-term planning data, the justification was that it was necessary to do our planning job. In the process, that database was an enabler for portfolio analysis. It was not practical to go directly into a significant organizational change from my role, but the database laid a foundation for portfolio analysis and management.

Detail – Some Important Definitions

Company, firm, organization, and enterprise all refer to the entity attempting to manage or improve its performance. It can be an LLC, LLP, partnership, or a publicly or privately owned corporation. It is an entity on behalf of which we are making decisions to improve or optimize performance.

Referring to the Strategic Execution Framework graphic.

When the portfolio ellipse in the SEF informs operations and management and explicitly links project actions with enterprise aspirations, it is **tactical portfolio** analysis and management.

I consider tactical portfolio analysis to be the workhorse of portfolio levels. Decisions that can be informed by tactical portfolio analysis include:

1. Project alternatives, asset investment emphasis
2. Working interest
3. Project timing
4. Sub-optimizations – best greenhouse gas mitigation program, best exploration program, best kidney research program, best growth program for a single business unit
5. Budget and resource allocations
6. Acquisitions and Divestitures

When portfolio analysis informs strategy and leadership and is contained mainly in the top bubble, it is **strategic portfolio** analysis and management.

SEF High-Level Perspective

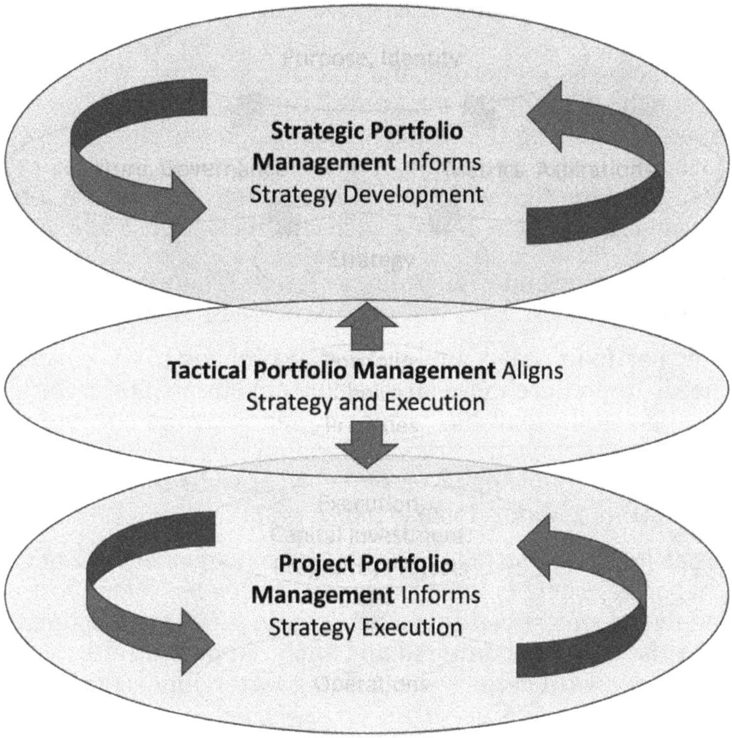

> *Look closely at this graphic, and you can see the Strategic Execution Framework in the background. Work that is done by and for the leadership team is Strategic Portfolio Management. Work entirely contained within the management circles is Project or Operational Portfolio Management. Work that links Strategy to Operations is Tactical Portfolio Management.*

Decisions that can be informed by strategic portfolio analysis include:

1. Asset class balances (upstream-downstream-renewables, deepwater, LNG, conventional vs. unconventional, etc.). Clinical area balance for pharmaceutical firms.
2. Time preferences (short- vs. long-term)
3. Resource replacement – acquisition, divestiture, exploration, Research vs. marketing emphasis in a pharmaceutical setting
4. Key metric tradeoffs
5. Risk aggregation – exploration success and business correlation

When portfolio analysis and management are wholly contained in operations and program management, it is **project portfolio management** or **PPM**. Project portfolio management is used mainly for sequencing projects given short-term limitations in people, capital, and infrastructure. PPM is more like queue management. A big part of PPM is aligning complementary resources so they mesh properly—like a zipper.

PPM often focuses on reporting and tracking progress. When is the product launch? When is the next phase gate? Is the project over or under budget? Knowing the status of a development pipeline is good, but it does not change a company's direction. It would seldom cause the type of thinking that will change a firm's strategy. By the time you are tracking your projects, the big decisions have been made

It adds a lot of value and is difficult to do well. There are many books and articles about PPM, so it will not be covered in detail in this book.

A strategic portfolio analysis might lead a company to the conclusion that it needs to produce more oil from unconventional reservoirs. Then the tactical portfolio analysis could encourage them to add two more drilling rigs in the (unconventional) Permian Basin. Finally, the project portfolio analysis could suggest a sequence of wells to maximize short-term value and minimize logistics costs.

These three levels of portfolio analysis and management are not strictly separate. There is lots of gray space between them. Portfolios can be analyzed almost continually as results occur and circumstances change, or they can be monitored and analyzed periodically. Imagination and skill become the limiting factors in determining portfolio uses.

"**Portfolio**" has several uses in this book. It can mean the overall portfolio analysis and management process, as in "The exploration team was going to do portfolio." It can also mean the calculated outcome of a specific set of asset decisions, e.g., "Portfolio 3 shows low growth." Some people use the word portfolio in the way I use inventory—as a listing of elements, e.g., "She was managing a portfolio of projects." Be aware of these different uses.

In this book, the **inventory** or c**omplete inventory** is a list of all assets and potential decisions and characteristics of the elements in the list.

The **working inventory** is the subset of the complete inventory used in the analyses. It is appropriate in many cases to deliberately exclude some potential decisions from the analysis, for example, a base-business optimization might exclude acquisitions. This is driven by the frame and purpose of the analysis.

We will generate **portfolios, hypothetical portfolios, portfolio scenarios,** or **candidate sets** by logically combining working inventory elements.

Those hypothetical portfolios will be generated to test their ability to achieve organizational financial and operational goals or targets.

A portfolio **strategy** may have an asset theme (e.g., focus on deepwater production or low development cost), a financial theme (high corporate return-on-capital-employed [ROCE], revenue growth greater than 5% over the next 5 years) as inputs to a model, or it could be the output of whatever emerges from the model to achieve desired performance.

Insights will be gained by analyzing and discussing the strategies and portfolios needed to achieve or balance goals.

Once a hypothetical portfolio is decided as the "final" set of actions and appropriate adjustments are made, that becomes the basis of the **plan**.

Detail – Harry Markowitz and the Efficient Frontier

This is not an action-adventure tale or a Hardy Boys mystery; instead, it describes the efforts of the Nobel Laureate founder of portfolio theory, Harry Markowitz. Markowitz, along with William Sharpe and Merton Miller, won the Nobel Prize for Economics in 1990 based on his work in finance.

Figure 6 from Portfolio Selection, Markowitz1952

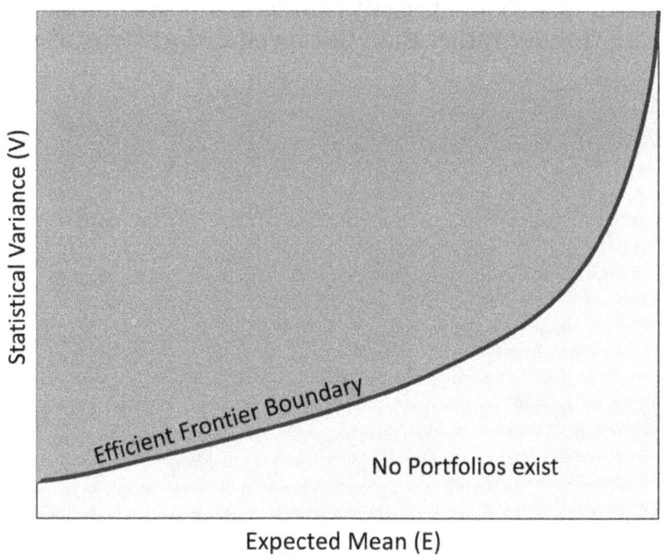

Figure 6 from Markowitz's seminal paper on portfolio optimization described portfolio combinations that formed the boundary of statistically possible performance. For any combination of securities (portfolio) that falls on the Efficient Frontier Boundary, there is no portfolio that can achieve both lower Statistical Variance and higher Expected Mean Return.

Markowitz's 1952 paper, "*Portfolio Selection*" in the Journal of Finance, introduced the idea of efficient combinations of securities to create portfolios. He showed that the most efficient combinations of securities are those for which a given return cannot be obtained with lower variance and a given variance cannot have a higher return. The boundary beyond which no combinations exist was later dubbed the efficient frontier.

In this context, E was the 'expected' mean value of a combination of securities, and V was the statistical variance.

Early asset portfolio analysis efforts in the oil industry used the same concept—looking for portfolios that maximized value with the lowest possible standard deviation. That approach never quite caught on. Executives care less about standard deviation than about financial and operational measures such as return on capital employed, revenue growth, and production levels. Investigating the trade-offs between important goals and values is essential, but the standard deviation of the corporation is not one of them.

People today still talk about efficient frontiers. In my experience, they often misuse the term. Markowitz's efficient frontier was an expected return versus variance frontier. That was useful in **his** context to measure risk and return for portfolios of financial securities. His efficient frontier is actually a Pareto frontier between these two metrics. When I talk about efficient frontiers, I usually mean the more general Pareto frontier rather than the specific Markowitz axes.

CHAPTER 2

Key Enablers of Portfolio Analysis and Management

The simplest types of portfolio analysis can be done with relatively little data and organization—in many cases, no more than the minimum requirements of corporate governance. The systems and processes can become overwhelming as you perform more sophisticated analyses and extract additional useful knowledge and insights from the information.

I saw a presentation in 2003 that showed three enablers of portfolio management. The presentation was meaningful and insightful, and it guided my work for many years. Over time, I realized that those three enablers—data, computing power, and visualization—covered only the mechanics of portfolio analysis. To use portfolio analysis and management to positive effect, two other elements are critical: framing the problem to be solved and leadership commitment to a portfolio culture.

The Mechanical Enablers

Organizing and conditioning data has a crucial enabling role in portfolio analysis and management. Many companies have planning systems that exist as linked Excel spreadsheets. That is adequate for limited implementations of portfolio analysis. However, as organizations grow, and needs become more critical and challenging, more efficient and robust systems become necessary.

Critical Success Factors for Portfolio Management

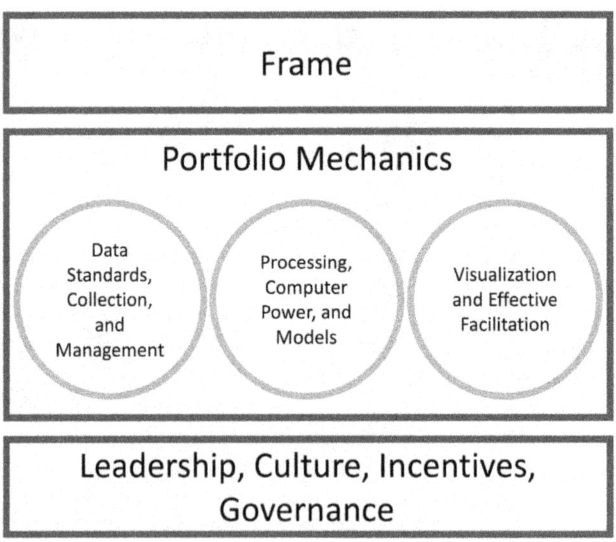

Historically, in the literature, asset portfolio efforts generally focused on the mechanical aspects of portfolio analysis and management—the how. That is a necessary but not sufficient component of managing a portfolio. Beyond that, you need a good frame for decision-making and leadership and cultural support for the analysis.

Computers, software, and network systems must be powerful and fast when there are large volumes of data. Besides storage, we also need software and hardware to perform the calculations for computer-intensive portfolio analysis.

Tools to display data or visualize the calculated results are also essential. Understanding trade-offs between multiple metrics across time and at an enterprise level needs not just excellent tools but time and becoming accustomed to and comfortable with the change in decision frame.

The Bookend Enablers

The first bookend is the frame. Framing your analysis is critical. It helps you determine the data, tools, and processes needed to solve the problem or answer the question. Framing sets the context of all work that will follow. It guides the efforts to ensure that decision-makers are getting the analysis they need to make high-quality decisions in time to capitalize on them.

Going beyond that, using the results of your analysis to make better decisions can be an enormous change management effort. Changing from a first-in, first-out decision-making style to one that synthesizes a larger group of decisions requires a change of mindset and strong facilitation. You will need a strong case for moving to a new way of making decisions, full management support and participation, and clarification from leadership on the firm's future.

The enablers of portfolio analysis and management are covered in the next five sections. First, we will talk about the frame.

Key Takeaways

Five elements are critical to support a portfolio analysis and management system. Data, computational tools, and visualization cover the mechanics of the portfolio, while framing and leadership commitment cover the needed cultural aspects. All five are necessary to maintain an effective portfolio practice.

The framing and leadership bookends of the enablers are where portfolio analysis and management most commonly run aground. Framing is straightforward if there is leadership commitment to using portfolio analysis to make decisions. Gaining leadership commitment for a change of process is the subject of many books, courses, and schools of thought. It is also the part that must be customized to the individual organization's leaders, culture, and governance. One of the reviewers of this book had hoped to see more on the cultural and change management aspects of portfolio management. I can add little to the conversation beyond the extensive work done in the change management field. Therefore, most of this book covers the three mechanical enablers and provides a guide to create a technically functional system. There is a section on framing with a decision tree to help inform the analytical frame. Throughout the book, there is discussion of how the frame influences the mechanical choices for data and models. Many of the war stories and detail sections throughout the book are about management resistance, cultural and framing issues.

Detail – Decision Quality and Decision Analysis

Throughout this book, I allude to the tenets of decision quality and decision analysis. I operated for many years believing that if I just nailed those three mechanical enablers, everything would fall into place. Eventually, I realized that it wasn't enough. I had built it, and they weren't coming. Something else was needed.

The first realization was to put the analysis into a frame. What is the question to be answered? What is the problem we're trying to solve? What decisions are in and out? How final was the decision? Sometime later, I also realized that the decision-makers, the management of the corporation, had to agree to incorporate this way of thinking into their decisions.

As I began to incorporate these two bookend enablers, I realized that the portfolio enablers echo the decision quality framework used by decision scientists. I didn't have to create a new science; it was right there in front of me. I just had to show how the frameworks meshed with each other. The appendix contains a more detailed description of these Decision Analysis (DA) and Decision Quality (DQ) issues.

In a nutshell, for those who do not want to go down that rabbit hole, high Decision Quality (DQ) is what we aim for with all our decisions, while Decision Analysis (DA) describes the tools and methods we use to achieve that end.

Frame and executive acceptance/commitment to action are two of the elements of both decision quality and the portfolio enablers. Three of the elements of DQ align easily with the portfolio enablers. The sixth DQ element, Creative and Possible Alternatives applies to both entity data and portfolio creation.

The appendix contains a more detailed description of these topics. In a nutshell, for those who do not want to go down that rabbit hole, high Decision Quality (DQ) is what we aim for with all our decisions, while Decision Analysis (DA) describes the tools and methods we use to achieve that end.

▸ Critical Success Factors and DQ

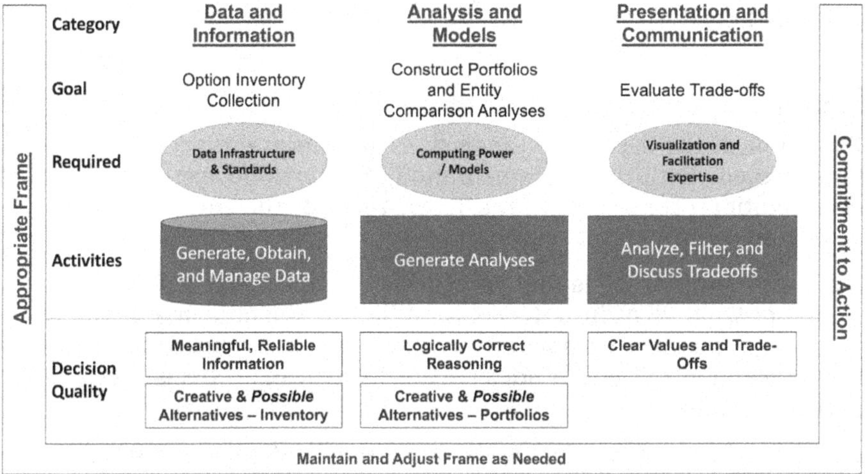

The three mechanical enablers for portfolio management must work in concert with Decision Quality in order to maximize the value of portfolio management.

The DQ framework contains six discrete elements to describe decision quality:

1. **Frame** – Understand the question we are trying to answer or the problem we're trying to solve.
2. **Meaningful, reliable data and information** – Gather factual data where possible and the best estimates from subject matter experts when facts are unavailable.
3. **Significantly distinct alternatives** – flesh out distinct potential decisions to choose between or to use to create a creative alternative hybrid path.
4. **Logical Thinking and Reasoning** – The mental or mathematical model containing the drivers of value. This shows us the consequences of our various alternatives.
5. **Values and tradeoffs** – There are always tradeoffs to consider—Short-term vs. long-term, risk-reward, and cost-revenue. Growth requires capital. How much of one are you willing to give up for another?
6. **Commitment to action** – Once you have achieved decision quality in the first five elements, are the decision-makers willing to commit the organization to a course of action informed by the analysis?

For material, complex, and high-consequence decisions, you should consider using formal approaches to attain and measure DQ.

The Society of Decision Professionals (SDP: https://www.decisionprofessionals.com) is a group for professionals and enthusiasts of DA and DQ.

Frame

The frame of the decision or analysis is an important piece that must precede both the implementation of a portfolio system and the operation of the system. It sets the tone for the entire analysis or system.

A primary tenet of DQ is that good decisions are measured by the quality of what went into the decision, not by the outcome. If you make high-quality decisions, your results will, on average, be better than if you don't. There is additional information on **Decision** Quality in the Appendix.

I imagine that most readers understand the fundamental analysis errors—false positive and false negative (types I and II errors, respectively). There is also a type III error. A common description for Type III errors is "asking the wrong question." Good framing may result in bad outcomes; poor framing may result in good outcomes. Good framing will never result in type III errors. Poor framing is the definition of type III errors.

Why does Frame get its own section? DQ is often pictured as a chain with six links, implying that each is as important as the other. I am breaking away from the DA dogma and elevating framing. I see the frame as more all-encompassing. If you get the frame wrong, the other five elements will suffer.

A poor frame can lead to:

1. Weak alternatives at both the entity and portfolio level.
2. Faulty model logic through overkill or over-generalizing.
3. Poor and incomplete data collection and standards.
4. Incomplete analysis for proper consideration of values and trade-offs.
5. Inability to drive commitment to action informed by the analysis. Action or inaction will happen based on the decision's circumstance and demands, but do not let it happen because of poor analysis and framing.
6. An analytical approach to the problem that is expensive or not complete enough to provide essential insights.

In other words, the frame is the "one ring" (to paraphrase Tolkien) that rules them all and [with transparency] binds them.

It may take time to get right, but failure in framing will significantly reduce the value realized from portfolio analysis.

The frame contains information that informs all other parts of the portfolio system or analysis. In creating a frame, the developers and analysts need to coordinate with portfolio subject matter experts, developers, and the managers and analysts who will be using and providing information and insights.

Elements of the frame include:

1. **Deadline** - When is the analysis due? This information will drive many other parts of the frame.
2. **Purpose** - What is the decision you are trying to make, the question you are trying to answer, the insight you hope to gain, or the problem you're trying to solve? Are we making a final decision that will be hard to reverse? Are the consequences of a mistake high or low? Bear in mind that even if it seems like there is just a question, (e.g., is it more expensive to grow with exploration or by acquisition), there is almost always an implied decision. "What is the decision?" is the mother of all framing questions.
3. **Decision Criteria** - How will we know a good decision when we see it? What criteria will be used to judge? What are we trying to accomplish as an organization? Is there a time component to the criteria? For example, there may be a five-year growth requirement, or a target set in the future (e.g., 1 million barrels per day 7 years from now).
4. **Stakeholder Analysis and Change Management** - This is especially important for the initial implementation of a portfolio system. Sharing information and changing certain decision rights, governance, and incentives are critical. Once implemented, the major stakeholder work will be with the execution teams.
5. **Values** - What are the measures we care about? What is the hierarchy of objectives? With a tool like an objectives hierarchy, you can understand the most important things you are trying to achieve—the Fundamental Objectives—and their drivers, the Means Objectives. (*Value Focused Thinking* by Ralph Keeney). Understanding these relationships will be especially important for optimization and interactions. Understanding values is critical, and it is a step that is often overlooked. The values help drive the structure of the analysis and required data. Values must align with the frame of the investigation. In the image below, Return on Capital, Cash Flow, and Corporate Continuity are Fundamental Objectives; the Means objectives below suggest the levers you can pull to achieve them. The top layer contains the fundamental objectives for the overall corporation and would be in scope for corporate-level decision-making.

▸ **Objectives Hierarchy**

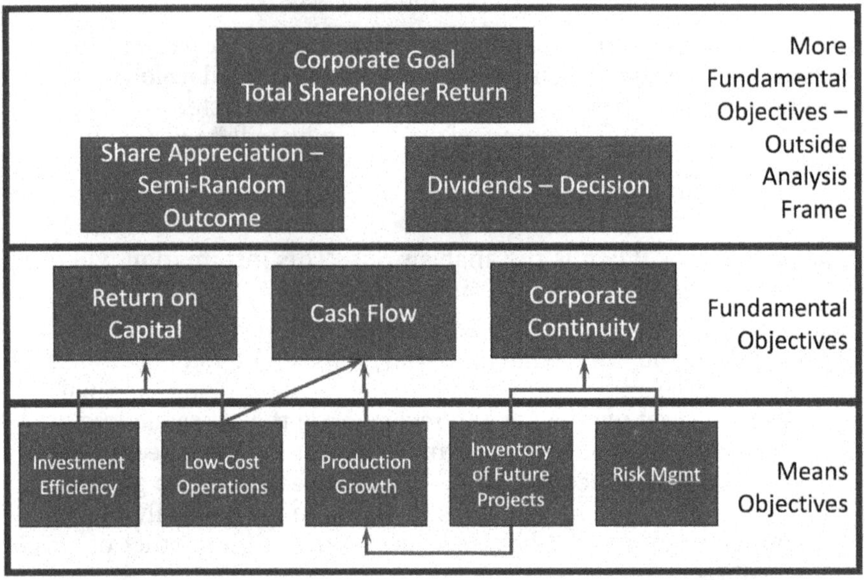

The level of the portfolio analysis informs the metrics of interest and whether they are truly fundamental to achieving the desired outcome. The tactical portfolio analysis example is driven by the means-objective components of the fundamental objectives of return on capital, cash flow, and corporate continuity.

6. **Working Inventory** - Which entities are in and out of the frame. Which ones may have different decisions, which are there only to provide context, and which decisions will be expressly excluded? Please note, it is a good analytical practice to test those exclusions. It may be that the given decisions or exclusions are not costly, but it is good to know.
7. **Entity Granularity** - What are the assets and parts of assets for which data will be collected, generated, and on which decisions will be made?
    a. **Entity Scope** - What is the complete set of entity data needed? Is this analysis global or local? Should unowned assets from Business Development be included?
    b. **Entity Optionality** - What potential decisions should be included in the analysis? What business logic and dependencies need to be structured into the models? What are the limits of possible decisions on the entities?
8. **Accounts** - What are the measures we care about? Are there essential sub-categories? These can be single-point metrics like NPV or time-series data like cash flow, capital expenditure, or human resources.

9. **Data Provenance** – Where will the data come from, and who will provide it?
10. **Timespan of inputs** – What is the length of time for which to collect data? Is this focused on the next budget, or is it a full asset-life analysis?
11. **Probability and Uncertainty** – How will we treat probability and uncertainty? Will results be deterministic, or is probability a critical attribute?
12. **Metadata** – What are the buckets or characteristics of the data for sorting and separate consideration? Metadata is particularly important when considering portfolio balance.
13. **Organizational Decision Process** – What will the process look like? Who makes the decisions?
14. **Visualizations** – How will visualizations be presented? Are the slides complete, or will additional interactions with leadership be necessary?
15. **Leader Interactions** – Will the leaders want to look at the raw data? How can you convince the leaders to appreciate the quality and consistency of the data? Will they want to participate in the portfolio generation, delegate that to the analysts, and then make final decisions?
16. **Output interfaces and accuracy** – What output from the portfolio process will be used to feed other processes? Can the outputs be directionally good and then require post-processing, or does the output from the portfolio tool need to reflect a high degree of rigor? (Be careful with this one.)
17. **Analytical Process** – Will this be standalone, comparison, simulation, optimization, or a combination? See this decision flowchart for further guidance on that.

The above list is reasonable for most portfolio problems. Stakeholder analysis and change management efforts are extremely important when implementing a portfolio practice, but generally less so when running a practice. Project and asset teams whose execution decisions are affected by portfolio efforts may have to work with stakeholders to effect those decisions.

Your initial frame should be updated as the analysis progresses. You will gain new information and insights that could render parts of the frame moot, or leaders sometimes have a change of heart about some elements.

Even with the best frame, outcomes may be poor. The goal is to ensure that the decisions are of high quality. Then trust the process and work to make good results a reality.

> **Key Takeaways**
> The frame will set the data processing, analysis, and decision foundation for the question or problem. As your analysis progresses, the frame will change. What starts as a simple standalone analysis may turn into a broader strategic analysis. That is normal. Early framing can help you anticipate these future changes. Failure to frame well will often lead to poor analysis, low data quality, and, unless you're lucky, bad outcomes.

Of Eagle's Beaks and Front-End Loading

In the distant past, projects were relatively simple. They required less planning and had fewer stakeholders to satisfy and barriers to push through. As the world became more complicated and interconnected, discipline in project management became critical. It was no longer enough to simply perform individual actions in isolation. Value was created by better sequencing and coordination of activities. Although it imposed costs, the discipline more than made up for those costs with better outcomes in project execution.

The gains from good project management were evident to the project world. Better control prevented untold losses from poor execution during the construction of ever more complex and challenging projects.

Companies became larger, projects had more partners, and competitive environments became even more difficult. In early 1964, Ronald A. Howard of Stanford University defined the profession of Decision Analysis (DA). DA, a derivative of Operations Research (OR), puts structure around the front end of project development or any other decision. DA, like project management, added some cost and delay to projects, but it quickly proved helpful, resulting in better-formulated projects. DA has evolved, and practitioners today think about delivering high decision quality (DQ) through effective decision analysis.

A common view of the distinction between the front-end DQ processes and project management is sometimes called the Eagle's Beak (or Seagull's Beak). When a project is identified, value is added in the early stages through framing, alternative generation, logical thinking, and value tradeoffs. This culminates in the preferred alternative being selected, at which time project management becomes key in preserving the identified value.

The Eagle's Beak

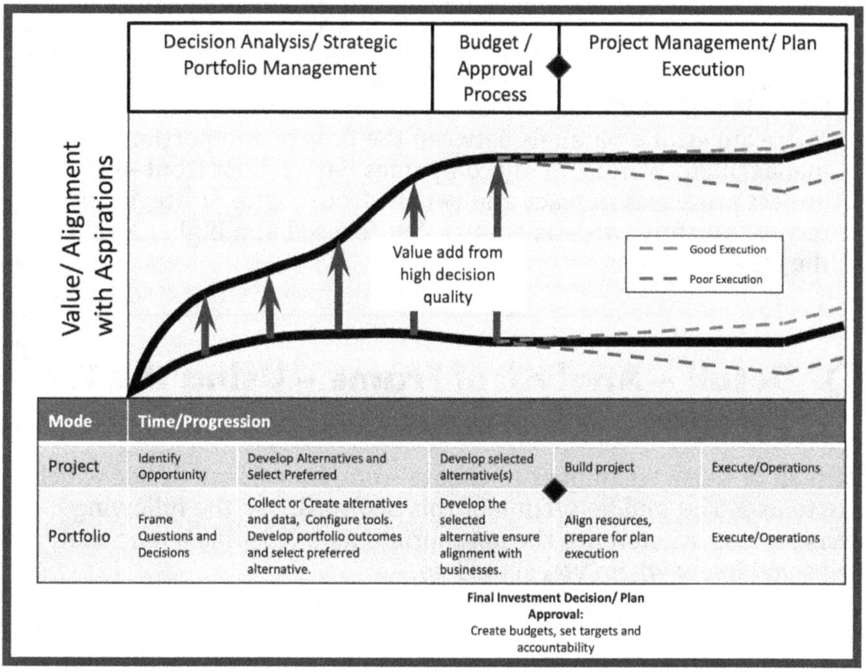

Good framing, data, logical thinking, and alternative selection are beneficial to project and other decisions. These elements are determined at the beginning of the project. Once decisions are made and the die is cast (the black diamond), there is little opportunity to capture additional upside. There is still plenty of opportunity to muck it up.

In the diagram, great execution will not save a poor project with little front-end loading, but defining the project well can overcome even subpar execution.

Bringing new front-end processes into an organization is difficult. When you already have a good, established front-end process, knowing what you would have done differently without the process is impossible—there is no counterfactual. Hindsight bias kicks in when projects go well, and **everyone** says, "that was the obvious right thing to do." The delay and personnel costs that these processes impart on a project are easy to measure. So, there is always an urge to do away with the hard-to-prove work.

Daniel Kahneman and Amos Tversky have demonstrated that humans are wired to emphasize prevention, regret, and fear of loss more than the capture of value. This is part of the reason that change is so hard.

Whereas project management and project portfolio management help prevent painful and very clear losses compared to our plans, DA and DQ help us align the project that comes into those management processes with corporate and leadership aspirations and values.

> **Key Takeaways**
> There are strong parallels between the project and portfolio management worlds. Many companies have robust front-end project processes in place and benefit from them. Strategic and tactical portfolio work is similar, but focused at a higher level in the organization.

Detail - Analytical Frame - Using the Tool Selector

With all of these techniques to choose from, how do we decide which one to use? The middle section of this book will use the following decision tree to reference the appropriate tool. It is like a map that helps you know where you should go.

To use it, start in the upper left and answer the questions.

1. Does management have an appetite for portfolio analysis (at least on this decision)?
2. Is there an inventory of assets and investment opportunities?
3. How urgent is this decision or question? Is there an existing model?

If the answer to any of those questions is no, it puts you onto the upper section of tools—**HIPPO** (Highest Paid Person's Opinion) and Chapter Three - **Standalone Analysis**. Standalone Analysis is critical in any case because it is the input source for all other portfolio techniques. I refer to the upper section techniques as implicit portfolio techniques because no explicit direct comparisons or interactions are considered. This is where many companies start.

If the answer to those three initial questions is yes, progress to the next question about **Data Availability**. We progress into the more extensive and varied part of the tree if your data is rich, granular, and has well-defined inputs such as fiscal terms and cost. Otherwise, we will examine simplified sparse data versions of those techniques.

▸ Portfolio Tool Selector

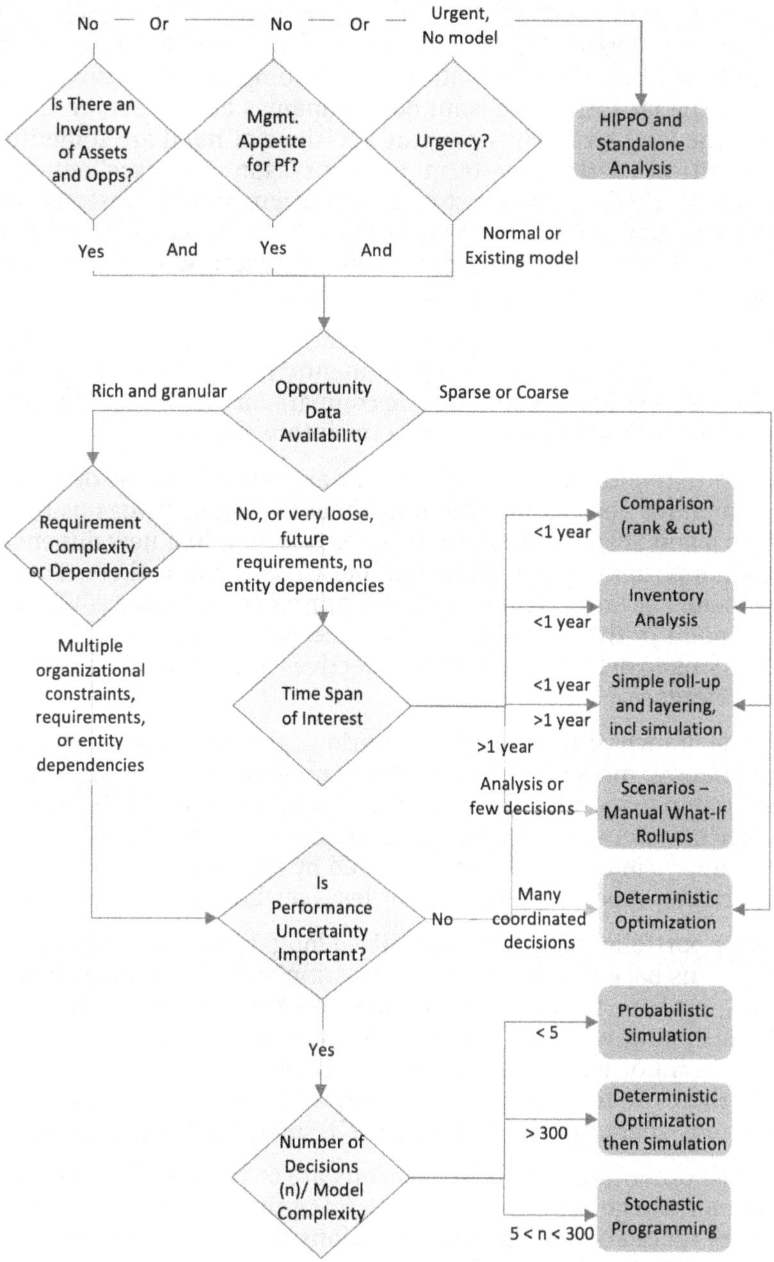

The best analytical tool for portfolio analysis depends on the context of the decision or question. The analysis should begin by addressing fundamental questions about process, culture, and data. The results that you reach using this selector will normally be a minimum tool. In many cases, you can use more advanced tools, especially if you already have them in place and have the time and autonomy to seek additional insights.

Let's first follow the Rich and Granular path. The next question is about the complexity of portfolio requirements. If the requirements are complex and extend far into the future, we would explore the further branch investigating the nature of that complexity. We always care about the far future; we want our companies and careers to thrive over the long term. However, the decisions at hand are sometimes less critical for the long-term. Budget season is an excellent example of this. If there are no strict future requirements or constraints (such as production growth five years in the future or long-term capital expenditures), we proceed to the next question: What is the time or focus of interest for this analysis?

Suppose it is short—less than one year. In that case, we can look at simple metrics like budget requirements, ratios of project performance (like NPV per barrel), and simple comparisons with other projects. This puts us into the Comparison and Inventory realm.

If future requirements beyond a year are relevant to the decisions at hand, we need to add the time dimension. This brings us to the Rollup and Scenario Analysis regime. Bringing in a new dimension is an important step and one familiar to decision-makers. They have all looked at long-term projections of production and cash flow. At this point in the portfolio decision tree, we are not generally altering decisions to achieve long-term objectives but rather showing them for reference.

A side branch of Rollups and Scenario analysis is Simulation. With simulation, instead of simply adding up our inventory, we aggregate the rollup using probabilistic or stochastic methods. This gives us a range of potential outcomes instead of a single answer. Simulation is not always understood or appreciated by decision-makers, but it can be critical, especially in riskier or less-certain parts of the business.

Using portfolio techniques to achieve long-term objectives and goals brings us back to the requirements complexity box where we answer, "Yes, we have future organizational constraints or requirements." At this point, we must also consider whether the uncertainty is significant or will be relevant in the decision-making process. If not, and there are few decisions to make, we have some overlap with a previous analysis type, and we revisit Rollup and Scenario Analysis.

On the other hand, if many decisions are to be made in a coordinated manner, we go into the Deterministic Optimization branch. This is where there are too many combinations of decisions to find an answer manually. Even large decision sets with complex requirements can be solved in seconds in this branch.

On the lower branches of the decision tree, we need to combine optimization with simulation, where performance uncertainty is a consideration.

Simulation alone can work only if there are only a few coordinated decisions. Otherwise, we look to Optimization with Simulation or Stochastic Optimization. This section can accommodate simple simulation models with a limited number of decisions, without the need for optimization. Optimization functionality is essential when there are more than a few decisions to coordinate.

Finally, working back up the tree to where our data is sparse or coarse, we get to Chapter Eleven - Sparse Data Techniques. These are similar to some of the other techniques already discussed, but with modifications to adapt to the sparse data.

Even if you find yourself on the lower branches of portfolio methods, you can and should use the methods in the upper portion. They are, at worst, interesting QC tools and can also assist with gaining comfort in your results and conclusions. They provide valuable and powerful views of asset attributes for stakeholders and decision-makers.

As a check, look at the result you get from the decision tree analysis in the context of the chart below. You're probably in good shape if you find yourself on a medium gray Good zone square. If Maybe, you might wish to reconsider. If it's a dark, Poor square, you should definitely reconsider.

Suitability of Analytical Method by Analysis Type

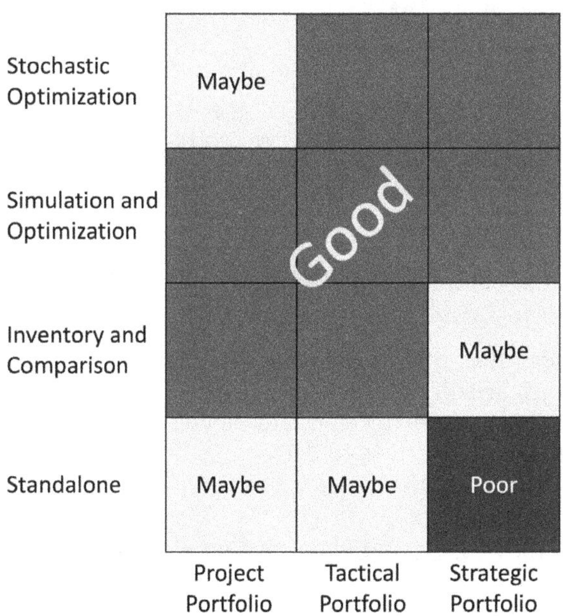

A very general view combining the level of portfolio work with suitability for portfolio analysis. You should aim to be in the good zone, but if that's not possible, the maybes are the next best option. Asset standalone analysis by itself is not suitable for strategic portfolio decisions.

I do not cover in detail multi-attribute scoring approaches like the Analytic Hierarchy Process, which combines many attributes into a single number that expresses the "goodness" of the decision. Like a cash flow model, this approach is essentially a way to do a standalone analysis. Once you have the scores for each of the entities, you can then use any of the portfolio methods to perform your portfolio analysis. I have seldom seen the standalone part done well with scoring approaches. Many nuances must be attended to, and it often requires highly skilled facilitation skills to get right. I generally do not recommend them for portfolio analysis, but they may have their place. Many people like the apparent simplicity and ease of understanding. While there is merit in these approaches, it is a complex field in itself, covered in detail in other places.

Key Takeaways

The selection of a tool or tools to be used for an analysis drives the quality of the analysis and the effort and data required. While no simple decision tree covers all possible permutations, this can get an analysis started in the right direction.

Detail – Fundamental and Means Objectives

Use Your Means Objectives to Create Different Approaches to Achieving Better Results

Means objectives are the levers you can pull by your decisions to drive better results.

Focus on Fundamental Objectives for Comparing Outcomes of Different Approaches

The fundamental objectives that define success and value are the best focus for the comparison of alternatives. When you generate alternatives, Fundamental Objectives should be your focus of evaluation. Using means-objectives to drive your decisions leads to sub-optimization and underperformance.

Means Objectives are Sometimes Fundamental Objectives Too

Capital expenditure is a means of achieving growth and sustainability for your business. It is necessary. At the same time, financial analysts judge corporations harshly for excessive expenditure. So even though an objectives hierarchy shows capital as a means to achieve better corporate results in the long run, subjectively, it can negatively impact share value in the short run.

When using capital as a lever, you may find that spending more gives you "objectively" superior outcomes. However, if "the market" believes that the expenditure is too high, then all of those outcomes will be for nothing. It is both a means and a fundamental objective for achieving corporate performance, but in different timeframes. You ignore it at your peril.

Finding Your Means and Fundamental Objectives

When you list your objectives, you can ask some standard questions about them. If you want to move upwards towards more fundamental objectives, you can ask questions like "What result does that drive?" or "Why is that important?"

To move downwards to means-objectives, ask "What elements can drive this metric in the right direction?" and "What factors can drive those elements?"

> **Key Takeaways**
>
> Select your metrics with care. Focus on the Fundamental Objectives, but don't ignore the enabling ones when they are used to assess your performance. Spend time understanding what you are trying to achieve and the means to get there.

Meaningful, Reliable Data and Information (Data)

Data is (are) Important

Many consider data to be the weak point of most portfolio analyses. There are always questions about accuracy, precision, comparability, noise, and predictability; we all know the expression garbage in-garbage out. They're good questions and raise valid concerns.

The key as an analyst is to understand the flaws and limitations of the data and to do our best to communicate the limitations of the data to answer the question at hand or provide insight into the decision to be made. I'll talk about several dimensions: data standards, data accuracy, decision-maker buy-in, and data storage and organization.

Data Standards

Before launching into a discussion of data needs and quality, the reader should have a basic understanding of the principles of finance and economics. Some essential basics are covered in the Appendix in the section entitled "Financial and Economic Concepts."

Data is one of the most disputed issues in portfolio analysis and management, probably not for the reasons you think though. Many complain that data is not of high enough quality, so we should not do portfolio analysis at all. We should just move forward with our usual decision processes.

But if data is not good enough for portfolio decisions, why would **anyone** think it is good enough for a standalone decision? The main difference between portfolio and standalone analysis is that portfolio analysis puts your data into an organizational context. In fact, with most portfolio work, you're looking for trends and exploring boundaries of performance at a rolled-up or aggregated level. Data quality is even less of an issue in portfolio analysis than it is with standalone work. This is especially true if you use simulation in your analysis. Consistency and standards in the working set of a portfolio analysis become the drivers of high-quality portfolio analysis, not absolute accuracy.

Principles of Data Standards and Acquisition

1. Use what you have at the start. We always have more information than we think.
2. Be aware of the ability of the data to answer the question being posed. For example, if your output requirement includes a probabilistic assessment of a measure, such as the probability of loss, you also need probabilistic inputs.
3. Data standards are critical. If your decision team does not trust that all data is at least consistent, it will undermine the effort.
4. Understand the costs and benefits of better data before paying for it. The accuracy and precision of the data is always contentious. For strategic portfolio work, you mostly care about relative values; decimal point precision does not add value. As the strategic planning process transitions to a tactical plan and budget, better short-term accuracy and precision may be required.
5. The granularity of the model needs to align with decision rights, a firm's preferences, and the questions being asked.
6. Alternatives within the working set of entities are needed and are an ultimate source of value from portfolio management. If there are no alternatives at a project or asset level, there are no portfolio alternatives.
7. There is magic in rolling up many entities. Minor errors in data tend to cancel. Strategic portfolio work is done for portfolio-level insights, not necessarily for specific project actions.

Data is important, but it is just one aspect of portfolio work. A tremendous amount of insight can be gleaned from limited and marginal quality data. Most important is that data be developed using consistent inputs and standards, be mathematically logical, and pass basic good sense tests.

"Here is a short list of the information that you will not find in data.

1. "Strategic Intent,
2. "Goals and Objectives, and
3. "Preferences and Tradeoffs."

(Credit: Rob Brown)

These must be determined by adequate framing, analysis, and leadership discussion.

In organizations that do not have a portfolio culture, data from the planning process is often used in the initial attempts at portfolio management. That's a good start and helps to understand the general issues.

There are some limitations to this approach. First, the granularity of such data is often relatively coarse. For example, it might be at a country level and offer no view into individual projects or programs. Second, even when the data are at a finer granularity, frequently fixed costs, such as corporate charges, are included in one or some of the templates. This is fine for planning and accountability, but it is not optimal for portfolio work.

In addition, since it is often used for accountability, planning data may be a negotiated value with lots of baggage rather than a statistically valid expected value.

If you **can** specify the form of the portfolio inputs, the following is a good set of standards.

1. Data should be on a statistically expected value (EV) success case basis with the probability of happening as a separate item.
    a. If range or probability data is important, available, or practical to collect, it may be helpful later.
2. Detail should be at the level of decision granularity. This will vary by industry and company. It is essential that assets over which the company has a significant amount of control are represented.
3. Best efforts (sometimes called unconstrained) basis is a valuable perspective for projects in a portfolio. This shows what the project would look like if significant constraints were removed. Often the basis for planning is more "realistic," incorporating certain decisions that have not yet been made, such as personnel or budget.
4. It is best if each piece is represented on a marginal basis. An excellent way to think about it is that if you removed the entity from a summation of all the elements of a corporation (a

"rollup"), the rollup would still be an accurate representation. This implies that allocations like corporate overhead, which would not go away if the asset went away, should be captured in a separate, fixed entity. Why separate overhead from the projects and assets? Why can't we just allocate it? Shouldn't an asset have to pay its own way? That is a sound bite interfering with good DQ. Often this is minor; for some assets, it is significant.

5. Data standards for asset or project alternatives in a portfolio context should be consistent across the portfolio. Input assumptions such as pricing, demand, and external scenarios should be the same, unless there is a genuine exception, such as contract terms.
6. Use real or constant dollars for portfolio analysis instead of nominal. Most budgets are prepared on a nominal or dollar-of-the-day basis. That is, the expenditure and revenue streams contain assumed inflation or escalation. This generally works well for rollups of short-term data, but comparisons of longer-term assets and investments can be distorted. Even though decision-makers sometimes believe they are calibrated to an inflation and discount rate, compounding interest can be tricky and difficult to compare.
7. "Accuracy" of the data can be an issue. Too many things can happen for it to be otherwise except by luck. However, the data must represent the point of view of the future shared by the enterprise's leadership.

The initial "preferred alternative" is the one the business unit has brought forward on a planning basis. It commonly represents an alternative that the business believes can be done with existing people and processes without significant risk. As the analysis progresses, you may find that other asset options yield superior results for the enterprise.

Depending on the purpose of the portfolio analysis and the tools used, you must consider how best to create or collect project or asset alternatives.

Data Accuracy

The data quality continuum below is a reality check on your data.

Reading from left to right, the fiscal regime and the gross resource distribution in place are the most reliable pieces of information you have (for upstream hydrocarbon analysis). I was criticized once because I was told that gross resources are unreliable. They were right, of course, but the point is that EVERYTHING else (except external assumptions) is driven by or derived from that data—everything.

▸ **Data Reliability and Derivatives**

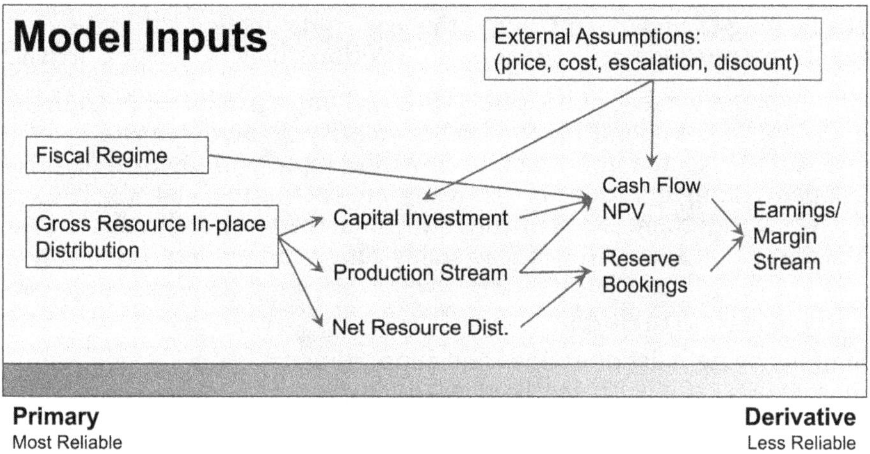

Cash flow, earnings, and reserves—considered fundamental objectives for many studies—rely on multiple inputs with a chain of assumptions. The arrows show the derivations. The fiscal and regulatory regime at the field and its gross resource in place distribution (left) are the most reliable inputs to a typical upstream petroleum project.

Your production profiles, capital investment, cash flow, and earnings are driven by gross resource in place and the historically wildly inaccurate external price and cost assumptions.

All the inputs and outputs in your entity models are subject to tremendous uncertainties. The outputs seldom create an accurate forecast. But they are the best ones you have. Consistency is more important than perfection for most portfolio work, especially strategic portfolio analysis.

General production and capital investment patterns by asset class (deep water, heavy oil, unconventional) are typically the most relevant drivers of portfolio solutions. If the numbers are internally consistent, use the same external assumptions, and are reasonably representative of reality, much can be done, even deterministically. If you capture uncertainty information, probabilistic methods can also provide better and additional insights.

Decision-Maker Buy In

This is a non-technical issue and so, of course, is frequently overlooked. For a leadership or decision-making body to make a group decision, it needs to be confident that the data is representative enough for the decisions at hand. This is an issue because of culture, biases in data standards and collection, and real or perceived incentives.

It is a good practice to get all the data in front of the decision body before much additional analysis happens. The analysis can be challenging to understand, and if the leaders do not agree that the inputs are representative, your portfolio efforts may be dead on arrival.

Unit managers may be unfamiliar with and unprepared to defend their own data. If they don't believe in the integrity of their own analyses, you're done, so at a minimum, review their input with them and ask penetrating questions before using the data in the analysis. In a perfect world, there is a step where the managers see each other's data and agree that everything is reasonably consistent and representative.

Entity Alternatives

Simply having a list of entities and supporting data is not enough to manage a portfolio. The entities on which decisions are being made in your working inventory need to have some form of flexibility defined. Management implies the ability to do something—to guide changes in decisions and actions. Understanding the possible choices that can be made for an entity is crucial to adding value through portfolio analysis.

Some alternatives could include the following:

1. Should we do the project or not?
2. Should we do a minimal development, a phased development, or a single large development?
3. Should we accelerate development by putting more people and money into it, or is a more measured approach appropriate?
4. Should we sell that asset or partial working interest?
5. Should we buy that other asset or partial working interest?
6. Should we continue to stem the production decline of an aging asset, spend more money to increase and maximize extraction, or abandon it?

Data Storage and Organization

Microsoft Excel can do much of the data management needed if your needs are modest. It can be used as a database, it can slice and dice, it can do graphics, and it contains a good calculation engine. In addition, with a few add-ins, you can perform sophisticated analysis such as Monte Carlo simulation or optimization.

However, Excel has limits for data storage. At some point, the internal logic of a spreadsheet can get so large, and the effort required to manage hundreds of linked spreadsheets across a network can get so time-consuming that you spend all your time and energy trying to manage data—and still fail.

Welcome to Excel Hell.

When a company descends into "Excel Hell," something must be done to help with data management.

Database Solutions

There are many commercial relational databases available. Microsoft Access is one that most people already have on their computers. In addition, some companies will happily sell you an off-the-shelf solution specifically for your industry. The data science boom has opened up new horizons in data management. There are many possible and reasonable solutions depending on your specific circumstances.

An especially useful database structure is a subset of relational databases called OLAP. Some people call these data warehouses, and they have been around since the mid-90s. An OLAP database or 'cube' can be designed to handle many or most of the needs for portfolio management and analysis, planning, and budgeting.

OLAP is an acronym that stands for **O**n**L**ine **A**nalytical **P**rocessing. It is a type of database that stores data in a multi-dimensional grid or virtual space. It allows for defining hierarchies in each dimension and pre-calculates values along the hierarchies against all dimensions to make reporting very fast.

The main dimensions that virtually all OLAP databases use are category, entity, account, and time. Additional dimensions can be added as needed.

1. Category is a marker for the provenance of the data. It could be strategic plan data; it could be budget; it could be active/evergreen, or even historical. This allows comparison between different complete data sets, such as actual results, last year's plan cycle, and this year's plan cycle.
2. Entity is the organizational structure. It would typically comprise multiple business units reporting to the overall company level. Then, each business unit would have numerous assets and regions. Additional levels of granularity can be included for important subtotals.
3. Account includes all the things we measure, such as revenue, expense, capital spending, and production, as well as all their subtotals. Like the entity dimension, it allows for important subtotals and any level of detail.
4. Time is where values are put in their proper place in time. Like other dimensions, it can be specified as a hierarchy. Month, quarter, and year are typically defined.

Some OLAP products allow for multiple hierarchies. This can be useful when individual entities must be looked at from different perspectives.

Example Entity Hierarchies

1. Company
    a. Corporate overhead
    b. Corporate business development
    c. Business Unit 1
        i. Asset 1
            1. Producing business 1
            2. Project 1
            3. Project 2
        ii. Asset 2
            1. Producing business 2
    d. Business Unit 2
        i. Asset 3
            1. Producing business 3
            2. Project 3

A classic business entity hierarchy.

Alternate Hierarchy within the same dimension (this perspective could also be its own dimension)

1. Company
    a. Producing businesses
        i. Producing business 1
        ii. Producing business 2
        iii. Producing business 3
    b. Projects
        i. Project 1
        ii. Project 2
        iii. Project 3

A hierarchy with asset maturity is often useful. If it is an alternate hierarchy in the Entity dimension, it has more limitations than as a separate dimension. For example, looking at Asset1 with the two maturities broken out as individual pieces would be difficult.

Other dimensions in an OLAP database can be used for other purposes, such as categorizing entities by maturity level. Most commercial OLAP databases can keep track of ten or more dimensions.

OLAP cubes built on row-based relational databases were an excellent solution in the 1990s and may have reached their peak. New data models such as columnar databases are emerging and can provide functionality like OLAP, but more efficiently. Even better models will undoubtedly be developed. These new models are well beyond the scope of this book.

Interfaces – Data and Model Integration

Storing input data is essential; moving data to and from models into analysis tools, and for visual representation, analysis, and discussion is necessary too. When designing the system and data storage, you must consider whether to use a single platform for everything or whether to use multiple tools for the different parts of the system. Fully integrated systems with project economics and portfolio tools all in one place can be convenient. The main advantage is the ease of integrating the system and the seamless sharing of information. The main disadvantage, aside from the potentially high price, is that, similar to a Swiss army knife, it has many tools, but none of them are exceptional on their own.

Key Takeaways

Data is always a contentious issue. It never seems "good enough." But if data is not good enough for portfolio work, it's not good enough for standalone decisions. Although your data will never be accurate enough to satisfy everyone, the more important goal is for the data to be on the same basis and to get agreement from decision-makers that such is the case.

Some people are hesitant to start their portfolio journey because they believe that without standards in place, there is no point in going further. This line of reasoning is flawed for a few reasons. First, decisions will be made based on the existing data. Putting that data into a portfolio context does not change the data or that decisions will be made, it just provides a basis for comparison. It might create the motivation to develop standards to ensure apples-to-apples comparison. Second, in most cases, you have more data than you think. Order of magnitude estimates are not perfect, but they are better than nothing. Moving in the right direction improves your decisions; better accuracy and precision can come later.

When managing data becomes too much for Excel, better tools should be implemented. OLAP is a proven solution for structuring data and may be a good conceptual starting place when considering an upgrade.

War Story – Time Horizon of Your Data

One question that often arises is what time horizon to use for planning and strategic work. When one company developed its upstream planning system, there was much discussion about this matter. Previously, the business plan was for three years, and the strategic plan had a five-year horizon. The planning team was in the final stages of the database design and development.

But the company was shifting to a more strategic view of the business, tying reserves and resources into its thinking and planning. Oil fields can have decades-long lifecycles, so five years was inadequate for a strategic plan. The database development team proposed a fifty-year horizon for the planning system on the assumption that anything beyond fifty years was effectively discounted to zero anyway.

There was pushback from some of the business unit planners.

"Everything beyond a few years is just guesswork anyway."

They were right, of course, which was the actual point. The planners had previously given the corporate planners five years of data, with a large NPV in the fifth year, to represent the future cash flows. Those NPVs were derived from a cash flow model, which incorporated corporate assumptions. That model existed on someone's hard drive. They had projections; however, they were not comfortable sharing them.

"We have not developed full-field lifecycle plans."

Everyone understands that there is uncertainty on prices, technology, and commercial terms, but again, a resource company can only produce the resource to which it has access. The company needs to know the plans for the remaining resources in each of its fields and have an idea of how likely the development is. Long-term continuity requires continuous replacement of resources. If they do not have full-field plans, they should.

The database was built to allow up to forty years of input data. In any planning exercise, there is a time horizon of concern. Decisions are always about what we will do today. To determine resource replacement needs through exploration and business development efforts, it is essential to have an approximate view of what will happen in the future 10–20 years from now. Having the long-term context is strategically critical.

Lessons Learned

1. The people managing assets should have at least an approximate or notional view of what the far future holds.
2. Some of the business units were hyperfocused on the near term, with little thought about the longer term. Forcing their focus to the longer timeframe helped them understand their assets and development alternatives better.
3. Business units, with good reason, were concerned that headquarters analysts might misuse their data. Mistrust of headquarters personnel can be a real and destructive force. This is exacerbated when working-level headquarters people do not have an opportunity to go to business units to meet, present, and discuss the standards and concepts being implemented. Developing trust and transparency is essential.

Detail – Ethics in Analysis

At some level, there must be an assumption that the data is objective, fair, and diligently modeled. This is not always the case. This book outlines some ways to adjust for biases and the ultimate fidelity of your data and models, but it would be better to have good data at the start.

Many professions have codes of ethics governing acceptable behaviors and encouraging giving back to the professional community. Finance and engineering societies have generally accepted principles and codes of conduct guiding practitioners towards proper behaviors and standards. As of this writing, there is no generally accepted code for analysts, planners, and portfolio practitioners.

Economic and portfolio analysts have access to decision-makers whose decisions are at least partially informed by economics. But there are complications.

Sometimes decision-makers believe that it is more important to push a project through than to do what is objectively best for the company. Self-interest and distortions in company culture often drive these behaviors. It is not unheard of for people in such positions to pressure analysts to alter the economics to make the investment look better than it is.

It seems innocuous at first. They might ask for a sensitivity case, e.g., "What happens if we can cut investment by 10%?"—a valid and reasonable request. It loses its validity when they say it is the new base case for approval without measures to effect the change.

Be careful. If you are asked to do this, do your best to resist and stick to the principles of appropriate and objective analysis.

In 2020, Chevron developed a Code of Ethics for Decision Analysts. It contained statements about following corporate behavior standards and service to our internal clients and the corporation. It encouraged accepting feedback, giving back to the function, and knowing our limitations. It mandates knowing the limits of knowledge gained from the data, providing a balanced, complete, and objective view (not simply advocating), and what to do when there are deviations.

A professional ethics code will not solve all potential problems, but it can help raise awareness and provide documentation and support if something is out of line. As with engineering, finance, and other professional codes, it can help prevent abuses and distortions in decision-making, thereby protecting corporate value.

See the Appendix for a sample version of an analyst code of ethics.

Significantly Distinct Alternatives (Entity and Portfolio Alternatives or Options)

Alternatives in a portfolio practice exist at two levels: entity and portfolio candidate sets.

Entity alternatives are the input to a model. They represent decisions we can make with the entity and are the base elements we combine to create a calculated or simulated portfolio outcome. These were covered in the Data section.

Portfolio alternatives are to explore the envelope of possibilities across our metrics and strategic targets of concern at the rolled-up enterprise level.

You can think of alternatives, like a menu at a restaurant. You can't have everything on the menu, so you might limit your choices to one or two items in each category. You can have that filet with green beans or that pork chop dish with garlic mashed potatoes. You then pick one. Maybe you chose the filet dish because, at that moment, it made your mouth water.

But there is another possibility. How about a hybrid where you substitute garlic mashed potatoes for green beans? Now you get the filet with the yummy mashed potatoes.

As your project teams generate entity alternatives, they should bear in mind that the wider the diversity of options they can provide, the higher the probability that their project will be funded. These alternatives, in turn, help drive improved portfolio outcomes that were unknown and are entirely unforeseen.

Portfolio alternatives, in turn, are best generated by the portfolio team, which works with enterprise leadership to frame and clarify **their** values and trade-offs. Next, we will cover the models that help create those alternative futures.

Portfolio-level alternatives are particularly relevant in the bottom half of the portfolio methods selector tool. Anything below rollups, in which the enterprise total results are a focus, must have portfolio alternatives.

Logical Thinking and Reasoning (Computing and Models)

Most of this section addresses models that are more sophisticated and complex than the simple conceptual models used in comparison. It applies mainly to quantitative portfolio models used in the Interactions techniques as well as many standalone analysis models.

High Powered Computing, Storage, and Communication Infrastructure

The large amount of data required to perform portfolio analysis implies robust digital systems. The effort to generate, control, and maintain big data is tremendous. Inefficient data retrieval, slow network speeds, and insufficient computer power for analyses can place immense stress on participants, cause errors, and prevent those involved from having time to understand the results.

Thankfully, high-performance computers and networks have become ubiquitous over the last several decades. We'll talk much more about data storage in a later section. For now, let's discuss models.

We all have models embedded in our brains and processes. Economists use supply and demand, petroleum engineers have reservoir models, and finance folks use the Capital Asset Pricing Model (CAPM) as a model for value. When we buy our kid a present, we have a mental model that says she will react with joy. Each of these models attempts to distill the most important aspects of reality in order to gain insight. Opportunity economic models are no different.

Model, Working Definition: A model is a representation of a thing or process that the model-builder hopes will accurately reflect essential aspects of reality. Usually, we speak of computer models, but they can also be mental models.

When you build a model to understand your portfolio, you should not consider it a prediction. Instead, consider it a tool to understand and model alternative outcomes to shape your organization's performance.

Portfolio models, especially strategic models, should reflect fiscal and physical processes in the business. They should be broadly accurate for the intended use. Precision can wait for later steps.

Strategic Portfolio Alternatives

Our strategic portfolio models aim to create meaningfully different portfolio-level alternatives, i.e., coordinated sets of decisions that deliver different results and consequences. Once we have *project-level* options, as discussed in the Data section, we need to combine those alternatives into different strategic themes.

Key Principles of Models

1. Strategic models do not give "the answer." They mainly help an enterprise test the limits of its performance and the tradeoffs between enterprise goals.
2. Any reasonable, internally consistent model is sufficient. Strategic analysis should focus more on the synthesized results and less on the decisions that lead to the results.
3. The granularity of your model is important. Granularity can be measured in multiple ways. The entities being considered, time granularity (annual, monthly), measure/account granularity (total revenue vs oil and gas revenue).
4. The model(s) must be able to generate appropriate outputs for consideration.
5. Precision vs. Accuracy is an issue. Models should be accurate enough to generate useful insights. If more accuracy or precision can be built without affecting the effort to build it or the model's speed, that's great. It's often not the case.

Finding the right balance between the speed and accuracy of a model is a challenge. Suppose you want to consider the impact of delaying a project. There are several ways to handle it.

a. Shift the project in time. All numbers simply shift to a new and later time without adjustment.
b. Shift the project and add carrying costs for vacated years.
c. Shift the project, add carrying costs, and multiply costs and revenues by the time-specific inflation and escalation factors.
d. Generate multiple realistic cases and make them mutually exclusive in your portfolio model.

Clearly, d) above is the most accurate representation of shifting projects; it also represents the highest amount of work for project teams. They will have to generate carrying costs and run the project through economic models. It is costly and takes time. It takes the calculations out of the portfolio model and puts them on individual economic models.

Method a) is the easiest for a model to handle. It is not precise, but if the project costs are much higher than the carrying costs, as is often the case, it's close enough for most strategic work. Method b) is straightforward to model and is an unnecessary detail in many cases. If that level of accuracy is required, you may need to move to c) or d).

Method c) may be a simple addition to a model if it's only for the primary inputs. The challenge is modeling the fiscal effects of escalation and inflation. Increasing revenues and costs will have an impact on earnings and cash flows when run through a tax regime. Often the results are not linear and can be complex. These details in a model can slow it to a crawl if precision is essential in your portfolio model.

"Generally, past some point of diminishing returns, adding features creates opportunities for modeling errors, heightens the need to simplify a model's mathematics, requires additional information, thus exposing a model to additional bias and noise, while providing pathways that propagate errors through the model to the objectives."

Gary J. Summers, Ph.D., Friction and Decision Rules in Portfolio Decision Analysis

Before adding more complexity with a new feature, ask yourself whether it will add clarity to the discussion of portfolios or whether it is more likely to add false precision.

Fiscal Systems

Tax and regulatory regimes are essential determinants of both risk and reward. Many industries simply follow standard local and national tax codes. Oil companies, however, often have an additional or separate layer specifically designed for resource industries. The structures can have infinite variety, and that's before bringing in the complexity of international taxation and financial structures. It is a topic all by itself. For this book, we will assume that fiscal, regulatory, and tax impacts are appropriately modeled.

Model Platforms

Excel is an excellent first step. For many, it is also the last step. Excel and other spreadsheet models have enormous capability, especially with robust, specialized add-in programs. In addition, there is a vast user base of people comfortable with the tools.

Other platforms to consider include:

1. Lumina Analytica - a visual, highly capable computing platform
2. Industry-specific platforms - Quorum Aucerna, Schlumberger Merak
3. General-purpose portfolio platforms - Planview, SmartOrg
4. Procedural language for analysis like R, Python, or Julia.
5. Hybrid systems that use multiple platforms for input, processing, and output.

In selecting a platform, there are trade-offs between speed, cost, training, transparency, maintainability, capacity, interfaces, and capability.

Key Takeaways

Computing tools and models are essential components in portfolio analysis. Computers greatly aid in the creation of alternative strategies and in creating meaningful insights from a set of decisions. Always treat models as relative indicators of your important measures and not as good forecasts. The purpose of portfolio management is to inform great decisions, not to make great forecasts.

Detour – AI Will Solve It All, So Why Bother

The principles outlined in this book transcend technology. The most powerful and well-organized computer and data system imaginable does no good if it answers the wrong question or if leadership ignores the insights.

As I write this, artificial intelligence and machine learning are getting a lot of press. Large language models like ChatGPT are all the rage. I do not claim expertise in the field. I can say that framing a problem and the local knowledge required to develop the logic to make models give credible answers are not AI issues. They are the inside, private information about the drivers of the business relationships involved. I see tremendous possibilities in using AI to improve the data inputs on investments, especially with regard to timing completion and cost. If AI systems can be trained on projects similar enough to the new ones, AI can be a neutral arbiter free of organizational and human biases.

AI technologies may improve modelers' productivity and lead to natural language interfaces for analytical tools. Those would be great additions. Getting there will require checking that the algorithms and models perform as expected. Obviously, there are numerous other possibilities for machine learning and AI in fields outside portfolio analysis. Undoubtedly, someone will come up with better optimization algorithms and data-driven models that forecast much more accurately than we can today. These will improve data flow, model accuracy, and model precision. That still leaves us with the issue of framing the problem we're trying to solve. There may come a day when our systems will control everything, and corporate leaders will relinquish their authority (and pay packages) to machines. Until then, the principles in this book will still be valid for portfolio management.

Detour – Model Errors – Red Alert!

When a model's result is used to inform important decisions, there **must** be a step to look for and correct errors. This holds true for both portfolio and standalone models. If the model seems correct only because the answer looks right, then why build it in the first place?

Important models must be checked in detail. Sorry, it's a fact. You should allow time and resources to do this.

Any model that is more than trivial almost certainly has errors and potential issues. They can be typos, named ranges that miss cells, improperly copied formulas, hard-coded values in the middle of a group of formulas, or a logic or math error. It can even be seemingly innocuous, such as hard-coded numbers that are assumptions embedded in formulas or having model inputs in multiple places. Some of the issues may be potential issues that do not cause problems except under specific circumstances. Trust me; those circumstances will occur.

The ubiquity of spreadsheet platforms, the wide diversity of user skills, and different programming styles and standards make spreadsheets especially prone to error.

Several commercial tools help detect and repair mechanical and reference errors in spreadsheets, but logic errors are often difficult to find. It is a good idea to run these tools during and after the development of a model or to have disinterested analysts review the model for both logic and structure.

The Actuarial Standards Board (ASB) has a set of standards (http://www.actuarialstandardsboard.org/asops/modeling-3) related to modeling, including documentation of the intended purpose, dealing with data and models provided by other parties, and evaluation of model risk. Following these guidelines is an excellent start.

Model errors can cost millions or billions in expenses or lost revenue. Spending time and effort to ensure high-quality models is well worth the effort. Simply holding people "accountable" after the fact does not prevent harm.

Detail – Precision vs Accuracy

As used in this book, precision and accuracy are two separate and independent characteristics of models and data.

Precision, as I use it here, means that a model is complete and internally consistent.

Accuracy means that it gives an unbiased "correct" answer with uncertain estimates (if any) centered around the actual result.

▸ **Accuracy vs. Precision**

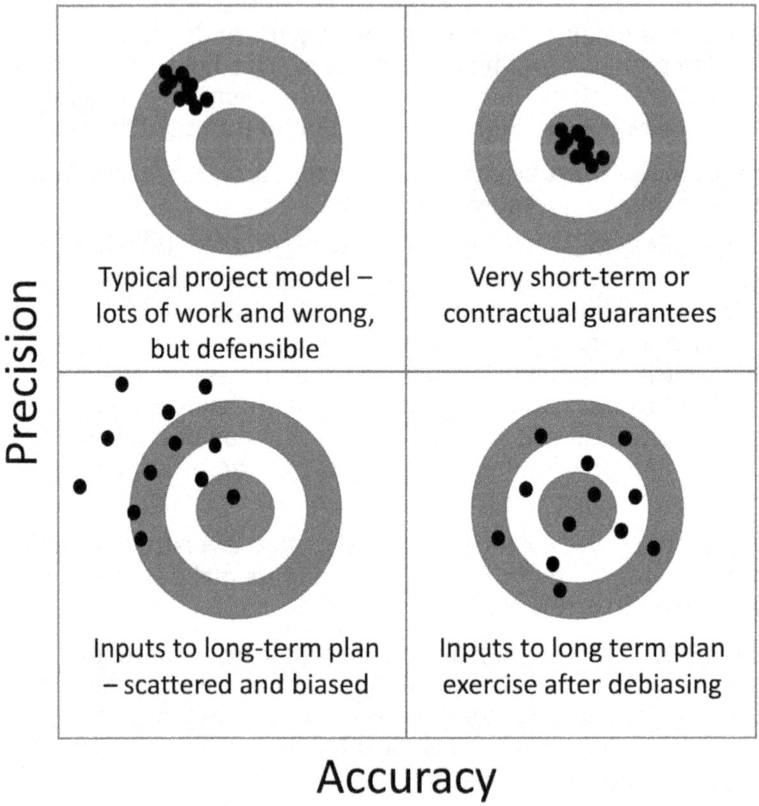

Precision and accuracy apply equally to models and input data. For much tactical prioritization work, models will fall in the lower left—neither accurate nor precise—but as long as standards are applied, they will be sufficient. The best you can generally hope for and work towards is the lower right, where you can get in the right general zone and express outcomes as ranges.

Precise But Inaccurate (Upper left)

I'll start with a precise but inaccurate model (upper left quadrant on the graphic). In the world of economic analysis, this is the norm. It is the world of business plans, budgets, and final investment decisions (FID). Analysts work tirelessly to ensure that the model is correctly programmed. They ensure that no stone is left unturned. There are multiple factors for cost and revenue escalation and reduction, and all tax consequences are considered. The timing of tax payments is carefully vetted, and the model is run on a monthly or quarterly basis to ensure that discount rates are appropriately applied. Precision in models is difficult and costly to achieve and maintain, and the models may be slow to run depending on the nature of the complexity.

This sounds wonderful until we realize that all corporations have poor track records of accuracy on price, inflation, cost, and timing inputs. Even the selection of the best discount rate to use has some uncertainty. So, while the model is credible, internally consistent, vetted, and complete, the answers are incorrect as *forecasts* due to flawed inputs.

This is not an unusual space for input data in the portfolio model. It has flawed inputs and a high cost to build and run. On top of that, if the biases are consistent across assets and projects, the rolled-up result will be wildly biased. Data in this quadrant is not too bad, because even though the results are biased, they are consistently biased, and there's hope to be able to differentiate and compare projects and portfolios. Do not believe that this quadrant will result in a good forecast.

Accurate and Precise (Upper Right)

This is mostly a unicorn. Accuracy and precision can overlap in a few circumstances, for example, very short-term projections or hedged positions. There is less uncertainty in the short term (weeks), so you **might** be accurate and precise in those cases. Short-term models are of limited usefulness for most strategic and tactical portfolio work, so this category has little relevance. It might be relevant for project portfolio management.

Inaccurate and Imprecise (Lower Left)

This is a relevant category for portfolio work because it is a common data type for strategic portfolio analysis and in sparse data scenarios. Inputs often come from other processes, e.g., budget and approval, where results carry incentives and other biases. Sometimes this data comes from third-party services that estimate costs and reservoir properties based on published results and intelligence.

The biases can be based on the project team's perceived incentives or sometimes deliberately induced distortions. For example, the near-term product price for budgeting may not be a forecast but may be shifted downwards to create barriers for sub-par projects or to test cash needs. Early-phase efforts, like oil exploration before the main discovery, and drug discovery and testing, will most likely fall into this quadrant.

Sometimes you will not have the means or basis to de-bias the models and shift them into the Accurate but Imprecise category. In that case, the analyst's challenge is to find consistent data elements and use those elements for comparison and input. This puts limitations on the conclusions that can be drawn from the analysis. It will be suitable for relative, but not for absolute decisions.

Portfolio analysts need to be careful not to over-interpret these inaccurate and imprecise models, but they are still helpful for strategic and tactical portfolio analyses. In later sections of the book, I also introduce the concept of post-processing of portfolio results. In that case, once you have used portfolio analysis to make significant relative decisions, data can be transferred into more precise, accurate, and more complex models to generate standardized outputs.

For portfolio work in this quadrant to be valid, the entities involved in creating the model must have been generated using consistent standards and inputs.

Accurate But Imprecise (Lower Right)

"Uncertainty is a more accurate representation of the world. And I'd like to argue that the more accurate your representation of the world, the better your decisions are, and the better you're going to propel yourself to success."

Annie Duke, Author of "Thinking in Bets: Making Smarter Decisions When You Don't Have all the Facts"

Given the uncertainty in the inputs, how can we hope to be "accurate"? We can if we define accuracy as being without bias **and** put ranges on the data to depict a reasonable range of outcomes. The very act of recognizing uncertainty in our models means that precision is meaningless. After all, how useful is a number like 17.228329 +/-7? The range of answers may be centered on the correct final answer, but there will be a large scatter in the answers. We can say that the answer is between about 10 and 24. Those decimals do not add meaningful information.

This is the standard to try to achieve with portfolio models as a rule. This implies that simulation or some other means of describing a range of outcomes is required. Of course, if your portfolio problem or question does not require testing of probabilities, the inaccurate and imprecise quadrant may be sufficient.

War Story – The Negative Consequences of Believing Your Models, Part 1

Misunderstood and Abused

The exploration economist conducted a study of worldwide fiscal regimes by imagining a representative 100-million-barrel oil field and its associated development and production. She plugged the costs and revenues into over a hundred different fiscal regimes to see which ones would generate the highest NPV. The idea was to look for areas in which there was a disconnect between the terms and geology. In most cases, favorable geology has more onerous fiscal terms.

She had a rank-ordered list, bar charts, etc., which she shared with executives around the company so they could see how the regimes compared. A number of interesting conclusions and counterintuitive insights came out of the study. This study was focused on exploration, where NPV was more important than the rate of return.

For example, OPEC regimes tended to keep the most money for the country (not surprising), but some OPEC regimes had quite progressive tax regimes allowing for relatively higher rates of return.

Some countries that allowed for a higher company take also had regressive regimes that incurred taxes earlier in the revenue stream, making them less attractive for investment despite the decreased government take.

In any case, an acquisition opportunity arrived at one of the divisions. The person who received the correspondence looked at the ranked list, saw that the country in question was way down the list, and rejected the offer.

However, this was not consistent with the intent or aim of the study. The analyst was happy that someone was using her work, but less happy that it was misused. Even though the country had a poor ranking on the NPV list, it was not a bad fiscal regime overall. In fact, it was a progressive tax regime, so development would have had an acceptable rate of return. In any case, since the company would be the buyer, they could ensure that the offer would result in an acceptable return.

Lessons Learned

1. Once a study goes into the wild, you have no control over how it will be used or misused.
2. Sometimes people look for excuses to say no.

Values and Tradeoffs (Visualization and Communication)

Visualization

In the dark ages (the mid-1990s), rapid, interactive computer graphics were a novelty. Many people still wanted to see tables of numbers. Color printers were not yet ubiquitous, and people were happy to wait until the next day while their assistants made line charts. Remember viewgraph transparencies?

Technology has come a long way. With programs like Spotfire, Tableau, and PowerBI, decision-makers can analyze portfolio and opportunity strengths and weaknesses interactively in a collaborative setting.

The analytical tools for even the most sophisticated analyses have existed for years. The graphical tools to digest the results are an important frontier of portfolio analysis.

Principles

1. Curating portfolios is essential. An analyst might create 20,000 portfolio scenarios for consideration, but the number of candidate sets must be filtered to the relevant, insightful ones that illustrate important tradeoffs to the decision-makers for their consideration and discussion.
2. Looking at portfolios is different from looking at individual entities. Decision-makers need time to shift their frame from projects to portfolios. It is not unusual for leaders to look at a display of portfolios and say, "Which ones of those are my projects." This is a bad start to a portfolio meeting. Each of those portfolios contain many projects.
3. There is a difference between analysis and presentation. Portfolio analysts will have analyzed and filtered out many portfolios. They may have become immersed in a universe of possibilities and spent days familiarizing themselves with all the details behind each portfolio. They will have complex sets of displays. There is a bit of "sausage-making" in the analysis and curation of portfolios. Decision-makers do not need to see all that goes on in that process. They need to see the conclusions and simple perspectives boiled down to their essence.
4. There is a tendency for some decision-makers to look for weaknesses in the analysis to discredit it. Again, there needs to be priming for decision-makers to have the comfort of using the insights from the analysis. It is essential to have the leader's understanding and support of the basis of the analysis. The Harvard Business Review paper, "*How SmithKline-Beecham Makes*

Better Resource Allocation Decisions" by Sharpe and Keelin, is a great paper that shows the importance of leadership buy-in plus other success factors such as having multiple options for each project and openness to consider alternate capital scenarios.

Regardless of the method used to create your coordinated set of decisions, you want to evaluate and understand differences in outcomes between the portfolios.

There are five general classes of information we want to be able to display: point metrics, stream metrics, decision representation, categorical (buckets), and qualitative information.

Point metrics include values collapsed to a single point. There are a handful of useful ones: NPV, Total Capital expenditure, negative cash flow from projects, value at risk, investment efficiency, and Average Return on Capital employed. These numbers can be derived from full-life data or data within a specific time period.

Stream (time-series) data shows measures as they progress over time. The time "granularity" will depend on the nature of the analysis, but it can be annual, monthly, or even weekly. Revenue, earnings, cash flow, ROCE, production, reserves, and capital employed, all across time, are useful measures. Strategic analyses will typically be on an annual basis.

Seeing the virtual asset decision display is important, especially in the interaction techniques where you are considering coordinated sets of decisions or using asset robustness as an essential insight. It is a representation, sometimes with a single number, of the best decisions that help achieve specific goals. Finding patterns in virtual asset decisions helps reduce the cognitive load on decision-makers. If one asset is always included in the best portfolios and one is always excluded, that effectively makes them "no regrets" decisions.

Categorical information can be helpful for either point or stream data. Category information can include data such as the percent of production coming from OPEC countries, oil production as a percentage of the total, upstream vs. downstream earnings, OPEC vs. Non-OPEC production, unconventional revenue vs. deep water vs. heavy oil vs. conventional, etc. For investment portfolios, we think about asset classes like stocks vs. bonds and industrial sectors. Pharmaceutical companies might consider the drug class, clinical focus, or manufacturing types. These views can help leadership understand trends and progress towards achieving strategic targets.

Finally, qualitative or intangible information can be applied to snapshots in time or shown over time. Qualitative information can include labels like "good" or "core" assets. These can essentially be coded to form categories, so they would fall into the categorical data type. Sometimes, people say they just "know something when they see it." This may be true, but there is something underlying that knowledge. If you can get to the root of the matter, you will be better off.

Doug Hubbard, the author of "How to Measure Anything: Finding the Value of Intangibles in Business," says that labeling a desired outcome as "intangible" is nonsense. If it's something you care about, there must be something you can see, and when you figure out what that is, you can find a way to measure it.

Modern visualization programs go far beyond static Excel graphs. Interactive views and graphical user interfaces allow for powerful analysis and insights and can handle large sets of data.

People consume information differently. The information must be customized for the audience and the question at hand. Well-constructed graphics can make the information compelling, draw in the decision-makers, and allow them to see and get a gut feel for the data.

There is a pdf file with tips and tricks for graphic analysis here. (graphicsprinciples.github.io/cheatsheet.html).

JunkCharts provides a three-point framework and taxonomy for testing your visualizations. https://junkcharts.typepad.com/junk_charts/junk-charts-trifecta-checkup-the-definitive-guide.html

The trifecta encourages you to ask a) what the question is, b) what the data tells you, and c) whether your visualization is consistent with those first two questions.

Edward Tufte, author of several books, including "The Visual Display of Quantitative Information," is a proponent of information-dense and rich visualizations. Besides his books, he offers classes—both live and online—that cover his methods. Tufte's work is amazing and insightful. It is worth investigating. Tufte likes rich graphic displays that take time to process and tell a deep story. The elegance of that approach is undeniable. The practicality is a problem. Executives and decision-makers most typically want information in bite-sized pieces. Furthermore, depending on the company's culture, you may not have the luxury of walking them through the logic or story that you have put together for them. Unless you are highly confident that the bosses will appreciate a sophisticated story slide, stick with what they know. Your mileage may vary.

Analysis of big data has created new tools and perspectives for visualizing and analyzing data. Almost any specifics that can be written about will be outdated within a few years. At this time, hypergraphs and topological transformations are recent developments in visualizing and analyzing relationships across multiple dimensions. As these concepts and tools are further developed, it is important for analysts and managers to be able to engage in creative play to test their utility.

One last comment on visualization. The canonical order of the best displays for comparison is bar chart, pie chart, stacked bar chart, and bubble chart. Bar charts dominate. But a recent paper (*The Risks of Ranking: Revisiting Graphical Perception to Model Individual Differences in Visualization Performance, Davis et al*) shows that some people's perceptions do not work that way. There are people whose perceptions are the exact opposite. Make sure your displays are suitable for your audience.

Communication

Beyond simple visualization, there is a communication and learning process that needs to happen with both analysts and decision-makers. The frame for portfolio analysis is different enough to be confusing to many.

This section will deal mainly with more advanced portfolio techniques. Organizations that currently use stand-alone techniques are quite familiar with and adapted to those techniques. Effective communication and facilitation of the portfolio framework and techniques is difficult. But in the final analysis, no matter how good your frame, data, analyses, and visualizations are, leaders must take action to realize value.

"Explaining things is easy; getting people to understand them is harder."
Sam Savage

Some concepts and ideas are difficult and complex. Leaders seldom care about all the contortions you perform to simplify the message—they just want the message. In fact, showing the innovative and clever work that went into it may look like bragging or distract from the message.

Despite communication being at the end of the chain, communication and understanding start early. Every organization has different challenges, cultures, and personalities. So, there is not a set answer to "What is the best way to communicate and convince our leaders of the validity of this portfolio analysis?" Rather, there are a series of guidelines that might help you find the key to your organization.

1. Know who is the decision-maker (DM) in a situation and who are the advisors. Portfolio analysts generally need to have an advisor mindset. The model is not solving the problem; it is merely informing the decision-maker and his or her other advisors.
2. Involve decision-makers in the business framing very early in the process.

3. Decision-maker involvement in analytic framing should focus on the key values and provenance of data. They will likely need to support and have confidence in the generation and standards of the data.
4. Start communicating early in the process with any of the decision-makers that will not be involved throughout.
5. Plant seeds. Seek out objections and criticisms early. It will help you deliver a better product. As they say, "Headwinds lift us higher."
6. Avoid technical discussion of the models and optimization algorithms. Emphasize that the purpose of any type of prioritization or optimization is to create a logical, coordinated set of decisions for comparison of results.
7. Some key concepts that leaders must understand:
    a. Portfolio provides insights, not answers.
    b. They are still the decision-makers; analysis can help inform their decisions.
    c. The single most important takeaway should be their vision of company performance. Specific decisions to get there are almost incidental.
8. Limit the size of the decision meeting. Fewer than about seven people is manageable. In a meeting larger than that, reaching alignment and understanding is difficult.
9. Tailor the meetings and all displays to the DMs' preferences. This requires preparation and, if possible, regular check-ins to ensure you are on the right track. Adopt a mindset that is agile.
10. Strive for engagement of the leaders in meetings. If you can create a user interface on a model that the leaders can manipulate easily and quickly and get instant feedback, or even if they can direct an analyst live, it could be a tremendous hit. Building engaging models is difficult for me in the cultures I have worked in. I have found it best for me to stick with static displays during leadership meetings. Dynamic graphic and analysis tools have often been more confusing than helpful. Your mileage may vary, and if you can pull it off, you have a big edge.
11. Ensure that decision-makers understand what you are doing, especially if you're showing rollups and interactions and they are accustomed to standalone analyses.
12. Decision-maker stakeholders must believe that the data is comparable and consistent.
13. It is especially important that the leader of the decision team be well-versed and supportive of the efforts. I have heard of meetings where, at the first hint of pushback, the leader crumbled.

Key Takeaways

1. Visualization and communication must be customized to something that works for your decision-makers; there is not a universal solution. Displays and tools that are useful for analysis may not be useful for presentation. Training or education may be needed to ensure that the decision-makers are in alignment about the purpose and outcomes of an analysis.
2. Do your best to create a story with your data. Humans are wired to respond to stories. They strike an emotional chord that objectivity and rationality often miss.
3. To implement a portfolio process or system, it is important to manage expectations. Portfolio tools can slice and dice, and inform great decisions, but they will not necessarily give good forecasts or budget-ready outputs. Think in terms of directional insights, not answers.

War Story – Simplify Your Visuals

My team and I were working on a complex analysis. We generated multitudes of files, graphics, and analyses as we worked. Fully documenting what we did and why was important to the team because the analysis was somewhat controversial and a new type of analysis for the company.

Finally, we showed it to our boss. We walked him through the logic to ensure that he supported the approach and conclusions and did not see any holes.

As we walked through the slides, he became noticeably impatient. He said, "Yeah, yeah, but what's the answer?"

We skipped through 90% of the slides and showed him the answer. His only comment was to trim the 20-slide presentation to three slides to show to the executives.

Sigh.

Lessons Learned

1. Set expectations – He was expecting a quick rundown of the answers, not documentation of the brilliance of his analysis team. We should have made it clear if we wanted a critical perspective of our work. We erroneously thought that the informal setting and slides would sufficiently indicate informality. Make your purpose and expectations explicit and clear.

2. Read the room – He knew we were thorough and professional and would do a great job. His time was precious. We didn't need to remind him of our mad skills.
3. Established credibility is a great thing—use it. Once your credibility is established, people no longer care about how you do very clever work. They want conclusions and recommendations.

Management Commitment, Facilitation, and Portfolio Culture

Managing a portfolio requires the ability to analyze it and determine its quality. Tools and processes that can help you find better courses of action are vital to exploring the portfolio. But regardless of the quality of the analysis, if your enterprise leaders do not have confidence in the tools and workflow and do not have incentives aligned with the recommendations that emerge from the investigation, that superb analysis is a waste of time.

Management commitment, like the frame, is a separate element of decision quality. The commitment part of portfolio management is vital as a firm establishes a portfolio practice.

Incorporating portfolio perspectives into formal governance guidelines can ensure that the processes persist. The use of portfolio perspectives drives value only when management is committed to action.

The Portfolio Mindset

"Plans are nothing; planning is everything."
Dwight D. Eisenhower

Shifting from a project to a portfolio mindset is crucial. It brings a dimension of thinking outside the usual corporate financial budgeting framework. But it's not just a mindset; there is also a necessary willingness to dive into the strengths and weaknesses of your assets and projects, to break away from an operational focus and dig into what you have, where you want to go, and how to get there from here.

Portfolio analysis and management is planning done well. Sadly, for many companies, the planning process looks something like the following:

a. Make promises to the market analysts.
b. Tell your businesses to provide budgets that exceed the promises.
c. Twist arms when the received plans are expensive and underperform.

d. Massage the final budgets and hold people accountable for impossible outcomes.

A better process flows something like the following:

1. Determine where you are in your current state.
2. Determine where you want to be in the future. This is not a precise definition of specific metrics but is more general. You want to compile the list of metrics that you will use to judge your results, but not necessarily exact targets for the values of those metrics.
3. Create possible project/asset options. Is it possible to sell, harvest, go slow, accelerate, or adjust the working interest of your assets and projects? In the early stages, keep your funnel open (at least for analysis purposes). The purpose of the initial step is to understand what you would do if you controlled all the decisions regarding your assets.
4. Create coherent sets of decisions following strategic themes and use goal-seeking optimization or other means to define a cloud of meaningfully different operational and financial possibilities.
5. As you create and analyze the coherent decision sets, learn from the results. If you see inconsistencies between stated goals and possible combinations of decisions, then expectations or options need to be changed.
6. Fine-tune your goals. You may find unintended consequences—both positive and negative—to your initial thoughts.
7. Develop your preferred path with realistic, doable actions. Acknowledge that there are some results that are beyond your control and be ready to adjust your approach when the outcomes do not meet your expectations.
8. Now, make those promises to the market and hold people accountable for their actions—not only for the results.

The process above can be likened to a funnel that begins with a wide range of options and gradually narrows them down to the best action plan. John Howell has described this process as "running the funnel."

▸ Running the Funnel from Open Options to a Plan

When doing portfolio work, it is best to start with your potential decision options as wide open as possible, then work towards realistic answers. Closing the funnel too fast removes the ability to gain insights about your asset base and performance limits.

It is easy for a portfolio process to short-circuit steps 2-5 and go straight to step 7, developing the preferred path. It's even worse when a firm leads with 8—promises to market and accountability—before doing the vital background work. Portfolios will be managed. The key is to manage them with good insight and understanding. Gut feeling has a place, but it should not be everything.

Key Takeaways

The best way to ensure no insight is to rush straight to the answer. A more thoughtful process allows leaders and stakeholders to better understand a company's strengths, weaknesses, and possibilities. Even the best, most experienced leaders miss opportunities for improved performance by rushing to judgment.

Detour – A Historical Perspective on Portfolio in the Oil Industry

The oil industry had a wave of portfolio work in the literature around 2000. The literature focused on how to do portfolio work, but not on the reasons for doing it. Leadership was implicitly assumed to know exactly what they wanted. During that period, analysts would set their constraints and requirements, run the optimization, plot standard deviation vs. NPV, declare victory, and get ignored.

Leadership knew generally what they wanted to achieve. And they needed to see their alternatives and trade-offs with metrics they cared about. (Narrator: They didn't care about standard deviation.)

The comparison of Agile project management and Phase Gate (waterfall) methodologies provides a good analogy. With Waterfall methods, the team determines all the required specifications, then goes off and creates the perfect product. This works well until the requirements change, the world changes or people think they want something that they actually do not. With Agile, a team takes a step, receives feedback, adjusts it, receives feedback, and so on.

Agile is a more interactive version of the Dialogue Decision Process discussed in the Decision Analysis Appendix. Instead of long time-gaps between pre-defined touchpoints, Agile allows for more frequent and less formal interactions. The touchpoints in the Decision Dialog Process are sometimes called snaking. You can think of Agile interactions as 'micro-snaking.'

As advocated in this book, portfolio analysis and management is more like Agile project methodologies. Test a metric, see what it does to other metrics and overall performance, get feedback, and then try another. Keep going until you get close to what the leaders want. Business performance goals emerge from interactions rather than being set in stone at the start.

SECTION TWO
Portfolio Methods

Portfolio Techniques Overview

There are three broad classes of portfolio techniques: standalone, inventory or comparison, and interactions. The three classes either assume or explicitly model an inventory of alternative uses of resources. There is a significant jump between the classes (plus a jump within interactions) in terms of data, tools, and skills required. Each of these jumps changes the frame of the analysis.

Stand-alone techniques include cash flow analysis and more general opportunity assessment. In addition to the standard development alternative comparison, these techniques add portfolio insights by incorporating opportunity cost, which implicitly carries a portfolio perspective. They are practically universal, and much has been written about them elsewhere. They are generally done for any economic decision, and every company has standards for this work. You need an economic modeling tool, opportunity-specific information, and simple graphics, for example, Excel charts, to display results.

Jump 1 to comparison and rollup compare different opportunities and assets within an enterprise against each other and the overall firm. Rollups aggregate plan elements to the enterprise or firm level to show the synthesis of plans. The fundamental input is the analysis from stand-alone methods plus metadata, for example, country, asset class, and so on.

This jump requires detailed information about the inventory of opportunities, strong business domain knowledge by the generators and consumers of the information, and is significantly aided by more advanced graphical, sorting, and filtering techniques. The input for this step comes from the standalone analysis and data.

Jump 2 brings us to simulation and optimization interaction techniques. These techniques roll opportunities up to the enterprise level and explicitly consider limitations, strategic direction, uncertainties, and enterprise aspirations and targets, typically across years into the future. With optimization, you can test and compare different combinations of assets and asset decisions. With simulations, you incorporate probabilities and uncertainty to provide a different perspective on the rollup. It is a different way to aggregate data considering uncertainties in the inputs.

The second jump requires different tools, such as simulation and addition of probabilistic and entity interaction data, detailed knowledge about assets, and access to leadership for guidance about enterprise strategy and aspirations.

Discrete Jumps in Portfolio Analysis Methods

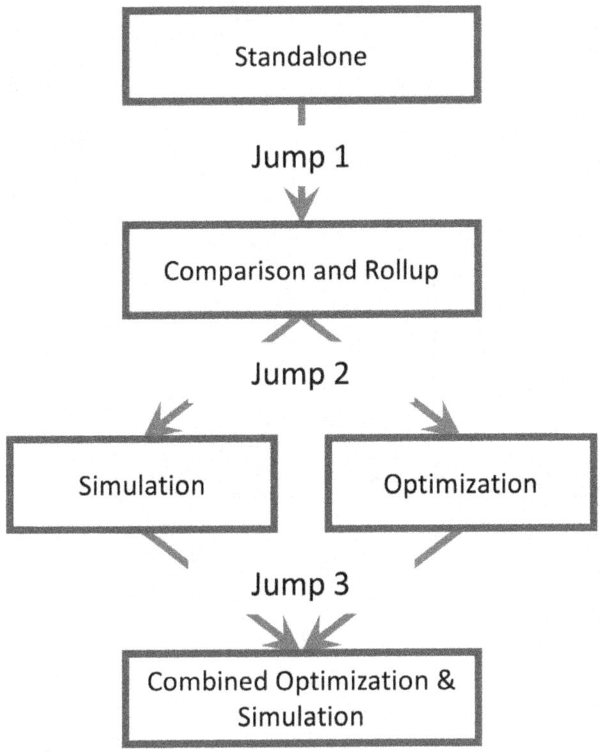

> *The large categories of portfolio methods contain three significant jumps that require different data, tools, and skill sets. Jump 1 requires comparative data plus some graphics skills. Jump 2 is substantial, requiring one or more new tools and skillful modeling. Jump 3 requires additional modeling skills, an additional program, all the data from the previous level, and decision-makers who are attuned to the concepts of probability and risk.*

Jump 3, combining optimization and simulation, is still in the interactions realm. This step requires smart configuration of models, as well as leaders prepared to consume the analysis. It also offers the best insights. Bringing in the concept of finding decision sets focused on the probability of achieving enterprise targets is a significant step-change that few organizations are prepared for. But even if not done at an enterprise level, it can be helpful for sub-optimizations of exploration, research, or acquisition, divestiture, and development.

This final jump brings us to a more advanced type of interaction analysis, which requires probabilistic thinking by leaders, additional quantitative analysis skills, all the data from the previous jump, and tools to support the actual number crunching.

Portfolio Tool Selector

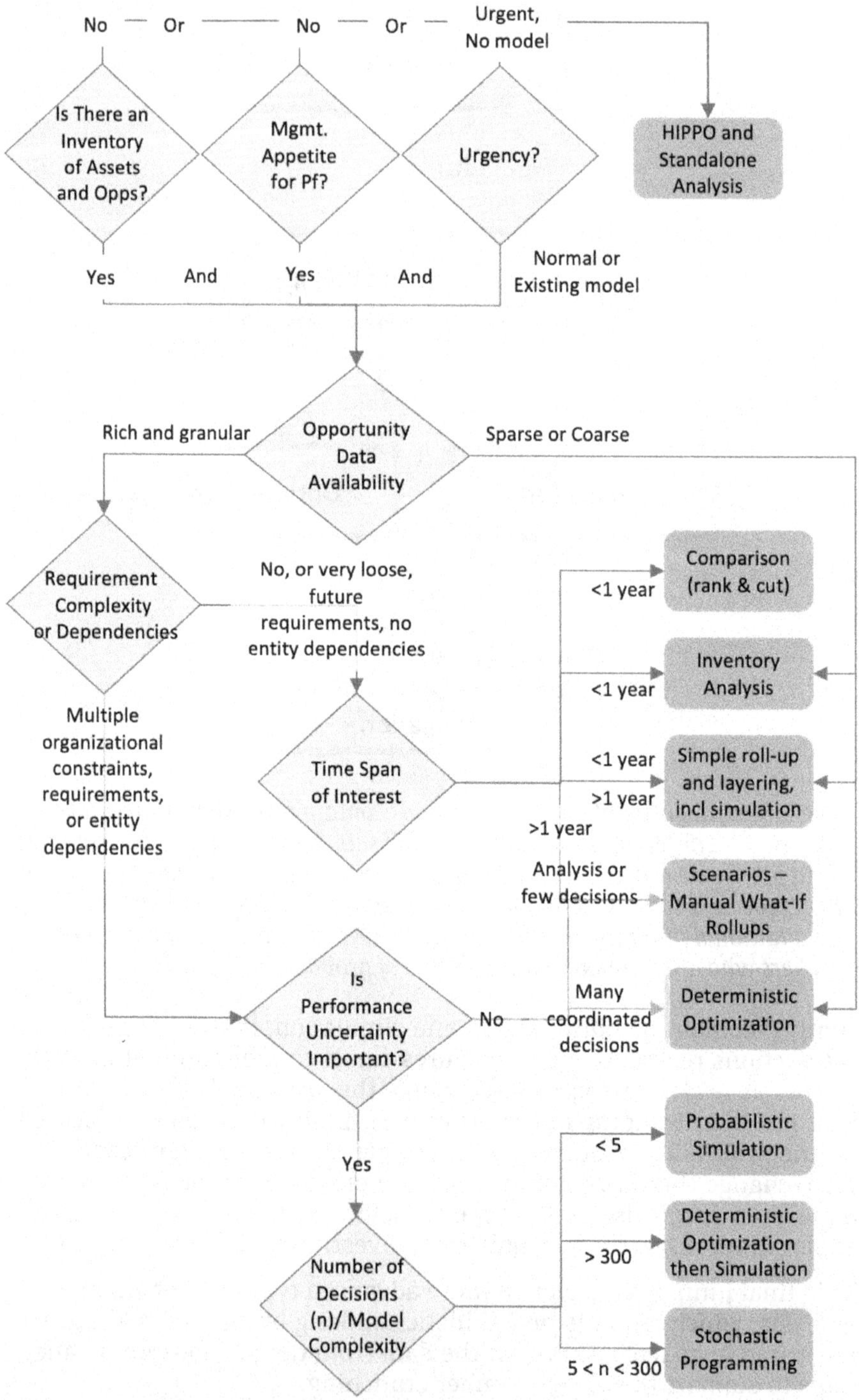

A repeat of the portfolio tool selector for reference.

For completeness, I will write about all the levels of portfolio techniques, but I will spend the most effort on the interaction techniques. They generally require more knowledge and tools beyond simple Excel.

As we progress through this second section of the book, we will continue to refer to the decision tree introduced in the analytical frame section.

A Note on Scalability:
I speak of projects throughout this second section. I am using the project as a proxy for appropriate decision granularity. You may also think of it as an investment, program, initiative, asset, product line, or business unit. The concepts are still relevant, but the analysis should be conducted at an appropriate level.

Detail – Cheat Sheet of the Methods and Their Limitations

Stand-alone analysis provides good information about an opportunity. Would most people consider it a good investment? It does not tell you if it is a good opportunity for your organization specifically. How certain are you about other opportunities "thought to exist" inside your organization? Furthermore, because in most companies, opportunities arrive when they arrive, if you fund the current opportunity in question, what opportunities will not get funded? What if they are obligatory investments? Wouldn't it be better to know those answers directly?

Nonetheless, if you have cash flow economics, do not have data on other competing opportunities, and only have an estimate of the returns on other opportunities, Standalone analysis becomes the best information you have. Use it.

All other methods require an inventory of opportunities.

Comparison Methods

Simple single-dimensional comparisons are the next simplest method. These are reasonably popular and effective for similar opportunities, especially when there is a short-term (less than one year) investment and a single limitation, e.g., budget. This method will tend to over-predict outcomes, but it is good, simple, and generally accepted.

Rank and cut methods fall apart in a few circumstances: multi-year programs, multiple dimensions of interest, dissimilar investments, and when patterns of production and capital expenditure over time are important.

For cases in which the time dimension is not critical, use multi-dimensional graphics to display tradeoffs between opportunities. They can be qualitative or quantitative. Often, they take the form of some sort of 2x2 matrix. These graphs are great to see how investments compare when collapsed to several point metrics of interest such as NPV or Rate of Return. These methods are most useful to create "short lists" of investments for funding. The opportunities in the one quadrant might become your no-regrets execution projects. The opposite quadrant contains the no regrets non-funded projects, and the other quadrants are 'on the bubble.'

But there is still the time dimension to consider. Rank and cut and multi-dimensional graphs collapse a stream of numbers into single points. But those streams of numbers represent the future of the company. Most firms must continually renew themselves to sustain the business. This is especially important for resource companies, which are strictly limited by the volume of resources held. Investments have some kind of production, investment, or cash flow profile over time associated with them. It starts with discovery or research, followed by investment, and then operations.

Rollups and Slice-and-Dice

The sum of all the business profiles into time is a representation of the future of the company. Proper balance across time is critical for all companies. Over-investing can lead to cash flow shortages; under-investing may give up a competitive advantage. The balance of product lines or asset classes is important as the external world changes as well. For example, energy companies are now conscious of the carbon emissions of their businesses, pharmaceutical companies need to track demographic changes with aging and ever-longer-lived populations, and mining companies have shifted away from coal and towards minerals suitable for low-carbon energy systems. Seeing how your current portfolio fits into those trends and making changes are important strategic considerations.

Rollups (sums) of all the cash flow, earnings, production, operating expense, R&D, and other time-series data by year are used regularly by many companies as a part of their planning and budgeting processes. The details and standards vary across companies, but it is a major tool for judging direction.

Rollups will do a good job of helping you understand whether your direction is consistent with your beliefs about the business and external environment, but they fall down in two significant ways. First, when you have uncertain aspects of your business, demand for product, price, and probability of successful R&D or exploration, it may be important to know what a range of outcomes will look like rather than simply hanging your hat on a single number. Second, rollups generally do not inform on corrective actions.

Simulation

When your challenge is the uncertainty of your firm's results, Monte Carlo Simulation is the next step to take. This method has been used in many fields and can yield powerful insights into the likelihood of achieving your goals and targets. Simulation is a fancy way to add up numbers. It is a rollup that takes uncertainty into account. Like arithmetic rollups, you can gain important insights, but simulation alone will not inform or test corrective actions.

Testing corrective actions is the next step in portfolio analysis. In simple cases it can be done manually. For example, when doing simple rollups, if you find you are falling short and need an acquisition to fill a gap, you can simply layer the acquisition on top of your existing plan and see if it would improve your outcomes. That's easy.

But you may find that an acquisition is too much, so you would have to make other adjustments on top of the acquisition to make it work for your company. Perhaps some investments would need to be delayed, accelerated, downsized, divested, or developed with an alternative approach.

Optimization

For these more complex cases with interactions that reach across an organization, mathematical optimization becomes a practical and important tool to see very quickly and at a low cost what coordinated sets of decisions would improve your firm's outcomes across various dimensions.

Modeling interactions requires some degree of modeling skill and probably the creation of specialized tools. It is also the most powerful method for increasing the value of your investments. Experience and technical papers show increases from 10-40% of the value of an investment program by considering alternative developments and prioritizing investments to increase your chances of achieving targets. There are many flavors of mathematical optimization, and you should walk before you run. If your portfolio journey takes you here, start with simple forms of optimization that give approximate solutions and insights. Add complexity only if the increased precision can be justified by the nature of the decision and the cost and time to increase the complexity of your tools and processes.

As I wrote this section, I thought this might have been the whole book. Portfolio methods are mesmerizing to the quants and seem like they are the world. However, there are lots of details that need to be attended to in implementing methods, and the methods are only one of the five enablers in establishing a successful portfolio practice. You still need a valid frame, data and a way to manage it, visualization and facilitation to enable the tradeoff discussions, and the change management and leadership commitment to using portfolio insights.

Now, on to the details behind the methods.

CHAPTER 3

Standalone Analysis

Standalone project evaluation methods are standard and straightforward in most cases. They tell you a lot about a given project. They do not directly provide robust information about how well a project fits the firm's strategies and aspirations over time.

Following our flow chart, we see that if you do not have an inventory for comparison or combining, if management has no appetite for portfolio, **or** if there is not a portfolio model that is ready to go (or can be built in the required timeframe), we go straight to the standalone approaches—**HIPPO** (**H**ighest **P**aid **P**erson's **O**pinion) and Standalone Analysis.

In all likelihood, the highest-paid person has at least a qualitative portfolio model in their head. They may believe they can do all the relevant calculations or do not need calculations; their gut knows the answer. I will not cover HIPPO in this book. Gut feelings (often the basis of HIPPO) can be powerful, but they are inarticulate (credit to Dave Evans). Seeing real goals and tradeoffs will help communicate and understand the decision drivers. We all know that gut feelings are not repeatable and it's impossible to distinguish luck from skill.

Standalone Branch of the Tool Selector

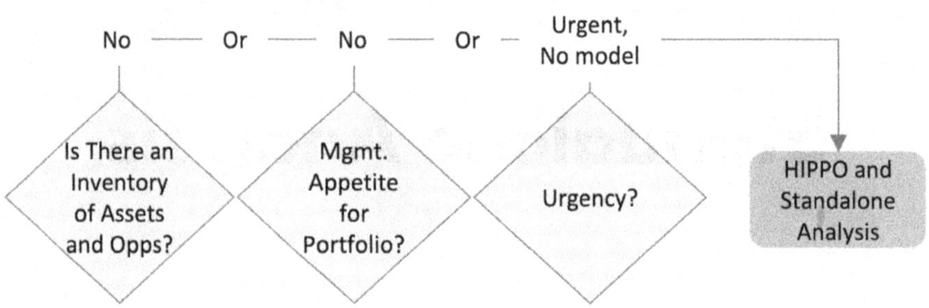

> *If you do not have an inventory of relevant assets, OR if there is urgency and you do not have a model or data prepared, OR there is not management appetite for more explicit portfolio techniques, you are in the standalone zone.*

Leaving aside HIPPO, historically, most companies have looked at projects on a stand-alone basis. If a project met hurdles and it was not stupid, the project would be funded.

Indeed, the standard practice is to evaluate projects and initiatives on a stand-alone basis. This is adequate in many cases and is the approach in most project management and finance circles. In any case, standard economic analysis becomes the input for all other types of portfolio analysis.

Portfolio management does not take the place of individual project management. Projects still need to be scheduled, estimated, and managed. The difference is that with portfolio management in place, the project team receives better guidance on the development alternative best aligned with corporate needs.

An excellent way to think about project alternative selection is to look at the net value the project adds to the company. In other words, what does the company look like if we do this project, and what does it look like if we don't do the project? That is the true value of doing the project. In some cases, the difference is the same as the standalone case; in others, it is very different.

Decision Analysis and Project Management

Many firms use a robust project management and decision analysis process to assist in making better decisions. Typically, the process flows through several phases that look something like this:

1. Framing – Is there an opportunity? How should we approach it? What will be the criteria used to make decisions?
2. Alternative Development – What are the scale of the facilities, the scope of the development, and the market focus?
3. Alternative Selection and Front-End Engineering – Choose and develop the selected alternative – Given the frame, which option provides the best answer? Is there a superior hybrid solution? Develop your construction and execution plans.
4. Construction – Make it happen once the engineering and project plans are complete and approved.
5. Operation – Construction is complete. Now operate.
6. Lookback – What went well? What didn't?

This methodology has demonstrably improved the ability to execute projects and make better decisions. These techniques, which are well-aligned with the decision quality framework, have added enormous value.

Even without a robust project process, financial theory says that a project that results in a positive NPV will add value to a firm.

In project analysis, an action's value is typically measured against a baseline. For example, what is the value of this project if we do it compared to the value of the project if divested? This is part of the alternative selection. Simple subtraction of the cash flow values between the baseline and alternative gives a good understanding of the relative values. In cases where the alternative to development is neither to develop nor divest, discounting the cash flows compares the project to an alternative, for example, the cost of capital or opportunity cost.

This can be a practical approach in an opportunity-limited environment, i.e., where a company is struggling to find suitable investments. Every project with a positive NPV will add value to the company.

However, firms prioritize when there are constraints, such as organizational capability (people) or capital limitations. In constrained environments, every decision is a decision that affects the portfolio. The question is whether it will be an **informed** portfolio decision.

The Discount Rate Makes It Portfolio Analysis

In financial theory, the Net Present Value of the cash flow of an investment, discounted at the firm's weighted average cost of capital (WACC), is the value a project adds to a firm. If the firm has no constraints in capital, people, or other resources, this will provide the net value of the investment to the firm.

But "no constraints" is seldom the case. When there are constraints, the implication is that taking one action precludes or delays another. The lost value from this cancellation or delay is generally referred to as the "opportunity cost." Portfolio methods adjust values for the opportunity cost. When your investment capacity is constrained, the rate of return of alternative opportunities believed to exist within the firm is the appropriate discount rate to create a portfolio perspective. This is often referred to as a hurdle rate. This hurdle rate essentially incorporates an imaginary inventory of alternative investments.

Key Takeaways

1. Standalone analysis is the first class of portfolio analysis, with the next step being comparison methods. But standalone **is** a comparison. The discount rate chosen makes standalone an **implicit** comparison to either the cost of capital or an opportunity cost hurdle rate.
2. Standalone analysis is the primary input for all other methods. Some companies never move beyond standalone. They risk making under-informed decisions—the cost of incremental steps of portfolio analysis is low compared to the insight and value they provide.
3. Regardless of whether to move beyond standalone analysis, a firm should, at a minimum, have a consistent financial framework, inputs, and standards to be used even for the most basic analyses.
4. Standalone analysis changes the context of the decision when you can make informed assumptions about alternate investments within the company. If this is as far as you go on your portfolio journey, it is better than never having started. You will make better-informed decisions.

Project by Project Decisions

Before starting this section, the reader should possess basic knowledge of economic analysis, finance, and the terms used in those fields. Please see the Financial and Economic Concepts appendix for an overview of theory and practice. These concepts and terms will be used throughout the book.

Project by Project Decisions

Many would not consider standalone economic analysis a portfolio technique because there is little attempt to establish the context of the decision. Nonetheless, this is how many companies make decisions and it's essential to know this approach's strengths, weaknesses, and appropriate decisions for managing a portfolio.

Description: Projects are submitted to decision-makers by project teams. The decision-maker accepts the project or rejects it based on its characteristics.

If there are no perceived constraints or barriers, such as capital or personnel, to execute the investment, the decision could in theory be made on an NPV basis. However, there are always constraints—even if sometimes they aren't apparent.

It is common for budgeted capital or qualified personnel to be the main constraints. When the constraint is people resources, companies often use budget as the proxy for people. Other constraints include external resources, such as steel, or limitations of a supplier. Essential targets, such as future growth, may also act as constraints.

Methodology: For project-by-project decisions, it is generally appropriate to use a discount rate other than the firm's weighted average cost of capital (WACC). If the corporate average rate of reinvestment is known, that is appropriate. For any going concern, the rate of return on future investments will be higher than the WACC. The implication is that funds can be diverted to other projects if the project being considered does not have a positive NPV (discounted at the investment return of opportunities believed to exist). This approach compares the opportunity to the cloud of other investment opportunities.

In many cases, companies will specify the discount rate to be used in the approval and analysis process. As a side note, it does not have to be a percentage rate of return; the hurdle rate for opportunities thought to exist can be expressed as a benefit-to-cost ratio as well.

"Strategic" Investments

Sometimes, projects that do not meet minimum thresholds are brought forward for approval. The proponents then claim that the project is "strategic." Unfortunately, the strategic label is often applied to mask the fact that it's simply a bad investment. The word "strategic" gets thrown around without clear criteria.

For a project to be truly strategic, it typically needs to have one or more of several characteristics:

1. It is long term.
2. It is in a new area.
3. It is huge.
4. It helps fill a performance gap.
5. It adds value to another asset or set of assets but is undocumented in the current analysis.

A "strategic opportunity" investment that lacks any of these features is simply a poor investment.

Standalone Analysis Attributes

Data: Cash flow projections (generally annual), physical characteristics of the opportunity

Tools: Spreadsheet or commercial fiscal modeling tool

Common Relevant Measures: NPV as a value metric, IRR or discounted cost ratio as an efficiency metric, cost per unit, margin per unit

Decisions: Which alternative should be selected for this project? How much to pay for this opportunity? Should we invest?

Why Standalone Analysis is good:

1. Least expensive approach.
2. It is the first step to all other approaches.
3. There's a long history in many companies; people understand the approach well.
4. It is good if there are no enterprise-level time series requirements or targets like production or earnings growth within the frame of the analysis.
5. It is straightforward and typically has clear criteria.

Why Standalone Analysis is not good:

1. Compression of numbers like cash flow and investment into single values obscures essential details. For example, if the plan for the project has spikes in expenditures, it may cause budget or financial problems. The metrics used for this analysis may not be good proxies for what the company is trying to accomplish.

2. When there are performance requirements such as production growth across a timeframe, it is crucial to know how a project contributes. You can see what this project gives you, but is it enough as part of the aggregate to contribute to enterprise targets?
3. You do not have an explicit comparison with other projects that may be coming. What if this project uses all your available project staffing, and then two months from now, an even better project comes in?

Economic and Data Standards

Cash flow and financial models are the foundations of all economic and portfolio analyses. There are books about how best to perform these analyses, so I will not delve deeply into how to build a model. Most companies have standards that govern economic calculation. Sometimes the standards are loose, other times exacting.

The following are some standards that will help facilitate the use of economic models for portfolio work.

Probabilistic Basis: Most companies use mean values or some version of a mid-case—neither over- nor under-optimistic. Companies may create probability distributions on key metrics such as total production, NPV, and earnings per barrel. Others may generate sensitivity cases, such as a low product-price version, to test robustness.

Incorporate future contingent or "real" options or not: Many projects contain points at which contingent decisions can be made. Good financial modeling incorporates these contingent decisions. This is typically modeled with Monte Carlo simulation or decision tree modeling. However, not all opportunities contain future managerial options. Sometimes there is little optionality. How should those scenarios be incorporated? The people working on projects without options may argue that letting other projects use options is unfair, but the point is to reflect reality, not simply be consistent.

Discount Rate for NPV Calculation: There are two main camps: (1) "pure" CAPM and (2) different discount rates based on project or other diversifiable risks (e.g., country risk). It is better to separate project risk elements from value. This allows for a better comparison. If you must use different discounts, each entity in the portfolio will need its own discount rate, which can then be summed, rather than adding the cash flows and discounting at the rollup when you combine them.

Product Pricing and Volumes: Many companies have committees or economists who provide price outlooks. The prices are used for both short and long-term planning. There may be biases based on perceived needs. Also, different assets respond differently to price changes based mainly on the fiscal and commercial regimes in place.

Discount Rate Basis (End or Mid-year): It is unusual for a change in the timing basis of a discount rate to change the relative ranking or perception of an asset. Even if it does, the difference is likely within the uncertainty band of the asset. The NPV function in Excel uses end-of-year discounting. All things considered; I favor a mid-year basis for individual analysis. The fix in Excel is to multiply the result of the NPV function statement by (1+ discount rate) ^0.5.

Efficiency Metrics (Denominator basis): There are two primary schools of thought on efficiency metrics: net cash-flow-based denominators and accounting capital/budget-based denominators. Net cash flow-based denominators are consistent with financial theory and are the gold standard. Denominators based on accounting-capital are inconsistent with corporate financial theory and practice, but they have the advantage of simplicity in some cases. These capital-based systems create blind spots, false positives, and false negatives. It's not hard to identify them, but we must be aware of the blind spots to prevent errors in our analysis.

Other issues include when to switch the starting discount year, using point-forward versus full-cycle economics, treatment of leveraged economics, whether to use a dynamic real options framework or rely on static models, and so on. Many other issues affect our view of a project.

The question of the forward basis of economics is especially important. In decision theory, ALL decisions should be made on a point-forward basis. There is no opposition to that concept. However, it is useful to see the full-cycle numbers to understand corporate or project performance and contribution. When we rely on full-cycle numbers instead of point-forward ones for decision-making, we introduce the sunk cost fallacy into our decision-making. If people in your organization spend without effective governance, it can lead to poor full-cycle results. This is not an economics or decision-making issue; it's governance.

Allocations of corporate **fixed** costs should not be included in investment economics. The rule of thumb is that if the cost does not change because of the decision at hand, it should not be included. Some people will argue that a project must "carry its weight." That is not logical. Marginal economics is. If a project will result in higher fixed costs, e.g., a new office to support it or additional tax accountants, those costs **should** be included.

Speaking of sunk costs, suppose you have a project with high capitalized sunk costs. When you run your economics, should you include the tax benefits of the sunk costs? It depends on the tax framework of your firm and the project. Remember, implicitly or explicitly, we always have a comparison basis in our economics. So, if you can expense and deduct those capitalized costs in the stop-project case, the deductions should not be reflected in the go-forward case. Including them would be a false benefit of doing the project. Remember, we are always looking for the marginal benefit. What happens if we do the project minus what happens if we don't do it?

Leveraged versus unleveraged economics is another tricky area. Corporations make decisions about how to fund the company. They can use corporate bonds (debt), cash flow, or accumulated cash (equity) financing. A firm's financing structure determines the overall cost of capital under the CAPM framework.

But what if a company decides that for this one project, they will use project financing, i.e., a third-party finance company will provide funding for that specific project? Using other people's money (OPM) like this is a form of leveraging or gearing. The interest rates a firm would pay for this type of project financing is usually higher than it would pay for corporate debt, but lower than the cost of capital under CAPM. Therefore, the project realizes a higher NPV, and because it uses OPM, the investment efficiency is outstanding relative to internal financing.

But here's the catch. **Any** project could use external financing, and if they all tried to, it would skew the company's overall debt and equity profile, which is important. Projects of mediocre quality would appear much more appealing if someone decided to seek funding from a third party. Allowing this destroys comparability between projects.

In other words, the firm should first focus on making the best investments. The decision of how to pay for it is then a secondary consideration. To break it down, making suitable investments is the fundamental objective; financing is a corporate-level means objective.

Key Takeaways

A good way to begin your portfolio journey is to ensure that your standards are consistent and generally compatible with the above economic and data standards (if practical). At the very least, this makes your analyses reasonable and comparable. Simply adhering to standard inputs (being consistent) is not enough in some cases, as different assets and decisions respond differently to various external world outcomes. Standards, while necessary, may not be sufficient, depending on the frame of the decisions to be made and the analytical techniques selected.

Detail – Incremental Analysis

No decision is made in a vacuum, even though it appears to be so sometimes. A comparison is always an implicit part of the decision.

When you look at a new project and calculate all the economic parameters, you see NPV, efficiency metrics, and production and revenue streams. That is great. But you are comparing that to an implicit base case of zero. Your assumption is that you will either do this or receive zero value, revenue, cost, etc.

This is fine for some decisions. But many potential investments have value even if you do not execute the project under consideration. For example, you may be able to sell it to another party. An exploration discovery, or a drug compound with some promise outside your expertise would fit this profile. So, the investment case should be explicitly compared to the sales case.

Another important and obvious case is the expansion of an existing asset. Investing in the asset would increase production, but you can only claim the difference between with and without the investment. In my experience, the easiest way to do this is by running economics with the investment and subtracting the cash flow without the investment from it. Then run all your routine analyses on the difference between the two.

The frame of a decision always includes "Compared to what?" Make that question explicit for both standalone and portfolio analysis.

Detail – Efficiency Metrics

Net Present Value (NPV) is a value metric. It measures how much an investment is worth. It helps to compare absolute size.

Efficiency metrics are another class of metrics that help you understand what it takes to achieve that NPV.

Efficiency metrics are typically expressed as a ratio, such as value divided by cost (bang per buck), or as a percentage, for example, a 15% rate of return.

The following is a list of some standard efficiency metrics and their benefits and pitfalls. I will use the following annual cash flows as an example.

▸ **Sample Annual Discounted Cash Flow**

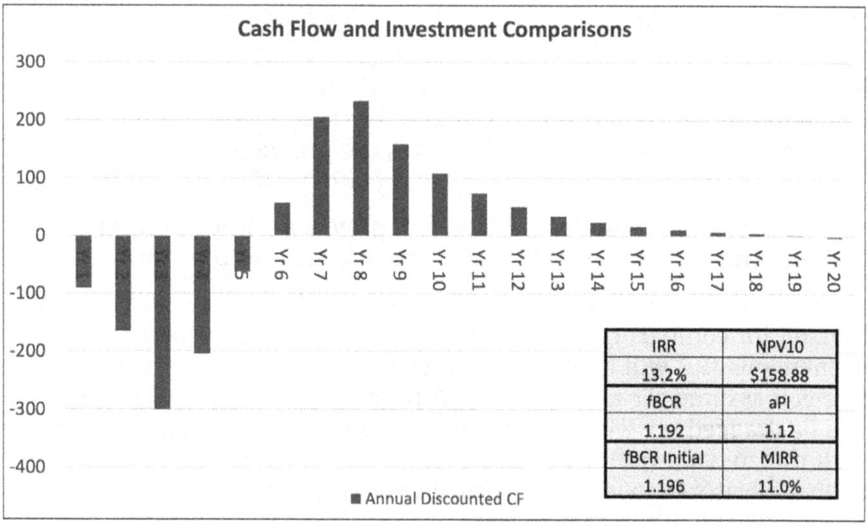

Annual discounted cash flow for use in this section, along with several typical metrics.

Internal Rate of Return (IRR or ROR)

IRR is a cash flow metric that measures, as a percentage, the effective interest that a negative cash flow receives across the life of an investment. It is an iterative calculation, like a goal-seek. Its definition is "the discount rate at which NPV = 0." Because the NPV10 is positive in the above chart, the IRR must be greater than 10%. This holds true only for "normal" cash flows without multiple pulses of negative and positive cash flow switches.

It has two technical pitfalls and misleading characteristics. The first is that it is the **internal** rate of return. It makes no assumptions about the rate of return on reinvestment of the returned cash. This makes a high rate of return (ROR) appear unrealistically high, and a low ROR appear unrealistically low. The cash returned to the corporation will be used for something.

The second pitfall is with complicated cash flow streams. Every time the annual cash flow crosses zero, there is another potential solution to the IRR equation. Which one should you pick? All are correct mathematically, but they may be nonsense logically.

Many people use IRR despite its flaws and issues with using it to compare projects.

Growth Rate of Return or Modified Internal Rate of Return (MIRR)

Like IRR, MIRR is expressed as a percentage. MIRR explicitly incorporates a presumed rate of return for other investments, which compensates for the main flaws of IRR. First, by incorporating a presumed rate for reinvestment, it fixes the problems with IRR. Secondly, doing so compensates for the mathematical flaw of IRR.

It is a better metric for comparison and provides a more accurate representation of the investment's rate of return for the firm.

However, there are two caveats. First, you need to set a standard time horizon for comparing projects. A five-year life cycle project with a tremendous IRR will be drawn asymptotically towards the discount rate you assume for reinvestment. A poorly performing IRR project will be dragged up. This is a feature, not a bug. In our example above, with the 20-year horizon of this project, the MIRR is 11% compared to 13.2% IRR. It's because the returned cash is assumed to be invested at a rate lower than the project itself.

The second issue is related to that feature. If you use a long time-horizon as the standard for this calculation, for example, 50 years, there may be little apparent differentiation between projects as everything approaches your reinvestment rate. Again, it's probably good technically, but it may need some explaining.

Benefit to Cost Ratios: Financial Benefit to Cost Ratio (fBCR) and Other Ratios (aPI)

This section is complicated because companies use and interpret these metrics differently. Generically, all the different flavors of this metric take the form of a value divided by an investment. The definitions of both Value and Investment are where the complications lie.

In this section, I will focus on the financial definitions of bang per buck, but other analyses are possible. An exploration team might look at the statistically expected barrels per well; a marketing team might look at increased sales per advertising dollar. These are sub-optimizations but certainly useful ones for organizations with specific budget or operational scarcities.

The numerator for these metrics is usually NPV at the corporate (or other) discount rate. NPV is straightforward, as discussed previously. It's the investment part that gets hairy.

fBCR - Financial Benefit to Cost Ratio

Let's start with the gold standard definition of investment as defined in every financial textbook written in the last fifty years. I will call it the financial Benefit to Cost Ratio (fBCR) in this book. Its definition is the (discounted positive net cash flow) divided by the (absolute value of the discounted net negative cash flow). Discounted net negative cash flow (DNNCF) is the finance field's definition of capital. This metric is well aligned with financial theory.

Sometimes, this calculation is simplified as 1 + NPV/ABS(DNNCF). A common omission with this paradigm is that negative abandonment cash flow is not included in this calculation. It's easy and consistent with financial standards to include late-life costs.

You can see why people use the "1 +" expression in that picture. It is because it can be approximated as fBCR = (NPV + ABS(Cost)) / ABS(Cost), which simplifies to 1 + NPV / | Cost |.

▸ Calculation of fBCR

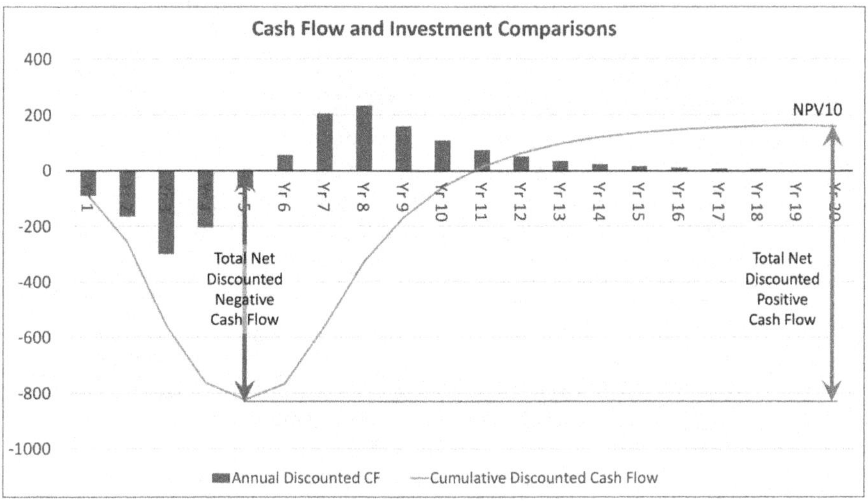

The financial standard efficiency metric is called fBCR in this book. It is defined as the sum of the discounted positive annual net cash flows divided by the sum of the discounted negative annual net cash flows. The negative investment should have a positive sign in the equation. People often simplify it as 1 plus the NPV divided by the initial negative pulse. That mathematical construct ignores abandonment or future negative cash flow. Those are often small but may be relevant, especially for phased projects.

In setting standards for this metric, there is a temptation to put extra work into the transition year in which net cash flow becomes positive, while still making expenditures. For example, what should you do if your investment expenditure ends in June, production starts, and overwhelms the expenditure, ending as a positive cash flow for the year?

In terms of defensibility and precision, you "should" go to a smaller time interval for your analysis. This could create extra work for analysts. Does it improve the picture? Does it improve decision quality? Maybe. In terms of accuracy, other questions could easily override this detail. How certain are you of the timing and magnitude of revenue? How confident are you in the pattern, timing, and magnitude of expenditures? Those factors tend to overwhelm the transition year issue.

If the investment in the transition year is large or if the project has an unusual pattern of investment and revenue compared to other projects under consideration, there may be some variation. Whichever way you choose, pick a standard and stick to it.

Related to the transition year issue above, the fBCR metric can be complicated to calculate when the investment cycle is very short, e.g., if a project investment takes place over a few days at the start of a project. For that and other reasons, when comparing similar short-cycle investments. NPV/I metrics may be more helpful.

NPV / I or aPI – Accounting Profitability Index

Another common denominator is accounting capital (or Capex). This is money that will be spent and booked as an asset rather than an expense. This is the same as budgeted capital expenditure. This number is often discounted for long-term projects. This denominator is practical when the investment time is compressed into a very short period and when comparing similar investments. It has some blind spots compared to fBCR relative to financial theory. When the denominator for these metrics is based on undiscounted budgeted capital, I will call the metric NPV over I. It is some form of the NPV of the opportunity divided by the sum of investments. When the metric uses discounted capital budget in the denominator, I will refer to it as aPI for accounting Profitability Index. These metrics are fine for a single business unit with similar assets and for very small, short-cycle investments. They're simple and good enough. Outside of those circumstances, these metrics have blind spots relative to fBCR.

First, projects with large ongoing budgeted Capex requirements can show relatively less efficiency than would be indicated using fBCR. This long-term Capex, as you might see in a phased project, gets counted against the project even if it is covered by cash flow from operations. aPI creates an artificial burden relative to fBCR.

The second common situation is in countries that allow tax consolidation to depreciate investment against profitable operations. This reduces the effective investment of the development.

In the chart below, rather than a denominator of about 800 with fBCR, this metric would have a denominator of over 1300. You can see in year four and beyond, there is an offset to the capital expenditure that is reflected in the cash flow but not in the Capex.

I have seen this formula calculated in several ways: NPV divided by discounted Capex, NPV divided by Undiscounted Capex, and NPV / (Discounted Capex + abandonment and other costs), and any of these with the +1.

▸ Calculation of NPV/I

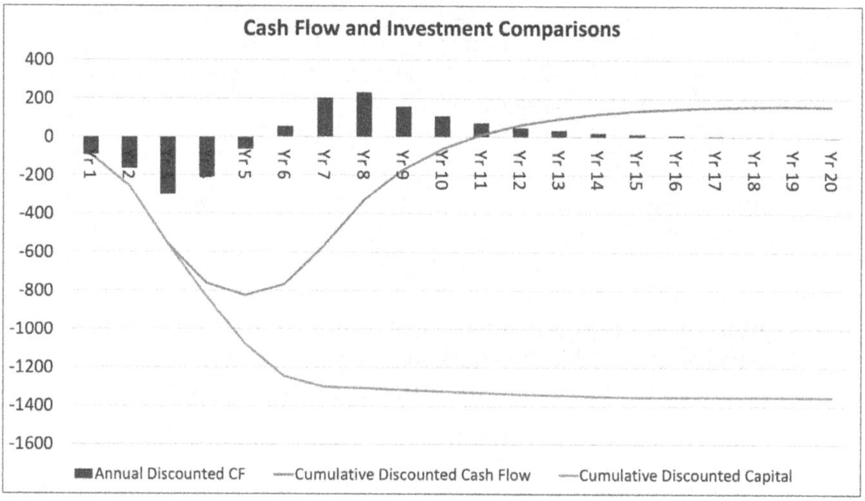

> *The NPV over I metrics depart from the financial textbook standard by including budgeted capital spending even when the net cash flow is positive. This usually results in a lower mathematical value than fBCR, so aPI and fBCR are not directly comparable. More importantly, projects with future budget capital needs or with early tax benefits show up as less efficient than others when measured by aPI. This creates an inconsistency between the aPI metric and financial theory. It can lead to flawed decisions (false negatives).*

The math of the calculation for NPV / I can cause division-by-zero issues for incremental economics and leads to distortions relative to financial theory for comparing investments with distinct cash flow patterns or in different fiscal regimes.

Despite the issues, NPV / I metrics are popular due to their perceived simplicity and their clear utility with short-term projects.

Other Ratios

I have seen other ratios proposed, e.g., 1 + NPV / (Total Capex plus Opex). Or additions to the denominator for specific expenses or costs, or credits for other specific types of payments or costs. These complications serve to turn what should be a simple metric into a black box that does not tell a clear story. On top of that, each one of these complications gets further away from the financial gold standard of net negative discounted cash flow.

Key Takeaways

MIRR and fBCR will give relative ranking recommendations consistent with financial theory. Other efficiency metrics suffer from mathematical and conceptual quirks that may yield different and misleading conclusions. If your company has standards for doing these calculations and ratios, you should follow those standards. But especially when comparing investments in dissimilar asset classes and fiscal systems, cross-check against fBCR. If it does not make a difference in the decision, do not worry. If it does make a difference, raise a red flag.

Countries seem to create fiscal regimes that give good investment efficiency to existing companies in the country. They do this by allowing for consolidation of results across a firm's businesses within the country. This allows earlier expensing of capital investment and lower cash exposure to the firm. The ability to recognize this lower exposure can make or break an investment in comparison with other ones in the portfolio.

Detour – Real Options

Real Options were a thing in the mid-to late-1990s. I saw two main paradigms in the literature of that time.

The first paradigm is related to a very algorithmic quantitative approach that attempts to use price volatility to apply different discount rates and even prices to products. This was sophisticated, somewhat esoteric, and could be challenging to calculate. The main flaw is that it did not incorporate the CAPM framework to help understand the value of the investment to the firm. I see some theoretical utility of these approaches in determining a market price for a project or asset without comparable sales to help calibrate.

In my opinion, one flavor of this first paradigm was more about marketing than options. The strategy was to use a lower discount rate for the project while also using futures prices in the models. The thinking was that because management can hedge oil prices, it allows for the use of a lower discount rate. Project managers with weak projects really liked this one because it made their projects look good.

This paradigm gained credibility when some of the largest consulting firms put their good names behind it. This approach was flawed in many ways. I heard of at least one project approved on this basis.

The second paradigm relates more to future management decisions that could be taken depending on previous outcomes. This approach is also sophisticated and costly to implement, but it makes more theoretical sense. It is more of a brute-force modeling than an algorithmic approach and links to potential real-world outcomes. The initial attempts used decision trees and traced optimal paths through probabilistic outcomes.

This is a detailed standard economic modeling approach that should be used when appropriate.

Options thinking is essential in business. Some investments open up more optionality than others, and it is valuable to incorporate those options into your thinking and quantitative models when practical.

But Should the Project Be Approved?

Science says, "I'll believe it when I see it." (IBIWISI.) Confirmation bias says, "I'll see it when I believe it." (ISIWIBI.)
Tony Kenck, 2022

Now we get to the crux of stand-alone decision-making. You have followed your standards and come up with a tremendous analysis. You may have generated some probability and sensitivity diagrams. Now what? Should you do the project?

Go vs. no-go decisions are sometimes black magic. There may be hurdles, like "IRR must be greater than 15%." Or perhaps that's the general rule, but exceptions are made for "strategic" assets or projects.

If you live in the perfect world of the Finance MBA textbook, you should do all projects with a positive NPV. In other words, all projects with a rate of return higher than your firm's cost of capital.

▸ Conceptual Ranking by Return

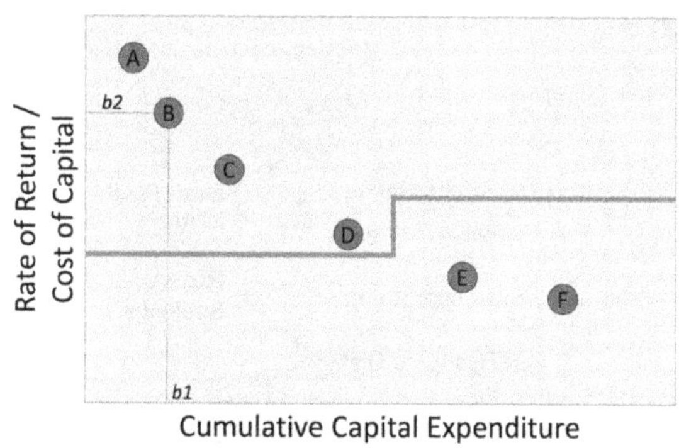

In a perfect world, projects with rates of return higher than the corporate cost of capital should be done. They will add value to the firm. As total financing costs increase, the cost of capital may also increase. You should, in theory, do A, B, C, and D, but not E or F. Forecasting the actual future performance of uncertain assets is impossible, so firms cut off projects well before they reach the cost of capital (e.g., at b2 rate of return or b1 cumulative capital).

There are several problems with this. First, not having constraints is unrealistic. Second, even if there are plenty of resources, at some point, the cost of capital will increase—as a firm takes on more and more projects, its cost of capital rises to reflect the risk that the company will overextend. Those first two are both important, but the third is the real kicker. Our calculated economics never accurately represent what will happen. The basis of the cost of capital chart above is that the dots represent how the projects will perform.

It has been a mantra in many industries across many years that projects tend to be late, over budget, and underperform. In the oil industry, during the first fifteen years of the 21st century, there was a fourth consideration. They were then "saved by the oil price." I call this the project mantra. These four uncertainties presented themselves in two ways: first, there is a wide uncertainty band around the economics of any project, and second, there is an optimism or confirmation bias inherent in projects, exacerbated by cultures that perceive that moving a project forward will be rewarded, even if the project is less than stellar in reality.

The diagram below (introduced here) shows an important reason why there is so much uncertainty. The best, most certain inputs in an upstream economic model are the fiscal regime and the estimate of the total oil and gas in place in an underground reservoir. The arrows show the derivatives. In general, the boxes on the left are the most reliable. The boxes on the right are either derived from the left or rely on unreliable inputs, such as future price and macroeconomic indicator estimates.

▸ **Data Reliability and Derivatives**

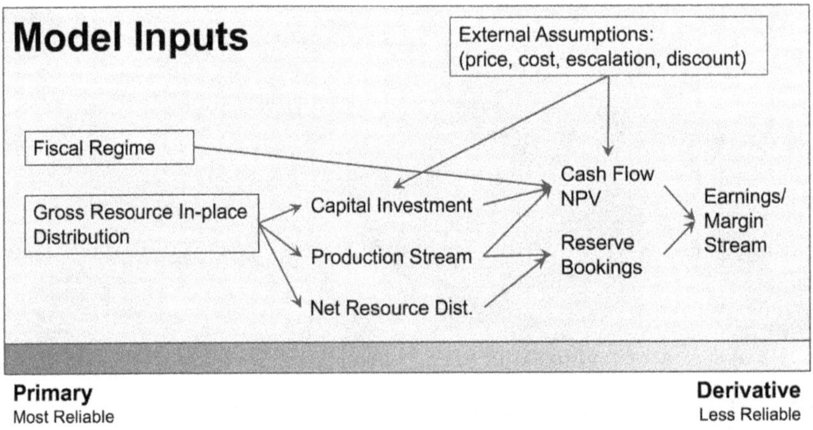

With so many assumptions, there is a good chance that a single value—the number—will be flawed. In addition, organizations have multiple biases. In standalone analysis, the only comparison is to a theoretical number based on projects thought to exist (with the same assumptions).

Calculations from highly uncertain and biased inputs are often optimistic, so companies are careful not to overextend. That is one reason why they apply budget constraints or an artificially high hurdle rate. In the cost of capital graph above, they might set their capital expenditure as no more than "b1" or set the "b2" rate of return for any project as the "must exceed" rate of return.

Finally, if your company has constraints, you should be discounting your cash flows at the rate of the next best project you can do, not at the (usually) lower cost of capital.

Now let's answer the question, "Should the project be approved"? If you do not have a listing of all the current projects, the answer is that you should approve the project if it makes sense strategically, fits with the company's mission, and exceeds your internal hurdle rate.

If you have a listing of internal projects, consider moving on to the comparison approaches of portfolio management.

Why is Standalone Analysis Not Sufficient? Opportunity Cost!

The good news is that Standalone Analysis is a prerequisite for every other type of portfolio analysis. The level and detail can vary, but there is always helpful information at the project level to incorporate into portfolio analyses.

The previous section goes a long way towards answering why standalone may be inadequate. Here I will expand on the concept of Opportunity Cost.

Opportunity Cost is a core concept in decision-making. If you live in a world of limited time, money, and attention, you already know this concept.

Consider this scenario. Your friend calls you and invites you to go skiing on Saturday. You really want to ski, so you say yes. But by saying yes, you have said no to everything else you could have been doing on Saturday. You're going to miss your kid's soccer game. You miss your parents' anniversary barbecue. You lose the opportunity to make a few bucks by driving for Uber.

When you say yes to one activity, you say no to everything that conflicts with it.

This is the essence of all economic analysis, including portfolio analysis. It is the reason for having a discount rate, and the reason for having a hurdle rate higher than the WACC.

Suppose you have a business that makes money. Business is good, and you are considering an expansion investment. The economic analysis would start with your base case—what your business is currently doing. Then you run a hypothetical case in which you invest in expansion. This will tell you what your business will look like after the investment. Finally, you would subtract the base case from the expansion case to see what it shows on an incremental basis.

In some cases, the standalone economic case is equal to the difference described above. But there are often interactions that occur, sometimes unnoticed. Think of a case in which you have two similar projects, both of which need your best project manager full-time. Trying to do both projects at once would result in delays in either or both projects. The same goes for cash or other scarce resources in an organization. Looking at the projects separately, without considering organizational restrictions, yields an optimistic view. The Appendix section on Portfolio Specific Value discusses these concepts in much greater detail.

When we look at standalone opportunities, we often increase the discount rate relative to the corporate WACC. With this higher discount rate, we have an implicit assumption that we are foregoing other good projects. Obviously, this discount rate adjustment does not help us with the shortage of project managers. **When you raise the discount rate to reflect opportunity cost, you make an implicit portfolio adjustment.** You are doing a crude form of portfolio.

This is the line where portfolio analysis starts. Standalone economics with cash flow discounted at the corporate WACC is just standalone. When you increase the discount rate to compensate for the other opportunities thought to exist, you have crossed into portfolio analysis territory.

Graphics and Communication in Standalone

Graphics for Standalone Analysis are straightforward.

Decision-makers will need to see relevant information along with a discussion of risks, costs, rewards, and graphs showing how an investment is expected to perform over time.

Companies will often have standard graphs, colors, and formats so that the decision-makers do not need to re-orient themselves with every project.

Usually, there is a table with key metrics and multiple time series graphs showing how they would progress over time.

▸ Eight Pack of Standalone Performance

Metrics Panel			
NPV8	$ 162,758	NPV12	$ 8,254
IRR	12.3%		
MIRR (8%, 12%)	11.7%		
fBCR8	1.27		
aPI8	1.16		
Average Earnings per BOE	$ 5.22	Total Barrels Produced MMBOE	142.5
Total Cost per BOE	$ 38.97		
Capital Cost per BOE	$ 11.02		
Average ROCE	15.86%		

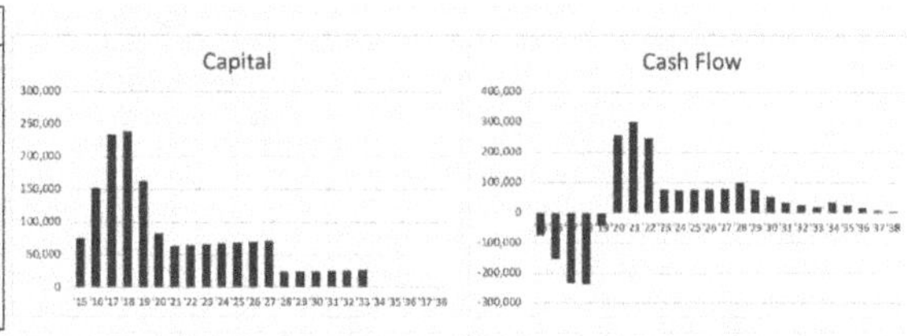

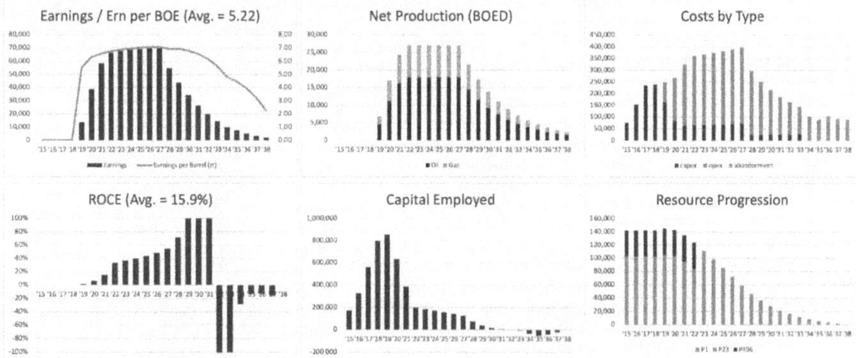

Stand-alone graphs and metrics displays can contain any number of metrics in any order. Most firms have formal or informal standards for reporting and decision-making.

The project above certainly looks promising. It has a high NPV, excellent efficiency as measured by several metrics, and it makes almost $13 per barrel in average earnings margin. It is a low capital-cost development, but the total cost per barrel is high due to high operating expenses.

Decision analysts who make comparisons of different timing, scale, and scope options for a project have their own sets of tools and displays. Those specifics are covered in other books and literature.

This is an example. Every company has standards for what the leaders want to see for stand-alone decision-making.

CHAPTER 4

The Broad Process Beyond Standalone Analysis

This is our first jump past standalone analysis. The process gets more involved. All other methods rely on an inventory of opportunities and investment alternatives with their associated information.

Inventories

Listing of entities or competing investments, time series data, metadata, and decision possibilities of the entire business under consideration. A *Complete Inventory* in a perfect world would include, at least, a high-level sense of decisions thought to be off the table.

The complete inventory of a company would be sizable and potentially include many decisions that are not being considered at a given time. Such an inventory is difficult to develop and maintain. We need to reduce the complete inventory to something more manageable. The Working Inventory is the subset of the complete inventory determined by the frame of the analysis. It is the data for all the entities or parts of the business to be incorporated into the study.

For comparison methods, you want the investments to be comparable to and competing with other investments. Rollup and interaction techniques will also include base entities, which are relevant because they provide the context for the firm's overall performance, even though there may be no decision to be made on them. The working inventory must also include limits and other information about the decisions or potential decisions that should be taken into consideration.

Inventory Analysis

Next, we can compare and combine entities from the working inventory in meaningful ways.

Comparison and Inventory Methods require the tabular or graphical display of comparable or competing opportunities.

Portfolio Candidate Set Generation in Rollup and Interaction Methods

Rollups require the addition of portfolio pieces and meaningful segmentation. Rollup portfolios are generally simple and have most of the decisions pre-determined, often with an extra entity or two.

For *Simulation* and other probabilistic work, it is necessary to have representations of the risks and uncertainties involved in your entities. You can perform simulations using Excel or a specialized tool.

For *Optimization*, you'll need a goal-seeking tool to find the best set of coordinated decisions that achieves organizational targets. The set can also be created by manually selecting the elements using rules of thumb, strategic themes, or intuition to guide selection. A group of coordinated decisions is known as the Candidate Set.

▸ Process Flow Beyond Standalone Analysis

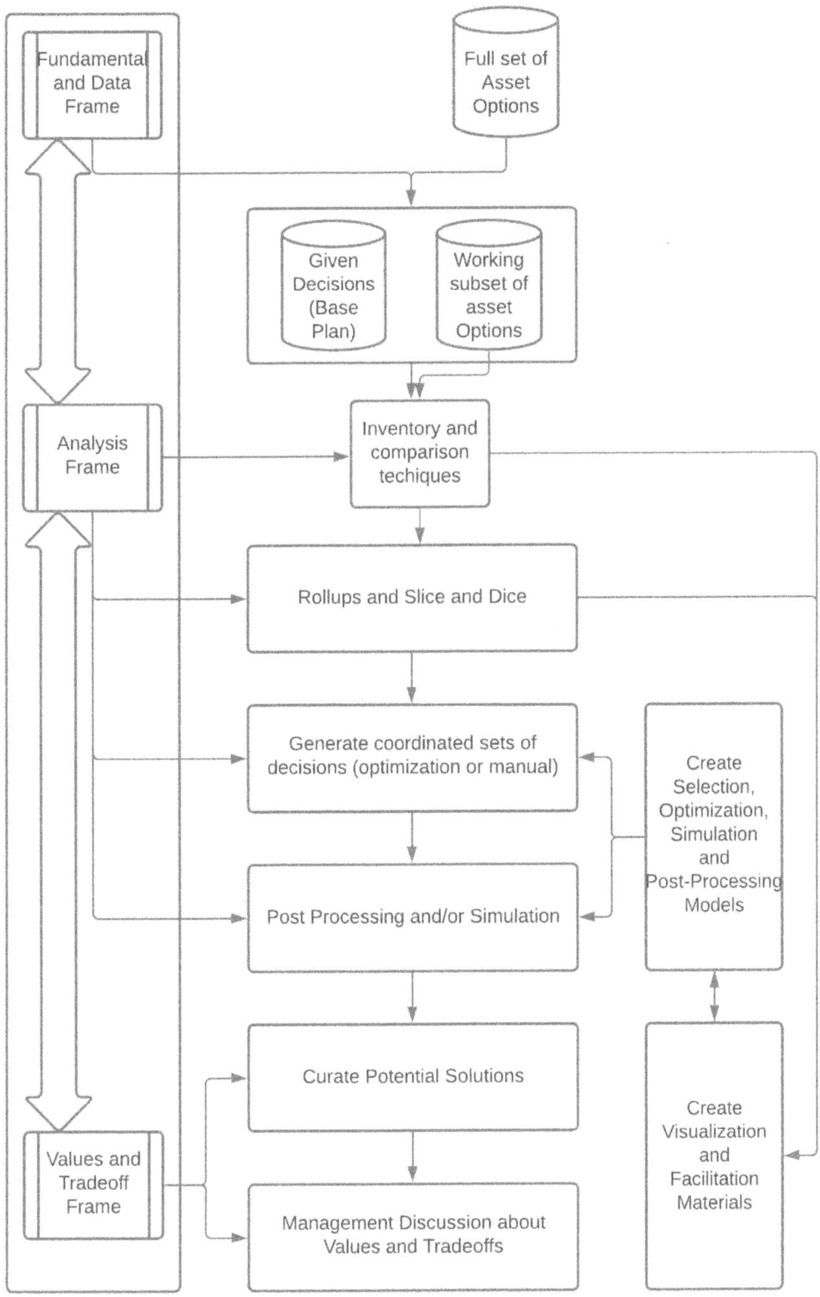

> *The processes beyond standalone require tools, skills, and a different decision-making perspective. A firm that wishes to make portfolio decisions needs to properly frame its needs and appetite for additional complexity and nuance.*

Post-processing of portfolios

Use Monte Carlo or other means to simulate results and to incorporate complex dependencies (such as tax consolidation) and statistical relationships that would be overly complex for quick optimization. Additional processing may result in material differences in outcomes and decisions. Alternatively, the post-processing step may align the data with corporate needs for planning and forecasting.

Visualization and Decision-making

Finally, you need to display the analysis in a way that provides insights to the decision-makers.

The overall framework of the analysis on the left is always present and always live. Insights gained during portfolio analysis and discussion can modify the frame.

> **Key Takeaways**
>
> Moving beyond standalone implies having data for multiple opportunities for comparison and aggregation. The framing of the decisions or questions is vital in selecting the entities and data to include. To be clear, many decisions do not need to incorporate all of the steps in the chart above. It is a fairly complete view of what could be done and how the process would flow.

CHAPTER 5

Comparison and Inventory Methods

Now that we are past standalone analysis and the assumption of unlimited funding and resources, we can move on to the concept of constraints and requirements. There are **always** factors that prevent us from doing everything we might want to do as fast as it can be done. Whether it's people, money, government approvals, or specific targets or goals, there is always something that limits how much we do.

Comparison methods is the first step towards providing an explicit context for portfolio decisions. Data without context is information malpractice. Moving to compare portfolio techniques is a small technical step for a firm. After all, the data exists for each of the projects under consideration. Organizing the data already generated for approvals provides a great start to this step. Cultural barriers to transparency and sharing of data are sometimes an issue.

Portfolio Selector Focus on Comparison Methods

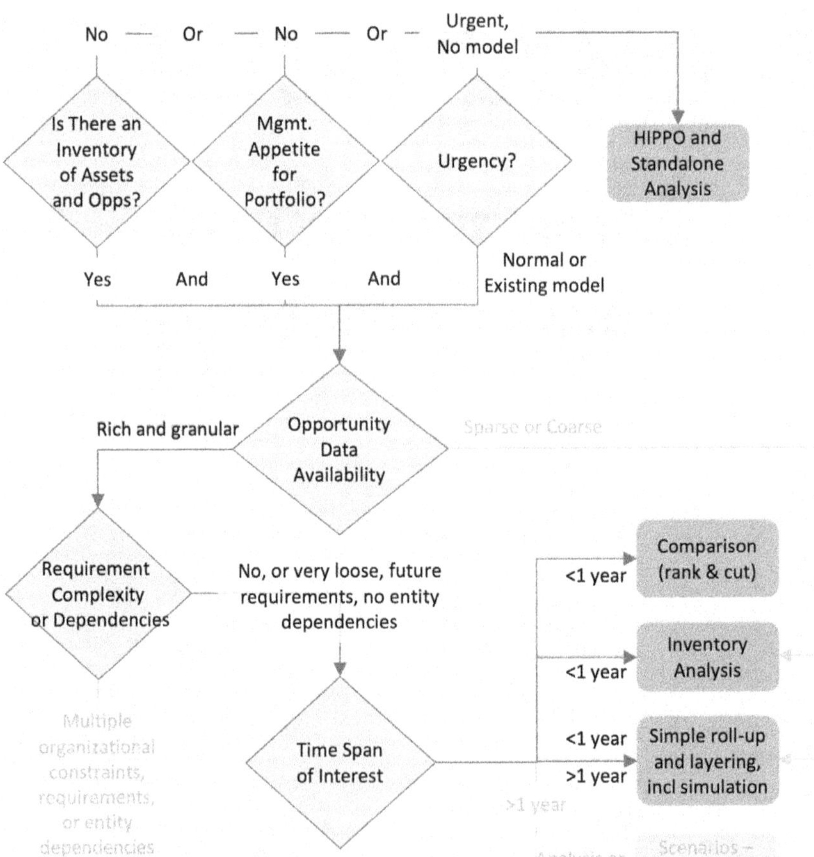

Once there's time, data, and an appetite for more, the next step is the jump to simple inventory and comparison. These methods are easiest when your metrics of interest can be reduced to a single value, such as NPV, IRR, or total production.

We use these approaches when there is good inventory and portfolio data, potential optionality in assets or outcomes, management appetite for portfolio work, and adequate time to do the work.

Please note that for many companies, the availability of data from throughout the company is difficult. Asset and project managers, sometimes with good reason, resist sharing "their" information without knowing the specific purpose for sharing or being compelled to do so because of the culture. They may have been burned by a zealous but unskilled analyst who misused or mischaracterized projects in the past. Decentralized organizations are especially prone to these suspicions.

Getting past the closed culture and moving towards a more open and sharing culture is a prerequisite for the more powerful portfolio methods.

Key Takeaways

1. This first class of techniques beyond standalone analysis requires data across multiple entities. Once past that hurdle, the analytic methods of this class are relatively simple. Data organization and management are more important than sophisticated analytics. Graduation to this class of portfolio tools helps decision-makers go beyond the simple question of whether the investment is good, and into the context of "Compared to What?"
2. This analysis class is foundational for more sophisticated classes because the skills used to compare individual investment opportunities will also be applied at a portfolio level with interactive techniques.

Rank and Cut

Simple rank ordering of projects by a metric is an excellent start to understanding your portfolio. There is nothing mechanically tricky about doing this. Picking the right ranking criterion and then using the information is trickier.

If ranking on a single criterion, the best one is usually an efficiency metric using your constrained resource in the denominator. For example, if you have more projects than capital budget, NPV divided by project capital budget might be a good criterion. You would sort the projects in descending order of efficiency, then fund the top projects until the cumulative costs exceed the budget.

Finance textbooks often recommend that when ranking multiple projects to select a subset of them, they should be ordered by internal rate of return (IRR) or an efficiency metric like NPV/Investment, where

Investment is the discounted negative cash flow stream. As detailed elsewhere in the book, other measures of cost are used and have a practical aspect that is valuable to consider.

For many people, and in many cases, this is an excellent way to rank and select investments. Let's look at a simple example using the data set below.

Working Set of Example Opportunities

	Cost	Value
Opp 1	1	7.1
Opp 2	3	4.1
Opp 3	5	9
Opp 4	8	19
Opp 5	2	3
Opp 6	4	7
Opp 7	6	1
Opp 8	9	3
Opp 9	12	8
Opp 10	4	10

The working set of opportunities for the examples in this section. Cost and value are generic. Value is the net realized value after all costs.

We get this if we sort the table above by the value-to-cost ratio (VCR).

We can see that the best project is Opp 1 with a VCR of 7.1, followed by Opp 10 with a VCR of 2.5, and so on. The worst opportunity is Opp 7, with a VCR of 0.17.

Sample Opportunities Sorted by Efficiency

	Cost	Value	Value/ Cost
Opp 1	1	7.1	7.1
Opp 10	4	10	2.5
Opp 4	8	19	2.38
Opp 3	5	9	1.8
Opp 6	4	7	1.75
Opp 5	2	3	1.5
Opp 2	3	4.1	1.37
Opp 9	12	8	0.67
Opp 8	9	3	0.33
Opp 7	6	1	0.17

Sorting the working inventory list based on the value-to-cost ratio yields a prioritized list based on efficiency.

This view is interesting and valuable. You can see which projects provide the best bang for your buck.

Another perspective is provided with the so-called 'CFO chart,' which is a line plot of cumulative value on the Y-axis and cumulative cost on the x-axis. It shows visually how efficiency changes across the inventory of opportunities.

The projects to the left have the highest efficiency, as measured by the value to cost ratio. Consequently, the slope of the line between the points is the incremental efficiency of the project on the right.

By inspection, you can fund the best projects by selecting the ones on the left until you reach your total budget on the x-axis. This view shows the **Rank**; then you **Cut** everything to the right of your budget line.

▸ "CFO Chart" of the Sorted Opportunities

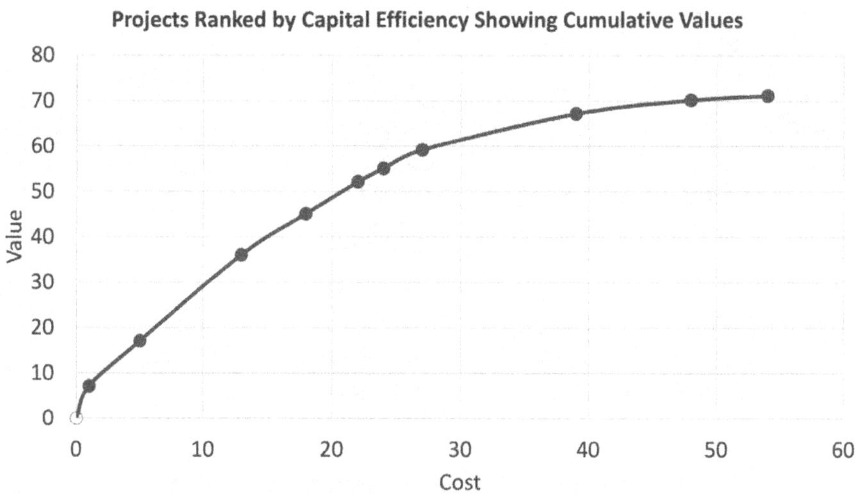

The 'CFO chart' shows the efficiency-ranked opportunities as a chart of cumulative value on the y-axis and cumulative cost on the x-axis. In principle, you can cut off the list at the cost that reflects your budget, then fund the projects that fall to the left of the budgetary constraint. Each point on the chart represents a set of projects—a unique candidate set (portfolio) of funded activities.

People often believe this approach gives "the answer"—it may or may not, but it is often a good starting point. There may be other considerations not depicted on this graph. For example, the worst-ranked project on the right may have some risk mitigation that is not shown on the value side and which leadership believes outweighs the value addition of the other opportunities.

Alternatively, investments can be given combination scores that contain some form of goodness or utility metric. Some decision-makers favor a multi-attribute or multi-objective scoring system to create a single-point score for ranking. You could then select your projects based on this combination metric until you run out of money to fund them.

When using an investment efficiency criterion, the numerator is a value measure (e.g., NPV), and investment in some form is the denominator. This may be a reasonable assumption, especially when the projects are small and payouts are in the near term. When the investment and revenue stream occur over multiple years, any approach that collapses strings of costs and benefits into a single point can mislead.

Rank and Cut Attributes

Data: Usually, cash flow and investment time series data collapse to a single value—perhaps using NPV calculations. Alternatively, data for the numerator and denominator of whatever metric you plan to use.

Tools: Spreadsheet with graphing capabilities, advanced graphics program

Decisions: Most appropriate for projects with a short implementation time, generally within the budget year. Also used for comparing similar investment types or asset classes.

Advantages:

1. Simple.
2. Useful for considering opportunities with similar cash flows, risks, etc., such as with a development drilling program.

Disadvantages:

1. It does not show the effects of projects across time.
2. Optimizers Curse and other unforeseen consequences (see following sections).

Key Takeaways

1. Many people who read this section will probably think, "This is good. This is what I do, and it is portfolio management. What could possibly be beyond this?"
2. If you are doing this in your business, that is a good start. Your, perhaps unstated, premise is something like "the efficiency of my investments as defined by multi-year cash flow discounted at our standard rate divided by multi-year investment discounted at the same standard rate is all my company should care about."

3. If you work in a business with an inventory of similar opportunities that are reasonably comparable, that's probably acceptable. Strategic decisions have been made, and you are executing. Good job.
4. If you compare dissimilar assets with investments and benefits that stretch across many years, you are missing insights with this approach.
5. Rank and Cut is the first step in comparison methods. It is especially useful in budgeting, and there are pitfalls. Besides Standalone, Rank and Cut is probably the most common form of portfolio analysis and management. It is technically simple, and the most significant difficulty is ensuring that data is comparable.
6. Standalone analysis makes an implicit assumption about the inventory. Rank and Cut views the relevant projects explicitly in the context of other projects in the working inventory that are being considered. If this is as far as you go on your portfolio journey, it is better than never having started. You will make better-informed decisions.

Detour – Planning Model vs Portfolio Model

People in planning and strategy organizations often focus on near-term planning and budgeting. While strategy is essential, budgeting and planning become urgent based on the calendar, and require a lot of time, attention, data, and executive focus.

Planners want a model that produces precise and internally consistent summations of the plan, including all the tax consequences across countries and different fiscal regimes. They want the precision required when submitting budgets on which people will be judged next year. The inputs to those models contain implicit decisions and assumptions.

The precision of those models may be necessary when judging short-term performance. But such a model, which I refer to as a planning model, is the opposite of what is useful for portfolio modeling.

With portfolio modeling, speed and ease of manipulation are much more important than precision.

With a planning model, everything is locked into place and decisions are predetermined. Incorporating changes in an asset, such as delays, acceleration, testing a different development concept, or changing working interest, can be difficult and are typically not considered.

A rough-and-ready portfolio model can make those changes with the flip of a switch. They allow for quick portfolio tests that do not have a budget's false precision but are insightful nonetheless.

The ability to quickly model widely varying decisions and strategies is an essential early step in portfolio analysis *before* the decisions are made. Once the insights are gained with **portfolio** tools, lock in the actions for detailed modeling for budgeting and accountability.

Detail – Optimizer's Curse, aka The Law of Inevitable Disappointment

Rank and Cut methods are standard in business. It is common to have more opportunities than the capacity to execute them. Rank and Cut provides a simple way to make the selection. Rank the projects by some metric, then select the best ones that fit within the budget.

It will be the best answer in a perfectly predictable and deterministic world. Sadly (or thankfully), we do not live in that world. One negative consequence of single-dimensional rank and cut approaches is "Optimizer's Curse," aka "The Law of Inevitable Disappointment." It is a tendency to inadvertently overstate forecasted rollup results, even if the underlying forecasts or projections are very reasonable and unbiased.

Let's start with a list of ten projects. They all have the same cost to keep the illustration simple, but they have different values. The value-to-cost ratio is here defined as 1 + Value / Cost. It is effectively the positive cash flow stream divided by the investment.

▸ **Sample Projects for Optimizer's Curse**

Project Name	Value	Cost	Value to Cost Ratio
Alpha	12.9	10	2.29
Bravo	14.9	10	2.49
Charlie	6.6	10	1.66
Delta	9.3	10	1.93
Echo	5.7	10	1.57
Foxtrot	2.5	10	1.25
Golf	18.2	10	2.82
Hotel	2.7	10	1.27
India	15	10	2.5
Juliett	12.2	10	2.22

The input set of projects used to illustrate the Optimizer's Curse. Please note that the costs of the projects are all the same. The distinction in these projects is on the value side.

Golf is the best project in this sorted list, with a net value of 18.2. Foxtrot is the worst, with a value of 2.5. If you were given a budget of 50, selecting Golf, Bravo, India, Juliett, and Alfa would be quite reasonable. The expected program value would be 73.2.

But I forgot to mention something... Oops!

The projects are identical. They will each, in reality, have a cost of 10 and a value of 10 for a Value to Cost Ratio of 2.0. The calculated values came from the assessments by different project teams. They had different personal biases, education, and information. As a group, they were unbiased; the total estimated value was equal to the total actual value. Five of the opportunities were overvalued and five were undervalued.

If you had completed all ten projects, your lookback would indicate that your technical staff is unbiased and, given the uncertainties, good estimators. But once there is a choice to be made and a single-dimensional criterion, a form of survivorship bias kicks in.

To explain the table below, if you were to do only the best project, you would forecast a value of 18.2. However, you would realize an actual value of 10. So, the forecast error resulting from the optimizer's curse is 8.2 or 45% of the forecasted value. Adding Bravo—the second-best project—reduces the percentage error to 40%. By the time you are back to all ten projects, the forecasting error on the program will have disappeared.

Table Showing Optimizer's Curse

Project Name	Calculated Value	Cost	Value to Cost Ratio	Total Cumulative Calculated Value	Total Cumulative Actual Value	Optimizer Curse Error	Error as a % of program calculated value
Golf	18.2	10	2.82	18.2	10	8.2	45%
Bravo	14.9	10	2.49	33.1	20	13.1	40%
India	15	10	2.5	48.1	30	18.1	38%
Juliett	12.2	10	2.22	60.3	40	20.3	34%
Alpha	12.9	10	2.29	73.2	50	23.2	32%
Delta	9.3	10	1.93	82.5	60	22.5	27%
Charlie	6.6	10	1.66	89.1	70	19.1	21%
Echo	5.7	10	1.57	94.8	80	14.8	16%
Hotel	2.7	10	1.27	97.5	90	7.5	8%
Foxtrot	2.5	10	1.25	100	100	0	0%

The harsher the cut in your rank and cut analysis, the further your forecast of results will be from the actual outcome. This is a form of statistical survivorship bias.

The stricter the cut, the larger the error. You can see in the last column that the lower the number of projects in the rank and cut selection, the larger the error of actual results as a percent of the forecast. This is a contrived and overly simplistic example to illustrate the concept, but the principle applies.

What's the solution? As of this writing, I have not seen a satisfying answer. Perhaps a business could generate a function based on past rank and cut exercises to understand empirically the amount of uncertainty in their estimates and then use that to back-calculate a correction factor to align the expectations with reality.

Expanding this framework a bit more, it is similar to the Winner's Curse. I wonder if this sort of survivorship bias is partly the source of Planners' Bias with all the projects that were prematurely rejected due to erroneous value or cost estimates.

Detail – Wonky, Unintended Consequences of Using Rank and Cut and Standalone with the Wrong Frame

Taking uncertainty out of the picture, I want to talk about the frame in which rank and cut is applicable and how it might lead to other unintended consequences.

Optimizers Curse shows a survivorship bias based on the inherent uncertainty of an inventory of potential investments. It is a statistical artifact of uncertainty combined with the selection process.

Rank and Cut is applicable when comparing similar, typically small, projects within a single business unit. It loses fidelity when a firm aspires to do more than simply maximize the investment efficiency of the company's individual projects.

Many efficiency metrics contain biases. For example, the internal rate of return (IRR) will exaggerate the effective rate of return of a short-term, relatively low investment project. It does not technically exaggerate the IRR, but it **does** implicitly assume that the project is one of many similar projects. The calculation of IRR does not take into account the reinvestment returns of cash that is spun out of a project. This was covered in more detail in Detail – Efficiency Metrics.

Why is this a problem?

If a firm has goals beyond simply executing the highest returning projects, those goals may be compromised. Many firms want to increase their earnings or production over time and achieve longevity. In the oil industry, the most efficient projects are often low-investment, short production-life extensions of existing operations. These are excellent investments. But there is not an "endless" supply of them. As the best ones are drilled and produced, the remaining ones are more expensive and less productive.

This leads to a firm needing to do more and more to maintain cash flow and earnings. This business model is effective for a limited time. Ultimately, assets that last longer and can carry production without significant additional cash investments are required to get through the low periods.

Consider this contrived example as an illustration.

A firm has several small opportunities and one large one that is reasonably long-lived. The firm's WACC is 8%.

▸ **Cash Flow Time-Series for Big Project**

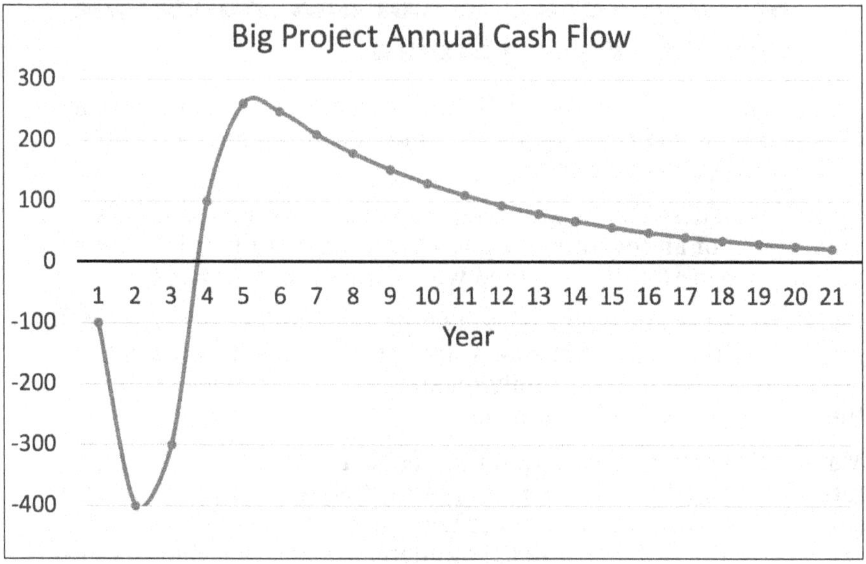

Annual net cash flow for the big, low-return project

▸ **Cash Flow Time-Series for Small Projects**

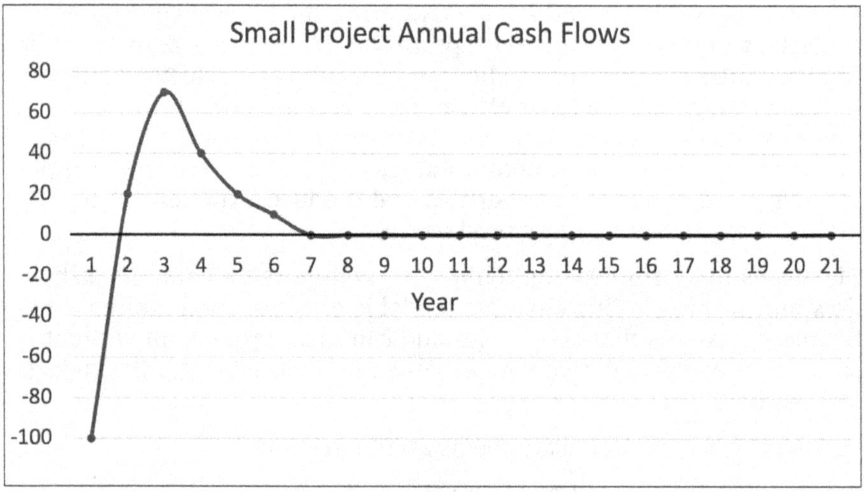

Annual net cash flow for the small, high-return project

Each of the small ones has an excellent rate of return of 21%, while the large project has a rate of 15%.

The firm has ascertained that 16% is its opportunity cost of capital, so it uses 16% as the discount rate hurdle. Remember that this reflects management's belief in an endless supply of 16% opportunities.

Comparative Metrics for Single Big and Small Projects

	NPV8	NPV16	IRR
Small Project	$29.44	$9.22	21%
Big Project	$291.82	($19.92)	15%

Comparative metrics for Big and Small project

Standalone Analysis with 16% Hurdle Rate

Using NPV16, you would reject Big Project because there are better places to spend money in the company according to your beliefs about internal alternatives.

Rank and Cut Analysis

In comparing Big Project with Small Project, we see that Small Project has a higher rate of return. We'll **compare the results of an equivalent investment in multiple Small projects with the Big project**.

To do this, we put one small project in year 1, four in year 2, and three in year 3. This gives us the same initial investment profile.

Summing the small projects together gives the result in dark line compared to the lighter single big project.

You can see the difference. While small projects give us a tremendous bang for the buck in the short term, they do not last. In order to continue as a viable firm, there would need to be a deep pipeline of projects. There's nothing wrong with that if a reliable pipeline of projects exists. If not, the lack of a relatively stable base cash flow could put the firm's longevity in peril by pursuing returns without considering other program attributes.

But wait, there's more!

▶ Outcomes for Comparable Capital Outlays

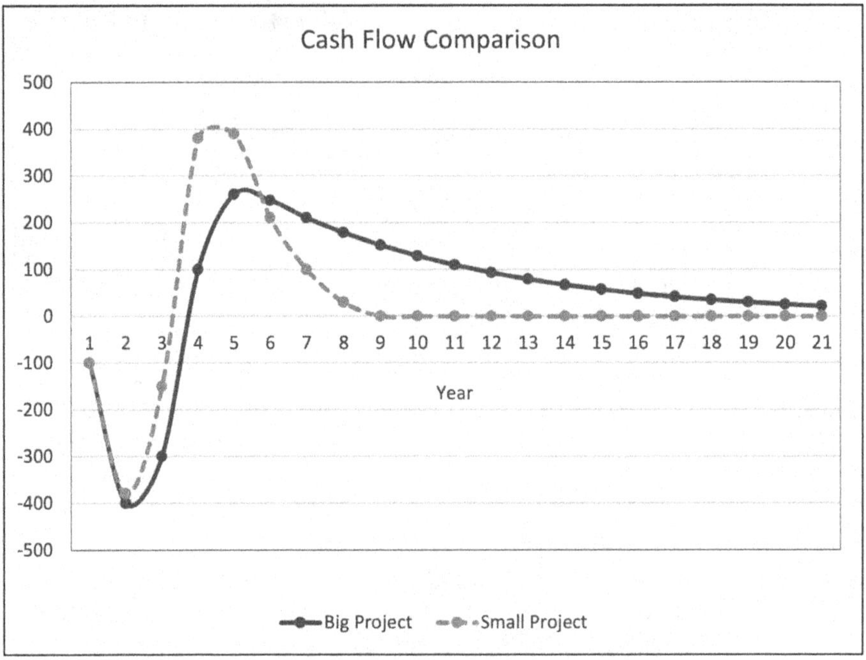

Equal budgeted capital results in a similar cash outlay for two years. The main contrast is in the positive cash flow. The big project has a much slower decline after its peak production, while the combination of multiple small projects has a higher peak cash flow but is gone after 9 years.

▶ Comparison of Comparable Program Metrics

	NPV8	NPV16	IRR
Small Project	$214.18	$16.57	21%
Big Project	$291.82	($19.92)	15%

Although the Small Project has great metrics, it has no longevity. The firm would need to continue investing large amounts to show the same longevity from small projects as from a single big project. This example is obviously contrived to make the Big Project look bad at the hurdle rate. The ability to take a longer-term view with rollups could prevent this sort of situation.

By pursuing higher returns, you may also sacrifice corporate value. Remember, the ultimate value of the corporation is determined by its NPV at the **WACC** (8%). A program that emphasizes investment efficiency using a higher opportunity may sacrifice value as an unintended consequence.

As mentioned, this is a contrived example. Planning and budgeting processes may help prevent this outcome. But it illustrates the perils of pursuing a singular focus on a metric that is not in good alignment with a full suite of corporate aspirations. It is seeking a means objective (IRR) at the expense of the fundamental objective (NPV at WACC).

Adding Dimensions to Rank and Cut

As we saw in the Rank Ordering section, there are many ways to rank order projects or assets. They can be ordered by NPV, Benefit Cost Ratio (BCR), Strategic fit, or any other parameter. Of course, the world is seldom so simple that a single metric tells us everything we need to know, so we extend the framework. This single-dimensional view can be extended into multiple dimensions or axes.

Boston Consulting Group (BCG) popularized the Growth Share Matrix as a strategic portfolio tool to help companies sort and categorize their assets to inform decisions. Market growth and market share are two factors companies should consider when deciding where to invest. We see that the "Star" assets are those with high market share and high growth. A "star" asset should be significantly invested in as it has high future potential. The "Pets" (also referred to as "Dogs") are those with low market share and low growth, companies should divest from, or reposition, these products. "Cash Cows" are products with low growth and high share and should be "milked" for cash to reinvest. "Question Marks" are those whose future is uncertain and should be invested in or discarded depending on their chances of becoming "stars." Managers would then plan their actions according to the general needs of holdings in that quadrant. *Description provided with permission by Boston Consulting Group.*

The axes of this graph are useful in a retail or consumer market environment, but less so in a global fungible commodity market, such as the oil industry. However, there is an essential lesson from this chart that can be generalized. It compares an external attribute (overall market growth) with an inward-looking one (our market share). This type of perspective can be valuable in many circumstances.

A powerful example from my experience was comparing potential acquisition targets. We plotted 'do-ability,' which is the external competitive focus on whether we could capture it, versus desirability, which is the strategic fit to the company.

▸ **Boston Consulting Group Growth Share Matrix**

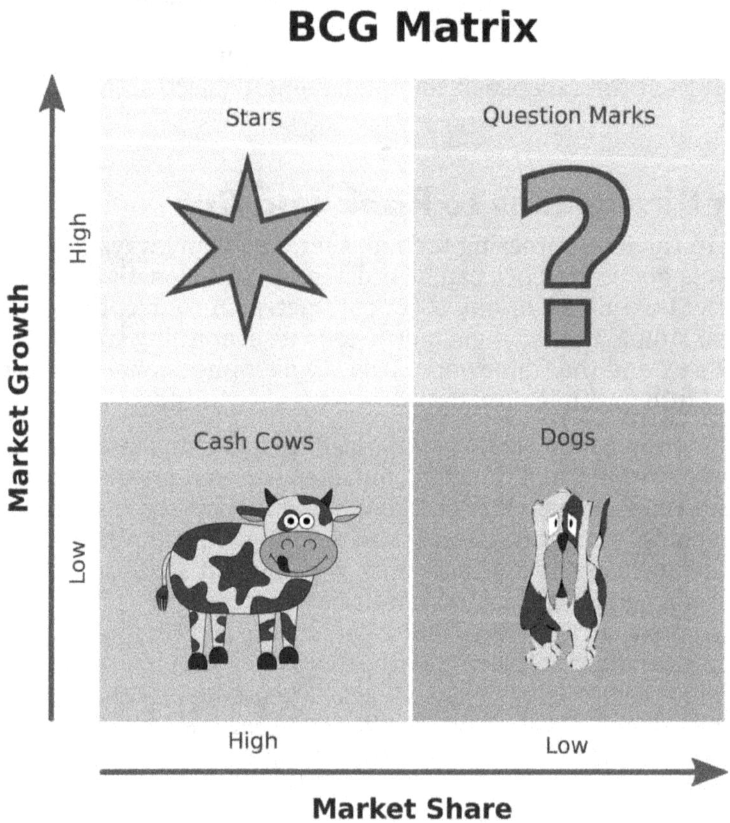

The Boston Consulting Group's famous 2x2 matrix shows the stars as the winners, dogs (now pets) with low growth and low market share as the losers, and the cash cow and question mark quadrants as needing improvement. The cash cows are reliable cash generators in a slow sector, while the question marks need to increase market share in a hot sector.

Anytime there are two variables, they can be plotted against each other to help understand the relationships and possible trade-offs between the variables. The two-dimensional plot can be thought of as two superimposed rank-and-cut lists (seriatim ranked lists). The y-axis shows the ascending order of one metric, while the x-axis shows the ascending order of the other.

As an example, the following two graphs can be combined into a single scatter plot.

Operational Metric – Total Production by Country

▸ **Rank Order by Future Production**

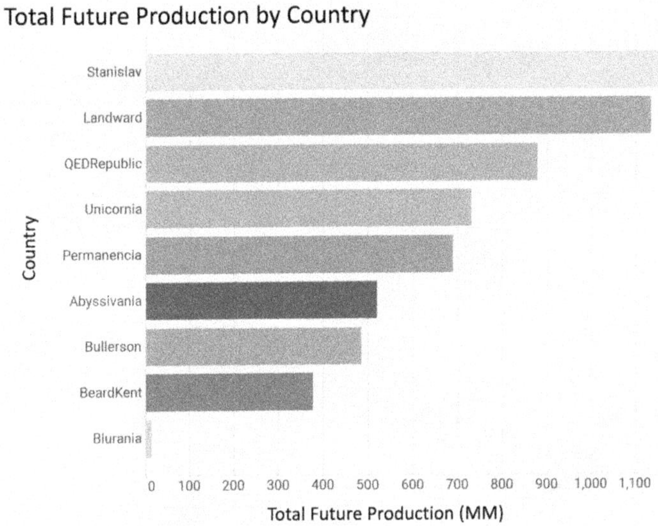

| *Shows the rank order by country of total future production.*

Financial Metric – Avg Earnings per Barrel by Country

▸ **Rank Order of Profitability**

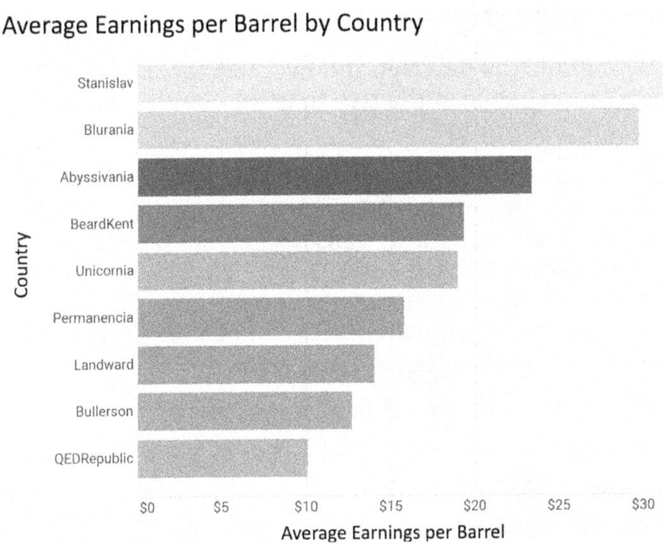

| *Shows the rank order by country of average lifetime earnings per barrel.*

Earnings per Barrel and Total Production Cross Plotted

▸ Cross-Plotting Production and Profitability

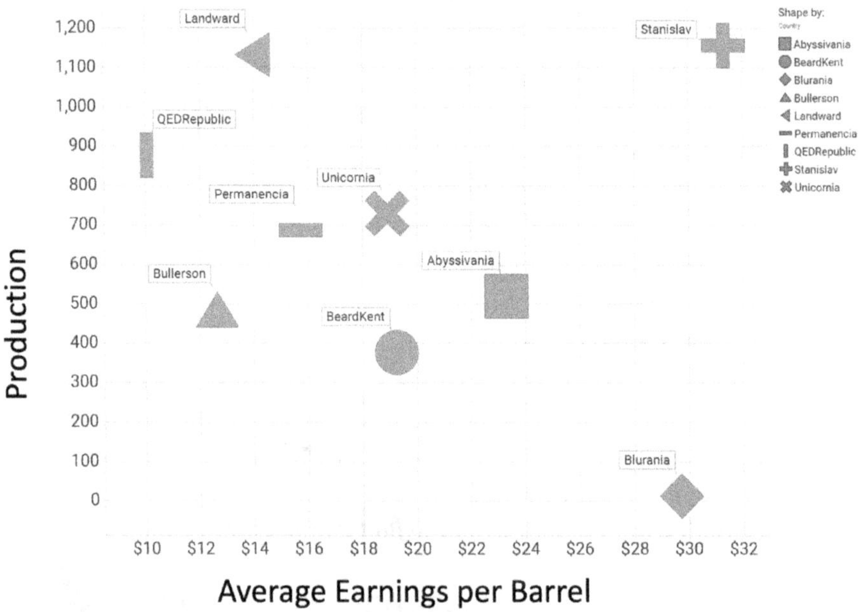

2D charts are effectively two one-dimensional charts at right angles to each other. This allows us to see relationships between the variables or to find exceptionally good or bad assets. The shapes are by asset.

This plot shows the relationship between the two metrics. There seems to be a negative correlation between the two metrics. Stanislav is an outlier and is both large and profitable.

It is a best practice to create multiple charts with different axes to see and understand relationships between metrics. In addition, using modern graphical visualization software, selecting a data point in one chart will highlight the same entity in other charts. With these types of tools, you can create a dashboard that can show you at a glance the strengths and weaknesses of individual entities. Some other examples of potentially interesting goal comparisons are:

1. Short-term v long-term profitability and cash flow.
2. Next year's earnings vs. long-term NPV.
3. Return on Capital Employed vs. NPV.
4. NPV vs. discounted capital investment.
5. Success case NPV vs. Probability of Success (research or exploration).

6. Risked NPV vs. Success Case Rate of Return.
7. Return vs. risk.
8. Time horizon of efforts vs categories.
9. Profitability at high prices vs. profitability at low prices.
10. Economic value vs. strategic importance.
11. Do-ability vs. desirability.
12. Total lifetime production vs. the NPV of the asset.
13. Viability (economic) vs. Fit (strategic).

Another example is a simple chart showing NPV on the x-axis against total resources (Risked P1-P6) on the y-axis. Gray shade is an indicator of the hydrocarbon type, with lighter gray being more gas-prone and darker more oil-prone.

▸ Adding a Third Dimension with Shading or Color

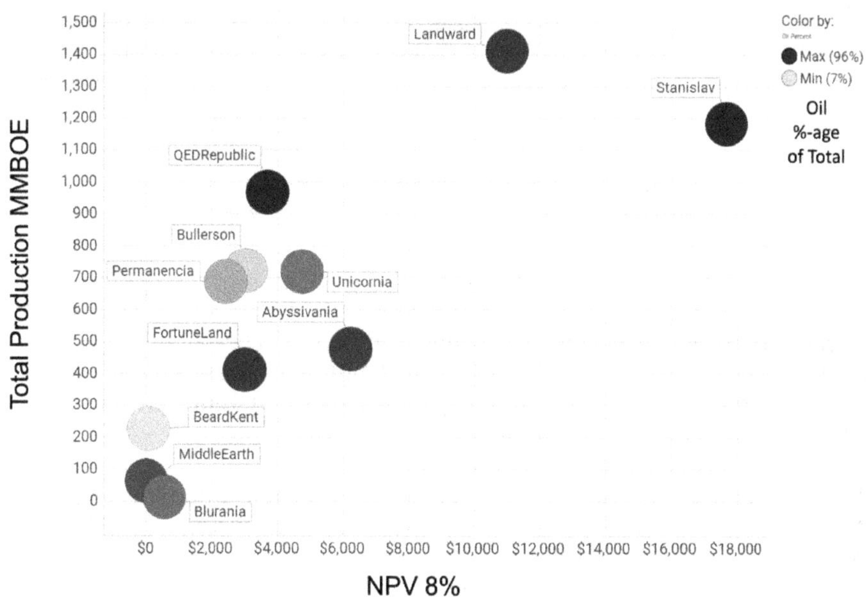

Adding color or shades of gray is great for showing categorical differences. Shades are more difficult to interpret than position, but are often insightful. In this case, we use gray shades to show a gradation of oil vs. gas production.

It is possible, but a really bad idea, to show eight dimensions on a single two-dimensional plot. X and Y are easy. Z can be brought in as a 3D projection onto the screen or paper. Bubble size, shape, color, rotation of the shape, and labels can all be added.

Here's an example with five dimensions. Avg Earnings per BOE is on the x-axis, 10-year production on the y-axis, color shows hydrocarbon type, and size shows total lifetime production. Finally, the shape shows the country. This chart lacks a 3rd dimension, marker rotation, and labels to thoroughly saturate the view.

▸ Busy Busy Chart – Five Dimensions

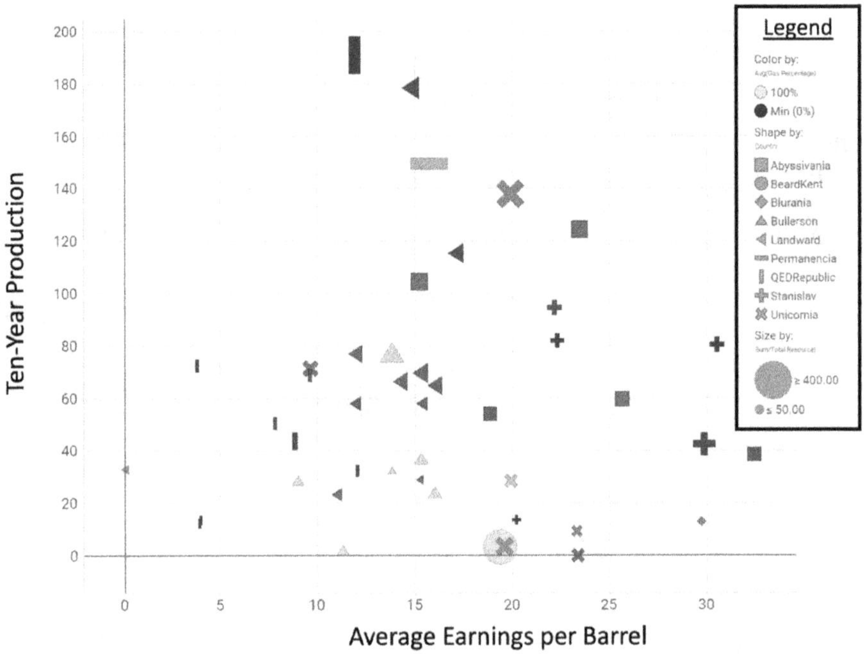

> *Graphs that show more than three dimensions quickly become extremely busy, and for analysts with my design sense, quite ugly. Showing off the insane capabilities of your graphics package may not lead to effective communication.*

Now forget you ever saw it. Just remember that it's a bad idea. It is too complicated for anyone to wrap their head around meaningfully, especially in a limited time.

Some people prefer to put the dots into buckets, like low, medium, and high, rather than assigning a value. This makes sense if the axis is a category by its nature, such as asset class. When the axis is a value, step functions between buckets mislead. There can also be significant differences within a category from one limit to the other. In my experience, unless the boundaries between buckets are meaningful and crystal clear, with no possibility of independent judgment or gaming, there may be problems. This bucketing issue could be eliminated by defining more and smaller buckets-but then why bucket at all?

The horizontal bar charts above, which show total production and earnings per barrel by country, are examples of bucketing metrics into a category. Note that the buckets (assets) are discrete, but the values are just the values.

Value Estimation When Uncertainty is Large

Organizations hate to change. Asking people to estimate numbers precisely when accuracy is impossible can seem counterproductive. Why not just put the numbers into broad buckets and be done? As mentioned, this creates distortions due to incentives to over- or under-estimate to fit a better bucket. Another issue, which is probably worse, is that when presented with buckets, some people turn off their brains and don't think hard about the case for the bucket location. The consumers of the analysis (rightly) lose confidence in the inputs when people assign values without a logical rationale.

Key Takeaways

As a rule, adding dimensions to rank and cut is a good idea, and it helps management understand the roles different assets play in the portfolio. They can also be insightful when comparing a decision to others made recently or that will likely be made soon. For example, you can compare a project's NPV and investment efficiency against other projects in the portfolio. It helps to inform questions and can form the basis for a final investment decision.

Multiple Dimension Attributes

Tools: Interactive graphics platform, spreadsheet, or database to store inputs and outputs.

Decisions: Portfolio balances across different strategic objectives. Creating shortlists of assets for further investment or divestment. Investments can be similar or dissimilar.

Advantages:

1. There is usually little resistance to developing these types of perspectives.
2. Transparent to the decision-makers.
3. Simple to put together from existing data—even third-party data can be used.
4. Good basis for comparison with competing firms.
5. Meeting with decision-makers encourages collaboration and transparent sharing of business needs and targets.
6. Tells you where you are and what your asset base looks like.

Disadvantages:

1. May not create optimal portfolios.
2. Scaling large numbers of attributes and entities is difficult.
3. Provides little information or insight onto a better path.

> **Key Takeaways**
>
> 1. The addition of dimensions introduces the idea that there are multiple values that are important. When these values are inversely related, such as with investment and NPV, it creates tension in our trade-offs.
> 2. Interactive visualization techniques make it straightforward to see the tradeoffs and create hypotheses for further investigation. Multiple dimensions bring us into a more strategic realm than single-dimension rank and cut. Once you have created your hypotheses, testing them with rollups or optimizations is an excellent next step to confirm or reject them.
> 3. Using multiple dimensions to view individual assets takes simple comparison up a level. Now you're looking at multiple measures of quality all at once. It takes the context from a simple ranking and explicitly shows some of the differences and tradeoffs between assets. If this is as far as you go on your portfolio journey, it is better than never having started. You will make better-informed decisions.

Detail – Capital Efficiency Charts

Many possibilities for multiple dimensions are available for strategic analysis, such as NPV vs Total Reserves by project. One axis is value, and the other relates to the enterprise's sustainability. You want assets that are generally high and to the right; those are your best assets, but others have their place. Lower left quadrants are less important assets that you may consider for divestiture. The war story in this section covers this type of scenario.

However, one chart in particular deserves more detail for its general usefulness. It is sometimes called the capital efficiency chart. It is a plot of value (typically NPV on the y-axis vs an investment measure (often discounted investment) on the x-axis. It shows individual projects, not portfolios.

Let's start with the basics.

This plot shows a series of projects plotted as Value vs. Investment.

▸ **Value vs. Investment Project Comparison**

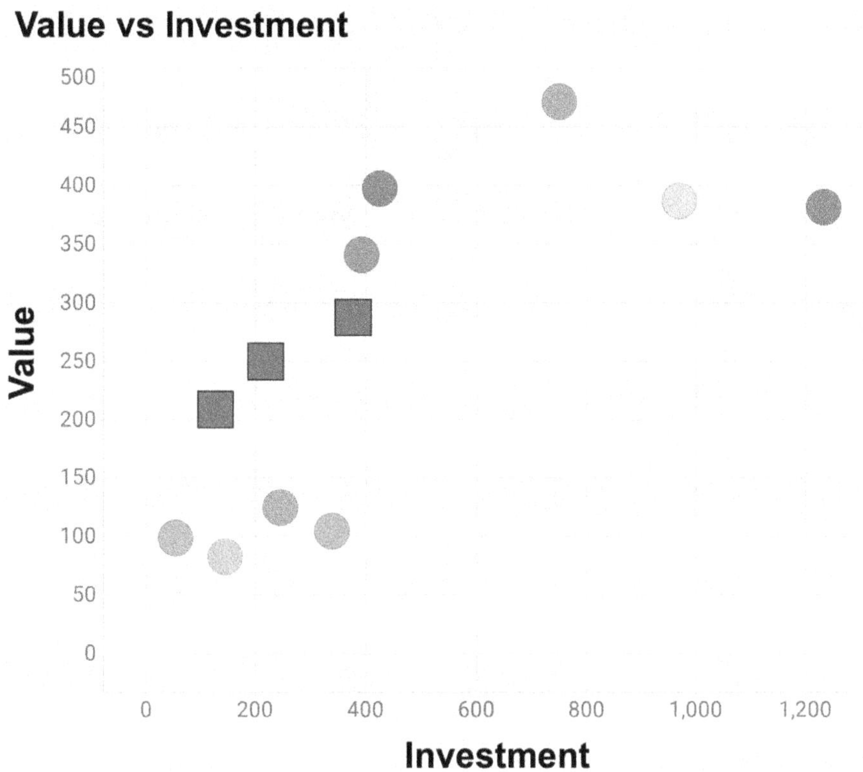

This is a basic investment efficiency plot. The x-axis represents the investment, while the y-axis is the value. Each point represents a single project or alternative development. The investments high and to the left provide the most value relative to the investment.

You want the projects that cost less and deliver more, so high and to the left is the preferred direction. That's fine, but what is the **precise** tradeoff between investment and value? We know we want more for less, but how much value will we give up to save money? In this case, we go back to our economic evaluation textbooks and realize that the slope of the tradeoff line is generally considered to be based on the investment opportunities thought to exist otherwise.

We can insert a line at the 1.5 investment efficiency threshold on the graph using the formula Investment efficiency = 1 + value divided by investment.

▸ **Value vs Investment Comparison with Reference Line**

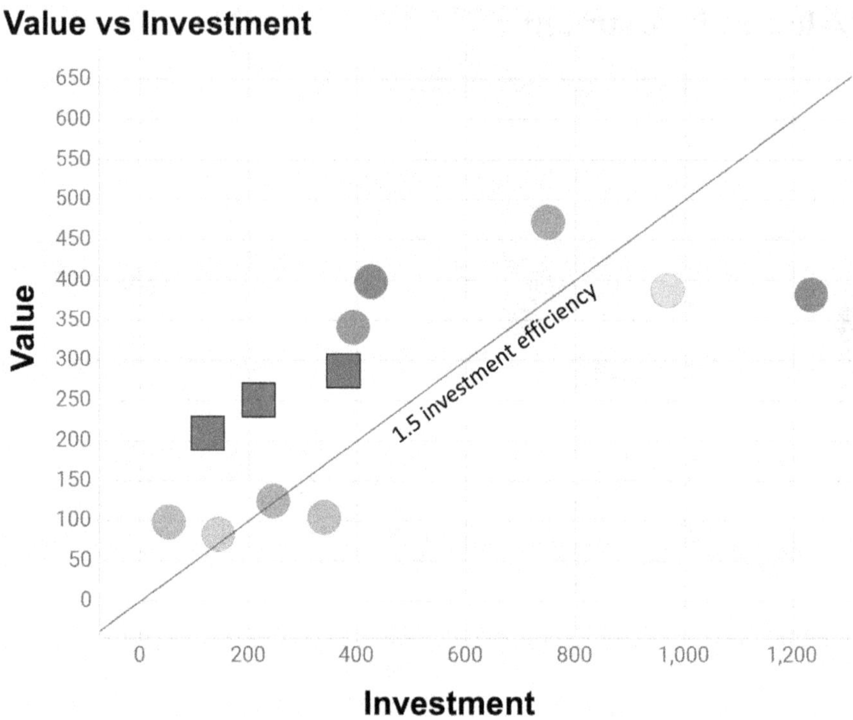

Adding a line representing a hurdle rate based on opportunities thought to exist in the organization provides a reference. Investments above the line exceed internal undisplayed/undocumented investments. Each investment will have its own efficiency as a function of value divided by investment.

The projects below the line are less efficient than projects outside this set that are thought to exist. This doesn't mean they should not be done. The two projects below the line on the far right would add a lot of value, but they would need something more than economic efficiency to justify their execution.

Which are the best ones? It's tricky to read the offset from a diagonal line, so we can determine this mathematically and see how they rank.

▸ **Value Above Enterprise "Hurdle Rate"**

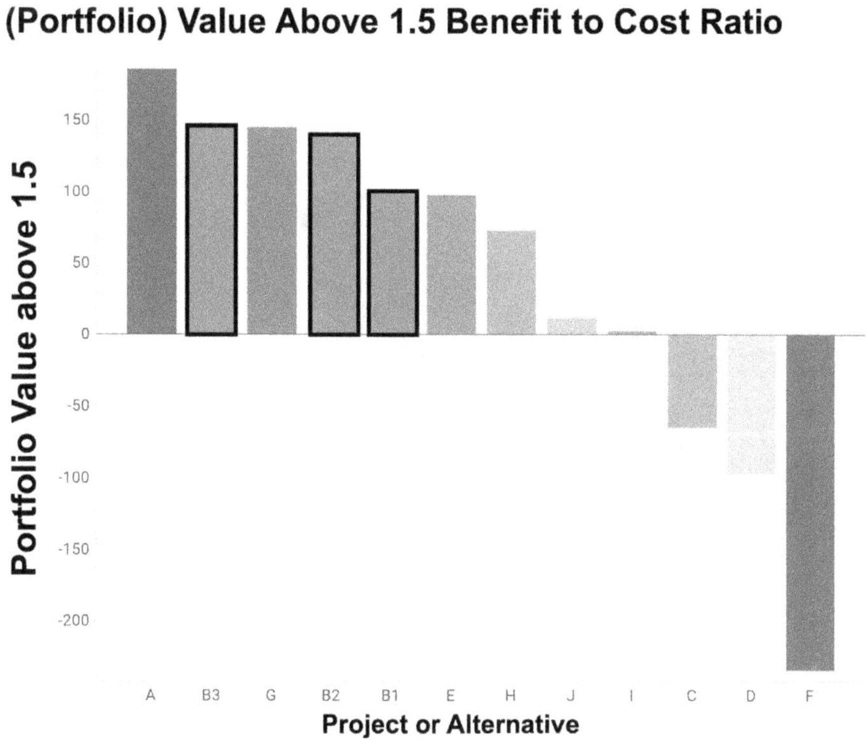

> *The vertical difference between the diagonal hurdle line and the dot shows how much value a given project adds relative to the 1.5 investment efficiency reference. Knowing that value allows us to rank the opportunities by portfolio-value-addition, considering opportunity cost.*

This value above or below the 1.5 line measures the value of the opportunity compared to alternative projects "thought to exist." I'll call it the portfolio value of these opportunities. We will discuss other ways to measure portfolio value later, but this is a first pass at the value above the implicit opportunity cost of the portfolio.

However, the investment efficiency of "projects thought to exist" may be fuzzy, so we can plot additional preference lines and see if they change our decisions. This creates a perspective on the sensitivity of our selections relative to our estimate of alternative uses of capital.

▸ **Sensitivity to Hurdle Rate Comparison**

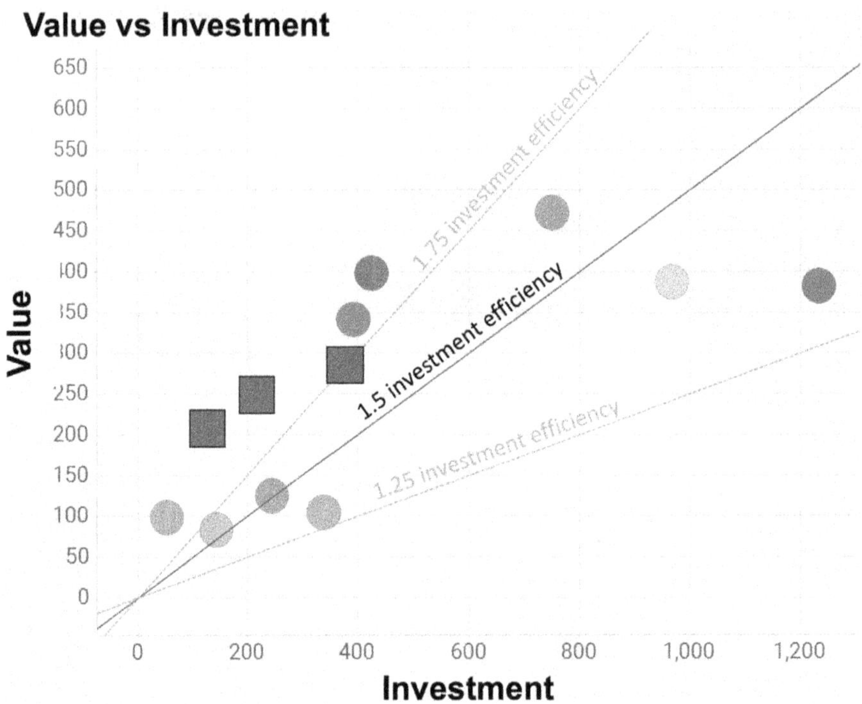

When we have uncertainty or disputes about the investment efficiency of opportunities thought to exist, we can plot alternative possibilities to see if that would change our decision. For example, in the 1.75 efficiency context, three more projects would not add value, whereas at a 1.5 threshold, they would.

This graph can be used to compare development alternatives for a single project. Although we have been referring to a set of projects, the three square points represent different development alternatives for the same project.

▸ Detail Comparison of Single Project Alternatives

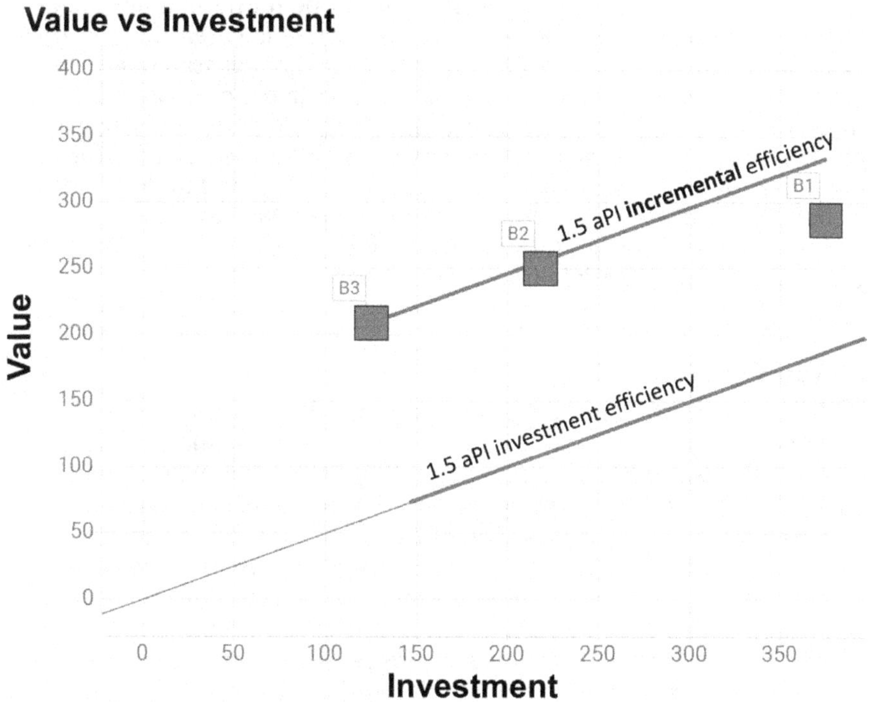

> *The square dots represent three different development alternatives for a single project. B3 has the highest efficiency with a 2.67 ratio. B2 is second with a 2.15 ratio. B1 is last with a ratio of 1.77. Even though B2 is less efficient, it adds more value than B3. However, it would be slightly erosive to portfolio value if the 1.5 slope is correct. A lower slope would make B2 more valuable to the portfolio. B1, despite having a higher value, requires too much more investment to compete, but remember that these are just two dimensions. B1 may have other attributes that would overcome the pure efficiency calculation.*

We can see which alternative adds the most portfolio value (above the opportunity cost of 1.5 efficiency) by moving the 1.5 line up to the alternatives. Alternative B1 adds slightly more portfolio value than B2, while B3 adds much less.

As a side note, each point on the graph can be assumed to be near the center of a cloud of possibilities. Value and cost are highly unlikely to fall precisely at any given point. But when comparing different alternatives of the same project, the outcomes will likely be well-correlated. Whichever alternative is chosen, they all share the same reservoir, oil quality, project managers, and external economic environment. It is usually safe to treat the values as points when comparing different alternatives of the same project. Your mileage may vary, so if you have reason to believe that the options would carry different risks, you may wish to put probability bars around the points.

If you are comparing similar opportunities—investments with similar magnitudes and cash flow patterns as might be found in a particular basin or country—consistency of the axis values is essential. Specifics of the measure you use are less important. If the investments are markedly different asset classes, fiscal regimes, or phased investments, avoid blind spots in your x-axis selection. I discuss elsewhere in the book why net negative cash flow (fBCR) is better aligned with efficiency calculations in finance theory than accounting or budgeted capital (aPI), which is blind to specific beneficial circumstances of development or taxes. Whatever you use, make sure you understand potential blind spots.

Key Takeaways

Investment efficiency plots are common for a reason—they provide a robust view to compare investments. In addition, they can help us see how projects do on these two dimensions, which, when negative cash flow is used on the x-axis is consistent with financial theory. The selection of the x-axis metric can make a significant difference, and even the discount rate used for value can matter. Some companies use budgeted capital for the x-axis, while a technically more rigorous approach would use net negative cash flow. In your early stages, it's best to use values and metrics that people are familiar with, but run sensitivities with other values to see if they would make a significant difference in your decisions. The context here is leadership's belief about opportunities that are thought to exist elsewhere for the company.

Detail – When is an Efficient Frontier Not an Efficient Frontier?

The views described in this section are sometimes erroneously referred to as Efficient Frontier Plots. An Efficient Frontier is a specific plot type showing the relationship between mean return and variance. Other similar plots are more appropriately referred to as Pareto Frontiers. Leaving that aside, Efficient Frontiers are meant to compare multiple **mutually exclusive courses of action**. Each point on the frontier is a unique set of actions, only one of which may be chosen. Efficient Frontier is not a grouping of independent items, some, or all of which may be selected.

Take this example of projects shown on a cost vs. value graph. We generally want our projects to be in the upper left-hand quadrant, i.e., high value and low cost. If **we could select only one project,** it would be appropriate to call that line an efficient frontier.

▸ **Projects Plotted by Value and Cost**

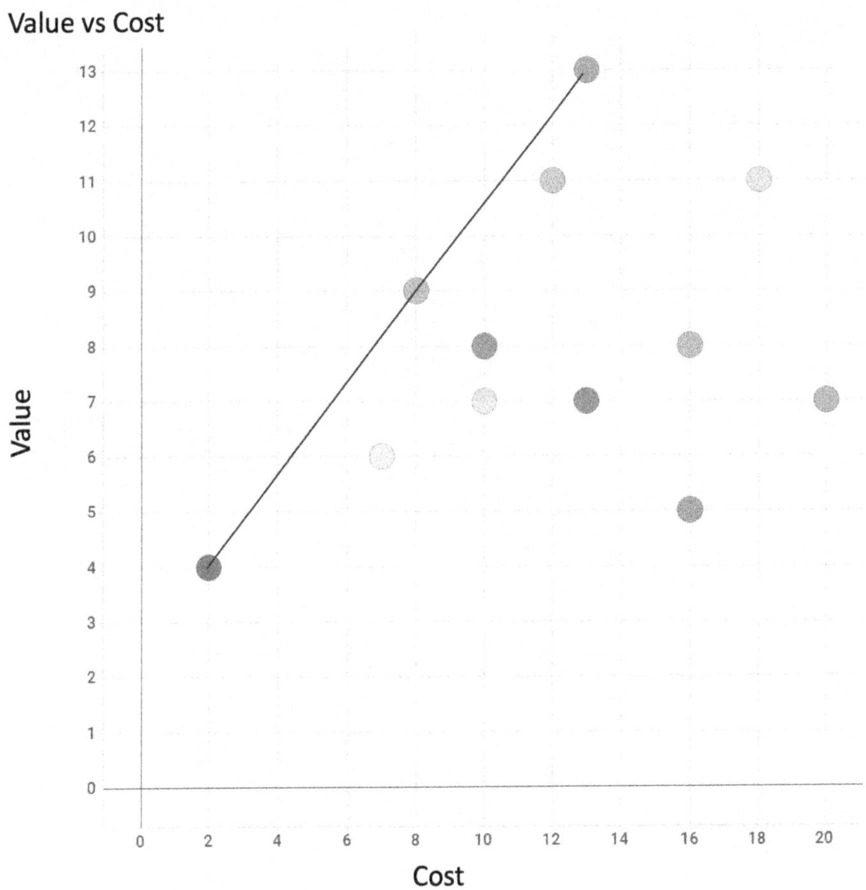

This graph shows individual projects. You can say that given this set of projects, there are none that are above and to the left of the line. But there's nothing magical about that line. A project could be added to the mix that would plot above and to the left. If all of these projects are mutually exclusive, then it could be argued that this is an efficient frontier.

However, when people compare projects or assets, they may intend to select several of them. Don't get me wrong. Plotting your projects on a value vs. cost plot is appropriate. But it's not an efficient frontier.

The next plot **is** an efficient frontier. See the cluster of light dots in the lower left? Those are all the individual projects from above. To plot the efficient frontier of **portfolios**, we sort the projects by efficiency, which is the descending order of the bang per buck. Then we create a plot of cumulative value versus cumulative cost.

An Efficient (Pareto) Frontier of Portfolios with Input Projects Shown

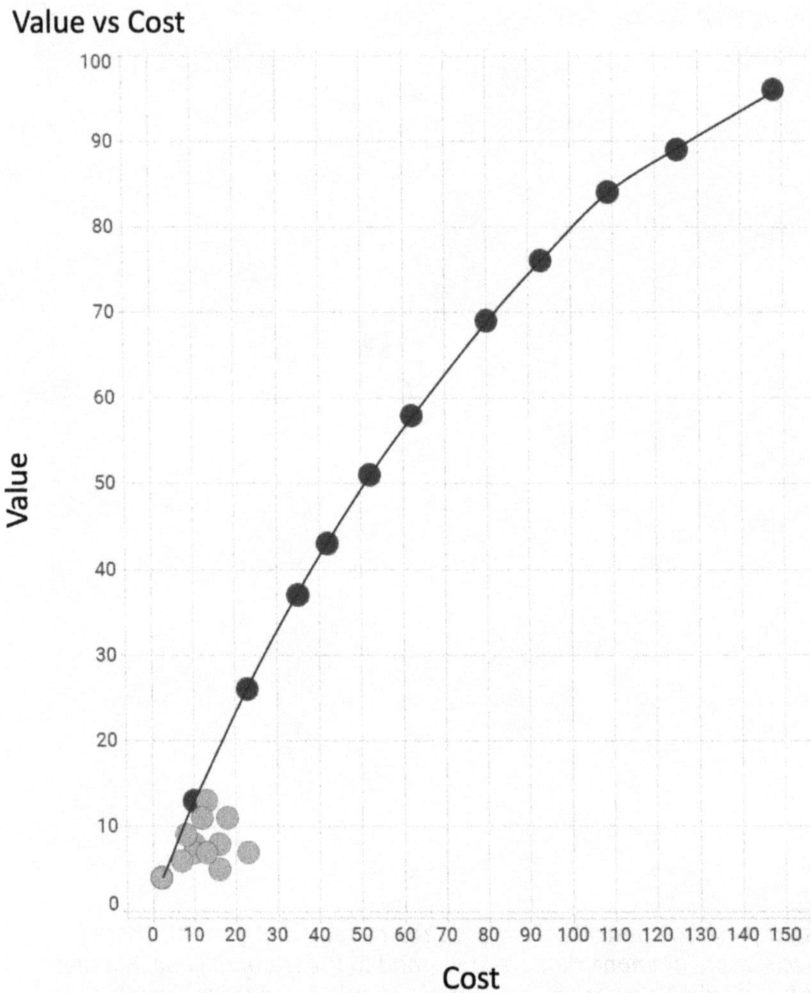

Efficient frontiers result from mutually exclusive ***sets*** *of projects. The light dots on the lower left are the same projects as in the previous graph. The dark dots are the most efficient* ***portfolios*** *comprising one or more of the light dots. The lowermost light dot is also a dark dot. It is a portfolio with only the single most efficient project. The next dark dot includes the two most efficient projects. In a typical efficient frontier analysis, you pick the portfolio, then the components are revealed. Given that set of light projects, there is no possible portfolio that is above and to the left of the line.*

The dot in the lower left is the portfolio containing only the single most efficient project. The dot at (10, 13) on the efficient frontier adds the cost and benefit of the second most efficient project to the first point. The next dot (23, 26) adds the third-best project, and so on. Each of the dots along the line is a summation of projects, not a single project.

This should look familiar to you. It is the same as the CFO chart discussed in the Rank and Cut section. We have now shifted the focus to thinking about the points as portfolios, rather than individual projects.

A plot of projects is not generally an efficient or Pareto frontier. If someone shows you a graph of non-mutually exclusive projects and claims it is an efficient frontier, they may not understand the concept.

Hypothetical Case Study - Multiple Dimension Short List

The executive had good reason to be reticent about selling assets. Once you sell an asset, you lose the resource forever. Moreover, selling assets was rarely tax efficient.

With high oil prices, her boss wanted to know what we should consider selling. The order came down to create a shortlist of assets to divest.

There were several key attributes that they wanted the portfolio to deliver. The first was value (NPV). High NPV assets carry big economies of scale and form the core of the corporation's value. The second was production. The corporation had oil production targets (a proxy for revenue growth in oil and gas). Finally, they needed assets for the future. Many assets contained significant resources (future reserves) but had relatively low NPV because of the time and money required to develop them. Once online, they would be material.

The analysis team gathered the data, put it into TIBCO Spotfire, and began sorting through displays to see what insights they could gain. The following graphs represent three parameters for each asset. The x-axis is total NPV (used as a proxy for sales proceeds); the y-axis is total future production across the asset's life. The colors represent production over the next five years, with white indicating zero or relatively low production, grading through medium gray, and then up to the darker dots indicating the highest production in the 5-year timeframe.

This is the working set, which includes all the assets under consideration for divestiture. Pieces of the business that were difficult to separate were roughly defined as assets. This graph has axes that are linear. With linear axes and a wide variety of assets, the smaller ones tend to clump together on the low end, while the larger ones spread out.

▸ **Assets Plotted as Production vs Value**

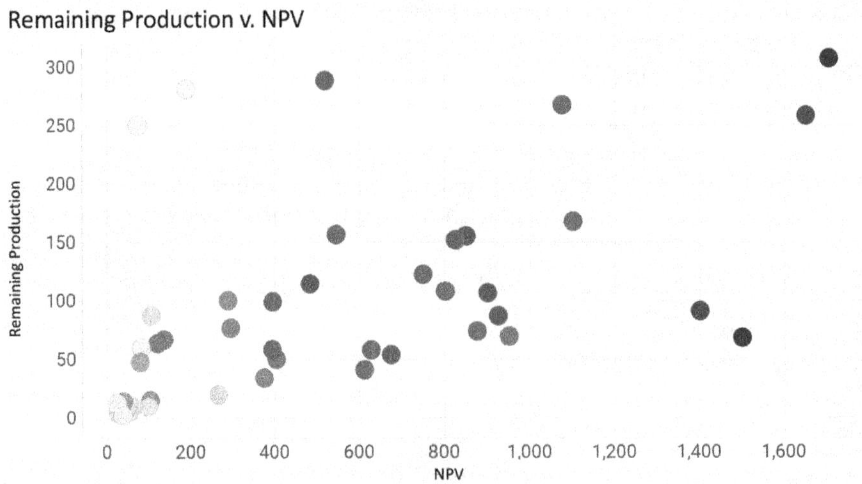

The working set of assets for divestiture consideration. Executives wanted the analyst team to create a shortlist of assets for divestiture consideration. The two main criteria for creating the shortlist were value, as expressed by NPV, and remaining production. Please note: These assets are fictitious. The scale units are arbitrary and are for illustration purposes only.

The team converted the axes to log-log, which evened out the appearance of the data and made it easier to work with. This gave us a more even picture of the assets. They had to remember that the small assets were **much** smaller than the largest ones.

▸ **Logarithmic X and Y Axes**

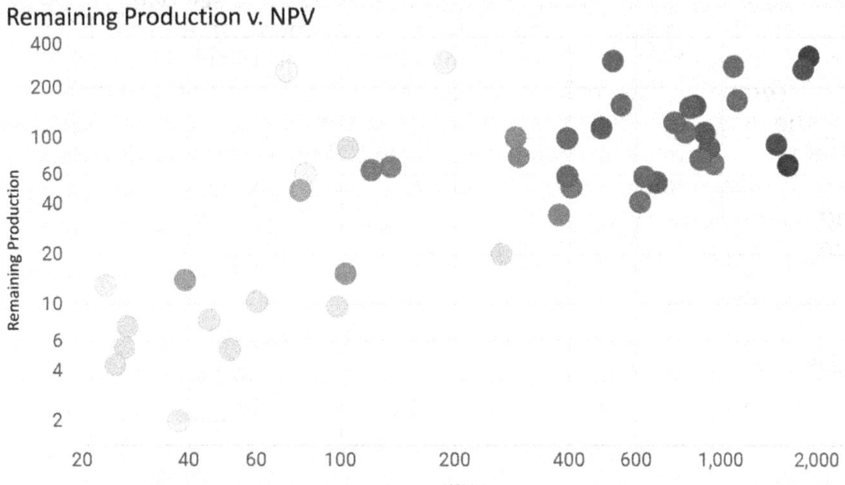

> *Converting the graph to logarithmic axes made it easier to see the details. Very large and very small assets became more evenly spaced. Analysts must remember that the smallest assets are quite small.*

Let's discuss a few observations. This log-log graph shows a clear correlation between NPV and production. There is a significant scatter and some outliers in the top center portion of the chart. Generally, production and NPV are strongly related. In the upstream oil industry, there has always been a production focus. The engineering culture of most companies drives it, but it works because of the strong relationship between production and financial results.

Three main components cause the scatter: field properties, fiscal regime, and field or development maturity:

1. Field properties include oil-to-gas ratio, well productivity, and oil quality.
2. Fiscal regimes are driven by the governments that control or oversee hydrocarbon production. OPEC countries tend to have high tax rates and onerous terms, while non-OPEC countries tend to have more lax and business-friendly terms.
3. Field maturity feeds into the time-value calculation in NPV, while the production axis is not discounted. Future developments will have low NPVs relative to their total production.

After graphing the data, we began filtering and grouping.

First, the team eliminated the most significant assets with the most production from consideration (labeled as "Core"). This was about trimming the sails, not sinking the ship.

This leaves a much smaller candidate set. What else do we see?

Looking at the group to the left of Core assets, there see two groupings of assets. The darkest symbols have very low production in the near term, but very high total production. These projects are the future of the company. The low valuations reflect low investment to date and the long-time `horizon. Selling these would significantly reduce future production. The dots have substantial near-term production, large future production, and lower NPV. These may be in countries with onerous fiscal terms. They have labeled this grouping as "Future Core." That leaves "Assets of Interest."

Assets Grouped

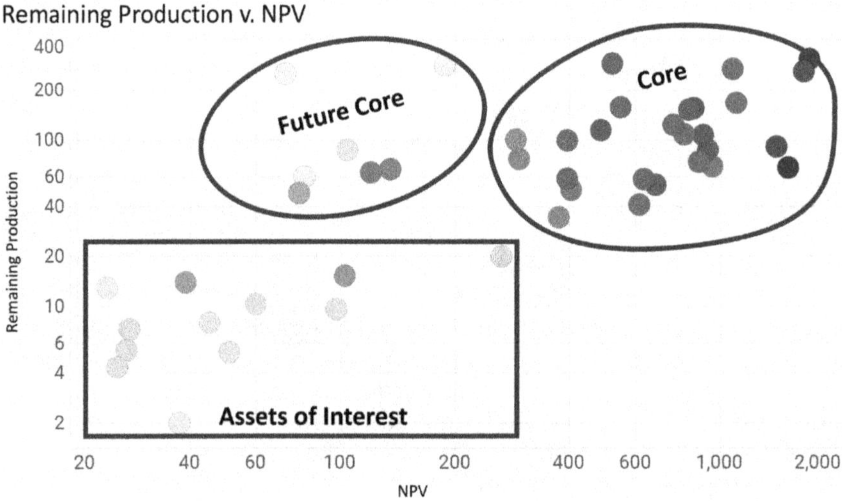

> *The assets were divided into three main categories: Core Assets, Future Core Assets, and Assets of Interest. Core and Future Core assets were removed from divestiture consideration.*

The Tier 1 assets have the highest valuation for the lowest production. The firm could receive the most revenue for the smallest production drop. The Tier 2 assets are not as efficient in receiving value for lost barrels, but the barrel loss would still be minor. The two remaining dark dots outside the ellipses were eliminated because they have high current production.

▸ **Detail Divestiture Groupings**

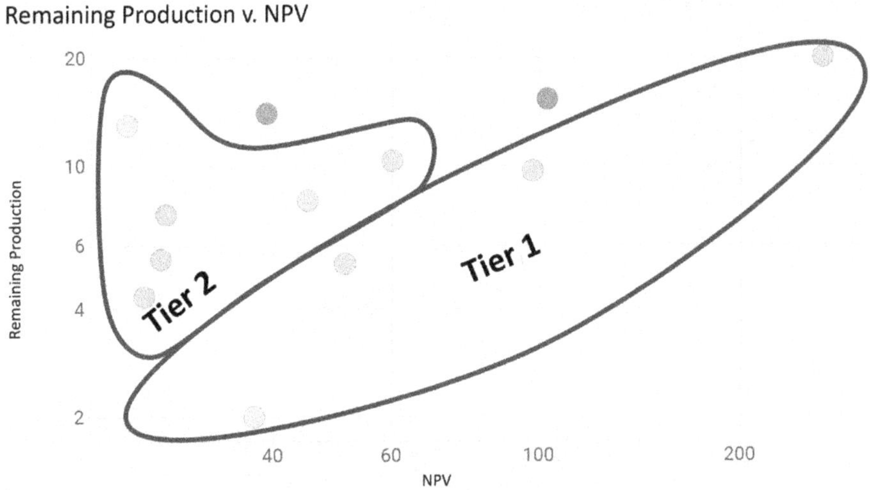

Among the assets for consideration, the analysts focused on the swath of assets with the highest NPV and lowest production. The Tier 1 assets had likely benefited the most from the high oil price and would have minimal impact on the ability to achieve production targets. Tier 2 assets were generally quite small and barely worth selling. The two dots outside the tiers had more significant near-term production, so they were eliminated from consideration.

These ten assets represent a short list of opportunities submitted to corporate executives for consideration. This analysis did not attempt to answer do-ability questions of a sale, tax consequences, or strategic or intangible aspects. But in a short time, they came up with a list of divestiture candidates from an initial list of dozens of assets.

Below is the initial linear plot with the final area of interest marked for reference. I believe filtering would have led them to the same place.

▸ **Linear vs. Logarithmic Revisited**

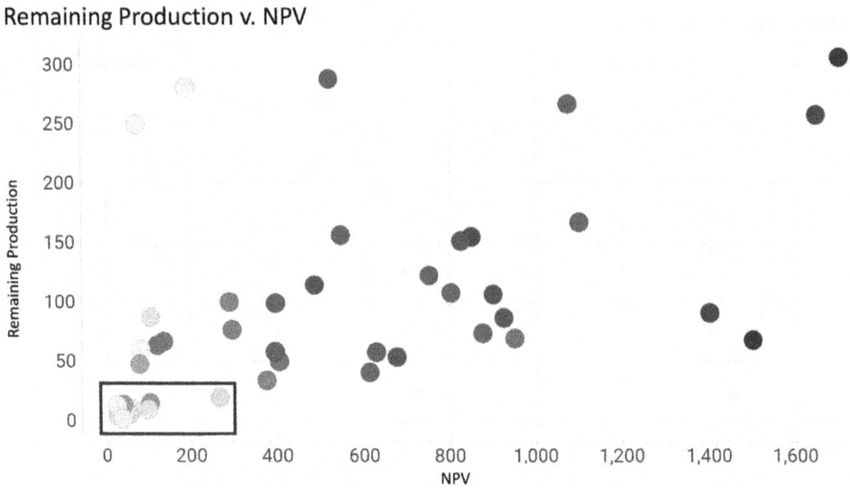

> *Looking at the linear-linear plot again, the lower left rectangle contains all of the assets under consideration. This view helps ground decision-makers on the scale of the assets under consideration.*

The presentation to the executives went well. They understood the concepts and walked out with a resolve to investigate further. However, before any decisions had been made, the price of oil dropped precipitously. The opportunity to sell high had passed.

Lessons Learned

1. It turns out that the assets with the lowest production and highest NPV had the lowest effective income tax rate. It stands to reason that each barrel had a higher value.
2. Framing the decision in terms of corporate objectives helps executives see the wisdom of considering some highly profitable but small assets for sale.
3. Spotfire is a wonderful analysis tool. The ability to filter, rescale, and gain insights is impressive.
4. The assets in tier 1 and tier 2 were not a final decision to sell. Making a sell decision would require additional internal due diligence on tax positions, understanding operational and tax synergies with other parts of the business, understanding the impact on corporate goals, and investigating multiple legal and regulatory hurdles.
5. Resizing, rescaling, and switching between live views can cause something akin to vertigo for the audience. It can be hard to keep track, even for well-choreographed interactive sessions. Static images may be better than live analysis, unless the audience is fully engaged and familiar with the tool. Go slowly.

Multi-Attribute, Multi-Objective Scoring Methods

Multi-Attribute Decision Making (MADM) or Multi-Objective Decision Making (MODM) methods, such as the Analytic Hierarchy Process (AHP) or Multi-attribute Utility Analysis (MUA), straddle the border between Standalone and Rank and Cut techniques. Most people consider them a means of ranking opportunities, so I put them in the comparison section. These are actually standalone analysis techniques that can be used with portfolio techniques to prioritize. I will refer to them as MUA generically.

Most of the work in MUA lies in developing a single value that represents the goodness of an opportunity by combining multiple attributes or objectives. Once your entities are scored, you can analyze them with portfolio methods. The most common portfolio technique with these techniques is Rank and Cut.

The main difference between common standalone and MUA is that instead of choosing a single parameter (like NPV or Bang/Buck), you select several of them, apply a weight to the parameters, and sum them up. This results in a single score that reflects company preferences or overall utility.

There is controversy regarding MUA. Many people like the simplicity of generating a single number that gives the answer or insight. However, getting to a valid single number requires skill and experience, and it adds a layer of opacity to the process. My approach has generally been to explore the value metrics and requirements explicitly and separately, then facilitate the leadership team in discussion about their tradeoffs.

That said, the discussions and facilitation to discover leadership and enterprise preferences through MUA can create tremendous value. Done well, it can augment your framing activities. My main objection is the final black-box step of consolidating it into a single value.

These approaches can be helpful for making initial decisions. For instance, if you are reviewing a list of opportunities, you can narrow down the list to a more manageable size for additional consideration.

Keep a few things in mind. These methods can be very tricky to set up. It can be difficult to accurately weigh scores, guarantee that categories are mutually exclusive and collectively exhaustive, and comprehend the results and their validity. Non-linear utility functions and dependencies between the utilities of the attributes or objectives add complexity.

While the approach may be statistically valid, making it work in practice can be difficult. Turning a multidimensional problem into a single-dimensional one is the very definition of a black box. In my experience, it is better to take a more granular approach. Interactive graphics programs can facilitate rich discussions of tradeoffs between different opportunities and help narrow them down to a relevant subset by elimination.

I have often seen simplistic approaches put together by non-statisticians or inexperienced analysts, who apply their personal weighting scores or equal weightings, and then present it as an approach. This may help to eliminate the worst decisions, but it lacks the accuracy required for high-quality decision-making.

Done poorly, MUA and similar approaches will be:

1. Arbitrary - Assigning proper weightings throughout a relevant range of preferences can be daunting.
2. Opaque - 2x2 charts can show tradeoffs, but when one of the dimensions is a black box, it loses meaning.
3. High-level indicators at best - MUA might help screen out the worst.
4. Misleading at worst - MUA might wrongfully screen out good opportunities. Without good facilitation and knowledge, metrics can inadvertently be over-emphasized or mistakenly ignored.

A somewhat comparable concept, risk matrices, which combine two axes into a single score, have been criticized for their weaknesses. *The Risk of Using Risk Matrices* by Thomas, Bickel, and Bratvold, published in the SPE Economics and Management Journal in 2013, was particularly critical of some of the details of how risk matrices are used in the petroleum industry. Although some of their conclusions do not apply to MUA, the paper illustrates the challenges of these approaches to multi-attribute problems.

MUA and other multidimensional metric approaches can be used as an objective function in optimization. Even if the metric is not spot on, using the overall approach as described in the optimization section, a MUA metric will provide the tension required for an optimization model. Results can then be compared on individual dimensions.

A word of caution. If you choose to use a weighted combination function, please ensure that your portfolio selection provides what you want—in the aggregate—from each of the elements that go into the weighting, i.e., don't use it blindly. Even the best and most carefully controlled statistical analyses might yield undesirable results when combined and rolled up to the enterprise level.

Key Takeaways

1. MUA methods are mathematically elegant but fraught with peril for the inexperienced. However, discussions about explicit and implicit tradeoffs during the discovery framing are invaluable.
2. Multi-Attribute and Multi-Objective methods are commonly used in many applications. Applying portfolio analysis once you have generated the scores is similar to applying any other value metric. It is a number that reflects utility and can be used as the primary value metric/objective function or alongside others.
3. Scoring systems can help screen a large number of candidates. In my experience and practice, I prefer showing attributes with color or numerical indicators for each rather than combining numbers to come up with a single value. This approach is more transparent, and leadership can discuss individual attributes rather than arguing about weights.

War Stories – Multi-Attribute Value Function

The leadership team of a research organization that covered a wide range of specialty areas needed a way to compare their efforts across multiple research centers. Previously, they had attempted to use economic analysis to estimate the statistically expected value of the projects. However, they believed that the effort entailed too much work and did not produce reasonable, consistent, or useful results.

There had been many discussions, but little progress.

They decided to hire former high-level scientists from a government agency that specializes in scientific and engineering research to help them. The scientists were tasked with developing a value function that everyone could agree on.

The scientists met and interviewed executives and technical people for months, and finally rolled out a value function. The leadership did not have confidence in the value function and rejected the work when they ultimately tried to use it to optimize their spending. The results did not pass their smell test.

Another multi-attribute project in a different company was an effort to rank assets of a certain type. They ranked twenty assets across 12 attributes, and then assigned equal weights to each attribute. The leadership rejected the results and methodology because they believed there were "too many categories" and that the weights could not possibly be correct.

A third effort to rank projects was led by an experienced Analytic Hierarchy Process (AHP) practitioner who was aligned with the approach of transparency and participation. He did a demo project for the leadership team, who were initially very enthusiastic. Then nothing. The leadership team were apparently quite happy with the status quo.

Lessons Learned

1. Even with the best intentions and really smart people, value functions are not useful unless the leadership completely buys into them.
2. Too many categories turn a ranking system into a black box.
3. Even when done well, leaders have to want to use these types of tools to help guide them.

CHAPTER 6

Rollups – Simple Mathematical Aggregation

Until this point, we have mostly ignored the time dimension. NPV, rate of return, and other single metrics take a long time series of data across time and collapse them mathematically into a single number. These are reductionist metrics; they simplify our view of the world by removing detail. It is simple to look at the individual parts or metrics and assume that if they're good, the enterprise will be good. This misses the perspective of how those parts combine to create the whole *over time*.

Rollups bring in the time dimension. Looking at the time dimension is useful, even for individual opportunities, but it is even more useful within the enterprise context.

Portfolio Selector Focus on Rollups

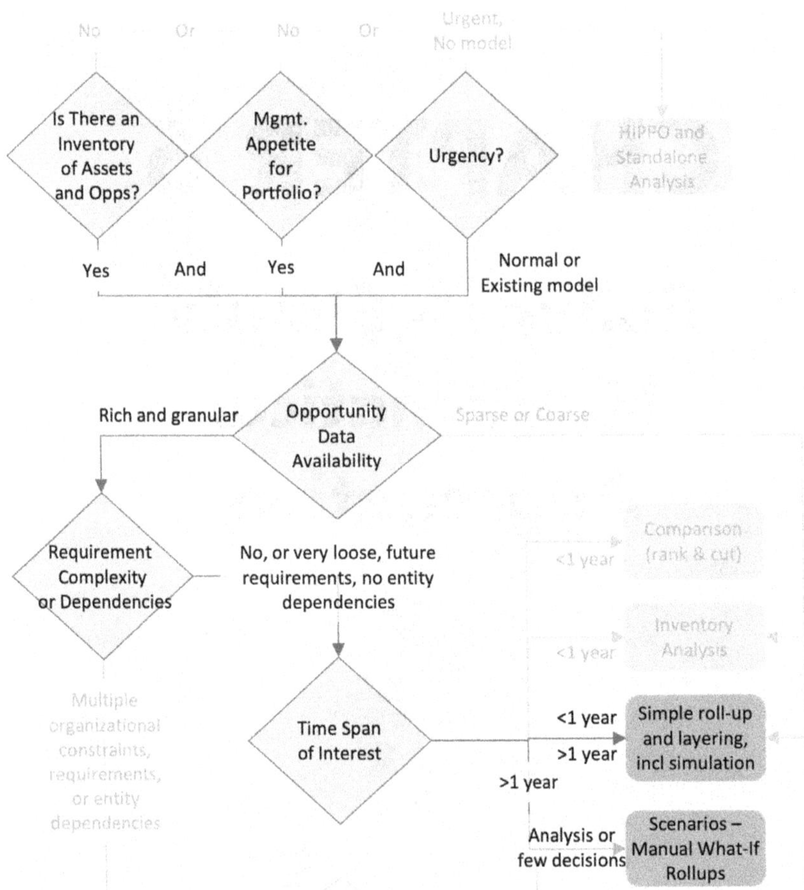

Rollups are the next level of portfolio work. On the Selector tool, rollups become important when we increase the time span of interest beyond one year. Rollups can be either for information or for comparison of a few alternate decisions, such as when considering the purchase of an asset. At this point, rollups are still deterministic. We have not introduced probability yet

Increasing the complexity of the system occurs when we move beyond individual consideration of opportunities as standalone entities. This step may be a barrier to portfolio analysis for some firms.

However, most firms have a rollup planning and budgeting process. Take the individual parts, add them up, make a few adjustments, and voila! You have the budget. It can be a one-year or five-year budget or even a life-of-asset view.

Fortunately, taking this next step is *mechanically* simple. Whether or not the long-term data are added together is a matter of company culture and governance. Regardless of what the firm collects, asset managers have a longer-term view. Data exists on the individual pieces. Now roll them up to see what the sum of the parts gives you at the higher level.

Remember that firms are judged based on annual results, annual spending, the annual return on capital employed **at the enterprise level**, and how those play out over time. The collapsed numbers provide no insight into those aspects and, therefore, can mislead.

Rollups provide the next level of context for our decisions.

Key Takeaways

1. Simple mathematical aggregation (the rollup) is the first significant step in combining a set of decisions. Rolling up data is especially important when taking time series perspectives of our decisions. Looking at the different layers provides an essential view for strategic decisions.
2. Rollup with guided selection, as I will describe, combines comparison and inventory methods with rollups to provide both strategic and tactical guidance for decisions about programs (multiple coordinated decisions).
3. Rollups put any incremental decisions explicitly into the larger context across time. Rolling up is an important concept that will continue to be used in the more advanced methods. The manner of selecting the entities to include, and the mathematics of the rollup will change, but it is still an aggregation of performance across time. If this is as far as you go on your portfolio journey, it is better than never having started. You will make better-informed decisions.

Detail – Rolling Up the Data, Layering On, and Slice and Dice

Most companies have a planning process that generates a perspective of the future. It consists of collecting data at a low level and summing it to see what happens at higher levels. For example, starting with an individual asset and combining it with nearby assets gives you a regional picture. Combining regions gives you a country picture; combining countries gives you a worldwide view. These plans can be for one year or multiple years.

Adding data to achieve a synthesized view of the firm is a fundamental building block of planning and portfolio. This synthesized view of your business is the first step to interaction portfolio techniques.

The following is an example of production rolled up over a ten-year period. There is no decision to make yet, but there are a few things to note. First, there is a pronounced decline in production over the next four years. Then production begins to turn up again. Even so, production at the end of ten years is lower than the starting point.

Base Plan Rollup

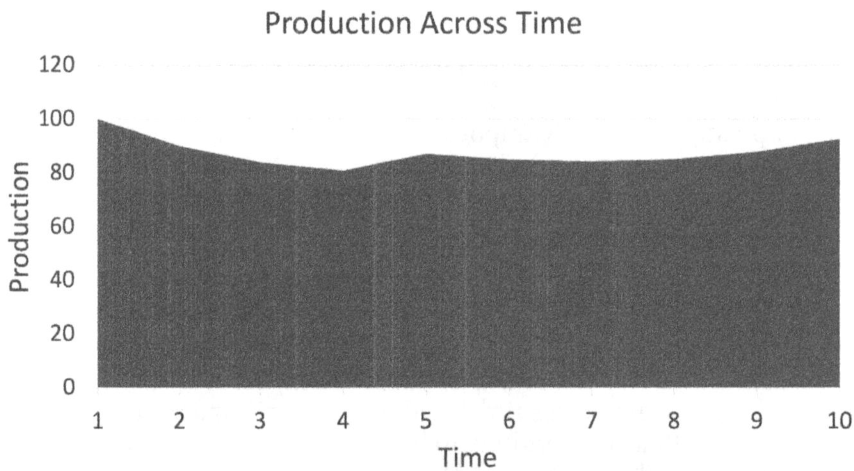

This is a notional plan for a resource company. They see a short-term decrease in production, but starting in year 5, they see an increase. The market is concerned about its growth prospects.

Management decides that this is unacceptable—they want to show growth or at least stay even across the entire ten-year timeframe—and considers an acquisition.

Below is what an acquisition would do for their production.

▸ Base Plan with Acquisition

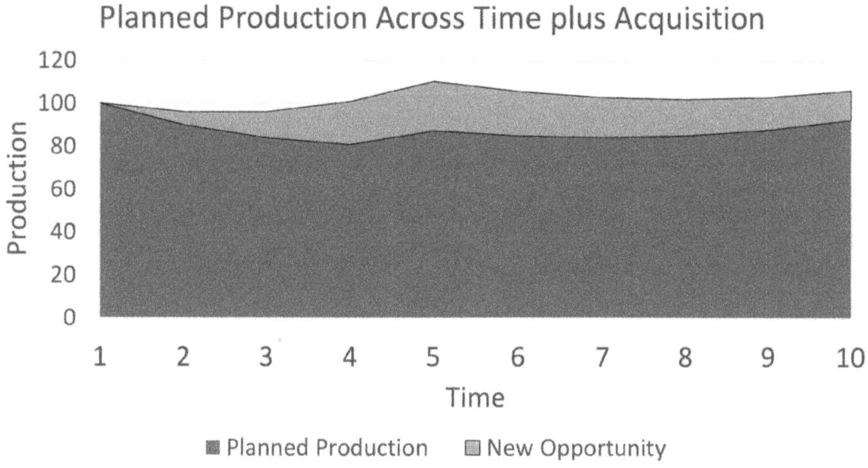

> *The company is considering acquiring an asset that will fill most of the near and medium-term gap.*

Now, we see how we can use a rollup to understand this top-line impact on the company. While the purchase will not fill the dip in the next two years, it is a significant addition that will leave us better off in ten years than if we had not made the purchase.

This type of perspective is commonly referred to as "gap analysis." Management looks at what it has, and then compares it to what it wants. The difference is "the gap." Determining how to fill the gap is a big part of portfolio analysis, whether it be production, margins, ROCE, or reserve replacement.

These are area charts. What if you had more opportunities to consider? It may be more beneficial to use line charts for comparisons.

The chart below shows the base plan (the lower line) and the rollup of two alternative acquisitions. Notice the change in scale of the y-axis.

▸ **Comparing Acquisition Alternatives**

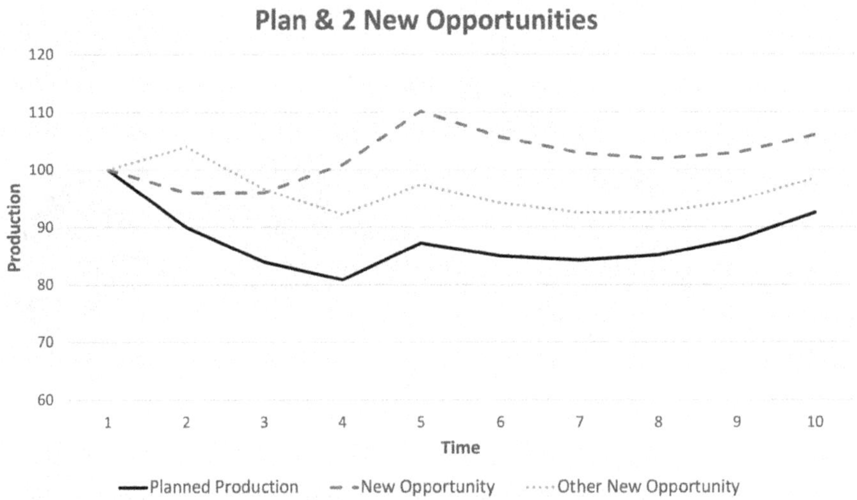

> *The leadership team is considering another acquisition that would add some production next year but would result in lower overall production beyond year 2. Comparing the two acquisitions would give the leadership team insight into their ability to help the company.*

The "Other New Opportunity" yields a different profile than the first one. It shores up the near term but is weaker in the longer term. Management should have a preference among the three shapes. It may also be possible to purchase both with a lower working interest.

Of course, I haven't shown any other information at this point. Acquisition cost will be an essential consideration, and the finance department will opine on whether either acquisition would be accretive to earnings, etc. Also, the opportunities themselves will generate capital expenditures, reserves progression, and earnings.

Slice and Dice

Simply adding up your information to get the synthesized whole is seldom enough.

Let's look at the original production graph over the next ten years.

▸ **Base Plan Rollup**

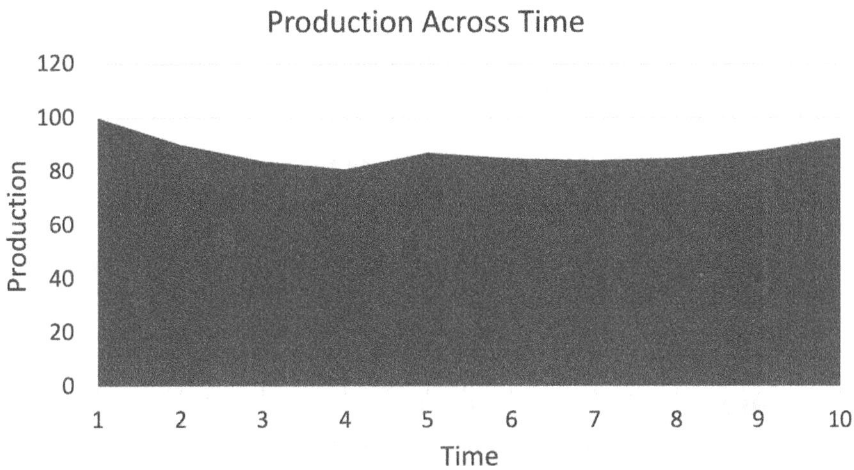

Revisiting the original profile.

Let's look at another view of the data. This time the upper wedge is showing the exploration component of the future production.

▸ **Components of the Original plan**

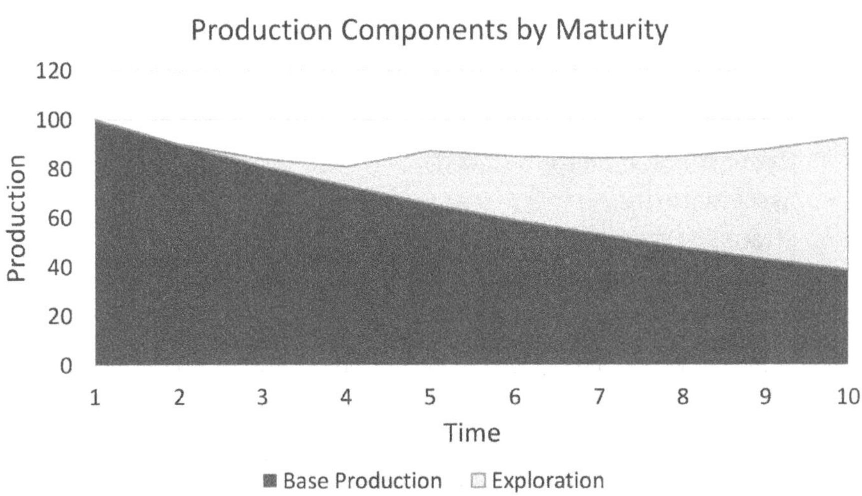

All the organic growth of the organization prior to the acquisitions was due to exploration. This may change the view of the leadership team regarding the type of asset it would need to purchase.

This is an example of slicing and dicing time-series data. Rolling up the time-series data to only the top line is nice, but it provides little context. The stratification in lighter gray creates essential context.

Your producing assets are declining. All of the growth is triggered by exploration. Therefore, the growth wedge is a highly uncertain piece of your future production that can't be counted on. Although the statistics show a relatively level profile, we know that the context of exploration may reveal that the profile is actually much more or less than what is shown.

For this definition of slice and dice, we add the time dimension to the bucketing approach described in the comparison and inventory section. The example above is a slice and dice by asset maturity. Anytime you can categorize the individual elements, you can create slice and dice analysis.

Slice and dice then is a rollup, over time, broken out by categories.

Metadata - Data About Data

All assets have permanent and temporary attributes that define, describe, or categorize them. They can be geographic, business class, clinical focus, organizational position, asset class, maturity, or any other class or category that makes sense.

Looking at slice-and-dice wedges informs you where your current (or proposed) strategy is taking you. The graphs are easy to create, but the main challenge is to extract meaning.

Some metadata categories:

1. Country
2. Country category, e.g., OPEC, OECD
3. Business Unit
4. Hydrocarbon type (oil vs. gas)
5. Asset Maturity
6. Strategic Category
7. Asset Class - deepwater, heavy oil, unconventional, shelf
8. Reservoir - carbonate, clastic, tight
9. Drug class - biologics, mRNA, chemical
10. Clinical focus - cancer, diabetes, kidney
11. Country Risk categories

Any of these can be helpful depending on the frame of the problem and the insight desired from the analysis.

Slice-and-dice is mechanically simple once you have your time series and metadata. It can be a formula in Excel, or you can organize your database to automate the categorical extraction. How does it help?

What Are Rollup and Slice and Dice Good For?

Looking at your rolled-up plan across time tells a lot about the depicted strategy—not necessarily the stated strategy, but what you are **actually doing**.

Based on the actual or proposed program, you can see how much you're doing in which countries and asset classes and how that will impact your financial metrics over time. Sometimes, executive management does not have a clear vision of where they want to go beyond "more production, more cash flow, less cost," but these slice-and-dice views can bring worrying trends to light.

Leaders may say, "Look, I may not know exactly where we want to go, but I know where we **don't** want to go. I would make a course correction if that graph showed a worrying trend."

Data Quality and Bias

Planner's Fallacy is a tendency of planners to make optimistic assumptions about cost, timing, and results. We all do it, and it's hard to overcome. This is exacerbated and complicated when implicit or explicit incentives push the bias even further. Some companies see project size as a symbol of responsibility, trust, and competency—a badge of honor. Bigger is better, so small or pilot options are sometimes eliminated from consideration. We also see cases where marginal projects are exaggerated to attract funding. The opposite also occurs because people do not want to be held to high expectations if they can avoid it. Sandbagging either way is not unusual in arriving at a budget.

If you have data for comparison, you have data for rollups. Rollups are mechanically simple and should be done as a matter of course. They help you understand where you don't want to go, they're easy to do, and there is no harm in doing them. Incorporating strategic measures, such as total hydrocarbon resources, provides essential insights into where the company is headed.

Key Takeaways

The mathematical aggregation of time-series data is insightful. It provides directional information about the strategy being executed or proposed. Splitting the time series out using categorical data is even better. Often, executives do not have a clear view of where they want to go, but they usually know where they do not want to go. Rolled-up data based on planning exercises often contains biases based on human nature and company culture. Care must be taken to treat the projections as directional—not as a forecast.

Detail – Combining Comparison and Inventory Methods with Rollups (Rollups with Guided Selection)

When discussing rollup, we focused mainly on using it for slice-and-dice analysis or to add a single opportunity into the mix. A hybrid method captures the intuitiveness of comparison with the aggregation and slice-and-dice perspective of rollups.

Using interactive graphics tools like Spotfire or PowerBI, decision-makers can use a comparison approach to select projects and aggregate them into the rollup with desired slices displayed. I refer to this approach as *Rollups with Guided Selection* (RGS).

It is an excellent approach that allows decision leaders to see the impact of their choices interactively. They can test different strategies, look at what a pure rank and cut approach does for them, and see how everything will play out. With some forethought and preparation, the system can even do probabilistic rollups. It is an excellent approach and is great when management is hands-on and prefers open and transparent processes.

Planview has an excellent short video showing how to combine these approaches for an intermediate-size working inventory. For scale, let's say less than 50 entities to select from, with no dependencies between projects (https://blog.planview.com/portfolio-prioritization-best-practices/ or https://www.youtube.com/watch?v=pV4kxB5OwfA).

You'll see a seven-minute video at the link that walks through the "why" of portfolio management and shows the "how." It captures a sequence, including rank and cut, a CFO chart, and category information about the maturity and clinical areas of the working inventory and candidate set selection.

A single screen can show several important views for the decision-making team. One panel can show the efficiency of the projects as a CFO chart. Selecting multiple projects as a candidate set shows its location relative to the efficient frontier. Another view can show the working inventory and candidate set compositions regarding the focus areas of the work or project maturity. Another panel can show a time series, such as revenue, and an indication of targeted values over time.

It is an interactive dashboard that a decision-making team can use to make decisions that balance strategic objectives, efficiency, revenue targets, and any other metrics of importance.

▸ Rollup with Guided Selection Dashboard

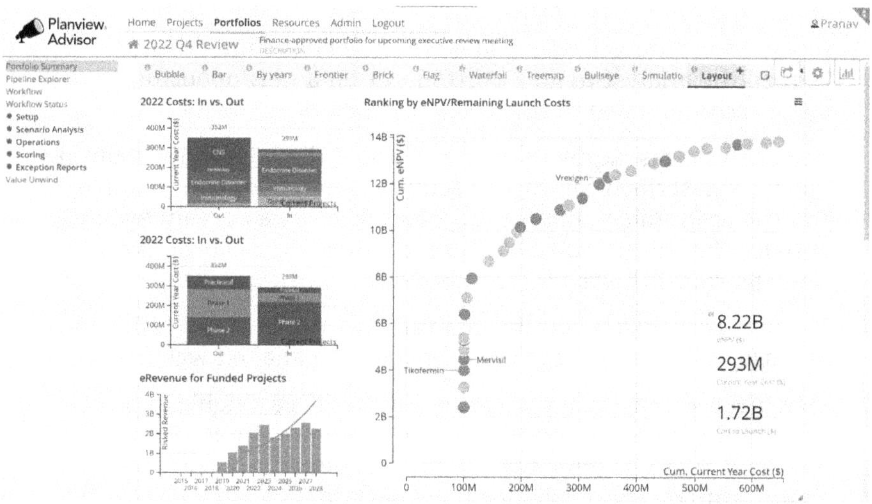

The following image from Planview Advisor (formerly Enrich Analytics) shows a powerful perspective on a group of projects for funding consideration. The right chart is a CFO chart, sorted by project goodness, but on a budget axis. The left side graphs show how the selected projects fall into strategic categories and the expected revenue. These types of tools provide granular control and insight to decision-makers and help balance tactical and strategic considerations.

RGS can run into a challenge with a larger scale and complexity of the portfolio problem. If the number of potential choices is relatively low and uncomplicated, (e.g., less than 50 decisions without dependencies), the number of value metrics is low and straightforward, (e.g., growth over five years, NPV, budget requirements), balance. This approach can yield excellent results.

As the complexity and size of the problem increases, finding good portfolios using RGS can be difficult, and finding excellent or optimal portfolios is nearly impossible.

Put another way, if the working inventory is large, the value measures are many, and dependencies in the data become important, you will need a better way to find suitable candidate sets for consideration. These methods are covered in detail in the interactions section.

War Story – The Big New Project

It was an ordinary Tuesday at work. The boss came in and wanted the analyst to do a portfolio fit on a new opportunity being recommended to the decision-makers at the top.

The analyst was happy to do it and asked the boss more about it. The boss described the cost to acquire, the size of the resource, and the economic parameters. It sounded like a bargain even at twice the price. (*Narrator: This is a serious red flag in business development (BD). Nobody gives good assets away.)*

The analyst asked when the analysis was needed. "By tomorrow. At close of business," the boss replied. The analyst was floored.

They needed to examine the economics for reasonableness, prepare the portfolio model, and check assumptions. There was no way it could be done with rigor—required because it was a significant commitment for the corporation.

The boss told the analyst to do what they could by the next day. With such a short timeline, the analyst could only look at the economics and layer the opportunity on top of the official rolled-up business plan. (It showed nothing particularly good or bad.) Even a significant opportunity layered on top of an already enormous company provides little insight. The width of the lines on the graph was practically enough to obscure the impact.

It turned out that despite the flaws with the economics and the lack of rigor in the portfolio fit analysis, the decision had already been made.

Lessons Learned

1. Do what you can with what you have and do your best to communicate the shortcomings.
2. Governance or lack of governance around portfolio decisions jeopardizes portfolio insights.
3. Although BD opportunities and the work around them are secretive, there still needs to be a review to ensure the quality of the analyses.

CHAPTER 7

Simulation – Stochastic Aggregation

“

Doubt is not a pleasant condition, but certainty is an absurd one”

Voltaire

The world is unpredictable. Something may happen or not. Whether or not it happens, there are many possible outcomes. Volatility can be considered a subset of uncertainty that includes the time dimension. Failure to acknowledge, understand, and manage this enormous, uncertain gray space can be disastrous to a business.

Uncertainty is a difficult concept for many people. To start, a lack of certainty creates discomfort in most people. We all want to know what will happen accurately. Unfortunately, despite efforts to try to forecast better, success remains elusive. Statistics and computer simulations provide us with a framework to think about and manage uncertainty.

In the Rollup section, we talked about mathematical summation or aggregation. Now, we shift to stochastic aggregation, which is a way of adding **uncertain** numbers to understand the range of what may occur. We perform this stochastic aggregation by using Monte Carlo simulation or other statistical methods to combine the inputs. Simulation is used in many fields, and there are books, tools, and consultants who can help with it.

▸ Simulation Appears Twice in the Portfolio Selector

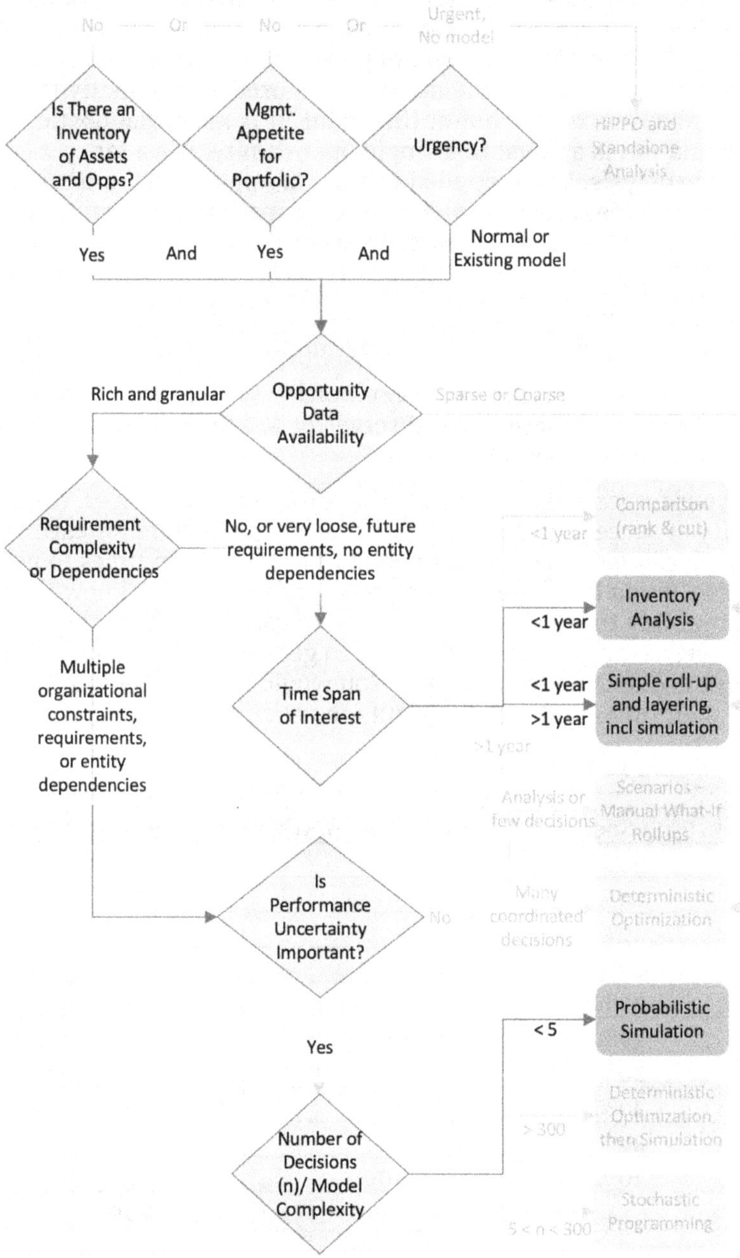

There's an ambiguity to simulation in the selector. It is easy to reach the inventory analysis or simple rollup box and need simulation. A single-year exploration drilling program might be in the less than one-year (inventory analysis) category, and a stochastic rollup of a firm's production would be in the simple rollup category.

As with mathematical rollups, simulations may not give firm guidance on what to do, but they might tell you that you should do **something** different. For the purposes of this book, simulation by itself is generally a portfolio **analysis** tool, not a portfolio **management** one. We will later explore how simulation can be used with sensitivity analysis and optimization, but at this point, it is more diagnostic. When simulation is applied to a single opportunity, it's a fancy standalone analysis. When applied to a set of opportunities, it's a fancy rollup. The fanciness carries important information. Simulation has many other purposes besides portfolio analysis.

The obvious example in the oil and gas business of portfolio simulation is its most probabilistic one—exploration. The analog in pharmaceuticals is the Research and Development (R&D) program.

Suppose you have a program of 10 exploration wells, each of which has a 20% probability of success and reserves of 100 million barrels of oil (MMBO) in case of success.

What is your forecasted outcome for that program? Remember, the 20% probability of success means an 80% probability of failure for each well. You know intuitively that you cannot add 100 MMBO ten times to get the answer. If you know something about probability, you know that you can multiply the likelihood of success of each well times the success case reserves and add them all together to get the [statistically] expected value or risked outcome in the table. You would need to multiply 20% times 100 ten times and add the results to get 200.

▸ Table of Example Wells

Well	Prob Success	Success Case MMBO	Risked Outcome
1	20%	100	20
2	20%	100	20
3	20%	100	20
4	20%	100	20
5	20%	100	20
6	20%	100	20
7	20%	100	20
8	20%	100	20
9	20%	100	20
10	20%	100	20
Total		**1,000**	**200**

This example assumes ten exploration wells, each with a 20% probability of success and holding 100 million barrels of oil if successful. The statistically expected value from this program is 200 million barrels, but the final outcomes could be anywhere between zero and 1,000 million barrels (or more). This example assumes that all wells are statistically independent of each other.

Your risked outcome or "expected value" (a probability-weighted mean value) is 200 MMBO. But that is not a guarantee. This example assumes that all wells are statistically independent of each other. In this scenario, there is still about a 10% chance that none of the wells will be successful. Or perhaps you will have three or four discoveries.

▸ Gambler's Ruin

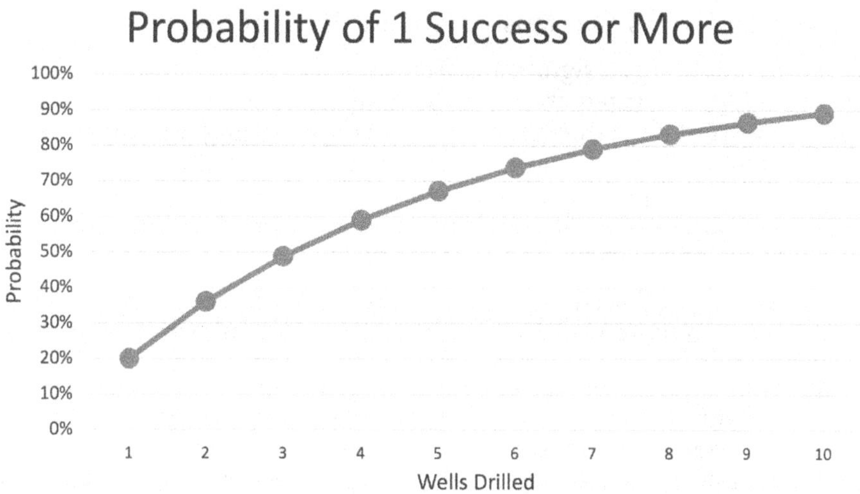

The Gambler's Ruin chart shows the probability of at least one success. Even with ten wells drilled—each with a 20% probability of success—you still have only a 89% chance of at least one success, which means an 11% chance of failure (ruin).

It's not unreasonable that this program would yield anywhere from zero to 400 MMBO discovered. This example is a simple calculation; in reality, there will be different probabilities of success and ranges on the outcomes of each of the wells.

Simulation attempts to test the future across a wide range of inputs, given that those inputs are uncertain. It supports understanding the expected range of outcomes and may help drive decisions to improve the results. Although simulation by itself does not tell you the best course of action, it may show you that a change is needed.

Key Takeaways

1. Simulation is conceptually similar to rollups: combine a set of possible decisions to see what it gives you. The challenge is in the particulars. Rather than simply adding the numbers and seeing the answer, simulation incorporates probabilities and ranges into its input values. The outputs include compilations and statistics of those different results.
2. Simulation is a significant step, in practice, from simple rollup, and it requires data that may not exist under your standard processes. This means that generating consistent inputs for simulation will require the creation of a new set of data generation and communication standards. It will also require that decision-makers be comfortable with probabilistic views in decision-making.
3. Even with flawed input data, simulations almost always reflect a more realistic worldview than deterministic views.
4. Simulation incorporates probabilities to place your decisions and directions into a context that reflects the reality of uncertainty in the world. If this is as far as you have gone on your portfolio journey, it is better than never having started. You will make better informed decisions.

Detail – Risk vs. Uncertainty Aversion

The word risk conjures visions of danger. In many contexts, risk equates to danger. Jumping out of an airplane without a parachute is a fine example. But sometimes, the word "risk" indicates uncertainty or variability.

Consider a pharmaceutical compound research or an oil exploration well. There is a good chance that the investigation effort will fail. There may be a 90% probability of failure and loss of our investment. In that sense, it is risky. You are risking the money to acquire more information, with the hope of converting that investment into income. Those funds define the limit of your loss unless additional funds are invested.

But business is about recognizing when those risks are more than offset by the opportunity. Spending one million dollars on a project with a 90% chance of failure would be considered risky by many people. But if the firm can withstand that kind of loss, it is worth the attempt **if** the reward for success is large enough. This is especially important if there will be multiple similar opportunities that are **independent** of each other.

This is an example of risk diversification. Unfortunately, many companies are set up in compartments where the failure of even a low-probability effort is seen as the manager's failure. This creates a strong disincentive to even consider low-probability investments.

Some companies take pride in being risk-takers, while others have a culture of being "fast-followers."

It would be foolish to propose a test similar to other failures and with a modest reward relative to the risk. Risk aversion is smart business. This is like the fear of snakes. You know that they bite and if they do, it will be bad. So, you stay away.

On the other hand, it is not foolish to test an **untested** area that could have enormous potential. You have no way of knowing how likely an untested concept is, but if the test works, it could be huge. This is not like the fear of danger. This is like the fear of darkness, in which there might possibly be danger. You are not afraid of the risk; you are afraid of not knowing—afraid of uncertainty. Companies that shy away from uncertainty become fast followers. Those who do not are the risk takers.

In some statistical and management circles, the word risk implies both upside and downside. I consider this to be misleading jargon. **Nobody** in the real world considers potential gain as a risk. This is wonkiness run amok.

Key Takeaways

1. Risk aversion is avoiding something you have good reason to believe will hurt more than help. It is generally healthy. Uncertainty aversion avoids something that might hurt you, or help, but is not well defined. Uncertainty aversion hinders the ability of a company to participate early in new ventures. It generally prevents innovation and leads to stagnation.
2. Smart risk plus the ability to absorb failures equals success. Bad risk plus no ability to absorb failures equals disaster.
3. Usage of the word risk in business and finance is very different from typical English usage. This has led to misconceptions and poor frameworks for decision-making and valuation.

Estimation of Probability and Uncertainty Inputs

One of the most common questions in my portfolio classes is how to deal with probabilities and uncertainties. They add complexity to portfolio analysis. It is essential to decide on the purpose of the study before deciding how to use probabilities. Therefore, as always, proper framing is necessary. The main questions you're trying to answer, and the analytical frame drive the data and tools you'll need. Handling probabilities is an integral part of that analytical framework.

Probabilities and Uncertainties

There is a series of critical probabilities of success in the upstream oil industry: Probability of Capture, Probability of Exploration Success, Probability of Commerciality or Development (Given Exploration Success), and Probability of Divestiture. Some may never be relevant. For example, assets may be abandoned rather than divested.

▸ Upstream Probabilities

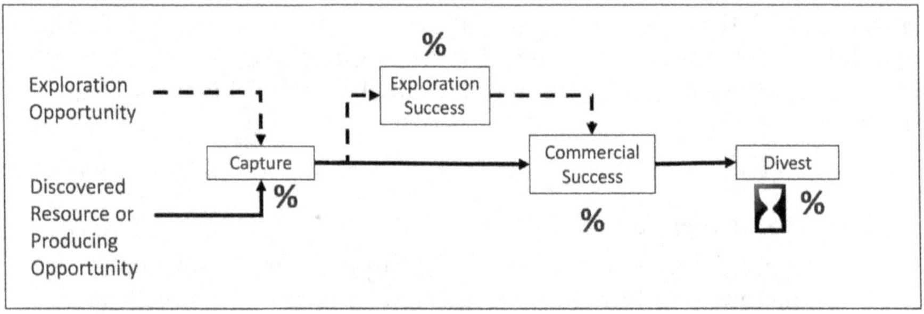

There are four main probabilities across the lifecycle of probabilities in the oil upstream, Capturing the right to derive economic benefit, technically successful exploration well, commercial success, and divestiture. The hourglass indicates that time is often an issue in divestiture analysis.

The success case of each of these probabilities may contain many uncertain variables and, therefore, wide uncertainty in the success case outcomes.

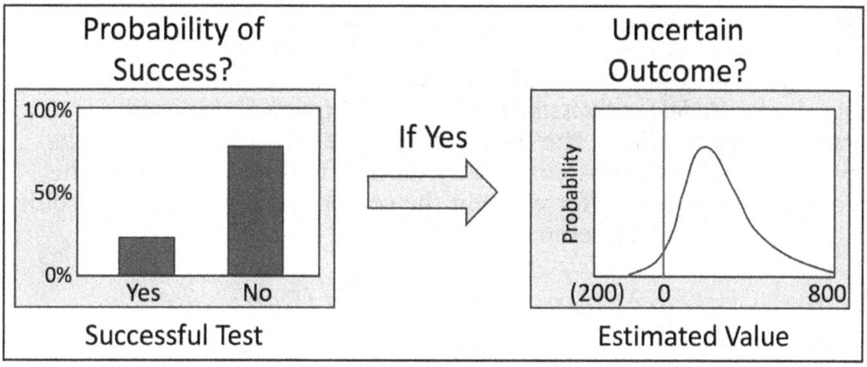

Each probability of occurrence generally contains two distributions: the Bernoulli (Yes-No) distribution on whether the effort will succeed and the uncertain outcome. The Yes-No is a binary distribution, and the sum of the two probabilities is 100%. The uncertain outcome may be of any range or shape. Consider the numbers on the x-axis to be economic value. The specifics dictate its form.

Probabilities

Each probability may also have a factor related to decision-maker support. For example, a project may have all the metrics that would make it good, but management does not like the Operator and is unlikely to support the project or opportunity. Or perhaps, an investment may look good, but there are better investments to make in the portfolio. From a portfolio standpoint, that is not a probability—it is a decision. When management commitment is not assured, separating that factor from the actual probabilities is useful. The framework of the analysis will determine whether and how to include that factor.

The four probabilities are themselves the product of the decomposition or disaggregation of factors or conditions required for the event to occur. These decompositions require a deep knowledge of the subject area. The factors for probability estimates must be mutually exclusive and collectively exhaustive—all the factors considered, but only once. Care must be taken in the definition and assessment to ensure that there is no overlap or omission. Creating such a framework is not a trivial matter, but once it is done, it is quite robust.

Over time, the risk models can be calibrated using standard statistical calibration tests like the Brier Score or other approaches that measure the accuracy or calibration of probability predictions.

Probability of Capture (PoC)

There is one published framework that I am aware of for estimating the Probability of Capture of a new unowned venture. It is in an SPE paper published in 2013, written by Kenck et al., called "*A Proposed Four-Factor Model for Assessing Probability of Capture of Unowned Resource Opportunities.*" The four factors assess the probability of the owner selling, the probability that your firm will make an offer, the probability that your offer will win the competition, and the probability of reaching a final agreement.

Probability of Exploration Success (PoS)

Many companies in the oil industry already have standards for assessing the probability of exploration success. Pete Rose, Founder of Rose and Associates, was instrumental in popularizing the techniques for upstream assessment. It is a four-factor framework that assesses hydrocarbon charge, reservoir quality and producibility, the existence of a favorable trap geometry, and a seal rock to prevent hydrocarbons from leaving the reservoir rock.

Exploration drilling may compete with more immediate commercial considerations, so the management commitment factor in exploration may also be applied to the probability of drilling the exploratory well. Finally, exploratory wells may be located in complex and poorly understood geological circumstances. When this is the case, it may be appropriate to include a factor for the probability of successfully drilling and testing the geologic target of interest.

Probability of Development (PoD)

Once a discovery is made and the exploration probability is resolved, the question remains whether it is a good project to develop. There is direct subsurface information at this point, and much more is known than before. However, even at that point, much remains uncertain. Sometimes there is technology that needs to be developed and tested. Sometimes, the reservoir does not flow as well as hoped. Sometimes, the world changes with prices or costs going up or down. And as always, there is the management commitment factor. Is management willing to spend the money to commit to this development?

Probability of Divestiture (PoDiv)

The Probability of Divestiture is similar to the Probability of Capture. But now your firm is the seller. Previously, the probability of "buy" was a decision; now, attempting a "Buy" is the probability that the asset will attract earnest offers. "Win," instead of looking at how your bid would compare to the rest of the world, needs to consider whether any of the buyers might be willing to meet your internal minimum price. The probability of final alignment remains similar.

The PoDiv framework can add another factor—timing. Divestiture programs are often tied to a market commitment to maintain cash flow or receive proceeds from a buyer. In prioritizing which assets to divest, it may be important to consider the timeframe of the transaction. This can be especially true for large assets in countries with stringent regulatory or legislative requirements for this type of transaction.

Note: Bayesian vs. Frequentist Probabilities

The probabilities described above apply to an asset, well, or property. Each one is a special snowflake. There is no reasonable way to know the actual probability. So, we use Bayesian methods. With these methods, we assess the quality of our information and in which direction it pulls us. As more information arrives, we revise our probabilities.

For much portfolio work, accurate and precise probabilities are **not** the most significant driver of decision insight but rather the **relative** probabilities within the working set are. We are looking to make great decisions, not necessarily great forecasts. Having said that, these probabilities can be reasonably calibrated with experience using statistical tests.

As your organization's analytic capabilities improve, you may find that getting your probabilities right and accurate in the aggregate is increasingly important. Doug Hubbard has written several books on probability estimation and measurement *(How to Measure Anything, The Failure of Risk Management)*, and runs courses, through his company, Hubbard Decision Research, to debias subject matter experts (SMEs).

Input Uncertainties and Distributions

Every parameter that goes into estimating the size or value of an asset contains uncertainty. Many decision analysis and quantitative estimation books cover how to estimate that uncertainty. For this book, we assume that uncertainty estimates are reasonably well-calibrated and have definable probability distributions. The uncertain inputs are put into a quantitative model, such as an event tree or a Monte Carlo simulation, resulting in a distribution of outputs. Each output from one of these models can be represented as an uncertainty distribution.

The input distributions can be tricky. Geek religious wars have been fought over which probability density function to use for different purposes. Fortunately, for most portfolio work, because we tend to combine multiple elements, it is more important to represent variability than to capture the distribution's shape perfectly.

In this vein, input uncertainty distributions can be represented using standard distributions such as normal, lognormal, triangular, or uniform distributions depending on the nature of the uncertainty. If you have an agreed basis for the shape of the distribution, use it. If you don't, keep it simple.

There are some interesting recent developments in this field. Probability Management is a non-profit organization devoted to the mathematics of probability. This organization espouses auditable, additive, actionable, and agnostic approaches to using distributions. The Metalog or Keelin distribution is a recent development that can closely approximate complicated distributions, even when the data does not fit smoothly with common distributions. Data standards and Metalog distributions can allow for compact and repeatable communication of uncertainty.

Detour – Bayes vs Frequentist Concepts

Frequentist statistics is what you likely learned in your probability and statistics class. It is helpful in many fields, especially when large numbers of observable events can be reasonably grouped. It is excellent for repeatable processes.

The upstream oil industry is seldom like that. Every oil field is different; every exploration prospect is different and has different data available. Much of the interpretation is inferred from remote sensing rather than direct measurement. You never repeat experiments with the same conditions.

Bayesian statistics are the solution. Bayesian statistics are a way to start with a "prior" probability and then update based on available information. Because of the non-repeating nature of these unique evaluations, it may be helpful to think of Bayesian probabilities as a measure of plausibility rather than probability. The use of the value is the same either way. You may have seen some surprising Bayesian statistics when people talk about the effectiveness of medical testing.

Frequentist statistics give an answer, but they cannot answer the probability that an effort will succeed given the data. There is no way to compute that without a prior probability. So, frequentist statisticians answer a different question: If the null hypothesis is true (e.g., the drug is no better than a placebo or the well is a dry hole), what is the probability that we would observe this outcome?

Portfolio and decision problems require the probability that a project will succeed. Frequentist statistical data with enough information may be able to provide enough information to establish a prior probability.

Ron A. Howard, a founder of the field of Decision Analysis, said in his seminal paper (*Decision Analysis: Applied Decision Theory*, Howard 1966) that Bayes Theorem is seldom applied rigorously but that an important implication is that probabilities of this sort are a "state of mind."

Bayesian concepts are fundamental in evaluating the probability of occurrence and value of information (VoI) analyses.

This link https://www.youtube.com/watch?v=GEFxFVESQXc takes you to a 7-minute video that demonstrates the difference between Bayesian and Frequentist concepts from Cassie Kozyrkov, the former Chief Decision Officer for Google, and current CEO of Data Scientific.

A full explanation of the differences, uses, and generation of Bayesian and frequentist concepts is beyond the scope of this book. This website provides a good overview. https://arbital.com/p/bayes_rule/?l=1zq

This site contrasts Bayesian and Frequentist concepts, focusing on the difference between the probability framework and the probability elicitation. https://www.cantorsparadise.com/the-two-schools-of-probability-theory-76d0c0c8198d

Key Takeaways

I'm not a statistician or a mathematician, but I have built and used probability frameworks to make probability estimates. I differentiate Bayesian from frequentist statistics in the following way. We use frequentism when we have repeatable events that we can track. An obvious example is bolts coming off an assembly line. Some percentage of them will be fine, but there will be an occasional defective one.

With Bayesian statistics, as I have used it here, we start with a non-repeatable event, understand the underlying process or circumstances that will lead to success, and then estimate our subjective view of those underlying circumstances. Oil exploration wells and pharmaceutical research are classic examples. We start with an estimate. Then, as we gather more information and do more research, we update our estimate of the conditions. Ultimately, though, each one will never be repeated.

As with selecting the correct probability distribution to use in simulation, there are nerd flame wars between Bayesians and frequentists. I don't participate in those. I will say that the above approach provides a useful perspective for portfolio analysis and management. With time and calibration, the estimates of probability might even be accurate. However, because the discrete events are not repeatable, they may never rise to the level of "science."

I don't care. It helps us make better decisions.

Detail - Management Commitment

Considering management commitment, the likelihood that management will commit to an action as a probability—deserves special mention and discussion.

I stated previously that the use of the management commitment factor depends on the frame of the problem.

It boils down to the following:

1. If you are using the numbers for a forecast model, the management commitment factor should be included as a probability factor. Until the question of whether to move forward on something is fully resolved, it **is** an uncertainty.
2. If you are using the numbers for portfolio decision-making, i.e., to help guide those decision-makers in whether to do something, management commitment should not be included.

Management commitment is in our **firm's** control, even though it isn't in the analyst's control. Portfolio analysis will inform management on what they *should* do. The perspective of the decision on an investment or asset should not be distorted by someone's estimate of how likely management is to approve something.

On the other hand, the management commitment of a different company that will affect us, for example, a partner in a venture, is a probability because it is not in our control. Estimating this type of probability can be guided by past interactions and their stated and understood priorities. The application of Game Theory concepts may help with efforts to influence government and industry partners.

War Story - Acronyms

The Probability of Capture is PoC. The Probability of Development is PoD, so Probability of Divest had to be PoDiv. PoS is the common acronym for the probability of exploration success at Chevron. Unocal used PoH for Probability of Happening.

But before we had these different probabilities defined, there was one that stood in for all of them, Probability of Occurrence. Yes, POO.

We would be in meetings with some of the highest-level people in the company discussing what the POO factor was or should be set to.

I have permanent scars on the inside of my cheeks where I bit them to prevent myself from immaturely cracking up like a third grader. Sometimes we are too serious for our own good.

Modeling Uncertainty – Monte Carlo Simulation and Decision Trees

Ed Capen, formerly with Arco, described compositing multiple events and combining them into an expected value as essentially calculating a betting odds number. The probabilistic results may never match the actual outcome (half "heads" does not exist in a coin flip), but before the fact, they may tell you if it's a good bet.

The first and most straightforward way in which people typically incorporate probabilities and ranges is by calculating an "expected" value and ending up with a single number. For example, in a game where someone flips a coin and gives you a dollar for heads and nothing for tails, the statistically expected value is $0.50. It is simply the value of success times the probability of that happening minus the cost of failure times the likelihood of that happening ($1 x 50% + $0 x 50%). This expected value can never possibly happen with a single coin flip. There are only two outcomes: $0 or $1. In this case, the expected value (EV) is not a possible outcome but rather a statistically adjusted value to help you understand the wisdom of the bet. You might "rationally" be willing to pay up to $0.49 to play the game. This is essentially calculating the betting odds for a given proposition.

To develop further insights from uncertainties and probabilities, you need a process or model to convert them into an output to organize and understand the results. Two common approaches to modeling uncertainty are event (or decision) trees and Monte Carlo simulation (MC). Monte Carlo generally scales better than event trees for portfolio problems, but event trees are also helpful in small-scale portfolio problems.

Monte Carlo

Monte Carlo (MC) is another approach to generating outputs from uncertain inputs. MC samples a possibility from the probability distribution for each random input, runs the underlying mathematical model, and then generates and saves the output. It returns to the beginning, selects another set of random inputs, executes the model, and stores those outcomes. It repeats this process as many times as specified. It could be hundreds, thousands, or millions of times. Each iteration (or trial) is a virtual experiment—it calculates a possible outcome of the system or process that you are modeling. Ultimately, you are left with a complete set of statistics about possible outcomes or consequences.

There is an art and science to selecting the best parameters for the type of sampling and number of trials but specifying Latin Hypercube sampling and 100 trials is often a reasonable starting point while troubleshooting a model. Latin Hypercube is a technique for distributing samples evenly across a probability space instead of relying on random processes. Trying different parameters will give you a sense of the adequacy of those settings, but it is likely that you will want more than 100 trials. There are tradeoffs between time to solve and desired precision.

There are several commercial Monte Carlo programs (Crystal Ball, @Risk, Analytica, Vose, Frontline), or you can use native Excel. Probability Management, a non-profit corporation, has a free Excel toolbar, plus instructions and examples.

Decision or Event Trees

Conditional probabilities can be expressed in a tree format too. Indeed, many people prefer it. It has the advantage of being visually tractable for small problems. Note: When there are decisions within the tree it is usually called a decision tree. In the case below, where decisions are assumed, it is an event tree.

▸ **Oil Well Simple Decision Tree**

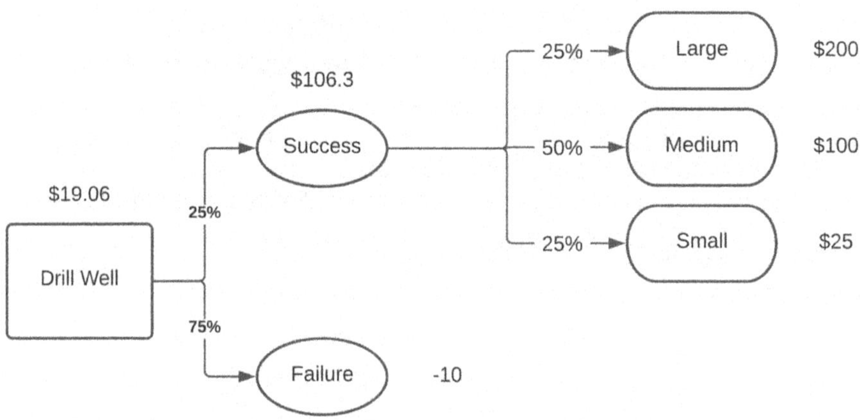

An oil well will be drilled. Working from left to right, we see a 75% probability on the failure node with a value of -$10 and a success node with a probability of 25% and a value of $106.3. The success value is a weighted average of the Small, Medium, and Large outcomes. The statistically expected value of the well before the fact is $19.06. This is the weighted average of the Success and Failure branches.

The success branch on the right has a 90th percentile value of $200, a 50th percentile value of $100, and a 10th percentile value of $25. The node values in the tree, when multiplied by the percentages (using an approximation of 25%, 50%, 25%) and summed, yield an approximate mean value assuming a normal distribution.

The end nodes of decision trees are usually expressed as discrete value outcomes. But each end node may be expressed as a probability distribution instead. That approach allows the visual power of a decision tree with the more continuous depiction of outcomes or input variables of Monte Carlo. It can be especially important when distributions have long tails, which might not be visible in discrete trees.

Output Uncertainties and Distributions

For a set of probabilities and uncertain inputs, the output of a system or model will have a range of outcomes. This range of outcomes can be expressed as a probability density function (such as a bell curve), or it can be expressed as a cumulative probability function (sometimes called an S-curve).

▸ Comparison of Probability Distribution and Cumulative Probability

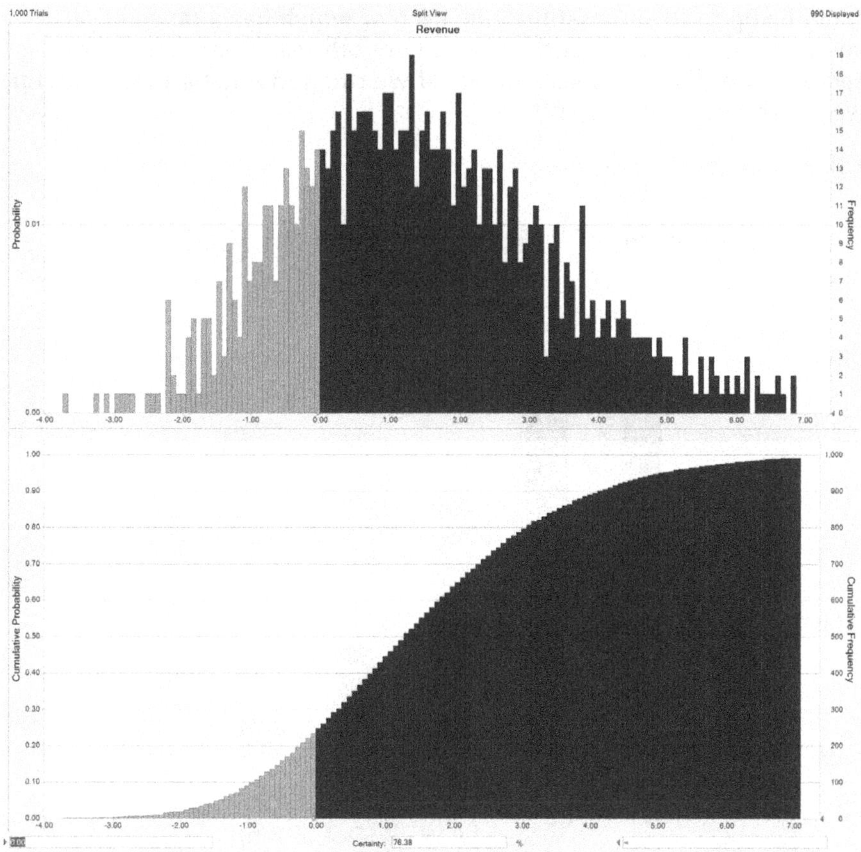

The upper diagram shows a probability density function from a model with 1,000 trials, and the lower one shows a cumulative probability distribution of the same data.

The graph shows two different depictions of a range of outcomes. The upper one is like a bell curve—for each value bin on the x-axis, we can see the probability that the outcome will fall into that bin. This is a useful way to compare different scenarios for how uncertainty is distributed. It shows the details.

The cumulative probability curve is the accumulation of probabilities from left to right with each value on the x-axis. It's valuable if you wish to express the likelihood of being above or below a specific outcome. In the figure, reading up from the zero value on the x-axis shows about an 25% probability of being below zero and a 45% chance of being below 1.

Our previous example of ten wells was simplistic, assuming that each well would yield 100 million barrels if successful and showing only the probability of one or more successful wells. The reality is that there could be up to 10 successful wells, each of which has a range of oil volumes that fall on a continuum of possibilities. There may be zero successful wells or as many as ten. If we run a Monte Carlo simulation, we see the following results.

▸ Depiction of Outcome Probabilities

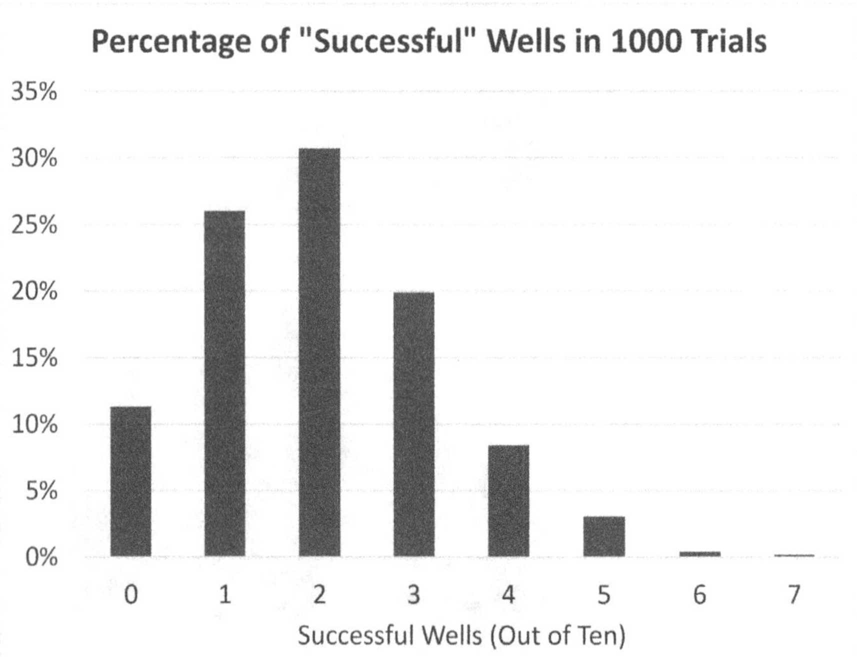

The bar chart shows the number of virtual successful wells in 1,000 Monte Carlo trials. Note that two wells (20% of the wells being successful) is the most likely, with an 11% probability of no successes. There is a slim possibility of six or seven successes, but none of the trials had more than seven successes.

The cumulative probability chart of oil volume gives us a picture of the likelihood of a given volume of oil from our drilling program. There is still an 11% chance of no oil, while the previously calculated mean of 200 (or greater) would occur less than 40% of the time. Often, people think of the 'mean' as a midpoint, but in this case, we incorporated a lognormal (skewed) probability distribution reflecting typical geological outcomes.

▸ **Cumulative Probability of Outcomes**

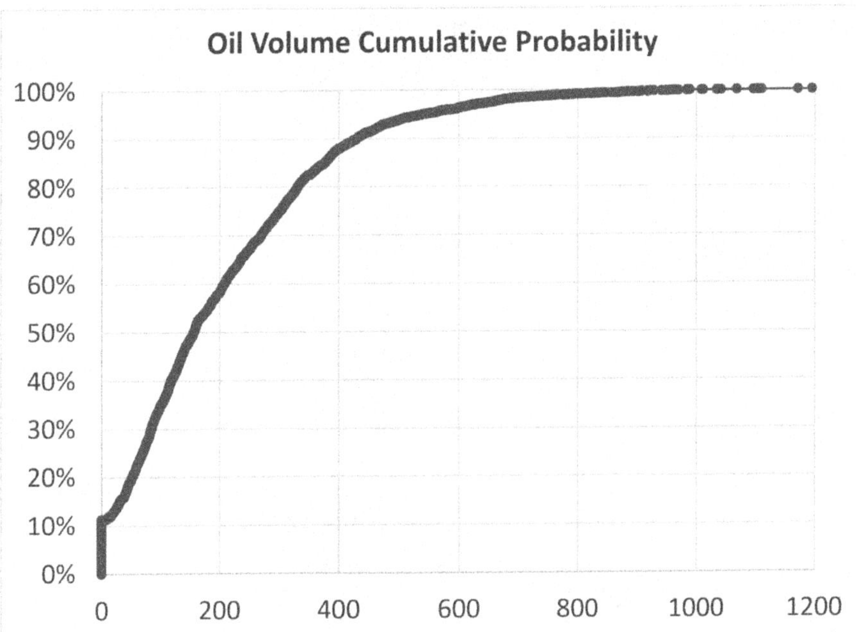

The cumulative probability chart of oil volume gives us a picture of the likelihood of a given volume of oil from our drilling program. No successful wells at 11%, has no oil volumes, and the previously calculated mean of 200 (or greater) would occur less than 40% of the time. Often, people think of the mean as a midpoint, but in this case, we incorporated a skewed probability distribution that would have small possibilities of large volumes.

The tool selection for simulation will depend on several factors: budget, problem complexity, and familiarity with the tool. For beginners on a budget, use native Excel with free tools for either simulation or event trees. Commercial products have advantages that can override the cost factor as the analysis gets more complex.

Elements of Simulation Modeling

For portfolio work, there are three significant steps towards recognizing portfolio-level risks. The first is acknowledging that there is no "the number" [*Why Can't You Just Give Me the Number?* By Patrick Leach]. The second is finding (and ultimately correcting) consistent biases in the numbers you have. The third is recognizing correlations between the drivers of uncertainty.

Recognizing Uncertainty

Start with the fact that every number used in the input of economic comparisons is variable (before mitigation or hedging). You know that you can sell your oil, but at what price? Will it be $25 per barrel or $50? Or $75? Will it cost $500 million to develop a field or $1 billion? Will it take three years to build or seven? How many appraisal wells will be required? Will the tax regime stay the same? Can we get an extension of our production license? At what cost? These uncertainties can drive a project to wild success or abject failure. Many of them are uncontrollable. A Monte Carlo analysis with even the simplest distributions can reveal tremendous insight.

Adding uncertainty to a model is the transformative step. Recognizing that distribution shapes are not usually determinative is a step-change in mindset. I will paraphrase an analogy by Dr. Sam Savage from his book *"Decision Making with Insight."*

Consider what happened the last time you climbed a ladder. You leaned it against the house and set the feet. Then you gave it a shake.

Let me ask you. Did the shake you gave the ladder mimic the forces that you were about to put on it?

Of course not. Did it provide insight into the stability of the ladder? Yes!

Distributions are the same. For strategic portfolio work, the distributions are metaphorical ladder shakes.

It is essential to understand and model when and how non-linearities and step functions occur in your models and the real world. Probabilities of Success are a common type of step function. Exploration wells or clinical trials are bimodal distributions with a high probability of a negative outcome but a considerable, highly uncertain, success-case upside.

Biases

Data used as input for analysis often has biases. I'm not talking about uncertainty, but rather when the ranges or mean of the data are skewed away from the true value.

A common bias in portfolio work is planners' bias. Plans generally lead to budgets, and every planner knows that we are punished for exceeding the budget. On the other hand, underestimating the cost or exaggerating the speed of a project can increase the likelihood of approval. However, it is important to try to avoid these pitfalls. Budgets and long-range plans contain a mixture of optimism and pessimism rather than realism. We used to joke about the project mantra—the project was late, over-budget, and underperformed, but we were saved by the oil price. That is until the oil price no longer saved us.

Every organization has processes and a culture that may distort input data. Over time, you see how these distortions play out, and you can use probabilistic means to better forecast outcomes at an enterprise level.

Correlations

Leading up to the 2008 recession, many finance companies had put together packages of loans. A big assumption behind those packages was that each loan was independent of the others—if one loan defaulted, that event was a private misfortune for someone, but all the other loans were related to that one. It turns out that the overall economy and housing market were the mechanisms that connected them. This correlation took away the power of the supposed diversification of the loan packages.

In the oil industry, this plays out in a few ways. A change in oil price has a global impact on the entire oil-related part of a portfolio because oil is a globally fungible commodity. The price of liquefied natural gas is often correlated with the price of oil. Natural gas sold into local markets is often unrelated to oil price swings because prices are set contractually or driven by local conditions.

In the hydrocarbon exploration world, the first well in a basin can lead to a reassessment of the area's potential and risk, leading to a cessation of work or a land rush. In other words, success can upgrade nearby prospects, while failure downgrades them. The basin's future wells have the common characteristics of the basin.

In the Shell example in the Appendix, correlations were important to the executives. The portfolio team created streams of correlated data that illustrated the response relationships of the assets to changes in the external environment. For example, the plots show that Ventures 6, 7, and 8 respond randomly and similarly to Region 1 Gas Price, while Ventures 4, 4A, and 5 show a linear response to the same price.

▸ Scatter Plots Showing Correlated Outcomes

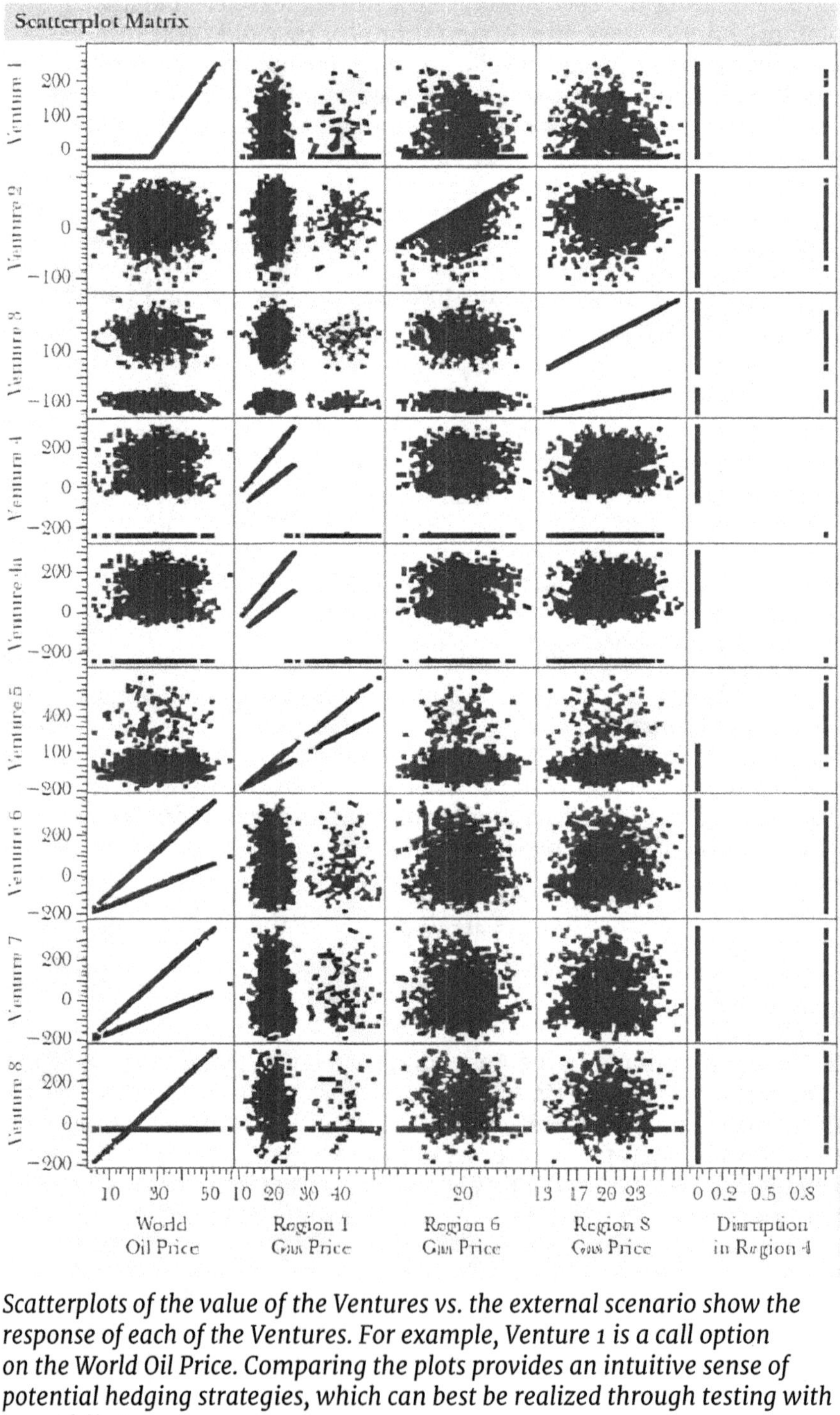

Scatterplots of the value of the Ventures vs. the external scenario show the response of each of the Ventures. For example, Venture 1 is a call option on the World Oil Price. Comparing the plots provides an intuitive sense of potential hedging strategies, which can best be realized through testing with a portfolio too.

To the extent you can, when creating correlations, try to understand the drivers. As an example, in the upstream oil industry, all oil-producing assets are dependent on oil prices for profitability. This means that their profitability is related to the oil price rather than to each other. Look for the causality and model that where practical.

This style of defining relations based on results modeled with identical sets of input parameters provides more realistic information well beyond what a simple mathematical correlation matrix would capture. It shows real-world relationships, including all the messiness of step functions and other non-linearities.

Correlation is not always of immediate concern. Some oil companies seem to actively seek correlation with oil prices either as a hedge for investors, because they are bullish on the macroeconomic conditions, or because they are opportunity driven. Understanding and tracking alternative macroeconomic scenarios can be critical to profitability and corporate survival.

Key Takeaways

As you progress on your simulation journey, you may find that simulation parameters and nailing the correct distribution can make a difference. However, the three factors in this section: recognizing uncertainty, understanding biases, and incorporating correlations, are a great start.

Which Uncertainties to Model?

The Project Mantra

I mentioned earlier that projects tend to be late, over-budget, and under-perform, and if we're lucky, the oil price saves us. We need to consider at least those four factors, as well as the probability of even having something to develop. For portfolio work, you can usually address those four factors at the project or asset level. For individual project work, more detail is required.

Probability of Occurrence

The most straightforward uncertainty to model is the probability of success. The probability is binary, either yes or no. The bar chart below shows a 30% chance of success (1) and a 70% chance of failure (0). When your simulation runs, 30% of the time, you expect a 1; 70% of the time, you expect a 0.

Depiction of a Yes-No Distribution

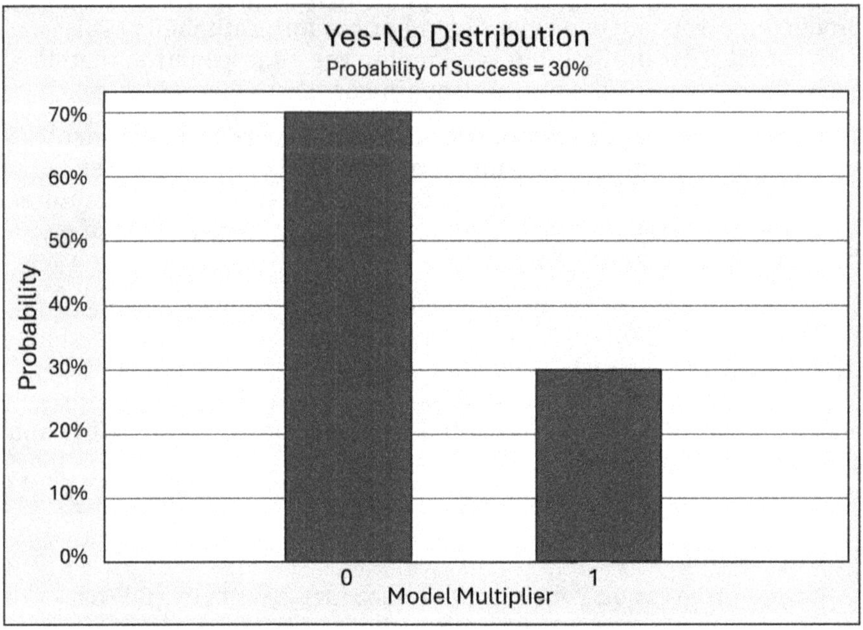

Each bar represents the probability of the result on the x-axis. The shorter bar at x = 1 will occur 30% of the time; the longer bar at x = 0 will occur 70% of the time. This event has a 30% probability of happening.

Continuous Inputs for Development Projects

The next type of uncertainty is a continuous distribution of inputs to the economic model. In terms of NPV in the oil industry, the most prominent drivers of uncertainty are typically oil price, oil volume/production rate, cost of development, and timing of first production.

There are many ways to model oil prices, and an exhaustive review is beyond the scope of this book. The main consideration for multiple opportunities, is that the opportunities use a consistent basis for oil, gas, or other product prices across time.

The cost of development and the oil volume are usually correlated. When considering multiple opportunities, it is important that the opportunities use consistent oil prices, whether deterministic or probabilistic. More oil means more production, leading to larger capacities and more expensive production costs. The cost per barrel is typically lower for more significant developments due to economies of scale. In addition, there are step functions in development concepts.

Single numbers with ranges can express capital cost, total resource, production, and opex for development projects. Total cash flow and total earnings (across the project life) can be approximated for simple fiscal regimes from the previous numbers plus fiscal regime information.

A small field would call for one type of development, while a larger one would call for another kind. Moreover, the cost is affected by inflation/escalation rates, scope changes, foreign exchange, and delays. Modeling the interplay between volume, external factors, cost, and fiscal regimes can be complex. Depending on the frame of the desired results, it is often sufficient to use a simpler cost model than to incorporate all the rigor.

Modeling development projects is complicated, but doable. A portfolio model would be bogged down by the complexity required for a detailed single project analysis, combined with numerous other projects.

Declining Production

Every oil field goes into decline from the moment production begins. Not only does the remaining oil production decline, but the pressure in the reservoir depletes, and more water is produced with the oil. Temporary shutdowns can be caused by weather and as facilities age, there is a higher chance of unexpected problems and planned maintenance that causes temporary shutdowns, thereby affecting production "uptime."

Furthermore, a drop in oil prices could render a field uneconomic, or a government may decide to seize a field or increase the government take (e.g., tax rates). These factors could be linked to oil prices and the likelihood of sudden production loss in any given year.

A complex model would handle all the interactions as described. A simpler one might make a chained assumption of a greater or lesser decline rate.

Development Delays

Remember the project mantra above. How do you model timing to first production? First, know your company's tendencies. Most companies and project teams exaggerate development speed, especially for complicated projects with many moving parts. Early estimates will tend to be less reliable than later ones. Congratulations if your company does better and tends to have unbiased timing estimates. Keep in mind that this positive bias is the norm.

Although there is technically a continuous distribution of project start-up timing, you should consider using discrete probabilities (like months or years) instead. Annual steps work well for strategic portfolio models. Tactical and operational models might require smaller time steps.

Probability step functions can be easily created in simulation programs. The next section discusses time delays in more detail.

If you have timing adjustments in the form of P10-P50-P90 inputs, you may want to fit them to a known distribution, such as lognormal or even use an algorithm with two functions combined in a piecewise fashion. With this approach, 0-50% is one distribution shape, while 50-100% is a different one.

Above Ground Risks

Many other risks can be modeled. Currency fluctuations are important in some cases. Political events such as coups, changes in tax rates, government seizure of facilities, or obsolescing bargain risk, in which a sovereign state gains negotiating power and changes your deal as the enterprise invests money, can have a significant impact on business operations. Events like weather or Acts of God, environmental disasters like Macondo, and other high-impact-low-probability (HILP) events are all possibilities. What to include and how should be explicitly stated as part of the frame of the problem.

Complex Portfolio Simulation Models

The complexity and rigor normally required for a single project analysis would bog down a model containing numerous other similar projects. Simplifying the models significantly or importing a stream of pre-calculated uncertainty data using SIPs and SLURPs are the main practical approaches for simulating portfolio results.

Key Takeaways

1. This chapter gives you a sense of the complexity that **can** go into a simulation model. A person could spend a lifetime trying to build a comprehensive model that perfectly models the full range of possibilities. This book is about **practical** portfolio methods, so you must develop your model complexity appropriately. It needs to contain enough accuracy to show a wide range of outcomes but not be so complicated that it takes too long to get insights.
2. Start with the most straightforward assumptions for strategic modeling and cut out as much complexity as you can. Always remember that the big win is in recognizing that leadership must understand and consider uncertainty, not in getting the fifth decimal place correct.

Rigor in Time-Series Outcome Modeling

I think of four different levels for showing time-series uncertainty. Each level requires additional work within the model or the inputs. The frame of the problem and data availability should drive the decision of which to level to use.

Level 1: In cases where the probability of success is the overriding risk element, as with pharmaceutical research or oil exploration, entering only the mean case time-series information may be adequate. Development timing and the range of outcomes will change your probabilistic outcome range, but in my experience, the effort may be higher than the gained insight. This is the easiest and quickest approach but understates the range of outcomes.

Use a single multiplier across your time range if it is practical and reasonable. Incorporating annual uncertainties on multiple metrics across many years can slow a simulation model to a crawl. Specific requirements will depend on the frame of the analysis.

Level 2: The next step in complexity is to scale the time series to the initial outcome. As an example for hydrocarbon exploration or pharmaceutical research, there is often a forecasted range of outcomes based on either the nature of the reservoir or the efficacy and safety of a compound. Those initial outcomes are material drivers of future financial results. Timing uncertainty can also be part of Level 2 modeling. It is typically incorporated as a probability of shifting in time.

For oil and gas developments, a helpful approach is to create a "type curve," a pattern of production of the field's resources. For example, expressed as a percentage of total hydrocarbons, the type-curve may have 0 for four years during development, then 5%, 20%, 20%, 17%, 13%, 10%, 7%, 5%, 3% (adding up to 100%). You would multiply those percentages by the total resource found (as an uncertainty). Then the mean time-series information would be scaled by the magnitude of the success, and timing would be shifted based on project issues. This is probably not a realistic perspective, but it is only a small step above Level 1 in complexity and improves the deficiencies of Level 1.

Level 3: This step incorporates different project outcome scenarios, for example, small, mid, and large cases. There can be as many levels as required by the problem at hand.

Level 3 modeling is relatively simple to model using Boolean expressions but requires additional work on the inputs. Again, the frame of the problem will determine whether the extra effort, generally performed by project teams, is worth the effort. Level 3 modeling of timing can incorporate additional scenarios, timing shift probability as in level 2, or a middle ground that would insert additional carrying costs for delayed projects.

Level 4: With Level 3 modeling, you may also incorporate decisions that have not been taken yet. As an example, suppose two different development concepts are still under consideration—one with a sharp increase and a very short peak production, the other with a very broad and lower peak production. You can assign a probability to each of the decisions and allow the Monte Carlo tool to select one or the other randomly. This approach provides a probabilistic outcome, but you will not see a distinction in terms of which development would be preferred.

The most rigorous approach would incorporate an economic and even a reservoir model parameterized to generate outcomes from a set of random inputs. This level would integrate a version of the input models used for level 3 modeling. Many standalone models incorporate this level of rigor.

With a moderately extensive portfolio, the added detail and rigor would be lost in the stochastic noise. The added precision of a Level 4 model is unlikely to justify the time and effort required to go from Level 3 to Level 4.

I presented the four levels above as discrete steps, but there is gray space and the possibility of mixing and matching.

▸ Main Simulation Factors for Upstream

Factor to Model	Decisions	Comments
Probability of success	Which risky investments to pursue or prioritize	The probability of success is part of an expected value framework for investments that may never pay out. Exploration, research, and front-end engineering are common investments in this category. The high probability of failure is the primary driver of outcomes in these cases. These models generally run fast.
Flow rate/ resource, sales volume, product price	Which investments to pursue, revenue sensitivity	Once the probability of success is resolved, this next level of uncertainty takes on added relevance. It can be modeled with continuous or discrete distributions.
Capital and operating cost	Which investments to pursue, cost sensitivity	Capital is easy to model as a total cost but more difficult to model in a time series. Modeling can be tricky. Project delays usually increase costs because of escalation and overhead. Acceleration may also increase costs. For portfolio work, stick to high-level assumptions.
Production and revenue timing	Promises to market, economic viability	Production timing can be important when considering commitments to stakeholders. Simulation can compensate for planners' bias, perhaps the most common bias in planning and portfolio. Delays affect revenue and timing and commonly cause problems in the project. Those problems drive costs higher. Delays may erode competitive advantage and positioning.
Full stochastic	Risk management, large, highly material efforts	Fully stochastic models should be considered when making bet-the-company types of decisions. Deciding how to handle prices and correlations between sectors in a company, e.g., upstream vs. downstream in petroleum, is important.

Portfolio modeling generally requires less rigor than individual project modeling. When combining many unrelated projects, diversifiable risks tend to cancel. Keep your models as simple as possible, introducing additional complexity only as needed.

Modeling the Probability of Project Delay

One decision in modeling project production/revenue delay is time granularity. Timing uncertainty is infinitely variable. However, modeling infinite variability is quite involved and adds complexity to a model.

For strategic and tactical models, incorporating annual delays provides good utility in understanding the effect of timing on performance. The result of a Monte Carlo run, especially with multiple projects, will be smooth enough, and the Excel logic is a simple lookup-style command.

Below is an example of a probability distribution of delay. This can be determined with analytics using delay models, empirical data for similar projects, rules of thumb, or gut feel. More important than a perfect distribution is any distribution at all.

▸ **Probability of Delay**

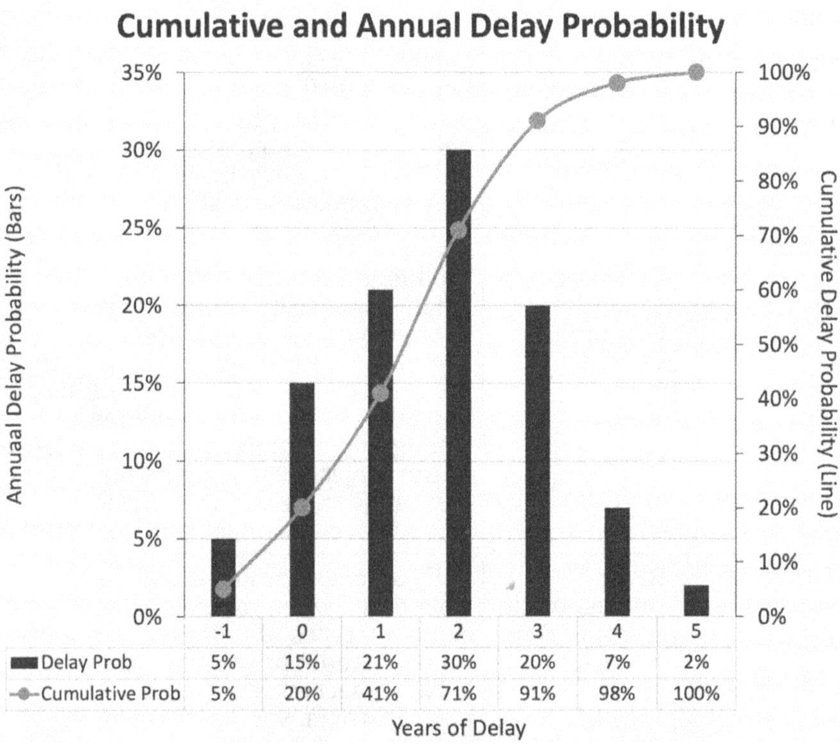

Model the start of production (revenue) based on the project's size, complexity, and novelty combined with your knowledge and data of organizational tendencies.

In the above example, there is a 5% chance of coming in one year early and a 15% chance of being on time. Which, combined, translates to a 20% probability of being early or on time (right axis). In this case, the probability distribution goes up to 5 years of delay. This would be considered a worst delay success case. Your definition of success must tie to the distributions of the success case for both delay and value. So, if you consider a seven-year delay to be a success, you need to expand your timing distribution.

> **Key Takeaways**
> 1. The frame of the problem drives the required detail for time-series simulation.
> 2. For portfolio work, strive to use the lower levels of detail unless forced to incorporate the complexity.

Detail – Challenges with Simulating Monetary Time-Series in a Portfolio Context

Simulation is simple when values can be aggregated across a project's life. Distributing those numbers across time creates additional challenges.

Revenue

Modeling the top-line number is straightforward. Pick your approach for modeling production levels and delays. Model the product price uncertainty across time however you see fit. Revenue in a given year is the product of those two sums.

Capital Cost

Timing issues confound capital cost simulation. Project delays usually increase total costs and distribute the money differently over time. Finishing a project sooner than scheduled compresses the expenditure and may increase or decrease the total cost.

Operating Expense

Opex is typically not a significant driver of discounted economic results before the fact—it comes later than capital costs and is immediately tax-deductible. It does make a difference in your time series. Opex is often expressed as two components: fixed annual and variable costs tied to production. The fixed and planned components can be modeled as separate multipliers. The planned part could have a delay model. The variable cost component is tied to production.

Depreciation

Tax depreciation is typically statutory and straightforward. Timing would be keyed to the production startup timing unless the regime allows consolidating capital costs with already profitable projects.

Earnings depreciation is either on a unit of production (UOP) basis tied to annual production and booked reserves or to time in service. If your model incorporates variable annual production or production across different time spans, it will affect earnings depreciation. Some tax regimes use or allow UOP depreciation.

The timing of post-startup capital costs will affect depreciation timing for both tax and earnings depreciation.

Net Cash Flow and Earnings

A well-constructed and robust model should keep all the earnings and cash flow calculations intact. Complex logic may be required for exceptionally high or low cases to accurately represent fiscal and accounting circumstances. This type of detailed model is useful for a single project perspective but would weigh down a typical portfolio model.

Key Takeaways

Simulating the money components correctly can be complex. Portfolio models should make as many simplifications as reasonable while still complying with the analysis frame. There is a huge tradeoff between precision, model calculation time, and complexity, so choose or develop carefully. Your frame and the necessity of defensibility and precision in the results will help determine where you can give up precision for speed. If all else fails, you can build your approximate portfolio model for speed, then add a post-processing step to incorporate the complexities. When in doubt, return to your frame—are you seeking insights or answers? Get the insights fast, then work the answers in detail.

Detour – Uncertainty Distribution Selection May Not Be Critical

As discussed in the Elements of Simulation Modeling section, the most important aspect of simulation is the recognition of the existence and general form of uncertainty. After that, deciding on the appropriate distribution is *typically* less critical in portfolio modeling.

It is common knowledge that if you have a fair six-sided die, there is an equal chance of each number coming up. That would be described as a discrete uniform distribution. Normal curves have their distinctive bell shape. Lognormal distributions have the same form but on a logarithmic value axis. Weibull, Pareto, beta, and triangular are some other distributions you may have heard of.

They each have strengths, weaknesses, and specific uses. Nerd religious wars have been fought over which distribution to use in what circumstance. People spend much time figuring out which distribution to use for uncertain variables. It can make a difference, especially for a single opportunity where you are trying to find the best course of action and for uncertainties with very long tails (low probability-high consequence). Especially at a portfolio level, recognizing all the many uncertainties in the broader perspective, the distribution is seldom a significant driver of decisions and insights.

Some will object to my casual treatment of the probability distributions. I agree with them to some extent.

If your organization has high analytical maturity, you may have a good sense of the correct distribution for your uncertainties. Maybe you have historical data or experience. And you may already know that the precision of your distributions and parameters is an important driver of good decisions for your frame. More power to you. Use the good stuff.

To be clear, I'm not saying that the distribution selection is completely unimportant. But if your firm is just starting to use probabilities, do not sweat those details. Distribution shape is much less important than figuring out why you care about and how to use uncertainty. As your organizational capability for analysis matures, you may find that better models of the probability distributions **do** make a difference. This is especially true for risk management, where the size of the tails can be enormous.

Get started, see what coarse distributions give you, run sensitivity-to-distribution-type, and see what you discover from that. Odds are you will find that for individual opportunities, those factors make a difference, while at the organizational level, they don't.

Key Takeaways

1. If you have data representing the risk in question, the type of distribution can be statistically derived using best-fit tools. Many simulation packages also allow sampling directly from a defined data set.
2. When the distribution is based on high- and low-value estimates, with only a handful of points, we resort to parameterization. Given two or more values and knowledge of the physical situation, we can test various probability distribution construct parameters and see which ones provide the best match. The Metalog distribution is like a Swiss army knife in that it can generate an infinite number of parameterized distributions.
3. Finally, your firm or professional function may have defined distributions for specific cases. For example, in oil exploration, many companies use the log-normal distribution along with point estimates of the 10th and 90th percentiles.

War Story – Risk Measures and MBAs

Twelve people attended a meeting about developing a portfolio tool for the department. A freshly minted MBA who had done some work previously on portfolios mentioned several times that the new tool should incorporate Value at Risk (VaR). It seemed to be an obsession for her.

Finally, a director asked her to tell them more about VaR, describe what it was and explain why she thought our leaders should focus on that metric as a critical measure. She stumbled a bit and confidently responded that the calculation of VaR should use the standard formulas and that, of course the executives care about VaR. It is an important concept in finance.

It turned out that she had read an article about how banks and financial firms were using this technique to assess reserve needs. It is not a generally helpful metric for global supermajor oil companies.

One crucial reason investors put money into oil companies is to provide diversification with other holdings. The classic example is that airline stocks suffer when the price of oil increases and vice versa. So, a significant risk to an oil company's profits may benefit its owners. Reducing oil price correlation would make the company less attractive to some investors.

Oil companies can choose how much they want to tie their fortunes to the price of oil. It can be done by selecting a different mix of assets or by using financial instruments to manage it.

There is a germ of insight in all that. Most risk measures contain two essential dimensions: the probability of a loss and the size of the loss. Loss can be relative to zero profitability, or it can be relative to a different limit, such as a production target or cash reserve limit. The probability of loss in a model can be seen on cumulative probability curves or extracted from the underlying data. It is simply the percentage of simulation trials that result in a value less than the threshold.

The simplest expression of the magnitude of loss is probably the mean loss, which is the average of all trials that are less than the threshold.

Lessons Learned

1. A trending metric being important in one industry does not make it important for yours.
2. Finding and defining practical risk measures to use is not trivial.
3. Many noteworthy trends and metrics written up in the financial press are based on simple concepts for typically skilled quantitative analysts. The financial press usually does a poor job of describing and covering them.
4. The three magic letters (MBA) are a signal of having learned something. They are not a badge of infallibility. (I have an MBA).
5. True confession – when I started my portfolio journey (shortly after completing my MBA), I had a conversation with a planning manager in which I expressed my certainty that we should use efficient frontiers. When he asked me what measure we should use for risk, I replied with standard deviation or variance. It seemed so right at the time.

War Story – Simulating Plan Biases

The business unit (BU) strategic plan was finalized, and it seemed unrealistically optimistic.

The BU had a reputation for optimistic plans, even on a project-by-project basis. Lookbacks showed that early-phase projects were typically two years behind the forecast, and even the projects already in construction were often six months late or more.

"But not this time," they assured the analysts. "The project teams were aware of the delays and built them into their plans." The analysts thought that maybe they had not considered Hofstadter's Law which states, "*It always takes longer than you expect, even when you take into account Hofstadter's Law.*"

The BU took its very aggressive plan to the corporation for approval. Although it was based on their long-term outlook, the business unit managers had 'sandbagged,' reducing the total production level to be safe.

An analysis team built a simulation to incorporate the known optimistic biases and other uncertainties. The team was not a part of the forecasting team, so they were doing this work to help detect and understand future performance gaps.

The analysis team hurriedly finished the simulation model and produced results. They talked with the BU forecasting staff and broke the bad news. Even with very generous assumptions about delays, their plan—even after their production reduction—had a very low probability of achieving its goals.

The forecasters were quite upset and said the analysis team models were wrong. (*Narrator: They weren't.*)

A few years later, despite seemingly adequate funding, they were on course to miss their targets by a lot. The simulation model was much better than their biased plan, with actual production coming in somewhere around the 40th percentile of the simulation model, which was more than 10% less than the original prediction.

Lessons Learned

1. The expression "accurate deterministic forecast" is an oxymoron. Only by incorporating a probabilistic model with ranges can we hope to have a reasonable context in which to make strategic decisions.
2. Once something important has been released, the people who released it do NOT want to hear how wrong they are.
3. Hofstadter's law is right. You ignore it at your peril.
4. Simulation, even using seat-of-the-pants distributions, doesn't give a single, accurate forecast; it provides a range (there is not a correct answer except after the fact), but it beats the heck out of not simulating.
5. Biases are real and common. If every project has only a slight bias, when you add them together deterministically, there is a good chance of being hugely wrong in the aggregate. Put another way, the sum of slightly optimistic forecasts does not yield a slightly optimistic aggregation; it generates an insanely optimistic one.

War Story – Expected Value

The team had flown in for a presentation to headquarters. They were looking at an opportunity to participate in an exploration license that contained a new play in a prolific basin.

The company had started using risk analysis and incorporating statistical concepts into its exploration business two years earlier. The analysts confidently stood before the upstream vice president and his assistant and talked about the economics and other parameters of the main prospect.

They said, "The risked NPV of the first prospect is 50 million dollars, the risked IRR is 18%, and the expected reserves are 15 million barrels. Other prospects around the block provide follow-on potential if this one works. This is all for a cost of entry of 5 million dollars. The operator is experienced and knows the basin as well as anyone. This is an extraordinary deal."

The executive's assistant piped up, "Wait. We expect only 15 million barrels? This isn't strategic at all; it is too small."

The analysts tried to explain that expected value was the multiplication of probability of success and success case reserves (closer to 100 million barrels), but it was too late. Apparently, he had not received the fancy risk training yet. His eyes glazed over with the math, and the verdict was in. Rejected.

Lessons Learned

1. **Never** assume that your audience understands even simple, statistical concepts. The assistant was an engineer.
2. The first time you discuss "expected value" with an audience, say, "statistically expected value," so they know you are not speaking English.
3. These particular executives may have been just looking for an excuse to say no.

Scaling Uncertainty – Probability Management, SIPs, and SLURPs

Dr. Sam Savage has developed and led the development of tools and techniques for creating, storing, and combining uncertain inputs and outputs.

His non-profit organization is Probability Management at http://www.probabilitymanagement.org. From their website:

"Probability Management is a nonprofit dedicated to transforming uncertainty through education, best practices, and our open PM SIPmath Standard.

"The discipline of probability management uses an open standard for making uncertainty actionable through arrays of auditable data known as SIPs. It is compatible with virtually any software platform, including native Excel. It has created an Excel toolbar to make Monte Carlo simulation readily available at no cost. There is also a version with advanced tools available for a fee."

Sam has espoused three main concepts in his work.

The first is the standard for Stochastic Information Packets (SIPs) and Stochastic Library Units with Relationships Preserved (SLURPs). These standards allow sharing, combining, and distributing inputs and outputs for simulation models. Combining SIPs and SLURPs is a simple mathematical exercise.

The second is using the standard Excel table function to provide speedy Monte Carlo simulation without expensive software. A part of this is creating highly usable and intuitive models that encourage engagement.

The third is focusing on education and getting the word out to the world about uncertainty and how to use it in assessing business and life.

Recent (2023) developments at Probability Management are exciting. Douglas Hubbard (The author of How to Measure Anything) has created a random number generator that creates rigorous and repeatable random values; Tom Keelin has developed the Metalog distribution, which allows for flexible parameterization of probability distribution functions.

The combination of the Hubbard Random Numbers and the Metalog distribution means that a full distribution can be "compressed" into a handful of numerical parameters rather than storing a vector containing thousands or millions of discrete trials. As Sam describes, a complete distribution can be expressed with a tweet rather than a book. The standard for this abbreviated format is called SIPmath 3.0.

This will be an exciting area to watch in the coming years.

Scenarios

In preparing for battle, I have always found that plans are useless, but planning is indispensable.

Dwight D. Eisenhower

Pierre Wack, the father of Scenario Planning, has stated that scenarios are not about getting the right forecast but rather changing the mental map of decision-makers. It's more important to improve the mental model than create a forecast.

The word "scenario" is used in a few different ways, so I want to clarify how I think about and use it in the context of portfolio analysis.

The first way is a very narrow description of one or more input assumptions. You might have a "low-price scenario" to test project robustness or a "high-cost scenario" for the same. Or you can have a "worst-case scenario" in which the project is late, over-budget, and underperforms, then is not saved by the oil price.

These types of scenarios are common in the planning, budgeting, and decision worlds. I usually call them sensitivities rather than scenarios.

Scenarios, in my mind, go further into the drivers of the sensitivities. For example, a low-price scenario may arise because of lower demand due to increasing legislation to remove greenhouse gases or increased supply, as we saw in 2010 with fracking in West Texas. Each of those scenarios carries other impacts that become a part of the scenario. Our greenhouse gas legislation scenario might drive costs down, while the West Texas scenario leads to less volatility in oil prices. I think of these as big-S Scenarios vs. the little-s sensitivity scenarios.

In this framework, a scenario is a broader view of the world reflecting big trends and their impact on economies, trade, politics, and energy.

Sometimes people want to apply weights to scenarios to calculate a mean or expected value case. This mean would have little validity unless the scenarios were constructed with unusual statistical and macroeconomic rigor.

In my experience, these sensitivities and scenarios can help drive decisions by helping project, investment, and leadership teams focus on "what-ifs"—what they would do differently if the future unfolds in different forms—rather than pretending to have exact percentages. Leadership teams can make "no-regrets" decisions that do not change across the scenarios, while focusing on signposts and decisions that may change as the world unfolds.

An astute observer might have realized that the growth in Permian oil with its associated gas production was a death knell in the short run for US natural gas production in other parts of the country. But it would not have helped if someone had put a 10% probability of that happening and created EV economics. The power lies in thinking through the implications, not creating a mythical expected scenario with different weightings.

There is a hybrid between the wide net of scenarios and the detail of sensitivity analysis. This approach creates a two-by-two matrix to combine bookends of two different aspects of the business. As in typical scenario generation, the two dimensions may be uncontrollable, e.g., hydrocarbon supply vs. greenhouse gas legislation. Also, instead of two uncontrollable dimensions, you could create a hybrid with one dimension based on alternate strategic directions your company may consider. There's a war story of this approach in a later section of the book.

Key Takeaways

1. Some organizations embrace scenarios—others, not so much.
2. The principal value in scenarios is helping you think about which assets will thrive in different circumstances. These then pre-load your way of thinking when circumstances change.
3. The hybrid approach provides a practical way to test asset robustness and decisions against external environments.
4. There is extensive literature on how to use scenarios for strategy analysis.

High-Impact, Low-Probability Events

Most of this book deals with common business problems. For completeness, I want to address a class of events you should know about—high-impact, low-probability (HILP) events. These rare events may not be practical or possible to address analytically, but if they happen, they may be catastrophic or incredibly good.

HILP event analysis is used extensively in the risk management field. Think about a hurricane that affects the entire US Gulf Coast oil production or an earthquake in California. The probability of one of these events at a catastrophic level in a given year is relatively small. Failure to adequately prepare can be extremely costly.

On the bad side, consider an oil well drilled in the deepwater Gulf of Mexico. Very few wells have significant operational problems, there are backup systems and controls, processes are generally well-established, and empirically, there are few significant incidents.

If you were modeling it with Monte Carlo, you might insert a 1-in-10,000 chance of a catastrophe with a mean cost of 100 million dollars and a lognormal damage distribution with a long tail. Modeling this event with 10,000 trials means that, on average, it will occur once. The cost may be high, but divided by 10,000, it doesn't hit your awareness unless the one failure case in that 10,000 was so massive that it overcame the 0.0001 multiplier and rose out of the noise of other uncertainties. Many other risks are significant and much more likely to worry about. So perhaps you should run 100,000 simulations. Even then, the (average) 10 failure cases may not adequately sample the outcome range.

But this describes the Macondo disaster. It weakened and almost drove British Petroleum out of business. Few companies could have survived it.

If you are using portfolio methods as described in this book to do work on risks with fat tails, you should do more work to understand the nature of those tails. Corporate existential-level events are possible in this domain and need special care and attention. The risk of not achieving a production target is entirely different from the risk of existential disasters.

The flip side is in exploration or pharmaceutical research, where there is significant potential but a low probability of success. In both cases, decisions are often driven by the near-term cost of avoiding the disaster or gaining exposure to an unknown upside. Avoidance of cost is a strong motivator; gaining upside is less so. This is human nature and a difficult problem to solve and communicate.

Ensuring you have the correct probabilities is impossible. With a large range of outcomes, it becomes intractable analytically and practically speaking, because of the multiplication of very large and very small numbers, may not even show up.

So run a Monte Carlo, but if there is even a slight possibility of a survival-threatening catastrophe, you should also take a different approach. Talk about the probability, admit that precision is poor, focus on the range of outcomes, and take measures to avoid the long tail of the loss. The short-term costs may hurt, but remember that you probably have an exaggerated bias against those near-term, certain costs.

As I write this, there is a trend of companies not being willing to spend money on risk-prevention. Instead, they do all they can to squeeze every penny out of operations. These systems become super-critical and fragile; one small problem can create a domino effect and lead to disaster.

If you want exposure to a low probability beneficial event, ensure you have exit options, but participate. In your plans and forecasts, it may be convenient to treat it as a cost with no benefit; but stay in the game.

The analytical branch will not be precise and might not even be visible, given other uncertainties. The communication branch is the best place to show the risk or upside.

A field called "importance sampling" addresses how to handle these problems. Dr. Sam Savage has done significant work on the creation, storage, and aggregation of these events (see his patent application (WO2017185066 – SPARSE AND NON CONGRUENT STOCHASTIC ROLL-UP). Lumina Analytica handles importance weighting as part of its simulation library. Full details are outside of the scope of this book.

Portfolio Management in Exploration, Business Development, and Pharmaceuticals

Risky front-end parts of a business share a risk and reward structure regardless of the industry. Typically, there is a very low probability of success at the start, followed by various feasibility studies and research, a declaration of success, a decision to develop, and the actual outcome.

Failure can occur at any step. The prior probability of success for an exploration prospect or a single pharmaceutical compound is remarkably low. There are several keys to success in these businesses—have a large set of possibilities, do what can be done to increase the probability of success, minimize the cost of testing each one, and smart development and commercialization.

The pharmaceutical world addresses this challenge by screening thousands of compounds across a broad spectrum of possibilities, then reducing the possibilities as compounds do not pass the screen. Ultimately, only a few combinations go through rigorous and expensive human testing and approval processes.

The exploration model is similar to pharmaceuticals. Prospective basins first have inexpensive remote sensing surveys, followed by regional seismic grids, then more detailed grids to fine-tune details. Even with millions of dollars of research, the test well, which can cost tens or hundreds of millions of dollars, may still have between a 60% and 90% chance of **failure**.

Finally, in Business Development (BD), the cost of "testing" an opportunity is relatively low. It might be a phone call from one BD executive to another or perhaps sending a small team to a data room to understand the technical and economic details of the opportunity. Acquiring assets that have resolved key risk elements (been de-risked) is expensive. The owner knows what they have and is not interested in providing charity.

When drugs or exploration prospects are successful, they must be very successful. Companies need to be able to pay for all the failures from the few successes, plus have room for additional profit. On the other hand, BD is not expensive to test but is costly to purchase. Much of the value in the opportunities is from de-risking.

Simulation approaches are helpful in these parts of the business. They give you a sense of what your current efforts may yield, and you can test other levels of effort. Simulation can be extended into more rigorous decision-making using other portfolio tools described in the interactions section.

Value of Information Under Uncertainty in a Portfolio Context

So far, we have discussed probability in the concept of a "known" probability. Sometimes it is possible to acquire more information that can alter probabilities or our perception of probabilities.

Consider this situation. You have an exploration well that will cost $10 million to drill and, if successful, will be worth $100 million.

▸ Simple Exploration Decision Tree

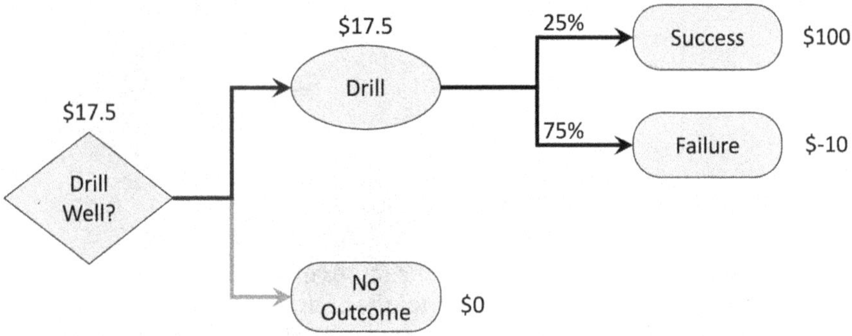

Deciding to drill the well in question is a good bet. Its value overcomes the cost and probability of failure. This would probably be a drillable prospect. Acquiring additional information may increase the value of the prospect, but only if there is an option not to drill the well.

The decision is whether to drill the well. The "No Outcome" branch shows what happens if you decide not to drill. It is worth $0—you're not investing; you're neither gaining nor losing. The drill branch has two possible outcomes a success branch worth $100 and a failure branch that costs $10. Your earth scientists have determined that based on the best information available, the probability of success is 25% (therefore, the likelihood of failure is 75%).

The probabilistically combined value of the two branches is 25% * $100 + 75% * -$10 = $17.50. This is statistically a good bet—it has an expected value greater than zero. If you could make this investment 100 times, you would, on average, come out $17.50 ahead for each one.

But suppose a magic technology exists that will tell you before you drill whether the well will be a success or a failure. We think about applying our magic technology. If the technology says "yes," the well will succeed 100% of the time. If the technology says no, it will be a dry hole.

This changes our decision tree. The decision tree below shows that running the magic test results in a different decision flow. We drill the well only if the magic test is positive. We do not drill if it's negative.

▸ Decision Tree with Additional Data

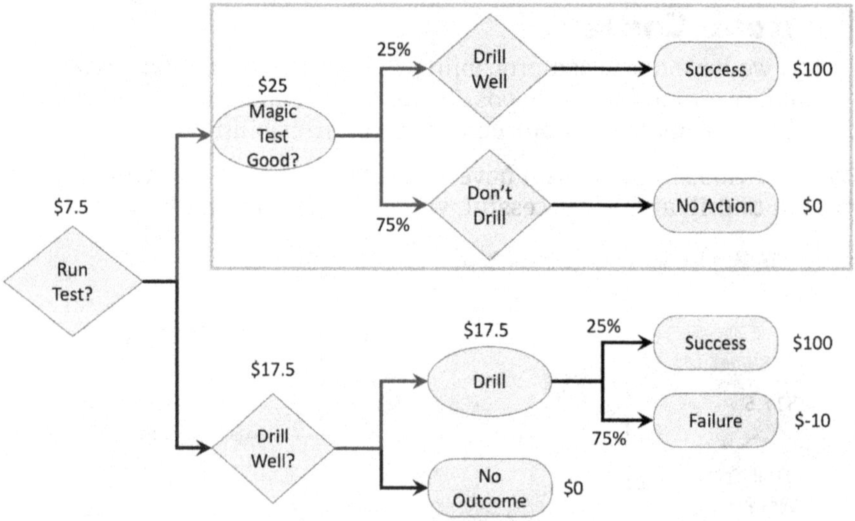

The question becomes whether to run the test or drill the well. The nodes inside the box show how the test changes the decision and its value. If the test is positive, we drill the well; otherwise, we don't. We rely on the guidance of the magic test because it is definitive. Performing the magic test adds $7.50 to the prospect. Please note, it adds value only if the well is optional. If it is a must drill, this magic test adds no value, because "Don't Drill" is not an option. If the magic test costs more than $7.5, you should not purchase it.

Because we have the **option** to drill or not, the value of the perfect magic test is $7.50—the difference between drilling the well blind ($17.5) and drilling the well once you know it will be successful.

In this example, the magic test (information) is free. In real life, that is seldom the case. Seismic data costs money; testing a drug costs money. How much is it worth then to run the magic test? In the example case, it would be worth up to $7.50 to acquire a test with perfect information. In principle, you should be willing to pay up to $7.49 for the magic test.

Many people are confused about something here. They say, "Wait, once we get the test back and it's positive, the well is now worth $100." That is true. However, your original 25% assessment (your prior probability) must carry through in a decision tree like this. If you were to run the magic test on four wells, only one would have a positive outcome. So out of your inventory of 100 wells, 25 would be positive, leading to a total value of $2500—an average of $25 for each well in the inventory.

This is a simple example of the Value of (Perfect) Information. Treatment of imperfect information is similar but incorporates probabilities of false negatives and positives. The full discussion is beyond the scope of this book and ties into the Bayesian concepts discussed previously.

Why is this in a portfolio book? From a portfolio decision standpoint, we are always looking for alternative courses of action. Remember, if we do not have alternatives, we are operating the portfolio—not managing it. A fundamental assumption built into the above example is that you have the option not to drill the well. This is sometimes not the case. Always remember that information has no value if decisions cannot be changed.

With portfolio tools, you can incorporate data acquisition vs. drilling a well as an option. For a given exploration budget, you need to show results, but buying information can lead to better future results by reducing your exploration portfolio's overall riskiness. In the example case, you may find that you would be willing to pay up to $4 for the perfect information, given other opportunities in the portfolio. Opportunity cost is still, and always will be, an important concept.

If you find yourself in a situation where there is no ability to change either the decision to drill or the location of the well, additional information provides no value. The opportunity will be successful, or it won't. Changing your subjective probability has no effect on nature. No test, regardless of the outcome, will change the reality.

Probability Visualization

One of the challenges in bringing in probabilities is getting used to a new set of graphs and concepts. This section will cover both the uncommon and common displays.

Probability Distribution Functions (PDF) or Bell Curves

We have all seen bell curves. The one below is a log-normal bell curve. Note the long tail to the right.

When plotting PDFs, there must be bins on the x-axis. With a Monte Carlo simulation (assuming continuous variables, it is unlikely that a resulting number would repeat at the precision of your simulation tool if we tried to plot every single sample.

Uncertainty programs may give options on how to draw the bell curve. Some common ones are the width of the bins (bars), how much gap to show between the bars, and whether to include **all** the data, including outliers.

▶ Lognormal Probability Distribution Function

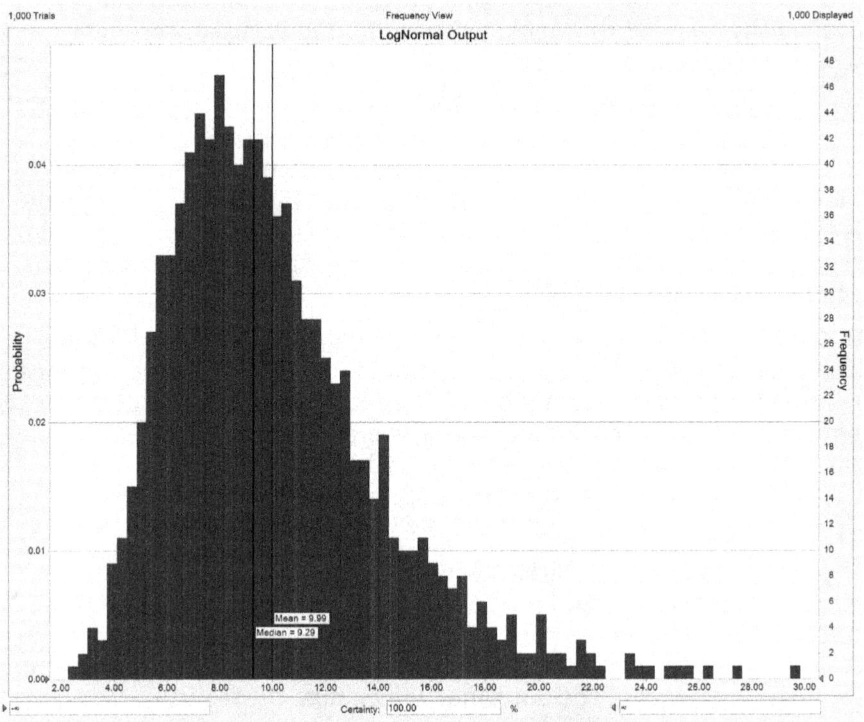

A lognormal PDF. The X axis is the values of a variable segregated into bins; the y-axes show the percentage of the values on the left and samples on the right that fall into the x-axis bins. This display truncates some of the very high and low outlier values.

▸ Lognormal PDF with Narrow Bins

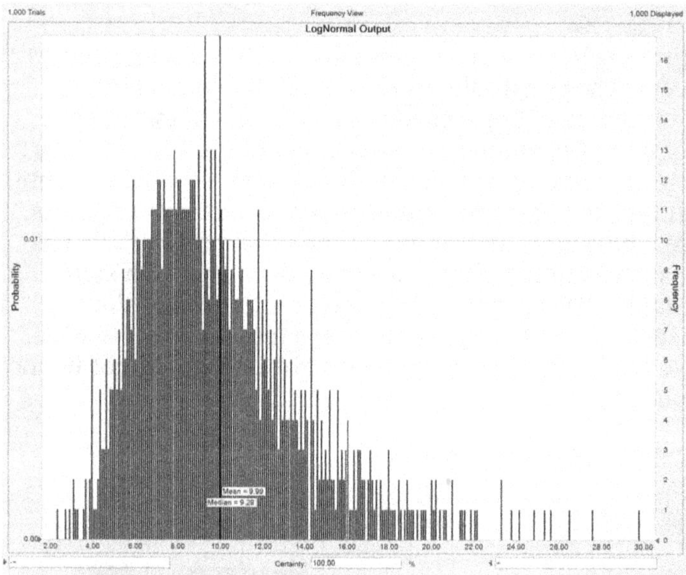

This is the same data as the previous plot. The narrower bins lead to a more jagged appearance. There is also spacing inserted between the bins.

▸ More Simulations Means More Outliers

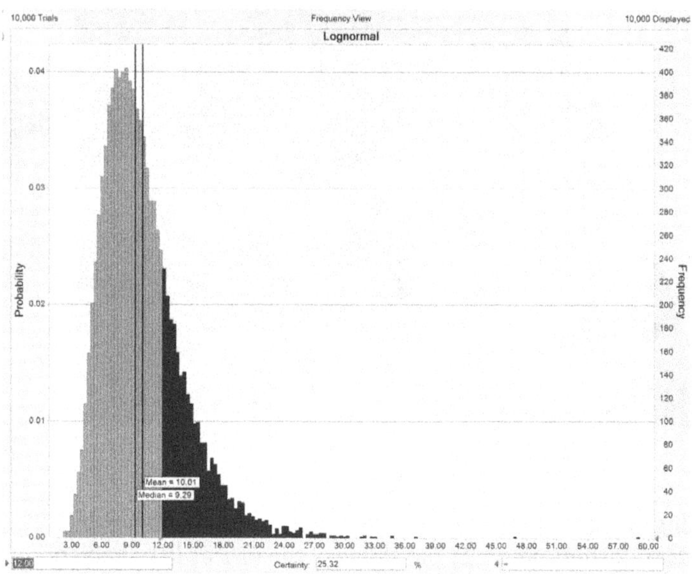

This run has ten times more data (10,000 vs 1,000 simulations). Note the longer tail on the data. This graph has values segregated based on their value. Everything below twelve is the lighter shade. Above 12 is the darker shade. 25% of the samples are above twelve.

Cumulative Probability Distribution Functions (CDF) or S-Curve

CDFs are sometimes called S-curves (not to be confused with product maturity s-curves). The y-axis shows the cumulative probability of achieving the x-axis value. These curves are often lines, rather than column charts of bins. Depending on the manner of generation, they can either appear continuous or have a series of step functions. Monte Carlo simulation typically generates hundreds or thousands of points, so the curves are continuous. (Of course, if the underlying model has a step function, such as probability of success, there will be a step function in the data.) CDFs generated by decision trees may show relatively large steps. In fact, because the steps tend to be quite wide, they **should** have these steps. Drawing a straight line would not honor the model behind it.

Cumulative Probability Distribution

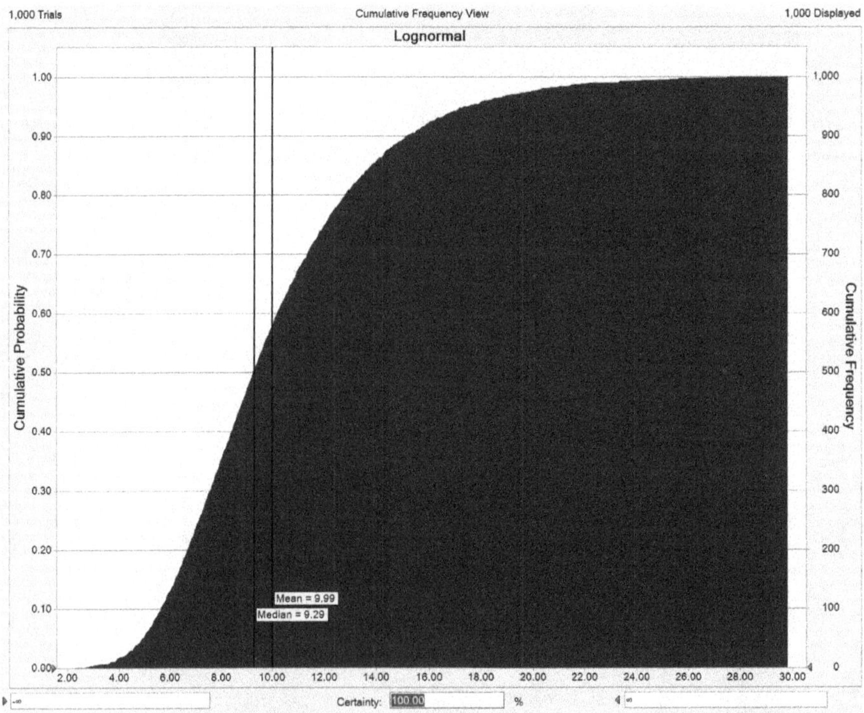

This CDF contains the same information as the first two PDFs above. It is difficult to extract information about the shape of the PDF or likelihood of a given bin, but it is much easier to see the percentage where a given value lies. It is clear from this graph that the median is at the 50th percentile, while the mean is at about the 57th percentile.

▸ Cumulative Distribution with Relevant Shading

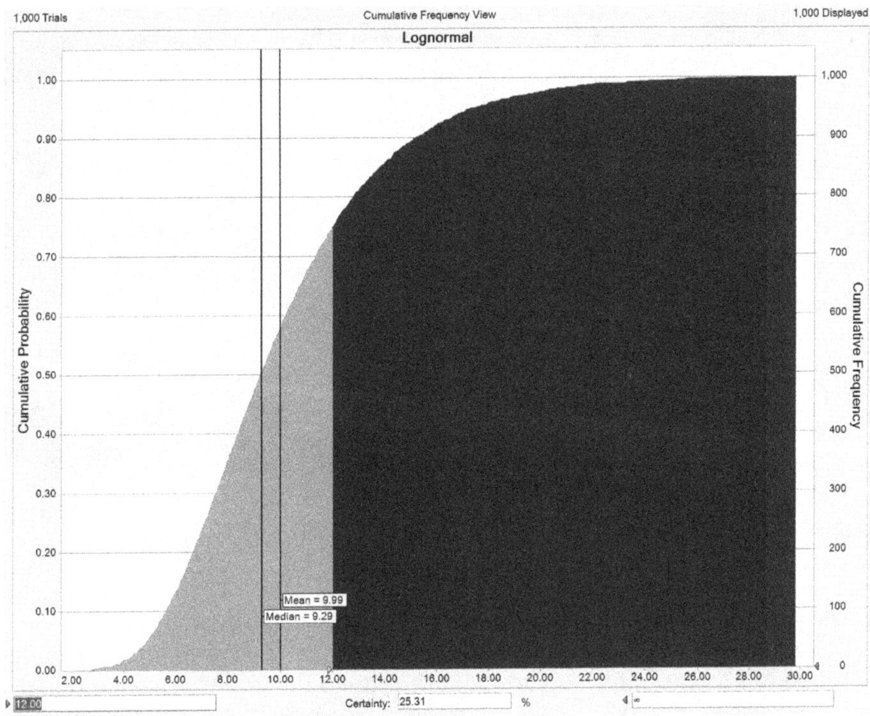

> *As with the PDF, Crystal Ball allows the user to specify a value to highlight values above and below. By observation, we can see that the value of 12 is at the 75th percentile of the data.*

Conclusions – Probability Distribution Graphs

Bell Curve Views will tend to emphasize the value axis (x) and highlight the statistical mode of the data. Cumulative probability distributions will tend to emphasize the probability (y) axis and give you an easy way to estimate the likelihood of achieving different levels of performance.

Time Series

You could show a series of CDFs or PDFs to show the uncertainty of a metric in a number of years. In fact, if there is a specific important target year, that might be the best way to do it.

If the progression of a time series and its peaks and troughs are important, the series of individual year plots may be difficult to follow and mentally track. One way to show this then is to show the high and low ranges of your metric across time.

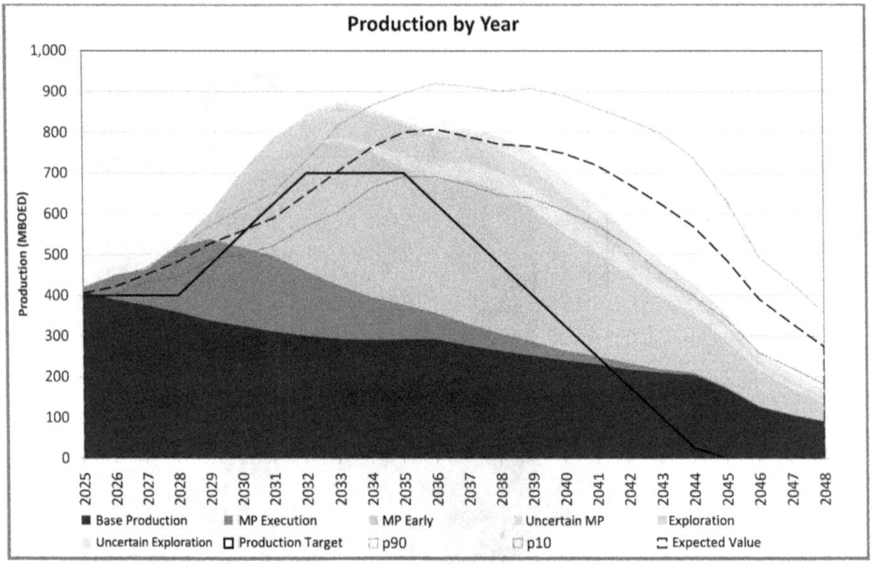

The solid black line shows the production target across the years. The decrease in later years reflects the limits of data, reserves, and foresight or "planner's droop." Most important in this case is the corporate commitment to achieve 700,000 barrels per day by 2032. The area plots show the long-term forecast from the strategic plan, which historically is biased towards optimism. The portfolio team used a Monte Carlo model to de-bias the forecast. The Upper dotted line shows the P90 production probability, while the lower dotted line shows the P10. The dashed black line is the average (expected) value. Note that the probability of achieving 700,000 barrels in 2032 is somewhere around the 75th percentile, meaning that the corporation has a 75% chance of missing the target, despite its plan, which shows around 850,000 barrels per day.

A common question when looking at time series probabilities is whether the 10th or 90th percentile line represents a possible outcome. The short answer is "no" for resource industries and "perhaps" for manufacturers.

With resource industries, production is governed by (uncertain) inventory of resource (oil or minerals). If the uncertainty is driven by the volumes of resources, those lines could possibly be achievable. More often, a large part of the uncertainty is driven by project delay. Project delays have little impact on resource, but in those cases, a 10th percentile outcome in early years could lead to a 90th percentile in later years. Mass balance must be honored.

For industries that are not resource-limited but in which the uncertainties are driven by market capture, the percentile lines are more likely to represent a discrete outcome.

Efficient Frontier Graphs Incorporating Uncertainty

The classic Markowitz Efficient frontier has uncertainty as one of the axes, so uncertainty is built into the graph. Other portfolio frontiers, such as NPV vs Capital Investment shown below, do not have the same luxury.

▸ **Basic Pareto Frontier**

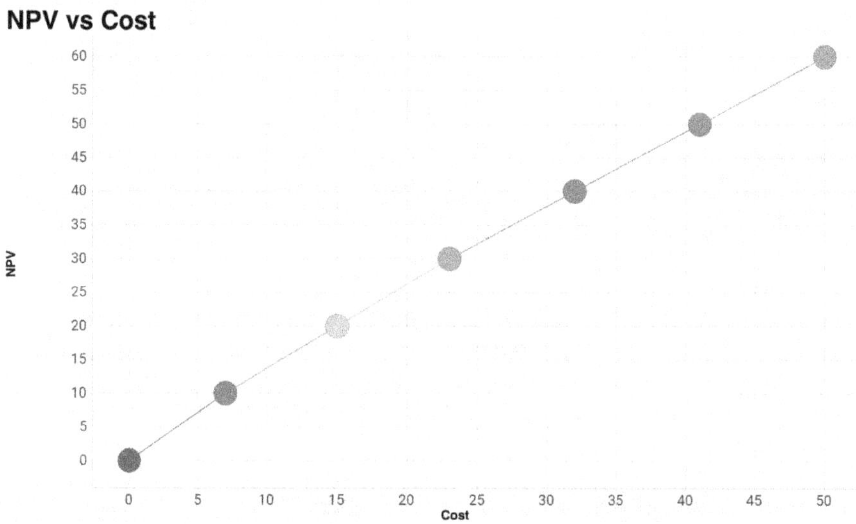

A simple Pareto frontier. Each dot represents a portfolio with its cost on the x-axis and value on the y-axis.

This box plot can show multiple statistics from a cloud of points. In this case, it is showing various statistics of value for each point.

▸ **Pareto Frontier with Y-Axis Uncertainty**

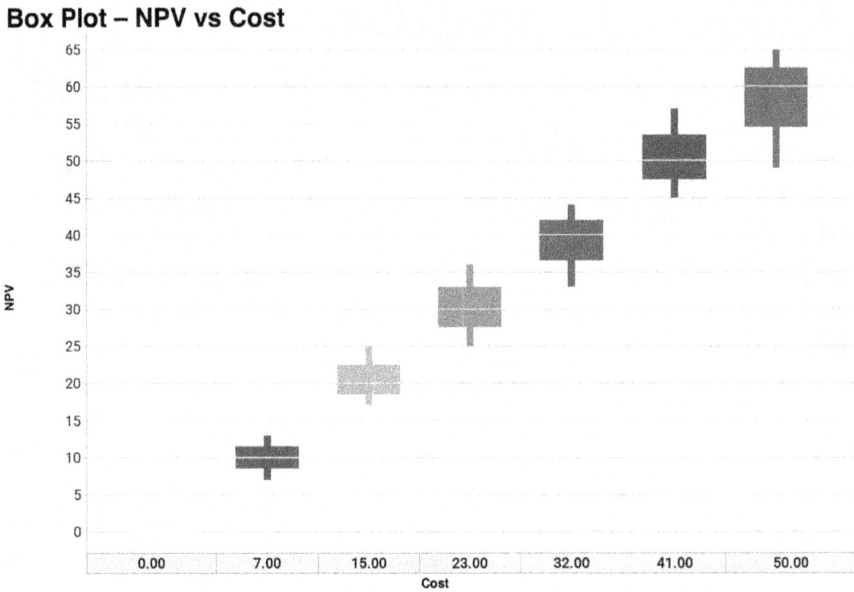

A box plot with the same data but showing the value uncertainty. In this specific plot, the x-axis is plotted as categories, rather than being spaced in proportion to the cost value. This perspective, but with a proportional x-axis, would work for a Markowitz efficient frontier because the uncertainty is already encoded in the x-axis.

The graph below shows the limits on the axes of each of the two variables. Notionally, the markers surrounding the points are the 10 and 90 percentiles. You could use any relevant percentiles, plot contours around the points, or even put a color-coded cloud of smaller dots, which might better represent the density of outcomes.

▸ **Pareto Frontier with X and Y Uncertainty**

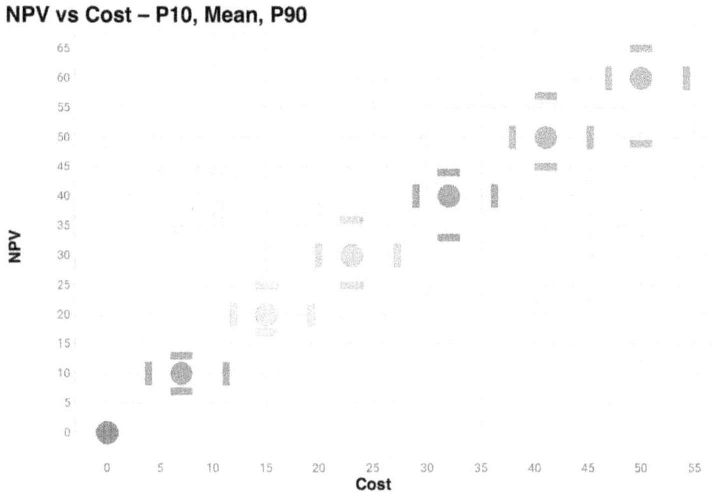

An efficient frontier showing the 80% confidence of falling within the bounds for each of the portfolios on both axes. In essence, each portfolio is a two-dimensional probability distribution function with the mean value at the dot and a region of probabilities surrounding it.

When you connect all the outlying points, you get an efficient zone rather than a sharp frontier.

▸ **Pareto Frontier Zone**

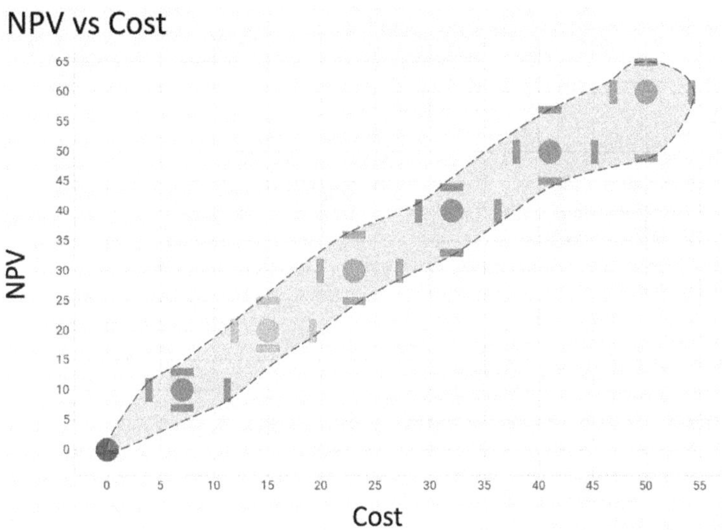

The Pareto frontier, in this case, is an efficient zone rather than a sharp frontier line.

Key Takeaways

1. Representing uncertainty is critical when it is a metric of importance to the decision-makers. On top of that, it sends a clear message that the single deterministic values are not a true forecast.
2. Many leaders are not trained in probability and statistics, so might have difficulty interpreting and using uncertainty in their decision-making. Make sure you have reviewed with them in advance to give them soak time to incorporate uncertainty into their thinking.

CHAPTER 8

Interactions

Up to Simulation, we focused on mechanical techniques that should always be done if you have an inventory of opportunities. There is no downside in those because the methods are simple and cheap to develop. There is a benefit to each of the previous steps because the information may be insightful to leadership.

The comparative techniques run out of steam for several reasons:

1. Incorporating the time dimension stretches the limits of comparison techniques. Having multiple, time-based goals and metrics makes comparison techniques ineffective.
2. Multiple alternatives for a single project make rank and cut and other comparison approaches difficult in a portfolio analysis context.
3. Logical dependencies and constraints, such as Phase 2 must follow Phase 1, adds complication.
4. For a large inventory, finding good candidate sets (combinations of complementary decisions) can be daunting. Automating and using algorithms to find better combinations becomes much more effective than manual means.

The presence of **any** of the above factors means you should consider interaction techniques. More than one factor makes it a must.

Interaction techniques are the second big jump in the methods. Instead of simply comparing or layering new opportunities on top of the existing ones, we broaden the perspective to examine coordinated decisions across assets.

Interaction techniques bring new dimensions, tools, skills, and a different mindset. This is a step-change from the inventory methods. It is also the highest potential value add. While inventory methods are good because there is no downside, interaction methods are powerful **because** of the upside. And if you already have an inventory, the downside is not too steep.

What Do We Mean by Interactions?

In a company, interactions occur whenever one asset influences others. Sometimes these interactions are apparent—you can't do phase two of a project unless you do phase one first. In many cases, they are less obvious, especially when a company is large enough to have multiple semi-independent business units.

Capital budgets are one example of interaction. For a given budget, every dollar you spend in one SBU results in one less dollar you can spend in another SBU. Developing a long-term investment may have cash flow effects that prevent shorter-term projects from going forward due to capital or capability constraints. Increasing your firm's return on capital employed may reduce your revenue growth trajectory. Opportunity cost is real in a constrained environment and must be considered.

An example of an opportunity cost is the following: You make an hourly wage of $100 per hour. You need to paint your house, and you get a bid for $500 from a professional painter. You estimate that if you were to do the work yourself, it would take 8 hours, so you would lose $800 in revenue. That is your opportunity cost. You can spend $800 in lost revenue or $500 in cash. You're better off hiring the painter. Proper economic analysis always contains an implicit or explicit difference between the proposed and base cases.

In the chapter on standalone analysis, we discussed the idea of using a higher discount rate to factor in the other opportunities "that are thought to exist." In the interactions space, we explicitly see what those opportunities are (they are our working inventory) and factor them into the frame of the decision.

Risk also interacts. Correlations to the external environment can increase the uncertainty of a corporation's profit streams. So, if you are an oil producer or a diabetes drug producer, without diversification, changes in external environments create exaggerated uncertainty and variability in results.

Finally, there is a diversification effect with risky investments like oil exploration and pharmaceutical research. Although a single investment can have a high chance of failure (for example, 75% with an exploration well or a new drug compound), having additional independent opportunities reduces the probability of failure of your investment program.

▸ Portfolio Selector Focus on Comparison Methods

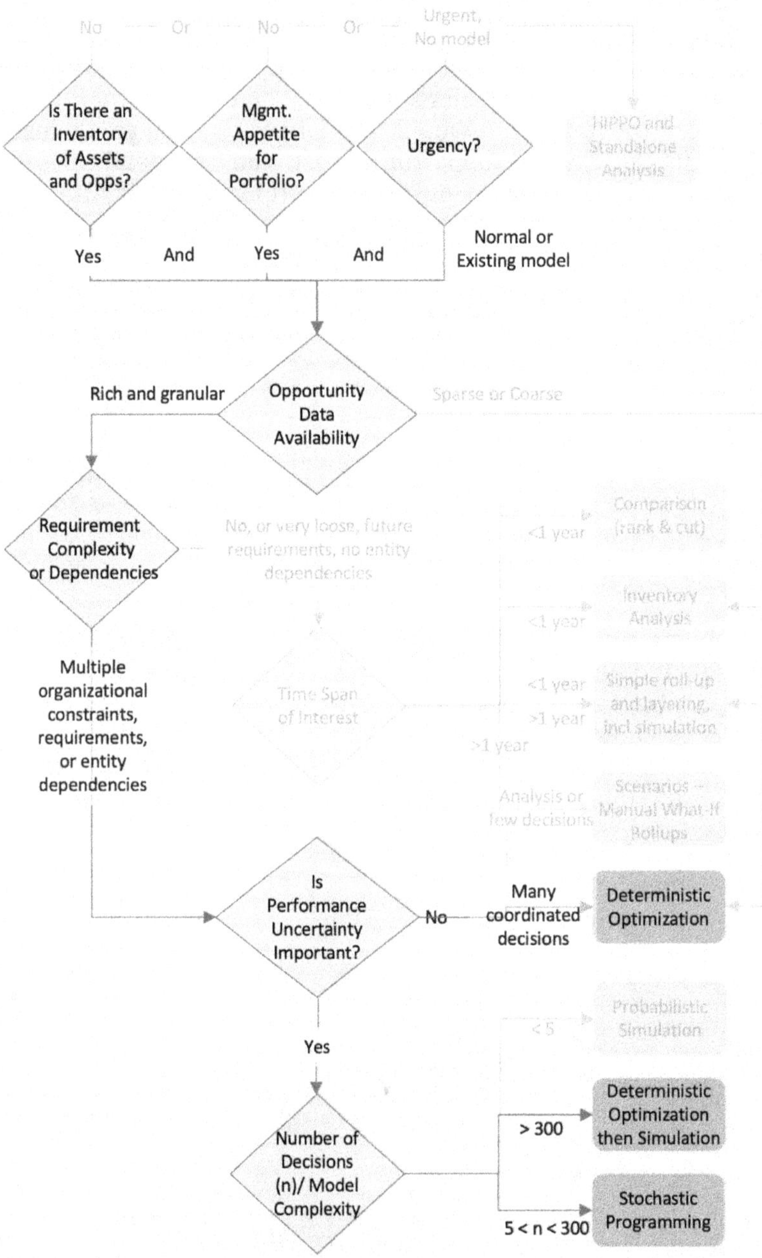

Complex requirements and many coordinated open the door to interactions. Interactions, along with simulation, are the second big jump in methods. Interactions comprise various flavors of optimization, including optimization with simulation. Achieving full value from interactions requires an organizational culture and structure that supports coordination.

Multiple Decisions are in the Frame

The coordination and management of interactions require cooperation. With interactions, we begin to test more than a single decision as we tend to do with simple rollups. It's not about how we look if we just layer on an asset; we also need to understand what other asset actions we should, therefore, consider.

Optimization is a valuable tool for combining those decisions into a coordinated whole. I'll say it here and repeat it later. Optimization does not give you the answer. It gives you a reasonable, internally consistent solution for comparison with other solutions. These solutions yield insights into a firm's performance envelope, its capabilities, and the true contextualized value of its investments.

Detail – Some Reasons Interaction Approaches are Necessary

Periodically (daily, weekly, monthly, yearly) or at arbitrary times, a firm must decide which investments to initiate, stop, modify, accelerate, delay, buy, or sell. This decision is nontrivial for a variety of reasons. The most important reasons are:

1. **Investments "compete" for scarce resources:** Cash, available external resources, staff, etc.
2. **Finding the right balance between important goals:** Investors expect growth and high returns. Growth requires investment, which decreases returns in the short term. What is the right balance?
3. **Some investments are complementary:** Building a new pipeline makes drilling near it more attractive, and a liquefied natural gas (LNG) plant may require dedicated ships to transport the product.
4. **Some investments are mutually exclusive or must be done in a specific sequence:** You can't develop an asset with both a minimum case and one with all the bells and whistles; phase two of a project must follow phase 1.
5. **Different cash flow patterns:** Cash flows of potential investments and investment programs have patterns across time that may or may not fit the overall cash needs of the firm. This is comparable to asset classes in the securities investment world.
6. **Uncertainty:** Many investments have considerable uncertainty associated with them. Will it succeed? How big will it be? When will returns arrive? How many risky investments should we make? Can we spread out or mitigate the risk?

7. **Correlation:** Some asset classes respond differently to changes in the external environment. Do we want our firm's results to move with the changes, or do we want the changes to be moderated? A pharmaceutical company can invest in a single clinical area, but if that clinical area becomes less promising, the firm could find itself in financial trouble. Or perhaps an oil company could consider investing in solar or wind power, which, while correlated with the overall economy, may be negatively correlated with oil.

Portfolio analysis methods that incorporate interactions can provide clarity to decision-makers on all the above and more.

(Modified from a private note from Mark Wiley of Lindo Systems).

Optimization General

Previously we discussed rollups combined with inventory and comparison methods (see Rollups with Guided Selection). That is a semi-quantitative approach to optimization that can result in much better results than simpler methods. One drawback to that approach is in scaling the technique. If there are many decisions, requirements, and constraints to consider, it becomes difficult to see and manipulate the variables and outcomes manually. For the larger and more complex cases, mathematical approaches to optimization are helpful. Please keep in mind that optimization, especially strategic and tactical optimization, does not provide the answer but rather the means to generate different coordinated sets of virtual decisions for consideration and insights.

A company of any size will have an almost infinite number of possible combinations of decisions. The key to portfolio analysis is to find and test combinations that may align with the needs of the enterprise. Discovering the best decision combinations manually or with rules of thumb is intractable; we can find feasible solutions in seconds with optimization software. Given the uncertainty and variability in the world, optimization might not find a specific needle in the vast haystack, but it can get us to the closest 1-inch cube that contains it.

An critical building block of creating a better outcome for your firm is understanding your asset and project options and the choices you can make about your business.

Optimization is used in many parts of business and personal life. It is a way of balancing competing needs, wants, and constraints to devise a good solution. There are many types of formal and informal optimizations that we all do.

What is Optimization, and How Do We Do It?

Optimization is a mathematical technique that helps you achieve more with less, all while ensuring that you meet relevant targets. A simple mnemonic is to make sure you follow the ABCs. **A** is for **A**djustable (decisions to be made); **B** is for **B**est (the objective function—the value you are trying to maximize or minimize); **C** is for **C**onstraints and Requirements (physical or logical limitations and goals you are trying to accomplish).

Let's think about a common optimization we all do—using GPS for driving directions. When you fire up that GPS program, you run an optimizer. **A**djustables are the turns you make and the streets you take. The **B**est (objective function) is to minimize the time (or distance) driven. **C**onstraints are both implicit and explicit. Explicit can be parameters like avoiding dirt roads, highways, toll booths, or left turns; implicit constraints are to stay on roads and drive legally. The Requirement is to get from where you are to your destination.

Given all those factors, the GPS program will find a route for you that gives you the best outcome for your objective function. Also, internet-connected GPS systems can tie into traffic data and reroute you as conditions change.

I think about optimization at three levels: operational, tactical, and strategic.

How do we distinguish these? It boils down to knowing the question you are trying to answer. Let's refer to the Strategic Execution Framework.

SEF High-Level Perspective

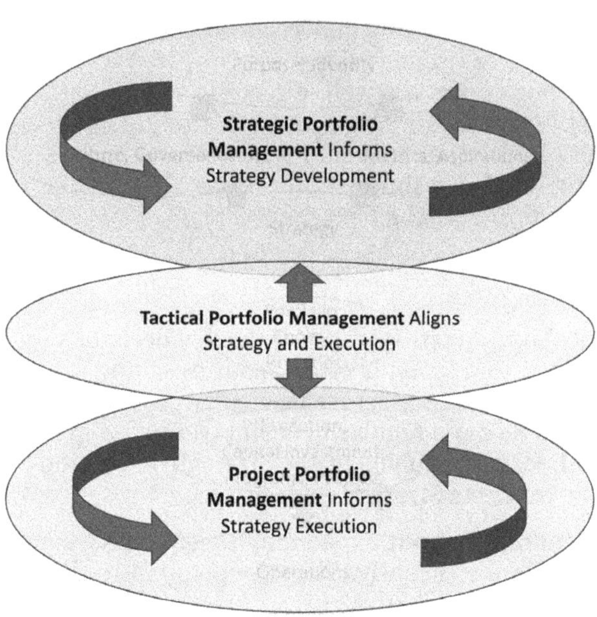

Optimization can apply to any of the three levels of portfolio management.

Strategic Optimization

Strategic optimization and strategy exploration occurs in the top parts of the diagram and inform ideation, the vision of what success looks like, and the structure and culture of the organization.

The word strategy is used in many ways. In the context of portfolio analysis, we'll think of it as a direction or position to help a firm achieve its goals. Goals are usually cast in terms of a metric and a timeframe, so, for example, you may wish to achieve 15% production growth in four years. It's an aggressive target, and something must change. You can test different strategic themes, such as increasing unconventional activity or reducing exploration budgets that do not provide production within four years, focusing on a country, or taking an opportunistic approach and using portfolio tools to select the best opportunities. The good news is you can test all of them quickly.

With our unconventional example, a strategic optimization could include how much unconventional production a firm wants in its portfolio compared to deepwater, heavy oil, LNG, and conventional.

Strategic optimization is about ensuring that you are focused on the right areas, projects, and business sectors to achieve strategic goals. Not next week, not next year, but in the future beyond what is already in action. It is about doing the right things to make sure you are positioned well into the future.

Strategic optimization can transform a company and add hundreds of millions or billions of dollars in value.

Tactical Optimization

Tactical optimization is used to help inform decisions over the next one to five years. It's about tweaking decisions that are already made and ensuring that your efforts are well-directed and efficient. Examples include budgeting for drilling rig contracts, finding an optimal exploration drill program, or redirecting next year's budget funds. It's about ensuring that your short-term actions align with what you hope to tell investors over the next few years.

Tactical optimization ties your business asset decisions directly to your strategies.

By the time you do tactical optimization, most of the key decisions are already made. Tactical optimization is often about tweaking specific expenditures and performance across particular years. Tactical optimization, which should be done regularly, is an essential step in alignment. It is the small portfolio bubble in the Strategic Execution Framework diagram that connects Strategy to decisions.

Tactical optimizations generally lay out a road map to get you to your short-term goal effectively and efficiently. They are prescriptive but seldom account for changing conditions. Yearly budget processes often include an element of tactical optimization.

In the context of a firm, a tactical optimization would include activities like near-term capital allocation, budgeting, and people assignments over the next year or two. We might consider how many rig lines to run for our unconventional basin and when.

Tactical optimization can add tens of millions to billions of dollars to the firm.

Project Portfolio Optimization

First, we'll talk about operational optimization or project portfolio management—the bottom bubble. If an optimization occurs entirely in the lower part of the diagram, it is likely operational optimization. It is happening to inform near-term decisions that are purely at the discretion of managers or individual contributors in business units. Your GPS is an excellent example of operational optimization. Supply chain optimization or SCO is in this bubble as well.

With operational optimization, real-time decisions are being made. Turn here. Increase the temperature of the coking unit. Put in more catalyst. They may automatic controls rather than computer programs. That project deadline is two months away; we need more people. There is important real-time value in this type of optimization.

Our driving example above is operational optimization because it gives you directions to be followed in real-time. Other examples are control systems for refineries or plants where temperature, throughput, and catalyst are all changed in real time to alter outcomes to yield more efficient use of inputs to the system.

In the oil industry, scheduling drilling rigs in an unconventional producing basin like the Permian Basin of west Texas, is a good example of operational optimization. Where will they go when they finish this well? It incorporates mobilization and demobilization costs, preference for drilling better sites first, utilization of producing infrastructure, leasehold requirements, and personnel.

Operational optimization is valuable. It can increase value by millions or tens of millions of dollars. There are books written about it, consultants dedicated to helping companies do it better, and entire areas of study around it. It is well-covered. This book will not deal extensively in this area. The focus is on tactical and strategic optimization.

The following table shows some differences between the three levels of optimization work.

Data Needs for Strategic, Tactical, and Operational Optimization

Attribute	Strategic	Tactical	Operational
Data	Real Data and Surrogates for business lines	Mostly real data, with some surrogates early in the process	Real
Time Horizon and Granularity	2–50 years Granularity: Years	1–10 years (focus on early years), Granularity: Years, Quarters	Weeks and Months, Granularity: Weeks, Days
Types of Questions and Decisions	Which asset classes should we focus on? What should be our long-term goals and aspirations? What is the ongoing level of capital?	Should we bid on this acquisition; how much to offer? Which project alternative for a major project? What is the best set of decisions to align assets and corporate goals? Which assets are critical for achieving targets? Project prioritization and sequencing.	Order of operations? Allocation of people? Capacities.
Metric Types	Resource replacement, Level of investment, percent of funding or revenue from different geographies. Corporate fundamental objectives. Production/ revenue growth, total cost basis, price sensitivity	NPV. Production/ revenue growth, capital allocation, return on capital employed, reserves/ production (R/P). Portfolio fit. Ability to grow the resource base, resource addition needs	Equipment and facility downtime. Utilization rates, safety, doability

General requirements for data, time granularity, the types of questions and metric types based on the level of the portfolio work.

Optimization Types and Algorithms

Perhaps you have heard of some of the many types of optimization. Linear programming, stochastic programming, non-linear programming, genetic algorithms, metaheuristics, particle swarm optimization, branch and bound, scatter search, simulated annealing, hierarchical risk portfolio parity, mean-variance optimization, and quadratic programming are some terms you may be familiar with. There are many flavors of optimization and algorithms, each with its own characteristics.

Which ones you use depends on your needs, expertise, and the nature of the problem you are solving. As with probability distributions, there can be a religious fervor over the selection.

The right optimizer for your needs will have several characteristics.

1. **Accuracy** – optimization engines or "solvers" will give you mathematical solutions to feasible problems. In some cases, it will be able to know that a problem is analytically the best possible solution. Even when that is not knowable, whichever tool you use will almost certainly provide a better answer than can be achieved manually. If a globally optimal solution cannot be found in a reasonable time, that's ok. The standard is whether it is better than you could have achieved manually with similar effort.
2. **Speed** – your model needs to solve quickly enough to apply to your needs. Linear problems can generally be solved quickly (< 5 seconds). Models with non-linearities, step functions, and conditional logic may take very long (hours or days) to solve. Your problem may need reframing at that point.
3. **Flexibility** – tools and platforms that can handle a wide range of problems are best until the problem or platform solution is tightly defined. Many optimizer tools must be configured for the size of the problem.

In general, linear programs are fast and accurate if a problem can be linearized or adequately estimated linearly. For more complex problems, you may need to hunt for the right one.

Detour – Why Use an Optimizer Tool? Isn't that just overkill?

Compared to rollups, optimization is a big step in capability and analysis. And it's not for everyone.

Once the time dimension comes into play, most companies use a planning process to roll data together and then twist arms to deliver more output with less input. Leaders may say that it has served them well. It's the same thing most competitors are doing; they have all done just fine without it. Besides, the most important assets will become apparent in the planning process, so nobody has to resort to that black box geekery.

I get that.

But you probably have no idea how much value you're losing by not using these advanced tools. Optimization unlocks the possibility of enormous value in the following circumstances:

1. Decisions about treatment (invest, hold, delay, accelerate, divest, size, etc.) of assets and investments are not a given.
2. There are many assets and alternative treatments. Once past about 20 assets and treatments, it becomes impossible to remember all the rules that govern and limit them.
3. With fourteen assets or elements that can be in or out, you can generate all possible portfolios (16,000) and use graphical tools to sort them out. By the time you get to 20 assets, there are over 1 million possible combinations. This gets worse if there are multiple treatments or alternatives for each one.
4. A simple optimization tool can find the best combination of assets and investment alternatives in seconds, allowing for a deep understanding of capabilities across time and multiple measures.
5. Maximizing NPV with time preferences and multiple value measures is impossible without that combination of human insight and computer algorithm.

The human-machine partnership can unlock enormous value. If your competitors are not using these techniques, it will give your firm a competitive advantage. If they are already doing it, you have some catch-up.

War Story – The Eureka Moment

Corporate did not have ready access to powerful optimization tools, so the exploration portfolio team was creating coordinated sets of wells manually. (This was in the dark ages of the late 1980s.)

There were about 100 prospects, and the portfolio team was trying to balance cost, expected hydrocarbon resource addition, future production, and the depth of the Capex hole they would be digging with their probabilistic discoveries.

With 100 wells, there were effectively an infinite number of solutions. The team decided on some limitations, such as the number of wells in the program and wells by area, but still, the task was daunting. The three portfolio team members decided to take 8-hour shifts around the clock on the department's mainframe computer terminal.

This went on and on. After four days, they had not found a solution that was even feasible, much less optimal.

Suddenly "Eureka," cried the analyst.

He had found a feasible solution. With this solution as a guide, they were able to find some other feasible solutions. There was no way to know if they had found an optimal one.

The following year, they convinced the corporation to purchase a linear optimization tool. It solved and found a better solution in seconds.

Lesson Learned

This is why we use computer tools.

CHAPTER 9

Deterministic Optimization

As used in the following sections, optimization is a mathematical approach to making a set of decisions that balances your objective, goals, and limitations. It allows you to test a coordinated set of decisions that maximizes your strategic driver (e.g., NPV) while achieving important goals like revenue growth, increasing Return on Capital Employed, or business continuity.

It would be easy enough to optimize your set of decisions if there were only four or five decisions in the company, but typically there are 100s or thousands of decisions made by people across the organization.

Nothing stops a person from manually combining different decisions to create logical, internally consistent sets of decisions. In fact, if a problem is small, it is simple. As we saw in the Introduction, two assets with three options have only nine possible solutions. Life is seldom that simple.

The statistics of this problem are daunting. I worked on a project in which an organization had 34 assets. Each asset could be handled in five ways: speeding up investment, slowing down investment, selling the asset, and a few other alternatives. We were maximizing NPV and needed to hit some targets at specific times. The math of this problem says that there are 5 to the 34th power possible combinations. That is 5.82 x 10^23, or 582 sextillion combinations. It would take until the heat death of the universe to solve this problem using random means. The magnitude of the statistical challenge is why computer tools are necessary for optimization. We need a way to eliminate all the poor portfolios to see the interesting ones. This optimization solved in under 5 seconds on a laptop PC.

Optimization tools provide the means to create portfolios that give us insight into the impact of different strategies and decisions. Computers are so fast that you can develop one candidate solution, observe what it tells you, try another one, see what it tells you, then lather, rinse, repeat. The process can also be automated. It is fast and easy to develop hundreds of different candidate solutions that achieve different goals and illustrate the impact of different financial or operational strategies. There is a multidimensional cloud of possible outcomes contingent on decisions made. It is our job to sort through this cloud and find the best solutions and plans for the future.

▸ Portfolio Selector Focus on Deterministic Optimization

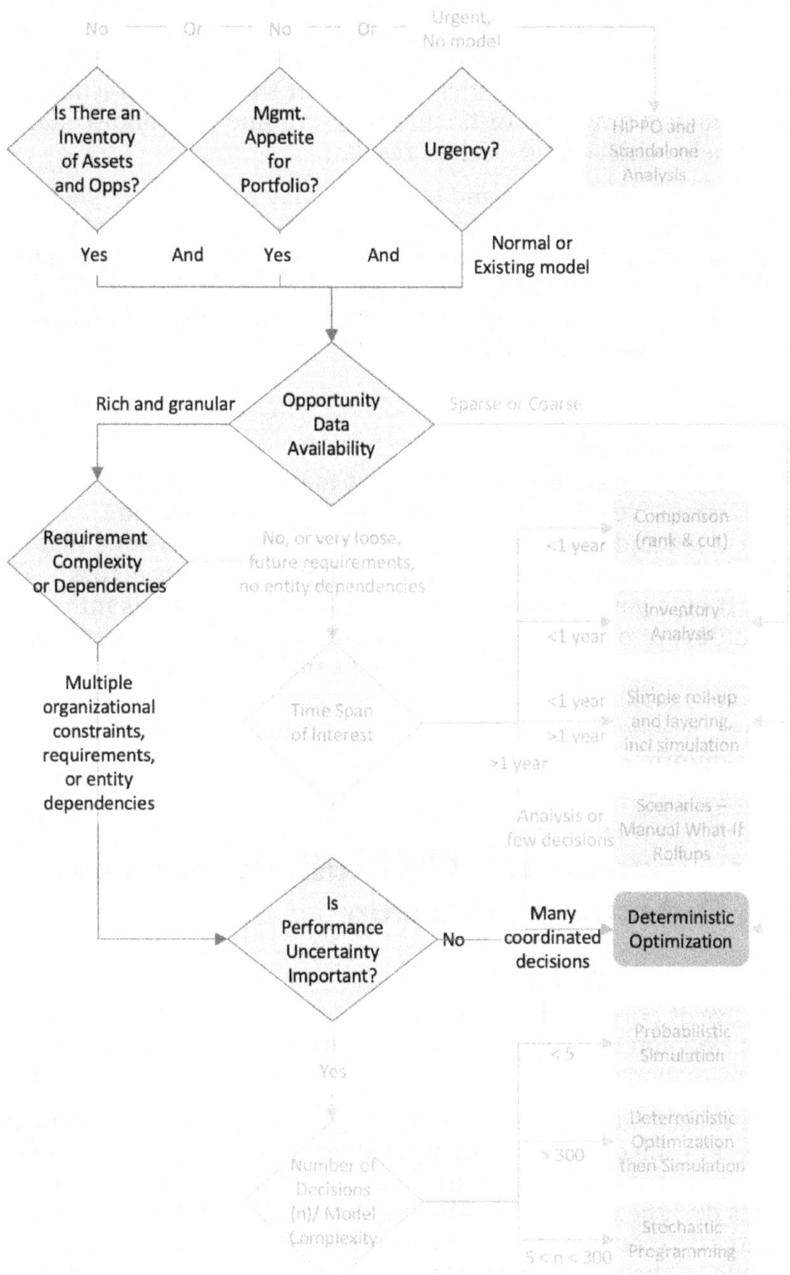

Deterministic Optimization is the first step into optimization. It is a powerful step when the frame includes multiple coordinated decisions. It enables perspectives of the envelope of organizational performance across multiple metrics that would not be practical without it.

There is a special case where optimizations are unnecessary—only the generation of answers. That is the case when the number of decision combinations is limited, e.g., a few thousand. In those cases, you can generate all the possible candidate sets. Process the results deterministically or probabilistically, then sift through the results using interactive graphical or tabular filters to find portfolio scenarios that best help achieve your desired results.

As you develop your process and tools, you may find that people push back on the idea of "having a computer run their business." Manual selection will always be an option, but finding good solutions is hard for anything beyond trivial problems. For this reason, I have often counseled analysts to de-emphasize the computational technology process (amazing as it is) and focus on the results for the firm.

> **Key Takeaways**
> Deterministic optimization is the first major step into the 'interactions' realm of portfolio methods. It goes beyond comparison and into creating coordinated sets of decisions that allow your firm to achieve multiple competing targets across time. It puts your complete set of coordinating decisions into the context of overall company performance. With deterministic optimization, you can gain tremendous insight into many portfolio problems. If this is as far as you go on your portfolio journey, it is better than never having started. You will make better-informed decisions.

Inputs – Investment Alternatives, Business Logic, Outcome vs Decision

Input Asset Alternatives

The essence of portfolio management is choice. If you do not have a choice or decision to make, there is no portfolio management, only operations management.

In decentralized companies, the full suite of choices available is often not known in the corporate center. Each business unit may keep many of its options to itself. They do this because this is how the company process is designed. Portfolio thinking needs to transcend that mode of operation. To realize the most value from portfolio analysis and management, the suite of projects and alternatives should be as open and transparent as possible.

At an asset level, there is always a choice. You can keep the asset, or you can sell it. If you choose to keep it, you can operate at normal capacity, slow down and operate at reduced capacity, upgrade and increase capacity this year, upgrade and increase capacity in two years, etc. Each of these choices has a cost, benefit, and risks.

Often, the question of whether we truly have a choice becomes critical. For example, suppose your firm has a partner in an asset, and the course of action is determined by a vote. Should we consider that an option even though we do not control it?

The short answer is that you should keep the decision in your portfolio working set. Even though it is not strictly a choice, it is an alternative decision. Your portfolio analysis will then inform you what you **should** do. The difference between what you would do given a choice and what you are forced to do is known as the "Value of Control."

In this non-control case, if your analysis shows that you should do something different from what is already happening, you will then consider actions to align the partners with your preference, knowing full well that your alignment efforts fail. If they fail, the asset decision reverts to the less advantageous one and life moves on.

Business Logic – Project and Asset Dependencies

Dependencies are constraints on inputs. When multiple assets or decisions are being considered, there are often dependencies between the assets that must be understood.

Here is a list of the major dependency types for portfolio work.

▸ **Type of Dependencies (Constraints or Business Logic)**

Type	Description	Example
Independent	You can do either, both, or neither.	Investments that have no direct logical connection to each other at the project level.
Mutually exclusive	You can do one or the other, but not both.	This is typical for different choices around a single asset. Alternatives for a single project are typically mutually exclusive.
Direct dependence	If you do one project, you must do the other.	If you build a factory, there must be roads and utilities feeding it. The responsibility for different parts is sometimes budgeted across organizational boundaries.
Contingent dependence	If you do one project, you may do the other, but you don't have to. If you don't do the first, you can't do the second.	Drill an exploration well followed by field development, phased projects.
Combination dependence	If you do one project, you must do one of several alternative projects (combining direct and mutually exclusive).	Build an LNG plant, and you must lease or buy ships or choose a combination. But you must factor in shipping.
Temporal dependence	In addition to whether to do a project, there is often a timing issue.	You can't do phase 2 of a project before you do phase 1. If project A is delayed by two years, project B must be delayed by two years (or more).

The dependencies can also be combined. Complex selection constraint logic can be expressed with all optimization tools. Experience and creativity are useful traits for the optimization modeler. Other constraints may include working interest, delay maximum, and the entity is locked in or out.

Action Alternative vs. Outcome Variability

Please note that when I talk about alternatives, it is not about different outcomes but the choices that precede them.

Decisions:
Consider a decision to build a widget factory with three mutually exclusive capacity decisions:

1. Low capacity - 250,000 widgets per year
2. Medium capacity - 1,000,000 widgets per year
3. High capacity - 2,000,000 widgets per year

Pick one of those. That's your decision. The outcome is what happens after that.

Outcomes:
Demand for the entire production run may exist. Or perhaps the market is only 500,000 because a competitor comes out with a new, improved widget. The product may be a total flop because of tainted materials from a supplier. These outcomes are independent of your capacity decision.

Decisions Contingent on Outcomes:

In the high-outcome case, you can model a second factory or an expansion of the original one as a potential additional business value.

Some Examples of Alternative Investment Options

Ongoing business alternatives

1. As Is (Base case)
2. Cash Cow Case (minimize investment, return as much as possible to the company)
3. Grow Case (High investment to increase or maintain production)
4. Divest Case

Project alternatives

1. As Is (Base Case)
2. Stop the project
3. Minimum case that achieves objectives
4. Acceleration case (fastest it can be done)
5. Reduced capacity
6. Increased capacity
7. Delay case (1 year to understand the carrying cost of the project)
8. Delay case (4 years to understand the mothballed perspective)
9. Reduce working interest/divest
10. Acquire additional working interest

Market Alternatives

1. Low Price, High Volume
2. High Price, Low Volume
3. Global Rollout
4. Local Rollout, Phased rollout
5. Focus on a Single User Class or Clinical Use
6. Expand to Additional Clinical Uses

Research and Development Alternatives

1. As Is (Base Case)
2. Reduced expenditure
3. Increased expenditure
4. Acceleration or Deceleration
5. Fast Fail
6. Different emphasis (any number of scenarios)

Acquisition

1. As Is (Base case)
2. Lower working interest
3. Higher working interest
4. Lower purchase price (affects the probability of capture and NPV)
5. Higher purchase price (affects the probability of capture and NPV)

This list is not exhaustive. In the final analysis, every business or asset has its unique set of potential decisions.

An axiom of portfolio optimization is that locking in a decision in your model can only reduce value. The more options on each of your assets, the more opportunities there are to add value. A working paper by Jeffrey Keisler called "*The Value of Refining Buy-up Alternatives for Portfolio Decision Analysis*" (2010) postulates that once you have three or four alternatives for each of your assets, you may be close to maximizing the possible value from your portfolio. There's not a magic number, but more options lead to more insights. Empirically, it is not unusual to see 30% increase in value by having adequate alternatives defined.

Detail – Real Assets or Surrogates?

How good does your data have to be? How much granularity should we include? What if we do not have data for certain parts of our inventory? Can we use poor to marginal data? Is there anything we can gain from that?

Those questions are typical of those encountered when first embarking on the portfolio journey. The answers to those questions are always the same—it depends.

Strategic Portfolio Analysis

For strategic portfolio analysis, the purpose is to inform the leadership of the high-level tradeoffs facing the firm. Should we push for growth? How much? Should we focus on deepwater developments or unconventional ones? Should we enter a new country? Should we broaden our pharmaceutical portfolio into a new therapeutic area? If we go for returns instead of growth, what are the implications for the sustainability of the dividend?

For these kinds of high-level and open-ended questions, you would start with your basic inventory of assets as a baseline, but you must branch out well beyond that to test different strategies. Once you go beyond your known assets, you have two choices: spend time, energy, and effort to develop detailed projections of real-world assets, or you can generate scalable estimates that capture the "spirit"—the approximate fundamental patterns of cash flow, production, earnings, capital, and risk—of the new areas you're considering. I have heard these scalable estimates called proxies or surrogates.

For strategic portfolio analysis, it's OK to use surrogate projects that reflect the character of a broad class of assets and use appropriate multipliers to test your appetite for the class. A model incorporating average discovery, testing, and development costs is reasonable for exploration or drug discovery. Outputs from this model can be inserted as a scalable wedge or entity.

There is an essential caveat with surrogates. If you are doing time-series optimization, unless you have a powerful reason to do otherwise, you should set up the surrogates to have small, positive (like $0.1) nominal NPVs. Price, acquisition cost, and other input assumptions and uncertainties can have unrealistic impacts on outcomes. Optimization models will always tilt towards the highest value, so the optimization results would be skewed by biases in uncertain variables. Setting your NPV near zero forces the optimization tool to seek other reasons to select entities besides your fictional NPV (objective function). Rather the optimization will emphasize other drivers and requirements, such as production or cost, to create insights.

Tactical Portfolio Analysis

Tactical portfolio analysis is a different matter. Yes, you can get high-level insights about strategy and metrics, but typically, tactical decisions are more specific. Given a set of choices for this owned asset or project, which one do I pursue? In the tactical realm, the first question is to understand "What decision **should** I make?" Given the choices in front of me and the goals and targets we are pursuing from the strategic analysis, what is the best course of action for this asset?

If you are confident that the data you received from the assets is diligently modeled, it's easy enough to copy it and make surrogates to test whether to strive for more rig lines or a higher working interest. If your analysis indicates that you should make a different decision, request a tighter model from the business unit. This assumes enough time cushion for iterations of the analysis.

But as discussed previously, asset decisions are not always a choice. There are joint ventures that require approval by other firms, government approvals, and sometimes unexpected resource constraints. With tactical portfolio work, leadership might express the opinion that project alternative A is preferred, but operations and project management need to be able to respond that this alternative may not be doable. Often, influence can be exerted to push projects in a more desirable direction, but success is not a given.

This two-way communication of expectations and aspirations is critical and requires aligned incentives and a high degree of trust between strategy and operations.

Operational Optimization

When you're at the operational level, you need precision and accuracy. For example, optimizing a well program requires precision in the timing of drilling, logging, mobilization and demobilization, etc. There will always be uncertainty in this space, but it's uncertainty in terms of hours and days, not months and years. Even with resource and reserve estimates, if you are drilling enough independent prospects and your estimates are unbiased, the statistics revert to the mean because of a high number of wells.

For operational optimization, you need accurate, granular information. There is seldom the luxury of multiple iterations. The analyses have to be good from the start.

Detail – Managing Your Portfolio vs Operating It

When your working inventory is equal to the candidate set, you have a problem. It means that you are doing everything that you are considering. At that point, you are not managing your portfolio; you are simply operating it. Your portfolio is a to-do list. Without alternatives, there is no opportunity to add value by managing your portfolio.

You can do simulations and slice-and-dice analyses to the extent that those are important to your business, and you should. But without decisions to make, there is no ability to add value with portfolio analysis.

If you find yourself in this situation, there are two things to do: operate efficiently and find options. Leadership's job is to find options.

Lest there be a misunderstanding, efficient, safe, and cost-effective operations are essential to business. They add measurable value and keep the lights on. They reside in the bottom half of the "Strategic Execution Framework" diagram. For most strategic and tactical portfolio work, those values are a given.

Detail – Deterministic Optimization Process

The idea of optimization is that for any working set or inventory of assets, there is a collection of decisions that maximize the value of the firm subject to adherence to constraints and targets. Optimization can help you find the efficient frontier of your value and risk parameters—whatever they are.

Remember, the primary purpose of the optimizer in portfolio work is to create reasonable, coordinated candidate sets to test the consequences of different sets of decisions. It's good to test a wide variety of objective functions and requirements. Ultimately, you will look at and compare the enterprise's total outcomes. Treating the optimizer as the one correct set of answers is a mistake. It's mathematically correct, but businesses have more complexity than can be accurately portrayed solely by a computer model.

Instead, use the optimization results to help understand the key metrics, which assets and projects are the most critical, what are the overall capabilities of the portfolio, what are reasonable goals to set, and the robustness of the resulting plan.

You'll be looking at and comparing NPVs and all the values that are a part of your frame. Don't sweat too much about the parameters you use to create the different portfolios. Remember, you're comparing the outputs, not the mathematical manipulations that made them.

However you build the candidate sets, you need to ensure that you collect the output data you care about. Optimizing the portfolio with an NPV objective function 5% higher than your WACC may provide an interesting perspective, but make sure to capture the NPV at WACC or whatever rate is representative of corporate value so you can later compare your portfolios on an apples-to-apples basis.

The basic process is the following:

1. Put data into an optimization model - your frame should include whether you require precise answers or whether approximate methods suffice.
2. Specify decision flexibility limits for each entity - as you start the analysis, it is best not to over-constrain the model. Constraining is easy—someone can always find a rationale for not allowing project flexibility. Allow constraints initially only for impossibility, not for difficulty.
    a. Time shift constraints - Maximum delay and acceleration
    b. Commitment constraints - Entity may not be rejected
    c. Working Interest (WI) constraint - The project may be a different WI
3. Set up the dependencies and business rules between all the entities.
4. Specify the objective function to maximize (usually NPV) or minimize. Be willing to test different objective functions to test other approaches and paths.
5. Set the input constraints (usually capital or people).
6. Set other output targets and requirements (production volume, cash flow, ROCE, risk, etc.).
7. Run the optimization.
8. Discuss and save results; if needed, return to Step 3.
9. Once there are sufficient portfolio candidate sets, compare them using tables, graphs, or statistical analysis and narrow them down to five to ten distinct portfolios with meaningfully different outcomes for leadership to discuss.
10. Discuss with decision-makers to better understand **their** tradeoffs between portfolio attributes.

At the end of all this, there must be a validation step and fine-tuning. Step 2—decision flexibility—is a particular challenge. Initial passes may have allowed more flexibility than is practical. You now know what options are preferred—what the assets **should** do. Next, there has to be validation with the asset managers for practical matters and planning. What can they do to attempt to change decisions on those assets? Is it something they decide, or are there others that need to be convinced?

As you work through a portfolio, it is helpful to think like a scientist. Start with a hypothesis. For example, if I do everything I have as fast as possible, that will yield the best result. That first pass is not even an optimization—it's maximization. It's possible that this will give you an acceptable answer. I have never seen that happen; there is always room for improvement.

Build Optimizations Outside the Box

Once you see the results of that first pass, you can generate a hypothesis of how that can be improved. For example, you might believe that holding capital flat for five years could give you a good outcome. Optimize with that requirement and examine the answer. Did it give you the expected result? Try different hypotheses. Test limits on production, ROCE, reserves to production ratio. Each time, before you run it, think through what you think it will do or show you. This helps you create a mental model and gives you immediate feedback about its validity.

Detail - Practical Notes for Optimization

Model Linearity

There are many types of mathematical optimization. The mathematical structure of the problem drives which type of optimization you should use. The different mathematical structures suggest different solver types to reach good or best answers quickly. You may have heard of linear programming (LP), genetic algorithms, heuristics, and global solvers. When building or preparing an optimization model, as part of the frame, you need to know the tradeoffs between the solver's speed and the model's accuracy.

Modelers often (always?) include additional detail to make the models correct, defensible, and internally consistent. That extra detail and complexity can add hours or days to an optimization calculation. Consider carefully whether the purpose of the model is to gain strategic insights or to create budget or business plan-quality output. Long optimization times limit the number of candidate sets and strategies that can be tested.

As a rule, LP is the fastest and easiest approach to optimization, but it may be less accurate because the world is seldom genuinely linear. In practice, simplifying a model to run using LP allows for broad investigation of strategy with "good enough" answers.

A simple example of linearizing is when using a metric like return on capital employed (ROCE) as a requirement. ROCE is earnings divided by the capital employed in a given year. You may want that to be greater than 15%. But since it is a quotient, so it's not linear.

To convert it to linear, do the following:

Start with ROCE >= Earnings / Capital Employed.

Change the formula by multiplying both sides by the capital employed.

Now it is Earnings >= ROCE times Capital Employed, which is linear.

Your requirement then would be expressed as Earnings >= 15% * (Capital Employed).

Even the NPV calculation should be treated as a SUMPRODUCT of the cash flows and discount factors by year. The NPV function in Excel is non-linear.

Another example is project delays. Shifting a project's stream data by two years does not capture factors like the change in costs, prices, carrying costs, and fiscal effects. Incorporating those factors would add complexity and precision to the model but would not yield insight in many cases. Projections of future prices and cost changes are scientific wild guesses at best, and carrying-costs and incremental changes usually are much smaller than the impact of the shift in the first place. You will probably recalculate everything eventually for conformance with corporate requirements, plans, and accountability, but don't let it slow you down.

One approach is to keep your model linear but directionally accurate, then post-process the candidate sets using a more precise model. This may not yield the perfect optimized solution, but given the uncertainties inherent in the world, it will be a much better plan than what you are doing today.

Objective Function

In general, NPV at the weighted-average cost of capital is appropriate. Adding 1-5% to your discount rate may be appropriate if you are not optimizing at the firm's highest level or do not have a full slate of alternatives. At least test different discount rates to see if it gives an appreciably different answer—often it doesn't. Your decision-makers may have a prescribed discount rate to use. Use it. But run tests with other discount rates to see if it makes a material difference in the decisions. You can also calculate the NPV at various rates to see if the best answers change based on the discount rate.

The reason not to use a higher hurdle rate when optimizing at the enterprise level is that when you have enterprise-level data, you do not need to compensate for the opportunity cost of opportunities "thought to exist." You have them in the model.

Remember, the objective function provides the "North Star" for the optimization. Requirements and constraints create tension in the model and incremental insights. And often those requirements and constraints are more important to the decision-makers than the objective function.

Requirements and Constraints

As you develop different portfolio scenarios, you will find some that look great and hit all your targets across the years. There's still a question. Are these the right goals and constraints?

Use your frame as a guide. When you thought about the things you care about, some were fundamental objectives; some were means objectives. Use the means objectives to drive results. For example, if your fundamental objective is to increase shareholder value, you may have cascading means objectives: increased revenue can be caused by increased production. So, you can use revenue or production as requirements.

It is worth testing the restraining impact of your goals and constraints on the value of your firm. What does this mean? Let's try an example. Your bosses have said that they want at least 40% of production to come from gas. And they are firm about that. They are bullish on the long-term role of gas in the world economy. All your portfolios generated have achieved that requirement.

But you have a nagging question. Why 40%? Is it truly a requirement in all years? The requirement could be relaxed in the short term while waiting for signposts.

Test those requirements!!!!! Try a few things. First, relax the near-term requirement to 35% gas production. You still achieve 40% eventually, but the near-term requirement is relaxed. Another practice is to put requirements every five years, leaving no requirements in the intervening years. The 40% number is not magic—it is an arbitrary round number. Let the portfolio drift down or up a little. It can go to 38% for a few years, and as long as it continues to "seek" that 40% level, the strategic intent is being fulfilled. You will get added value from the softer constraints, and the optimization will solve faster.

The objective function drives the model in a specific direction. The constraints and requirements set the boundaries of the feasible solution. With minimal constraints, the feasibility region is large, bounded only by the possible solutions. As you add constraints and requirements, the feasibility region shrinks until you add the one that reduces the area to zero. The problem is mathematically infeasible when there is no set of solutions that meets all the constraints and requirements.

Non-Value Objective Functions

If someone asks what the maximum that can be attained of a metric in a given year, e.g., production in 2030, it's certainly ok to set that as the objective function to see what it tells you. The overall run may not be useful, but the number is.

There is a glitch you will see when you do this type of exercise. Setting a maximum on a single year will ignore any entity that does not influence that year. So, with NPV removed as the driver, great projects may have nonsense decisions applied to them. A great project might be eliminated because it has no impact on 2030 production. The decision becomes random.

The workaround is to run the different objective function and note the value (for example 1 million units in 2030). Then set that value (minus 1 or 999,999) as a requirement, change the optimization to your normal objective function, and rerun.

For example, the maximum value for ROCE in 2025 is 17.2%. Change the objective function to NPV and set 17.15% in 2025 as an optimization requirement. That way, you are at or near the maximum ROCE and making value-producing decisions on all your entities.

Granularity

The model granularity should be consistent with the insight and decisions being made. For example, suppose you are working on the composition of your portfolio concerning countries, asset classes, or lines of business. In that case, you do not need granularity at the individual well or reservoir level. Excessive granularity is more work, slower to optimize, and will lead to modeling errors.

Business Logic

Build the business logic for the initial portfolio insights.

You need to ensure the logical consistency of the model. It should not allow impossible decisions or actions but may allow difficult ones.

Examples of impossible decisions: doing phase 1 after phase 2 of a project, delaying a currently producing asset, and impossible acceleration of a project schedule. Difficult ones include delaying a project that requires approval from others and divestiture of assets with government hurdles.

The business logic in the early iterations should be left as open as practical; allow projects to delay more than you think is realistic or allow the model to exclude an asset with no compensation. In the real world, you would never give away an asset, but if the model's math tells you that that is the best answer, it is a crucial insight about that asset.

Model Decision Flexibility

Some types of flexibility can be modeled easily, while some require a separate independent economic run. It depends on the requirements and purpose of the optimization and the time available for the work.

Project Delay: What kind of delay granularity? (month, year), what is the first year that can be delayed (for example, if the budget is already committed for this year...)? Is there a cost to put the project on mothballs or carry it through the delay time? For purposes of the analysis, is a simple bulk shift adequate, or should it also inflate revenues and costs? A bulk shift is simple but less accurate. Developing specific case economics costs time and money and distracts people from their primary jobs.

Often it is beneficial to separate an entity into two separate ones with different flexibility or riskiness. The classic example is an exploration well that **will** be drilled next year, but the follow-on development is contingent on success and may be delayed. Likewise, you may have already budgeted front-end engineering work on a discovery, but the project itself may be delayed.

Asset Out: If the optimizer rejects an asset or project, how should it be handled? If the optimization tool continually rejects an asset, even without receiving compensation for it, it is sending a strong message—this asset does not fit your portfolio. Real-world actions include simply releasing it, selling it now, or selling it at some time in the future. Perhaps a partial sale of the asset Is possible.

The alternative is to keep the project as is and compromise on your strategic goals. There's nothing wrong with that, but it should be done consciously.

Detail – Options vs Outcomes

Options are decisions; outcomes are results. I have heard the word options used when discussing outcomes. This creates fog and confusion in discussions.

Consider a project with three defined possible outcomes and economics. The outcomes are based on the total volume of hydrocarbons in the field. There are low, middle, and high outcomes. Those outcomes are based on a currently unknown state of nature. There is an accurate answer, but it is unknown to us.

With full knowledge of these three possible outcomes, a decision-maker may decide not to develop, develop with a minimal concept, or develop with a large capacity concept. Those would be three options. The two development options will have very different economic outcomes depending on the volume of hydrocarbons and how the future unfolds.

Alignment of Development Alternatives with the State of Nature

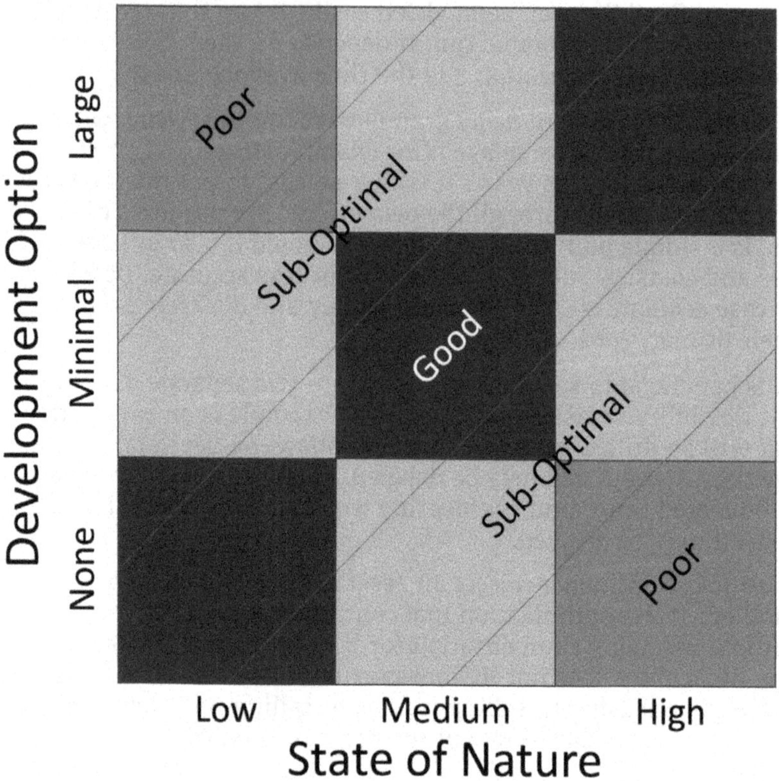

The development options that align with the state of nature (reality) have the best economic outcomes black the worst misalignments have the worst economic consequences (medium gray), and the intermediate cases have middle-of-the-road economic consequences (light gray).

Perhaps you can acquire more information about reality to better align your development options to the updated view of reality.

Testing potential outcomes against different options is a great practice. It can help you stress test a proposed development and help you understand how a large or small outcome will affect the company differently. It can also help you know when and how much you would be willing to pay for information that narrows the range of outcomes.

The separation of decisions from outcomes applies to individual opportunities and portfolio-level analysis.

Detail – Why Your Objective Function May Not Matter (Much)

Many arguments have taken place regarding the proper objective function for portfolio work. Those arguments miss the point. They assume that optimization gives you **the** correct answer.

In a complex and unpredictable world, it is challenging to select the one true perfect course. As soon as you set out, you encounter barriers and bumps. Optimization provides mathematically consistent but possibly impractical answers given a set of assumptions. It is more valuable to use optimization as a means of creating different virtual outcomes that show the tradeoffs inherent in your goals and targets.

As covered elsewhere, Net Present Value (NPV) is a very obvious objective function. I would argue that it is the key overriding value. But stock market analysts who judge your company and its results care about discipline in your capital program. They want revenue or production growth and increases in reserves for a resource company. Operational aspects of business, like safety and environmental responsibility, are also important. Future growth prospects matter.

A multi-objective technique like the Analytic Hierarchy Process (AHP) may seem like a suitable objective function approach. As discussed earlier, these techniques are challenging to do well. But there is no harm in even bad objective functions as long as you look at the total results, not just the highest answer. Using the approach outlined here, **the objective function serves mainly to create tension** when building sets of coordinated decisions for further analysis. You can use the weighting factors derived from an AHP analysis and create some sort of "Franken-objective function" for optimization. But again, look at the components of it after the fact to ensure you like the specific, detailed results.

Optimization models then use the ABCs to ensure that we mind all that our leaders care about. The value of using optimization to create multiple virtual portfolio outcomes quickly is to see how all the values interact. The optimization parameters provide mathematical parameters for the model to create outcomes.

You should test different parameters for objective functions as well as the constraints and requirements in your optimization, then look through the portfolio-level **results** and find the ones that best balance the values you care about in important periods.

When you take this approach, the optimization objective function, constraints, and requirements do not matter. The optimization parameters set up only the **mathematical** conditions. So, use NPV at the weighted average cost of capital, use NPV at a higher hurdle rate, or use any other metric that puts a sensible, directional **tension** into the model and see what you get.

Detail – How Many and Which Portfolio Candidate Sets to Create?

Before answering the title question of this section, let's consider where we're going.

Use your analysis frame as a first clue. If this is a simple one-off "What If" case, maybe one candidate set will suffice. But often, even simple What-If questions, like "what if we cut capital 10% for the next three years?" deserve more nuanced analysis, e.g., what do 5% and 15% look like?

Thinking about this simple case, you could generate three portfolios and display the results compared to your 0% base case, and leadership can have their discussion.

Small Working Sets

Many portfolio problems have a binary structure. An entity decision can be on or off. In the simplest of cases, where it can select any number of the decisions once and only once, the number of possible combinations is 2 to the nth power. If there are ten entities, the number of combinations is 2^10 or 1024. Only 1024 possible candidate sets (portfolios) can be generated from this small working set. These 1024 portfolios test the entire universe of possibilities.

For many tools, this is a trivial number of different portfolios. The analyst does not have to think about the objective function or requirements—run them all, then sort them out later using filters and graphics.

Larger Problems

When you have even more entities, each of which has multiple alternatives, the numbers get massive quickly. A set of 30 entities, each of which has three mutually exclusive options, would require 200 trillion portfolios to test all possible combinations. The generate-them-all approach is impractical.

Instead, you will need a more intelligent search function focused on outcomes. It would be best if you had some definition for exploring the envelope of possibilities. Do some pre-work to determine reasonable outcome ranges in various measures. Every measure you care about adds a multiplicative dimension to the number of portfolios to generate.

You may wish to test ten levels of capital investment, five trajectories of production growth, different scenarios of acquisition and divestiture, asset class mix, country mix, and sensitivity to changes like a government takeover of an asset in specific years. It depends on the frame, but you could easily end up with 50–200 different candidate sets to consider.

See the detail section for an approach to automate a part of this process. That automation will set up the edges of the envelope of possible and relevant performance for the measures that matter to you. You will undoubtedly be able to gain insights, but there will be quirks in some of the portfolios, and you will need to fill in gaps on your most important metrics. After that, you can set up a new automation or optimize manually. I suggest a significant amount of manual work. There is still insight that requires human knowledge. I do not doubt that sometime within the next decade, machines with artificial intelligence and machine learning will be able to automate more. Still, I believe that some degree of human intelligence and insight will always need to be applied.

As a practice, run a maximum NPV case, then think about what is wrong with it and change one set of requirements, e.g., capital expenditures. Create a mental hypothesis about how the model will respond. Then run it and see if you were right. Do this for multiple metrics across multiple years and with different objective functions. You will develop a sixth sense of how your company can respond to different strategies and approaches.

Then automate to fill in the entire envelope and find all the hyper-dimensional edges of performance. At this point, you may have generated between 10 and 1,000 different outcomes of the portfolio results. Now you need to see how they relate to each other and the tradeoffs.

Now What?

Once you get past a few portfolios, you must consider how to present and discuss the results. Few leadership teams have the patience or experience to work through tens, let alone thousands, of portfolios. There is a curation step that should happen before bringing results to the leadership team. But don't take this as a given; there may be ways to create an interactive tool that executives would enjoy exploring. This is not always easy or practical, but it's worth considering. See the Sam Savage Shell Portfolio Tool in the appendix.

The analysts will need to sort through the large set of portfolios and select a subset of portfolios that capture representative parts of the performance envelope and illustrate tradeoffs between metrics before bringing a reduced set of no more than ten portfolios for discussion.

We will discuss this more in the outputs and visualization section.

Detail – Setting Up Batches to Explore the Multidimensional Performance Envelope

We have discussed an iterative approach to portfolio optimization where the analyst iteratively works from optimization to optimization after reviewing the previous one.

Another approach is to set up and automate batch runs to ensure that you thoroughly test the relevant and interesting performance indicators.

Go back to the frame of the analysis. You need to know which metrics your firm cares about and approximate desired levels for each.

NPV will typically be your objective function—it is a corporate North Star. But metrics like ROCE in a target year, production or production growth, risk metrics, and capital expenditure in a target year or across years provide the multidimensional performance envelope to explore.

Here's an example: Suppose you have two metrics you care about (besides NPV): ROCE in 2025 and production in 2025. With 25 runs, you can explore a relevant swath of that performance envelope with some detail. You'll find that some of the easy portfolios are the same and some of the hard ones are infeasible, but that then defines the entire region between these two metrics.

Below is a visual of a two-dimensional set of indicators. On the y-axis is the production rate; the x-axis is ROCE. Each of the squares in the grid is a set of constraints to be tested—an optimization to be run. If you use a macro to set up an automation, the optimization tool can quickly generate candidate sets and show the outcomes and feasibility of each combination. This batch approach can be quickly run to help you understand your envelope of possible performance.

▸ **Portfolio Alternatives with Two Dimensions of Performance**

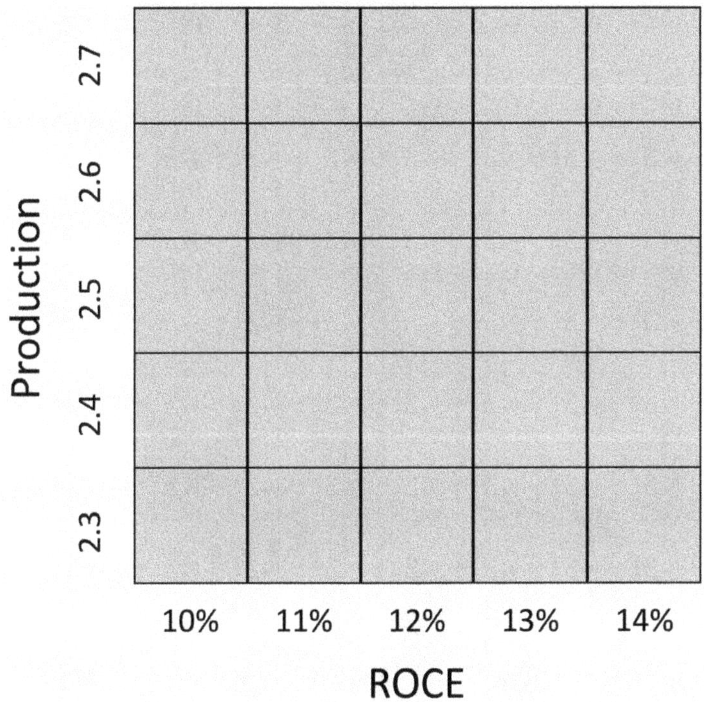

A simple two-dimensional grid shows how you can establish all the tradeoffs in relevant ranges of metrics. In this case, 25 optimization runs would be required to determine the rough envelope of possibilities between production and ROCE in a given time period.

Now add a third metric. Now you need 125 portfolios to completely define the space. As you add additional dimensions, you may want fewer samples across each dimension. The number of portfolios to test would be (Samples per dimension) to the power of (number of dimensions). In this case, 5 ^ 3 = 125.

This approach would define the boundaries of your firm's multidimensional performance envelope. You would know approximately where to focus.

▸ **Portfolio Alternatives with Three Dimensions of Performance**

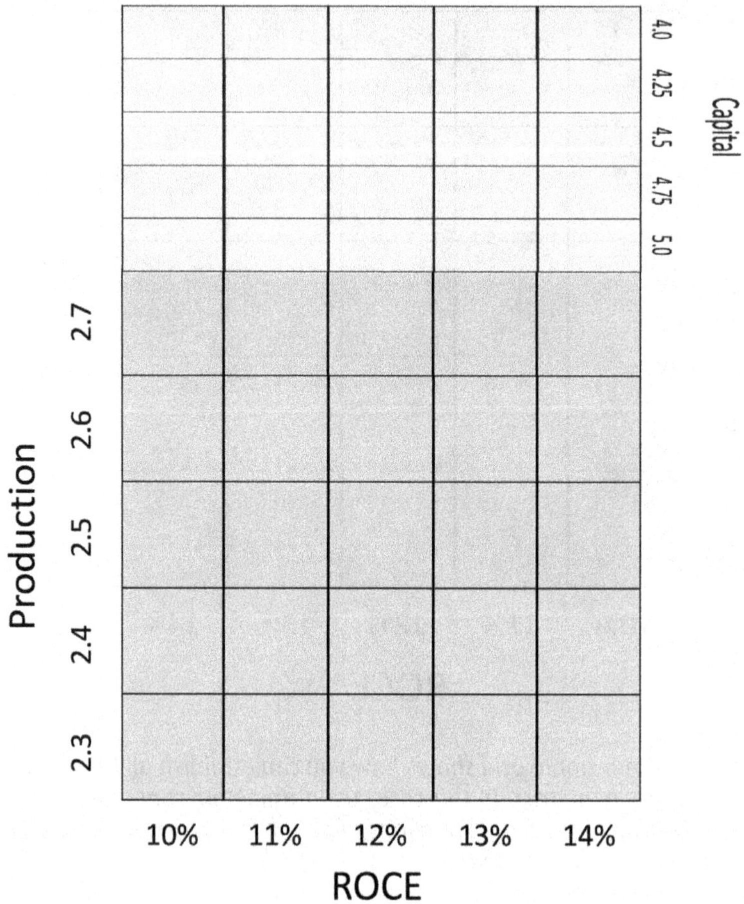

> *Adding more dimensions would require more portfolio runs to adequately characterize all tradeoffs. One more dimension with five targets increases the portfolio runs from 25 to 125. Consider smaller dimensions with a wider spacing between targets or narrowing the relevant range. You may wish to first test two metrics against each other, then use those results to establish a narrower relevant range for the third metric.*

You will need to know or determine what leadership's "must-have" metrics are. Those will be the focus of discussion. You will generally not want to show them all 125 portfolios. Instead, narrow it down to the 5-10 that best illustrate the tradeoffs.

Detail – Optimizing Portfolio-Level Weighted Proxies Like Political Risk

Optimizing uncertainty can take two broad forms. The first and easiest is to use proxies for risk and treat the problem as linear. The second is to use stochastic programming general solvers. The choice of approaches is determined by the nature of the risk you are trying to manage and the problem frame. This section covers aggregate proxies; stochastic optimization is covered here.

I'll provide two examples of using linear proxies: Country Risk and Price Risk.

Country Risk

Every entity is tied to a nation, its laws, and customs. The firm must sometimes deal with cultures and regulations that are unfamiliar and difficult to manage. Various consulting companies have created indices to measure or express relative riskiness at a country level.

These indices may include regulatory and tax system stability, probability of confiscation, currency issues, import and export restrictions, and currency transfer. One way to measure the overall risk would be a weighted average of the production, capital, or cash flow by the country risk index. The formula looks like below.

Weighted Country Risk Formula

$$Measure\,Weighted\,Country\,Risk = \frac{\sum_{c=1}^{n}(CountryRisk_c \times Measure_c)}{TotalMeasure}$$

> *Country risk can be weighted by capital employed, capital expenditure, revenue, production, or any relevant measure that executives care about.*

Where Measure is the thing you care about, e.g., production, and CountryRisk is the relative risk index. This is a simple formula that would change values across time.

Oil Price Sensitivity Framework

Another metric could be a production-weighted sensitivity to the oil price.

▸ **Weighted Oil Price Sensitivity Formula**

$$Production\ Weighted\ Oil\ Price\ Sensitivity = \frac{\sum_{k=1}^{n} \left(Price\ Sensitivity_k \times Production_k\right)}{TotalProduction}$$

> *Oil price sensitivity must be weighted by oil production to make any sense. This formula can be linearized and used to find portfolios that achieve specific sensitivities.*

This is the same form as Country Risk and can be a linear model. It would be especially useful if leadership wishes to increase or decrease price sensitivity. For example, when the oil price is hitting new lows and is expected eventually to turn up, a company might consider taking an aggressive posture for oil price sensitivity; likewise, when prices are high, they might consider a more defensive one through asset acquisition and divestiture.

This approach can then show you the trend. Are you getting more or less risky as measured by revenue (production) or capital employed? Business strategy determines which is preferable, but again, knowing where you stand and what your actions will drive you towards is a first step in determining if there is or should be a concern.

War Story - Over-Constraining is a Thing

There was a lot I needed to learn when I began my optimization journey.

Once I started using the optimization tool, it seemed the sky was the limit. Anything was possible with all the entities I had in the tool and the high degree of business logic flexibility.

I started modestly. What does a maximum NPV case look like? Can we hit 4% production growth through 2015? It was all so insightful. With the LP model and 500 entities, these simple questions would be solved in under a minute (even in 2004).

But I couldn't just leave it there. Noooooo! I just had to make optimization runs that showed growth in every single year, and achieved improved ROCE in every single year, and replaced reserves in every single year, and... and... and...

Like the frog in the pot of boiling water, I didn't notice that as I added those requirements, the runtime was getting longer and longer. First, it was a couple of minutes, then five, then fifteen. It was fun because the optimization program showed convergence between the best answer found and the theoretical maximum. There was a kind of suspense as the program worked away; sometimes, it would find the optimal solution with a few giant leaps, and other times it would nick away at it. While it was running, I caught up on email and did other work.

Finally, I started one that nicked away and, even after fifteen minutes, was still a long way from the solution. I decided to take lunch.

Returning from lunch, I found that there was still no solution. Finally, it found one, and it was ugly. There were no downs in any of the time-series data. Production, cash flow, and earnings showed an unnatural, straight-line upward progression for 20 years. It was mathematically optimal and totally implausible.

Eventually, I realized that by putting certain requirements at five-year intervals, the optimization solved faster and looked much more reasonable.

Lessons Learned

1. These tools are REALLY FUN!
2. The differences between the over-constrained and less constrained cases were irrelevant to the strategic insights we hoped to gain.
3. Let your frame be your guide. (I didn't have much of one.)

Detail – Isn't Portfolio About Comparing Risk and Returns?

I received a question about portfolio risk measures a while back:

"I was wondering if you could comment on the measure of portfolio risk. I see optimization of NPV (typically) is the goal, I am not sure how you normally take risk into account during any optimization. I would think chasing high NPVs would generate a riskier portfolio. Is there a standard deviation of the NPV distribution or other measure that better notes the value metric risk in a portfolio? Thanks."

My response was:
From a Decision Quality perspective, there are stated values that we care about that help drive our decisions.

Portfolio risk has been a fundamental portfolio analysis and management metric since Harry Markowitz did his Nobel prize efficient frontier work. He used the portfolio's expected variance vs. the portfolio's expected return as the risk and value measures. A subsequent extension of that work by William Sharpe established the Capital Asset Pricing Model (CAPM) as a guide to the appropriate discount rate to determine an investment's value-add. Sharpe, Markowitz, and Merton Miller shared the Nobel prize in 1990.

An implicit assumption in Markowitz' model is that portfolio returns and the variance of those returns are the two main drivers of the goodness of a portfolio.

Asset portfolio management is similar conceptually—we are establishing tradeoffs between conflicting drivers—but the specifics are different. Instead of annual return on investment as the positive value metric, we typically use NPV. The tradeoffs are often not risk metrics but rather other types of requirements and constraints like capital.

A corporation may care about capital expenditure, Return on Capital Employed (ROCE), production/revenue growth, reserve replacement, and cash flow in individual years over time. For each of those, we can make a graph of NPV vs. the metric and establish appropriate, efficient frontiers.

Within the Markowitz framework, a single company would not typically be considered a portfolio. But reducing the variability of outcomes can increase the value of a firm on the market.

What is the risk we care about at the firm level? Under CAPM, risk refers to the volatility of the underlying security relative to the overall market. A stock that moves in the same direction as the market, but more, is considered riskier and "requires" higher returns to offset the variability. But CAPM includes only non-diversifiable risks. Unless we change the company's nature, most of our risk is diversifiable.

So, what risks should the leaders of a company care about? Is the variance of the NPV something they should care about? Perhaps the ability to meet the dividend from cash flow is more important to them.

Those variabilities can be expressed as the variance of NPV or perhaps the cash flow in the next three years. But what should we include in the calculation? Production risk, price risk, cost risk, country, currency regulatory, and public order are all possibilities. The biggest one for an upstream hydrocarbon company is often oil price variability because it correlates broadly across its assets.

But how should we use that? Many oil companies are apparent risk seekers in terms of sensitivity to the oil price. This sensitivity may deliver a counter-cyclical balance to other parts of the market. If that's the case, do we really want to minimize that part of variability? Or is it up to individual investors to use our firm's securities as a hedge within their personal investment portfolios? Do we really want zero variability, or is there some optimum variance level? Using the probability of paying dividends from cash flow would bring oil price risk into the mix. Are there portfolio actions the firm is willing to take to change the sensitivity to price? What about market hedges or futures?

There are often more meaningful risks that can be modeled. For example, a firm may have a production target in the future. How likely is it to achieve that target? There are tradeoffs between that likelihood, NPV, and capital expenditure. Another firm may be proud of its exploration performance, so the probability of resource replacement through exploration may be important to them.

For every combination of metrics, there is an implied Pareto frontier. Sometimes it's a meaningful one. Each firm needs to know itself and what the shareholders expect.

As you advance you may discover that sophisticated statistical measures are a real driver for your firm. But start simple. Start with performance and effectiveness measures that people understand well—not the fancy statistical wizardry that someone read about in a journal.

War Story – Optimization for Scenarios and Sensitivities

The planning group had prepared all the Excel spreadsheets, linked everything together, and were poised for the onslaught of strategic data to arrive for the Strategic Plan exercise.

Then the corporation came down with an unexpected twist on the plan. Instead of a long-term view of only the mid-price case, they wanted to create different versions of the plan incorporating different price assumptions and corporate targets.

Arguments had been raging for months about whether to shoot for high growth or high returns. There had not been a resolution to this vital question, so it fell on the planning community to assist with the analysis.

The planning groups throughout the company quickly pivoted in their preparation work. They developed an Excel file network to incorporate three different price scenarios (Low, Mid, and High) with an initial focus on Low and High. One of the planners had an Excel optimization model that could be used to create different candidate sets of investment options.

Planners from around the company converged at corporate headquarters to participate in three days of optimization, discussion, and generation of suitable and different courses of action that would reflect the two strategies in two different price environments (Low and High).

▸ **External Scenario vs Internal Requirement**

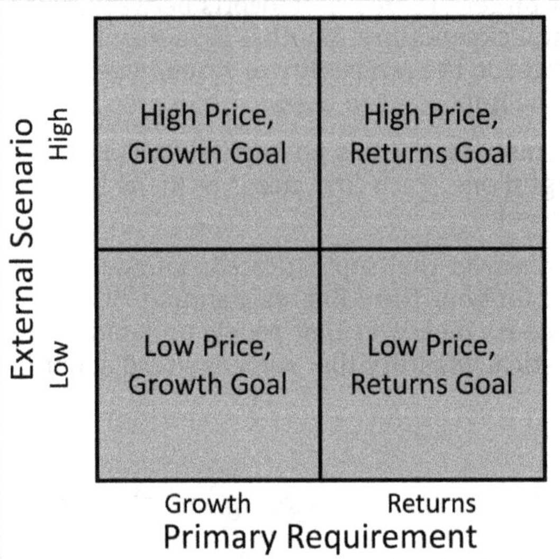

> *The analysts created multiple portfolios in each quadrant with different primary requirements. Executives were able to see and understand how the two main strategic goals would play out in different price environments.*

Nobody in the room had ever done this type of work, so there were many blind alleys and starts and stops, but at the end of three days, there were several possible plans in each of the four quadrants with different emphasis across the years.

The executives saw that for the company's portfolio of investment opportunities and assets and at the prices they had selected, the growth goal dominated the returns goal in almost every portfolio beyond a few years. The corporation decided to emphasize growth rather than returns.

This well-considered, high-quality portfolio decision transformed the firm and resulted in tremendous value growth. Oil prices over the next decade exceeded even the high-price sensitivity, and the company developed and purchased production at a low cost as prices soared.

Lessons Learned

1. Besides the multitude that did the work, this story has three heroes: the Corporate VP of Strategy who had the idea to do this test, the planner who had that optimizer model and worked it in front of a large crowd of highly critical people, and the GM of planning who brought all the planning managers together and made this happen.

2. Given the success of the process, the planning community believed that portfolio analysis and management had arrived. They developed a planning database that could be used for even a complex portfolio process. It would be ten years before the next crisis hit and the corporation did significant portfolio analysis like this again. But when it happened, they were prepared.
3. Because the optimization model was simple and linear, it ran fast. The planning team was able to test and learn rapidly. It was like an agile approach to planning. Although the results were never accurate enough for budgeting, the insights from these efforts were indispensable.

War Story – The Value of Tactical Optimization

The portfolio capabilities of a company had languished for some years. Only a small core of people used portfolio analysis regularly and had maintained the skills. But the infrastructure and data standards had been in place for a decade. Oil price was high, and management had not felt compelled to be super-disciplined or selective with the capital program.

When the price of oil fell from $110 to $30, compulsion kicked in in spades. Projects that "couldn't possibly be delayed" suddenly could. Entire programs and developments were canceled. The capital program had to be trimmed to extremes. But it had to be done in a way that did not destroy the company's long-term viability.

In the immediate aftermath of the price drop, headquarters created synthetic proxy alternatives, but business units provided better quality data over the next few years. Eventually, tactical optimization became a regular part of the business plan, and portfolio analysis and optimization sprang up in other places in the company.

Annual tactical portfolio analysis adds tremendous value and ability to achieve operational and financial performance goals

Lessons Learned

1. Never let a crisis go to waste.
2. The portfolio skills that had been preserved proved extremely useful in the teeth of the crisis. External consultants, even from the famous consulting companies, could not have stepped in and filled the gap.
3. Tactical portfolio analysis is valuable and, importantly, is seen as valuable.
4. Other optimization efforts that sprang up around the company added value and bolstered their portfolio function.

Detour – You Can Have Too Much of a Good Thing

Think of it this way. Suppose you have a project. It's not a good project; it's a great one. It has high value and a high rate of return in a stable fiscal and regulatory regime. It will cost a few billion dollars to develop, but it's a potential company-maker. You have one now. Would you like another one?

Of course.

Now, how about a third, fourth, or fifth one?

If you have five of them, now you are looking at putting over 10 billion dollars of investor money at risk before receiving a dime of revenue. And do you have the human resources to manage several large projects simultaneously? Of course, you could offset the projects to reduce the overlap, but then you are eroding value by delaying the projects. The bottom line is that too much of a good or even great thing can hurt you or inhibit the company's ability to achieve its targets.

Once you have a good queue of projects, adding to it may limit additional value creation.

(Loosely Adapted from a John Howell War Story)

Detail – Outputs of Optimization

Running a portfolio optimization gives two sets of output data: the summed or combined portfolio results and the candidate set of decisions that drove the results.

Decision-makers should focus on the portfolio results initially. You want them to determine their tradeoffs between the conflicting metrics in the frame. Although some will argue that leaders should know their tradeoff function before the work starts, that is often unrealistic.

Nobody knows their exact tradeoff between near-term and short-term, between capital discipline and growth. Only when they see real (simulated) results will they have a basis for even having that discussion.

It's like the test at the optometrist's office where they flip a lens, then flip it again. "1 or 2?... 2 or 1?..." You need more than that though.

You want more details, such as, "I like the growth in portfolio A, but B has a more doable capital program." Although you can guarantee they can't have everything for nothing, you now have critical information about a better outcome—a hybrid of A and B with a little more growth than B and a little less capital than A.

You may be familiar with the old joke, "How many psychologists does it take to change a light bulb?"

Answer: "Only one, but it has to WANT to change."

This is true of the discussion with your leadership too. Many firms have an internal negotiation process that governs budgeting and planning. Each manager controls a small part of the business, but nobody owns the overall plan. There is an implicit assumption that if each business unit comes up with its best plan, the comprehensive plan will be the best possible.

How do you have those conversations? They have to WANT to have those conversations. Then the portfolio analysts give them the information they need in a form they can and will digest. At one bookend is the live dynamic meeting with leadership participating in the comparison and one discussion of different portfolios. They could even talk about specifics for optimization and do the optimizations live. It is enormously powerful—and unusual—for a leadership team to be interested in that.

More realistic is putting together static slides with portfolio results and comparisons. The conversation will likely be less rich than the more dynamic meeting, but it is the process that many firms and leadership teams prefer.

I could include multiple line, bar, pie, and scatter plots here. But in the final analysis, the form of communication depends on your leadership team, their preferred form of receiving information, and the corporate culture of open discussion.

CHAPTER 10

Optimization Then Simulation

Optimization followed by Monte Carlo simulation takes the results from optimization in the above section and shows ranges of outcomes and probabilities. It adds a simulation process to the end of your optimization. This gives additional insights into your plan. It could allow you to say something like, "Our plan will double our mean earnings in five years. However, there is only a 25% chance that we will achieve our minimum production target. In addition, our earnings have a 40% probability of being negative three years from now."

As a general guideline, if the model is complex, it takes more than the blink of an eye to calculate a solution, has many potential decisions (more than 200–300), or if the model inputs can't be meaningfully constrained, optimization then simulation is a good approach. For smaller, simpler, faster models that can be constrained, stochastic optimization may work.

A straightforward approach was described in the Simulating Plan Biases section. In that case, it simulated the simple rollup without any synthetic portfolio decisions. The same process can be applied to optimized portfolios with virtual decisions already applied.

▸ Portfolio Selector Focus on Optimization Then Simulation

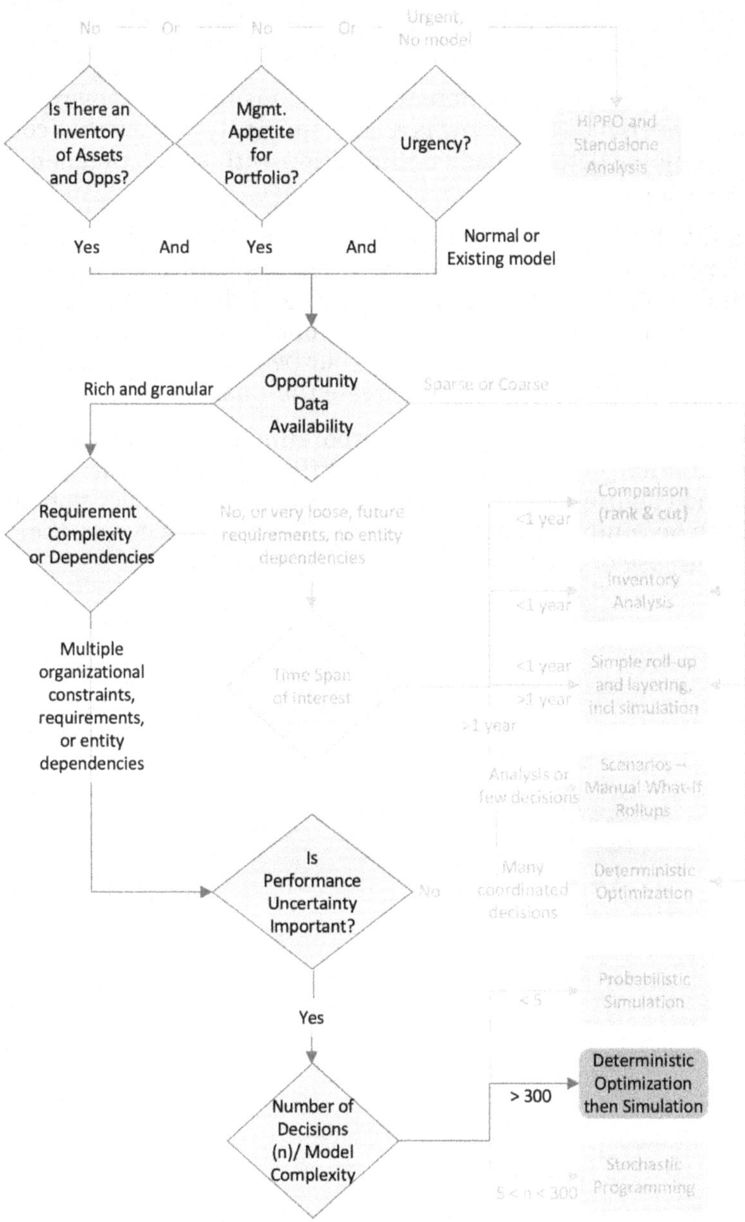

Optimization followed by simulation is a somewhat clunky hybrid between deterministic and stochastic optimization. It's a two-step process that requires deterministic optimization to set the candidate set, then simulation to see the range of outcomes from those decisions. Although cumbersome, it is a good option when the working inventory of decisions is large, or the simulation runs slowly.

It may be possible to use your Excel optimization file for simulation. However, the probabilistic routines add complexity and additional code to your model. It is often best to keep them as separate models but maintain similar formats for data and portfolio decisions.

Having different models for different calculations requires moving your data between models. Below is a data and analysis flow that could be used to combine deterministic optimization with simulation and result in a final plan.

Following this flow, your optimization and simulation models would contain the same input data. Virtual decisions are passed from the optimization model to the simulation model, and then both models feed the analysis of candidate sets. Finally, once you have a candidate set that meets your needs, you sharpen your pencil and incorporate any specific calculations you need to create the final answer.

Production modeling is simple, but incorporating other considerations like price variation, correlations between different parts of the business, and compressing and expanding production and development accounts can be computationally expensive. Keep a close eye on the scope and purpose of the model—it's easy to go overboard.

▸ **Process Flow for Optimization Then Simulation**

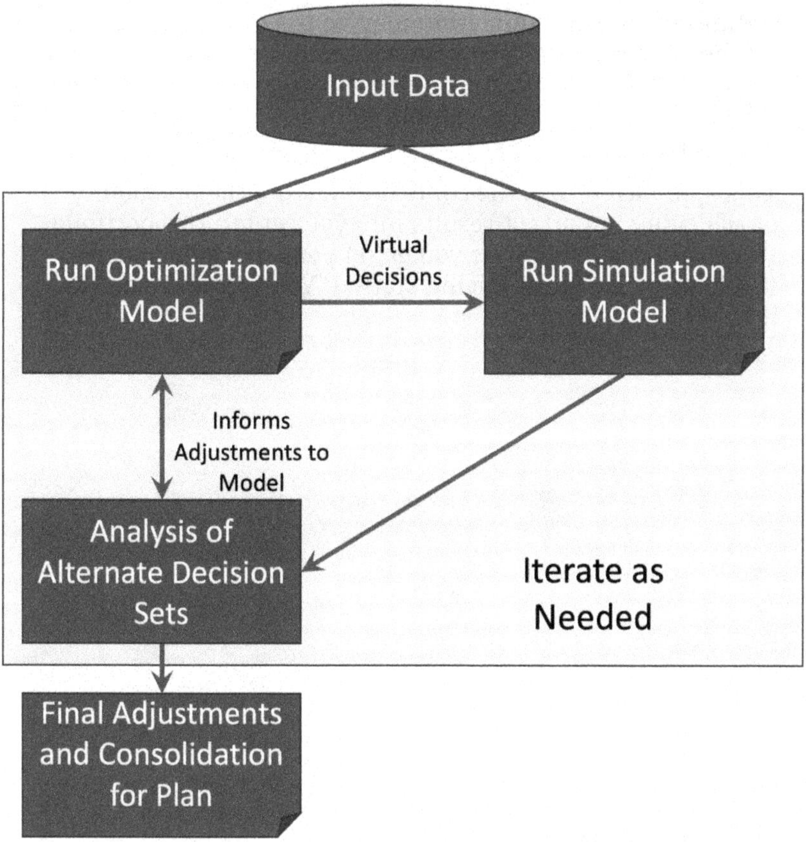

> *Be sure to use the same primary input data for the two models. The simulation model requires probabilistic information in addition to what's needed in the optimization model. The optimization model drives the decisions; the simulation model shows the range of outcomes. The models may be in the same file or not, depending on the platform and your tolerance for model complexity.*

Optimization then Simulation does not "optimize" probabilities, but it does help you understand outcome probabilities after correcting for risk and bias. If the likelihood of achieving specific targets is a key performance indicator, this is a good approach for large models and problems.

Key Takeaways

1. Optimization then Simulation may be the best analysis that can be done practically in your situation. Specifically, taking the next step to stochastic optimization may be impossible if your models are large, complicated, and have many decisions.
2. This approach brings the context of testing the probability of achieving important results into your enterprise portfolio results. If this is as far as you go on your portfolio journey, it is better than never having started. You will make better-informed decisions.

CHAPTER 11

Optimizing Uncertainty (Stochastic Programming)

Optimizing uncertainty can take two broad forms. The first is to use reasonable proxies for risk and treat the problem as linear (covered here). The second is to use stochastic optimization general solvers.

Optimizing Uncertainty is the third jump in the portfolio analysis techniques. Stochastic programming is a logical next step once you have used simulation and optimization. However, there is a learning curve when creating and using these models. That learning curve for both analysts and decision-makers is the third jump.

Stochastic Optimization

Stochastic optimization is the step beyond "Optimization Then Simulation." It is a simulation in conjunction with optimization. Instead of providing the results of an already-developed plan like "this plan will double our earnings growth, but there's only a 25% chance of achieving that target," we can create a set of decisions that will maximize our NPV while at the same time giving us an 80% chance of doubling our earnings in five years.

▸ Portfolio Selector Focus on Stochastic Optimization

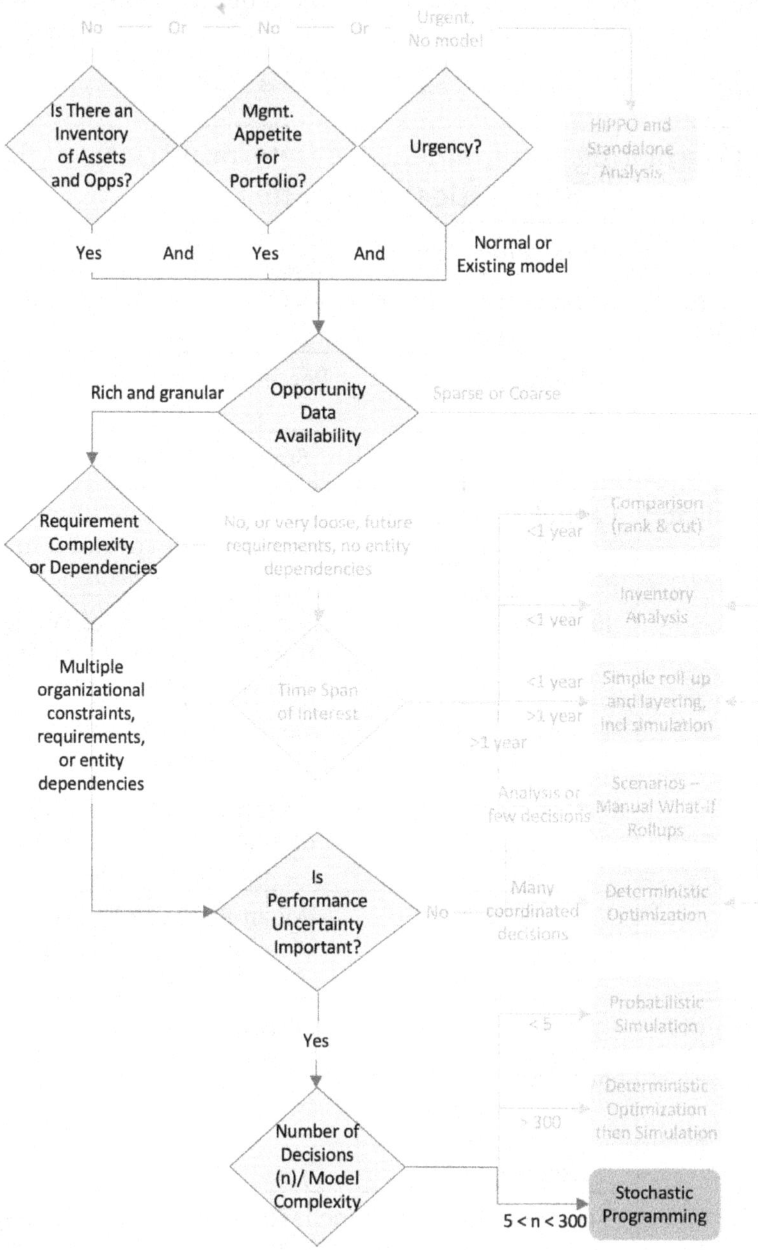

Stochastic optimization is the most challenging technical method we will discuss. It's better than Optimization-then-Simulation generally because it can seek probabilities explicitly. Stochastic optimization may not scale well to large problems. In the chart above, n is the number of variable decisions (adjustables).

The form is similar to any optimization, but the specification of requirements differs. Also, constraints on the input decisions become especially important.

▸ Contrasting Requirements for Deterministic and Stochastic Optimization

Contrasting Requirements in Deterministic vs. Stochastic Optimization		
	Linear/Non-Linear	**Stochastic**
Objective Function	Deterministic NPV or Score	Mean NPV, Percentile NPV
	Minimize Cost	Percentile Cost, Probability Cost
		Standard Deviation NPV
Requirements	Capital Expenditure by Year	Percent probability of surpassing the mean for any of those measures
	Production By Year	Mean Production, Probability of Achieving a Production level or growth rate
	Resource Adds	Mean adds, Probability of achieving
	Reserve Replacement	Mean adds, Probability of achieving, Reserves to Production ratio
	ROCE	Mean ROCE, Probability of achieving (need price/earnings uncertainty)
Constraints	Standard Business Logic	
	For linear, constraint expression is the same as requirements	
	For non-linear and stochastic optimization, linear constraints on decision inputs are needed to limit the solution sets	

Optimization parameter categories stay the same, but stochastic optimization allows objective functions and requirements to be expressed as statistical functions.

Linear problems are solved quickly using fast algorithms that parameterize the model and narrow the solution space analytically. Many non-linear, and especially stochastic programming problems, do not have this luxury.

They rely on an intelligent trial-and-error approach. For stochastic programming, the computer sequence looks something like the following:

1. Initialize the problem.
2. Select a candidate set (a miracle occurs) using the solver's algorithm and any saved data while honoring input constraints.
3. Simulate the model with as many trials as specified.
4. Determine if the solution is feasible (requirements satisfied).
5. Record the objective function and other relevant data.
6. Record the candidate set used.
7. If end conditions are met, then stop. Otherwise, go back to step 2.

Step 2 refers to the solver's algorithm. There are many algorithms available to generate the candidate sets to test. A full description of them is outside of the scope of this book.

Trial and error with large data sets could mean, effectively, an infinite number of possible solutions, so it behooves you to limit the potential candidate sets for the optimization tool. This is why constraints are so important. Constraints on the input decisions can significantly reduce the amount of solution time by eliminating consideration of cases outside the constraints.

Constraints and Requirements

Earlier in the book, we defined constraints as applied to the inputs while requirements are on the outputs. This is the payoff.

For example, consider a binary selection of 50 entities. Each one can be selected or not. The total number of possible solutions is 2^50 > 1 quadrillion possible combinations. Your answer set must contain no more than four entities.

Without constraints on the possible inputs, the world is its oyster. It may, for example, select 40 entities, run all the simulation trials, save the answers, add it to its database of solutions, **then** reject the answer because it violated the requirement of more than four entities selected. It would take until the heat death of the universe to be sure you have found an optimal or even feasible solution.

By entering constraints on the inputs, the solution set will be significantly reduced. Suppose you set the condition to select no more than 4 of the 50 at a time, perhaps because of personnel constraints. Your model will know not to consider all the quadrillion potential solutions but only the 251,176 possible solutions that are within the constraints. In other words, this constraint removes 99.99999998% of solutions that are not feasible. It's still a significant problem, but the algorithm can narrow that down much quicker.

Types of Problems

Stochastic programming may be appropriate when your frame includes the probability of something. Stochastic programming works best when models are not too large (less than 200–300 decisions) and can be well-constrained. If this is not possible, it may be better to try optimization followed by simulation.

There are broadly three flavors of stochastic programming: i. uncertain environment, ii. uncertain decision outcomes and effects, iii. removable uncertainty (recourse decisions).

i. In the uncertain environment style, the uncertainties are independent of the decisions. The simulation is done once, and then the outcome is parameterized. The optimization engine structures the problem and can solve it quickly. Even though simulation is involved, the optimization engine may exploit the underlying structure for efficient solving.

ii. When there are uncertain decision outcomes and effects of sequential decisions in play, the problem becomes too complex to simplify. The optimization tool will rely on a brute-force simulation and optimization approach.

Approach ii is the most general and can also be quite slow. Practically speaking, you should structure your problem as required, solve it with what you have (your tool might be able to structure it better), and if it takes too long, consider ways to restructure it or use a different optimization tool.

iii. Recourse decisions flip the order of decisions and uncertainties. Rather than making a decision, then simulating the outcome, recourse decisions simulate an outcome, then optimize decisions. This approach is most useful for standalone real-options analysis. It is a way to place a more realistic value on an uncertain asset or set of decisions with future flexibility. Effectively, the recourse decision approach builds a cloud of possible outcomes, then optimizes each scenario. This then shows the value of managerial flexibility.

As uncertainties narrow based on additional information, our view of an investment will change. We often need to make irrevocable decisions before resolving uncertainties, but many decisions based on the outcomes remain. Recourse optimization provides a means to estimate the value before the fact, incorporating the optionality inherent in the opportunity.

Recourse optimization sets up a two-stage simulation. The first stage contains the uncertainties that will be better resolved as you make future decisions. The next step optimizes the decisions with resolved uncertainties and simulates the remaining uncertainties.

For those who have little desire to dig into the guts of different types of stochastic portfolio optimization, the second case—the brute force method—is the most generalized. Frontline Systems (solver) and Crystal Ball with the OptQuest add-in are examples of tools that can handle this type of optimization.

Stochastic Programming Takes Practice

Standard deterministic linear programming is tricky. It requires a different way of thinking about strategic planning and value. Stochastic programming takes that one step further. Some or many problems can ultimately be solved using deterministic approaches, even though they appear to be stochastic. That should not stop you from trying these approaches.

The combination of optimization and simulation is more than most people are interested in even trying to grasp. As such, you may be well advised to treat stochastic programming as a skunkworks problem, show people the portfolio results and virtual decisions, but leave the black magic out of the picture.

Specific Use Case Examples

Oil Exploration

A. Given an inventory of 50 wildcat wells, what is the best program to select this year that has a 90% probability of exceeding our resources-discovered target this year?

You could use the following parameters:

1. Objective: Mean NPV.
2. Requirement: Probability >= 90% of exceeding resource discovery target this year. You may also wish to consider probabilistic production targets for future years.
3. Constraints: Exploration drilling budget of $200 million, no more than ten wells.

B. Exploration can take years to progress from geological concept to drillable prospect. Along the way, there are likely to be bid rounds and data acquisition. One challenge in exploration is developing enough of an inventory of opportunities to maintain a proper flow of wells. This exploration assembly line or factory is always tricky to model well. Still, as discussed previously, Value of Information (VoI) concepts can be part of the exploration value proposition.

Acquiring information across an immature area seldom adds to this year's drilling queue but may be a big part of your future program. Likewise, drilling in areas with the potential to upgrade prospects can bolster the future prospect queue. If you care about creating the chain of future wells, this should be a consideration in your exploration portfolio work.

You could use the following parameters:

1. Objective: Mean NPV.
2. Requirement: Probability >= 75% of exceeding resource discovery target this year.
3. Constraints: Future drilling queue will be 80% full over the next three years. (Any extra can be generated through ongoing activity and potential farmins.

Divestitures

This example has been expanded into a fictional case study. See Selecting Divestiture Candidates Using Stochastic Programming.

Which opportunities should we put on the market to achieve a > 90% probability of attaining public divestiture sales targets next year?

You could use the following parameters:

1. Objective: Mean NPV = Expected Sales Price - Asset NPV Value.
2. Requirements: Probability >= 90% that total deals closed next year exceed $2 billion.
3. Constraints: We can pursue the divestiture of 5 or fewer opportunities simultaneously.
4. Working inventory: Identified assets currently being considered for divestiture.

Key Takeaways

1. Stochastic Optimization is the bookend on the completeness scale of portfolio analysis. It requires specialized knowledge of programming tools and is overkill in most situations. But if you need it, you need it.
2. Stochastic optimization helps you find solutions that maximize the likelihood of hitting targets. This approach takes you out of the context of relying on averages and into the world of probabilistic thinking. If your portfolio journey takes you here, congratulations. You will make better-informed decisions.

Frontline's Description of Three Types of Probabilistic Optimization

Frontline Systems created the Solver tool that is used in Excel. They also have a full suite of optimization and simulation tools. They describe three different classes of Probabilistic Optimization as follows. Thanks to Frontline for granting permission to use their text in this book.

"In some models, the uncertainty or variation in the parameters may be small enough to be ignored, or it may be sufficient to address it using the sensitivity reports or parametric analysis covered earlier in this course. However, in some business cases, the uncertainty is so large that it is a major feature of the problem, and thus it is important to incorporate the uncertainty directly into the model.

[A] "In many real-world problems, the uncertainties being modeled are independent of the decision variables. For example, in a crop planning model where the acres to plant of different crops are decision variables, and the rainfall in a future period is an uncertainty, the uncertainty is independent of the decisions (i.e. the rainfall is not dependent on how much of each crop is planted). *Stochastic optimization* is the perfect tool for these problems.

[B] "In other real-world problems, the uncertain parameters being modeled are dependent on the decision variables – they change if the decisions change. For example, in a market response model that includes competitor actions in a future period, where your product prices are decision variables, and your competitors' product prices are uncertainties, it is quite likely that the uncertainties will depend on the decisions. As described in the next section, stochastic optimization cannot be used in the presence of decision-dependent uncertainties. Instead, another feature of Analytic Solver Platform, called *simulation optimization*, must be used.

[C] "In some real-world problems, we are uncertain about the value of a parameter today, and we will remain uncertain about its value in the future; we have to make decisions in the presence of this uncertainty. In other real-world problems, we are uncertain about the value of a parameter today, but we will know its value with certainty at some point in the future. In such cases, we might be able to make some decisions 'here and now before the uncertainty becomes known, while other decisions can be made on a 'wait and see' basis, after the uncertainty is known. Such models require the use of *recourse decisions*, which are included with Analytic Solver Platform but are outside the scope of this course."

Author Commentary

Real options analysis is described in several ways. One of the descriptions is to incorporate managerial flexibility explicitly. Modeling recourse decisions is an interesting method to quantify option value. Recourse decision modeling recognizes that there is uncertainty inherent in the outcomes of actions. We adjust when those outcomes are not precisely the same as our expectations or hopes.

In A and B above, decisions are made, then stuff happens. In C, recourse modeling, stuff happens, then decisions are made. Recourse decision modeling first runs the uncertainties, then optimizes as if those uncertainties were resolved as shown in the model.

The Flaw of Averages

The "Flaw of Averages" by Dr. Sam Savage is an excellent read, and the author has many stories that illustrate concepts in human terms.

Dr. Savage tells the story of a factory considering an expansion. They believe the market will be between 50 and 150 widgets per day. The boss says I need a number, so they settle on 100, the mean.

▸ A Normal or Bell Curve of Outcomes

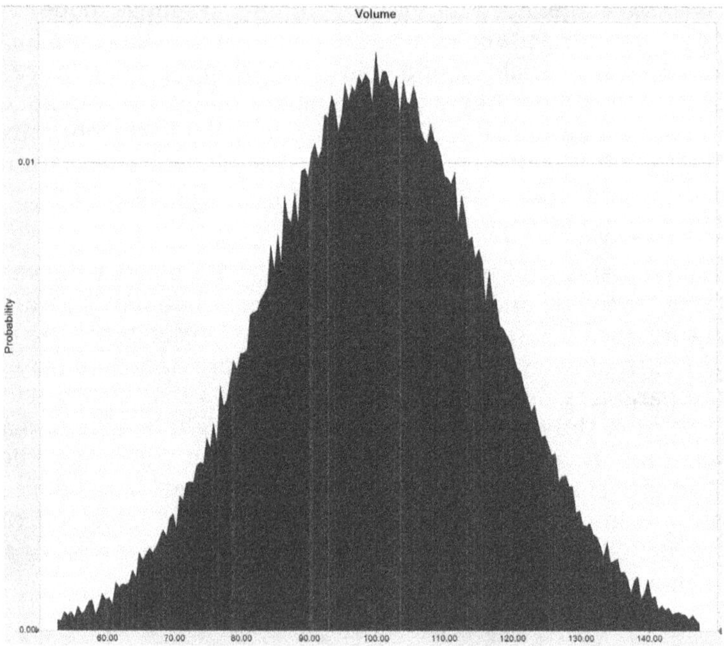

Start with the concept that a single number does not represent the full range of outcomes.

They build the expansion with a capacity of 100. But the expansion never achieves average production of 100. When the factory is down for maintenance or demand slacks off temporarily, there is no production. Once maintenance is complete, or when the demand has temporary peaks, they do not have the capacity to over-produce.

▸ Truncate the Bell Curve to Reflect a Capacity Decision

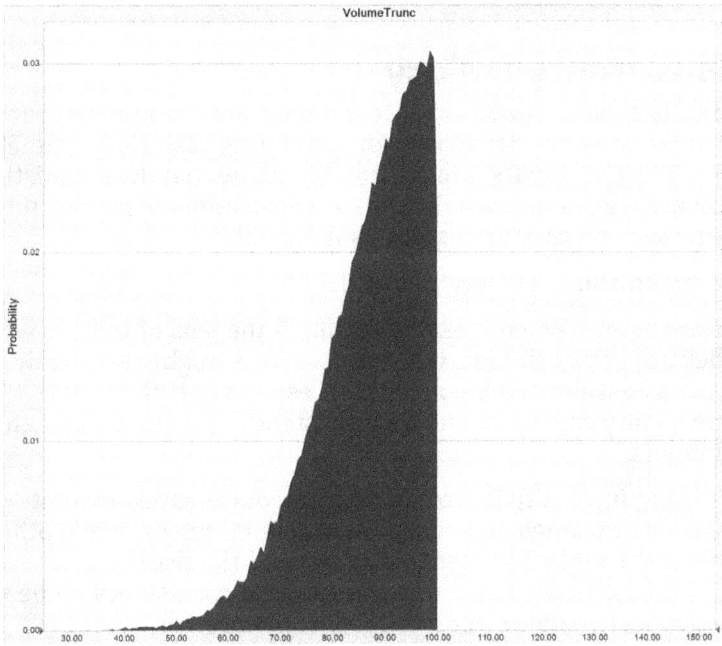

Making a decision changes the range of outcomes. The mean demand was 100 before making the capacity decision. Once the capacity decision is made, in this case, it removed the upside obviously but also reduced the mean production because of downtime and periods of low demand.

The point is that once you make a capacity decision, you have removed the upside that a larger facility would provide. Of course, you've also spent less on the facility, reducing the downside.

What should the facility size be then? As always, it depends on many factors. The marginal cost of capacity, how much the firm is willing to risk on the investment, the nature of their demand probability distribution, the nature of the product, and what the firm is trying to accomplish are essential factors.

Facility capacity decisions fit nicely into a probabilistic portfolio framework too. You can have single-phase expansion, or you can consider multiple phases, so build a first phase with a capacity of 60 (which reduces both downside and upside), but plan for a second phase for additional capacity if demand is higher. These two distinct decisions can be programmed into a portfolio model as mutually exclusive alternatives.

Most importantly, your assessment models must reflect the removal of parts of the distribution based on your decisions. Always make these decisions with your eyes open and an understanding of the consequences.

The Consistency Fallacy

Consistency is always a good start. It is a minimum requirement for doing portfolio analysis. Standards for generating cash flow estimates, including consistent inputs, are critical. We know that deterministic results are not a good forecast, but we use deterministic models for many purposes, and they are useful. Is it enough?

Are there circumstances where the model breaks?

Consider two assets. When looked at through the lens of today's oil prices, they are pretty similar. Outside observers might reasonably say that the assessments are comparable, especially if they have undergone quality control to ensure consistency of methodology and standard inputs.

Now let's bring in sensitivity to the oil price. Some assets exhibit relatively stable earnings and cash flow across oil prices, while others don't. This is driven by the cost to produce and the fiscal regime. Changes in the external environment mean that consistency alone may not lead to robust analyses and desirable outcomes.

Although the projects are equal at today's prices, if the price increases, the dashed-line project with higher sensitivity will be more valuable, while the solid-line project will be worth more at a lower price. It is essential to recognize that if there is bias or uncertainty in your price forecasts, consistency may not be enough to deliver a good outcome.

▸ **Relative Asset Outcomes May Change with the External Environment**

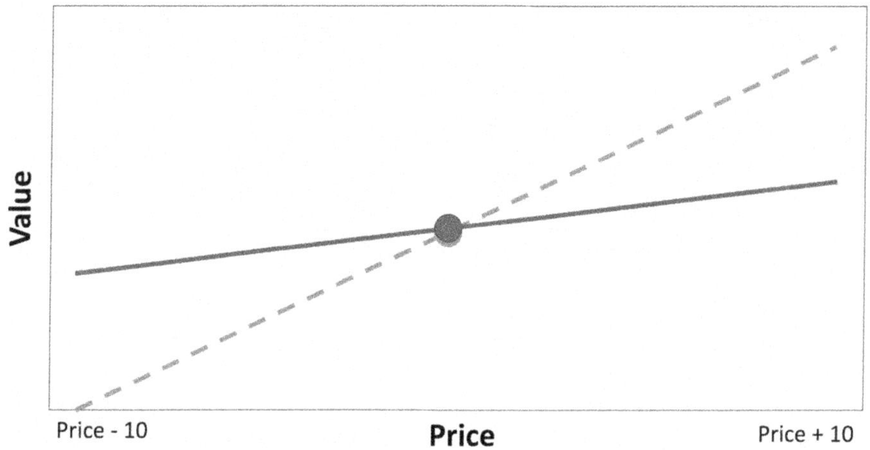

> *Consistency by itself does not achieve good decision-making. You can be perfectly consistent by choosing any one of the three price bases (Price, Price +10, Price -10). Choosing the dashed-line asset, then having a price drop would be a consistent decision with a bad outcome, if the price goes up, it's a great outcome. The solid-line asset provides a relatively consistent result. If the consistency of the result is important, there may be another metric you care about—the first derivative of value with respect to price.*

Dealing with his type of situation is a challenge. My rule of thumb is that if prices are at historic highs, you should overweight assets like the low-slope project. If prices are at historic lows, go for the high-slope project. Beyond that, unless you have a compelling reason to believe in the direction of the price, consistency is good enough for most purposes.

CHAPTER 12

Sparse Data Techniques

The sparse data techniques are variations of Inventory Analysis, Opportunity Cost Analysis using Deterministic Optimization, and Simple Rollups.

Let's discuss sparse data. In many cases, especially when contemplating the purchase of assets owned by others, there is often little detailed information available. Sometimes you don't even have a fiscal regime or commercial terms for a cash flow model. Fortunately, some info is usually available through public and private sources that can give at least a rough basis. Companies like Wood-Mackenzie or IHS Energy typically have reasonable estimates of discovered resource accumulations, including their productivity estimates and capital and operating expenditure.

You can perform stochastic operations, treating the known unknowns as uncertain variables. That may let you know if the standalone opportunity is even worth considering. But what else can be done?

If all you have is capital expenditures (CAPEX), operating expenses (OPEX), and production, you can compare the asset with your existing portfolio. You'll see how the opportunity compares on the cost and production sides. Inventory techniques can be a good start. It can also give you a first-pass earnings breakeven price.

The other simple thing is to add the opportunity to your time-series rollups to see the impact on your planned metrics.

The Opportunity Cost approach is more powerful and worth considering if you already have an optimization tool. You can see the impact of bringing the opportunity into the fold—even *without cash flow or NPV*. Exclude any cash flow information for the subject opportunity and run your optimizations with the opportunity locked in to see how much impact the opportunity has on the portfolio's value. It is often negative because funding for a zero NPV opportunity would displace positive NPV investments—a zero NPV opportunity hurts your portfolio because, in a capital-constrained world, you would have to delay better opportunities.

There are cases in which a zero NPV opportunity will add value to a portfolio. See the next War Story for details.

For more information about this type of optimization, see the Portfolio Specific Value section.

▸ Portfolio Selector Focus on Sparse Data Techniques

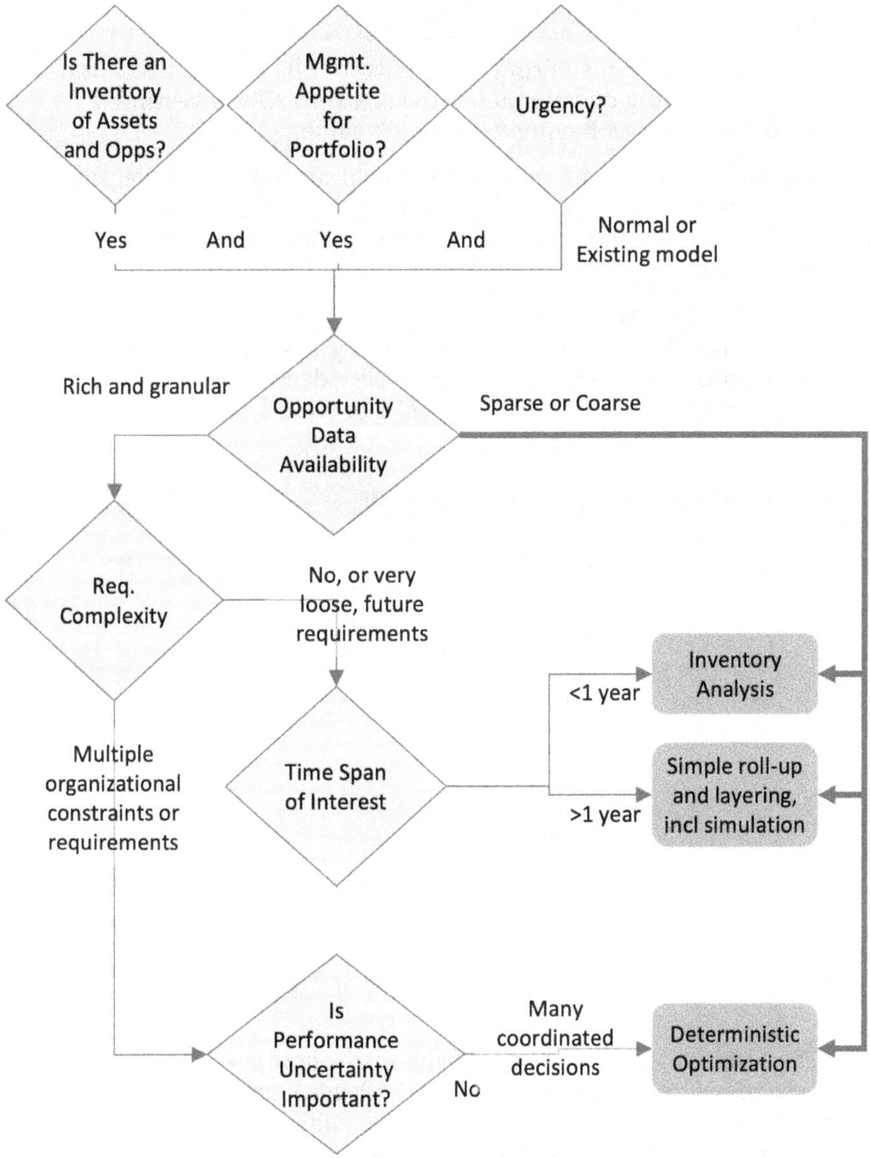

Often, data is sparse. Even so, there are still insights to be gained from portfolio. Inventory analysis with limited metrics, rollups, and even optimization can yield important insights.

War Story – How Can a Zero NPV Opportunity Possibly Have Value in a Portfolio?

A company was considering a divestiture. The project was large, but economically questionable. It was a zero NPV investment, but some saw it as having "strategic" value.

The business unit was reluctant to put it on the market because their guts told them it was still an important asset. They asked the portfolio team to look at the project from a portfolio perspective.

The portfolio specific value (PSV) of an NPV = 0 asset will almost always start at zero (on the right in the graph below) and go down from there. Locking in a zero-NPV decision can only take away from the better opportunities. You would expect to see a marginal value curve as below.

▸ **Standard Portfolio Specific Value (PSV) of an NPV = 0 Investment**

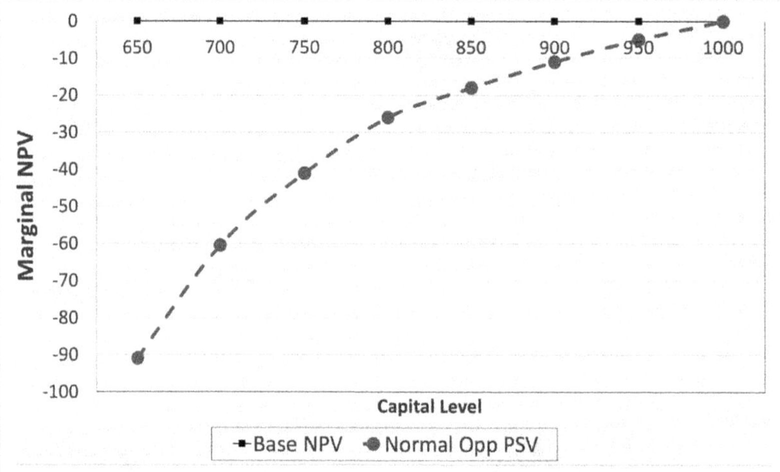

The dashed line is the difference between the base portfolios and portfolios with Normal Opp locked in. With adequate portfolio funding to do all projects (the rightmost portfolio), adding a zero NPV project does no harm. As the funding level decreases to the left, the zero-NPV project displaces positive projects. The more capital is reduced, the better the delayed projects, leading to a steeper downward slope.

In the case with entirely adequate capital, the opportunity adds no NPV. As the capital level decreases to the left, the opportunity erodes value.

But that's not what happened.

▸ PSV of a "Long-Term" NPV = 0 Investment Opportunity

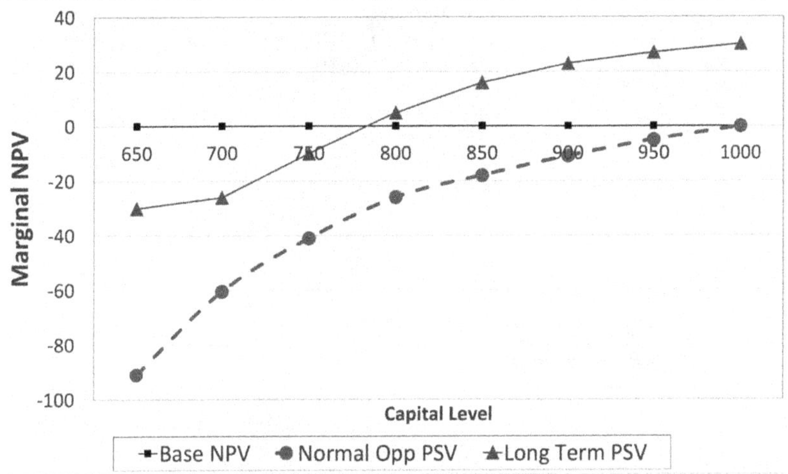

> *The upper, solid line (Long Term PSV) shows a long-term opportunity with an NPV of zero. It shows positive portfolio value despite its zero NPV. The company does not have adequate hydrocarbon resources to fulfill its long-term targets, so the base portfolio delayed some projects to hit growth targets. This would not likely happen in real life. Companies do what they have as fast as they can do it. Although not realistic, it is insightful—more hydrocarbons are needed to grow the business over the long term—if not from this project, another one.*

The opportunity depicted had a positive PSV for capital levels above 800 (see the graph above). How could this be happening (see the graph above)? Think about it and make a hypothesis before continuing.

In this case, there was a long-term production target. This particular asset had a long-term, steady production level. When the team created the base portfolio, although it could achieve the long-term production target, it had to delay projects, resulting in a decrease in NPV. Adding the project in question, those delayed projects could be executed sooner, increasing the portfolio NPV.

Lessons Learned

1. This is mathematical optimization; nobody would delay projects to hit some distant production target.
2. This analysis shows the impact a lack of a robust inventory of assets (future hydrocarbon production) can have on your activities.
3. Although this specific asset was not a keeper, it gave clues about the type of asset that would fit well.

4. The asset was divested. Some years later, the project ran into significant technical issues. Portfolio fit is just one of many inputs that should go into decision-making.
5. It may have occurred to you that this seems odd in the sparse data section. Here's the rub. Often, early in the evaluation of acquisition opportunities, we are asked for the portfolio fit of opportunities with little data. Maybe we have capital spending and production streams. We can leave off the cash flow (zero NPV) and assess the fit before the cash flow. This tells us how much drag (or benefit) the opportunity will exert on the portfolio. Ultimately, its NPV should exceed the opportunity cost drag for the acquisition to work.

Build Your Own

We have explained the Why and the What of building optimization tools but not the How. You have seen that modeling interactions are much more involved than comparison and simple rollup techniques. I believe that it is important that you build your own model at some point in your career for several reasons.

First, knowing a model's nuts and bolts is invaluable. It helps you understand the model's limitations and how to fix the model **when** it breaks or when you need to make changes.

Second, adapting someone else's model NEVER works. There are always nooks and crannies to trip you up, as well as model errors and undocumented assumptions. They are always there. Having confidence in a complicated model built by someone else is hard.

Third, you will improve your Excel skills.

Fourth, the satisfaction of DIY.

Fifth, this gives you an alternative to spending millions of dollars on an off-the-shelf tool that checks all the boxes but doesn't do what you want.

Finally, it gives you a *Jedi-Knight-builds-his-own-light-saber* credibility. You will see the fundamental simplicity of the model and that it will take only a few days to build it.

Not everyone wants to build a big spreadsheet from scratch. Contact me through my website at https://www.practicalportfoliomanagement.com if you wish to discuss further.

CHAPTER 13

Outputs and Visualization – Comparing Portfolio Strategies

Visualization of outputs is the final step in determining which tradeoffs are worth making. There is no objectively correct answer to this question; it varies by company, by the nature of its challenges, by shareholder needs, and by executive preferences.

On top of that, data visualization has two very different purposes: data analysis and exploration, and data presentation and communication. Those two purposes will be separated by a curation step where the analyst reduces the total possible portfolio candidates from many (perhaps hundreds or thousands) to 5-10 for leadership discussion.

The following is paraphrased from Juice Analytics https://www.juiceanalytics.com/writing/5-differences-between-data-exploration-and-data-presentation:

Visualizations and Purpose

Dimension	Analyst	Leadership
Audience	Data exploration - make hypotheses, analyze, repeat	Show results and conclusions, guided insights
Message	The journey is important. Goes down blind alleys	Avoid blind alleys, stay on track
Explanations	Data is self-explanatory to analysts	Diverse leadership teams may require grounding in the significance of metrics and results
Visualizations	Easy to create and modify, may include complex dimensionality	Simple and intuitive. No more than three dimensions, e.g., x, y, color
Goal	Ask better questions; learn the boundaries of performance and drivers	Answer specific questions; inform particular decisions. Gain strategic insights
Personal Interactions	Data clarification, organizing, and building relations. The analyst role is often solitary or a few people at most	Leadership discussions should be interactive and questioning. Displays that support a rich dialog and discussion is the goal

Juice Analytics has great explanations of visualization and purpose. They distinguish between exploring data and presenting it, with a happy place in the middle—data storytelling—for leadership exploration.

It may be possible to have a more interactive and detailed analyst-style discussion with leadership. In my experience, it is rare. Preparing and priming data and background can take a lot of time. But that interaction can also give insights to leadership that they could never achieve through a standard presentation.

Ultimately, executives should be able to see the results of different portfolio candidate sets and understand the tradeoffs between the key corporate drivers. That way, when they decide on a course of action, they know how much they are getting and how much they are giving up to pursue their targets.

Each executive will bring a point of view based on their specialty, knowledge, experience, and perspective of the external environment. It is best to have a decision team with the balance, experience, and expertise to understand the implications of the proposed tradeoffs to the company and shareholders.

There's no single way to do this, so we'll walk through a fictional case study.

Branco Petroleum: A Fictional Tactical Analysis Case Study

The asset data in this fictional case study are based on internally consistent but fictional models. The study depicts a company with various asset classes ranging from deep water to heavy oil to unconventional. The names of the assets and the company are fictional. The fictional data assumed an oil price of about $100 per barrel. All the characters are fictional and not based on anybody living or dead .(except one, yours truly, who is obsessive-compulsive about metrics). What'sBest! from Lindo Systems was the LP platform used in the case.

The Scenario

Branco Petroleum was preparing for its annual tactical portfolio analysis. They collected data on all their significant assets and some different project alternatives generated in their decision analysis process. Each business unit expressed through their submittals what they believed was the best alternative for their unit. The development scenarios were not forecasts but depicted "best-efforts" plans, assuming the projects and assets could get personnel, funding, and other resources needed to succeed. Branco had recently acquired companies with excellent projects but little funding, so the portfolio was heavy on projects. The company needed to assimilate the new assets into its portfolio plans.

Let's start with a rollup of the company based on its current assets and preliminary plans.

▸ Branco Petroleum Base Portfolio

Base Plan as Submitted

Portfolio	NPV8 ($MM)
Pf1	44,324
Pf2	46,231

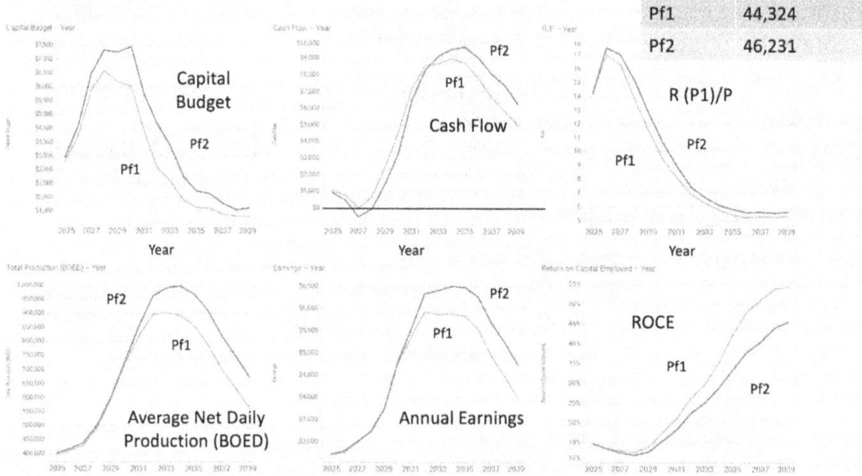

The base portfolio, as submitted by the business units, shows extreme growth in capital and production. Branco is opportunity-rich. Leadership must determine how much they can spend without overextending. They also see long-term challenges as their projects are developed. Portfolio 2 dominates Portfolio 1 in all measures except ROCE.

The two portfolios shown are the certain expenditures (Port 1) and certain expenditures plus risked actions taken as a consequence (Port 2). As we advance in this analysis, the lighter-colored line, Portfolio 2, will be considered the base case.

The initial pass from this opportunity-rich portfolio showed a considerable increase in capital expenditure with a corresponding increase in production. The leaders recognized that the company did not have the organizational capability to ramp up its capital expenditure as quickly as depicted. Worryingly, although the reserves-to-production ratio increased sharply, it also fell sharply. There were no solid plans to replace the hydrocarbon resources being produced or to expand those efforts as production increased.

They had the good kind of problem—they were opportunity-rich. If they pursued the SBU-recommended programs, they would see tremendous growth in production and value. They would also rapidly draw down their resource and reserve base and spend beyond their capacity, wasting funds and efforts.

The leadership team wanted to understand how much organic growth they could reasonably fund and how that would balance their desires for growth, capital discipline, and continuity.

The portfolio team went to work generating portfolios with different capital levels.

The data were loaded into the optimizer tool, and all business logic was set and checked. The portfolio analysts went to work. First, they manually entered the base plan decisions into the optimizer and saved that set of decisions and outcomes as the base plan. The Base Plan included only the expenditures that were certain to happen but did not include uncertain follow-on efforts. So, there were some pilot projects and feasibility studies but no uncertain success cases. They also built a case with the risked follow-up development. Those probabilities of success were generated using a standard tool developed by the corporation to ensure consistency.

Next, they developed a no-constraint maximization of NPV (Branco uses an 8% discount rate for portfolio work).

▸ Add a Maximum NPV Case

Base Plan as Submitted Pf2 and Max NPV Pf3

Portfolio	NPV8 ($MM)
Pf2	46,231
Pf3	46,494

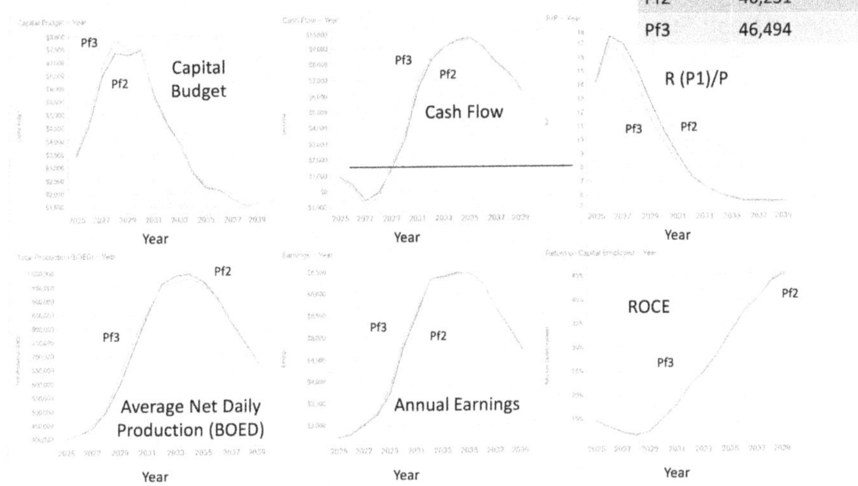

The analyst team developed a Maximum NPV case using their optimization tool. It is almost identical to the submitted case, except it requires more capital early on. This tells you that the SBUs' decisions are aligned with maximizing the NPV of their assets. That is normally good, but in an opportunity-rich company, it may cause problems with allocating people and funding.

We see little difference between the two cases overall. The main differences appear in the first three years of the plan. The max NPV case requires more capital and, therefore, has a worse negative cash flow in the early years. Over three years, the overall capital requirement doubles from about four to eight billion dollars per year in both cases. Production growth is enormous in both cases, increasing from about 400,000 barrels per day at the start to about 1,000,000 per day in ten years. Future cash flow and earnings are tremendous. Although the reserves-to-production ratio increases in the early years, it declines rapidly. There is no plan to replace hydrocarbon resources and reserves to ensure the firm's continuity.

From the portfolio analysis decision frame, the leaders knew that NPV, production growth, ROCE over the next five to ten years, and resource and reserve profiles were essential for the corporation. The board of directors had expressed concern about the potential of softening oil prices, so they also wanted to understand the corporation's sensitivity to a decrease in price.

The portfolio analysis team went to work. They first developed a case that kept cash flow over $500 million per year in all years. It improved the short term but made little overall impact compared to the Base and Max NPV Cases.

▸ Test a Cash Flow > $500 Million Case

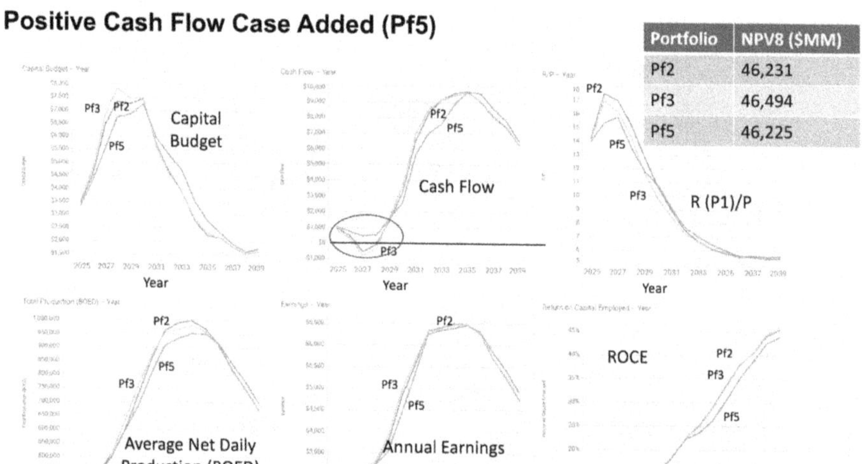

After Max NPV, the first case developed provided for $500 million cash flow in all years. It helps a little, but it is far from where Branco needs to be. The main distinction, which was a requirement of the optimization, is seen in the ellipse on the cash flow chart. Stronger medicine was needed.

Next, the team developed capital limitation cases in increments to $2.5 billion capital investment annually. They developed hybrid cases. In the end, they developed about 50 portfolios. While that was useful for their work, they knew they needed to curate to a manageable number for discussion with leadership. This view shows how the portfolios progressed as the analyst team worked through the different capital expenditure levels.

▸ **Multiple Capital Level Cases Developed**

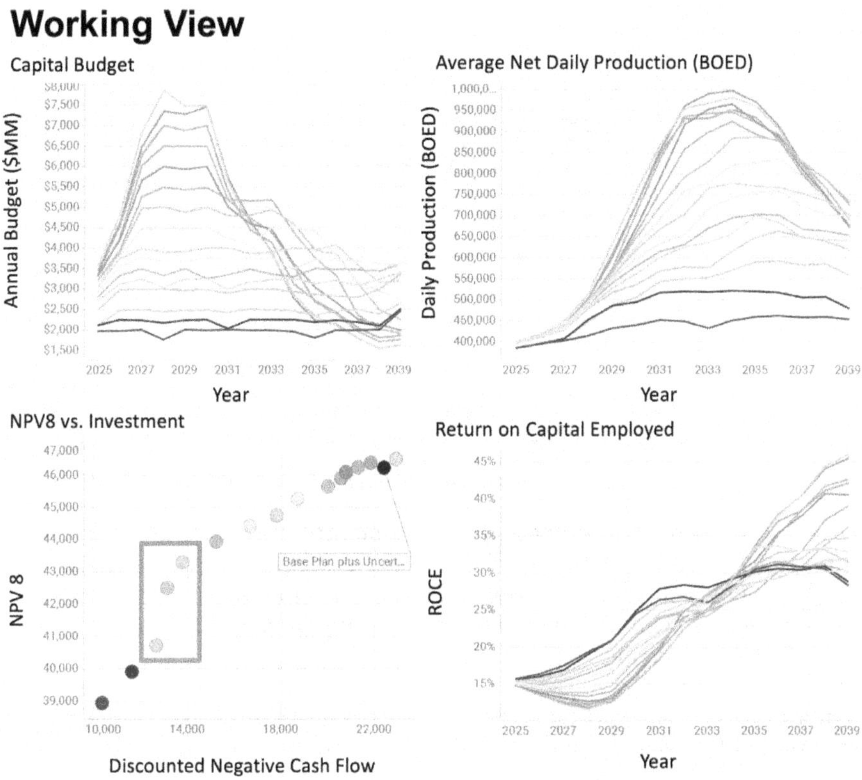

The working view showed the most critical time series and point data. The analysis team uses the sum of net negative cash flows across projects as the cost measure. Similar results are achieved with a budgeted capital perspective. The optimizations used budgeted capital, as shown in the capital budget display.

The Pareto frontier on the NPV vs. Discounted Negative Cash Flow graphic had an odd appearance. It is common for a string of similar portfolio optimizations to form a continuous line that defines the boundary between the possible and impossible. Slope changes are often not smooth because asset decisions can be lumpy. In this case, the points followed two distinct trends with a discontinuity inside the box above.

▸ **Pareto Frontier of Portfolios**

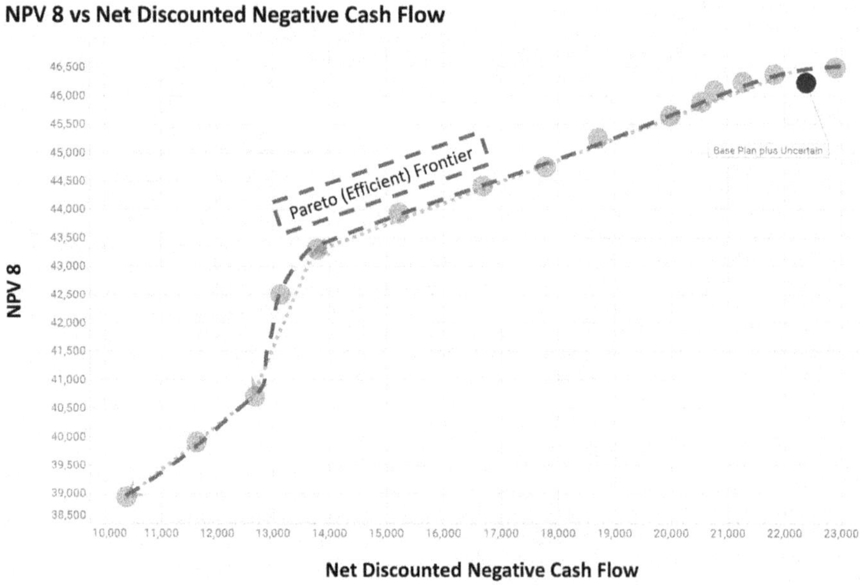

The development of different portfolios using capital expenditure as a limitation led to an unusual kink in the Pareto frontier. The cause of the kink was not clear from this display. The portfolio tool was configured to exaggerate significant changes by not including compensation for removing assets. In practice, they could sell interest in the asset.

Using Spotfire, when they select the portfolios of interest, they can also see which assets are included and whether development is delayed or rejected.

In the view below, the table on the right shows the in/out and delay decisions in two portfolios. The black cells with the number 10 towards the top show asset options not included in that portfolio candidate set. The cells with 0 towards the bottom indicate that the asset is selected with no delay—all other cells with numbers from one to nine show the years of delay before starting the investment. The higher the number, the less robust that entity alternative is in the portfolios.

We see several differences between portfolios 14 and 15. However, the big one that drives the discontinuity is removing the ShaleRes Basin asset. It is a sizable asset that requires large amounts of budget to finance. Compared with the other significant assets in the portfolio, this is the worst project remaining and must be removed to accommodate the required capital expenditure. Removing the ShaleRes Basin from the portfolio (without compensation) devastates long-term production and NPV.

▸ **Heat Map Shows the Source of the Kink**

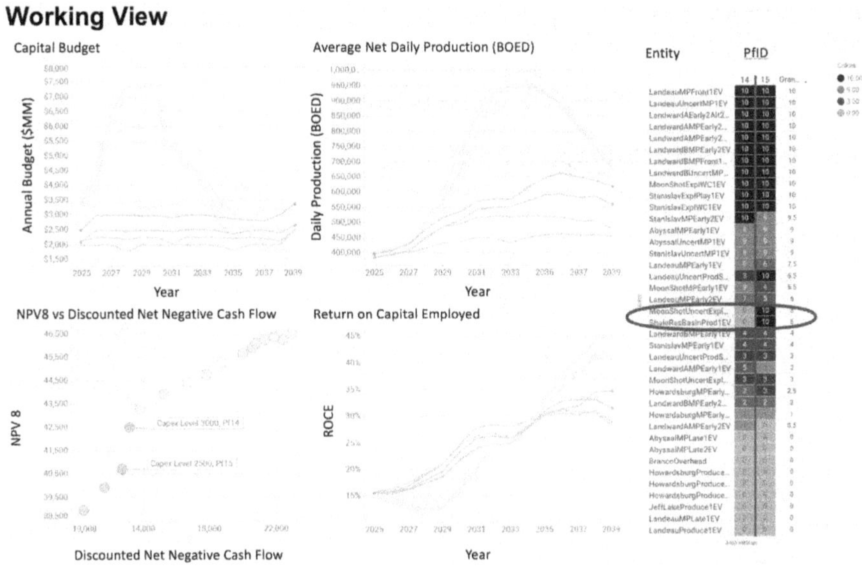

The heat map on the right shows the ShaleRes Basin asset being removed from portfolio 15. This causes a significant drop in value and production

Reaching the 2.5 billion dollar annual capital expenditure level and keeping the ShaleRes Basin asset in the portfolio will require a broader range of actions that would be taken on either the ShaleRes Basin (reducing the annual drilling program, reducing working interest) or other asset decisions.

This conundrum was presented to the CEO, who decided that lower capital programs were off the table and that portfolios below three billion dollars per year could safely be ignored for the upcoming discussions.

When doing portfolio work and using budget capital as the limitation, it is crucial to remember that budgeted capital is seldom the true constraining factor. Financially strong companies can get additional financing if they need it. Instead, capital expenditure is a visible component of reports to market and financial analysts, so being stingy with capital signals great virtue and hard-nosed business sense. More importantly, it acts as a proxy for project development capability. Given their available people, it helps them understand how much money the organization can spend intelligently.

The CEO wanted to see portfolios that increased capability at about 3% above the baseline, so they directed the portfolio team to include increases in capital across the relevant plan years. They felt that flat capex, while an interesting view, did not reflect reality as well as a capability growth scenario.

Additional Portfolios

The portfolio team developed about 50 more portfolios covering a full range of their key metrics.

▸ **Spaghetti Plots to Show Coverage of Tests**

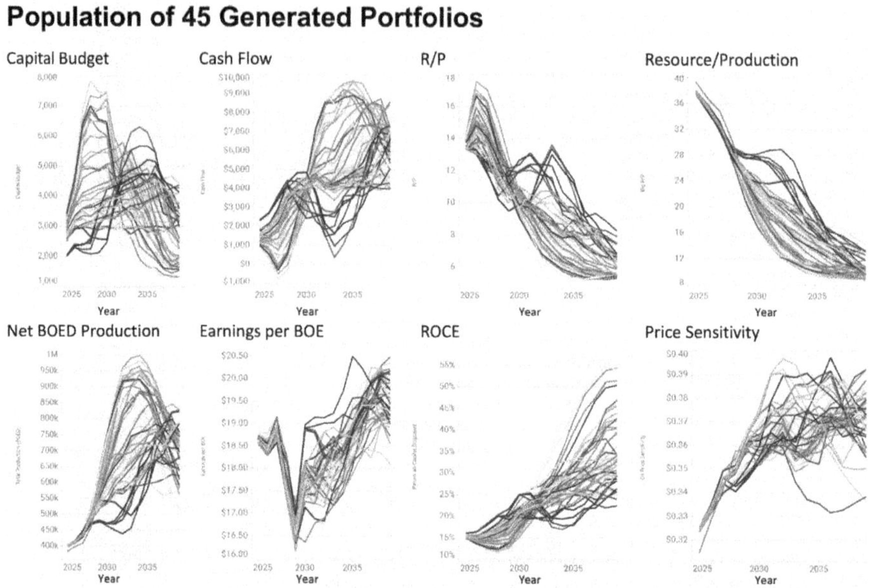

> *"Spaghetti" plots are useful but overwhelming. Given the asset flexibility in the portfolio tool, they show how much terrain the generated portfolios cover and reveal insights about the firm's full capabilities.*

These spaghetti plots were not helpful by themselves, but they show that the team has covered a wide range of outcomes for Branco's essential metrics.

The team selected a working view for the analysts to help them understand the generated portfolios and critical value tradeoffs.

The analysis team used the optimization tool to create other portfolios that put requirements on production levels, ROCE, and capital expenditures.

After eliminating the portfolios that rejected the unconventional play, the team also eliminated portfolios that showed extreme jumps in capital expenditure. In particular, they found that the portfolios constrained on ROCE in the early years needed to keep expenditures very low for several years and, in some cases, almost double expenditures overnight.

▸ **Curated Portfolios for Analyst Consideration**

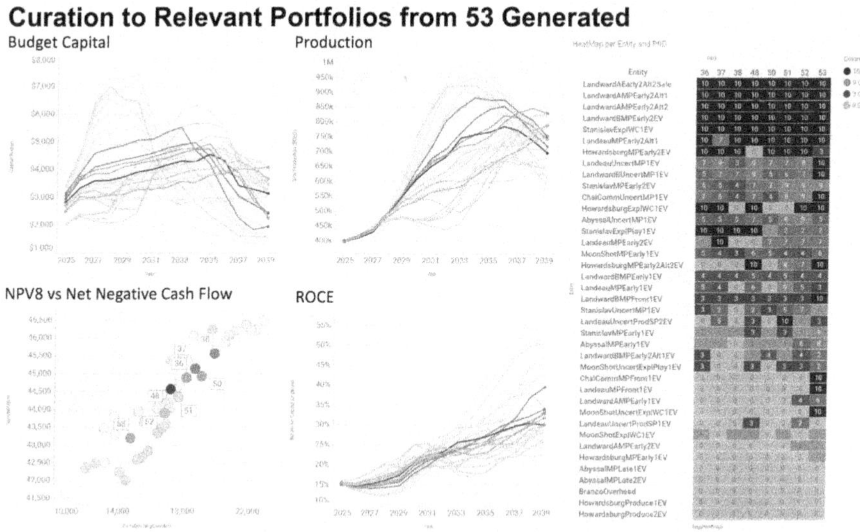

> *The team selected the most relevant capital levels, sampled from the production profiles, and analyzed several ROCE-focused portfolios. From the set of 53 candidate portfolios, the portfolio team selected eight for discussion at the next leadership meeting.*

The Next Meeting

The analysis team used the working view as a prompt for leadership team discussion. Those tradeoffs could be seen directly with capital, production, and ROCE as the primary metrics. Other, less critical metrics could also be examined as a tiebreaker or for cases of significant damaging unintended consequences.

Although the leadership team was generally optimistic about the industry's health and overall economy, there was significant concern about the potential for a softening market and oil prices.

▸ Further Curation for Management Discussion

Working View of Eight Curated Portfolios

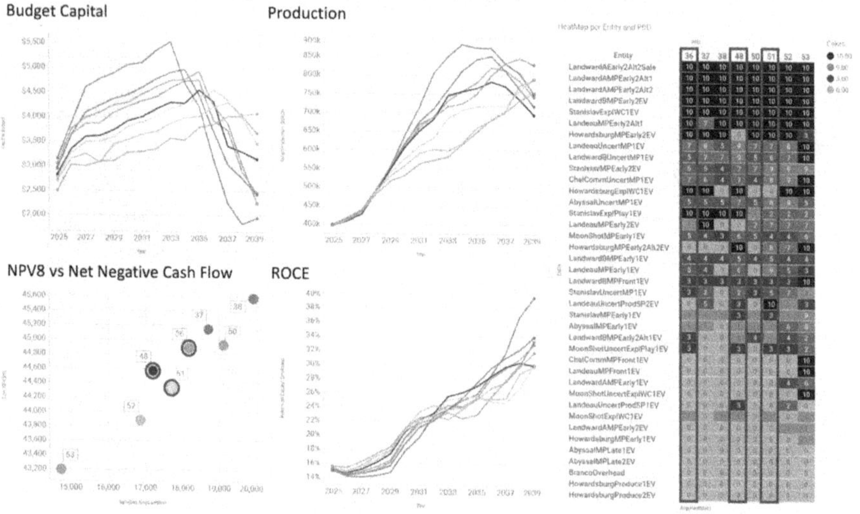

The portfolios for final consideration provided diverse perspectives on the possibilities, including NPV tradeoffs associated with achieving different metrics.

The leadership team examined and discussed the above working view and others they had been given on paper. They decided that achieving substantially higher ROCE with their asset base and legacy decisions would be prohibitive. The moderate path would be most appropriate for the forward plan. It balanced the need for returns and reduced the corporate sensitivity to oil prices.

They made several observations looking at the portfolio information.

1. The portfolios showed different performances, but relatively few decisions caused those differences. The heat map view shows about twenty assets driving the differences. Look for changes across the columns.
2. The NPV ranged from \$45.6 billion to \$43.2 billion NPV at an 8% discount rate.
3. Given the assets' decision flexibility, there was little room to increase production in the next three years.
4. The difference in ROCE in the early years could be four percentage points and has a negative correlation with capital budget levels.
5. 2025 shows low capital requirements, but they immediately ramp up because of the rich queue of projects.
6. The firm had enough hydrocarbon resources to grow at 5% for years. Portfolios 51, 52, and 53 all maintained that level of growth but with a decrease in NPV. Good projects were delayed to finesse the timing and achieve that growth rate.

7. Faster growth would result in higher NPV. The highest capital programs with the highest production growth had the highest NPV.
8. Faster growth would require additional hydrocarbon resource capture efforts, and leadership would need to decide where best to direct those efforts. In the fastest-growing portfolio, investment opportunities declined precipitously in 2033.
9. The highest ROCE portfolio had the slowest growth and lowest total production. Assets needed to be shed to exceed 18% ROCE in the next four years.
10. ROCE goes way up, and capital goes way down in the later years. This "planner's droop" is indicative of a bare long-term cupboard. By 2035, little would be left to develop, even at a measured pace.
11. Leadership noticed that the portfolios with the harshest capital constraints also had the highest sensitivity to oil prices. Even though the absolute bang per buck of those portfolios was high, they reduced NPV while at the same time exposing the firm to drops in oil prices, (as well as lost revenue from delayed production should oil prices fall).

Some companies try to take a do-everything approach. It can make sense when opportunities are limited. When there is a rich project queue—more projects than the ability to do them all—prioritization choices must be made. Failure to make those choices will lead to underperformance. Developing a queue of potential farm-outs of Branco assets seems to make sense. Projects will be deferred, like it or not, without ready project capacity. But selling interest has its own risks. You are exchanging potential future value for cash in hand. If prices go up, you look like a fool; if they go down, you look like a genius. Not investigating those alternatives is ignoring a potentially important choice.

A. The executives charged the portfolio team with developing a case with the CFO and business unit leadership to achieve a production level of more than 650,000 BOED per day barrels per day by 2032. However, they wanted the total discounted capital to remain under or close to $18 billion while keeping the annual budgeted capital under $3.5 billion per year plus escalation at 3%.
B. They also asked the human resources department and the project functions to develop a staffing plan to achieve the ramp-up in project work.
C. It was apparent that Branco bit off more than it could chew. While its acquisition efforts were wildly successful, maximizing the value of its assets would require monetizing some of the projects to operators with the organizational capability and ability to fund their share.

D. Business unit leaders would put together a short list of assets in which they could sell some working interest and operatorship. This way, they could at least partially monetize some time-delayed projects while accelerating development.
E. Midstream and trading departments needed to be prepared to handle the volume growth.
F. Exploration and M&A/Business Development needed to develop plans to increase the acquisition and discovery of resources to support longer-term growth. At over 600 MBOEPD, they would require resource additions of about 200-250 million barrels annually.
G. The finance department would develop a white paper to consider changing the efficiency metric to one that is more consistent with financial theory and would be straightforward to implement.
H. Given the biases inherent in the plan submissions, the leaders understood fully that this rolled-up set of entities did not represent a forecast. At the same time, they believed they had a tremendous story to tell shareholders and stock market analysts. The portfolio team would develop a model to remove significant biases using a combination of sensitivity analysis and simulation to create a more realistic forecast.

Key Takeaways

This is a fictional example of a tactical optimization analysis. Discussion of asset quality, location, and match with in-house capabilities was intentionally not within the frame. The result is not a strategy but a plan of action to guide managers and leaders around the company. There is a suggestion for future strategic work, especially regarding resource replacement.

This story depicts a remarkably well-behaved and disciplined leadership team and a well-oiled portfolio team. However, your actual process will likely be less smooth and involve more complicated personalities.

The interactive graphics tools made the analysis simple for the portfolio team and gave the leaders the information and insights they needed to have a good discussion and reach conclusions.

The portfolio team was flexible enough to modify its model and quickly develop multiple additional portfolios requested by leadership.

Branco – A New Business Model May Break Existing Metrics

During the initial portfolio meeting, the leadership team decided to understand the existing assets better. They would later determine inorganic (acquisition) opportunities and adjustments to their exploration strategy at a later meeting.

The chart below shows the NPV of the individual investments available vs. the discounted capital. Branco typically likes its investments to have an efficiency ratio greater than 1.4 (using the formula efficiency = 1 + NPV/Discounted Capital).

▸ **Asset Plot Showing Accounting Capital Efficiency**

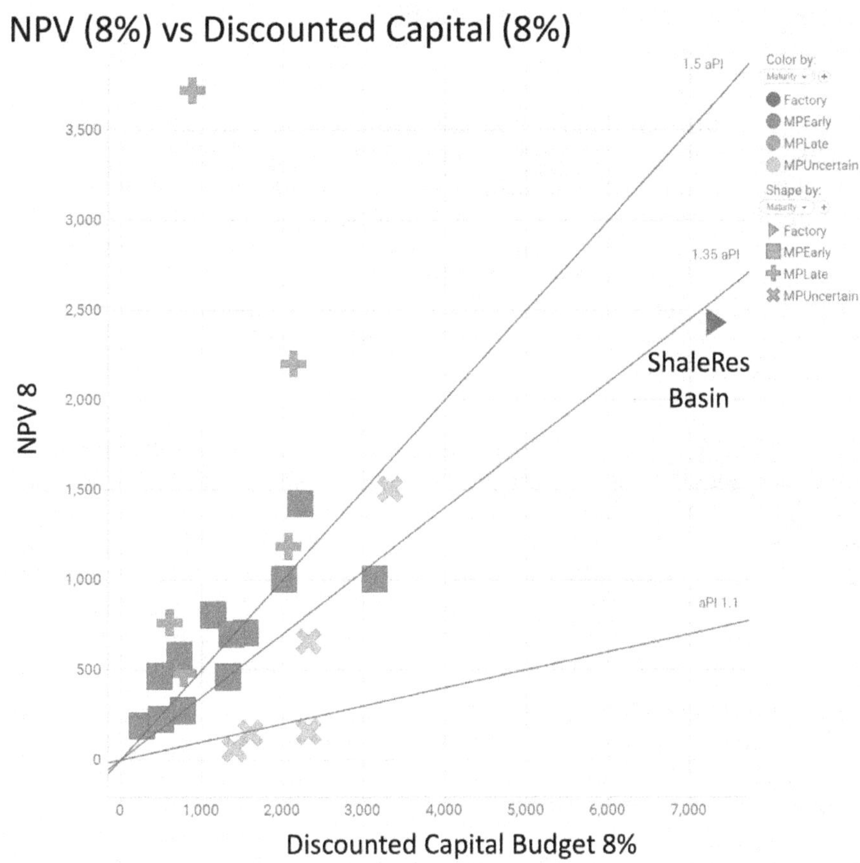

> *Most producing assets and major projects have aPIs greater than 1.5 or even 2.0. The ShaleRes Basin, a producing asset, is below 1.3. This poses a conundrum for the Branco leadership team. What's going on?*

They made a few observations:

1. Late-stage projects (MPLate) were very capital efficient. The development manager pointed out that they typically had sunk a fair amount of capital and were, therefore, highly efficient on a point-forward basis.
2. Producing assets (not shown above) that required capital for reinvestment, workers, etc., were also highly efficient. The marginal assets tended to be early-phase major capital projects (MPEarly) and immature projects (MPUncertain).
3. The ShaleRes Basin unconventional producing investment was an exception and appeared to be a poor investment overall.

With the third observation, the room erupted. The ShaleRes operations manager talked about how great the play was as an investment, while the heads of heavy oil and deepwater touted how great their assets were. Finally, the Chief Financial Officer (CFO) spoke up.

"There is confusion in our company with the word capital and how we use the metrics. The external market judges our company on our stated budgeted capital program. That context uses a standard accounting definition of capital. In the finance and investment world, there is a different definition—net negative cash flow. In many or most cases, the distinction makes little difference. There are a few exceptions: projects with phased capital expenditures and projects in countries that allow consolidation between assets in their fiscal terms. In those circumstances, our standard definition of capital efficiency can understate investment efficiency.

"The ShaleRes Basin is an unconventional fracking basin. Each well we drill is wildly efficient and economical but short-lived. Every time we expand to a new area, we must build infrastructure for gathering and operations. It is, in essence, a continuously phased project. As we expand operations, it shows up as a cash drain until it reaches a critical mass; then, it's a great cash flow generator. In long-established corporate investment practice and theory, once it reaches that critical mass, it is no longer considered a drain on the corporate funds.

"But our efficiency metric sees it as a drain because it uses accounting or budgeting "capital." To be fair, we do need to watch our budgeted capital because the market expects it. But we must take care not to overreact because of a blind spot in our metrics. Looking at our investment through the lens of net negative cash flow, we see a different picture for ShaleRes Basin. If we want a hurdle rate for our opportunities using net negative cash flow, it will need to be set at a higher value than for accounting capital. In any case, ShaleRes Basin drastically improves compared to other assets. Thank you for letting me rant about this."

▸ **Asset Plot Showing Financial Efficiency**

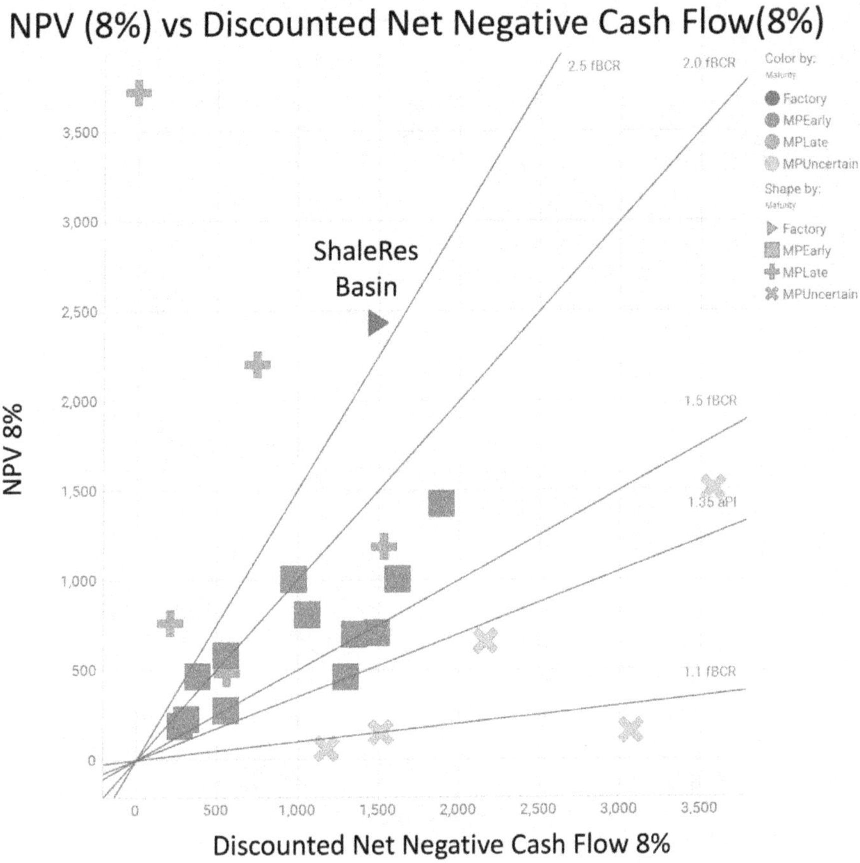

Redisplaying efficiency using the fBCR denominator shows the ShaleRes Basin asset in a different light. Because it has some negative cash flow at the start, it is less efficient than other producing assets. Its short-lived investments act more like opex than capex, so it's an unfamiliar asset type. Nonetheless, it competes favorably with conventional major projects in the portfolio.

Thank you for letting me rant about this.

Branco – If We Can Get More Money from Selling Than Our Calculated NPV, Why Not Just Sell?

The analyst team noted that Branco could sell the ShaleRes asset for more than it is worth in their NPV calculations. Several other assets could also fall into that category. Shouldn't the company then sell the assets? Isn't that the path to maximizing shareholder value?

This question hinges on the premise that an asset's calculated NPV represents an unbiased value. But Branco's planning assumptions serve many purposes. Let's consider oil price, which is often the most prominent and impactful metric.

Corporate Treasury and Finance focus on short-term safety. They need to know if the corporation may need to access external markets for financing. This means that the near-term price is often somewhat conservative (low) compared to an unbiased price estimate. They use the price basis as a near-term stress test.

Beyond the plan's first few years, Branco typically inputs an inflation assumption and lets oil prices rise along with inflation. Nobody believes that price assumption. It is entirely unrealistic and at odds with the historical trends and uncertain and volatile forward path of oil prices.

In real life, companies make adjustments as external conditions change. Unconventional production, as in the ShaleRes Basin, is uniquely valuable when conditions change. The short turnaround from drilling a well to putting production into a pipeline allows flexibility to increase or decrease activity based on varying external conditions. It is an option on the oil price.

All this is to say that the static, calculated NPV based on an unrealistic oil price deck understates the asset's option value, and the conservative near-term price assumption understates its near-term cash flow.

Another factor in many companies is that the discount rate for opportunity analysis is typically higher than the weighted average cost of capital (WACC) dictated by CAPM. This is a good practice for standalone analysis but may distort valuation decisions in a portfolio context.

Finally, although the analyst team suggested that the assets could be sold at an advantageous price, that would depend on finding the right buyer with the right motivation and ability to absorb an asset. There is always capriciousness in these small and opaque markets.

A more rigorous approach to analysis would incorporate managerial options and flexibility and likely show a higher value for most assets in the portfolio. But even that is not the end of the story. Branco has been a strong company with reliable dividends for many years. Its management is skilled and has received support from the Board of Directors. The Board has long believed in the company's assets and management and that Branco is worth more to the owners as an ongoing concern. Selling long-lived assets for quick cash does not support that perspective and strategy.

Branco – What Happens When the Displays Use Different Metrics Than the Optimization

When the team created the view of NPV8 vs. the discounted net negative cash flow, it raised red flags because it had an unusual and unexpected pattern. Instead of a smooth concave downward efficient frontier, it showed two distinct trends and a prominent kink.

▸ Portfolio Pareto Frontier with Kink

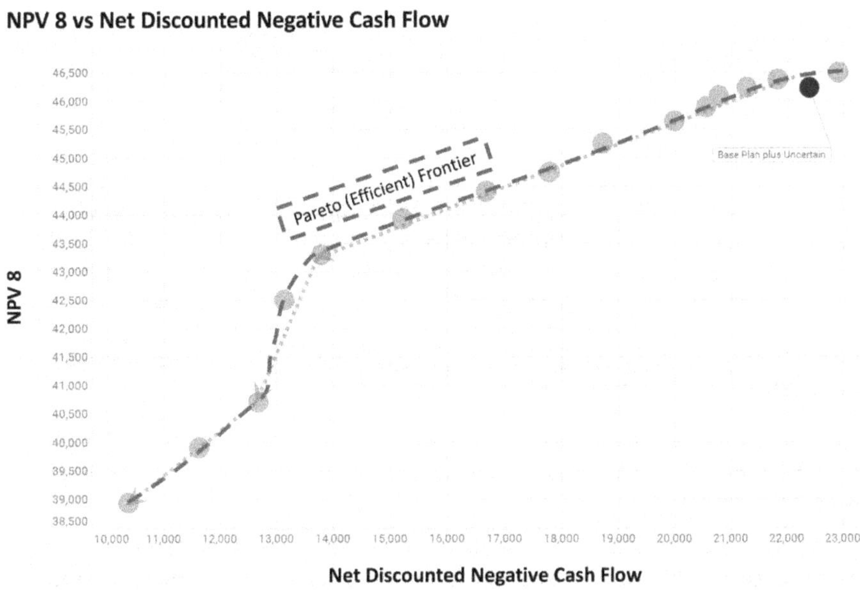

> *This is the same visualization we used when discussing the large kink caused by the optimization tool rejecting the ShaleRes asset. But the issue goes beyond that. Our optimizations used the annual budget limit as a requirement, but this view is based on discounted net negative cash flow.*

An alert analyst pointed out that the optimization had been done using budgeted capital. That plot shows a smooth concave-down continuum on an NPV vs. discounted budget capital graph. In contrast, the original displays used the standard finance definition of capital (discounted net negative cash flow). Whatever you believe about that particular metric compared with discounted budget capital, the view provides an example of how using a metric for optimization might give a different outcome. Indeed, the NPV vs. Budget capital plot is not alarming at all.

Comparison of Two Different Pareto Frontiers of the Same Portfolios

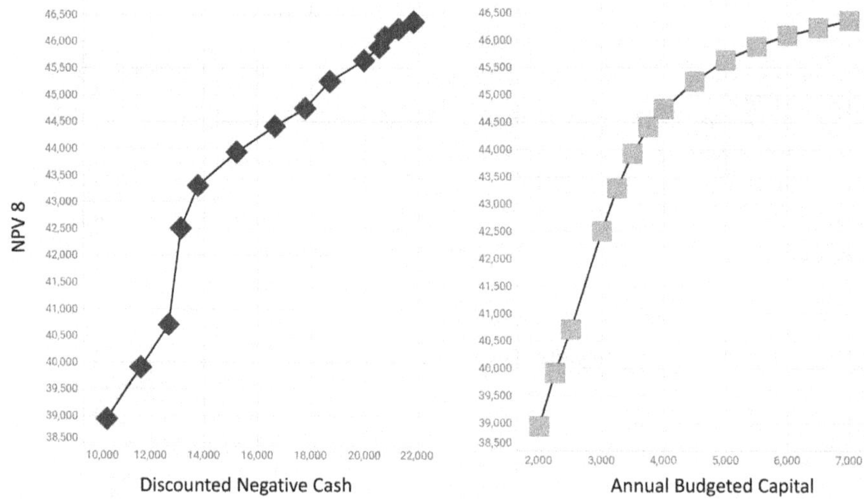

Changing the x-axis to discounted budgeted capital cleans up the Pareto frontier. It's now smoother and concave-downward. To be clear, discounted budgeted capital was not our portfolio requirement, it was annual budgeted capital. The two metrics are closely related, so the graphic behaved.

So, should your displays and optimizations be the same? Should they be different?

The short answer is that this is a multi-dimensional problem. Every perspective and trade-off you use to view the data has the potential to provide insights.

In this case, viewing the data using a lens different from the optimization and with a time-tested corporate financial perspective was enough to raise a red flag and provide insight into the importance of the ShaleRes Basin asset.

Branco – The Slope of Your Efficient Frontier Tells You the Marginal Investment Return at a Given Point

An important insight can be gained from the NPV vs. Discounted Capital chart. You can see that the efficient frontier slope changes as you increase the capital. The slope of the efficient frontier at any given point indicates your portfolio's opportunity cost.

▸ Determining Hurdle Rates for Opportunities "Thought to Exist"

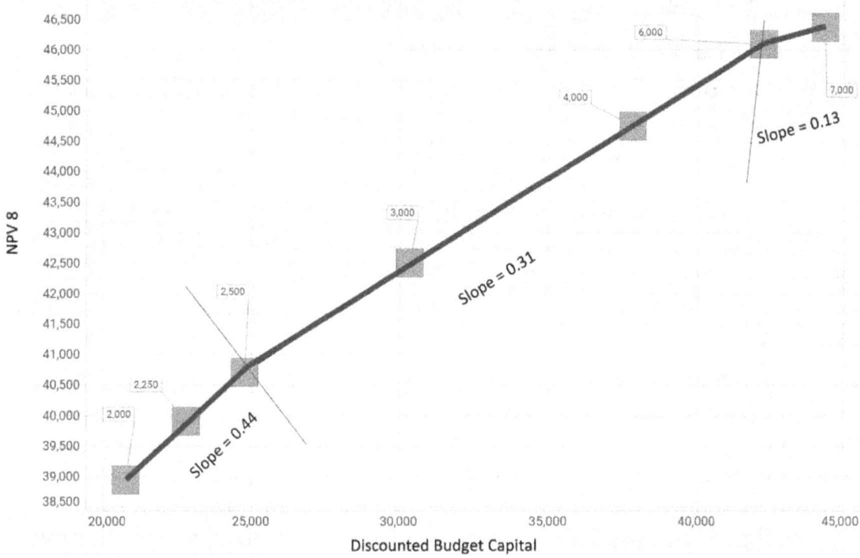

Companies assign hurdle rates based on opportunities thought to exist either implicitly or explicitly. If you have an inventory of opportunities and alternatives and an optimizer, you can derive the opportunities that actually exist. The slopes are based on the total discounted budgeted capital. The labels on the points show the corresponding capital budget levels.

If your portfolio funding level were at 30,000 (x-axis), corresponding to 3,000 in budgeted capital, your incremental investment would, in theory, be 1.31 (using a typical formula of 1 + NPV/ Discounted Capital. That would be a reasonable hurdle rate for a new opportunity.

This assumes that you use accounting capital for your investment efficiency metric, fund your opportunities based on portfolio optimization, and take advantage of your portfolio flexibility, e.g., changing development options when it is reasonable. If you use discounted net negative cash flow as your efficiency denominator, the methodology is the same, but with that as the x-axis. Using discounted budgeted capital as the denominator is common and, in some cases, more straightforward to calculate, but discounted net negative cash flow aligns better with financial theory.

You may remember that, in the standalone section, we discussed opportunities "thought to exist" as an appropriate hurdle or discount rate. The perspective above empirically gives you that rate. Assuming you have a robust inventory, you now see the incremental investment return that additional projects must achieve to add value to your portfolio.

Branco – Setting an Objective Function to Maximize a Yearly Value

The production manager wanted to know how high production could possibly be 7 and 10 years out. He asked the team to maximize net production in 2032 and 2035 (set objective function to 2032, then 2035 production). When the team ran those cases, a few things happened. First, the production was very high. (Yay!) But the NPV decreased considerably. The team noticed that many excellent projects were deselected. Excellent projects, otherwise scheduled to come online sooner, were delayed in the tool to ensure peak production occurred in 2032 and 2035.

Setting production as the objective function had some strange effects. Portfolio NPV decreased markedly. The optimizer no longer "cared" about NPV, so if a project did not have or could not have production in 2032 with a delay, it might not be selected. Or maybe it would be. Those choices became arbitrary. The analysis team pondered this. They realized that once they knew the maximum possible production in a given year, they could set a requirement for production just a hair under that and set the NPV as the objective function again. This creates the required tension in the model to ensure that all good projects are still selected, even if they are delayed unrealistically to satisfy the production objective.

This technique is useful when a decision-maker has unrealistic expectations about targets over time. If you can show that a goal is impossible to reach, you may be able to guide the objective to a reasonable level.

BHAGs (Big Hairy Audacious Goals) are motivational; impossible goals are not.

Detail – The Emergent Strategy

It's great to have a strategic hypothesis. By this, I mean that your leadership may have a belief about what strategic theme the firm should pursue. In oil and gas, it can be a geographical theme (e.g., North American assets), geological (e.g., heavy oil or unconventional production focus), market (e.g., Asian LNG dominant), or sourcing (e.g., exploration as the primary manner to add hydrocarbon resource). Pharmaceutical development might focus on a class of compounds (e.g., mRNA), a biological system (e.g., heart and artery, kidney), or a sub-population (e.g., people exposed to malaria).

But there needs to be a reality check. Just because a company is good at a specific business line does not mean it will propel the firm to achieve its financial and operational goals. As analysis progresses, a leadership team may discover that the emphasis will unlikely lead to the financial results needed for competitive success. They then need to test strategies that will lead to success.

A strategy table (example below) can be a powerful tool to help guide strategy development.

▸ Sample Petroleum Upstream Strategy Table

Sample Petroleum Upstream Strategy Table

	Financial Target Focus				Balance Focus		
Strategy Name	Cash Flow	ROCE	Capital Expenditure	Revenue/ Production	Geographical Focus	Exploration/ Research	Asset Class Focus
Max Value	Positive in all years, sufficient for dividend	Stable	$5 Billion	Flat real through 2030	US	No Change	Deep Water
As Is	Allow negative cash flow in some years	Drive for 15% by 2030	$6 Billion (As Is)	1% real growth through 2030	Americas	Increase 15%	Unconventional Reservoirs
Core Up		Drive for 20% by 2030	$7 Billion	2% real growth through 2030	OPEC plus US	Decrease 15%	Onshore
Int'l Diversification			$8 Billion	3% real growth through 2030	OECD		Natural Gas/LNG
Vertical Integration			$9 Billion				Midstream
Capital Efficiency							
Revenue Growth							
Cash Flow Growth	Emergent	Emergent	Emergent	Emergent	Emergent	Emergent	Emergent
Long-Term Sustainable							
Decrease Exploration							

For each strategy name, select one goal or virtual decision from each column. The bottom row, "Emergent," means that you do not set anything else for that column; just let the column fall where it may. The Max Value strategy is always a good baseline; everything is emergent, and it maximizes NPV. Any other decision represents some form of compromise or sub-optimization and can only reduce NPV.

With a tool like this, leaders can describe specifics about what they mean when they say we must "core up" or "vertically integrate." Keep in mind that hybrid strategies are also possible. For example, the leaders may wish to test a vertical integration strategy that decreases exploration expenditure by 15%. However, as they further develop the strategy, they find that the company needs to replace its reserves faster. In that case, they can increase the exploration expenditure or test various acquisitions.

One approach is to use optimization to find the most value-adding ways to achieve financial results. But just because a financial result is possible does not make it a good strategy. Financial results are goals for most strategic portfolio work. The strategy to accomplish those goals needs to incorporate the culture and capability of the organization.

If your firm is very strong in one area, but your math model tells you that area will not achieve your financial goals, you may need to modify your goals or develop other strengths. If your model tells you that you should change to a different area entirely, that's interesting, but check your assumptions. Changing focus to a different area may not be aligned with your culture, organization, or capabilities.

Simple number crunching is necessary but insufficient to create a strategy. Strategic decision-making has to go beyond math. You **can** calculate a range of outcomes from a particular strategy. You **can** quantitatively determine sets of decisions that would be more likely to result in success or unlikely to lead to success.

Ultimately models don't give the answers; models provide insights to leaders that can be used as a framework for future decisions and setting strategy. In my worldview, by combining the power of computers with real-world business insights, better strategies **emerge** from the human-machine combination.

Leadership teams with some degree of humility and a culture of honest inquiry will see portfolio analysis as an opportunity to improve and fine-tune their strategy hypothesis. Other leadership groups may circle the wagons and criticize the analysis, treating their strategic hypotheses as something to be protected, sharpshooting every perceived minor inconsistency.

May you be blessed with the former. The latter behaviors drive flawed analysis and faulty conclusions. Care must be taken to ensure that communications are strong enough to drive sound decisions and soft enough to save face. It is not an easy place.

Detail – Efficient Frontiers

You may recall the "CFO chart" introduced in the Rank and Cut section.

▸ CFO Chart Revisited

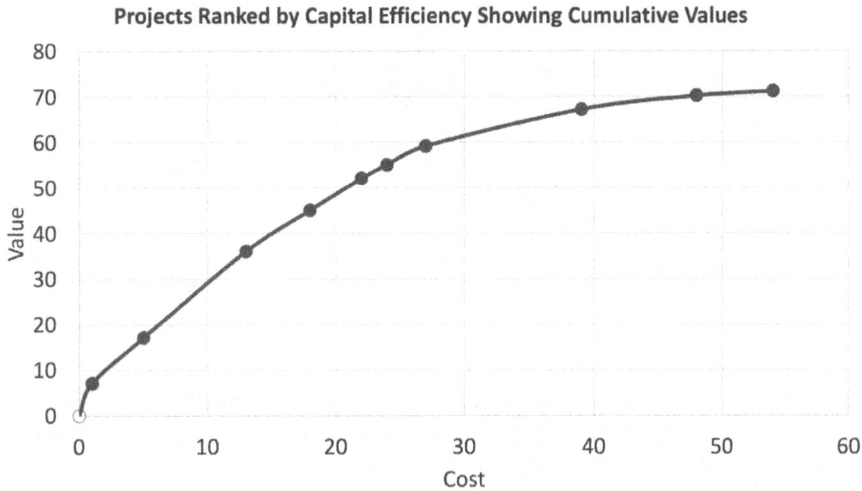

The rank and cut section described this as seriatim-ranked projects. In fact, each dot is a portfolio consisting of the most efficient portfolios by the axial metrics. That means that this line is an efficient frontier.

It is a plot of Cumulative Value vs. Cumulative Cost. I introduced it then as projects accumulated along these axes. In reality, each dot represents a candidate portfolio set. The first dot on the left is a portfolio with a single investment. The next dot to the right is a portfolio with two investments: the first and the second most efficient. It continues to the right, with each dot adding a single project to create a new portfolio.

Given this set of ten projects, the CFO Chart represents the efficient or Pareto frontier for the two metrics. With those ten projects, there are 2^10 or 1024 possible portfolio combinations. They would create a virtual cloud in the area underneath the curve. The lower bound of the complete set of points would be the "inefficient frontier"—the least efficient portfolios.

Let's walk through the idea of looking at multiple measures. The figure below shows an efficient frontier based on a tiny sampling of the billions of possible portfolios from even a modest set of investment options.

▸ Conceptual Portfolios, Including Those Below the Frontier

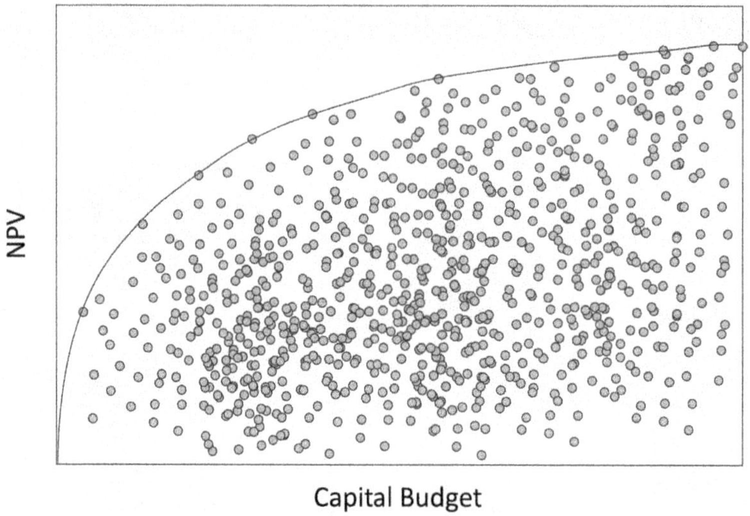

The empty area in the upper left contains no possible portfolios given the working inventory. No constraints have been applied, so the frontier is a true frontier beyond which no portfolio exists that has both a lower budget and higher NPV.

Bringing in another measure, for example, "ROCE in three years," adds a dimension. The above budget vs. value chart includes all values of ROCE. It is effectively a projection of a three-dimensional volume onto a 2-D plane.

▸ 3D Version of Cloud of Portfolios Projected to Two Dimensions

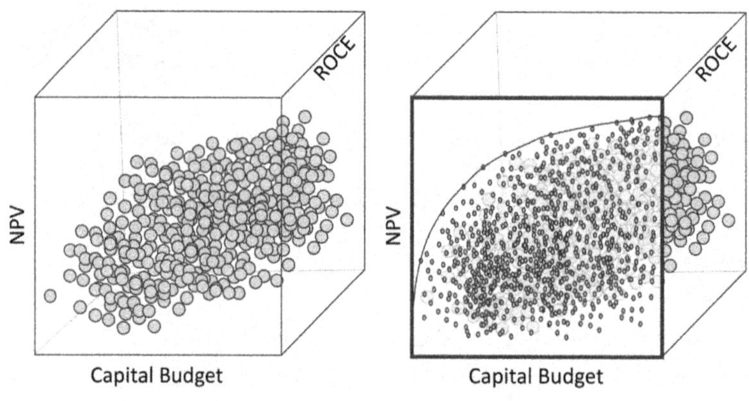

We see efficient frontiers as two-dimensional plots. They can be visualized as a projection of a multi-dimensional cloud of portfolios onto two axes. Each of those portfolios has many metrics that would be of interest. The front window into the cube is the projection of all the portfolios.

Setting a requirement in the third (ROCE) dimension (filtering out all portfolios below a certain ROCE) eliminates some possible portfolios. Although the efficient frontier may remain the same, a high ROCE threshold will likely move the efficient frontier down. A requirement or constraint in the third dimension could keep your efficient frontier the same at best or make it worse.

Adding a Constraint Moves the Pareto Frontier

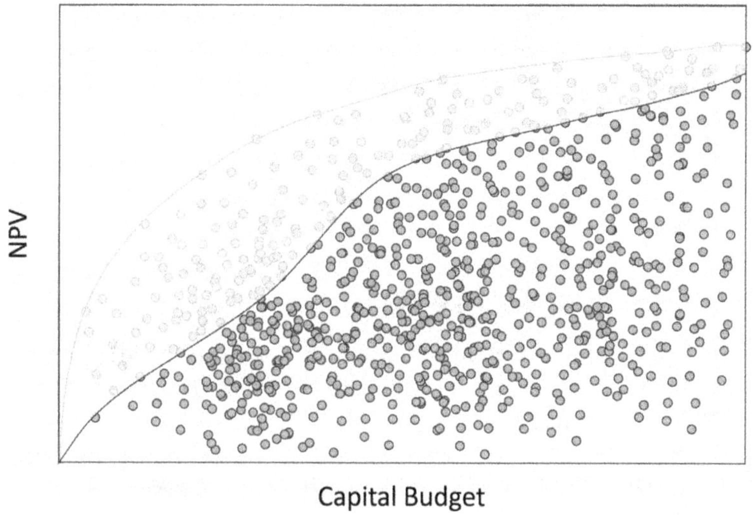

In this case, a minimum ROCE limitation eliminated many of the highest-value portfolios by inserting a virtual screen or wall in the hypercube, creating a new efficient frontier projection.

Now let's add another requirement based on the maximum negative cash flow exposure resulting from the program. This will move the Pareto frontier based on a different third dimension. Notice that this filter cuts out some of the portfolio upside. You have to spend money to make money.

▸ **Additional Constrain Lowers the Frontier in Some Places**

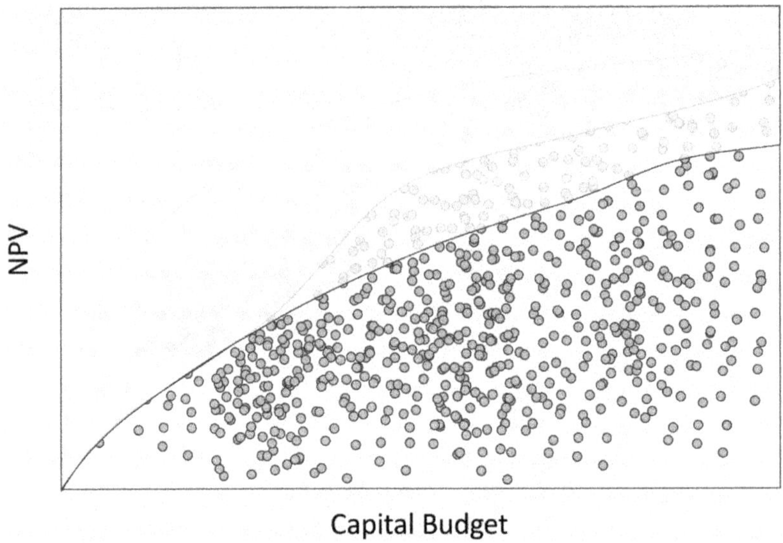

Adding another constraint, this time on the cumulative negative cash flow exposure, eliminates even more of the high-end portfolios. The lower-cost portfolios mostly remain intact.

The final filter is applied within the below 2-D view by setting a maximum on the Capital Budget.

Bear in mind our unconstrained efficient frontier was at the dashed line originally.

▸ **Vertical Line to Reflect Capital Limitation**

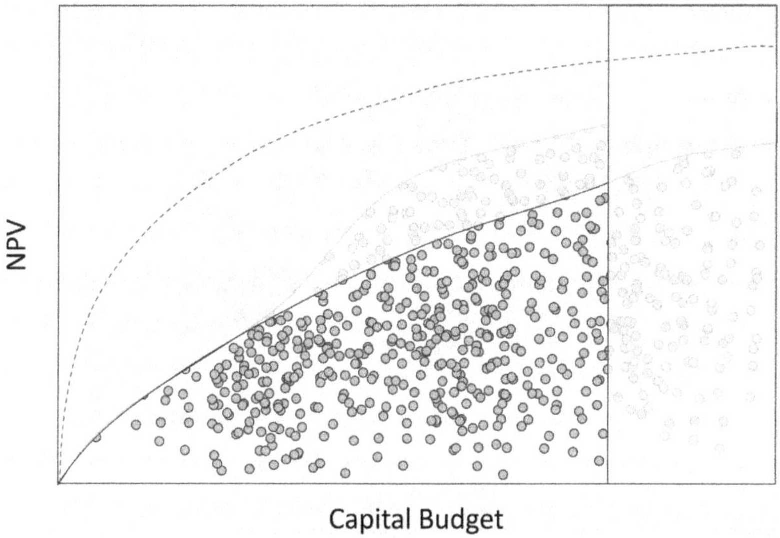

> *Finally, we'll add a capital budget requirement. Because the capital budget is one of the axes in this display, the screen is perpendicular to the projection, resulting in a vertical wall. These constraints have significantly reduced the possible value that can be derived from the working inventory. It's time for a leadership gut-check on whether the budget and metric constraints justify the loss in value.*

These views make it clear exactly how much requirements and constraints cost a company in terms of NPV (corporate value).

Constraints and requirements are important. But set them with your eyes open; know what value you sacrifice to achieve the constraint.

Detail – Sig Figs

In high school and college science classes, they teach about the relevance of significant figures (Sig Figs). It has to do with factors like measurement error and the ability to draw precise conclusions in the presence of that measurement error.

For example, mathematically, 17. x 22.4436719 = 381.5424223. Significant figure practice tells you that all those decimals are irrelevant because your least precise value—17 in the above equation—lacks the precision to allow for using those decimals. You should therefore use 382—the rounded value of the mathematical answer.

All that is well and good. Then came Excel.

It is so easy not to do all that rounding and truncation. In fact, it takes extra effort to remove the values after the decimal.

Now segue to the probability of success of a hypothetical project. Perhaps you have a four-factor probability framework. You assess each of the factors separately, do your best job to fit your numbers to the standards in place, and come up with 70%, 85%, 65%, and 40%. Multiplying these gives you a 15.47% probability of success.

Under sig fig thinking, you might say that it is 15% (or perhaps even round up to 20%). Remember, this is a before-the-fact relative estimate of likelihood of a unique circumstance, so there's not really a correct answer.

So now you have this number, and you copy and paste it, plus others, from Excel into PowerPoint and show it to a group of decision-makers so they can use the probability to help them prioritize.

I promise there will always be someone in the group who does not want to make collaborative decisions and will shoot arrows at the sig figs you did not clean up. Their strawman is that you believe that those hundredths of a percent are meaningful.

You know that when you multiply the percentage by the success case value, those decimals make no difference in the outcome. There is no harm in showing them. Let's be clear. This is a personal attack on **you** to discredit the methodology.

▸ **Meaning is in the Groupings—Not the Exact Numbers**

Opportunity Probability of Success

Entity	PoS
Opp 1	15%
Opp 2	15%
Opp 3	10%
Opp 4	33%

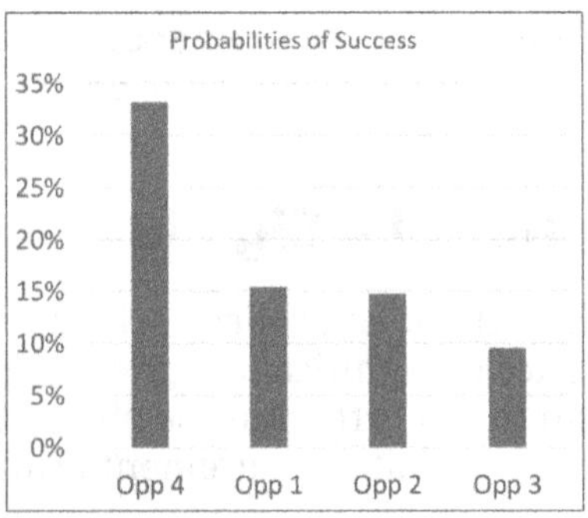

Three groupings are clear: high, middle, and low. There is an apparent conflict between the values on the table and the bars. The bar for Opp 1 is higher than the bar for Opp 2. Even though Opp 1 shows a higher bar than Opp 2, they are clearly quite close. PoS should not be a distinguishing metric between those two opportunities.

Key Takeaways

1. There's always someone ready to shoot you down.
2. Stay calm and thank them for pointing out the typo.
3. When you show numbers, round them, but make sure the graphs continue to show the differences. For every five people who complain about sig figs, there's one person who does the math in their head and will point out that those two equal graph bars should not be equal. For every one of those, there's another one who will now complain about the inconsistency between the numbers and the graphs. Just nod knowingly and tell them the numbers are rounded.
4. At some level, you have to trust your leaders to understand that minor differences from quantitative models that contain hundreds of assumptions and contingencies are not material.

War Story – Data Entry

An issue related to significant figures occurs with data entry. I favor entry in thousands of dollars for my personal decisions, e.g., the cost of my kitchen remodel is about fourteen thousand (I wish). Larger projects may be entered as millions, and I know of a company that typically enters data in units of billions of dollars.

The input units are completely unimportant as long as everyone agrees on the units and they're consistent. I spoke with an analyst complaining that the cost inputs required entry in dollars. They complained that it was unrealistic precision. Nobody knew their project costs to the dollar, so it was silly.

I had worked with the system developers who had experience with people being confused with the conversions to millions or thousands. They insisted that the entry be in dollars. I knew from those conversations that there was no expectation of precision. In fact, some of the inputs were almost always talked about in terms of millions or billions, but the developers were adamant that not going to dollars would lead to QC issues.

Lessons Learned

1. There's not a right answer to this.
2. The people responsible for QC should be the ones who determine the standards; they're the ones who have to live with them.
3. Regardless of how well expectations are communicated, someone will always complain about accuracy and precision.

SECTION THREE

Use Cases, Implementation, and the Last Word

CHAPTER 14

Specific Use Cases and Examples

Much of this book has been devoted to portfolio work on typical, highly profitable projects. Portfolio techniques let us sequence and sort investments to achieve value measured by NPV.

We'll discuss four use cases in this section:

1. Portfolio fit using linear programming optimization - discusses how to quantify and think about whether an opportunity fits with your corporate aspirations
2. Cost centers - optimization can be a great tool, even for departments that have unclear or difficult-to-measure value propositions
3. Divestiture using stochastic optimization - shows an example of using the most potent type of optimization
4. Risk management - an established field that uses many of the same tools and skill sets

Portfolio Fit

One of the most common questions in portfolio analysis is, "How does this opportunity fit my portfolio?" It could be an acquisition, a divestiture, or a development; it doesn't matter. Ultimately, the objective is to know whether this asset or project decision adds value to the company.

When you boil it down, portfolio fit is the subject of this book. Whether you are trying to understand the role of an asset, which development alternative is best aligned with corporate aspirations, deciding on a harmonious set of actions, or deciding how much to pay for an acquisition, you, in the final analysis, make decisions that further the goals of the firm. Every one of the methods illustrated in this book can help answer that question.

Many analyses boil down to the simple question of "What we look like if we do this thing" vs. "What we look like if we **don't** do this thing." Rollup, simulation, and optimization are simply different ways of answering that question. Standalone and Comparison and Inventory methods answer a different and simpler question, "How does this compare to what we are already doing?"

As always, the frame is the key determinant of which methods to use. The following section shows an optimization technique to answer questions about portfolio fit.

Detail – Portfolio Specific Value (PSV) – Tactical Optimization

Decision, economic, and risk analysis strive to answer the question, "What is this asset or decision worth to my company?" This is especially important in the acquisition and project development worlds. How does the purchase of an asset or this development fit into my portfolio?

There are a few components to the answer. First, what is the intrinsic standalone value of the opportunity? On a standalone basis, will the investment efficiency at least exceed your corporate WACC? If so, is it a development you would do if you had it? Look at the opportunity with your proposed purchase price and on an after-purchase basis. Will this opportunity compete for funds within **YOUR** portfolio?

When using optimization to determine portfolio fit, we compare two working sets: the set of everything you own and that set with the new opportunity added.

The base portfolio then depicts a hypothetical momentum case, while the addition of the opportunity to the inventory is the incremental case. As with standalone economics, there must always be an explicit alternate course of action. When we determine the value of a decision, we must always ask, "Compared to what? The below graph provides insight into the answer.

Please note that the units are meaningless and arbitrary in the graph below. In this case, it shows the value of the opportunity without an acquisition payment (cost to acquire).

▸ **Portfolio Value at Different Capital Levels for Two Working Sets**

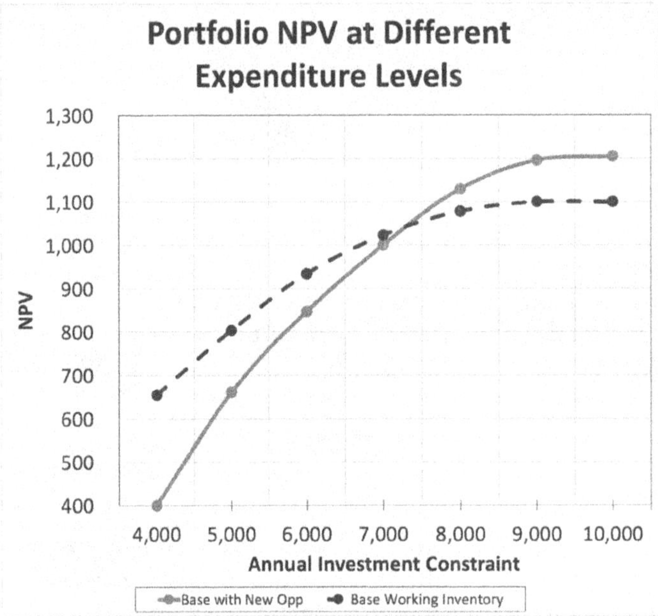

The dashed line represents the optimized net present value (NPV) of the base portfolio working set compared to the annual capital investment level. The solid line locks in the decision to develop new opportunities within the working set and re-optimizes. If capital funding exceeds 7,200, the new opportunity would add value to the portfolio. Below 7,200, the new opportunity exerts too much drag on the portfolio despite being a positive NPV investment on a standalone basis.

The dashed line shows the value of your base portfolio (y-axis) with different annual investment constraint levels. Looking from right to left, as your constraint changes from 10,000 to 9,000, there is no change in value. Even if you could spend that much money, you are opportunity-poor at that level. Reducing investment further erodes the value of your portfolio. When the investment constraint reaches 4,000, the portfolio's value is reduced to about 650.

Then, you lock a new opportunity with a standalone NPV value of 100 into the mix. We again see that if you have 10,000 to spend, there is no value erosion. But now, when the investment goes to 9,000, the portfolio value realized—the difference between the two lines—begins to decrease.

Below an investment level of 7,200, you would be better off not having the New Opportunity in your portfolio. (The New Opportunity was locked in place with no room for delay. If there had been flexibility, it might have fit better.) Its presence requires other, better investments to be delayed or removed from the program. As the firm's investment level gets smaller, ever-better projects are delayed.

The answer that leadership should be asking is beyond "What is the value of this project?" The project team will tell them $100. Instead, they should ask, "What do I believe the investment capacity of my firm is, and under what conditions does this opportunity make sense?"

This portfolio perspective also provides insight into how much you are willing to pay for the opportunity. If you believe the firm's expenditure capacity is around 8,000, you will not pay more than $55. By doing so, the value of the opportunity would shift from positive to negative within your portfolio.

You could also create another set of portfolios with a lower working interest or a different development concept on the new opportunity. Those would have different portfolio fits and provide insight into your capture strategy.

Viewing the graph above as a single line that represents the difference between the two lines offers a clearer, more incremental perspective on the value. It allows for comparison with other working sets and project alternatives.

Difference in Portfolio Value Between Base Inventory and Analysis Inventory

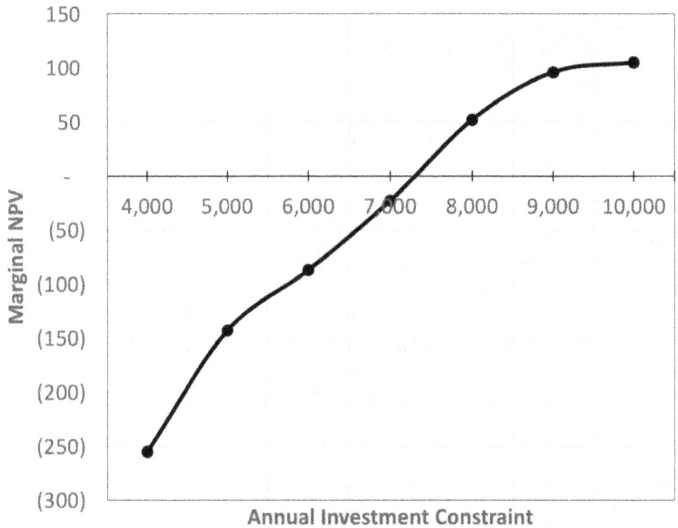

Calculating the value difference between the two curves clearly shows the portfolio value (PSV) at each capital expenditure point. This opportunity can result in a gain of 100 or a loss of 250, depending on the company's investment capacity.

This approach is not limited to acquisition opportunities. It is also an excellent framework for comparing development alternatives for a project you already own. The procedure takes you out of the project frame and puts the decision into the frame of enterprise value.

You probably have a plan in place with capital expenditure budgeted into the future. If you incorporate the opportunity without increasing the current limitations in your optimization, it will almost certainly show a poor portfolio fit. This is an easy way to say "No" and to make people question the value of portfolio analysis. If the answer is always going to be "No," why bother?

Significant acquisitions generally require increases in budget numbers or changes to existing investments. The question changes from "Does this opportunity fit my portfolio?" to "Under what assumptions would this fit in my portfolio?"

Besides the usual caveats about model accuracy, this has an additional one. More flexibility in the model leads to a higher portfolio value. If your firm is unwilling to act on the flexibility, the true value to be realized will be lower.

The Portfolio Specific Value section in the appendix describes a methodology (including a sparse data method) for answering that question and prompting that discussion among decision-makers.

Detour – Strategic and Opportunistic Investments

Strategic Investments

Periodically, a business development leader pitches a project by stating that it is strategic. The long-time joke is that the strategic moniker means it has lousy economics—that part is often true.

But what does it even mean for an investment to be strategic? My shorthand thinking is that it meets some goal invisible to standard economic and financial analysis. Portfolio analysis combined with decision quality is a great way to coax out the meaning of "strategic" and perhaps even find an objective value for it.

Exploration in the hydrocarbon upstream and R&D in pharmaceuticals are often like this. An individual exploration project may have an internal rate of return below 10% when considered across its full life. This pales in comparison to development projects at 12%-25%. But without the front-end expenditures, companies would be unable to grow or sustain themselves. Immature investments with a low probability of success and long-term potential will never stack up to near-term revenue opportunities.

The key then is for companies to consider their long-term outlook. Given what they have and know about, at what point do revenue and production roll over and begin to decline? The gap between the rollup with existing assets and growth targets becomes a strategic objective.

Companies must either assess the potential of a scenario where they go out of business and return money to shareholders or decide on the optimal way to allocate investments that support the long-term sustainability of the firm. This is also discussed in the section, War Story - How Can a Zero NPV Opportunity Possibly Have Value in a Portfolio?

Opportunistic Investments

Opportunistic investments are the opposite of strategic investments. Regardless of whether they help fulfill strategic targets, they have a high return on investment. They usually will be funded unless the investment is entirely out of line with the company's business or values.

It's OK to do the standard portfolio fit exercise. Outstanding investments will still show up as suitable and displace projects that are not as good overall. Optimization is unlikely to cause a rejection of one of these investments.

Bringing in a project that is a great investment but is not well-aligned with other values the corporation holds may lead to different decisions in regard to other assets and investments.

For example, suppose a company has goals around capital expenditure, production growth, and reduction of greenhouse gases. A project with great NPV and low capital cost but high greenhouse gas emissions is being considered. Optimizing the portfolio with parameters aligned to those values may tell you that you should do this project despite its emissions but make other portfolio adjustments. These other portfolio adjustments may materially dampen the portfolio value of the project.

Great investments are rare. A corporation needs the flexibility to accept them, even if doing so hinders the achievement of some of its goals and targets. The object is to do so with eyes open and ensure that progress towards those other goals continues at minimum cost.

The Broader Context

All of the above assume that the firm's leadership has a common perspective of its long-term vision, strategic position, and the future of the company and its industry. The most important question is whether a corporation should make marginal investments to continue the business rather than paying investors directly. Dividends and share buybacks generally fill that goal.

But even if leadership has had those discussions and the board has approved the direction, decisions can become disconnected from the stated strategy. For example, leadership may determine that they want the company to stay in business for a long time and decide that they need to invest in long-lived assets. But then, if they set an unrealistic hurdle rate, they will not make that long-lived investment because it "erodes value." Misalignments between stated aspirations and internal hurdles to achieving these aspirations are not uncommon.

Detail – Phased Projects and Economic Metrics

An important topic is how to frame decisions for investments with multiple phases. This is important for standalone investment metrics (NPV and efficiency) and comparison and interactive portfolio methods.

It goes beyond efficiency. Which case or combinations of cases should be used to make decisions? How you look at this depends on where you are in the asset's life cycle and the decisions at hand.

Consider an upstream oil and gas acquisition. The post-acquisition development of the investment is optional (but considered highly likely at 100%). The second phase is optional too but is not certain to occur as there are remaining technical risks, but the team believes it has a 75% chance of development.

There are three decisions in this case:

1. Whether to spend money to acquire the asset.
2. Whether to do the initial development.
3. Whether to do the second phase of development.

These decisions do not all need to be made prior to acquisition (decision 1), but they should be vetted for reasonability.

For the following discussion, we will use the following cash flows.

Cash Flows of Individual Project Phases

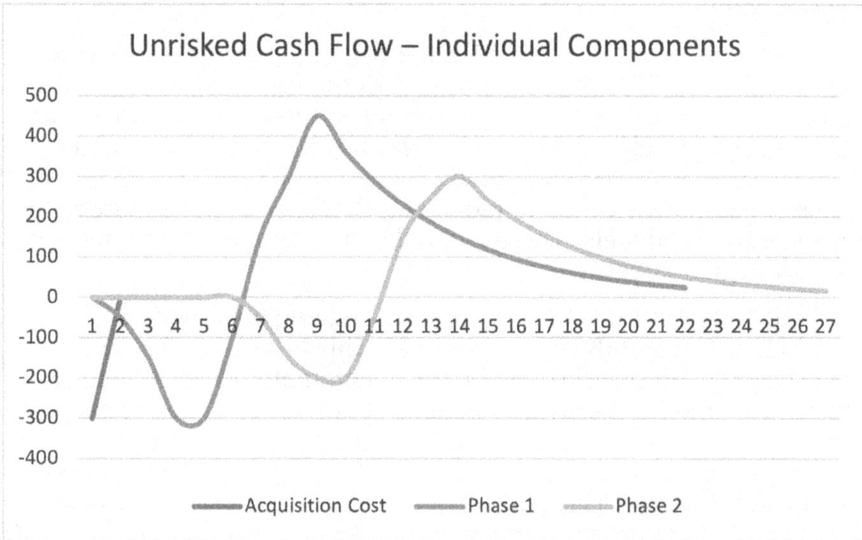

The three individual cash flows of the acquisition. The acquisition cost is the initial negative pulse. The Phase 1 development is the second set of cash flows. The Phase 2 development is the third.

Let's start with the acquisition decision. When you acquire an asset, typically, you purchase from someone who has done their internal analysis and found that it does not fit their needs well. The logic is the same whether the owner is selling all or part of the asset.

In my experience, acquisitions are seldom, if ever, **efficient** investments. The acquisition cost drags down the efficiency. The cost of entry is early and certain to occur, so it disproportionately affects time-discounted efficiency metrics. In fact, if an acquisition looks good even with the acquisition cost, it is likely over-optimistic. After all, the owner, who presumably knows the asset better than the purchaser, is selling an interest, not giving it away. Efficiency metrics are fine to calculate but should not be the primary driver of an acquisition. Usually, acquisitions fill some perceived gap in the company's goals.

The Acquisition Decision

At the acquisition point, there are two main questions:

1. Will this asset add value, including the acquisition cost?
2. Once we have the asset, will it fit our portfolio?

What scenario and discount rate should we use for the NPV? Start with the corporate WACC as a screening discount rate. If the NPV is negative at WACC, it's a no-go. The project would reduce the value of the company.

As a second screen, test the NPV at the corporate hurdle rate (higher than the WACC). This implicitly compares the full opportunity to the current investment opportunities. You hope it has a positive NPV at that rate but consider additional factors. If your internal investment queue is shallow or if it may serve a longer-term goal (like growth or resource additions), withhold judgment. You should incorporate time-sensitive portfolio tools. Those will tell you if the opportunity falls into the "strategic" category.

As a side note, future phases paid for by ongoing operations will have higher IRR and fBCR but lower aPI. This is because the former are driven by net cash flow, while the denominator of aPI is budget capital. IRR and fBCR provide a holistic perspective, while aPI better indicates if the future phase might be competitive in the portfolio. Looked at holistically, fBCR and IRR benefit from free NPV—additional value without a cost. This perspective would be representative only if the entire investment were in scope, i.e., Phase 2 was not an optional investment. It seems like a paradox that making a phase mandatory improves economic metrics. This is because standard deterministic economics often ignore option value.

Looking at the opportunity, including the acquisition cost, is where we are now, but the acquisition expenditure will be behind us in the future. It's important to know if the development will be attractive to fund once the acquisition funds are sunk.

Will It Fit Our Portfolio After Acquisition?

Most companies have standards for how they want to document the economics used for decision-making. For this section, I will ignore those and focus on what is needed to make high-quality decisions.

▸ Probabilistic Basis of the Components

Wedge Definitions		
Label	**Description**	**Risking**
A	Acquisition Cost	Unrisked
B	First Phase	Unrisked
C	Second Phase	Unrisked
D	Second Phase	Risked

Labels and descriptions of the cases for discussion.

Which cash flow cases to use? There are several considerations and possibilities:

1. Phase 1, including acquisition cost.
2. Phase 1 plus Phase 2, including acquisition cost.

Should we apply a probability of development to either or both phases?

The initial screening decision of the opportunity at the WACC should look at two cases: A + B and A + B + D. A + B is a somewhat conservative case. If it works, it passes the screen easily. Looking at A + B + D provides your best, most representative perspective, while A + B + C is optimistic.

▸ When to Use Which Basis

Portfolio Methods and Wedge Cases		
Standalone Decision Making/ Screening		
Acquisition plus First Phase	A + B	Provides a conservative view of the opportunity. Answers the question, "Does this make sense even if the second phase never works?"
Acquisition plus First Phase plus Risked Second Phase	A + B + D	The theoretically proper case to justify the acquisition. This reflects your current state of knowledge of the opportunity.
First Phase Standalone	B	An important perspective even before capture. A downside case that answers the question, "Will this be better than other projects in my portfolio?" If it can't compete on this basis, it becomes a "dog catches car" problem. You have it, but there's nothing that makes sense to do with it.
Comparison		
Acquisition plus First Phase	A + B	Screening step
First Phase standalone	B	Same as standalone
Second Phase Standalone	C or D	Can be risked or unrisked, depending on decision context and metrics.

Deterministic Rollups		
Acquisition, initial development, and risked second phase as separate wedges reflecting different types of activity	A, B, D	For the interaction techniques, it is best to separate the wedges.
Simulation (Stochastic Rollups) and Stochastic Optimization		
Acquisition, initial development, and unrisked second phase as separate wedges reflecting different types of activity	A, B, C	Separating the wedges allows for independent application of delays and probability of success.
Deterministic Optimization		
Acquisition, Initial Development, and Risked Second phase as separate entities	A, B, D	Allows for potential delay decision of first and second phases. Risking the second phase can lead to strange outcomes, because it will show lower coast and benefit. If second phase is outside of the current decision window, it's fine as a placeholder for context.

> *Which wedges and combinations should be used based on different portfolio methods?*

As always, the specifics depend on the frame and specifics of the decisions, standards, processes, and expectations of the decision-makers.

Sensitivity to Probability

A colleague once stated that we wouldn't be considering an opportunity if not 100% certain to be developed. I beg to differ. Our **intent** may be to develop the project, but stuff happens. New information comes to light, or the business environment changes. Besides, this is not an unusual concept. Every exploration block purchased or wildcat well drilled is done on that same basis. The intent is to develop the discovery, but a dry hole would make that an absurd decision.

Although we can assess the probability of development, it is sometimes easier to do the calculation that answers the inverse question, "At what probability of success would this opportunity be a no-go?" This is called sensitivity to probability analysis. In this case, considering only Phase 1, the probability of development would have to be less than 61% for the acquisition to be a bad bet.

This opportunity succeeds on all counts.

The Development Decision

Now that you have purchased the asset and it's in your portfolio, it's time to make the development decision. Which value and metrics should we use?

For decision-making, the acquisition cost is now irrelevant. You should be looking only at the point-forward case. But which one? Both phases or just the next one? As shown in the table above, both are relevant. The Phase 1 standalone view provides a downside case, while the Phase 1 plus a risked version of the Phase 2 case shows a more representative picture of the value lost if the project is not approved.

One of the arguments often cited for NPV/I type metrics (where "I" is defined as budget capital) is that future, phased investments are not free money, even if cash flow from operations covers the investment. That much is true.

When looking at the second phase, it should be viewed on an incremental basis. What is the investment relative to the do-nothing case? When a supplemental development is part of another operation, the best way to look at the incremental case is to create a do-nothing case, create a combined case, then subtract the do-nothing case from the combined case. Those are the incremental economics.

▸ Incremental Cash Flow Should Be the Basis for Decision-Making

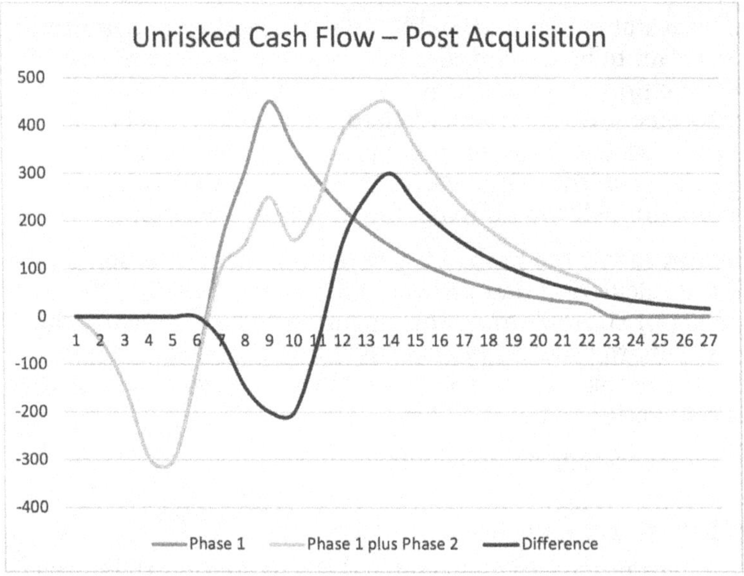

The Phase 2 investment decision must use the difference between the curves to determine its viability. Looking only at the Phase 1 plus Phase 2 curve yields little insight about the Phase 2 investment.

Beyond that, you should use the portfolio methods that allow for a fair and proper assessment of portfolio fit.

> **Key Takeaways**
>
> Phased projects introduce complications to investment and portfolio analysis. There is tension between the need for conservatism (from looking at only the first phase) and the importance of understanding the cost of a potential lost opportunity by including the second phase in decision-making.

Managing Cost Center Portfolios

Cost centers are departments within an organization that provide a service or good. The quantification of the value of these services is often irrelevant. This is a common situation. Auditing, computer technical support, and assurance groups are common examples.

In the oil industry, environmental remediation, field abandonment, basic research, and greenhouse gas reduction have tangible outputs but are also seen as cost centers. Standards for the value calculations are sometimes challenging to define, and with wide variability in the outcomes, standalone analysis has little utility.

Comparison and optimization techniques **can** help us get clarity on those decisions. Being a good corporate citizen is essential to most firms in the long run. If a company neglects that responsibility, over time, it will lose its "license to operate" in a country or area. Corporate citizenship includes cleaning up after yourself, abandonment and environmental remediation, and following relevant laws and regulations. Capital stewardship creates the opposite incentive—reduce spending as much as you reasonably can.

Greenhouse Gas Reduction

Reducing greenhouse gases in oil company operations comprises mainly flaring and venting reduction, energy efficiency investments, and carbon sequestration. These types of projects are seldom as good an investment as production. Companies have strong incentives to limit their expenditures on these types of activities.

The trick is to find an investment program that allows a firm to meet implicit and explicit commitments while at the same time being smart with cash expenditures. In the case of greenhouse gas emissions, many firms make explicit commitments to regulators and shareholders for future reductions. Portfolio analysis can help find the right balance between the two forces.

This simple time-series optimization problem has a few wrinkles and additional considerations.

Optimization requires something to provide "tension" in the model. If the objective function is to minimize expenditure or maximize NPV (of negative NPV projects), there must be drivers that create requirements to do more than nothing. When you have commitments to the market, it becomes an important requirement.

The appropriate discount rate to use may also be a question. Many in the sustainability community argue that we should use very low discount rates or even none. Their frame is different from that of a typical firm. The sustainability community is focused on the good to society; a firm should be looking at what is good for the owners or shareholders of the firm. Use the corporate weighted average cost of capital; that minimizes financial costs to the firm.

Another key issue is dependencies. Many sustainability projects are directly linked to oil fields and their production levels. A two-year delay in a mitigation project may have a very different greenhouse gas profile than the same project done now. Consider collecting a few delay cases for fields with steep declines or scaling the greenhouse gas impacts to production levels. There are a few ways to deal with it, find the one that fits best in your frame.

Less Tangible Requirements

When requirements are implicit, like risk reduction or customer satisfaction, it can be challenging to find and model measures that help understand the goodness of an effort. It's a challenge outside the scope of this writing. Douglas Hubbard's book, "*How to Measure Anything*," has excellent advice about finding those measures. They're probably right in front of you.

In any case, you should still be able to get good prioritization lists from optimization, then do reality checks to validate the outcomes.

Selecting Divestiture Candidates Using Stochastic Programming

There may come a time when your company decides to do multiple divestitures because of changing conditions, cash flow needs, or even a change of direction of the firm.

This example *fictional* case will illustrate a stochastic optimization approach to selecting a set of sales candidate sets to minimize value lost through divestitures (maximizing delta NPV minus after-tax proceeds). It will meet calendar-based market promises and limit the number of sales efforts due to organizational constraints.

The Setup

The price of oil had taken a tumble. The fictional company needed cash flow to avoid accumulating excessive debt from paying dividends and was reluctant to reduce the dividend again. It had done so two years earlier after an environmental judgment.

The business units responded quickly to the call for potential divestiture candidates. There were some old but excellent assets, old but poor assets, and newer but less strategic assets. The assets were scattered around the globe with differing regulatory and fiscal regimes.

The CFO wanted to know two things. What is the best way to raise money (net cash) this year and next, and what should be the public commitment for divestiture proceeds? Our initial target for proceeds is $400 million this year and the same amount next year. He wants to express high confidence estimates to the market.

The COO wants to minimize the impact on 2027 production, which is also an important consideration.

Here is a list of the divestiture candidates:

▸ **Short List of Divestments with First Pass Selections**

Asset	Mgmt. Selection	Internal NPV	Expected Proceeds	Tax Rate	Probability of Successful Divest
A	1	$ 526	$ 600	50%	81%
B	0	$ 388	$ 450	42%	54%
C	1	$ 27	$ 40	25%	77%
D	1	$ 33	$ 33	25%	77%
E	1	$ 19	$ 24	25%	72%
F	0	$ 82	$ 133	25%	29%
G	0	$ 35	$ 15	80%	37%
H	0	$ 47	$ 15	47%	37%
I	0	$ 252	$ 326	25%	60%
J	0	$ 181	$ 289	45%	44%
K	1	$ 377	$ 620	61%	61%
L	0	$ 111	$ 120	41%	73%
M	0	$ 348	$ 202	32%	40%
N	0	$ 62	$ 103	44%	56%
O	0	$ 67	$ 78	71%	65%
P	0	$ 112	$ 129	46%	47%
Q	0	$ 61	$ 40	43%	38%
R	0	$ 114	$ 155	38%	85%
S	0	$ 172	$ 244	56%	81%
T	0	$ 198	$ 217	63%	37%

The assets with a 1 in the second column were selected by management as a first pass at the list of divestitures. It's reasonable and based mostly on their perception of strategic fit with the company's needs.

Management believes in their first pass review that divestitures of assets A, C, D, E, and K would fill the bill. But there are misgivings. Some candidates might take a long time to set up and sign a deal. Also, even though some of the candidates are ready for divestiture from a maturity standpoint, the market for these older properties is unclear.

They ask your team to look at the complete list of potential divestitures and assess them.

You determine that the analysis must incorporate probabilities on before-tax (BT) proceeds by year and after-tax (AT). Given twenty divest opportunities, each one of which can take 1 of three decisions (keep, divest now, and divest later), there are 3.5 billion possible combinations (three to the 20th power). This problem is intractable manually. You decide on a Monte Carlo stochastic programming approach.

The ABCs of This Optimization

Adjustables: Decision to attempt to divest. We need two different years for this with three possible decisions: don't divest, divest attempt in year 1, and divest attempt in year 2.

Best: NPV Is usually good. For this purpose, you need to look at AT Proceeds minus NPV. AT Proceeds are BT Proceeds minus Tax due. Tax due is (Proceeds less depreciation remaining) times capital gains tax rate. For simplicity, tax consolidation effects will be ignored.

Constraints, Requirements, and Important Indicators: Limits on people available to work the various efforts, mean BT Proceeds A total and by year > 400, probability of achieving BT targets by year, 2027 production reduction. The model selections will be binary, and constraint logic will prevent the selection of divestiture of a single opportunity more than once.

You need multiple pieces of input information for each asset:

1. Internal calculated NPV
2. Expected sales price from market analysis and a range, if available
3. Minimum acceptable price
4. Probability of successful divestiture
5. Time range for successful divestiture
6. Capital gains tax rate
7. Remaining tax depreciation/cost recovery
8. 2027 production estimate
9. A measure of the effort required to prepare and close divestiture

The model took a few days to build in Excel, and the OptQuest add-in on Crystal Ball was used for the optimization.

Modeling

The first step is to model the management selection as the base case for comparison. We will track NPV, total proceeds, proceeds by year, expected 2027 production drop, total resource effort, probability of $400 in BT revenue in each year, and AT Proceeds.

Creating a base case is crucial for several reasons.

Decisions are always framed as "compared to what?" Given that someone has given thought to what is in the base case, there needs to be a comparison of that case against others.

Some will defend the base case as the only practical or possible one. That may be true, but the decision-makers need to see how much value they are giving up on which metrics to pursue that case.

Here is the base case:

Total Proceeds if All Sold at their average value of $1317.

Total statistically expected proceeds are $940.

So far, so good. Superficially these opportunities will be sufficient to achieve corporate targets.

But digging a little deeper shows some issues. Assets C, D, and E should sell quickly, but A and K may take substantially longer. Even though, on a risked basis, total proceeds appear sufficient, the timing of the asset sales would be in question.

The First Pass Short List Does Not Meet Objectives

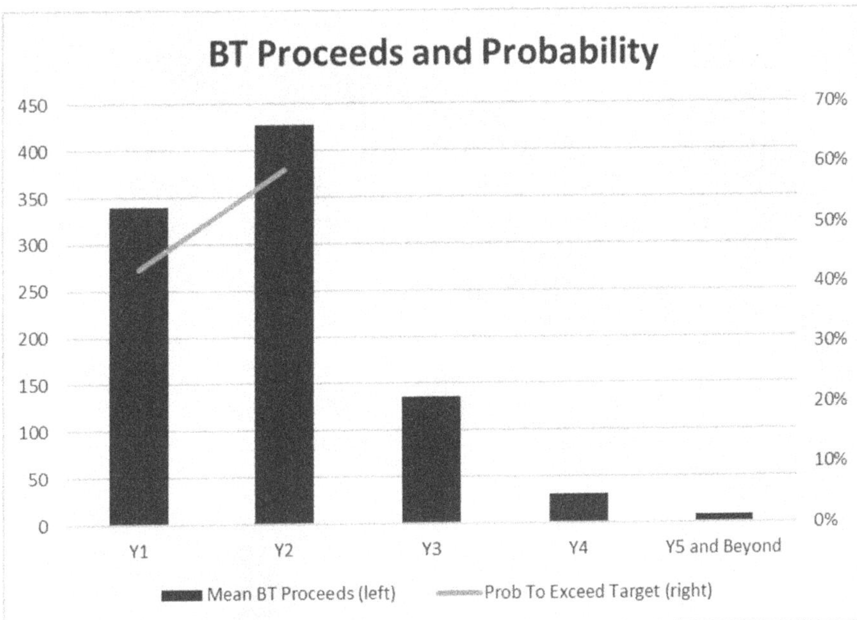

The management list, the Base Case, is expected to generate proceeds that would meet the total proceeds target, but there is relatively low confidence in achieving the annual targets. The timing of the sales and the low probability of achieving promises to the market are concerning.

Year 2 exceeds the requirement of 400, but year 1 comes up short at 340. There is about a 42% chance of achieving 400 in year one and a 59% chance of achieving it in year two. This selection would require staff resources of 12 full-time employees starting in year 1.

The 2027 production loss is about 70 thousand barrels of oil equivalent per day (mboed), so that parameter looks good, and the COO is happy.

The CFO isn't happy with the outcome. We need a better case with better chances of achieving the targets. The analysts used the optimization engine to create a few new scenarios. First and simplest, to maximize the value gain from the divestments and ensure that the mean before tax proceeds would be greater than $400 million each year. PfID 2 lost 163 mboed in production, so the requirement was added to keep production loss less than 100 mboed.

▸ **Table with Results of Three Decision Sets**

PfID	Strategy	Net Value Change	Y1 Proceeds	Y1 Prob > 400	Y2 Proceeds	Y2 Prob > 400	Lost Prod	Total Before Tax Proceeds
1	Base Case, Mgmt. Selection	$ 106	$ 340	42%	$ 428	59%	70	$ 942
2	Mean > 500 each year	$ 255	$ 683	71%	$ 574	61%	163	$ 1,544
3	Mean > 400, less than 100 prod reduction	$ 107	$ 414	52%	$ 405	49%	84	$ 1,002

The tabular representation of the first three portfolios shows distinctions. Perhaps a graph would be better.

The graphics below show some of the critical metrics for these three candidate sets.

▸ **Graphic of the Three Decision Set Outcomes**

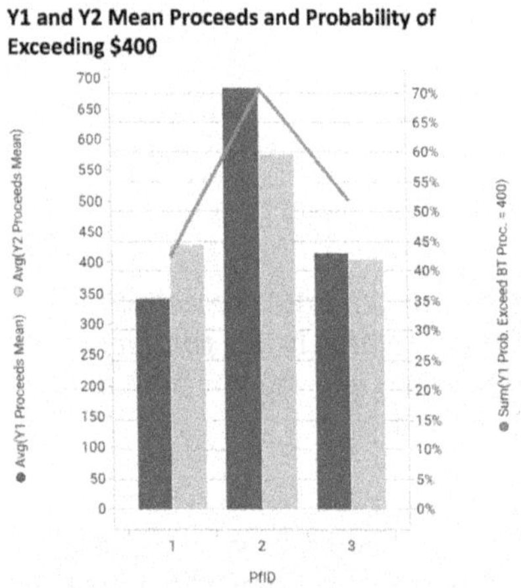

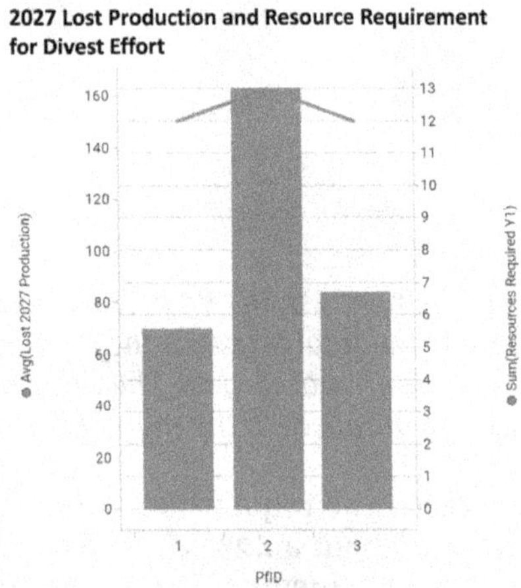

The first three portfolios deliver different results. The graph on the left displays the average proceeds over a two-year period, while the line represents the likelihood of generating over $400 in proceeds in the first year. According to the results, Portfolio 2 yields the highest proceeds and has a 70% chance of exceeding $400, but it requires more resources and leads to greater production loss, as illustrated by the graph on the right.

Portfolio (PfID) 2 and 3 are better than the base case on some dimensions, but there are still harsh compromises. Portfolio 2 hits production very hard but shows a better chance of achieving the proceeds targets. It also has a higher net value to the company. Portfolio 3 has a positive net value, keeps lost production low, and improves the chances of achieving the divest targets relative to the base case.

The analysis team continued looking for better answers. For the next set, the team added 16 portfolio candidate sets stressing different metrics and aspects of the problem. When viewed in the same format, it looks very crowded.

▸ **Plot Showing Outcomes, but Too Busy**

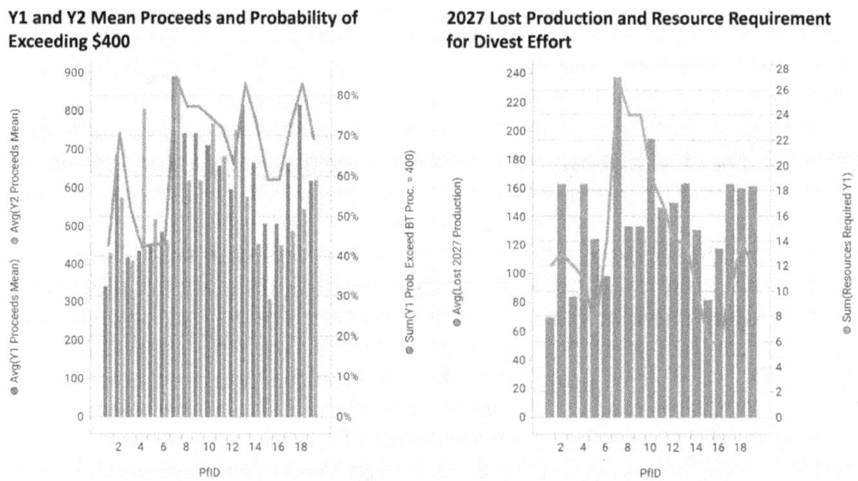

We can see a reasonable diversity of outcomes, but the display is a bit crowded. Let's try something else.

The team created a dashboard for analysis and graphical filtering to create a small subset for the leadership team to discuss.

Dimensional and Probabilistic Portfolio Comparisons

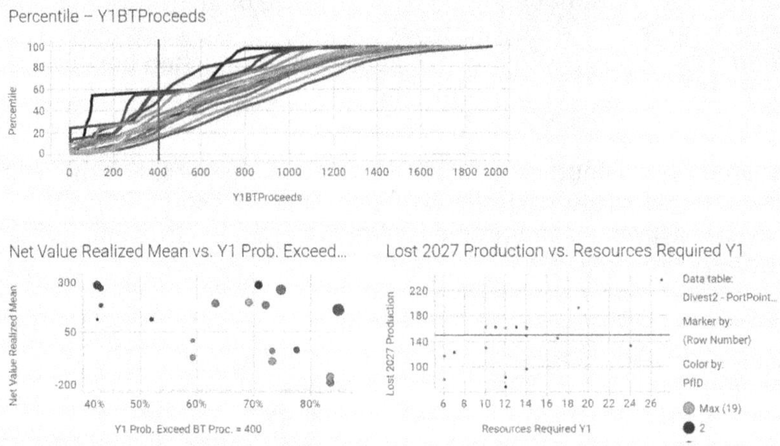

This dashboard is still busy, but it breaks out the important aspects of the different candidate sets more cleanly.

The dashboard shows results for 19 portfolio candidate sets. Each chart element shows the results of the specific candidate set plotted on the graph. The black dot and line represent the original divestiture proposal; the rest were developed analytically. The upper left chart shows the cumulative probability distribution for Year 1 Before Tax Proceeds (Y1BTProceeds). The lower left is a plot of the net value realized on the Y-axis vs. the probability of exceeding 400 for Y1BTProceeds. The lower right shows 2027 lost production on the Y-axis, and Y1 required divestiture resources on the x-axis.

The first filters removed the candidate sets that required more than 15 people in the first year and the ones that reduced 2027 production by more than 150 mboed. The VP of business development and negotiations was not confident she could devote even that much effort in the short term. The VPs of operations and finance believed that 150 was the upper limit on production loss. This left eight candidate sets.

▸ Curate Portfolios to Reduce the Busyness

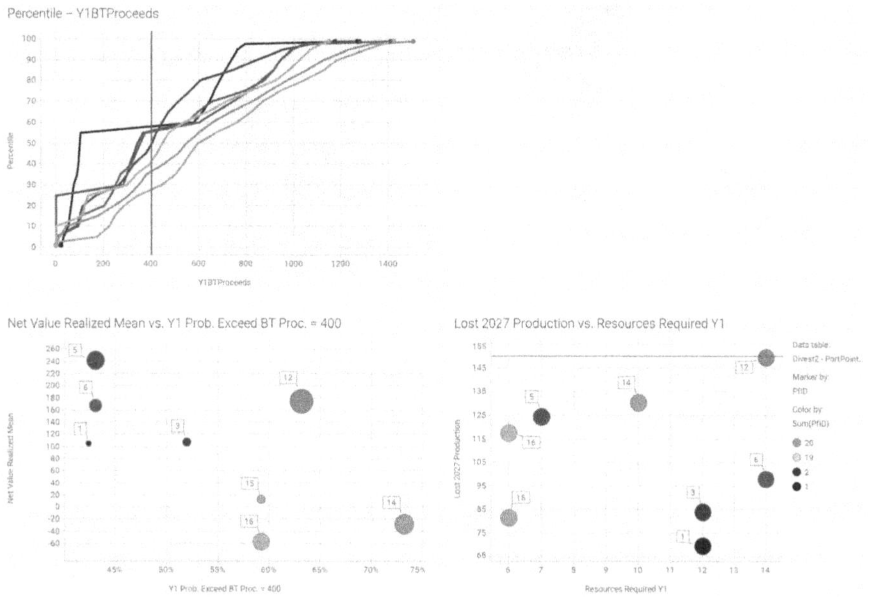

Curating the candidate sets to a smaller group begins to make the tradeoffs clear.

The initially proposed divestiture portfolio is represented by the black line in the upper left, the black dot at 42, 100 on the lower left plate, and the black dot at 12, 65 on the lower right. You can see that all of the remaining portfolios are better on one or more metrics.

Leadership removed the four portfolios on the left because they wanted a higher probability of hitting the year one target. This left portfolios 12, 14, 15, and 16. They liked that these portfolios had a higher likelihood of achieving the year one proceeds target. We are also introducing a new display below on the upper right. It is a portfolio entity heat map display. A light gray with a number 1 means that the entity on the left is selected in that portfolio (top labels) for divestiture in year one. Darker, with the number two, signifies a year two divestiture. Black, with the number ten, means it is not selected for divestiture. The entities are sorted by divestiture preference.

You can see that all four portfolios select assets A and I for divestiture in the first year. These two assets then become "no-regrets" divestiture candidates. Assets with all 10s become "no-regrets" keepers.

▸ Further Curation to Four Portfolios for Consideration

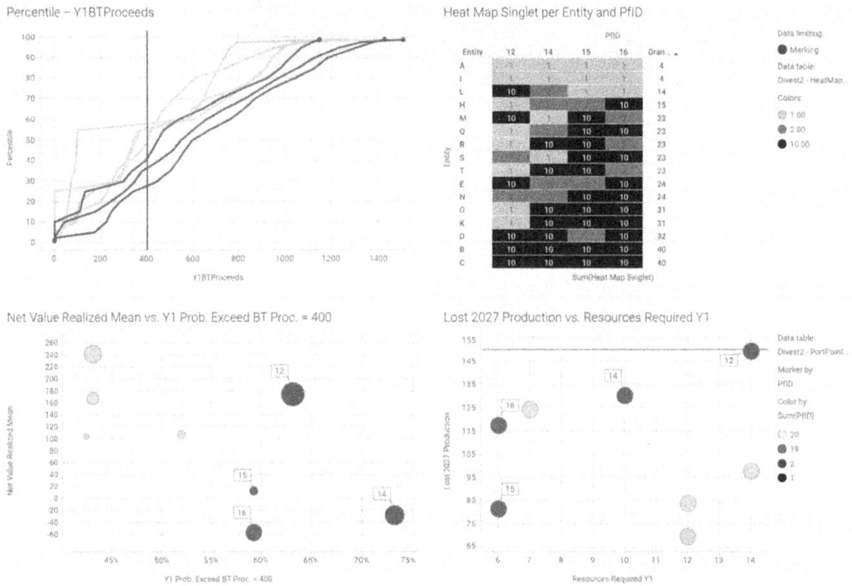

Narrowing down to four portfolios and adding a heat map, allows us to see both tradeoffs and the decisions driving them.

Although the leadership team was not thrilled with any of the outcomes, they liked the Portfolio 14 results best on balance. It had a high chance of achieving the target without significant personnel commitment or production loss of portfolio 12. Portfolios 14, 15, and 16 were all approximately break-even on value. Leadership had a suggestion. Rather than divest all of asset A, they decided to sell half the asset. While this reduced BT proceeds and did not affect the resources needed, it also increased the probability of sale because stakeholders would be less worried about a complete change of ownership.

The leadership team realized that their views on marketability and proceeds would change as the sales processes progressed. They could always stop or accelerate the sales processes if the environment changed.

The following shows the difference between the original proposed sales queue and the updated version (now portfolio 20).

▸ Final Decision Compared to Initial

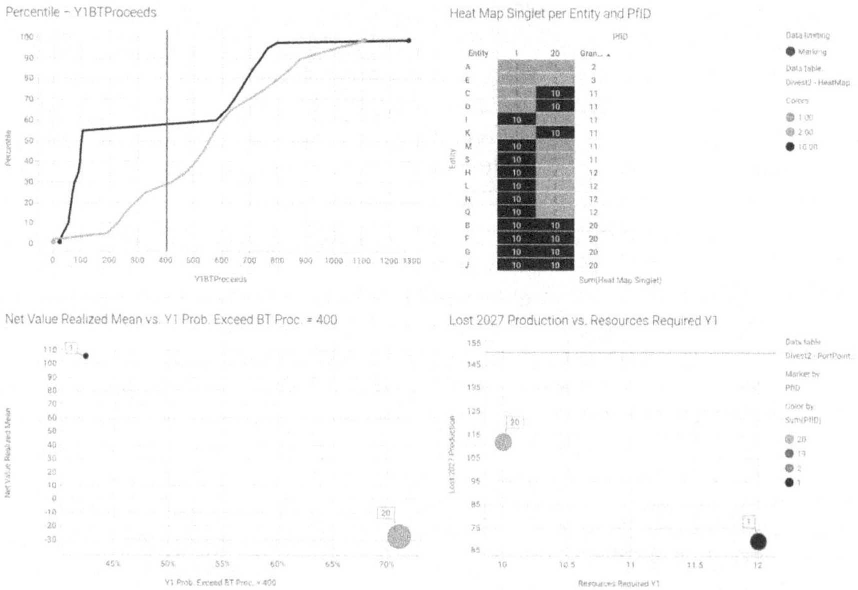

> *The leadership team picked and chose the best aspects of the final four portfolios and created a hybrid they liked even better. Portfolio 20 was selected as their go-forward case. Undoubtedly, as events unfold, they will make further adjustments, but given what they knew at the time, they made a high-quality decision.*

Portfolio 20 shows a slight loss from the sale, and more production is lost. It requires fewer sales resources and is more likely to achieve the target. On top of that, looking at the s-curves in the upper left, there's about a 20% chance that the sales efforts **in the first year** will cover the two-year proceeds target of $800.

Lookback on Model and Process

1. Value and NPV are fast and loose in this example. Time value of money adjustments based on divestiture timing is largely ignored. It is possible that those could have some impact. More worrying for this model is the possibility that someone in a meeting would spot the flaw and use it to discredit the whole analysis. Some corporate cultures work that way, which drives tremendous non-value-adding work.
2. Production progress is not incorporated into the values. In reality, purchase prices are often reduced based on realized production between the time the asset is put up for sale and the sale closes, especially for considerable lags. Divestiture value next year would technically need to be reduced by this year's production. Other factors like price and interest rates

will likely have much more significant effects, but there is a credibility issue to consider. An adjustment for "sunk revenue" incorporating time to close could be useful.

3. Remaining depreciation is often a guesstimate until additional resources are engaged. Accounting book values for depreciation, capital employed, and deferred income tax can be combined to estimate remaining tax depreciation or cost recovery. It's not precise, but it is close enough for screening.
4. Resources required are a relative indication of the effort to divest. It might have been more straightforward to limit the number of entities to attempt to sell. Each divestiture attempt takes effort, and your firm has limited resources to devote to these efforts, so there must be a way to restrict this in your model. There may also be financial disclosure requirements when an entity is chosen for divestiture, which would cause leadership to prefer fewer attempts rather than more.
5. Corporate executives and the negotiating team tightly hold minimum sales prices. Despite tremendous modeling rigor, many of the input assumptions are simply assumptions. It has the veneer of science and finance but is also often political and qualitative.
6. The model was not created to incorporate partial divestitures. Logic to allow fractional divestitures might have been insightful.

Risk Management

Risk management is an important field with many opinions about how best to analyze and manage the risks of a firm or project. As with portfolio analysis, there are many different meanings, levels, and specific uses for risk management from project to enterprise level.

The risk management field has many books, meetings, and societies compared to portfolio management. I speculate this is due to the common and powerful human bias against loss.

As with portfolio analysis, risk assessment can be qualitative or quantitative. It can be project-specific or rolled up to a higher organizational level. Also, as with portfolio analysis, few organizations do it well. Many organizations prefer a simple, cheap, and ineffective qualitative "risk-theater" approach that checks the perception box that the firm is managing risks.

The ISO 31000 manual on risk management standards discusses three large practices: Risk Analysis, Risk Evaluation, and Risk Treatment. Risk Analysis is analogous to standalone analysis. Practitioners strive to understand the characteristics of specific individual risks. Risk Evaluation addresses the ranking and prioritization of risks. Finally, risk treatment is about taking specific actions to reduce risk.

Portfolio Analysis and Management, as described throughout this book, focuses on maximizing gains and balancing factors like cost and delivering on promises. Risk management focuses on minimizing loss—monetary, reputational, or human life. Increasingly risk management professionals focus on balancing risk with returns. In the end, risk and portfolio management are at their most effective in the enterprise context. There is a convergence in risk and portfolio management, with the gray space between them shrinking daily.

Key Takeaways

1. Risk management and portfolio management have similar tools, aims, language, and skill sets. In both cases, although they can be done strictly at the project level, we care most about aggregated performance at the enterprise level.
2. Risk should be a part of the overall framework of portfolio management. If your task is portfolio management, incorporate risk if it makes sense in your context, and reach out to risk professionals in your organization.

Uses of Portfolio Management in Other Contexts

My practical experience has all been in the oil industry, which is why it's the focus of the examples. But portfolio analysis and management is useful whenever you want to determine the best combination of investments or assets.

The portfolio principles are fungible, creating a useful perspective across many fields. I have some examples of three of them here: financial investments, baseball, and government policy.

We'll start with the granddaddy of portfolio—investment analysis of stocks and bonds.

Securities Investment Portfolio Analysis

Harry Markowitz kicked off the portfolio era with his work on efficient frontiers. He used optimization techniques to find mixes of stocks that would deliver the best performance with the lowest risk. Since 1960, financial investment analysis tools have used variations of the concept. The tools have improved since 1960, so now when you go into a financial advisor, they use Monte Carlo simulation to help you understand the likelihood of achieving any number of financial goals under different investment and saving strategies. But what about the other elements of decision quality?

Frame – You complete an extensive questionnaire that lists your assets, aspirations, plans, hopes, and wishes. The analytical frame is set in advance. They will use their Monte Carlo tool to analyze, which is reasonable given the relatively high volume of clients. The questionnaire almost always has a few questions about risk tolerance. Family partners often have varying risk tolerances, which poses a challenge to this question. Based on my experience with these analyses, the definition of risk is often vague or absent. The good news is they tend to handle it better when they start talking about tradeoffs.

Reliable Data – Investment Analysts (IAs) have decades or more extended histories about all the securities in the world, and how they relate to each other in up, down, and sideways economies, making their data reliable. Data is not an issue as long as you have provided them with valid information. Remember what they always say though, past performance is not a guarantee of the future.

Logically Correct Reasoning – Mostly sound. They use sophisticated models to help determine probabilities of achieving goals and show you where you will end up with a given candidate set. The clients must understand that they are not receiving a forecast or prediction of their outcome. If the IA tells them something like, "You have a 98% probability of achieving your goals, it is not a guarantee."

If you see that you may not make a goal five years into your plan, you adjust. You do minimum wage work, drive an Uber, or eat at home, a few extra days per month. The models are not built to incorporate the risk of black swans—extreme events that come out of nowhere and behave like nothing seen before, so building in conservatism or even keeping counter-cyclical or antifragile investments as a part of your portfolio may be prudent.

Creative alternatives – Financial investments are infinitely scalable, so there is nothing but alternatives on the input side. Often the models used by the IAs reveal "the answer" to the client. You should ask for other approaches; for example, try higher or lower-risk candidate sets and examine the outcome. There may be an asset class you don't like, such as cigarette companies, or you may want to see more of an asset class. They can dial all of that in and let you see the results.

Tradeoffs – Return is obvious. What makes you the most money? But understanding the likelihood of different potential outcomes is also essential. Is there adequate diversification, or is there a risk of utter ruin in the portfolio, as people who had their life savings invested in Enron found out? There is also the question of your willingness or ability to see a significant paper loss play out when markets fall. Many people sell everything after markets fall (to prevent further paper losses), only to buy back in once the market has recovered. This ability to withstand paper losses seems to be mostly aligned with the IA definition of risk.

Commitment to Action – This is up to you and your partner or other stakeholders. Are you willing to act on the advice of the IA, or do you have overriding concerns not addressed in the quantitative analysis? At times, it is sufficient to validate your current path and there may be no urgent need to alter your investment allocation. You were probably open to it, or you wouldn't have put effort into providing data.

Results – Investment portfolio analysis clarifies the reality of plans' financial aspects. It does not make a precise forecast, but it helps people understand whether their hopes will likely become reality. It involves high-quality decision-making and positively impacts real lives.

War Story – Portfolio and Retirement

Let's say you saw the word portfolio in the book's title and thought, "This is great! I have stocks and bonds, social security, and a lump sum from my employer. This will tell me everything I need to know."

Sorry to burst your bubble. I unreservedly recommend the book, *The Only Investment Guide You'll Ever Need* by Andrew Tobias. It is not a fancy technical efficient portfolio optimization book, but it's chock full of common-sense tips.

I had an insight not too long ago that helped me. It's one that some investment advisors seem to overlook.

I was fortunate to have an excellent retirement program. There was a defined benefit annuity, which can be taken as monthly payments or a lump sum, a 401k that I contributed to, plus some other programs.

I managed my 401k using Financial Engines (FE) from Nobel-laureate William Sharpe on Vanguard through the years. I had always invested in the higher volatility (risky) side. The FE models usually showed a bit of upside with almost no downside in the long timeframes I was using to plan.

I also received periodic calls from independent financial advisors who offered to run my numbers to help me determine if I was on track for retirement. The offers were free, so I did it several times.

Every single one suggested a "balanced" approach to my 401k. Some stocks, some bonds, some cash. Often, they would recommend specific sectors of stocks or bonds as well. Their analyses seemed sound, but I did not pull the trigger on their advice. Instead, I kept the entire 401k in highly diversified index-type funds.

Interest rates went to zero in 2008 and remained low into the early 2020s. Following the 2008 crash, stocks boomed. You may be aware that when interest rates decrease, bond-fund values increase and vice versa. Keeping my investments in "riskier" investments paid off for me.

In 2019, I had an insight as I investigated the prospect of retirement. I would be getting Social Security (cash), collecting an annuity or a lump sum from the company (cash), plus my 401k. This meant that, even with all of my 401k being in stocks, **over 50% of my retirement portfolio was already in cash.** If I had followed the advisors' advice, I would have had lower returns through the years.

Please remember that this is not an analytical or quantitative problem, but rather a framing problem. The frame needed to be large enough to capture other sources of funds that were not then in my possession. And yes, I realize that those funds may never have materialized due to corporate financial ruin, an economic implosion, or through massive fraud or defunding of social security.

Lesson Learned

If you have multiple sources of retirement income, ponder whether they can be thought of as cash or risky investments and plan accordingly.

Moneyball

Perhaps you saw the movie Moneyball with Brad Pitt as General Manager Billy Beane of the Oakland A's baseball team. It was based on the book "*Moneyball: The Art of Winning in an Unfair Game*" by Michael Lewis.

Billy Beane was in a bind. He had just lost a star player and was trying to figure out how they could possibly replace him. Oakland is a secondary market, so he didn't have the kind of money to spend on big salaries that teams from New York and Los Angeles had.

There was a scene in the movie where Billy and his leadership team (scouts) were trying to decide how to replace some players they were losing to free agency. They were talking about one guy's swing, that other guy was good-looking, and that guy over there's wife was a 'six' at best. Locker room banter and outdated rules of thumb, what I call 'bro-vice,' seemed to be their main decision criteria.

Brad Pitt says that they didn't need to replace three key players. They needed to be competitive with a lower budget than most other teams in the major leagues.

Their star first baseman, Jason Giambi, was unique and irreplaceable by anyone in baseball. Therefore, it wasn't about just getting a new player.

Jonah Hill played the analyst in the movie. He said the goal shouldn't be to buy players but to buy wins. Which means you need to buy runs! Baseball thinking was medieval; they were asking all the wrong questions.

My epiphany came at 32 minutes and 15 seconds.

Brad Pitt says that we don't need to replace Giambi; we need a team that, in the aggregate, will deliver what they were losing with Giambi.

Boom! I realized that Moneyball was portfolio management.

And that's what portfolio management is in a nutshell. Not focusing on the trees but standing back, looking at the forest, and applying those six levers of decision quality. Brad/Billy was framing the problem and looking at alternatives.

He realized he didn't need to replace Giambi one to one; he just needed to replace what he gave to the team. That could be accomplished by changing the team's strategy and making several smaller moves.

He brought in great analysts who understood baseball and a management team that was willing to follow the strategy, but it required a lot of 'change management' in the process.

You can think about this in terms of the six elements of decision quality:

Frame – We don't need him; we need what he gives us. We also have limits on how much we can pay. Winning the World Series is the fundamental goal; scoring runs is enabling. Staying within budget was the requirement.

Reliable Data – The sabermetric revolution in baseball allowed for the compilation and analysis of enormous amounts of data.

Logically correct reasoning – Taking the scads of data from sabermetrics allowed modeling of the outcomes of different strategies. They appeared to be using a rank-and-cut methodology in selecting players. However, they were using different metrics for ranking than had been used before.

Creative alternatives – Consideration of replacing the star, changing the lineup to bring in similar skills and changing game tactics.

Tradeoffs – Budget, risk, results. The solution ultimately selected by the Oakland A's allowed them to stay within budget and get good results. There was a risk because the approaches they were taking, while supported by the data, had not been tested in real-life play in the major leagues. In fact, the approach directly contradicted a century of baseball tradition. There was professional risk to Beane and his leadership team, as well as a non-zero probability that the approach would not work.

Commitment to Action – The proposed changes required people in operations (coaching staff) to change the calls they made daily during games. Those who refused to go with the strategy were no longer welcome.

Results – The approach worked! The Oakland A's got farther than anyone expected before losing in the World Series. Every professional baseball team now uses similar approaches.

Even in 2020, there was an article in the Wall Street Journal about the Tampa Bay Rays and how the team manager, Kevin Cash, is bucking intuition and "trusting the system" they have set up.

Social Good

Bjorn Lomborg did a Ted Talk in 2005 about how best to improve the world's ills, given that there are not unlimited funds to achieve it. His organization, the Copenhagen Consensus, gathered high-level experts across several fields, including public health, environment, climate change, energy, and economics. Within each specialty, the experts assessed potential investments that could improve the world and estimated cost and economic benefit to come up with a ranked list in terms of the cost-to-benefit ratio. His Ted Talk is inspiring and exciting.

He starts by framing the question as prioritizing solutions, not simply prioritizing problems, which is an important distinction. His methodology was to distill benefit to a single economic benefit number. While that is an excellent and valuable step to communicate and introduce people to the concept, it can be expanded further. Sure, we care about economic benefit, but what else do we care about as a measure?

It's important to frame this problem correctly. What are the measures we care about?

The highest-level goal of the system, the fundamental objective, is something like promoting human flourishing, but the Copenhagen Consensus uses increasing monetary value as a proxy for that.

The Strategies and Means Objective for achieving that goal can be broken into three main categories:

A. Preservation of habitat and environment
   1. Fewer extinctions in the animal kingdom
   2. Healthy ecosystems
   3. Prevent overuse of natural resources

4. Preservation of natural environments
5. Preventing climate catastrophe
6. Prevent the emission of harmful substances

B. Economic growth
1. Ability to defend ourselves from adverse natural events, whatever the cause
2. Finance human flourishing

C. Reduction of poverty and attendant human suffering and death.
1. Lower mortality and disease
2. Lower poverty
3. Less starvation
4. Adequate food
5. Adequate shelter/Safe environment
6. Adequate medical and health care

The timing of achieving all the above is also an issue, so that is a consideration of both the cost and the benefits.

Frame – I believe they can use more work on the frame, including the analytical frame. While rank and cut is useful, we also care about how things play out over time. Reducing benefits and costs to a point value oversimplifies. At some level, every one of those measures contributes to human flourishing.

On the analytical side, I believe that the models they use to assess should include a time component and let "decision-makers" see the subcomponents before converting to economic benefit.

Reliable Data – It was great to bring in top experts across multiple fields, each to evaluate the cost and benefit of approaches in their areas. I noticed uncertainty in the estimates but did not see any evidence of explicit consideration of this uncertainty. I assume they used similar assumptions for their base scenarios.

Logically Correct Reasoning – This is about the model used to generate different coordinated sets of actions and to create estimated outcomes. Trying to model a planetary ecosystem and estimate human impacts, including all the feedback loops and ranges of outcomes, is unimaginably complex. For this type of analysis, simpler is better for the initial generation and screening of potential strategies. The pencil can be sharpened later. They used a single-dimension rank and cut approach. This is great for illustrating the problem and pointing in a direction.

Embedded in their analyses was not just money but also lives lost, the timing of those lives, illness, and many other factors that decision-makers should care about. Seeing explicitly how those play out should be a part of the next phase.

Creative alternatives – Most of the proposed interventions are scalable. There may be interventions outside of the scope of the specialties or that cross into different fields, but as a first pass, it is good on the entity level.

Lomborg uses simple maximizing economic benefit per dollar spent (bang per buck) as his sole strategy. For example, a program that emphasizes the reduction of human misery might look worse than one that emphasizes healthy ecosystems. They would both be beneficial beyond the direct focus, but their outcomes would address different values.

They did not show how combinations of solutions would play out. There may be value in retaining funding and expertise in the lower priority areas in case they worsen or as the higher priority solutions succeed.

Tradeoffs – These are hard. How much human suffering would you impose to save a species of fire ants halfway around the world? The tradeoff functions are critical, and there is no good way of knowing what they are. Until we see what might be possible and understand the absolutes of what might possibly be done, it's not practical to get a handle on tradeoffs.

This is a case in which generating different strategies and seeing the hypothetical outcomes can help drive an understanding of the true values of the decision-makers. For example, perhaps spending money to prevent temperature rise in 2050 will cost one billion premature deaths from starvation and preventable disease. Is this a good tradeoff if we can't do both? Who makes that tradeoff? Which brings us to...

Commitment to Action – This is the crux of the matter. There is no world government coordinating any of these potential actions or enforcing implementation. Therefore, the frame of the problem **has** to be at a very high level and hypothetical. There's nothing wrong with that; a thorough portfolio analysis could better inform future agreements through the UN or legislation in individual countries. That legislation may ultimately pull in somewhat different directions and reduce overall effectiveness compared to a coordinated response to the world's ills, but it is more palatable to sovereign nations.

To be fair, Lomborg has used this approach with sovereign nations in which he does have the attention of the decision-makers.

Additional Thoughts

Lomborg's approach shows how portfolio problems with multiple disparate values can be worked. He captured the economic essence of the solutions as the primary driver for his ranking. In my view and framework, this is a good start and stimulates thought about these issues, but it is too reductionist to mount a well-informed policy response.

To his credit, he did not ask the specialists to rank the solutions. Their job was to characterize the solutions to lay out cost, timeframe, and benefits. The ranking of the solutions was then performed separately. I will assume that the teams assessing each problem areas had a similar set of assumptions about the future world as inputs to their assessments.

For many, the loss of human life is more than just an economic issue; the loss of a species can have second and third-order effects that unfold over time. Therefore, it's crucial to consider the temporal aspects and incorporate them into solution strategies.

His overall message is that you can't do everything, so prioritizing will happen. Do it with your eyes open and in a coordinated manner.

Lomborg and Climate Change

One of the criticisms of Lomborg comes from climate scientists who do not believe that Lomborg has been fair with his treatment of climate change. Climate scientists believe that Lomborg has understated the benefits of mitigation of carbon dioxide, which to them explains why those measures rank so low on the benefit to cost ratio.

I am certain that there is some degree of motivated criticism in there, but there's a bigger lesson. Surprises from a model are a good thing. If the answers from models were totally predictable, we wouldn't need to bother with models, would we?

My question from the portfolio perspective is whether climate issues were treated on an even playing field with the other issues. When appropriate did they use similar inputs assumptions on both the cost and benefit sides.

Perhaps the issue is that the benefits of climate mitigation are in the distant future and uncertain, while many higher-ranking benefits are immediate and certain. The heat Lomborg has faced is indicative of the challenges that portfolio analysis and management can face.

When a portfolio model suggests a surprising result, interested parties may object strongly, the shocking results **should** cause those interested parties to take notice and understand where the numbers came from and why the results are so surprising. Sadly, the response has mostly been ad hominem attacks on Lomborg's qualifications, Paul

Krugman simply stated that the Copenhagen Consensus methods are not how those decisions are made.

That surprised and saddened me. Whether one agrees with the results, Lomborg's method is how decisions should be made or at least informed. Indeed, the alternative is arm-twisting and power plays. That seems like a poor way to run the world or a country.

CHAPTER 15

Implementing and Managing Portfolio Analysis and Management

"

I can only do the amazing. I can't do the impossible."

Harry Houdini

I hope you now believe portfolio analysis and management will be beneficial for your firm. But there are still many specifics about what to do, who should do it, and when.

I'll start with my answer and work backward:

1. You should do your own portfolio work with your in-house data for owned assets.
2. You should build the capability in-house to perform analysis, set standards, and construct or evaluate models.
3. You should start with simple approaches and work towards skilled practitioners and executives who understand the framing of portfolio analysis. Let the ultimate level of portfolio develop as leaders gain additional insight and see the power that further steps can deliver.
4. Strategic portfolio work should be done at least every two years and as needed. Tactical portfolio management should inform your budgeting process and also inform decisions regarding significant changes in the business.

POINT 1 is to do your own work with your own data. It has two aspects: whether to hire consultants and where the data comes from.

Consultants, especially the big consulting firms, lack skills, sometimes produce sloppy work, charge high fees, fail to adapt to corporate culture, and sometimes tend to upsell their services. In my experience, they simply lack the skills and tools to do advanced portfolio analysis. They will seldom have responsibility for running the tools, standards, and processes once the system is developed. They may sell you a 'one-time' product, provide an answer, then walk away. If continued use of portfolio management is your goal, you need to train your people.

Data for your owned assets – Hopefully, nobody has better data than you do for your assets. If they do, that's a problem for your company. It means either that the people generating the data are not skilled at their work or they are not sharing it with the corporation. The exception is in cases where your firm does not have strong standards, so even internal projects have different assumptions. If you choose not to use your internal data, perform checks to ensure consistent assumptions and broad alignment with internal perspectives.

POINT 2 is about building and maintaining capability and standards to build models and analysis flows that fit your process and governance. Portfolio work tends to ebb and flow with the planning cycle and mad rushes when acquisitions or divestitures become prominent. In between the rushes, there is a lot that a strategic portfolio management group can do.

1. Build and maintain economic and probability standards.
2. Build and check portfolio models.

3. Work with business units to train people and build support for the all-important alternatives and data sharing.
4. Work with project teams to advise on the portfolio fit of different development alternatives.
5. Build strategic portfolio models of competitors. See if they have poor strategic fit assets or projects that your firm might be interested in.
6. Work with executive teams to help them frame questions they ask the organization, informed by analysis types available.

POINT 3 recommends a phased approach. Walk before you run. Doing portfolio work requires cultural changes, education of practitioners and leaders, and tools that do what **you** need them to do. Implementing a portfolio process, like any improvement, requires change management to be successful.

Taking small steps is good because it allows time to assimilate the frame change required for portfolio thinking. But keep an eye on ways to improve tools and processes.

Leaders seldom know the extent of what is possible with portfolio tools. They believe all they need is one small step to something they know about, read about, or had a consultant pitch to them. They are blissfully unaware of the diverse approaches and tools that may be useful to them.

POINT 4 emphasizes the advisability of regular checkups and ad hoc work in between. It maintains portfolio capability and better aligns intent with decisions.

Use Excel or develop tools to manage quantitative and qualitative data and create data tables for reports and graphs. Work on categorizing your assets and generating simple rollups. Explore your current direction based on your programmed actions and plans.

Create your own optimization tool for business plan and budgeting tactical analysis; build portfolio simulation models for your exploration and research teams.

The right steps to implementing and managing sustainable portfolio analysis, whether at a corporate or business unit level, will depend on culture, governance, and leadership. The sections on implementing and managing a portfolio process begin with an overview of general pitfalls—those actions that can bring your efforts to a halt (hopefully just a temporary one).

Key Takeaways

1. Implementing a portfolio system and processes is a marathon, not a sprint. Assembling the parts and capability needed for the simpler approaches is generally straightforward. Because of the annual planning cycle in most firms, you can anticipate about one step change per year. Assuming there are standards for standalone analysis in place, rank and cut, rollups, and slice and dice can be done within the first year or right now.
2. Moving beyond the simplest methods will take time, experience, and effort. Simulation and optimization are skills. Understanding the limitations and nuances of those techniques can be tricky. Assume a two to three-year journey from no portfolio to high decision quality using interaction techniques.
3. Starting slow is one good reason to build your own. Another is the premature purchase of a system before you know your needs. Much time, money, and effort have been spent on tools that were later scrapped.

Pitfalls of Implementing a Portfolio Process

Talking about portfolio analysis and management (PfAM) is tricky because the two phases—implementation and operation—overlap in many aspects. Implementation is the step where you initially develop the workflows, tools, future support, training, etc. In operation, you apply the tools, processes, and systems in place. This section deals with the implementation of portfolio tools and processes.

Change Management

All the Usual Change Management Stuff

Improvement is impossible without change. Moving to a more rigorous portfolio process is even more difficult than some other changes because it may reveal deficiencies in the current way of doing business. As a result, leaders sometimes point to the people who execute the plans. They explain, "We don't need a new process. We just need to do the old one better." Of course, the old one was created in 1985 before anyone had access to powerful personal computers. It is akin to if Steve Jobs had tried to build a better CD changer instead of an iPod or if Henry Ford had developed robots to pull carriages instead of using an internal combustion engine.

Sometimes the frame of reference must be shifted, or at least be willing to look at the problem differently.

I am not a big fan of external consultants, especially during implementation. However, before making the implementation decision, it may help to have a disinterested voice advocating for change and even assisting with selecting methodologies. An internal person may be seen or characterized as self-serving.

Underestimating the Change Management Needs of Implementing a New Way of Thinking

Not every change is an improvement, but every improvement is a change. You can't do anything better unless you can manage to do it differently...

Eliezer Yudkowsky

Portfolio thinking is less linear than looking at individual projects. The people making portfolio-level decisions have likely been around a while and have organizations aligned with the previous approach to decision-making.

There is an implication that if there is a better way to do something and they aren't doing it, they are derelict in their duties. This puts in place cognitive dissonance and organizational and psychological incentives to resist change.

When implementing portfolio management in an organization, the analysis phase may be imprecise yet relatively simple, but the results can yield valuable insights. But even the best and most potent insight is not worth anything if the decision-makers are unwilling to act on them. Commitment to action is a part of decision quality for a reason. The analysis must be credible and ultimately supported by the firm's leadership.

I have not found a great way to bring portfolio analysis and management to people who think that what they're doing is already great. Every organization is different, but there needs to be a high-level leader or manager who wants the company to do things better. Grinding it out may be the only option if you do not have that. Try small steps—move from standalone to comparison. Or do a simulation for exploration, or if you have business or strategic plan data, build an optimizer and play with it (in your spare time, of course). Demonstrations of usefulness or insight might leave them wanting more.

I'm not an expert in change management, but there are books and specialists in this field. One book that I recommend is "*Bare Bones Change Management: What You Shouldn't Not Do*" by Bob Lewis.

People who need PfAM the most are often the least aware that they need it.

Trying to Do Too Much Too Soon

Even though the portfolio method selector may suggest that you use advanced methods, getting to that point may require a slower path. Standards must be developed, data providers must be trained, and people may need to work those standards into workflows.

It's better in most cases to start with data they already have and do what you can with that data. Establish a few small wins and gain support for why it is worth the effort to get better data. This is an agile, minimum viable product (MVP) approach, but always consider where you want to take the analysis in the long run. When using existing, non-standard data, there is a risk of portfolio theater—people making decisions based on flawed data, even though the process follows the right steps.

Failure to Plan for Success

Not Developing Future Portfolio Analysts and Succession Plans

One beauty of PfAM is that a single person with access to data and a model can add insights worth billions of dollars. Ironically, this analytical efficiency leads to one of the major pitfalls. Unlike project management, you need only one person to compile all the projects. It takes some time and experience, but that person is precious. But even portfolio analysts have careers and aspirations.

Because you do not need an army of analysts, there is little incentive to have much backup, so it will be hard for that person to move into another role without leaving a sizable capability gap. On top of that, all it takes is for one manager of a portfolio analyst to decide that they can do it in their head anyway, so why pay someone to do it? In other words, because portfolio insights are often generated by one person, there is exposure to a single point of failure.

During the development of a portfolio process, it's important to include planning for success as a key component of your change management efforts. While it may be tempting to cut the budget and delay filling positions until the next cycle, this approach can hinder progress and success in the long run.

If you want to realize value from portfolio management beyond the short term, there must be a commitment to the practice.

Releasing the Development Team Upon Completion of the IT Project

Portfolio systems often have a significant IT component, but they should not be considered IT projects—they are business change projects. Even well-planned business change takes time. Portfolio projects are more difficult than most because they deal with leadership paradigms and new ways of thinking that few are familiar with.

One result is that portfolio projects often need change and improvement, even after victory is declared. Count on at least two planning cycles for people to get used to the data, tools, and procedures. You should keep the core people who developed the conceptual basis for the tool and the most difficult nuts and bolts on board for at least that time. Not doing so risks confusion and, at some point, people throwing up their hands and saying, "At least we knew what we were doing in the old system."

Unrealistic Expectations/Frame

A Belief That Portfolio is the Solution to All Strategic Problems

Using portfolio methods puts a firm in a position to be aware of the range of impacts of its strategic and tactical decisions. Leadership is essential in defining the values and outcomes the firm cares about.

For example, imagine a firm that invests heavily and scales up staffing during a good business environment. They return cash to shareholders through share buybacks and dividends. Perhaps they have overextended the firm, assuming that the good times will continue.

When the inevitable happens, they must sell assets at a loss, lay off people at a high cost, and cut dividends. They were forced to make costly short-term focused decisions to get out of their disadvantageous position. Could portfolio management have prevented this?

Portfolio capability would be a necessary but not sufficient enabler in preventing this kind of issue. With good portfolio analysis practice, the consequences of a downturn can be investigated along multiple dimensions. They might have been able to determine how far back they would have to pull, how much they would have to restructure their finances, and modeled the implications of selling below cost. But there is a necessary pre-condition.

They must first believe that a shift in the business landscape is a plausible scenario. They should then incorporate this type of risk into their value system, which reflects their priorities.

Nobody has a crystal ball. Nor does it take one to know that the business environment will change over time. An assumption of a continuing straight-line environment may be the easiest estimate. But, if leadership is unwilling to consider and incorporate other scenarios, they will not make high-quality decisions.

Letting the perfect be the enemy of the good

This applies to both input data and the outputs from a portfolio model. Strategic portfolio work is about aggregated performance at the enterprise or organizational level. The insights come from comparisons of organizational performance.

People in a company often expect the tools and processes to be perfect and seamless, to do everything they may possibly want quickly. Then when the new approach is shown to have flaws—even in minor or unimportant ways—the entire effort is discredited, and the organization reverts to a demonstrably worse approach.

Doug Hubbard, the author of *How to Measure Anything,* coined a term for this and similar cognitive errors—exsupero ursus—surpassing the bear from the old joke about the two guys in the woods, one of whom was putting on sneakers to run faster. The solution you select and move towards does not need to be perfect, just better than the alternative.

Culture

A corporate culture that frames internal decision-making as competition rather than cooperation

The fundamental premise of portfolio management is to put the decisions into the frame of the firm, not the individual or business unit. Some corporate cultures believe competition is the best way to spur productivity and value. Indeed, competition and related incentives are strong drivers. But, if the drive is too strong, it can lead to distortions that prevent value realization. When the incentive is "My project must be selected, so I benefit," rather than "The best project must be selected, so we all benefit," the firm may suffer.

Treating your portfolio system as a process rather than a practice

Related to the overall proposition is the issue of thinking that portfolio is simply a process without human input.

Bob Lewis has written exhaustively over the last few decades on the difference between processes and practices. To paraphrase Bob:

A process is like a recipe. You do each step in sequence and specification, and you come up with repeatable results. Think of building an Ikea cabinet. You follow a set of drawings, and in the end, you and 900,000 other people have the exact same cabinet. Ikea does its best to remove the person building the cabinet from the picture.

Practices are much looser. Each circumstance is different. It is more of a craft. You can do some of the same steps, but practitioners need a more holistic perspective to decipher the different circumstances. They need to know when to use which tool. The person is very much a part of a practice—their skill, judgment, and experience are critical factors in the effort's success. Cooks follow recipes; chefs learn the practice.

Processes and practices are the bookends. In reality, much of business dwells somewhere between them. Companies often strive to turn practices into processes to save time and reduce the need for highly skilled labor.

Another way to look at this is the difference between uncertainty and ambiguity. Uncertainty can typically be modeled mathematically, but when there is ambiguity, such as conflicting goals, more rigorous framing is required to make good decisions.

With portfolio, there's a lot of math, modeling, and running sophisticated algorithms. But context is what really makes the difference. Leadership moves on, the world changes, and technology evolves. Some aspects of portfolio analysis can be automated, but the derivation of insights—where most of the value lies—requires strong facilitation skills, creativity, and vision. You have to be able to coax meaning from the data.

Poor communication and understanding of the portfolio process needs

Organizations are used to their way of doing business. Project alternatives are designed to maximize the metric that they have always used. Portfolio tools require diverse asset alternatives to fully realize value from the process. The teams that generate alternatives for inclusion in portfolio models must provide diverse options focusing on different metrics and approaches, even when those alternatives are at odds with the previously used metrics.

Not using the data that you have

Another pitfall revolves around data. Again, you can invest much time and effort in generating or acquiring more data, but is it worth it? You probably have more data than you think, or you can extrapolate useful data easily.

Fast and cheap should be your default first pass. Get better data as justified by business needs. This is closely related to letting the perfect be the enemy of the good.

Converting a strategic portfolio model into a budgeting model

In our perfect world, all the data flows smoothly.

Budgeting implies accuracy and precision. This is possible only in the very short term. Once you look beyond one year (or less) into the future, it is impossible to accurately predict the state of the world. And if you're looking out in the 10+ year timeframe, even though accuracy and precision are absurd, insights can still flow. There are two issues beyond simple accuracy and precision: distortion and complication.

Distortion due to nominal analyses

Some will insist that you use corporate inflation and escalation factors. If you must, you must. I suggest you resist as a general rule. Here's why.

For example, let's start our time series data with a $50 oil price. Across 20 years of 2% inflation, what will that price be? What if inflation is 3%? What if your corporation thinks it will be 2% for five years, then 4% after that? Where does the price end up? If your plan shows revenue growth from 100 to 130 across that time, is it good? Does it show progress if the earnings margin changes from $10 per barrel to $20? Even more important, is this a sound basis for strategic decisions? Even though the nominal dollars go up, have you made progress in terms of "real" dollars?

If your analysis suggests that you do something different from what you are doing today, is it valid, or is it an artifact of your assumptions? In other words, is a decision being driven by inaccurate guesses about the future? If so, your analysis is likely to be distorted.

Complications of changing the future playing field

Volatile oil prices and cost escalation can require tremendous modeling effort to get an internally consistent and "accurate" cash flow for budgeting. If it takes 40 minutes to recalculate your portfolio model, the insights you gain from the analysis will be limited by the calendar.

Nobody can do these kinds of compound growth adjustments in their heads. They don't know whether the increases in revenue and price are showing progress of the business or numerical distortion. Some people believe that the form of an analysis and adhering to "standards" is more important than the insights from analysis. They believe they are calibrated to the inflated, variable, escalated numbers and metrics across different periods, even though those factors change yearly. They're not.

Perhaps there should be a set of standards (separate from budgeting and planning assumptions) that puts portfolio work on a "real" basis without the distortions of all the "scientific guesses" about the future. This approach would create consistency and constancy of perspective around project comparisons; the disadvantage is that two different sets of assumptions would have to be continually explained and clarified.

Development Process

Premature focus on tool selection

Often somebody with influence in an organization sees a demo of a tool or product that seems to do everything they could ever need to do with portfolio. It slices, it dices, it optimizes, and it recalculates the whole business based on changes in underlying assumptions. And it works so fast! They form a team to implement the tool and let them go at it.

Ten million dollars later, they have a tool that works but doesn't fit within their management or planning processes. It doesn't do what they need, and even if it does, leaders don't understand what it's telling them.

Significant software implementation must be accompanied by significant change management. Even better, work on the change management with a simple version of the software and get fancier with the software as there is a business need and justification. You may end up with the software package. Often that is not the case.

The book, "*There's no Such Thing as an IT Project*" by Bob Lewis and Dave Kaiser may provide insights for you.

Premature focus on efficiency and streamlining data flow

Peter Drucker said that doing the wrong thing with great efficiency is useless. One pitfall I have witnessed is when teams work in a phase gate approach and create their process development alternatives, but their steering committee pushes them away from high-value but speculative or difficult-to-measure approaches. They push towards low-risk and much easier-to-measure approaches. One process change team tried to drive project decisions towards a portfolio frame. The benefit could easily have been hundreds of millions of dollars in NPV. The steering committee forced decisions away from portfolio management and into the data flow path, where they could reduce the number of copy-and-paste actions by employees. It was a lost opportunity.

There is value in streamlining data flows and reducing the error rate for the plan rollup. However, those gains are typically measured in fractions of a full-time employee vs. many millions of dollars.

The value comes from insights leading to different decisions and directions—not by removing a copy-paste step from the process. By all means, streamline and remove steps once you have captured the big-value insights.

Going for a quick win with no follow-up plan

The world keeps turning. Annual processes come and go. In the midst of it all, implementing portfolio analysis and management can be daunting. Often, the managers want to sidetrack development efforts to get a quick win in the normal cycle. Resist this if you can.

If the data and tools are not prepared, the outcomes will likely be misleading. Even if the data and tools aren't bad, these quick wins can lead a project into a blind alley where it will get stuck or have to backtrack significantly to recover lost ground. Bob Lewis said, "Going after low-hanging fruit is a popular consulting recommendation. It's usually a mistake because it creates the illusion of forward progress while failing to set the stage for additional forward progress."

Quick wins are often simple steps like streamlining data flow or better efficiency. While they are important, excessive focus on those quick wins can easily lead to complacency (80-20), preventing big wins. If you must pursue a quick win, try to incorporate progress in related competencies, tools, or processes.

When using an agile development process, you must have a clear vision in order to achieve meaningful progress. Without a North Star, agile development may result in only minor improvements and short-term successes.

Not managing expectations well

Half of the people who want to do portfolio work hope it will solve all their problems; the other half fear it will solve all their problems. People who do portfolio work are often on the numerical spectrum of life. The tools are powerful, provide valuable insights, and, let's face it, are fun to use and develop.

Some people push back against letting a computer run the company and make all the decisions. In contrast, others expect the tools to solve all problems with the press of a button and spit out board-quality presentations and answers that are not just insightful but also accurate.

Optimization models and methods can appear opaque, as they are often seen as a black box that produces answers. They won't trust it. There must be good facilitation, smart presentation, and a keen awareness of the perceived threats that this kind of approach brings.

Portfolio tools will not solve all the world's problems, and they will not put a company on autopilot. Portfolio tools, perspective, and analysis provide support to make better decisions.

Not realizing that "good, fast, or cheap (pick 2)" is reality

You can't have everything. In a perfect world, we would have a tool that does everything you could possibly need stochastically and quickly. Such a system, although theoretically possible, would be quite expensive, relying on multiple processors and data farms. It would be good and fast, but not cheap.

You could build it cheaper with the same technical capabilities, but it would take a long time to calculate. Therefore, it's good and cheap, but not fast.

Or you could build a system that makes simplifications, so it becomes fast and cheap but not "good."

During initial development, I favor the fast and cheap approach. This comes with the significant disadvantage that you constantly need to explain why the tool does not "solve the world." The good news is that it may leave them wanting more. This approach is consistent with agile project methodologies, which have become popular in many companies.

Real or perceived organizational incentives sometimes gravitate against this approach. There is status that comes with managing a big expensive project, as opposed to an incremental one. I have also seen cases where projects continued **because** they were hard and expensive. This is probably the sunk cost fallacy in action. After establishing the necessary staff and technical infrastructure, it can be extremely challenging to remove something harmful.

There will always be tension between people who want to make a perfect, defensible, internally consistent model and those who want to get fast, approximate answers. There is a tradeoff, and sometimes, seemingly small decisions with a slight impact on precision can hugely increase execution time. The only way to find the right point for your firm may be to tinker, scale, and test before making final decisions.

Thinking that people are more advanced than they are (My wife says this is my only flaw)

This pitfall comes back to different definitions of portfolio analysis and the lack of knowledge generally about what is possible. When someone tells me they want to "do portfolio management," I assume they already do standalone analysis, probably do inventory comparison, and want to go to the more advanced techniques. This is often not the case. Sometimes, they just want to bucket their assets into a Cash Cow and Oyster 2X2 grid while I'm ready to give them stochastic analysis.

It is essential to probe early on about what data is available and what they are trying to accomplish with their portfolio tools and efforts.

Key Takeaway

Implementing a portfolio system and processes is not to be taken lightly. The easiest approach, building a system around existing processes, misses value that could be captured. The more challenging approaches, which change how the company thinks about itself, add more value and are more difficult. Your organization and your tenacity and patience will determine the direction you take. Good luck on your implementation journey.

War Story – Go Big or Go Home

Management was concerned that the planning process was too expensive and time-consuming. Planners throughout the company were spending too much time reconciling between the budget and strategic plan six months later. They were also doing the same for the following business plan, and so forth. Something needed to change.

A team was formed to eliminate extra work, and they began working on the task. During the framing of the effort, the team did their best to keep value delivered as a critical metric of the work and not just cost savings. The decision executives focused on reducing costs, but the project team continued to focus on delivering value.

The main objective and driving force behind the decision was to reduce costs. But the decision-makers threw the team a bone and let them do a portfolio pilot project, the results of which they would consider for the next stage of the effort. The pilot was successful, but there was a re-organization and institutional memory was lost. Portfolio management was not implemented at that time.

Lessons Learned

1. Incremental change and continuous improvement are essential. They are also relatively easy, which means that your competitors will quickly catch up if they haven't already. Consequently, incremental change is short-lived and has diminishing returns. There will come a point when a step change is needed.
2. If the best you can do is to get that weak incremental change, take it and try to keep the vision alive. But remember, if you don't even try for the bigger win, you definitely won't get it.

Detail – The 80/20 Trap

The Pareto Principle states that roughly 80% of the consequence or benefit comes from approximately 20% of the input elements or causes. This is a great insight and, in my experience, generally true. Getting to 90% of what might double the effort, 95% might triple the effort required, etc.

80/20 can serve as a guide for when you have hit the point of diminishing returns. After all, if 20% of the work gives you 80% of the benefit, you should move on to something else more worthy of your time. It's a very reasonable perspective—except when it isn't.

In setting up foundational processes or tools that will influence many people or large amounts of money, sometimes it is worthwhile to go beyond that 80% solution. The foundational elements affect many factors moving forward. If each aspect is done to the 80/20 standard, the result will not be 80/20.

Suppose you have five tasks to complete to build a system or process. If each is done to an 80/20 standard, that is 80% * 80% * 80% * 80% * 80% = 33%. This means that merely "adequate" work may compound and result in an inadequate final product. This is part of the reason that creating and updating the frame of a problem or effort is so important. Error in the frame will result in wasted efforts down the line.

I am not suggesting perfection. Instead, put thought into your tasks, and ensure that the most critical, foundational ones that will feed into all subsequent tasks receive extra attention and are completed to a standard well beyond 80%.

Key Takeaways

Applying 80/20 can be a lazy and damaging approach. Be especially wary if applying the Pareto Principle to **foundational** aspects of your work without a solid plan to revisit and improve on it. Changes beyond the first pass at a solution may be extremely difficult to implement in the future.

Detour – The Single Version of the Truth Fallacy

People sometimes believe it is important to have a "single version of the truth." This is a great idea when a single truth exists. The challenge we have in our uncertain world is that the truth exists only after the fact. Before resolution to an outcome, there is no deterministic truth.

Even the expression "Single Version of Truth" implies that there may be other versions of the truth. That in itself seems like a contradiction. Truth is truth, right?

Accountants recording outcomes know the answers to how the world resolved in the last accounting period. It is truth and there is only a single version.

There is no single version of a future outcome that is objectively correct. When dealing with future events, having a single reference version for comparison is convenient. But do not confuse that with the truth. It comes down to people wanting an **official** version of the forecast. That way, when new information emerges, someone can manage the communication of the next single version of the forecast.

There is value in telling a consistent story and consistency between planning, approvals, and presentation, but don't confuse that with the truth. There are good reasons for showing different versions of the future depending on the specific question being asked and internal incentives for being wrong.

We are all familiar with the expression "under-promise and over-deliver." Under-promising is a lie, but it can be rational and smart if you know you will be punished for not delivering. Before an event unfolds, all you know is that the future is uncertain.

This may be semantics, but I believe that words and concepts are important and matter. We see that when people think a plan is (or should be) the same as a forecast. A lack of clarity in communication is costly.

Detail – Change is Hard and Slow in All Fields

Perhaps you have heard the saying that progress happens one funeral at a time. I prefer to think that it happens one retirement at a time. Regardless, there still has to be groundwork. It doesn't happen by itself.

Existing leadership becomes entrenched and resistant to change, so incoming leaders must help to drive change. This is always hard. People rise through the organization to their leadership positions based on the existing paradigm. After all, if that paradigm worked for them and recognized their talent, it must be good!

This is why humility is essential. Although the current order has its benefits, it also has drawbacks that any potential changes should be addressed. Yes, there are costs to effect any change. And hey, the organization has survived and thrived all this time.

But it's not just your company. The article "*4 Ways to Make Evidence-Based Practice the Norm in Health Care*" by Margaret M. Luciano, Thomas A. Aloia, and Joan F. Brett in the August 2019 Harvard Business Review states that research suggests that it takes 17 years to adopt a new practice from the first positive systematic evidence.

Consider Ignaz Semmelweis, who championed hand washing to prevent hospital deaths starting in 1847. He had irrefutable evidence of the efficacy of hand washing. He published a book on the matter in 1860. It wasn't until around 1885, twenty years after his death, that the medical world became more receptive to the idea.

There are many possible reasons for this considerable lag, but it is an international concern. Some of the reasons include the effort required to change curricula and the power and confidence of established professionals.

My belief and hope are that good portfolio analysis and management will become the norm. It makes sense on many levels. In the meantime, we can continue to move our own organizations in the right direction, learn more about tools, techniques, and persuasion, and work towards training and inspiring the next generation of analysts.

War Story – The Dwindling Importance Trap

After a smashing success that changed the company's direction, the portfolio planners were eager to replicate it.

There was some confusion as a management group gathered to create a plan. The previous year had strong guidance from executives; this time, the management group was on its own. There was no motivation to explore alternative strategies. The group leader had not yet established a vision for this strategic planning exercise.

On top of that, there was a glitch in a data extract. The technical problems were straightened out, but over the next several years, the strategic planning exercise became less important and more superficial. The result was effectively a caricature or cartoon of what a plan would look like if they were actually to try to implement it, which they didn't.

The promise of portfolio management had not continued after the big success. The systems were still in place, and one or two practitioners continued to use the tools in isolated situations.

Eventually, as external conditions changed, the systems began to be used well again. But portfolio decision analysis was wandering through the desert for a decade at the company.

Lessons Learned

1. The leadership group was large and diverse in their vested interests. They were not a team, but a group thrown together to ensure representation.
2. Stronger leadership from the head of the function and a specific agenda to test strategies would have helped both the analysts facilitating the process and the managers. The meeting lacked specific planning and a compelling reason for the group to try different strategies. The group's aim became to produce a set of graphs that would please executive leadership rather than improve the underlying decisions. Without strong leadership, little value came from the meeting.
3. Without a strong endorsement and vision from leadership across the enterprise, organizations tend to revert to their former selves.

War Story – The Developer Has Left the Building

In the 90s, there were memes and little parables all over the place about how "change is good." Anyone with a shred of intellect knows that the statement is not necessarily true. I can't tell you how many people I heard using those words. (Remember "*Who Moved My Cheese?*".)

Change is change. It is a decision and the result—good or bad—is an outcome. We hope for a good one, but that is not a given. Improvement requires change. It is impossible to improve if you do not allow change to happen. Unfortunately, sometimes changes are for the worse.

▸ **Improvement Requires Change**

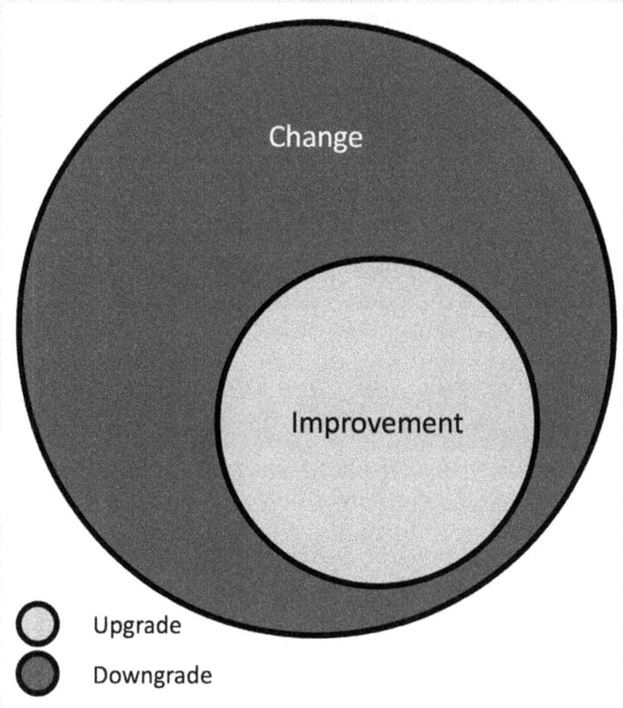

All improvements require change; some changes are not improvements.

At one company, developing the planning database had been a heroic push. In under one year, the project went from idea to implementation. The first cycle was rocky, but it went well overall. It was definitely better than the previous inefficient and error-prone Excel-based setup.

From the start of usage—the very first report pulled—the development team realized that there needed to be some significant improvements for the next planning cycle. The improvements would increase the complexity somewhat and improve functionality significantly.

The team did the work and got it running. It was a massive step in the evolution of the tool. The big strategic planning meeting was scheduled for the second week of April. The planners were busily chasing down the data, checking it for consistency, and preparing for the interactive session. Then in late March, the leader rescheduled the meeting for one week later.

A delay is usually welcome, but in this case, the key developer of the new features had an unavoidable commitment in the newly scheduled week. The developer did what he could to prepare all the reports needed to populate the models, but there was an error, with nobody on-site who had the technical skills to check or understand it.

The meeting started, and there was an obvious issue when they pulled up a report with the error. The effect on results was large, but the minor error could only be fixed by the one person who was not there and would only take seconds to resolve.

The leadership meeting was in disarray, with attendees deriding the significant improvements as unneeded complexity (it wasn't). They were able—eventually—to contact the developer, who walked the planning team through the fix. The meeting proceeded as planned.

Shortly after the issue, the developer shifted to another group but was still a phone call away. The leaders vowed that never again would anybody change the "now-perfect" system, so they set up a governance team to manage future changes. Fortunately, with the existing changes, the system was pretty good and much improved over the previous iteration. It could have been even better.

Lessons Learned

1. The improvement cycle was critical. If the developer had left after the initial implementation, the system would have been much less useful and would not have survived.
2. More effort and emphasis should have been put into training a backup developer.
3. Off-the-shelf tools or turnkey systems leave little room for change. Every company and leader approaches portfolio problems differently, therefore the system must remain flexible to accommodate changing leadership.

4. Early glitches can have a far-reaching impact. The governance board that formed after the fateful meeting prevented improvements to the system for several years. Even minor fixes were required to go through the governance board, which mostly said no. They allowed and promoted one significant change that made the system more uniform across business units. It is important to shape the mission of a governance board as more than gatekeepers of change prevention. There needs to be an improvement remit as well.

War Story – The Negative Consequences of Believing Your Models, Part 2

Overconfidence in the Process

The company had bought into portfolio management—really bought into it. So much so that they decided that they could accurately model and optimize their business and follow the advice from the model.

Everyone in the company gave his or her data to the center, the center would move the pieces, do a(nother) re-organization, and go their merry way.

Unfortunately, the advice from the models was not just counter-intuitive but detrimental. For instance, according to the model's recommendations, the company's controlling interest in an asset was reduced from 60% to an overly precise 25.5%, resulting in the loss of its operational control.

The yearly shifts were disruptive to the entire enterprise. The company had been completely re-prioritized before the previous effort had a chance to play out. This was terribly inefficient and also led to distrust with the company's partners.

There were a few faulty assumptions behind the philosophy of this work, including that all projects are fungible and the market for assets is efficient.

Lessons Learned

1. You can have too much of a good thing.
2. There is a Goldilocks spot for the pace of strategic work.
3. Large organizations with many projects do not turn on a dime.

Detour – Decision Science vs Decision Engineering—Be an Engineer

I listen to a podcast, "*Ask a Decision Engineer*," by Michelle Florendo. A recent episode got me thinking about how engineering is different than science generally and how that might apply to portfolio analysis and management.

Scientists do things like figure out how electrons work and the equations that govern them. Engineers, on the other hand, convert science into useful devices like electric can openers. (Apologies to Neal Stephenson, *Cryptonomicon*). That is a good paradigm to keep in mind as you develop a portfolio practice in your organization.

You can use the decision tree to select the best portfolio method. Read and learn about Decision Quality and how to achieve it. Maybe you could build a sophisticated model that solves the problem with aplomb. But in the final analysis, your organization has to agree to use it, agree to supply data, and develop a succession plan. Maybe your boss or one of their peers does not like the skillfully constructed displays you created. This is where engineering comes in. Organizational change breaks down in the theoretical realm. Only in practice does it have a possibility of working.

You will likely end up with a frankenhybrid of the approaches I have laid out. I know of one organization in which the attorneys and accountants would not allow numerical (dollar) estimation of risk, even on a what-if basis, for fear it would create a liability against the balance sheet. In another organization, a planning manager told their team that they would not allow the analysts to use mathematical optimization.

In both cases, the analysts found workarounds, which, although imperfect, provided insights that led to much better decisions. So have no fear. Don't let the perfect be the enemy of the better. You will find your path.

Detail – Practical Considerations – Cascaded Portfolios

In a theoretical "perfect world," the top level of a firm has access to all the data. It has probabilistic, accurate, and fast models that aggregate, simulate, optimize, and rerun everything as assumptions change. This would be a vast—impractical, if not impossible—undertaking for a company with any scale and diversity of business lines.

Companies delegate authority to push work out to the places with the knowledge needed to do detailed analyses. The people closest to the actual business know the business unit's needs best, while headquarters leaders know best what the enterprise needs. This asymmetry of information and difficulty communicating often leads to misunderstandings about the best role for a business unit.

There are some practical considerations as well. Many countries allow for tax consolidation between entities within the country. If you have two businesses, one profitable and one not, you can write off the profits of one against the losses of the other. While strategic-level portfolio work can often ignore these non-linear impacts, they may be material.

Business units need some level of autonomy and flexibility as well. Again, this is part of why there is a delegation of authority. Conditions can change rapidly, and local management needs the freedom to act quickly when required.

Time horizon also matters in portfolio modeling. In oil and gas, decisions are made months and years in advance—there is a long lead time between the inception of a project and execution. Trying to manage the next quarter's decisions from a portfolio model could contradict governance and common sense. Therefore, portfolio work should look far enough into the future to accommodate any necessary changes in direction and resource allocation.

All the above runs counter to the perfect world scenario. How does a company structure its portfolio decisions to reflect reality while not being an overwhelmingly complicated model?

Enter Cascaded Portfolio Management

There is a sweet spot for doing portfolio analysis. If a company has a small investment program, it may be difficult to justify the added expense and complexity of portfolio analysis. Medium-sized companies, meaning those that are not supermajor players in the petroleum or pharmaceutical industries, have the size and scale to make portfolio management worth the investment and can reap the most benefits from it. Super-large companies often have decentralized management and delegation of authority. While the companies could theoretically receive tremendous benefits from portfolio management, their size, complexity, and culture make it challenging to establish and manage. The idea of centralized portfolio management flies in the face of their corporate cultures.

Most companies have a rollup planning process, where each business unit generates a coherent investment and production scenario and submits it to the corporation for approval. Cascaded portfolio management is not much different. The main difference is that each business unit would offer a few meaningfully different scenarios for consideration and feedback from the center rather than just one.

Jeffrey Keisler wrote a paper that models the effect of having multiple alternatives to consider in a portfolio. If each of your projects were infinitesimally scalable, you could realize 100% of the total theoretical value of the investment program. Conversely, considering only one course of action per investment allows for no refinement above the base plan. One of Keisler's insightful findings is that with 3 or 4 options per investment, you could realize well over 90% of the maximum theoretical potential. His paper included different funding levels assuming smooth scalability. Asset investments seldom have that kind of granularity. But the lesson is the same— alternatives provide the opportunity to add value.

With that in mind, imagine a scenario where you have multiple business units with enough complexities that realistically modeling them is impossible at the higher level. With tools, standards, and training, the business units would submit their **integrated** alternatives to the corporation for consideration.

The corporation would process the complete set of options received and provide feedback to the BUs.

This takes advantage of the information asymmetry when local management knows the business while executive management knows the enterprise. The local groups can create alternative, integrated portfolio strategies with meaningfully different themes that would be accurate enough and doable with the constraints and complications of the local organization. The mechanics and feedback loops required for this to work are a function of the corporate culture and planning process.

Compare this to the planning process where each BU submits its answer. There is no value to be added through the planning process except for the usual arm twisting.

With the below organizational structure, the rollup could be done with three cascades:

1. Multiple project alternatives submitted to Asset
2. Asset generates several asset alternatives
3. SBUs develop SBU alternatives

Which then are submitted to the enterprise to sort it all out.

Sample Organizational Structure for Cascading Portfolio Work

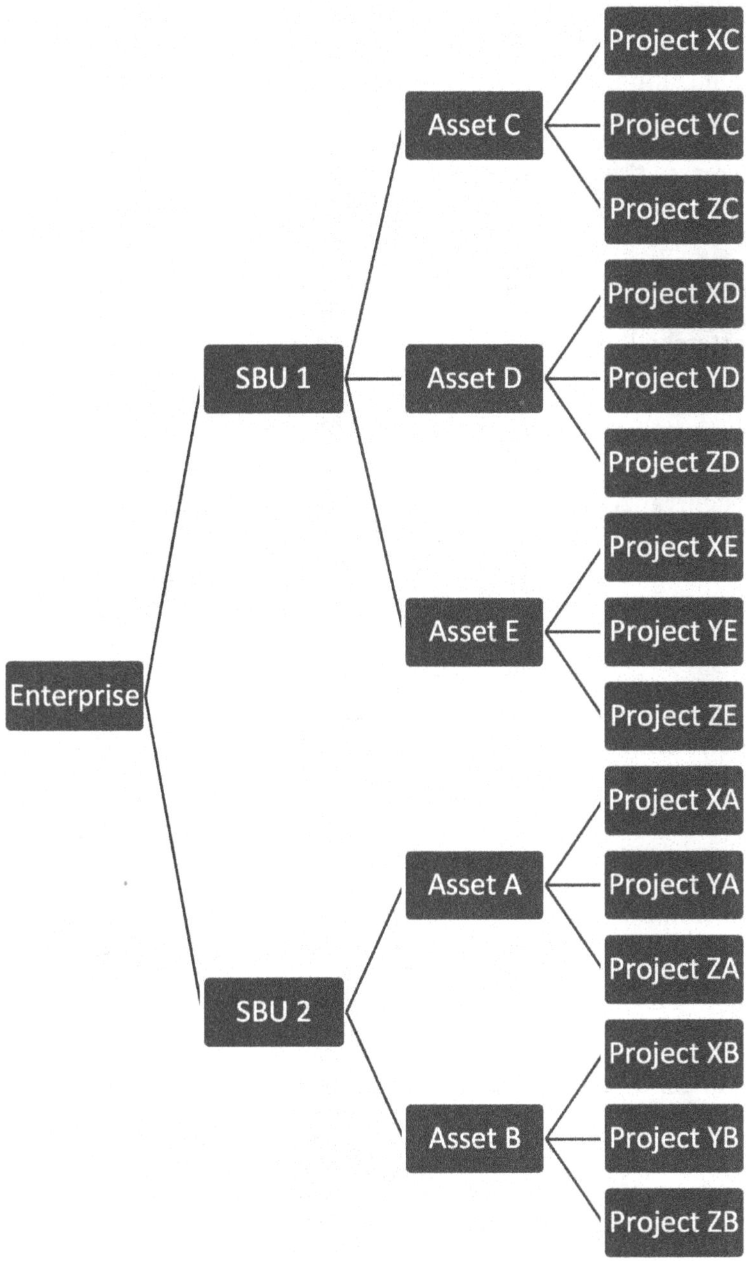

Organizations with multiple levels of hierarchy can cascade portfolios up the organizational levels rather than attempting to use a central model. This would be a bottom-up portfolio process. It differs from a bottom-up ***plan*** *in that the lower levels provide more than one project or asset alternative.*

This approach requires portfolio capabilities at the SBU and Enterprise levels, with knowledge at the assets. Depending on the structure of the business units and how they relate to taxation systems, it is often possible to cut out at least one level in this cascade. For example, SBU 2 could skip the Asset level entirely and generate multiple SBU alternatives directly from projects. Even better, skip the SBU and go directly from Asset to Enterprise. Keep in mind that with each cascade level decreases the potential value by 5-10%. Remember that each level of cascade reduces value somewhat. If skipping levels makes sense and can be managed, it is generally a better option.

The approach may also change local authority from a governance perspective. Now instead of selecting their preferred alternative, headquarters will be making that selection, while the business unit then has the authority to execute the selected alternative.

Contrasting Cascaded and Centralized Models

Centralized Model	Cascaded Model
Value	
Theoretically maximizes possible value	Some leakage in value (5-10%)
Value	
Extremely complex model or live with inaccuracy; Single large model (black box)	Accurate models, distributed
Asset Alternatives	
Very general, inaccurate, do not take some constraints and synergies into account	Accurate, doable, and include synergies and constraints
Capability	
Fewer portfolio experts needed, but must be **very** good	Need decent portfolio capability throughout the organization
Insights	
Business insights approximate	Business insights more accurate

Cascaded portfolio processes require more distributed capability and result in some value leakage. A single centralized model will be complex and will necessarily take shortcuts.

Cascaded Probabilistic Portfolio Work

All the problems with a single, centralized model are more difficult when you need to use probabilities. But Probability Management has developed standards that facilitate the sharing of probabilistic data across your firm by specifying inputs and outputs seamlessly and easily. It still requires preparation and standards, but the data can then be combined in essentially a big adding machine to create corporate-level probabilistic performance models.

Detail – Organizational Capability and Governance

Practical considerations lead to organizational ones. Depending on the structure and requirements for the work, you need both capabilities and standards. Capabilities include people with experience and training to facilitate and do the modeling necessary for portfolio analysis. Standards include data standards and the knowledge and expertise to frame the studies properly.

Many companies have a corporate planning department that ensures that projects and assets use consistent inputs on factors like price and inflation. Sam Savage has suggested that firms should also have a Chief Probability Officer (CPO) who oversees the probabilistic standards in a firm and ensures that people throughout the company are using consistent and aligned inputs to their probabilistic models.

Portfolio analysis and management sit at the intersection of finance, decision analysis, project management, and planning. Many companies have functional groups that manage that talent. You have to ask, "...should there be a portfolio function?" Possibly-but if I had to pick an existing one, I would want portfolio analysis to be a part of decision and economic analysis. Being a part of planning, particularly if it places the skills at or near the corporate center, is a very close second. Remember, portfolio management is a type of planning with high decision quality, or it is high decision quality applied at the organizational level.

I love the idea of having portfolio management as a part of finance. However, in my experience, finance tends to focus more on near-term and historical timeframes, and (rightly) focuses on accuracy more than insight. Of course, companies have different cultures and responsibility maps, so your mileage may vary.

Another idea whose time has come would be to have a planning and budgeting team responsible for near-term, obligatory, and generally low-uncertainty parts of the business, with a connected group with responsibility for the longer-term, higher variability, discretionary aspects of the business. The skills and mindsets of those two types of analysis are very different, and when a single group is responsible for both, the future perspective often takes a back seat.

Decentralized governance is often a stumbling block for portfolio management. *The main tension is between the authority to choose projects and the authority to execute them.* In a perfect world, the enterprise would decide which projects to do while the business units would execute them. But there still must be limits on that. Business units need autonomy for operations and relatively small investments. Setting the appropriate limitation on autonomy plays an important role in portfolio management.

Finally, portfolio analysis tends to be centralized, and as such, relatively few people become proficient. This leaves an organization vulnerable to loss of capability. Backup is needed to maintain a strong portfolio function.

Detail – We Can't Afford to Do Portfolio!

You can't afford **not** to do portfolio!

In resource industries, when times are bad and the product price is low, you should be looking at your assets and decisions in detail, understanding which ones can generate cash, and thinking hard about what you need to survive in the short term and recover.

When times are good and prices are high, you should be looking hard at your investments, figuring out which ones can generate revenues fast, looking at select divestitures, and prioritizing your operating vs. capital expenditures.

If you are at or near a price bookend, you should prepare for the inevitable wind shift.

Portfolio analysis, even done exceptionally well, has minimal incremental cost. You will need anywhere from 2-8 people working on portfolio analysis at a given time (depending on company size and asset diversity). Let's say this group costs $3 million per year in salaries. Smaller companies can get by with much lower effort, although I would never recommend fewer than two hands-on workers. But what value can they provide?

Let's look at a toy model of a single-year investment in a large oil company with those eight people.

The investment budget is $10 billion; the investment returns cash for another 20 years at a flat amount with no inflation or other adjustments. A simple goal-seek reveals that if that investment has a 12% IRR, it has an NPV of $1.27 billion.

The empirical data I have seen implies increases in NPV from 10% to 30%. Your results may differ, and other metrics such as increasing gas production, improving return on capital employed, or achieving a three-year production increase may also be important. But just on the raw NPV value multiplier on this $3 million team is between 42 and 126x.

The leverage from this type of analysis is spectacular.

War Story – What is Our Role?

The portfolio group was rolling out portfolio perspectives to the business units, and the leader of the group met with the head of one of the international divisions.

He had suffered from the ambiguity of the strategic role that his business unit was supposed to pursue. They had growth opportunities, or they could stop trying to grow and let their production run out as cheaply as possible, to milk those cash cows. He didn't really care. He wanted feedback from the corporation, which was hard to come by.

The portfolio leader realized that something like the cascaded approach would be helpful. His business unit had a specific tax regime that would provide benefits for growth amidst ongoing operations. Simply adding individual assets did not capture the benefits well.

They needed to put together their coordinated sets of decisions and submit three or four different versions.

Lessons Learned

1. Meeting with people who will be the victims of your new processes and methods can be highly insightful.
2. Even high-level executives sometimes are at a loss to know what is expected of them.
3. Understanding an asset's role allows an operating unit to create a strong message and direction.

Pitfalls of Managing a Portfolio Process

So now you have avoided the implementation pitfalls. Congratulations! You have a portfolio system and process in place. You have some additional hurdles and barriers that you need to get around, over, or through.

Once you have processes, skills, and tools in place, you must remain diligent to continue and improve. Portfolio Management adds a lot of value, but it is easy for that contribution to be ignored or undermined.

Lack of a Frame and Answer Seeking

Inadequate Frame

Nothing is worse than getting derailed by a decision-maker querying about an obscure metric that was never in scope. Or after a project is de-selected, the asset owner says, "Well, we have two other alternative development plans that might fit better." Do your best to question the core decision-makers and gain their support for the approach. Sometimes, the question to be answered is filtered through several people who may not even understand the concepts. It's like the telephone game that kids play around a campfire. Poor frames can lead to endless rework and wasted effort.

Locking in Too Many Decisions at the Start

Asset and project owners become attached to their portfolios and projects. Some firmly believe that their assets are valuable to the company, that their staff has made well-coordinated decisions, and that these decisions are the best possible. More cynically, some may believe that protecting their assets is vital to their own careers.

I have often heard objections like, "This project is very important to the business plan," "the government/partner/regulator would never allow this," or even "we do not have another alternative."

There are **always** possible alternatives. The best outcome for the firm is when the asset decisions combine to give the best overall performance across the firm's key performance metrics. A planning team in one business unit may not have the context and perspective to build the program that best aligns with the company's needs. Every decision that is locked in reduces the ability to add value.

It is best for analysts to run this less-constrained view before meetings with a larger group. This way, you know beforehand the assets that have the most impact. Reinforce the idea of portfolio analysis as determining what should be done (especially in the early stages) and how much it's worth. 'Doability' comes later.

Premature Closure to the Solution

Many people have an emotional or intellectual need to reach closure quickly. They are not interested in the logic or thought process but rather in getting to an answer. Others need to leave no stone unturned, get every piece of information, and come up with the perfect, no-risk solution, even if it comes too late. The fast-closure people tend to dominate a group.

Remember though, the fundamental goal of strategic portfolio analysis is to get insight into the business, not just to generate "the budget." Discovering performance limits given the inventory of assets and decision options is essential to understanding tradeoffs. With this approach, it is vital to mentally un-anchor the strategic analysis from the "business plan" that will be submitted for accountability and budgeting.

The decision quality framework posits that the maximum value-add occurs during the alternative generation stage. This is true for either individual project analysis or portfolio analysis. Do your best to make sure that alternatives are addressed adequately.

Staying Inside the Box

Related to premature closure is a lack of exploration—not thinking outside the box. Management and planning teams often narrow the analysis aperture quickly in the name of efficiency. This quick narrowing of the aperture prevents insights.

When running optimizations:

1. Test different objective functions with and without requirements
2. Loosen up the requirements, test across a range of requirements
3. Work to understand the impact of over-constrained business logic by relaxing decision constraints

Magritte has a painting, La Clairvoyance, in which the painter (himself) imagines the future of an egg on the table. Like the artist, it is your job to ensure that you develop views of what could be. Go beyond what you see in front of you and envision what the future could be.

▸ **Clairvoyance by René Magritte**

Magritte's "Clairvoyance" sums up the essence of portfolio analysis. Starting with raw material, the analysts, in concert with the decision-makers, envision what could be. © 2024 C. Herscovici / Artists Rights Society (ARS), New York

Not Considering Alternative External Scenarios

We like to think that our views of what the future will hold are a sound basis for planning. But much can happen that is off our radar. Shocks to the system occur regularly. It is a good idea to think through what your world could look like in alternate worlds and conduct "war games" on how you should respond in those worlds.

Expectations Management (unjustified belief in the accuracy of the model) and Data Issues

Falling in Love with Your Portfolio Model

It's most insightful to think of portfolio analysis as a "value of control" (VoC) exercise. VoC analysis is often focused on controlling the outcome. We are one step behind that with portfolio analysis; we model controlling the decision, which will, in turn, lead to a range of outcomes.

Portfolio models allow us to see how this candidate set would be different from other candidate sets—if we controlled the decisions.

You have seen many quotes about models. "All models are wrong, some are useful. "The map is not the territory." "The word is not the thing." "The menu is not the meal."

Perhaps you have seen the Magritte painting "La Trahison des Images" (The Tyranny of Images). Translated, the painting says, "This is not a pipe." Magritte later said, "...if I had written on my picture "This is a pipe," I'd have been lying!"

▸ Tyranny of Images by René Magritte

Magritte's "Tyranny of Images" reminds us that our models are not reality.

Like this mythical pipe, if people believe that somehow your model is reality, trouble will follow. Your portfolio model is an abstraction of reality, hopefully, a useful one.

We often have partners, governments, and other stakeholders who have a say. Sometimes the best we can do is attempt to influence the decisions. After our portfolio analysis, if we conclude that a different development concept would be better, we can influence the stakeholders to move in our preferred direction. Portfolio analysis can give us an understanding of the importance or value of that undertaking. It can help us understand how hard to push and what actions to take if we fail. A popular meme or bumper sticker from some years ago said, "What Would You Do If You Knew You Could Not Fail." This is the essence of value-of-control analysis.

In the end, no matter how good and complete your model is, it's still a model. Remember, the map is not the territory; when the map and territory are different, follow your feet.

Data / Data / Data

Overpromising on the insights gained from portfolio analysis can be an issue. The uncertainties are significant, and input data always has issues. Data quality in the best of circumstances can be questioned. Often there is resistance from decision-makers regarding the quality of the data. You might hear, "We can't even put together a budget for one year; why do you think this will be any better?"

It's a good question. The short answer is that it won't be. But...

There should be no better data for the firm's assets and projects than what you have generated internally. This is not always true, as discussed in the section on ethics. If a third party has better data than what is shared internally, it speaks to a much larger problem—either a lack of competence or a culture of distrust.

Always remember that, regardless of the data quality, **decisions will be made** on every asset. Your data will never be perfect, but data does not have to be perfect to gain insights.

The power of portfolio management—the value it delivers—comes from the change of the frame to the enterprise, not from the quality of the data.

Failure to Maintain Data or Keep It Aligned with Standards

"Everybody wants to go to heaven, but nobody wants to die."

The opposite of spending countless efforts trying to generate perfect data is ignoring it entirely. If it's worth doing portfolio management, it is worth spending time and effort preparing data to standards. I witnessed a case in which a business group did an exhaustive portfolio analysis and optimization, only to find out later that the data in their inventory was outdated and useless. It turned out that the group was doing everything in their actual inventory; there was no decision flexibility.

The insight that their data was useless caused the group to increase its emphasis on creating portfolio options.

Large Delays in the Post-Processing

In cases where you have either a simulation or a complex calculation that follows from your optimization, it is good to ensure that the post-processing happens as fast as possible.

It makes the work more interactive and helps manage leadership expectations. Sometimes the simplifications you make to make your optimization work fast reduces the accuracy or information content of the analysis. Quick iterations then become key to developing more optimal perspectives on actions. A slow turnaround on this count is damaging but not fatal.

The more significant issues arise when you have performed optimization work and management becomes fixated on a specific number. Now you do your post-processing, and that number has changed. In my experience, if the new number is a little better there's no problem, but if it's worse... Management has (erroneously) set their expectations on your approximate number. Now you're disappointing them.

Do your best to keep post-processing fast and with a quick turnaround.

Surprise!

The last thing you want to do is surprise your principal decision-makers during a meeting. This applies to both processes and results. The decision-makers should have a clear understanding of the process and approach. The analysis team should have done enough work in advance to know that when there are surprising conclusions, they understand where they came from and why.

Excessive Process Focus (too worried about the how)

Decision-makers Delving Too Far into the Details of How Portfolios Were Generated

Details around the method used to combine asset decisions are the least important issue in portfolio decision-making. Maybe you used a linear program; perhaps it was manual; maybe it was a genetic algorithm or stochastic programming. The outcomes of the generated portfolios matter, not the process of preparing them. More important is pre-work with the leaders to set them at ease that the business logic and dependencies are correct.

If you are the one who built the tool and the optimizations, you may be proud of your accomplishment. That conversation is for you and your supervisor. The leadership team assessing which decisions to make does not need to go into those weeds. When it's time for action, they will need to know which decisions are in and out; how they got there is not something they should care about.

Leadership may question if you have found the best solutions. That's fair. In all likelihood, your tools will not generate perfect solutions. They may be mathematically correct, but no model can capture the nuance and detail of the real world. The main question is whether the insights gained from the work drive better decisions than would have been made otherwise. Usually that answer is an emphatic yes.

Lack of Alignment, Focus, and Buy-in from Decision-Makers

Failure to Track the Value that Portfolio Management Adds

The initial implementation of portfolio management will likely involve a thorough comparison between the preliminary and selected portfolios that result from your process. Once a portfolio process is in place, there is little need to see the counterfactual. You're making good decisions using a robust process.

It's easy to forget the value of portfolio efforts once they are a part of your firm's DNA. Failure to at least attempt to establish counterfactuals can lead to defunding portfolio efforts. It's like closing your umbrella while it's still raining because you're no longer getting wet.

Failure to Get Leadership Alignment on the Reasonableness and Comparability of Data

The truth springs from arguments amongst friends.
David Hume

One of the most challenging issues is when the decision-makers go into a room and start questioning all the data, especially each other's data. Depending on the company culture, even one objection may be enough to render any subsequent discussion meaningless.

Before any meeting, the data standards must be clear, adhered to, practical, and checked off by the participants. This concept is an integral part of the process as laid out in the paper, "*How SmithKline Beecham Makes Better Resource-Allocation Decisions*," by Paul Sharpe and Tom Keelin, Mar-Apr, 1998, *Harvard Business Review*.

Focus on the Individual Decisions Rather Than Enterprise Outcomes

Often when a portfolio is generated, decision-makers will ask, "What happened to my assets?"

Combating this pitfall requires preparation with the decision-makers about what is or is not possible to include in the decision alternatives. Many managers think that "possible" is the same as practical. It also requires strong facilitation during the discussion to keep the focus on the portfolio results rather than the virtual decision that drove the outcome.

You need to eliminate entities and logic that are impossible. Beyond that, the focus of the initial passes should be on the portfolio outcomes. Much of this is about leadership buy-in to the process and strong facilitation.

Too Large a Decision-Making Body

A large part of the value of portfolio analysis is in prompting the discussion about tradeoffs among senior decision-makers. This is best done in a small leadership team, perhaps up to seven people. As groups get larger, there is not enough time to give participants a say, and often the discussion goes down rabbit holes of unimportant detail.

Inflexibility About Process

You may have a process in mind. Maybe it holds together really well and is totally logical in your mind. Then you start to work with one of the decision-makers, and it makes no sense to their way of thinking. They have something very different in mind. Now what?

Forcing your process onto an unwilling participant is not productive. If you can't get them to see the wisdom of your approach, you have to adapt. Their approach may not be good or make sense, so it may be incumbent on you to do extra work in the background to ensure that Decision Quality remains high.

Failure of Succession Planning

Portfolio analysis requires skills and perspective. The skills are developed working with leaders and models, while the perspective comes from a broad knowledge of business and the external environment. Few people can step into a portfolio analysis role and be successful from the first day. The value of portfolio management is immense; there is no excuse not to plan for succession in roles.

If you don't have succession plans, you run into what Bent Flyvbjerg and Dan Gardner called the Eternal Beginner syndrome in their book "*How Big Things Get Done.*" This is where the new person who fills a role does not have the depth of experience to be effective in the role. Large companies are especially prone to this as they move employees through short-term roles—seemingly to gain exposure to leadership—with little regard for the skill set required to do the technical work.

When Management Doesn't Like How You're Doing Things

You can follow all the instructions I have laid out, but in the end, your bosses need to like it. Apparently, many leaders believe that they should be able to manage portfolios in their heads. After all, isn't it their job description? But assuming you get past that hurdle, you now have many specifics to deal with.

Some leaders like to see displays and slides in the format they want, to the standards they want, and they want to see a forecast. They do not want to discuss issues in-depth or do hands-on planning and strategy work. You may not have enough access to them to walk them through the process and ideas.

If you can get an audience, try to tie the standards and methods you're using into the decision quality framework, ensure that they understand and have had input into the frame, the insights they can hope to gain, and the tradeoffs. Stress the importance of data that is meaningful to the decision or question at hand. For this to be effective, you need credibility with the leadership team.

This gets back to knowing your audience. If you can't get an audience, and they want to see results with an unrealistic discount rate and corporate distributed overhead lumped into even small assets, give them what they want.

Please ensure that they are aware of the work's limitations, and that due to corporate standards, there may have been shortcuts compared to the best practices of portfolio decision quality.

Not Performing Lookbacks on Your Portfolio Work

Lookbacks are important. To some people, they seem like a waste of time, but the ability to learn and improve is an essential competitive advantage. It's not just about looking at the result, though. Lookbacks for decision quality and portfolio management need to go beyond the simple results. Results matter, but the ability to repeat results becomes a sustainable competitive advantage.

There are two important implications. We need a counterfactual, or at least a sense of what we would have done in the absence of analysis, and we need to separate the results from the decision-making process. We need to know if we fell into the poor decision-quality quadrants because consistently falling there will ultimately lead to disaster.

I have seen cases in which a company missed its estimates of price, timing, and performance, was saved by the oil price, and patted itself on the back because the rate of return was higher than expected (saved by the oil price). But then, when the oil price failed to save them, they used that as an excuse.

That's one way to get a bonus when prices rise and to save your job in a down market. However, if you have a systematic bias in the four main inputs to an investment (cost, timing, performance, and price), you have a serious data problem. Fixing the systematic biases will give you a chance to improve your decision-making and forecasts.

Likewise, with portfolio work, even though portfolio analysis may not improve forecasting, we need to be continually aware of the value our efforts add. To that end, it is highly desirable to have a counterfactual before running the analyses.

Some of the specific questions to ask are:

Frame: Did we understand the problem? Did the decision-maker (DM) receive insights they couldn't have gotten outside the portfolio frame? Given the frame, data, and deadline, did we use the most appropriate analytic techniques?

Data: Did we have all the data elements we needed on the decision entities? Were the data consistent across all the entities?

Logically Correct Thinking: Was the model appropriate for the analysis? Was it too involved and complicated? Was it overly simple? Losing insights? Did the model capture the inputs adequately and provide insightful outputs consistent with the values of the DMs? Are the DM values appropriate to the decision at hand? Did disinterested analysts check the model for reasonableness and model errors?

Alternatives: Did you have reasonably distinct alternatives (or synthetic alternatives) for the input data? Did you create portfolios that explored a wide envelope of options across the stated and unstated values?

Values and Tradeoffs: Did the analysis honor the DMs' stated goals? Did the DMs understand the tradeoffs depicted and consider them adequately?

Commitment to Action: Did the decision-makers ultimately heed the insights from the analysis? Were the DMs involved in the framing and interim check-ins? Did the analysis lead to a decision different from the default/momentum decision? Did the DMs honor the insights?

Process: What went well? What didn't go well? Were the studies focused on the right questions? Was the data adequate to answer those questions? Did the analysis and communication enhance the discussion and lead to a richer conversation of values and tradeoffs? Were the decision-makers' expectations met? Were the conclusions consistent with the data and analysis limitations, or did they go beyond the logical bounds? Were the right people involved? Were the meeting behaviors good, with a focus on the decisions at hand, or did people spin off into criticism? These can be challenging questions, and even if your analysis team is not entirely in control of all of them, you may have some ability to influence them in the future.

Lookbacks help us ascertain whether results were driven by luck or skill. Skill is repeatable; luck isn't.

Lookbacks are not a formal part of the six-element Decision Quality framework. This may be appropriate because the DQ framework was made for single decisions, not an organization's overall DQ health. In my opinion, Lookbacks should be a seventh tenet of DQ, specifically applicable to driving organizational Decision Quality.

Having all your projects in one place, as is typical with portfolio analysis, is invaluable. It allows you to identify systemic issues within the organization. When you conduct lookbacks for projects, you typically compare results to forecasts, which helps the project team understand where they were right and wrong. However, at a project level, almost anything is possible. For instance, if your cost estimate has a P10 of 1 million and a P90 of 2 million, and the result for that project is 2.1 million, it's outside your 80% range but still plausible. This may not necessarily indicate bias or a flawed methodology. However, if all ten projects come in at 2.1, you have a systemic issue. This is unlikely to be fixable simply by better execution or working harder.

Key Takeaways

Expectations Management, proper framing of the problem being solved, data concerns, converging too quickly to a solution, misalignment among the management team, and failure to look back at what you have done are all fraught with peril. Make sure you have full support from management and the decision leadership to ensure successful efforts.

Detail – Facilitation Problems and Tips

What happens when the decision-makers do not understand strategy, portfolio, or financial measures? This is not unusual when leaders are great at their technical specialties but do not have experience or adequate training in finance and strategy. How can you ensure the appropriate mindset?

Before a meeting even starts, you must spend time with the decision-makers to have a shared understanding and agreement about the process and frame of the portfolio work. Meet one-on-one and address their concerns privately.

If they have a joint boss, the boss must understand and endorse your work. If the boss is willing to introduce the discussion with a description of the process and words of support, that's even better.

The principals also need to believe that the data from business units other than their own is comparable with theirs. Fair process and a level playing field are essential.

Let's discuss a few example issues.

Case 1 – Discounted Earnings

A business unit leadership team decided that discounted earnings was a better metric than discounted cash flow (earnings had become an important focus) for their optimizations. You have tried to direct the management team to focus on free cash flow, but they were not having it.

As a knowledgeable analyst, you know that discounted earnings are detached from any theoretical concept of value in financial theory and practice.

What should you do?

1. Realize first that optimization is to give insights—not answers. Optimization is simply a means to create portfolios for comparison. A poor choice of the objective function for strategic optimization is not the end of the world. Whatever objective

function is used for optimization, it is essential to compare portfolios based on a range of metrics.

2. Ensure that whatever objective function is chosen that you also capture a metric that captures **actual** value consistent with your corporate value guidelines (e.g., NPV at WACC), as well as other metrics that may also be important.
3. Develop portfolios using NPV as the objective function in addition to the ones they request.
4. Show them the tradeoffs between value and their chosen metric(s). An objective function or requirements on metrics other than value will erode value.
5. Create hybrid portfolios that minimize the damage caused by the alternative metrics. For example, you can maximize discounted earnings, subject to NPV being within 10% of the (pre-determined) maximum NPV.

Case 2 – Prematurely Locking-In Decisions

When the leadership team met to work on strategic and tactical portfolio matters, the planning managers reviewed the list of all the project investments to discuss potential project decisions. Most were cooperative and understood that the purpose was to understand the value of control. One of the managers dug in his heels. "These projects are very important to the business unit; you can't delay them!" The other managers tell you that if he's not allowing adjustments, they won't either.

Now what?

1. This sort of situation is not uncommon. Remember, "*A team is not a group of people who work together. A team is a group of people who trust each other.*" – Simon Sinek (https://www.simonsinek.com). Transparency and taking time to check, compare, and develop standards, as well as fostering a shared understanding, may help to build trust over time.
2. This is the type of objection that can sometimes be headed off with appropriate preparation and walking through the process, including how the transition from analysis to action might look.
3. Ask questions about whether delaying a project is impossible or difficult. Take notes. Understand if it is truly impossible or just a difficult ask for them to change it.
4. If you cannot get the manager to budge publicly, you may need to set up a different working set in private that has more flexibility. This is not about working around that person but understanding if the objections are important or material. If his objections are immaterial, communicate this to indicate that you will not oppose them. If they are material, clearly communicate the cost to the enterprise of those objections. If the boss and the peers do not object, move on.

Facilitation issues can often be headed off with good preparation before the meeting. Sometimes it simply is not practical. These can be difficult discussions, especially when they are not in private. That's why preparation is essential. When these issues arise in public, it is often best to address them privately rather than argue about details in a meeting. Then, work in the background to determine if the requested alterations are material.

How you handle your insights and communicate them to leadership will differ for every organization and person. As an analyst, you have a professional responsibility to help your "clients" understand what they are giving up and to help them move in a better direction if you can.

Key Takeaways

1. Giving the customers what they want is good commercial and career advice. Look, we can all read an organizational chart. You should give your boss what they want.
2. At the same time, if what they want is nonsense, you are not serving the ultimate customer very well. So, give them what they want, but also give them what they need to hear. Go beyond what they want and generate additional insights. If they listen, you have a better chance of becoming their trusted advisor. If they ignore you, well, at least you tried to do the right thing. Finally, if they shoot the messenger, maybe you don't want to work there anyway.

War Story – Envision Your End State, but Don't Start There

This is a cautionary sidebar of Stephen Covey's Principle "Begin with the end in mind."

Establishing a vision of your end state provides your teams and analysis with a North Star—a point to steer towards. It ensures that your plans are well directed towards achieving the desired ends. To do portfolio management well, we analyze first and budget later. Portfolio analysis is all about seeking an understanding of the value of control, then taking steps to achieve the best set of outcomes.

In a way, it is like a root-cause "why" analysis. You may believe that your ultimate goal is to crank out a budget. But ask why you need a budget, then ask again and again until you end up at "helping your enterprise achieve specific goals." The budget is essential, but it is a tool to help achieve better results.

Fairly early in my portfolio journey, I had the opportunity to work with an exploration group on their portfolio. It was a straightforward portfolio problem with one exception. There were many cases in which an exploration well had been planned, but the business unit would make the (very reasonable) decision to use the drilling rig for immediate economic benefit.

My team went straight to the budget perspective. If this was a factor, we had to include it in the optimization. Every potentially programmed well had to have a probability of drilling in addition to its probability of success. The exploration team implored us to remove the probability of drilling as a consideration. But we knew better. We were the experts. (*Narrator: The experts were overconfident.*)

We spent a lot of time and effort trying to calibrate probabilities and running big hairy optimizations before realizing that the advisors were right. We first needed to understand what we **should** do, **then** understand how those risks would impact program results. In that way, if a well was critical to achieving performance goals, they could make a course correction. We had not yet developed our value of control paradigm.

Ultimately, we came around and provided them with the product they wanted.

Lessons Learned

1. Listen to the decision-makers and their advisors. The "customer" is not always right. They are always important. And darn it, sometimes they're right.
2. Begin with a view of your ultimate goals; don't begin **at** the end. We tried to go straight to generating a simulated output/forecast rather than looking for insight first. Applying the risk of management commitment as an input to the portfolio analysis obscured the value of some highly valuable prospects.
3. Just because someone is considered an expert doesn't mean they will have all the answers. Everyone has blind spots and biases driven by their learning and experience. Mistakes and regret are great teachers for thoughtful people. They may also be expensive.
4. Learn from your mistakes. Extract reusable principles and incorporate them into your thought process.

Detail – Portfolio Theater

Somewhere between implementation and operation, portfolio analysis efforts may be challenged as unnecessary, too expensive, or too complicated. It may be that the leaders are challenging the development team to find a more efficient way to do the job, a key analyst moves to another position, or a new manager comes in who does not understand or believe the value proposition.

Without support from the organization, your efforts may devolve into portfolio theater. Portfolio theater is where the principals claim that they are doing value-based prioritization or portfolio analysis, but the structure or data of the analysis is so flawed as to be useless or even misleading.

Physicist Richard P. Feynman talked about Cargo Cult Science in his 1974 Commencement Address at Caltech. Following World War II, some South Pacific Islanders adopted the appearance of more technologically advanced nations to bring back the goods that had been delivered during the war. They salvaged uniforms and rifles, carved headphones out of wood, and made full-scale airplane replicas from straw in an attempt to bring back those goods. It looked like the real thing, but of course, it was ineffectual. The same thing happens with portfolio theater.

A typical symptom is a lack of control over the inputs, especially when developed by teams across the organization. Another one is a poorly constructed quantitative model.

And I get it. Cost is easily attributable to the bottom line of a firm. But if you want to ensure decent data or models—not perfect, decent—you may need to have someone whose job is to maintain standards. Their salary will have a known negative effect on the firm's bottom line. You can model what happens if you remove the salaries from your cost structure. High-quality portfolio management gains are often difficult to quantify due to the lack of a counterfactual and the challenge of envisioning their potential impact. Like a no-go decision, you will seldom track what could have been.

For example, I can give you a series of values for projects, {761.6, 670.7, 712.7, 515.3, 330.3, 276.6, 233.9, 486, 747.1, 533.1}. You can slice and dice, sort and rank, optimize, and simulate them. You can apply AI to them and get some fascinating results. That's all wonderful. But those are, in fact, random numbers. How useful could the output possibly be?

So even if the numbers aren't "accurate," even if they're not "precise," if they **have** been generated using common assumptions and global inputs, there is something useful there.

How do you achieve consistency of inputs and assumptions? Standards and some level of enforcement! One of the challenges with that is scaling the input analyses. If you have 10 projects in your portfolio and they are all simple and straightforward, no problem. If you have hundreds or thousands of investments, you need to develop a simple and straightforward approach to assigning value and risk.

If you are someday confronted with a situation in which the data are garbage, I hope you're in a position to state so. At the very least, if you are forced to do an analysis with poor data, make sure you caution the decision-makers that the data are inconsistent and that even though the displays and analyses look good, they may have little or no value.

Key Takeaways

Portfolio theater is, at best, a waste of time and effort. At worst, you can end up with worse results. It's easy to slide onto that path without diligence and at least attempting to show the counterfactual—the decisions that would have been made without portfolio analysis. The continual justification of the value of portfolio work may be a necessary evil.

Detail – How to Manage Portfolios When Decisions are Made First in, First-out

One of the challenges and objections I have heard to portfolio management is a strawman argument that goes something like this.

"*Our decisions do not all come in neatly at the same time. Therefore, if an investment opportunity appears after our planning cycle, running portfolio analysis might force us to change all the decisions that have already made during the budgeting cycle. Therefore, we shouldn't do portfolio analysis.*"

Let me break that down.

First, "Our decisions do not all come in neatly at the same time." That is absolutely true in many organizations. Every portfolio analysis contains a working inventory of all the decisions that are included in the effort. When an opportunity arises, it changes the working set and the frame. When the frame changes, we need to understand the new frame and how it may change decisions.

Next, "...if an investment opportunity appears after our planning cycle, running portfolio analysis might force us to change all the decisions that were already made during the budgeting cycle." Running portfolio analysis does not **force** anyone to change a decision that has already been made.

A portfolio analysis might highlight that, given your new frame, a different set of decisions would be more advantageous. What you then do is a choice. If a decision is worth the effort to change, then you change.

Unless a single project is quite large relative to the overall portfolio, there is little chance that it will materially change many decisions. That kind of scenario is certainly possible though. Remember, the optimization is not giving you answers. It gives you insights. If a new opportunity could significantly alter recommendations or decisions, it may be necessary to reassess your strategy.

Consider the example below. The list of investment opportunities is in the left column. The middle column is the set of actions determined during the budget cycle, and the right column shows the efforts that would yield the highest value by incorporating the New Opportunity. In the display, zero means that the project is in with no delay, 1 is a one-year delay, and 2 and 3 are also the years of delay. Ten means that the project is rejected or out of the frame.

▸ Late Additions to a Portfolio May Require Adjustments

Heat Map	Heat Map Before	Heat Map After New Opp
Opp A	0	1
Opp B	2	3
Opp C	0	0
Opp D	1	10
New Opp	10	0

Coordinating many decisions is easiest when all the decisions can be made at one time, for example, as part of a planning process. In the real world, decisions arrive arbitrarily. Oftentimes these decisions are not disruptive to plans. But if your plan and goals are aggressive, a new opportunity can cause significant adjustment. It is more work and will result in a better outcome.

Including the New Opportunity in "Heat Map After New Opp" causes calculated changes to several projects. Opportunities A and B should each be delayed by one year compared to the original plan, Opportunity C remains the same, and Opportunity D is rejected.

This scenario might require movement of people and funds from Opportunities A and D to the New Opportunity. Opportunity B would still be delayed, but a little longer, a small change. Perhaps it should be considered for divestiture.

In an optimization context, these are the decisions that **would** theoretically maximize the value of your portfolio. Leadership must consider the practicality of implementing the New Opportunity at this stage, as well as the level of disruption it may cause for organizations and project teams.

As a final note, the strawman conclusion "Therefore we should not do portfolio" is simply an excuse. Portfolio analysis is cheap and provides insights into what can be accomplished by making different decisions. It points leadership towards a path that would be difficult to see with conventional, standalone decision-making.

Portfolio analysis lets us see the path and decide whether to take it. Ignoring portfolio analysis removes value-adding options from consideration.

Detour – A Plan is Not a Forecast, Part n

I recently discovered that November 23rd is called Fibonacci Day by some. This is not Fibonacci's birthday or anything so obvious, but rather, it is a series of several numbers near the start of his famous sequence (1123).

The Fibonacci Sequence is an infinite sequence of numbers that begins 0, 1, 1, 2, 3, 5, 8, 13, 21, 34, 55... Each successive number is the sum of the two previous ones. It is useful as a model for natural phenomena.

If 11/23 is Fibonacci Day, I suppose 11/23/58 at 13:21:34 will be a super-Fibonacci singularity. My plan on that day is to pop a bottle of Champagne and toast the great man and his sequence.

Unfortunately, that's probably not a great forecast, as I would be 101 years old at the time. Odds are I will not be able to enjoy such an indulgence. This is a great plan but perhaps a low confidence forecast.

Detail – Organizational Requirements to Maintain a Successful Portfolio Practice

Much of this book focused on the key elements comprising the technical side of portfolio management. The soft side is every bit as important.

If the leadership, governance, organizational, and cultural support are not in place, the opportunity to add value from portfolio analysis is limited.

Leadership TEAM

Humility and a culture of honest inquiry are essential. A leadership team that works together, trusts each other, and is aligned with the needs of the firm can make all the difference. They are willing to consider results that are counter-intuitive and different from the current direction. They see portfolio analysis as a means to gain a deeper understanding before making decisions rather than as a means to support a decision they have already made.

Incentives are aligned to permit the give-and-take of portfolio decisions without punishment

In large organizations, a person's lateral position, i.e., which project or business unit they are assigned to, is often a function of random chance. Rather than advocate for their random slice of the world, corporations may be better served by systems that reward accurate or appropriate characterizations of the business. If a business or project fails to be funded despite proper characterization and execution, those in that business should not be punished. People respond to incentives. If they see their job as advocating for an internal outcome despite flaws, that is what they will do.

Perceived need to balance competing objectives in different time horizons

In our connected world, decisions often carry unintended consequences. Understanding the operational, financial, and long- and short-term implications of material decisions BEFORE commitment is crucial. Because the perspectives required to understand the portfolio view differ, some degree of coaching may be required.

Central perspective on making decisions

There are lines or gray space between simple, low-risk, low-consequence decisions and the large, high-risk, high-consequence ones. The choice of who has which decision rights can make or break efforts to achieve portfolio alignment in a firm. Some companies have strict governance on capital, while maintaining looser controls on operating expenses. Creeping sunk costs can result in unfavorable long-term decisions.

Governance Bylaws or culture that require a portfolio perspective

Most organizations have codified governance policies. As you incorporate portfolio thinking into the organization and processes, you must keep the current state in mind. There are several aspects to the portfolio thinking process that would need to be incorporated. Is there transparency into the potential queue of projects and decisions (including alternatives)? What is the decision governance process? Are projects submitted as they mature, or is there a more regular cadence?

Codifying the gray space in a way that requires taking the central perspective for important decisions can result in the great decision quality we strive for. Remember that interaction techniques often result in a lower value estimate than standalone analysis, so business managers may resist taking that perspective. Without something to compel that perspective, it is unlikely to happen.

Maintaining portfolio analysis capability

Finally, even if all the organizational pieces are in place, someone still needs to do the analytical work and development. The skills required to be a good portfolio practitioner are broad and relatively deep. It takes time to develop business, technical, financial, and computer modeling skills to be effective. This development is necessary to gain management and leadership support. For that reason, career progression as a professional portfolio practitioner must be possible.

Treat portfolio roles as a profession. This is especially true because of the relative immaturity of the field. Before this book, there was not a good resource for people to use to help guide them or develop an accepted set of descriptions of what portfolio management means. The alternative is to hire consultants who may or may not truly understand the business and culture of the firm. Develop a pipeline of talent and treat it well.

Detail – Data, One Last Time

Data is a never-ending non-problem in portfolio management. I want to talk about it one more time.

GIGO (garbage in-garbage out) is an important concept everywhere. There is a caveat in portfolio analysis though—if the garbage was generated with consistent standards, you can have garbage in and still get **insight** out.

Better data means that your insights will be more confident, resulting in more reasonable forecasts.

When Daniel Kahnemann and Amos Tversky invented the field of behavioral economics, they documented many cognitive biases that go into everyday thinking and decision-making.

A paper by Bent Flyvbjerg (Flyvbjerg, B. (2021) "*Top Ten Behavioral Biases in Project Management: An Overview*" in the Project Management Journal, 52(6), 531–546) documents his view of the ten most important biases in project management: strategic misrepresentation, optimism bias, uniqueness bias, planning fallacy, overconfidence, hindsight, availability, base rate fallacy, anchoring, and escalation of commitment.

The biases are not standalone; each can influence the others as well.

For portfolio analysis and management, the most important are probably planning/optimism bias, strategic misrepresentation, overconfidence, and escalation of commitment.

Planning Fallacy or Optimism Bias

Projects are late, over budget, and underperform (relative to plans). This pattern is consistent. There are many reasons for it—some good, some less good. When we put together a plan for a project, it is based on idealistic assumptions about resources and the world in general. Sometimes we do this on the first pass of a plan to get the sequence of events right. Unfortunately, that first idealistic pass becomes a psychological and political anchor. We hold that plan as a standard, and the organization remembers.

Then, instead of communicating accurate forecasts, people start to worry about the messaging and staying consistent rather than recalibrating the plan to reality. In some organizations, they shoot the messenger (or the messengers believe they will), so the messaging becomes all-important rather than the truth.

At its root, the Planning Fallacy is caused by the conflation of the concepts and definition of plan and forecast. Plans, which should be a roadmap, take on the added dimensions of cost, timing, and performance. It should be straightforward to fix this by benchmarking with similar projects and defining terms better. But it's a difficult and systemic problem.

If one project prioritizes realism in its plans, it would burden the project metrics compared to other projects in the organization. Suddenly their project would be worse than every other comparable project in the inventory. The result would be the untimely death of their project.

If the exaggerations are relatively small and still within the realm of the possible, portfolio work is helpful. Adding together a bunch of slightly exaggerated estimates unleashes statistical hell. When all of the many entities have even a tiny planning bias, the summed result can be enormously exaggerated.

Statistically, adding the mean of independent entities will give us the mean result. Any other basis for addition is statistically meaningless. Imagine that your firm has many projects with an objective mean value of 100 each, with a standard deviation of 10 (normal distribution). They are identified in the submission as having a predicted median outcome of 102, which represents a 2% exaggeration.

Your result is in the thickest part of the distribution for a single project. Sure, you know it's a bit of a stretch, but you have a great team in place, and everyone is focused on succeeding (uniqueness bias).

▸ Projects Often Have a Consistent Optimism Bias

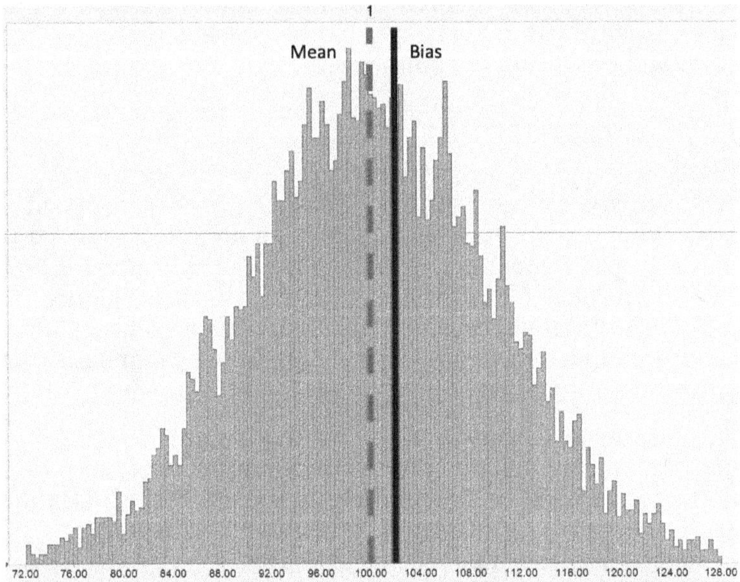

> *It is extremely common for project economics and submitted plans to contain at least a small bias.*

But the results are not so pretty when you add 50 slightly exaggerated projects. Now, you have about an 8% chance of meeting or exceeding the 2% exaggerated forecast.

▸ Summing Projects with Consistent Bias Leads to Overstated Forecast

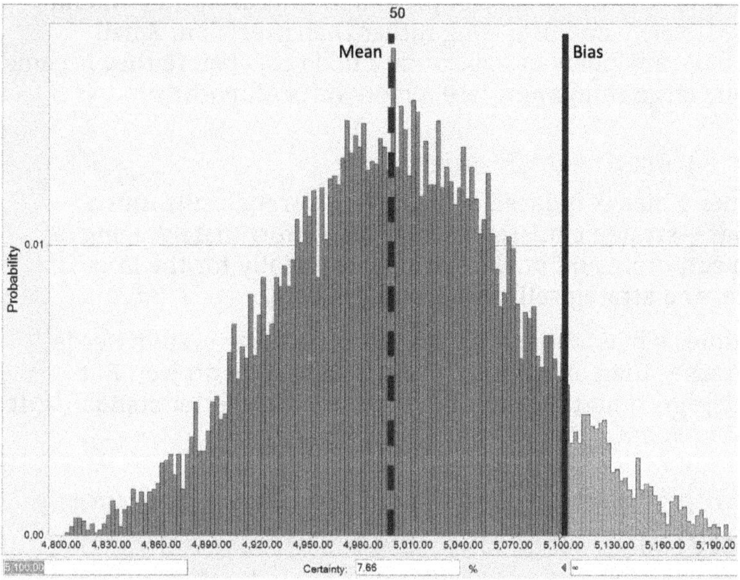

Summing 50 slightly optimistic plans results in a large optimistic bias.

Make it 100, and you are now under a 3% chance of meeting your 2% exaggerated forecast.

▸ The More Projects, the Worse the Overstatement

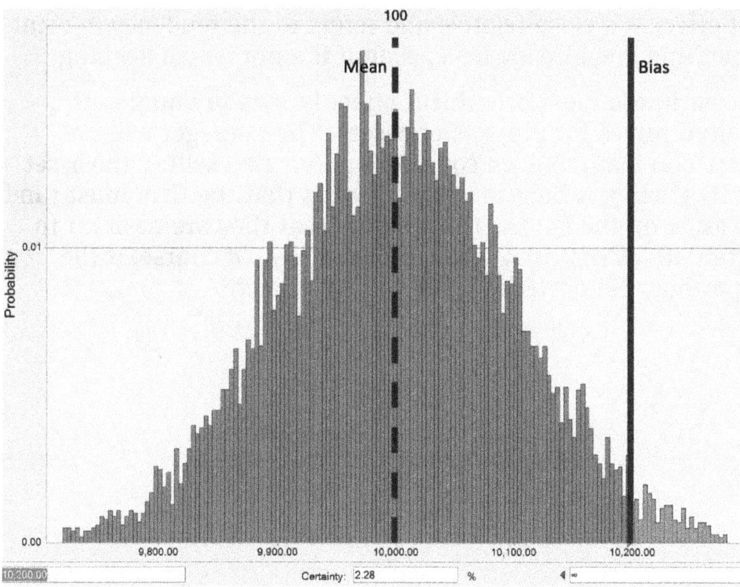

Summing 100 biased entities makes the forecast even worse.

The bottom line is that, unless an organization is ready and willing to revamp the way they do all project plans and forecasts, they should focus on consistency and debiasing rather than precision. Small companies have a window of opportunity to do this before they become too big, while large companies face a more difficult path.

Strategic Misrepresentation

When planner's bias is induced deliberately, it transforms into a different bias—strategic misrepresentation. Unfortunately, lying is common in corporate and public settings, especially for the largest, most visible, and strategically important projects.

As with Planner's bias, there is an argument that the system needs to be fixed rather than attempting to fix it project by project. But strategic misrepresentation can't be corrected with better standards. It is a cultural problem.

Escalation of Commitment (endowment effect/sunk cost fallacy)

Escalation of commitment is the belief that once significant funds have been expended, the show must go on, regardless. Sometimes, project managers strategically invest just enough funds into a project to hook executive leadership into providing funding. Then once a public commitment has been made, it becomes difficult to change course.

When done intentionally, strategic misrepresentation can lead executives to assume that they don't have a good fallback plan. The endowment effect is a close relative and refers to the tendency to want to keep something you already have, even if it's not worth keeping.

In portfolio work, the most prominent effect is seen in enumerating options or alternatives for projects or assets. The manager will not want the portfolio team to even consider options like selling the asset or delaying it. They may believe in their hearts that the firm must fund or keep the asset on the books. The result is that they are hesitant to generate alternatives that may weaken their baby. Of course, if the asset is important, the portfolio work will so indicate.

Key Takeaways

1. Given all this bias, as long as everything is consistent, we can answer the question of what the best course of action is given the input assumptions. However, the data we use for those decisions seldom results in a good forecast.
2. Ultimately, the question is whether it is "best" or even a "good" course of action when all the input assumptions don't pan out. Results still matter, and if the input estimates are too far off, value will erode.
3. This is where simulating the downsides is useful. This can be a valuable test, because some projects offer better mitigation options than others, so summing the means may not represent the actual outcomes well.

Detail – The Switch from What You Should Do to Execution

As already stated, you should un-anchor strategic analysis from your budgets. Budgets are a typical tool for accountability and directly communicating short-term actions. They clearly say what you will do now.

Portfolio analysis informs what you should do or would do if there were no constraints in your business. Results of strategic portfolio analysis inform the best course of action if you have control over the decisions. Often, outside parties can hinder that.

Let's look at a few examples:

Tactical Portfolio Analysis

You perform a tactical portfolio analysis. The analysis suggests that it is in your company's best interest to accelerate Project A's development, in which your company holds a 30% interest. Unfortunately, Project A is operated by one of your competitors, which favors a delay in the project. (In the oil industry, the operator is the firm that manages a project or asset subject to terms of a joint operating agreement. The operator has a strong influence on the development and operations of an asset.)

Some analysis is called for. If the operator holds a majority interest, it may not be practical to influence a change. On the other hand, if partners might be amenable to this change, you can attempt to persuade them to move or vote to accelerate. Therefore, the action coming from your portfolio analysis is to try to influence partners.

You would not have had this insight if you had locked the operator's plans into your portfolio analysis as a given decision.

The execution action coming from your analysis is to attempt to influence the development directly through the operator or with the other partners. You may also have a backup plan to attempt to sell all or part of your working interest. The project direction may not change, but your action does.

Strategic Portfolio Analysis

Executive leadership is concerned about the transition to sustainable energy. They believe that natural gas will be an important transition fuel. Yet when they look at the existing portfolio, they see the firm's oil production increasing and gas production declining. The corporation has been using a rank-and-cut approach, funding more oil developments than gas. Over-optimistic price inputs for oil probably drove these results.

The executives ask whether the firm has enough gas assets to reverse the trend. Analysts put the asset data into an optimization tool. Rather than only trying to maximize NPV for a given expenditure, they include a requirement that the gas production percentage increase over ten years.

The results are not encouraging. It is possible to increase gas production percentage, but not enough. There are not enough gas resources in the company. Given this insight, management has choices to make about the best approach for driving behaviors and culture that favor gas resource acquisition and development. Should they lower the oil price assumptions and increase the gas price assumptions? Should they instruct the M&A team to proactively pursue gas and bring in opportunities that have returns lower than the usual corporate hurdle? How should they communicate with shareholders and stock analysts about the change of direction without tipping their hand?

Leadership decides to attack this problem first by changing the price forecast to reflect their beliefs about the evolution of the oil and gas demand. Next, they instruct M&A to actively seek unowned gas assets, increase working interest in others, and consider corporate acquisitions that bolster production near demand centers.

Decisions Do Not Equal Success

At the risk of sounding like a broken record, portfolio analysis informs you what you should do or would do if you had control of the decisions and outcomes. It is a value-of-control calculation.

The decisions above—to try to put pressure on the operator and to emphasize gas development and acquisition—may not succeed. That's why it's essential to have contingency plans and milestones, track progress, and adjust.

Working hard on implementation, change management, and avoiding pitfalls is critical to developing the portfolio mindset.

Key Takeaways

This will be the most critical section of the book for many practitioners and implementers. Because engineers and quants are generally attracted to this type of work, the "softer" parts tend to be overlooked. My wife, who watched me battle organizational inertia for many years, tells me that this is the most important part of the book.

Each of the five critical success factors holds equal importance, but the difficulty of this management and organizational commitment piece is the most likely to be underestimated. Don't save it to the end. Begin to work on organizational change early

CHAPTER 16

The Last Word

This concludes the main body of the book. The lessons here easily apply to resource industries like petroleum and mining, and can be adapted to other sectors as well. When investments must be prioritized, it is valuable to put them into the proper context to extract the maximum benefit.

The appendices will be of interest to many. They provide further reading references, additional details around cash flow and earnings, a working paper, and some miscellaneous helpful information.

Writing and publishing this book became a life goal when I left Chevron in 2020. It's the book I wish I had when I started down my path to portfolio management in the late-90s. I would love to see it become required reading for anyone wishing to pursue the route of better analysis and portfolio management.

Critical Success Factors and DQ

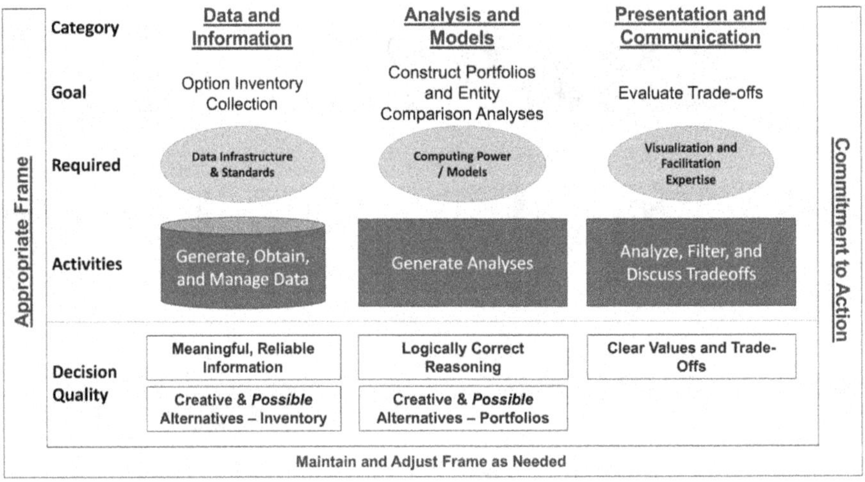

The three physical requirements for portfolio management must work in concert with Decision Quality in order to maximize the value of portfolio management.

This book has covered enough basics to get you started on your path to portfolio. It provides a foundation for conversations about portfolio analysis and management. I hope that the war stories, which are really more like historical fiction, are like cautionary tales to help guide you on your journey. I have no doubt that as you build skills and experience you will find better approaches for general and specific use within your organizations. I hope the book met or exceeded your expectations and that you found it helpful, insightful, and maybe even enjoyable.

I am always happy to discuss any of the concepts or specific questions or problems you have with any of the content. Best of luck to you, and may the odds be ever in your favor.

BIBLIOGRAPHY

Adams, Tom, Jeff Lund, Jack A. Albers, Michael Back, Jason McVean, and John I. Howell. 2000-2001. "Portfolio Balancing to Achieve Long Term Strategic Goals." Oilfield Review, Winter: 10-19.

Allan, Paul D. 2014. "Perspectives on Risk: Balancing Considerations of Financial and Operational Risks." SPE Hydrocarbon Economics and Evaluation Symposium. Houston: Society of Petroleum Engineers.

Allan, Paul D. 2001. "A Portfolio Management Approach to Assessing Acquisition and Divestiture." SPE Annual Technical Conference and Exhibition. New Orleans: Society of Petroleum Engineers.

Allen, Michael S. 2000. Business Portfolio Management. New York: John Wiley & Sons, Inc.

Arnold, Robin, and Carl Spetzler. 2004. "The Omission Ratio: Paths to Value Not Taken." Executive eBriefing. Strategic Decisions Group.

Back, M. J. 2001. "A Discussion on the Impact of Information Technology on the Capital Investment Decision Process in the Petroleum Industry." 2001 SPE Annual Technical Conference and Exhibition. New Orleans: Society of Petroleum Engineers.

Back, Michael J. 2003. "A Discussion on the Effect of International Fiscal Regimes on Portfolio Selection in the Petroleum Industry." SPE Hydrocarbons Economics and Evaluation Symposium. Dallas: Society of Petroleum Engineers.

Ball, Ben C., and Sam L. Savage. 1999. "Holistic vs. Hole-istic Exploration and Production Strategies, SPE-57701-JPT." Journal of Petroleum Technology, September 1: 74-84.

Barnard, Hannes. 2021. The Risk Matrix: horoscope or best practice? December 16. https://www.linkedin.com/pulse/risk-matrix-horoscope-best-practice-.

Begg, S. H., and R. B. Bratvold. 2001. "Improving Investment Decisions Using a Stochastic Integrated Model." SPE Annual Technical Conference and Exhibition. New Orleans: Society of Petroleum Engineers.

Beinhocker, Eric D., and Sarah Kaplan. 2002. "Tired of strategic planning?" The McKinsey Quarterly, 2002 Special Edition: Risk and resilience ed.

Bernstein, Peter L. 1996. Against the Odds: The Remarkable Story of Risk. New York: John Wiley & Sons, Inc.

Bickel, J. E., and R. B. Bratvold. 2008. "From Uncertainty Quantification to Decision Making in the Oil and Gas Industry." Energy Exploration and Exploitation 26 (5): 311–325.

Bickel, J. E., Larry W. Lake, and John Lehman. 2011. "Discretization, Simulation, and Swanson's (Inaccurate) Mean." SPE Economics and Management Journal 3 (3): 128–140.

Bickel, J. Eric, James E. Smith, and Jennifer L. Meyer. 2008. "Modeling Dependence Among Geologic Risks in Sequential Exploration Decisions." SPE Reservoir Evaluation and Engineering (Society of Petroleum Engineers) 352–361.

Blenko, Marcia W., Michael Mankins, and Paul Rogers. 2010. "The Decision-Driven Organization." Harvard Business Review, June.

Bos, C. F. M. 2005. "A Framework for Uncertainty Quantification and Technical-to-Business Integration for Improved Investment Decision-Making." SPE Europec/EAGE Annual Conference. Madrid: Society of Petroleum Engineers.

Brashear, J., A. B. Becker, and D. D. Faulder. 2000. "Where Have All the Profits Gone? Or Evaluating Risk and Return of E&P Projects." 2000 SPE Annual Technical Conference and Exhibition. Dallas: Society of Petroleum Engineers.

Bratvold, Reidar B., and Steve H. Begg. 2008. "I would rather be vaguely right than precisely wrong: A new approach to decision making in the petroleum exploration and production industry." AAPG Bulletin 1373–1392.

Bratvold, Reidar B., J. Eric Bickel, and Hans Petter Lohne. 2007. "Value of Information in the Oil and Gas Industry: Past, Present, and Future." 2007 SPE Annual Technical Conference and Exhibition. Anaheim: Society of Petroleum Engineers.

Brouwers, Max. 2004. "Managing." AAPG International Conference. Cancun, Mexico: AAPG.

Burton, Jonathan, and William F. Sharpe. 1998. "Revisiting the Capital Asset Pricing Model." Dow Jones Asset Manager, May/June: 20–28.

Campbell, Andrew, and Marcus Alexander. 1997. "What's Wrong with Strategy." Harvard Business Review, November-December: 42–51.

Campbell, John M. 1962. "Optimization of Capital Expenditures in Petroleum Investments." Journal of Petroleum Technology (Society of Petroleum Engineers) 14 (7): 708–714.

Capen, E. C. 2001. "Property Evaluation – A Return to First Principles." SPE Hydrocarbon Economics and Evaluation Symposium. Dallas: Society of Petroleum Engineers.

Capen, E. C. 1991. "Rethinking Sunk Costs – A Value approach." Journal of Petroleum Technology 1418-1423.

Capen, E. C. 1976. "The Difficulty of Assessing Uncertainty." Journal of Petroleum Technology 843-850.

—. 1984. "Why Lognormal?" Prospect Evaluation AAPG Course Notes. Tulsa, OK: American Association of Petroleum Geologists.

Capen, E. C., and R. V. Clapp. 1974. "The Ratio: A Possible Clash Between Science and Instinct." Journal of Petroleum Technology 483-493.

Capen, E. C., R. V. Clapp, and W. M. Campbell. 1971. "Competitive Bidding in High-Risk Situations, SPE 2993." Journal of Petroleum Technology, June: 641-653.

Capen, E. C., R. V. Clapp, and W.W. Phelps. 1976. "Growth Rate—A Rate-of-Return Measure of Investment Efficiency, SPE 4613." Journal of Petroleum Technology, May: 531-543.

Capen, Ed. 1995. "Dealing with Exploration Uncertainties." In The Business of Petroleum Exploration, by Richard Steinmetz, 29-62. Tulsa: The American Association of Petroleum Geologists.

Capen, Ed. 1985. "The Exploration Decision – How Much Luck? How Much Skill?" In Economics and the Explorer: AAPG Studies in Geology #19, by Robert E. Megill, 49-62. Tulsa.

Capen, Edgar C. 1995. "A Problem with Experts." SPE Hydrocarbon Economics and Evaluation Symposium. Dallas: Society of Petroleum Engineers.

Carpenter, Chris. 2015. "Chance of Development: Definition, Estimation, and Use." Journal of Petroleum Technology 57-.

Chen, M., and J. Dyer. 2007. "Inevitable Disappointment in Projects Selected on the Basis of Forecasts." Hydrocarbon Economics and Evaluation Symposium. Dallas: Society of Petroleum Engineers.

Chermack, Thomas. 2011. Scenario Planning in Organizations: How to Create, Use, and Assess Scenarios. Oakland: Berrett-Koehler Publishers.

Chin, Cedric. 2020. The Rise and Fall of the OLAP Cube. Jan 30. Accessed 2021. https://www.holistics.io/blog/the-rise-and-fall-of-the-olap-cube/.

Cooper, Robert G., Scott J. Edgett, and Elko J. Kleinschmidt. 2001. "Portfolio Management for New Product Development: Results of an Industry Practices Survey." R&D Management 31 (4).

Coopersmith, E. M., and P. C. Cunningham. 2002. "A Practical approach to Evaluating the Value of Information and Real Option Decisions in the Upstream Petroleum industry." SPE Annual Technical Conference and Exhibition. San Antonio: Society of Petroleum Engineers.

Coopersmith, E. M., P. C. Cunningham, and C. A. Pena. 2003. "Decision Mapping – A Practical Decision Analysis Approach to Appraisal& Development Strategy Evaluations." SPE Hydrocarbon Economic Evaluation Symposium. Dallas: Society of Petroleum Engineers.

Cunningham, Peter, and Steve Begg. 2008. "Using the value of information to determine optimal well order in a sequential drilling program." AAPG Bulletin 1393-1402.

Dalby, Michael, and Timo S. Smit. 2004. "A new look at diversification." The McKinsey Quarterly.

Dalio, Ray. 2019. Don't mistake possibilities for probabilities. https://www.principles.com/principles/5495ec6c-7d61-495f-a1e0-688bf6f11e7c/.

Danner, George E. 2014. "The Art and Science of Bidding for Offshore License Blocks." SPE Hydrocarbon Economics and Evaluation Symposium. Houston: Society of Petroleum Engineers.

Davidson, Lynn B. 2001. "Practical Issues in Using Risk-Based Decision Analysis." 2001 SPE Annual Technical Conference and Exhibition. New Orleans: Society of Petroleum Engineers.

Davis, Russell, Xiaoying Pu, Ding Yiren, Brian D. Hall, Karen Bonilla, Mi Feng, Matthew Kay, and Lane Harrison. 2022. "The Risks of Ranking: Revisiting Graphical Perception to Model Individual Differences in Visualization Performance." IEEE Transactions on Visualization and Computer Graphics 2022 (IEEE Transactions on Visualization and Computer Graphics 2022).

de Geus, Arie. 1997. The Living Company: Habits for survival in a turbulent business environment. Harvard Business Review Press.

DuBois, James R, William F Dunn, and John P Strother. 2016. "An Investigation into Uncertainty Correlation in Resource Plays." SPE/IAEE Hydrocarbon Economics and Evaluation Symposium. Houston: Society of Petroleum Engineers.

DuBois, James R. 2001. "An Investigation of Risk and Probability in a Portfolio Management Context." SPE Annual Technical Conference and Exhibition. New Orleans: Society of Petroleum Engineers.

DuBois, James R., and Andrew I. Quarles. 2003. "Insuring the Portfolio Against Large Project Failure." 2003 SPE Annual Technical Conference and Exhibition. Denver: Society of Petroleum Engineers. 674-680.

DuBois, James R., and John I. Howell. ca 2003. "Portfolio Management: The Probability Perspective." Oil and Gas Executive Report, 42-45.

DuBois, Jim. 2003. "Dealing with Questionable Data." Second PDI Portfolio Management Forum. Houston.

—. 2005. "Using Portfolio Modeling to Validate Long Term Inventory." Portfolio Decisions, Inc., December 8.

Eisenhardt, Kathleen M., and Donald N. Sull. 2001. "Strategy as Simple Rules." Harvard Business Review, January: 107-116.

Eisenhardt, Kathleen M., Jean L. Kahwajy, and L. J. Bourgeois III. 1997. "How Management Teams Can Have a Good Fight." Harvard Business Review, July-August: 77-85.

Epstein, Alex. 2014. The Moral Case for Fossil Fuels. New York, NY: Portfolio Hardcover/Penguin.

Erdogan, M., B. Mudford, C. T. Davis, and D. Stegemeier. 2005. "Going Beyond the Efficient Frontier Analysis Using an Integrated Portfolio Management Approach." 2005 SPE Hydrocarbon Economics and Evaluation Symposium. Dallas, TX.

Etherington, John R., Elizabeth J. Hunt, and Adebowale Adewusi. 2001. "Aggregating Reserves and Resources for Portfolio Management." 2001 SPE Annual Technical Conference and Exhibition. New Orleans: Society of Petroleum Engineers.

Few, Stephen L. 2007. "Save the Pies for Dessert." Visual Business Intelligence Newsletter.

Few, Stephen. 2012. Show Me the Numbers - Designing Tables and Graphs to Enlighten. Burlingame, CA: Analytics Press.

Feynman, Richard P. 1974. Cargo Cult Science - Caltech Commencement Address. Accessed 08 18, 2023. https://calteches.library.caltech.edu/51/2/CargoCult.htm.

Flyvbjerg, Bent. 2021. "Top Ten Behavioral Biases in Project Management: An Overview." Project Management Journal 52 (6): 531-546.

Flyvbjerg, Bent, and Dan Gardner. 2023. How Big Things Get Done: The Surprising Factors That Determine the Fate of Every Project, from Home Renovations to Space Exploration and Everything In Between. Currency.

Friendly, Michael, and Ernest Kwan. 2003. "Effect ordering for data displays." Computational Statistics & Data Analysis 509-539.

Fung, Kaiser. 2014. Junk Charts Trifecta Checkup: The Definitive Guide. May 26. https://junkcharts.typepad.com/junk_charts/junk-charts-trifecta-checkup-the-definitive-guide.html.

Galonske, Boris, Stephan Görner, and Volker H. Hoffmann. 2005. "When payback can take decades." The McKinsey Quarterly, January 3.

Grossman, Thomas A. 2004. "Spreadsheet Engineering of Crystal Ball Simulation Models." Proceedings of the 2004 Crystal Ball User Conference.

—. 2005. "The Business Analysis Lifecycle: Create Better Models, Analyses, and Presentations with Less Effort." Proceedings of the 2005 Crystal Ball User Conference.

Hamel, Gary. 1996. "Strategy as Revolution." Harvard Business Review, July-August: 69-82.

—. 2006. "The Why, What, and How of Management Innovation." Harvard Business Review, February: 72-84.

Hammond, John S., Ralph L. Keeney, and Howard Raiffa. 1998. "The Hidden Traps in Decision Making." Harvard Business Review, September-October: 47-58.

Harriman, Matt, and Josh Groves. 2023. Integrated Upstream Planning: The Essentials: The Ingredients for a Perfect Planning Process.

Haskett, William J. 2008. "Pain and Regret." SPE Annual Technical Conference and Exhibition. Denver: Society of Petroleum Engineers.

—. 2014. "The Myth of Sweet Spot Exploration." SPE Annual Technical Conference and Exhibition. Amsterdam: Society of Petroleum Engineers.

Haskett, William, Marco Better, and Jay April. 2004. "Practical Optimization: Working with the Realities of Decision Management." SPE Annual Technical Conference and Exhibition. Houston: Society of Petroleum Engineers.

Hawley, P. W., A. D. Bramley, J. M. Castellani, and Arthur D. Little. 1992. "Competitive Bidding Tactics for New Exploration Concessions." SPE Oil & Gas Economics, Finance and Management Conference. London: Society of Petroleum Engineers. 159-165.

Hofstadter, Douglas R. 1989. Gödel, Escher, Bach: An Eternal Golden Braid. New York: Vintage Books.

Horner, D. 1980. "On the theory of inevitable disappointment, Theoretical Note No. 21." Unpublished.

Howard, Ron A. 1966. "Decision Analysis: Applied Decision Theory." Proceedings of the Fourth International Conference on Operational Research. Wiley. 97-113.

Howard, Ronald A., and Ali E Abbas. 2016. Foundations of Decision Analysis. Pearson.

Howell III, John I. 1997. "Integrating Portfolio Management into Corporate Culture ...A tale of three meetings." Petro Annual Meeting.

Howell, J. I., and Peter A. Tyler. 2001. "Using Portfolio Analysis to Develop Corporate Strategy." SPE Hydrocarbon Economics and Evaluation Symposium. Dallas: Society of Petroleum Engineers.

Howell, J. I., R. N. Anderson, A. Boulanger, and B. Bentz. 1998. "Managing E&P Assets from a Portfolio Perspective." Oil & Gas Journal, November 30.

Howell, John I. 1997. "Integrating Portfolio Management into Corporate Culture ...A tale of three meetings."

—. 2003. "Monitoring Your Performance from a Portfolio Perspective." slideshare.net. Accessed February 2021. https://www.slideshare.net/portfoliodecisions/monitoring-your-performance-from-a-portfolio-perspective.

—. 2003. "Portfolio Management: Definitions, Options, and Organizational Challenges." Presentation at Chevron. San Ramon, CA.

Howell, John I., and Anita Howell. 1999. "Issues, Owners and Interactions." J. I. Howell & Co., September 8.

Howell, John I., and James R. DuBois. 2003. "Monitoring and Managing Business Performance from a Portfolio Perspective." SPE Annual Technical Conference and Exhibition. Denver.

Howell, John, Lillian H. Warren, and Anita L. Howell. 2002. Implementing Portfolio Management: Integrating Process, People and Tools. Houston: Portfolio Decisions Inc.

Hubbard, Douglas W. 2014. How to Measure Anything: Finding the Value of Intangibles in Business. Wiley.

—. 2009. The Failure of Risk Management. Wiley.

—. 2020. The Failure of Risk Management Webinar. July 22. https://hubbardresearch.com/wp-content/uploads/2020/07/The-Failure-of-Risk-Management-Webinar-22-July-2020-PDF.pdf.

Johnston, Daniel. 1994. International Petroleum Fiscal Systems and Production Sharing Contracts. Tulsa: PennWell.

Kahneman, Daniel. 2011. Thinking, Fast and slow. New York: Farrar, Straus and Giroux.

Kahnemann, D., and A. Tversky. 1979. "Prospect Theory: An Analysis of Decision Under Risk." Econometrica 263-292.

Kahnemann, D., P. Slovic, and A. Tversky. 1982. Judgment Under Uncertainty: Heuristics and Biases. Cambridge: Cambridge University Press.

Kaplan, Robert S., and David P. Norton. 2000. "Having Trouble with Your Strategy? Then Map It." Harvard Business Review, September-October: 167-176.

—. 1992. "The Balanced Scorecard—Measures that Drive Performance." Harvard Business Review, January-February.

—. 1996. "Using the Balanced Scorecard as a Strategic Management System." Harvard Business Review, January-February: 75-85.

Keelin, Thomas W., and Bill Shew. 2003. Three generations of portfolio management. Strategic Decisions Group.

Keeney, Ralph L. 1996. "Value-focused thinking: Identifying decision opportunities and creating alternatives." European Journal of Operational Research 537-549.

Keisler, Jeffrey M. 2006. "Portfolio Decision Quality Adds Value." Baltimore, MD: DAAG.

Keisler, Jeffrey. 2011. "Portfolio Decision Quality." In Portfolio Decision Analysis: Improved Methods for Resource Allocation, by Ahti Salo, Jeffrey Keisler and Alec Morton, 29-52. New York: Springer.

—. 2010. "The Value of Refining Buy-up Alternatives for Portfolio Decision Analysis." Boston, MA, 11 4.

Kelleher, John C, and Justin J. MacCormack. 2004. "Internal rate of return: A cautionary tale." McKinsey Quarterly, August.

Kenck, Anthony, Mal Wright, Jaime Alvarez Lopez, Steve Coulom, Todd Jonas, Terri Otzmann, Melina Simon, John Temple, and Bennett Williams. 2013. "A Proposed Four-Factor Model for Assessing Probability of Capture of Unowned Resource Opportunities." SPE Economics and Management.

Kim, W. Chan, and Renée Mauborgne. 1997. "Fair Process: Managing in the Knowledge Economy." Harvard Business Review, July-August: 65-75.

Kloeber, Jack. 2011. "Current and Cutting Edge Methods of Portfolio Decision Analysis in Pharmaceutical R&D." In Portfolio Decision Analysis: Improved Methods for Resource Allocation, by Ahti Salo, Jeffrey Keisler and Alec Morton, 283-332. New York: Springer.

Knaflic, Cole Nussbaumer. 2015. Storytelling with Data. Hoboken, NJ: John Wiley & Sons, Inc.

Koch, Franklyn J., John I. Howell, Jerry Brashear, Larry G. Chorn, James S. Dyer, James A. Mackay, Stan Cullick, et al. 2003. "Portfolio Optimization for Oil and Gas: Execute an Effective Analysis and Utilize Insights to Make Valuable Strategic and Operational Decisions." Houston: The Center for Business Intelligence.

Kokolis, George P., Boris L. Litvak, William J. Rapp, and Ben Wang. 1999. "Scenario Selection for Valuation of Multiple Prospect Opportunities: A Monte Carlo Play Simulation Approach." SPE Hydrocarbon Economics and Evaluation Symposium. Dallas: Society of Petroleum Engineers.

Kozyrkov, Cassie. 2020. Are you Bayesian or Frequentist? September 2. https://www.youtube.com/watch?v=GEFxFVESQXc.

—. 2021. MFML 020 - Decision Intelligence. August 31. https://www.youtube.com/watch?v=R51nueuAyIY&list= PLRKtJ4IpxJpDxl0NTvNY-QWKCYzHNuy2xG&index=26.

LaCosta, William C. P., and Andrei V. Milkov. 2022. "Petroleum exploration portfolios generated with different optimization approaches: Lessons for decision-makers." Journal of Petroleum Science and Engineering 214.

Laughton, David. 2007. "Draft: The Banff Taxonomy of Asset Valuation Methods: Lessons from Financial Markets for Real Asset Valuation in the Upstream Petroleum Industry." March 05.

Laughton, David, Raul Guerrero, and Donald Lessard. 2008. "Real Asset Valuation: A Back-to-basics Approach." Journal of Applied Corporate Finance 20 (2): 46-65.

Leach, Patrick. 2010. "Applying Economic Lessons from Unconventional Plays Back to Conventional Projects." AAPG Search and Discovery. New Orleans, LA: American Association of Petroleum Geologists (AAPG), April 11.

—. 2006. Why Can't You Just Give Me the Number. Gainesville: Probabilistic Publishing.

Lehman, John. 2012. "What the Mating Behaviors of Birds Can Teach Us About Corporate Decision Making." SPE Economics and Management Journal (Society of Petroleum Engineers) 190-193.

Lewis, Bob. 2010. Bare Bones Change Management. Eden Prairie, MN: IS Survivor Publishing.

—. 2006. Bare Bones Project Management. Eden Prairie, MN: IS Survivor Publishing.

Lewis, Michael. 2004. Moneyball: The Art of Winning an Unfair Game. W. W. Norton & Company.

—. 2016. The Undoing Project: A Friendship That Changed Our Minds. New York: W. W. Norton & Company.

Lindo Systems. 2016. "Linearization of Nonlinear Optimization Problems."

Lomborg, Bjorn. 2005. "Global Priorities Bigger Than Climate Change." Ted Talks. Internet. California, February.

Luehrman, Timothy A. 1998. "Strategy as a Portfolio of Real Options." Harvard Business Review, September-October: 89-99.

MacKay, James. ca. 2001. "Prospect Inventories and Portfolio Management." Rose and Associates.

Macmillan, Fiona. 2000. Risk, Uncertainty and Investment Decision-Making in the Upstream Oil and Gas Industry. PhD Thesis, Aberdeen, Scotland, United Kingdom: University of Aberdeen.

Mankins, Michael C., and Richard Steele. 2005. "Turning Great Strategy Into Great Performance." Harvard Business Review, July-August: 65-72.

Markowitz, H. M. 1952. "Portfolio Selection." Journal of Finance.

Markowitz, Harry. 1959. Portfolio Selection: Efficient Diversification of Investments (Cowles Foundation Monograph: No. 16). New York: John Wiley & Sons, Inc.

McGrath, Rita, and M Muneer. 2020. "Uncertain 2022? Well-Defined Strategy Can Help." peoplematters 27-29.

McVean, J. R. 2000. "The Significance of Risk Definition on Portfolio Selection." 2000 SPE Annual Technical Conference and Exhibition. Dallas: Society of Petroleum Engineers.

Megill, Robert E. 1988. An Introduction to Exploration Economics. Tulsa: Pennwell Corp.

—. 1979. An Introduction to Risk Analysis. Tulsa: PennWell Publishing.

Menke, Michael M. 2013. "Making R&D Portfolio Management More Effective." Research Technology Management 34-44.

Milkov, Andrei V. 2015. "Risk tables for less biased and more consistent estimation of probability of geological success (PoS) for segments with conventional oil and gas prospective resources." Earth-Science Reviews (Elsevier) 453-476.

Mintzberg, Henry. 1996. "Musings on Management." Harvard Business Review, July-August: 61-67.

Morgan, Mark, Raymond E. Levitt, and William Malek. 2007. Executing Your Strategy. Boston: Harvard Business School Press.

Multiple. 2022. Type III error. https://en.wikipedia.org/wiki/Type_III_error.

Newendorp, Paul D., and John R. Schuyler. 2000. Decision Analysis for Petroleum Exploration, 2nd Edition. Planning Press.

O'Reilly, Charles A., and Michael L. Tushman. 2004. "The Ambidextrous Organization." Harvard Business Review, April.

Orman, M. M., and T. E. Duggan. 1999. "Applying Modern Portfolio Theory to Upstream Investment Decision Making." Journal of Petroleum Technology 50-53.

Otis, R. M., and N. Schneidermann. 1997. "A Process for Evaluating Exploration Prospects." AAPG Bulletin 81 (7): 1087-1109.

Padilla, Lace M., Grace Hansen, Ian T. Ruginski, Heidi S. Kramer, William B. Thompson, and Sarah H. Creem-Regehr. 2015. "The influence of different graphical displays on nonexpert decision making under uncertainty." Journal of Experimental Psychology: Applied 37-46.

Panko, Raymond R. 2000. "Two Corpuses of Spreadsheet Errors." Proceedings of the 33rd Hawaii International Conference on System Sciences. IEEE.

Panko, Raymond R. 2005. "What We Know About Spreadsheet Errors." Journal of Organizational and End User Computing.

Pennypacker, James, and Sam Retna. 2009. Project Portfolio management. Hoboken: John Wiley & Sons, Inc.

Persinger, Charles, and Jay Andersen. 2025. "Probability Assessments to Support Portfolio Management at Eli Lilly." Foresight (2025:Q1): 6-14.

Pinkney, J. 2003. "An Approach for Characterizing Portfolios." 2003 SPE Hydrocarbon Economics and Evaluation Symposium. Dallas: Society of Petroleum Engineers.

Porter, Michael E. 1996. "What is Strategy." Harvard Business Review, November-December: 61-78.

Powell, Warren B. 2022. Reinforcement Learning and Stochastic Optimization: A Unified Framework for Sequential Decisions. Hoboken, NJ: John Wiley & Sons, Inc.

—. 2022. Sequential Decision Analytics. https://castlelab.princeton.edu/sda.

Purvis, D. C. 2003. "Judgment in Probabilistic Analysis." SPE Hydrocarbon Economics and Evaluation Symposium. Dallas: Society of Petroleum Engineers.

Rapp, William J., Boris L. Litvak, George P. Kokolis, and Ben Wang. 1999. "Utilizing Discounted Government Take Analysis for Comparison of International Oil and Gas E&P Fiscal Regimes." SPE Hydrocarbon Economics and Evaluation Symposium. Dallas: Society of Petroleum Engineers.

Rasey, Ph.D., Stephen M. 2002. "Faster and Better Exploration at ChevronTexaco with Spotfire." Spotfire. April 30. Accessed February 2021. http://www.spotfire.co.kr/userconference/2002/Faster%20and%20Better%20Exploration%20at%20Chevron%20-%20Chevron%20-%20breakout.pdf.

Rasey, S. M. 2005. "Visualization and Interactive Filtering of Strategy Driven Portfolios as an Alternative to LP Optimization." 2005 SPE Hydrocarbon Economics and Evaluation Symposium. Dallas: Society of Petroleum Engineers.

Rasey, Stephen M. 2003. WiserWays. May 20. Accessed February 2021. http://wiserways.com/download/030520Spotfire.pdf.

—. 2008. "Managing trade-offs between conflicting goals through a portfolio visualization process." AAPG Bulletin, October: 1337-1357.

Raynor, Michael E. 2007. The Strategy Paradox. New York: Doubleday.

Reinsvold, Chris, Eric Johnson, and Michael Menke. 2008. "Seeing the Forest As Well As the Trees: Creating Value with Portfolio Optimization." SPE Annual Technical Conference and Exhibition. Denver: Society of Petroleum Engineers.

Ricks, Richard L. 1985. "Acquisition of Information – Economic Considerations." Oil and Gas Journal, September 30: 68-69.

Rose, P. R. 1987. "Dealing With Risk and Uncertainty in Exploration." AAPG Bulletin, 1-16.

Rose, P. R. 1995. "Chance of Success and Its Use in Petroleum Exploration." In The Business of Petroleum Exploration, by R. Steinmetz, 71-86. Tulsa: American Association of Petroleum Geologists.

Rose, Peter R., and Gary P. Citron. 2000. "The "Prospector Myth" vs. Systematic Management of Exploration Portfolios: Dealing with the Dilemma." Houston Geological Society Bulletin, October.

Rose, Peter R., Gary P. Citron, and Mark McLane. 2002. "E&P Portfolio Management as a Corporate Best Practice." 2002 AAPG Annual Meeting. Houston, TX: AAPG.

Roxburgh, Charles. 2003. "Hidden flaws in strategy." The McKinsey Quarterly.

Salo, Ahti, Jeffrey Keisler, and Alec Morton. 2011. Portfolio Decision Analysis: Improved Methods for Resource Allocation. New York: Springer.

Sanwal, Anand. 2007. Optimizing Corporate Portfolio Management. Hoboken: John Wiley & Sons, Inc.

Savage, Sam L. 2012. The Flaw of Averages. Hoboken: Wiley.

—. n.d. Various Blog Posts and articles. https://www.probabilitymanagement.org/.

Savage, Sam L., Stefan Scholtes, and Daniel Zweidler. 2006. "Probability Management." ORMS Today (informs). https://pubsonline.informs.org/do/10.1287/orms.2006.01.10/full/.

Schollnberger, W. E. 1996. "A Balanced Scorecard for Petroleum Exploration." Oil Gas – European Magazine 2, 9–19.

Schuyler, J. R. 1997. "Best Practices on Project Evaluation and Influence of Company Performance." SPE Hydrocarbon Economics & Evaluation Symposium. Dallas, TX, USA: Society of Petroleum Engineers. 101–105.

—. 1995. "Rational is Practical – Better Evaluations Through the Logic of Shareholder Value." SPE Hydrocarbon Economics and Evaluation Symposium. Dallas: Society of Petroleum Engineers. 323–336.

—. 1993. "Slaying the Capital Budget Constraint." SPE Hydrocarbon Economics and Evaluation Symposium. Dallas: Society of Petroleum Engineers. 219–228.

Schuyler, J., and T. Nieman. 2007. "Optimizer's Curse: Removing the Effect of This Bias in Portfolio Planning." SPE Project Facilities and Construction.

Severns, William. 2002. Apples to Apples: Making Best Use of Portfolio Management in E&P. Cambridge Energy Research Associates, Cambridge: CERA.

Sharpe, Paul, and Tom Keelin. 1998. "How SmithKline Beecham Makes Better Resource-Allocation Decisions." Harvard Business Review, March–April.

Sharpe, William F. 1964. "Capital Asset Prices: A Theory of Market Equilibrium Under Conditions of Risk." The Journal of Finance XIX (3): 425–442.

Simpson, G. S., J. G. Ross, and T. Y. Ghazi. 2004. "The Importance of Rigorous Asset Analysis as Input to Portfolio Optimization: Practical Lessons from Recent Experience." SPE Annual Technical Conference and Exhibition. Houston: Society of Petroleum Engineers.

Skaf, Mazen A. 1999. "Portfolio Management in an Upstream Oil and Gas Organization." Interfaces 29 (6): 84-104.

Skinner, David C. 1999. Introduction to Decision Analysis. Gainesville: Probabilistic Publishing.

Smith, Daniel, and Richard Sonnenblick. 2013. "From Budget-Based to Strategy-Based Portfolio Management." Research-Technology Management, September-October: 45-51.

Smith, James E., and Robert L. Winkler. 2006. "The Optimizer's Curse: Skepticism and Postdecision Surprise in Decision Analysis." Management Science (informs) 52 (3): 311-322.

Sonnenblick, Ph.D., Richard, and Daniel Smith. 2012. "Eight Rules for Effective Portfolio Management: A Path to a More Valuable R&D Portfolio." enrich consulting. October. http://www.enrichconsulting.com.

Sonnenblick, Richard. 2008. "Prioritization vs. Balance: Aligning Your Early-Stage Portfolio for Success." CBI Conference: Early Stage Asset Valuation and Evaluations to Phase 1.

Spetzler, Carl, Hannah Winter, and Jennifer Meyer. 2016. Decision Quality: Value Creation from Better Business Decisions. Hoboken, NJ: Wiley.

Spradlin, Tom. 2003. "Decisions and Relativity." White Paper Nr. 12. Confident Choices, April 16.

Stanford University. n.d. Stanford Profiles - Ronald Howard. https://profiles.stanford.edu/ronald-howard.

Steinmetz, Richard. 1992. The Business of Petroleum Exploration. Tulsa: The American Association of Petroleum Geologists.

Stermole, Franklin J, and John M. Stermole. 1984. Economic Evaluation and Investment Decision Methods. Golden: Investment Evaluations Corporation.

Summers, Gary J. 2021. "Friction and Decision Rules in Portfolio Decision Analysis." (informs) 18 (2): 101-120.

Taleb, Nassim Nicholas. 2001. Fooled By Randomness. New York: Texere LLC.

Torkia, Eric, and William Klimack. 2024. *Decision Superhero Book 1: Driving Informed Decision-Making with Probability, Explainable Models, and Decision Science by Eric Torkia (Author)*. Technics Publications.

Tufte, Edward R. 2001. The Visual Display of Quantitative Information. Cheshire, CT: Graphics Press.

Vivion, Nick. 2017. There's no single version of the truth. April 17. https://towardsdatascience.com/theres-no-single-version-of-the-truth-fe4b9857a453.

Wang, B., G. P. Kokolis, W. J. Rapp, and B. L. Litvak. 2000. "Dependent Risk Calculations in Multiple-Prospect Exploration Evaluations." SPE Annual Technical Conference and Exhibition. Dallas: Society of Petroleum Engineers.

Wang, Ben L., B. L. Litvak, G. P. Kokolis, and W. J. Rapp. 1999. "Four Criteria for Selecting International Petroleum E&P Investment Opportunities." 1999 SPE Hydrocarbon Economics and Evaluation Symposium. Dallas: Society of Petroleum Engineers.

Washington, Tim. 2018. PPM 101: What Is Project Portfolio Management? September 6. https://acuityppm.com/ppm-101-what-is-project-portfolio-management/.

Welch, Jack and Suzy. 2006. "Stop the B.S. Budgets." BusinessWeek, June 26: 114.

Wideman, Max. 2022. Some Interesting Project Life Cycle Variables. July 1. http://www.maxwideman.com/papers/framework/variables.htm.

Willigers, B. J. A., and F. Majou. 2010. "Creating Efficient Portfolio That Match Competing Corporate Strategies." SPE Hydrocarbon Economics and Evaluation Symposium. Dallas: Society of Petroleum Engineers.

Willigers, B. J. A., F. Weis, and F. Majou. 2013. "Creating Portfolio Insights by a Practical Multimethod Optimization Approach." SPE Annual Technical Conference and Exhibition. Denver: Society of Petroleum Engineers.

Woolsey, Gene. 2006. "The Fifth Column: Homage to Doc Savage 1, or on Knowing Your Right from Your Left." Interfaces (informs) 140–141.

Woolsey, Gene. 2006. "The Fifth Column: Homage to Doc Savage 2, or "Yes I Know You Can Solve It with an Optimum Method, but What Are You Going to Tell Your Customer if He Asks, 'How Does It Do That?'" Interfaces (informs) 3422–342.

Woolsey, Gene. 2006. "The Fifth Column: Homage to Doc Savage 3, or on the Optimum Siting of an Airstrip in the Jungle, or I Did It With My Tinkertoy Set." Interfaces (informs) 470–472.

Yudkowsky, Eliezer S. 2003. An Intuitive Explanation of Bayes Theorem. https://www.yudkowsky.net/rational/bayes.

—. 2017. Harry Potter and the Methods of Rationality. http://www.hpmor.com/.

GLOSSARY

Disclaimer: *The following definitions are not super-rigorous in terms of statistics, science, or even the English language. They reflect the author's attempt to clarify terms as used within the book.*

Accruals (see also deferrals) – future activity that represents a future commitment to for cash expenditure or receipt that is recorded as revenue or expense on an earnings statement. Expenses recorded as a liability for the future abandonment of an oil field is an accrual.

Adjustables – potential decisions in an optimization model. Typically, an entity can be In or Out, timing can be adjusted, working interest may be changed. The rules for how adjustables act are set with constraints or business logic.

Agile project methodology – a project development approach that emphasizes quick iterations and feedback to the project team. Portfolio optimization can be thought of as an agile approach to planning. Generating virtual outcomes and comparing them with a desired state, followed by feedback is the essence of agility.

AHP, Analytical Hierarchy Process – a form of multiple attribute utility determination that uses statistically weighted value applied to various decision parameters.

aPI – accounting Profitability Index. An efficiency metric that is expressed as a ratio, similar to fBCR. aPI has a different denominator and is typically defined somewhat differently mathematically. aPI is typically defined as NPV divided by the discounted budgeted or expected capital expenditures (where capital is as defined by accountants). Some firms add a 1 toe this ratio value, which appears to make it comparable to fBCR.

Balanced scorecard – a performance measure with a perspective across multiple aspects of an organization's performance. Rather than simply measuring financial results, it brings in other aspects, typically customer, employee learning, and business processes. The expression may also be used anytime there are less-tangible investments (environment or safety) competing for funding with purely financial ones.

Bayesian Statistics – estimating the probability of success of an endeavor typically uses a Bayesian framework. An important concept of Bayesian Statistics is to develop an estimate of a "prior" probability. As used in this book, Bayesian thinking is more important as a mindset than as a formal statistical framework.

Biases, Cognitive Biases – factors that tend to distort decisions and forecasts away from an objective rational outcome. They are common in all walks of life. Estimates can be calibrated with training as provided by companies like Hubbard Decision Research. Even with great training, company cultural factors can interfere with accuracy.

Boolean Expressions – describe logical relationships and create a logical or mathematical operator. For example (sky is above and sky is purple) yields a 0, while (sky is above or sky is purple) yields a 1. Other operators include NOR, NAND, NOT.

Brier score – a calculation to determine the statistical accuracy of probability estimate compared with results

BU – see *SBU.*

BU plan – as used in this book, it is typically a budget created and submitted to the enterprise by a semi-independent business unit.

Business Logic – a type of constraint in an optimization model that relates to business reality. Business logic prevents an optimization model from allowing late project phases to be scheduled before early ones or allows two mutually exclusive projects to both be selected.

Candidate set or portfolio – when using interaction methods, it is a set of virtual, coordinated decisions to compile for comparison with other candidate sets. This allows performance comparison across various measures of interest.

CAPM (Capital Asset Pricing Model) – a model developed by Nobel laureate William Sharpe that assigns a value to a capital asset (like a company stock) shareholder's "required" return on the shares based on a portfolio perspective of the riskiness of the shares. Some form of CAPM is used by most companies in the US.

Cash flow or net cash flow – the sum of cash in less cash-out. Typically, cash flow is examined on periodic bases, e.g., quarterly or annual. Cash flow, as opposed to earnings, represents the reality of cash movements.

Capex – a common abbreviation for capital expenditure. Typically, capex refers to funds spent to purchase or upgrade long-lived assets (like equipment, buildings, or property) that will be depreciated over time.

CFO chart – a point or line chart showing cumulative cost on the x-axis and cumulative value on the y-axis. Projects or opportunities are plotted in descending order of efficiency ((value/cost). The CFO plot creates a set of the most cost-efficient portfolios, with each point to the right being the sum of everything to the left plus the next most efficient project. CFO charts are concave downward and are a Pareto frontier.

Constraints – the general term for bounding the inputs in an optimization model. Constraints can be logical and based on business realities, reflect preferences of the firm's leaders, or mathematical "housekeeping" to ensure the model runs properly. *Business Logic* is a subset of constraints. Sometimes people also refer to requirements as constraints. When an optimization model is non-linear or stochastic, the distinction is critical as a properly constrained model can run in minutes or hours instead of hours and days.

Data lake – a form of data storage that allows for flexible structuring for reporting. Rather than imposing a structure on the data storage, structure is applied for convenience in reporting.

Decision analysis or DA – a structured framework and tools to help drive high-quality decisions.

Decision Quality or DQ – a measurement of the completeness of the elements of a good decision. As used in this book, there is a six-point framework to consider for decision quality: frame, data, logic, values, tradeoffs between values, and management commitment. Decision quality is considered separate from outcomes in recognizing that uncertainty or luck may play a large role in outcomes.

Decision Tree – a type of visual model to express decision sequencing, often in the face of uncertainty. Decision trees have decisions embedded in them and can help guide the best mathematical and statistical decisions. IF there are no explicit decisions, it is simply and event or probability tree. See *Event Tree*.

Deferrals (see also *accruals*) – past activity that is recorded in the future as an expense or revenue on an earrings statement. Capital expenditure is a deferral that is recorded as an asset and then recognized as an expense at a later time. Another typical deferral is deferred income tax or DIT, which occurs when the cash income tax is often lower in the early years of a venture due to accelerated cash tax depreciation.

Depreciation – a means of spreading the recognition of a capital investment.

De-risk – improving the probability of success of a venture or reducing the uncertainty in the outcome. This is typically done by investing in additional information with activities like research and exploratory studies.

Deterministic Analysis – a form of analysis in which the modeler expresses the inputs to a system as a single number without incorporating any concepts of uncertainty The opposite of Monte Carlo Analysis.

Discount Rate – the interest rate used to express the time value of money of an investment. It can be set to the inflation rate, financing rate, WACC (weighted average cost of capital), or the return of opportunities thought to exist. The rate is dependent on the insight a firm hopes to gain.

Earnings (see also *Cash flow*) – a measure of profitability. Revenue minus expenses. Where expenses include variable and fixed costs, depreciation and other deferrals, accruals, and taxes, while cash flow shows the actual cash movement of a venture, Earnings are adjusted in time to put the cash expenditures and receipts in line with when the expenditures and receipts are incurred.

Efficiency Metrics – metrics typically associated with standalone analysis that provide a measure of the efficiency of the investment interns of a percentage rate of return or a ratio.

Efficient Frontier (see also *Pareto Frontier*) – a concept developed by Nobel Laureate Harry Markowitz. The efficient frontier is shown as a graph that demonstrates the tradeoff between riskiness of a portfolio and its returns of profitability. For a given set of investments under consideration, the efficient frontier shows combinations of investments beyond which no combinations exist that have less risk with higher returns. Efficient frontiers are a subset of Pareto Frontiers. It is not unusual for people to refer to efficient frontiers when referring to Pareto charts with different axes besides risk and return.

Event Tree or Probability Tree – a type of visual model to express probabilities. For example, "a couple has two children, what is the probability that they are both boys?" Since there is no decision involved, it is simply an event tree. If your tree has explicit decisions involved, it would be a decision tree. See Decision Tree.

Expected Value (EV) – a common statistical measure considering the probabilities of a range of outcomes. For activities with simple binary outcomes, it is the probability of success time the success value minus the probability of failure times the cost of failure. Continuous uncertainties commonly use statistical calculations or simulation to determine an EV.

EV – see Expected Value.

False positive, false negative – false indicators occur when a test is not consistent with reality. For all who have been through COVID-19, A false positive (Type 1 error) is when your COVID test indicates that you have COVID, but do not have it in reality. A false negative (Type 2 error) is when the test indicates that you do not have it, but you do. The same applies to clinical trials, seismic or well data, or other indicators or tests used to draw conclusions.

fBCR – financial Benefit to Cost Ratio. Considered the gold standard efficiency metric. It is the sum of the discounted positive cash flows divided by the sum of the discounted negative cash flows of an investment. If the number is greater than one, the investment is considered as accretive to value.

Full Inventory – all the potential assets, projects, or decisions possible within an organization (see also Working Inventory).

Game theory – a field of math and behavioral economics concerned with dynamic environments in which other parties' choices have an impact on your choices.

Gaming – a term for negotiation and political maneuvering used to influence decisions, especially internal to an organization. It is often manipulative, dishonest, or deceptive.

IRR, Internal rate of Return – a common measure of investment efficiency or "bang per buck." The result is expressed as a percentage rate of return. IRR is the discount rate at which the net present value (NPV) equals zero.

Latin Hypercube Sampling – a form of sampling random variables in Monte Carlo analysis. Instead of being a completely random sampling of numbers, it distributes the random variables evenly in bins. This generally means that a probability space can be modeled with fewer Monte Carlo iterations.

Leveraged Economics – incorporating third-party financing or cash contribution into the economics of a project. It can be insightful in some cases, but more often tends to distort the quality of an investment when compared with unleveraged ones.

Metalog Distribution – a flexible probability distribution algorithm developed by Thomas Keelin around 2011. The algorithm can mimic most common and even very complex probability distributions.

Monte Carlo Analysis, Monte Carlo Simulation– a form of computer simulation of a physical system that incorporates the potential variability of the inputs to the system—typically expressed as a range that follows a pattern known as the probability distribution. The Monte Carlo platform selects random points from the input ranges, calculates a solution for your answer function, records the results, and then goes to the next set of random inputs. It does this as many times as is specified in the model. Outputs from Monte Carlo analysis can be expressed as statistical values (like mean or variance) or graphically showing the range of outcomes. Monte Carlo analysis is the opposite of deterministic analysis.

Monte Carlo Sampling – completely random sampling of uncertain variables. Compare to Sobol Sampling and Latin Hypercube Sampling.

Multiple Attribute Decision Analysis, Multiple Objective Decision Analysis – forms of decision analysis that use weighted values for reaching a perspective of the "goodness" of an opportunity. See also AHP.

Net Income – see Earnings.

Net Present Value, NPV –cumulating cash flow across time by reducing future numbers to reflect opportunity cost or cost of funding. The formula to discount a cash flow from a future period is cash flow divided by (1 + discount rate) to the power of (time periods). As an example, $100 three years from now with a 10% discount rate would be $100 / [(1 + 0.1) ^ 3] or $75.13. *When you see an expression like NPV8, it is meant as the Net Present Value discounted at an 8% annual rate.*

Nominal or then-current dollars (currency) – an attempt to place dollars in time according to their actual numerical value.

Objective Function – in optimization work, the objective function sets the direction in which the optimizer tool should seek better solutions. It is always a factor to be maximized or minimized. Net Present Value is a typical objective function.

Obsolescing Bargain Risk – describes a risk common to resource industries in which the power relationship between a private company and a controlling government changes over time. Prior to investment in a country's natural resources, the company has more bargaining power. As it invests more and more capital, the power shifts to the controlling government. This power shift often leads to increased taxes or even expropriation.

Opex – a common abbreviation for operating expenditure. Operating expenditures tend to have a short life, e.g., rent, utilities, and property taxes.

Pareto Frontier (see also *Efficient Frontier*) –a chart that shows the relationships between two measures of interest. The frontier is the boundary beyond which one measure cannot improve without worsening the other. The data points must comprise mutually exclusive actions for the purposes of this book.

Pf – Simple abbreviation for the word "portfolio."

PfA – abbreviation for Portfolio Analysis.

PfAM – abbreviation for Portfolio Analysis and Management.

PfM – abbreviation for Portfolio Management.

Phase Gate, Phase Gate Process, Waterfall – A Phase Gate or Waterfall project management process is one in which a project goes through increasingly more difficult or rigorous tests prior to the final investment decision. Each of those tests is a Phase Gate. One defined Phase Gate process might include four phases: framing, alternative generation, project planning, project construction and execution, and operations.

Portfolio – a collection of things for consideration and possible action of some sort. Generally, in the context of this book, the things are assets, projects, oil or mining exploration prospects, or pharmaceutical compounds. We also refer to a *candidate set* of potential decisions as a portfolio.

Portfolio Analysis – explicitly using tools, methods, and systems thinking to guide decision-makers and project managers to decisions that best align with well-formulated business goals and constraints. Portfolio analysis helps guide better decisions by putting asset and project investment decisions into an organizational context.

Portfolio Fit – in the context of this book, it is a quantitative value that considers opportunity cost and benefits from executing a decision.

Many people use it in a more qualitative way referring to general alignment of an investment with the purpose of a firm.
(See also *Portfolio Specific Value*)

Portfolio Management – making asset, project, and strategy decisions, informed by Portfolio Analysis, that "stick" and improve the likelihood of reaching your organization's goals.

Portfolio Specific Value or PSV – PSV measures the value an investment adds to a portfolio after considering the opportunity cost or its ability to add quantified "strategic" value. PSV is often a strong indicator of *portfolio fit*.

Probability Density Function, Cumulative Probability Density Function, Probability Distribution – a description or depiction of the form of a set of potential outcomes of a system.

Probability – see Risk

Rank and cut, Rank and yank – a portfolio method that ranks an inventory of opportunities by a single metric and selects the highest-ranked ones for funding until a limitation is reached. The single metric can be a composite score as well.

Real or constant dollars (currency) – an attempt to put a currency into equivalent units based on its purchasing power.

Requirements – the required values of an optimization model's output. Many people call these constraints. When the model is constructed linearly, it makes no difference mathematically. When an optimization model is non-linear or stochastic, the distinction is critical as a properly constrained model can run in minutes or hours instead of hours and days.

Risk (Risk, Probability, and Uncertainty) – Probability is the chance of something happening between 0% and 100%. It can be tied to a discrete event like a coin flip (50% chance of heads), or a range of outcomes (70% chance that we will beat our sales target of $x). Uncertainty means that a precise answer is not known. As with probability, it can be either a discrete event (the success of a drug trial or wildcat well) or a range of outcomes (how profitable will the drug or well be). Probability can be considered to be a subset of uncertainty. The difference is that instead of a smooth distribution of outcomes, there are two or more higher probability groupings of outcomes (modes). Finally, Risk is the probability relative to an undesired outcome. If a venture may lose money, we might say it is risky. Just how risky is a function of the potential loss and probability of loss. It is popular in some circles to talk about the upside potential of a venture as "positive risk." I think the word uncertainty captures both upside and downside, while "risk" as usually understood in English is uncertainty in the bad direction. When we use expressions like risked economics, it means we have used statistically valid approaches to adjust values and outcomes for the perceived uncertainty.

Risked NPV – see Expected Value

ROCE – Return on Capital Employed. A measurement of capital efficiency, typically measured at an enterprise level. The formula is earnings divided by capital employed, where capital employed is undepreciated capital expenditure less current liabilities. When calculated at a project level, it is more accurate to say that it is the return on (undepreciated) property, plant, and equipment (*ROPPE*). This shows the impact of the project on the whole. ROCE is typically an annual calculation, but a weighted value can be calculated across a project or long timeframe by dividing total earnings across the life by the total capital annual capital employed across the life of the entity.

Rollup – Simple mathematical aggregation of entities of an organization to see the total results. Rollups typically incorporate a time dimension to allow decision-makers to see trends. When rollups show sub-totals within the rollup, such as asset maturity, or disease class, it becomes a slice and dice analysis.

ROPPE – Return on Property Plant, and Equipment (see ROCE).

ROR, Rate of Return – see IRR.

Sandbagging – A form of strategic misrepresentation of future results (lying). A business unit may understate their expectations of results or overstate the cost to achieve results, rather than provide their best estimate. It is also used in reverse to encourage funding of a difficult project. It is typically used during target setting for purposes of accountability. The incentive systems in some companies encourage sandbagging with few, if any consequences.

SBU – Strategic Business Unit. Typically, a semi-autonomous business that is a part of a larger corporate entity.

Sensitivity Analysis – a form of analysis that compares the results of a model's output from changing inputs. It is a hybrid form of analysis somewhere between Deterministic Analysis and Monte Carlo Analysis.

SIP – Stochastic Information Packet. An array of random numbers that is used for input to a Monte Carlo simulation.

SIPmath, SIPmath Standard – a form of Monte Carlo simulation that uses pre-defined arrays of random inputs. The standard results in simulations that are actionable, auditable, additive, and agnostic.

Slice and dice – a form of portfolio analysis that shows a whole as a sum of components. When viewed over time, it allows decision-makers to see where an organization is heading across important strategic dimensions.

SLURP – Stochastic Library Units with Relationships Preserved. A set of SIPs in which correlations between the SIPS is preserved by the order of the numbers in the SIP arrays.

Sobol Sequencing – a form of sampling random variables in Monte Carlo analysis. Instead of being a completely random sampling of numbers, it distributes the random variables evenly in multi-dimensional bins. This will generally mean that a probability space can be modeled with fewer

Monte Carlo iterations. Whereas Latin hypercube looks at each variable individually, Sobol looks at the entire multi-dimensional volume.

Stochastic aggregation – adding numbers incorporating uncertainty, rather than as a single representative (deterministic) value.

Type 1, Type 2 Errors – see *false positive, false negative*.

Type 3 Error – an error type in addition to Type 1 and Type 2. Type 3 errors indicate faulty framing of the question, so the answer may be correct but not valuable because the question is not relevant.

Uncertainty – see *Risk*.

WACC – Weighted Average Cost of Capital. In the CAPM framework, the weighted average cost of capital is an imputed interest rate of the cost of funds to a company. It is a weighted average of the simple cost of debt, and a more complex imputed return requirement for equity.

Waterfall – see *Phase Gate*.

Working Inventory – the subset of the full inventory that lies within the frame of a specific portfolio decision or problem.

APPENDICES

APPENDIX 1

Financial and Economic Concepts

Most portfolio work in business uses standard financial, economic, and operational data. Portfolio practitioners and decision-makers must understand the relationships between the metrics to create better outcomes for their businesses.

At the most basic level, a decision-maker might ask, "Will this asset be a 'moneymaker'?" While that seems like a very reasonable question, there are three distinct ways of thinking about that, as well as time sensitivities.

At its simplest, a moneymaker brings in more cash than it costs. During development, the project incurs expenses that exceed its income, but once it becomes operational and generates revenue, it should be profitable. Its status as a moneymaker changes over time.

If the costs are spread evenly throughout the duration of the project, such as being tied to production, then the cost may seem negligible during development but will become apparent once the asset is in production. Therefore, it is uncertain if the asset will actually "make money" based on this approach. We always hope that this 'smoothed' version of making money has more money coming in than going out over the project's life.

Summed across the life of a project or enterprise, these two versions of making money are equal. It is an accounting identity. The first perspective is cash flow; the second is akin to earnings or net income.

There is another perspective too. A firm must pay back its investors with some form of income (growth or dividends). This is where discount rates enter. Doing better than breaking even (as in the first two definitions) **plus** paying sufficient money to investors in the business is the third definition of making money. We use discount rates to describe whether an investment will make money and return something to the investors.

These three descriptions of making money and the quirks around measuring whether something makes money are a big part of the field of finance. Portfolio practitioners must understand these nuances to be proficient.

Executive Summary

It's a fair assumption that money is a part of virtually every portfolio problem. All organizations need to understand the resources available to accomplish their mission. One constraint common to almost all enterprises is cash. There may also be others, such as skilled personnel, but access to money is omnipresent. Thus, the portfolio practitioner must understand how cash flow and accounting work and interact.

Future cash flow discounted at the weighted average cost of capital is the definition of the value of a firm under the Capital Asset Pricing Model. If you get this right, good will follow.

Earnings across the life of a project will always equal cash flow. It is a mathematical identity.

Accounting for tax vs. financial books is very different. Financial accounting is principle-based and follows generally accepted accounting principles (GAAP) or international norms. Accounting for tax treatment varies by country and by the tax entities involved. This is because tax treatment is meant to provide incentives for specific actions, e.g., investing in a country, beyond simply keeping track of profitability.

Tax accounting is typically included in the cash flow model, but this book will not delve into it in detail.

While cash flow is the best decision metric for long-term value, it is essential to understand the interactions between cash flow and earnings and how they may affect the market perceptions of your firm.

Key Principles of Finance, Economics, and Value

The Cash Flow Estimate

The economic analysis of an investment or asset begins with an estimate of its cash flows across its full life. Revenues come from estimates or assumptions of sales volume and price. Capital costs may come from engineers skilled at construction estimation and economists who forecast future costs. Experts on operations estimate operating costs. All of that occurs within some tax and regulatory regime (a country or state). Tax attorneys ensure that the taxes are correctly characterized. An economic or decision analyst captures all the estimates in a quantitative model (built in software platforms such as Excel, Analytica, or a specialized procedural language, and produces outputs of estimated cash flow and other measures.

Some Basic Financial Concepts

Cash flow is the lifeblood of any company. Wherever it comes from, it is what pays the bills. Earnings are the scorecard to help analysts understand the basis of the cash flow. When you read about stock analysts' views of companies, they seldom talk about long-term cash flows; instead, they talk about the price-to-earnings ratio or the Price/Earnings-Growth (PEG) Ratio. They use earnings as a proxy for cash flow, then implicitly apply a factor based on their opinion of the ability of the company's management to deliver on their promises.

Throughout this book, the word "value" is used in the context of seeking what is desired. It could be net present value (NPV), growth rate, capital efficiency, or a combination of outcomes.

All modern finance textbooks cover the Capital Asset Pricing Model (CAPM)

1. Under CAPM, the value of a firm is the sum of the company's future cash flows discounted at the weighted average cost of capital (WACC).
2. WACC is calculated as a weighted average of the after-tax cost of debt, the imputed cost of common stock, and the cost of preferred stock. It is expressed as a percentage. The weightings applied to the WACC components are derived from the firm's balance sheet and reflect the sources of funds, mainly loans or equity investments.

Basic Framework for Financial Prioritization:

1. The sum of future cash flows discounted at the firm's weighted average cost of capital is the value of the stock.
2. In an unconstrained environment, firms *should* do all activities that will result in a higher return than the WACC.
3. In a constrained environment, firms *should* do the most efficient activities (highest benefit-to-cost ratio) with respect to the constrained resource.

Definitions of Capital

Accountants and finance professionals define capital differently. For an accountant, capital is money spent that is not immediately booked as an expense. It is recorded as an asset and depreciated over its useful life. On the other hand, your finance department considers any net negative cash flow to be capital. This distinction is especially important when assessing the efficiency of investments.

When I refer to capital, I generally refer to the finance definition (net annual negative cash flow), not the accounting one. When I refer to the accounting definition, I will call it accounting capital or CAPEX.The above refers to investment money that the shareholders provide to the company, directly or indirectly, to spend on future revenues.

Cost of Capital

Businesses need money to begin operations. Broadly, there are two ways to get that money: debt financing (a loan) or equity financing (as with stock). For a business to be viable, it must make enough money to pay the bills for operations and return money to the investors.

The investors have expectations. For a loan, it is the interest rate. They have a legal right to the money they gave the business plus the profit governed by the interest rate of the loan.

Equity investors, on the other hand, typically get a right to vote on the company's course but have few rights beyond that. Because they have little control and no contractual right to a set amount of money, they hope or expect that their payout will be higher than with debt financing. They want a return commensurate with the risk they have taken.

There is another common use of the word capital as in the expression Return on Capital Employed (ROCE). In that expression, capital is the accounting definition, and "capital employed" is the balance of capital that has been spent but not yet depreciated. Future obligations to spend money (accruals) show up as *negative* capital employed.

Here's an example:

You have a great idea for a business, so your Uncle Ollie agrees to lend you $1,000. The after-tax interest rate of the loan is 5%. At the end of the year, before paying interest to your Uncle, you have $1,100 in the bank. After paying Uncle Ollie his $50 (your 5% cost of capital), you find that you have increased the value of your business by $50. This is a 100% debt capital finance structure.

The cost of debt is generally simple to extract. It is the coupon rate of a bond on an after-tax basis. Therefore, assuming a 35% tax rate, a bond with a rate of 10% would be 6.5% after tax. Calculating the cost of preferred stock is relatively straightforward, as it is similar to a bond. Typically, there is a nominal interest rate for the shares. Common stock is more difficult to assign a cost to. There is no "coupon rate" or any other explicit rate of return. Investors hope to make money through. Developing the framework to estimate this 'cost of equity' won William Sharpe his Nobel Prize.

In Sharpe's Capital Asset Pricing Model (CAPM), the assumption is that investors are rational portfolio investors who want to maximize the return and minimize the risk of their portfolios. The cost of common stock is determined by several factors, including the risk-free interest rate, the market risk premium, and the beta of the company stock, which measures how closely the share price tracks the overall market. In principle, any project with a return higher than the WACC will add value to a company's stock.

Finance textbooks commonly illustrate the cost of capital as a value that rises in proportion to the amount of funds needed. At the same time, a firm's queue of projects can be sorted by decreasing return on investment. The firm would then fund every opportunity at which the rate of return exceeds the cost of capital.

This is a good framework for thinking about investment, but it has some serious practical shortcomings that can be solved through framing and portfolio thinking. The first is that the firm has access to information on all the opportunities available. The second is the assumption that the investment opportunities have all had risk applied appropriately to reflect the expected return on the projects. Thirdly, this method doesn't account for funding requirements that arise during multi-year project development. Nonetheless, it provides a reasonable standard for companies to use in assessing potential investments.

I have seen an argument that the cost of equity is not an actual cost, so it has no place in this analysis. Indeed, it does not appear on your balance sheet, earnings, or cash flow statements. I am sympathetic to this argument but do not concur. I think of it this way. If you make a return only high enough to pay off your bonds, you are earning a bare minimum. Yes, you will "make money." But your stock will not be a good performer if you pay your debts with nothing extra. To be attractive to investors, you must go beyond that bare minimum. The investors will expect dividends or above-market stock performance. Given the characteristics of the company's market behavior, investors need that additional return to justify the riskiness of your company in their portfolios. Exceeding the imputed cost of equity makes a company worth owning.

Selecting a Discount Factor

Many organizations specify a single discount rate for all project evaluations. It is often derived from the WACC calculation, then adjusted upwards to prevent marginal projects from coming for consideration. This upward adjustment of the discount rate introduces a short-term bias to decision making.

In practice, the discount rate is set using one of three philosophies in most firms: (1) to determine whether a project adds value to the corporation, (2) to adjust the NPV for risk, or (3) to use it for comparison with the average or marginal investment returns of the corporation. The first and the third are clear, valid uses for a discount factor, the second—adjusting for the riskiness of the investment—is less well-supported. What you set as the discount rate depends on the analysis's purpose. Let's take them in order.

1. Discount rate for determining the value

Most financial textbooks say you should use the WACC as the standard for determining value. If a project has a rate of return greater than WACC, it adds value to the firm.

2. Discount rate to account for risk

Some people believe that it is appropriate to adjust the discount rate used in calculating a project's NPV based on the project or country risk. This is often tackled from a purely financial perspective and uses a beta approach. One such perspective is to try to assess a beta for a country's stock market (which in many cases doesn't even exist) relative to the US market, then apply the required return formula to it. In my experience, this approach often stems from misunderstanding the word "risk" as used in the CAPM framework. There are better, clearer methods for addressing the country- or project-specific risk than by adjusting the discount rate. Adjusting risk with the discount rate, is somewhat arbitrary in most cases. Many countries do not have stock markets, and even if they did, a single project in a country is not analogous to the stock of a company in that country. If a project is faced with risks, it is better to understand them, determine how best to manage them, and then model the remaining risks explicitly in the context of the firm's needs.

The CAPM framework uses the variability of a company relative to the market overall as the measure of risk. This variability is driven by the nature of the firm and its assets. The risk in CAPM is the non-diversifiable risk of the company. When we apply a different discount rate to a single investment, that is diversifiable risk. Instead of drilling one wildcat well at 100% working interest, you could drill ten with each one having a 10% working interest. You have thereby diversified the risk.

3. Using the discount rate to adjust for "opportunity cost"

In cases where a company's investment effectiveness is known, comparing a new project to this rate of return can be enlightening. The rationale is that if a project does not exceed this rate, other investment opportunities are just waiting for the money. This is appropriate when making a project determination outside of a comparative context.

The first and third justifications for discount rate selection make sense in most contexts. The first, using the unadjusted WACC, is a pure number. It shows how much value an opportunity will add to the corporation, assuming the investment performs as characterized. The third, using WACC plus a factor for opportunities thought to exist within the company (WACC+), provides a "hurdle rate" that must be met for approval.

When adjusting for the opportunity cost, using the firm's average investment return is interesting, but a better standard is to use marginal return. What is the return on the next dollar the company would invest? The average is a reasonable proxy for this, but remember, roughly half your projects will end above and half below the average. This is useful for the single project standalone decision.

Specifying a discount rate higher than the WACC seldom filters out bad projects. A typical response to artificially high threshold rates is input fudging by project teams. This applies not just to high discount rates but also to artificially low price or demand numbers. Flawed corporate standards can drive rationalizing behaviors and ignore reality. If the industry standard rate of return for a type of project is 10%, instituting a 12% threshold will force people either to admit defeat and resign their positions or to subtly alter the numbers to make their projects look good enough. Why do you suppose companies are almost always too aggressive in their project timing estimates and overstate production estimates?

Using anything other than the WACC as a hurdle rate presupposes decisions that arguably should be made using portfolio methodology.

Variable Discount Rates Within a Standalone Analysis

There is another approach I want to mention in which each of the sub-streams of cash flow within an overall analysis is discounted at a market-based discount rate. In this approach, revenue, OPEX, CAPEX, and their sub-components are analyzed separately and discounted at different rates based on their variability. It's a somewhat geeky and interesting approach. I question in what circumstances it would be helpful.

First, it is not a company-specific measure like CAPM. Separating the individual cash flow streams into their appropriate risk regimes acts more from a market perspective. In many cases, individual elements can be hedged, either contractually or on the open market. Therefore, this approach yields an aggregated, external market perspective of value. In principle, it could generate an unbiased market value comparison as an alternative for an asset. Commercial professionals generally use comparable transactions that reflect the actual market, not a theoretical composited perspective.

Moreover, separating the individual streams and calculating their rates individually requires time and effort, and results in a black box answer. The method is not broadly accepted as a superior valuation method, but it is interesting.

Varying the Discount Rate Based on Project Risk Removes the Portfolio Context

The alternate discount rate approaches may reflect some kind of external market value but fall apart when considering the value of an investment to a firm. Here's a thought experiment. Consider two investments, identical in every way, except the country in which they are located.

Investment A is located in "Stableland," a solid country with centuries of political, economic, and social stability. Investment B is in "Landostan," an emerging republic with social, political, and economic unrest. Your financial professionals have figured out a way to make each of the investments worth $1,000 in NPV(WACC) through brilliant hedging and corporate structuring. They carry no risk at all.

The investments are not material enough to affect the corporate cost of capital or volatility in the market.

After the fact, each of the investments pays out its $1,000 NPV. Which one was worth more to the firm? This isn't a trick question. The only answer is that they each would add $1,000. The challenges and volatility of Landostan as a nation are irrelevant to the value added. But some people and firms believe it should have a higher discount rate. So maybe, before the fact, it would have shown a value of $750 at the higher discount rate.

If the NPV(WACC) of the Landostan investment had been $1,100, but discounted at the higher rate for analysis, you would have preferred the demonstrably worse investment because it had an unjustifiably lower discount rate.

If an investment is inherently risky by itself, there should be an adjustment to its value. I have not seen a good, logically supported way to do that with discount rates. Rather, it can be done with estimates of the probability of success and ranges of outcomes for the investment. For example, we routinely apply the probability of success to exploration wildcat wells, along with a range of outcomes if the well is successful. Similar analyses can be done on other investment classes, including financial ones.

Markowitz and Portfolio Theory

Generalizing from the Markowitz approach to security portfolio analysis, there is always tension in investment decisions. To get something, something else must be given up. In the case of securities, you give up low variance in exchange for a higher return. For asset portfolio decisions, other trade-off variables can be considered. The comparison of short-term profits versus long-term growth is one such tradeoff. Or capital is traded in exchange for growth. In the first case, you want to maximize both variables. In the second case, you want to maximize growth while minimizing capital expenditure. The perfect world would be infinite growth with zero outlay. That is not possible, so something has to give.

Growth is Important

People who analyze publicly traded companies look at the financials and how those financials change over time. They like to see growth. A company's price-to-earnings multiple and its value to equity holders increase with growth and a promising growth story. But what is "growth"?

In this context, growth is growing **earnings**. Yes, we still care about cash flow, but net income (earnings) is a version of cash flow (with adjustments or smoothing for the timing of the recognition of expenses and revenues). The smoothing makes it backward-looking, so it acts as a report card. Have past investments and decisions resulted in growth? Growth in earnings is an imperfect proxy for growth in future distributions to the shareholders.

Mathematically, there are two bookend ways to grow earnings. You can cut costs or increase revenues. In the short term, it is generally easier to cut costs. It is the go-to strategy when the business environment is challenging. But there are limits to how far you can cut costs and keep the business intact. If you squeeze a sponge, water will come out. Squeeze it again; more will come out, but less than the first time. At some point, you'll wreck the sponge. Top-line (revenue) growth requires investment, so cutting the wrong costs will hinder your future growth prospects.

Cutting costs gives only a partial benefit anyway. Depending on the tax regime, cutting costs can give you 75 cents on the dollar in the US or 15 cents on the dollar in Indonesia. Only top-line growth is sustainable over the medium term.

Revenue—the top line—equals volume times price. Oil is a fungible commodity. There is no opportunity for significant differentiation in the oil price. Oil price has been subject to the whims of the Organization of Petroleum Exporting Countries (OPEC) since about 1980. The result is that companies focus on production growth. They are price takers. The only factor they control in the revenue formula is volume. Other businesses like pharmaceuticals or appliance businesses can change price, inventory, and features/efficacy to modify revenue and profits.

OPEC lost significant power in the 2010s with the advent of unconventional non-OPEC oil production, especially in the Permian Basin of the US. Saudi Arabia was historically the swing producer that kept prices high and relatively stable; now, the Permian Basin producers in the USA have a large impact on the marginal supply. There is an enormous amount of oil in the region, and it seems likely that, barring significant disruption, the oil price will sustain at or above the $40 - $60 per barrel range for some time. Simply **growing production barrels without also increasing earnings is not good growth**. Chasing so called empty-barrels that do not increase profits is a good way to go out of business.

Balanced Scorecards and Non-Financial Measures

This section has focused on the financial and "hard," easily measured metrics. We recognize that certain metrics, such as employee retention and training, may be challenging to evaluate but are nevertheless crucial to our organization's success. In the 1990s, many firms tried using a Balanced Scorecard approach in running their business. Few of these efforts succeeded.

The Balanced Scorecard incorporated finance, customer metrics, internal business processes, and learning and growth as additional dimensions of a company's health. Although the intent was great, some firms found it difficult to implement and show value from softer, non-financial metrics. At the same time, it was easy to show value by reducing costs or moving the soft budget into hard investments. When the business climate shifts and profit margins become narrow, the longer-term efforts are often the first to be abandoned.

With portfolio tools, you may be able to see the costs and tradeoffs associated with those efforts. Importantly, as with the initial Balanced Scorecard efforts, there must be a commitment to those values and a belief from the leaders that they are important enough to justify the tradeoff with short-term performance. Losing employees is expensive. Keeping employees who do not have up-to-date training reduces their efficiency and effectiveness, costing competitive advantage. It is impossible to see this erosion in financial statements, so some of it must be taken on faith. This is where leadership and vision input are needed. Portfolio tools can potentially help make the tradeoffs visible and explicit.

Detail – Net Present Value and Internal Rate of Return Basics

Net Present Value (NPV)

NPV is a fundamental principle in finance and economics. It is a mathematical formulation expressing that something you have now is worth more than that same thing later: *"A bird in the hand is worth two in the bush."*

The formula reduces future cash flows using a 'discount factor.' It is usually a single percentage value that can be thought of as an interest rate. If you have $1 in the bank with a 5% interest rate, one year from now, that dollar will be worth $1.05. The future value of the $1 is the present value times (1+ interest rate). Doing a little algebra, you can change the formula to say Present value = Future value / (1+interest rate).

Therefore, the value of $1.05 one year from now, discounted at a rate of 5%, is $1 in present terms. That is the foundation of NPV. Now extend that same principle to compound the interest, and you can determine a multiplier for every year in the future.

The multiplier for money a year from now at a 5% discount rate is 1 / 1.05, or 0. Funds two years from now are multiplied by

1 / (1.05 * 1.05) = 0.9070. Funds three years from now are discounted at 1 / (1.05) ^ 3 = 0.8638, etc.

The NPV of a stream of cash flows then is the sum across time of the annual cash flows, each of which is multiplied by the corresponding discount multiplier. It's like an Excel SUMPRODUCT calculation.

Let's take an example cash flow series. The total cash flow across the years is 5.2. Twelve goes out in the first two years, then 17.2 comes in during the following four years. The NPV at a 15% discount rate is -0.93.

▸ Example Cash Flows

	Yr 1	Yr 2	Yr 3	Yr 4	Yr 5	Yr 6
Net Cash Flow	-8.0	-4.0	4.3	4.3	4.3	4.3

Simple short-term cash flows will be used to illustrate the relationship between the discount rate and IRR.

The chart below shows cash flows discounted and summed across time at two different discount rates 0% (NPV0) and 15% (NPV15). NPV0 is the same as the sum of all the cash flows without discounting. If your firm's WACC is 15%, this opportunity will not add value to the firm under the Capital Asset Pricing Model (CAPM), even though it appears profitable and would add earnings.

▸ Discounted Example Cash Flows

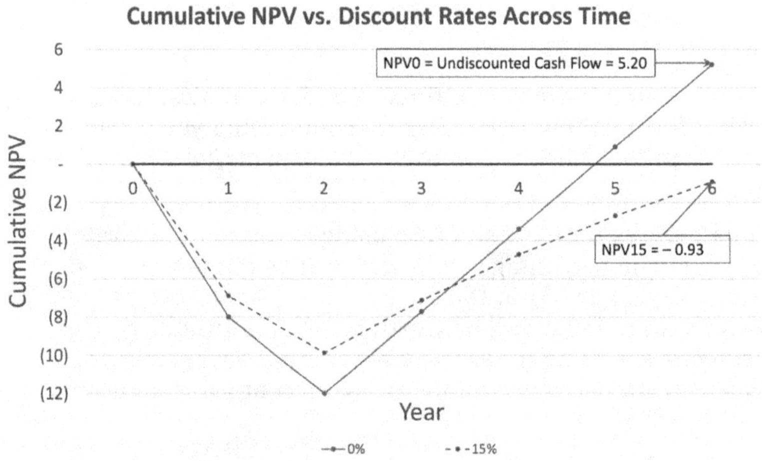

Undiscounted (NPV0), the cash flow above yields a positive value. Discounting at 15% shows a negative value.

Selecting the discount factor is an art as much as a science. Firms usually have some underlying model. CAPM is a common one.

Internal Rate of Return (IRR)

IRR is closely related to NPV. Rather than telling us the assets' value, it is an indicator of the efficiency of the investment. It indicates Bang per Buck. Investment is defined as the net negative cash flow for this metric (the finance definition).

The IRR definition ties directly to NPV. It is the discount rate at which the NPV of a set of cash flows is equal to zero.

Several cumulative discounted cash flows are shown below, with discount rates ranging from 0 to 20%. Note that NPV0, NPV5, and NPV10 are positive, while NPV15 and NPV20 are negative. The discount rate that ends at an NPV of 0 is 12.2844%. That is the IRR of the cash flow stream.

▸ **Discounted Example Cash Flows Highlighting IRR**

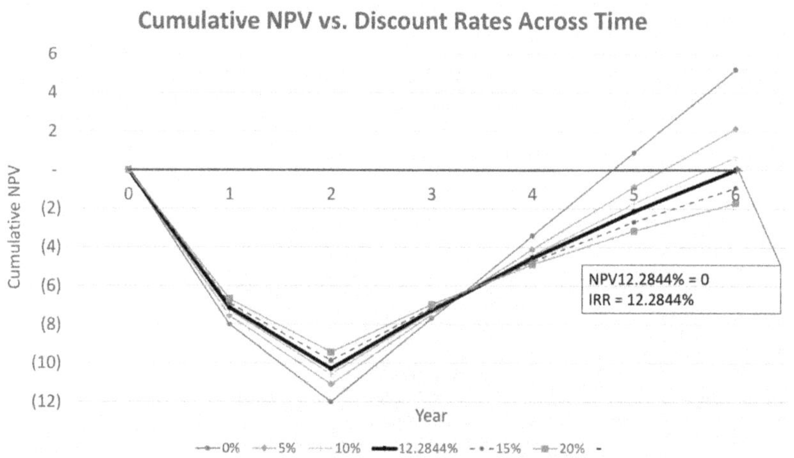

Applying a discount rate higher than the IRR results in a negative value. Lower than IRR results in a positive value. Discounting at the IRR gives an answer of zero.

IRR has some issues when used for analysis, but it is popular and well-known. The above examples use the Excel convention of end-year discounting, which means an assumption that all investments occur at the end of the year. Another common assumption is mid-year discounting.

Detail – Hydrocarbon Resource and Reserve Categorization

The reserves and additional resources held by a resource company are its lifeblood. Although this is not directly a financial issue, it is an underlying driver of results.

The volume of hydrocarbons that a company has the right to produce and sell may be the single most important and strategic indicator of the long-term strength of an oil company. From the day that production of an oil field begins, resources decline. They can increase only through exploration or acquisition activities. There is a physical limitation to the amount of oil in a field. If exploration and acquisition fail, the company will go out of business.

A popular framework to help manage those resources was devised by the Society of Petroleum Engineers (SPE) and has been implemented in some form by many oil and natural resource companies.

I'll refer to it as the 6P framework. The P stands for Proven, Probable, or Possible.

Commonly Used Hydrocarbon Resource Categories

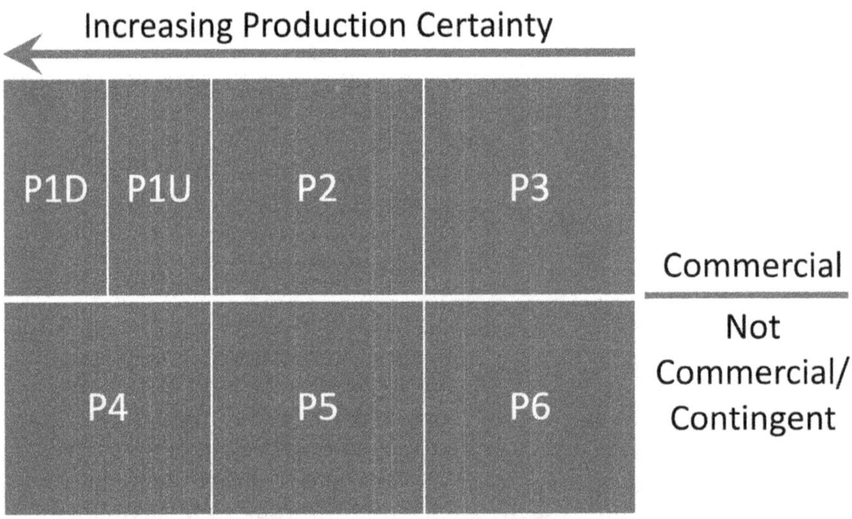

The standard categorization of hydrocarbon resources is sometimes known as the 6P Framework.P1D, P1U, P2, and P3 are all considered to be commercial with varying probability of being produced. P4, P5, and P6 are equivalent technically but suffer from an impediment to commerciality.

P1D(eveloped) and P1U(ndeveloped) in the upper left are "Reserves." There is a near certainty that those hydrocarbons will be produced **commercially**. P2 (probable) and P3 (possible) are less sure to be produced, mainly because of uncertainty in the physical volume of the "container" of hydrocarbons and reservoir characteristics. Once a field begins production, it is common for some P2 and P3 to move into P1. External markets strongly disapprove of any financial incidents caused by significant reductions in P1 due to price or recovery issues.

P1, P2, and P3 (P123) effectively define the successful development case. The uncertainty is how much of the total P123 will ultimately be produced. There are statistical methods to estimate how much will be produced from these categories to arrive at the estimated ultimate recovery (EUR) for a field. For reference, I will say "reserves" when referring to P1U and P1D. The sum of P1, P2, and P3 is "commercial resource."

The next layer of resources is P4, P5, and P6 (P456). These resources are currently not considered commercially developable. There may be several reasons for this: technical reservoir issues, high cost to develop, low product price, lack of market, or a combination of them. There may also be a management commitment factor. It is possible to estimate the probability of commercial success using these factors. I will call this layer "non-commercial resource" or "contingent resource."

I will call the sum of P1–P6 incorporating volume factors but not including the probability of success "total resource." Adding the P123 to the multiplication of the P456 by the likelihood of success is "total risked resource."

Some other layers may be considered if a company wishes. P789 may represent a hydrocarbon layer with potential for technical recovery, but extraction may be challenging or deferred due to current limitations. Exploration resources could be another possible layer.

Organizing and managing this assembly line of resources is at management's discretion based on the culture and organization of the company, but it **will** be managed either consciously or unconsciously. Consciously is better.

Sorting Out Cash Flow and Earnings

The distinction between the meaning and uses of earnings and cash flow is very important, and not as widely understood as it should be.

In financial theory, discounted cash flow is considered the most important measure of value. If a project has negative value discounted at the cost of funds (weighted average cost of capital or WACC), the project will not add value to the enterprise.

Cash flow is the reality of an investment. It is what pays the bills and returns cash to investors. The problem with cash flow is that it is usually uneven across the life of an investment. Typically, a large negative cash flow (investment) comes up front, followed by much lower investment but high revenue and positive cash flow. The results of any given year do not give a meaningful report card of the effectiveness of the overall investment.

Earnings across the life of an asset are exactly equal to undiscounted cash flow across its life. The difference is that earnings are time-shifted relative to cash flow. This allows a firm and investors to understand whether, on average, a company is making good, value-accretive investments.

Let's look at some examples:

Profitable Project:

Here's a profitable investment for a company with a 10% WACC. The NPV is $157, and it has an 18% rate of return.

▸ **Example Profitable Projects**

Profitable			Total	Yr 1	Yr 2	Yr 3	Yr 4	Yr 5	Yr 6	Yr 7	Yr 8	Yr 9	Yr 10
		Capital Expenditure	550	100	400	50							
IRR	NPV10	After tax Revenues	1,140			90	150	150	150	150	150	150	150
18%	$157	Cash Flow	590	-100	-400	40	150	150	150	150	150	150	150

Example cash flow.

If you were looking at year 1 cash flow, you might be quite concerned. It shows negative 100. Year 2 is even worse. However, looking at year 4, you might think that it is a stupendous investment. This is a simple illustration of the issue with cash flow as a financial metric—the value depends on where you are in the investment cycle.

Looking at earnings shows what the profitability looks like when costs are lined up with revenue.

▸ **Example Profitable Project Expanded**

Profitable			Total	Yr 1	Yr 2	Yr 3	Yr 4	Yr 5	Yr 6	Yr 7	Yr 8	Yr 9	Yr 10
		Capital Expenditure	550	100	400	50							
IRR	NPV10	After tax Revenues	1,140			90	150	150	150	150	150	150	150
18%	$157	Cash Flow	590	-100	-400	40	150	150	150	150	150	150	150
		Earnings	590	0	0	47	78	78	78	78	78	78	78
		Capital Employed (EOY)		100	500	507	434	362	289	217	145	72	0
	22.5%	ROCE			0%	9%	15%	18%	21%	27%	36%	54%	107%

Total earnings equal the total cash flow for the project. ROCE is shown as both an annual number and a weighted life-of-project average.

Here you see a project that adds to the bottom line and value (because the IRR of 18% is greater than the WACC of 10%).

Unprofitable Project:

This project has an IRR of 0% and an NPV of -$347. Although it is not *highly* unprofitable, this business generates zero earnings over its lifetime. If it were any worse, it would require writing down excess capital.

▸ Example Unprofitable Project

Unprofitable			Total	Yr 1	Yr 2	Yr 3	Yr 4	Yr 5	Yr 6	Yr 7	Yr 8	Yr 9	Yr 10
		Capital Expenditure	1,140	300	790	50							
IRR	NPV10	After tax Revenues	1,140			90	150	150	150	150	150	150	150
0%	($347)	Cash Flow	-	-300	-790	40	150	150	150	150	150	150	150
		Earnings	-	0	0	0	0	0	0	0	0	0	0
		Capital Employed (EOY)		300	1090	1050	900	750	600	450	300	150	0
	0.0%	ROCE			0%	0%	0%	0%	0%	0%	0%	0%	0%

> *Notice that after the initial investment, cash flow is positive in all years. Earnings are zero in all years. Because earnings are zero, the ROCE is zero. The negative NPV tells you that this project reduces the value of the company.*

If you were just looking at cash flow in individual years, you would have a similar tale as the profitable project—negative in early years, positive in later years. In this case, earnings tell you the real story. This project did not add anything to the bottom line and the negative NPV tells you that it eroded overall enterprise value.

The Value-Neutral Project:

This project has an IRR of 10% and an NPV of $0.00.

▸ Example Marginal Project

Value Neutral			Total	Yr 1	Yr 2	Yr 3	Yr 4	Yr 5	Yr 6	Yr 7	Yr 8	Yr 9	Yr 10
		Capital Expenditure	720	300	370	50							
IRR	NPV10	After tax Revenues	1,140			90	150	150	150	150	150	150	150
10%	($0)	Cash Flow	420	-300	-370	40	150	150	150	150	150	150	150
		Earnings	420	0	0	33	55	55	55	55	55	55	55
		Capital Employed (EOY)		300	670	663	569	474	379	284	190	95	0
	11.6%	ROCE			0%	5%	8%	10%	12%	15%	19%	29%	58%

> *The value-neutral project is neither good nor bad. Despite its NPV of zero, it has positive earnings and so contributes to ROCE. Notice that the average ROCE of 11.6% is different from the IRR of 10%.*

Cash flow in individual years tells a similar story as the other projects, but this would be accretive to **earnings**. The NPV of $0 tells you that this project does not add value above the cost of capital. Although it neither adds nor subtracts value directly, it may have other positive or negative characteristics. For example, it may help fill a gap in promised growth, or on the negative side, it might divert funds from better investments.

Key Takeaways

1. Cash flow is the lifeblood. The NPV of cash flow discounted at the WACC tells us whether the investment adds value to the firm.
2. Net income or earnings tells us whether the investment makes money in a minimal sense.
3. For a given investment, earnings always equals cash flow across the life of the project.

War Story – The Internal Interview

At one point I was interviewing for an internal role that would assist the company in connecting the technical aspects of exploration with finance and economics. One of the interviewers led with the question: "Cash flow or earnings?" I instantly responded, "Cash Flow!" I was certain then, but a little less certain today.

Remember that across the life of a project, cash flow is equal to earnings. It's an identity. Cash is king in financial theory and in practice. But... earnings matter. It is the key metric that drives comparison with competitors and judgments that affect the equity value of a company. It is therefore important.

Earnings is used in Price-Earnings analysis and Return on Capital Employed. In fact, almost any metric name that starts with "return" uses earnings in the numerator.

I still believe in the tenets of cash flow/financial theory, but when you make a decision, you must be aware of the earnings and other financial impacts that will follow. This gets even more difficult given the price uncertainty faced by the petroleum industry. See more information in the Margin-Price Framework section.

The Rest of the Story

By the way, I didn't get the job. Nobody did. Circumstances intervened, reorganizations happened.

Detail – In Defense of Growth

When oil prices drop, companies take a defensive posture, cut costs, and try to squeeze out every nickel of cost they can. This is appropriate and necessary given the volatility of the business.

Unfortunately, they hold on to those lessons for a long time even after prices recover. Then they overspend capital in an effort to grow production until the inevitable price collapse hits again. It's a story of swinging from irrational exuberance to crippling depression.

I want to talk here about that period as prices are recovering when companies should be focused on growth.

Let's refer again to the Strategic Execution Framework.

▸ Strategic Execution Framework

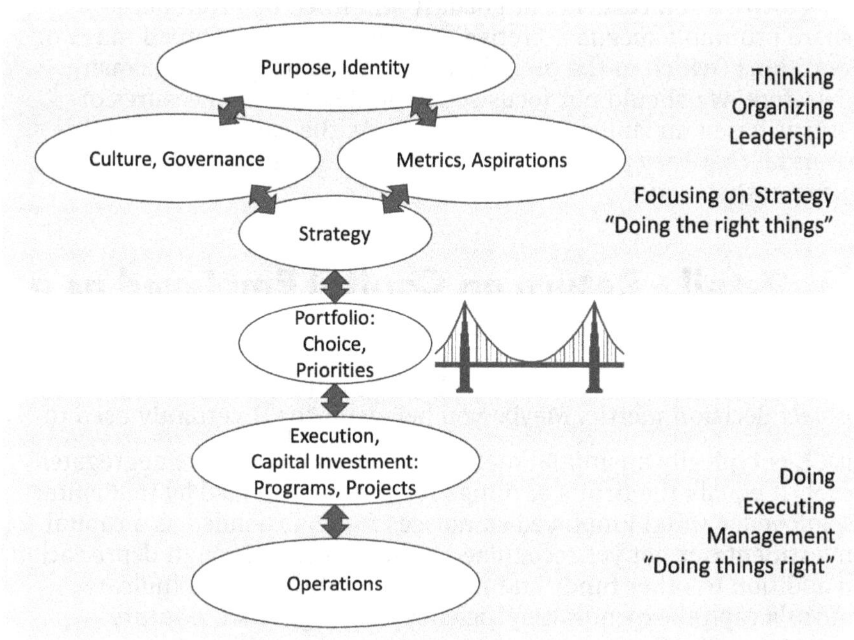

> *Let's go for growth! Henry Mintzberg, in Musings on Management, Harvard Business Review, July-August 1996, discussed Management's role as setting the "spirit of the hive." I have seen organizations that tried to improve profits by cutting costs and ones that have tried to grow by increasing revenue. It's like the difference between squeezing a sponge until it's so dry that you're just damaging it vs. growing wings and flying.*

The folks in the management bubble should be squeezing those dimes. That is their job. They should be ensuring that operations are run efficiently and safely. Leadership needs to monitor and understand their cost structure, but their main focus should be external, not internal. What are the trends showing? What are their competitors doing?

Adam Hartung, a columnist for Forbes Magazine has written extensively on the importance of top-line growth. Looking internally and trimming pennies off your unit costs is a good thing, but it does not lead to long-term prosperity. In fact, those pennies you trimmed may have led to your next future growth engine. You must beat your competition and increase your revenue. That growth can hide all manner of ills and allow for investment in new lines of business.

Growing the bottom line is necessary and important. Doing so without also growing the top line is a dead end. At some point, you run out of nickels, and you are stuck with your capital employed and a dying business until it all gets written off.

But growth at all costs is not good. It still must be profitable—where profitable means accretive to earnings under a broad range of conditions (which in the oil industry means during a price crash). Therefore, we should not focus solely on discounted measures of returns based on single price scenarios. As they aim to expand, it's essential that they consider the effect of the cost of growth on the entire cost structure.

Detail – Return on Capital Employed as a Project or Asset Metric

I have seen claims that Return on Capital Employed (ROCE) is a poor project decision metric. Maybe you believe it too. I certainly used to.

ROCE is typically an annual metric applied at a corporate aggregated level. It equals the firm's earnings for the year divided by its Capital Employed. Capital Employed comprises funds expended as a capital investment but not yet recognized as an expense through depreciation, in addition to other funds and negative liabilities. ROCE indicates a firm's capital expenditure efficiency and suggests the future robustness of a firm's earnings.

The arguments are something like the following:

1. ROCE is a financial metric based on earnings—not cash flow. Or,
2. Capital employed is only a corporate level financial metric. Or,
3. Annual capital employed swings all over the place across the life of the asset, so who knows what to do with it? Or,
4. ROCE changes from year to year, so it is not possible to calculate at a project level.

Although those arguments all have some merit, I am here to debunk them. ROCE **is** a financial metric. But I don't care. And the external market doesn't care. It **will** judge your firm based on ROCE. By definition, you better care about it.

While there are corporate-level considerations of capital employed having to do with financing, a project's impact on the overall corporate-level capital employed can be reasonably estimated on a comparative basis using the project earnings divided by undepreciated property, plant, and equipment. If you care, technically, I am referring to ROPPE rather than ROCE. But I'll still call it ROCE. The best way to think about ROCE (as I use it) is that it is your specific investment's contribution to the firm's ROCE.

Annual ROCE values do swing, sometimes wildly. The graph below shows how ROCE may progress. A few notes: ROCE in oil and gas at the asset level has two factors that drive the swings: Reduction of the undepreciated capital employed balance approaching zero and abandonment accrual reducing capital employed into negative territory At the point when the capital employed crosses through zero, the ROCE trends to positive infinity, then immediately approaches negative infinity. It seems hopeless to even try to do something with this.

ROCE Shows Wide Annual Variation

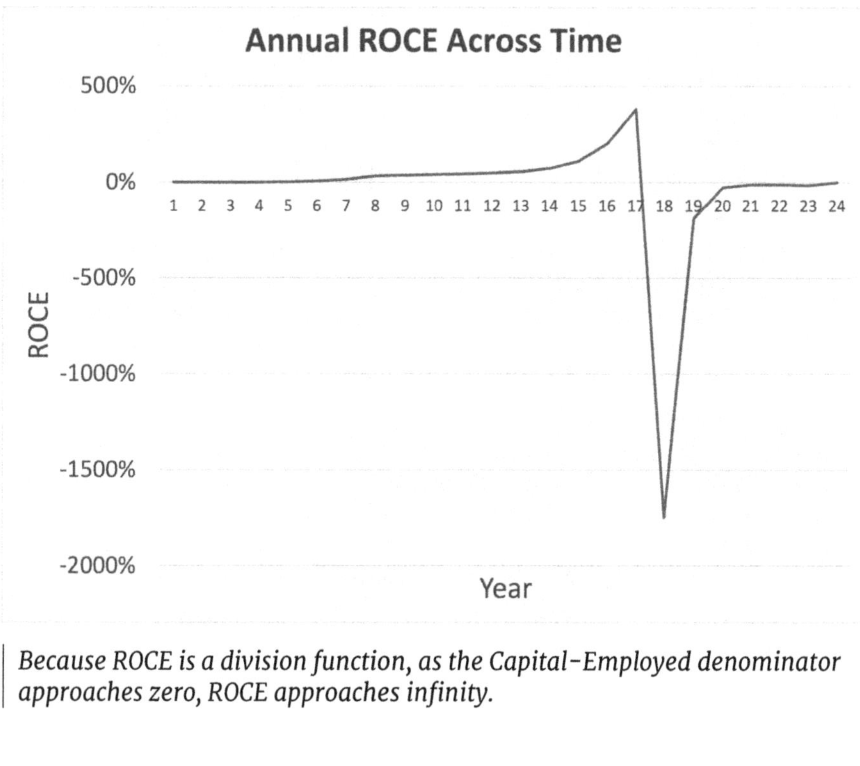

Because ROCE is a division function, as the Capital-Employed denominator approaches zero, ROCE approaches infinity.

It turns out there is something you can do. Although ROCE is an annual calculation, it can be compressed into a single, project-level metric based on a capital-employed-weighted average ROCE. By creating this average value, it shows the overall impact on the firm (on average). Those infinite values have no weight, because they are 0% of the firm's capital employed.

The formula for doing this is the sum of forward earnings across all years divided by the capital employed balances summed across all years. Dividing an annual metric by an annual balance metric may seem counterintuitive, but it is effective.

This average ROCE metric can be especially insightful when looking at and comparing assets with each other. I have used it to help screen candidates for divestiture.

War Story – Wait. Can Negative ROCE be Good?

Gregg, a geologist by training, was on a development assignment as a planning manager. That year, they were looking at divestitures. While in a meeting, one of his planners stated that negative ROCE was a good thing for an asset. Gregg sagely nodded in agreement.

After the meeting, Gregg came into my office and closed the door. "How the heck can negative ROCE be a good thing? I thought positive and high were what we are looking for."

I started to explain.

"Let's start with basics. ROCE is Earnings divided by the remaining undepreciated capital.

"Early in the life of an asset, capital employed is high and increases as the investment is developed. Until production starts, ROCE is zero because the earnings numerator is zero. Once the field starts producing revenue and earnings, the numerator is no longer zero, and yes, the bigger, the better.

"But with the start of production, something else happens—an obligation to abandon the asset at the end of its life accrues. Because it is a liability on our balance sheet, it is a *negative capital employed*. As the field is depleted of its reserves, the abandonment obligation becomes larger than the undepreciated capital, and the capital employed balance becomes negative.

"Although earnings are positive, the capital employed is negative, resulting in a negative ROCE. When we roll the earnings and capital employed up to the enterprise level, the effects of both the numerator and denominator positively influence corporate ROCE."

Gregg thought about it and said, "Wait. My head just exploded. Can you make a two-by-two chart?"

I went to the whiteboard and created something like the following:

Determining the Goodness of Capital Employed is Tricky

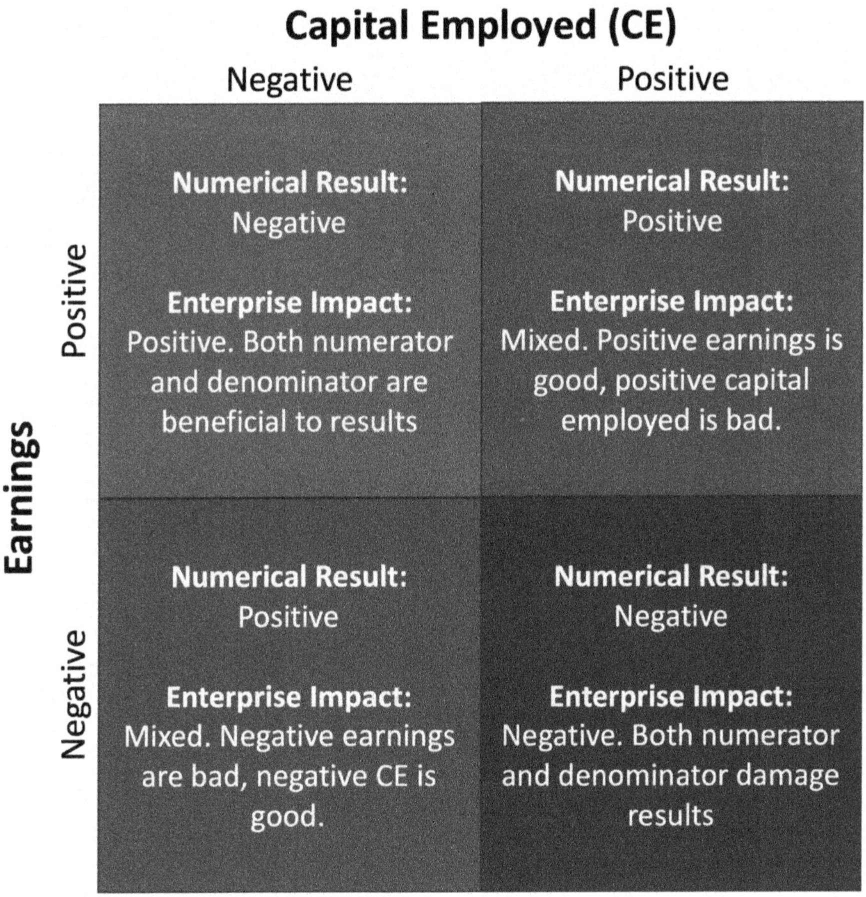

> *ROCE, by its nature, is complicated when using it to measure asset impact. Even really smart people can be misled without a deep understanding.*

Gregg took a picture with his phone and walked away. "Thanks. I'm going to have to think about this. Please erase your whiteboard."

APPENDIX 2

Decision Analysis, Decision Quality, and Project Management

"

...project management seems to be at odds with portfolio management. Project management is the backbone of accomplishment—it's how work gets done—while portfolio management is the brain of achievement. Stepping back from high-frequency project work to concentrate on portfolio work takes discipline."

David Matheson, SmartOrg, ValuePoint Newsletter, December 2019

Decision Analysis (DA) describes tools and procedures to structure decisions into logical components. The field is relatively new in the business world. It is an offshoot of Operations Research with some additions and distinctions. Decision Quality (DQ) is one way to measure that DA is effective and adding value. It is essential to include concepts of DQ in this book because portfolio decisions can be poorly defined and often contain a large amount of uncertainty. Clarity of purpose and transparency of thought are important in making good decisions. DA and DQ help us achieve that.

Project Management is a related field of practice with many books and courses of study. Details are outside the scope of this book. Project management processes combine nicely with DA to ensure that the right project decisions are made at the right time.

Decision Quality – Executive Summary

Immunity to outcome bias is the minimum requirement for decision competence.
Cassie Kozyrkov, former Chief Decision Scientist, Google, and current CEO of Data Scientific

Decisions should be measured primarily by the quality of what went into making the decision. The world is too uncertain and has too many variables to believe that a good outcome is the best sole criterion for judging decisions. The book "Fooled by Randomness" by Nassim Nicolas Taleb covers this in great detail.

One framework for making quality decisions comes from Strategic Decisions Group and includes six elements: frame; meaningful, reliable information; creative, doable alternatives; logically correct reasoning; clear values and tradeoffs; and commitment to action. This chain is only as strong as the weakest link, but the frame is a part of the decision quality framework that deserves special attention. It helps to understand the business problem you are trying to solve, as well as the specific details needed to perform a successful analysis.

Decision Quality is especially important for high-consequence decisions, but these six elements are worth considering for virtually any non-routine decision.

Decision Quality and Project Management

Decision Quality

One of the ongoing themes of this book is decision quality and its elements.

Decision quality is a framework for assessing how good a decision is. Rather than relying purely on the outcome to determine the decision quality, it looks at the thought process that goes into making the decision.

Think of a simple coin-flip game. I have a coin, which you inspect to ensure that it's fair. We made a deal that you will pay me $1 to flip the coin. If it comes up heads, I will pay you $10; if it is tails, I keep your dollar. You agree to play.

Before we flip the coin, think about it. **Did you make a good decision?** Of course you did, assuming you can afford to lose $1. You might lose a dollar or gain $10 on a 50-50 bet.

Now we flip the coin; it comes up tails (of course). You lose. **Now, would you say you made a good decision?**

If you said no, welcome to decision science.

Good Outcomes Do Not Automatically Result from Good Decisions

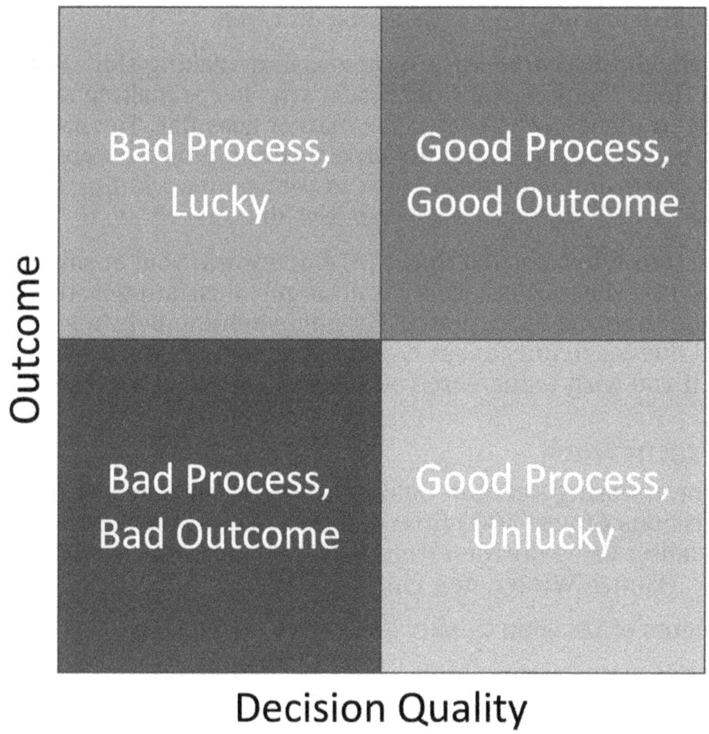

In general, we want to live on the right side of this graphic where we control our good decisions. Of course, some people seem to be born under a bad sign and make good decisions with bad outcomes in the lower right. Regardless, control what you can, trust the process, aim to be on the right side of the graph, and in the long run, you wind up in the upper right.

Many people would say, "No, it was a bad decision because you lost." This is known as outcome bias. With decision quality, we try to separate the quality of the decision from the outcome, on the principle that if you make better decisions, you will get better outcomes in the long run. This was a good decision with an unfortunate outcome (the lower right quadrant above).

Contrast this with a bet where you pay $10 to play and get $11 if you flip heads. It would be a bad decision to make the bet, but you might get lucky and end up $1 richer. You would then be in the upper left quadrant.

We know the expression, "I'd rather be lucky than good." Lucky is the top row; good is the right column. So yes, we would all like our outcomes to be good, but they're not controllable—your decisions are.

You want to live on the right side and hope for the top-right outcome. You want to avoid the left side, even though sometimes you might get lucky and make a bad decision with a good outcome.

It is often difficult to separate luck from decision-making skill. But we see it all the time. Think of the stock trader who keeps making tons of money day-trading stocks—until the market goes flat. The project manager's late, over-budget, and underperforming projects were saved by an oil price upswing. Suggesting luck to people on a winning streak can be a blow to their ego and cause cognitive dissonance.

Outcomes matter. When considering a DQ framework, you, at some level have to trust the process. There is an implicit assumption that you have more than one opportunity. For any potential investment that may fail due to circumstances beyond your control, you should have others if you wish to increase your overall chance of success.

The DQ Framework

One model for assessing Decision Quality has been published by the Strategic Decisions Group (SDG) from Palo Alto, CA, in the book, "Decision Quality: Value Creation from Better Business Decisions" by Carl Spetzler, Hannah Winter, and Jennifer Meyer.

The six elements of Decision Quality are:

1. FRAME – Adequate Frame – understand the problem you're trying to solve. What is the strategic decision on the table? How much risk, uncertainty, and ambiguity are involved? How does this decision affect and help move you towards desired organizational outcomes?

2. DATA – Meaningful, reliable information – collect information and facts that support different potential courses of action and that reflect the values by which you will measure success.

3. OPTIONS – Distinct possible alternatives – generate distinct project, asset, and portfolio alternatives that are possible and different enough to provide a meaningful difference.

4. LOGIC - Logically correct reasoning - analyze the alternatives using quantitative or qualitative models that explore the ranges of possible outcomes. Are the models internally consistent and follow real-world logic or an appropriate substitute?

5. TRADEOFFS - Clear values and tradeoffs - understand what elements are at play and relative values at stake. Yes, you want to grow your business, but not at any cost. How do you determine those tradeoffs?

6. ACTION - Commitment to action - Getting the first five elements in place is great, but the decision needs to be implemented to have the opportunity to succeed.

▸ **Decision Quality Broken Down**

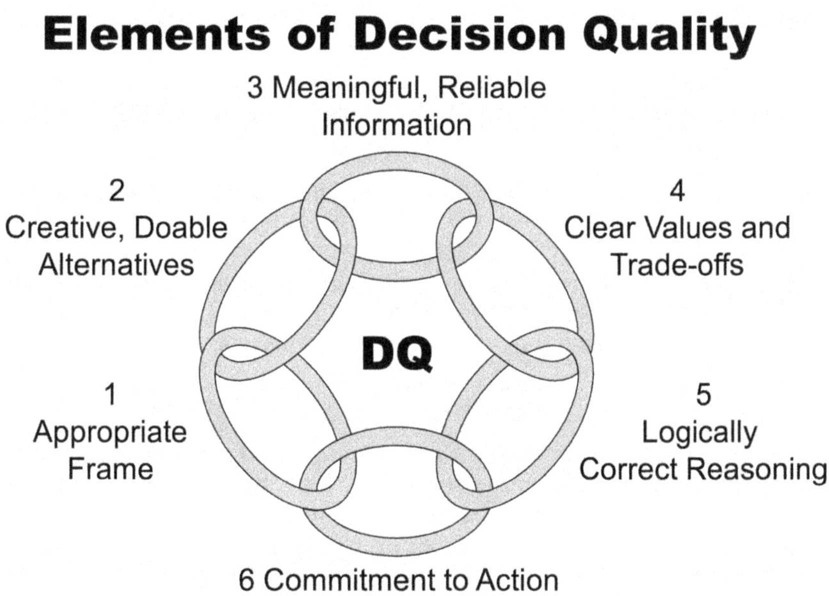

> *The Strategic Decisions Group has published a common framework for understanding and driving Decision Quality.* DQ is the why; DA is the what.

The Society of Decision Professionals (SDP) even has a decision-maker's bill of rights:

1. A decision frame that structures the decision in the context most relevant to your needs.
2. Creative alternatives that allow you to select from viable and distinct choices.

3. Relevant and reliable information upon which to base your decision, including the uncertainty of the information.
4. An understanding of the potential consequences of each alternative based on your choice criteria.
5. A logical analysis that allows you to draw meaningful conclusions from the information to reach clarity of action.
6. Effective facilitation to gain alignment and commitment to action.

The above Bill of Rights was originally developed at Eli Lilly and was further modified by the Society of Decision Professionals.

These six characteristics of decision quality work together. For instance, any options you create should be built to assess the tradeoffs between the value-measures in your frame. Data collection should capture the data needed to build an insightful model. The model should provide insight into tradeoffs as defined in the frame. The frame needs to explicitly state all of this, and the decision-makers need to be aligned with the frame and all the actions taken to reach a decision that gives them what they need to act.

The rigor applied to ensuring decision quality should be in proportion to the consequences, complexity, and ambiguity of the decision. If you are making a trivial decision, little rigor is needed. If you're making a billion-dollar, bet-the-company decision, it is worth the effort to ensure that you're doing the right thing for the right reasons and fully understand the consequences of failure and success.

Project Management and Project Decisions

The oil industry has focused on decision analysis and decision quality, mainly in the context of large projects. There are books on the tenets of decision quality, specifically in that context. Decision Analysis and Quality (DA/DQ) adds enormous value to the projects partly because of the stakes involved. In addition, the alternatives generated using DA/DQ are perfect inputs to portfolio models.

Exploration groups in the petroleum industry upstream and pharmaceutical research have utilized explicit portfolio techniques. Most companies use simulation to determine the robustness of their programs, and some take it a step further.

Besides decision quality, management of the decision-making process is important. One approach, also from Strategic Decisions Group, is called the Decision Dialog Process. It relies on a series of conversations between the working team and the management sponsors of the effort. These conversations are often called "snaking." It takes effort to ensure communication and alignment throughout the process. Not communicating takes more.

▸ "Snaking" to Align Project Teams with Decision-Makers

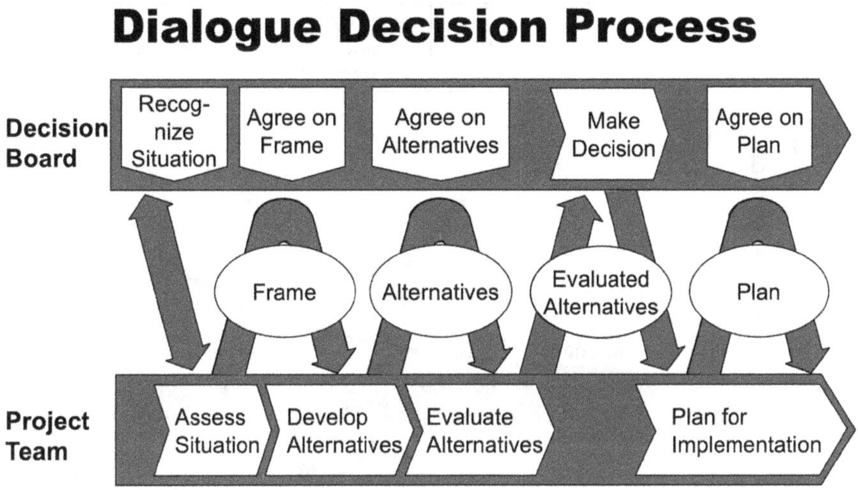

The actual decision situation dictates the appropriate number of interactions.

> *The Strategic Decisions Group has also encouraged people to use the Dialogue Decision process to ensure that project teams are aligned with management. The interactions between the project team and the Decision Board are often known as snaking. Agile processes are appropriate in many cases as well. In essence, Agile processes encourage micro-snaking with management, a very quick work-feedback cycle. This process, along with the many tools of decision analysis, is the "What" that drives high DQ.*

The above type of process, with communication between the project team and decision-makers at defined points, is often referred to as a phase gate or waterfall process. Whether phase gate or other project methodologies are used, the ability to add value is higher early in a project, and the cost to change is highest towards the end of a project. Therefore, it is important to ensure adequate "front-end loading." That is where the value is generated. Execution and operations are still critical and must be done well. Their most significant impact there is mainly in not eroding value.

We saw the Eagle's Beak earlier in the book and talked about the value of high decision quality, especially in the early stages of an investment. Here is another view superimposed over the original graphic.

▸ Front End Loading Increases Value

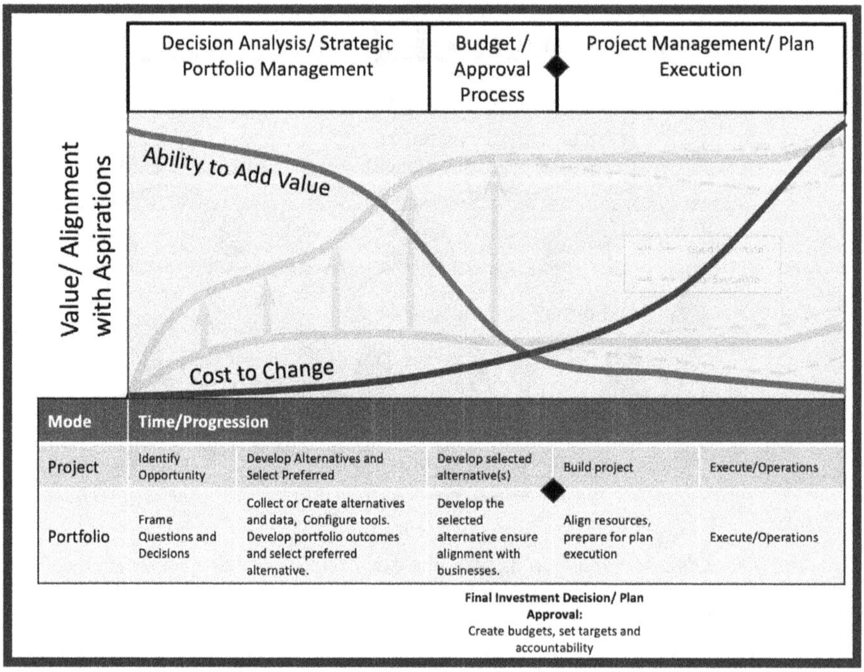

The front end of a decision process allows a high ability to change at a low cost. As a project progresses, the ability to add value decreases while the cost to change increases. Mind the early efforts.

The above graph shows that the most significant opportunity to add value is in the early phases. Once all plans are in place, construction is underway, and production starts, the ability to add value diminishes.

It is also important to note that the original design of a facility may limit the future changes that can or need to be made. Again, that front-end loading can affect values even far down the road. It pays to be thoughtful in the early phases.

People often feel rushed and move very quickly to decisions. There is a place for that. It is still always worthwhile to go through a decision quality checklist (at least mentally) with a trusted advisor.

Within this book, there is additional discussion of decision quality and project management as they pertain to portfolio analysis. Many excellent books and classes are available that cover DQ and project management in enormous detail.

War Stories – Decision Quality

Frame: The corporation commissioned a portfolio study with one of the big consulting companies. The study said the company should sell half its working interest in its largest and most profitable business operation. Executive management thought the result was absurd.

What was wrong with the study? Why would a consultant tell a company to sell half its most profitable venture? The frame of the study was reducing business risk. To the extent that business unit dominated corporate results, reducing interest in it would be a good way to reduce diversifiable risk. Somewhere along the line, management lost track that risk reduction was the frame of the analysis.

Meaningful Reliable information: In the first decade of the 2000s, projects in most oil companies suffered from the same fate. The project was late, over budget, and under-performed, but it was saved by the oil price. Think about it. Four main parameters drive the estimation of value: timing, cost, production profile, and unit revenue. Each of them had a systematic bias for about fifteen years. Everything was okay because it worked out as long as the price saved us.

In 2015 the price fell and stopped saving the industry. It could no longer count on the price to bail it out. But who got blamed? Mostly it was economic modelers and project management professionals. But did the fault truly lie with them? Were they incompetent, liars, or was something else happening?

More likely, there were real and perceived incentives in the system driving the poor estimates. On top of that, some of the forecasts, specifically price and inflation, were from the corporate center, so it could not have been the fault of project and decision professionals.

Speaking of planning assumptions from the corporate center, those numbers are developed by talented economists and econometric modelers and are often later modified to fit specific purposes. Executives can balance conservatism and optimism to make sound investment decisions and achieve growth goals.

The point is that although a set of future prices may have started as a best-estimate forecast, the forecasts can be modified to achieve specific purposes. I don't know the fix for this but given that cost and price—two of the four biased elements of the project mantra are at least partially driven by the center. You have not assessed Meaningful, Reliable Information until you include these factors.

Alternatives: Alternatives are often seen as either-or. And as long as you have multiple distinct options, that's a good start. I prefer to think of them as thought experiments showing how the alternatives can affect your essential indicators. Once you understand that, you can create a hybrid that achieves a better balance of those attributes you care about.

Logically Correct Reasoning: This is the realm of spreadsheet and model errors and improper shortcuts.

The project had always been seen as marginal. Although NPV had always been positive and the IRR was good, the ongoing requirement for budget funding was seen as a negative. The project was in an eternal loop of rework to drive costs lower. Then, when they found better ways to develop it, management gave the project team little credibility, assuming that the project team was suffering from confirmation or self-serving bias. In a last-ditch effort to get the project funded, the project team checked everything and found something ugly. They had applied a probability of success to the reserves and oil production but had not used the probability on the expenditure side.

Their model said that if they drilled a dry hole, they would spend the money to develop it anyway. This was a clear "logically correct reasoning" error embedded in the Excel model. It had not been checked because it was a "legacy" model that had been used by the business for many years (for other valid purposes).

1. Check and double-check the economic models. Perform model reviews by disinterested people who do **not** know your business, so they have no preconceived notions. This holds especially true for inherited models. Every model has built-in assumptions, simplifications, and shortcuts.
2. There's a more subtle lesson in this too. When errors lead to inaction, there may never be accountability or corrective action. Decisions to not invest seldom require lookbacks and do not cause financial incidents—just lost value that the firm never realized was lost.

Values and Tradeoffs: "It's an 'AND' world," declared the head of corporate strategy. "We need growth AND returns." Although this sounds great as a headline, it is not a mathematical possibility. Growth requires investment; investment drives return on capital down in the short term. We always need to be aware of reality and understand the tradeoffs. It is impossible to maximize diametrically opposed goals. The best you can do is find the point with the best trade-off.

Commitment to Action: Sometimes, there are meetings in which all parties agree to a course of action. The meeting is adjourned, and then nothing happens. This is a typical symptom of a lack of commitment to action. Lack of commitment to action is often seen in change management when a manager seemingly empowers a team to make changes, then refuses to follow through.

Detail – Analysts Code of Ethics and Professionalism

Chevron created the a code of ethics to help guide its analysis professionals. The modified version below has been generalized and made less specific. It is an excellent reminder to serve honorably and professionally.

Codes of ethics in general have two main impacts: they set the expectations for people in a profession, and they give people support when someone asks them to perform unethical actions. Codes of ethics may also improve the reputation of a profession and its practitioners, protect clients and employers, and create a positive work culture.

Code of Ethics

Portfolio, commercial, and decision analysts are expected to act in a responsible, ethical, and lawful manner. This helps to maintain the profession's integrity, reputation, honor, and usefulness.

This code will provide decision and analysis professionals with:

I. clarity on ethical and professional boundaries,

II. support for certified members to act ethically and morally, and

III. further guidance on professional responsibilities.

1. **Ethics.** Always operate with the highest ethical standards. Operate legally and transparently, avoiding conflicts of interest.
2. **Client.** Provide services consistent with the SDP Decision Makers' Bill of Rights and high decision quality.
3. **Stakeholder Interests.** Act in good faith toward stakeholders of the decisions. Ideally, the decision-maker's values and incentives are aligned with those of the stakeholders. Be wary of misalignment. Decision Analysts should act as balanced and objective arbiters to bring clarity, not as advocates of an outcome. When in a conflicted position, seek validation from a disinterested source.

4. **Requisite.** Conduct work with the quality and rigor required for the specific situation. Add complexity only when it adds quality to the decision. Carefully articulate the assumptions that underpin the analyses.
5. **Self-awareness.** Acknowledge the limitations of your knowledge, abilities, and experience, and actively seek assistance. Pursue continued professional development to learn concepts, tools, and techniques to improve your professional skills.
6. **Applicability.** Recognize the limitations of available data and models to answer the question or problem. Ensure that data is supported by disinterested subject matter experts if possible.
7. **Contribution.** Share your competency with colleagues. It is essential to the continuity and growth of the profession to contribute through participation in professional events, classes, peer reviews, and mentoring.
8. **Feedback.** Be objective, open to being challenged, and inclusive of diverse opinions. Accept that mistakes are a part of the work process and be willing to admit and correct them. Giving and receiving formal and informal peer reviews of models, inputs, and conclusions is a professional expectation and responsibility.
9. **Totality.** Provide a balanced and complete view of your analyses to the decision-makers. Prevent misrepresentation of data or conclusions. No deception by omission or commission.
10. **Redress.** Analysts should resist pressure to deviate from this code. Failing that, they should register their objections. Deviations from this code by colleagues and decision-makers should be reported through proper channels.

APPENDIX 3

Working Paper – Portfolio-Specific Value

One of the co-authors of this paper is Mal Wright. Mal passed away in 2023. His contributions to the thought processes in this working paper and the overall framework of portfolio analysis and management at Chevron were enormous. He was a good friend and family man. I think about him often.

RIP Mal.

Acquisition teams typically create their estimates of cost, production, oil price, etc., generate an economic model, and assume what the opportunity owner would accept as a purchase price. These economics on a standalone basis are then used to justify the purchase. That's a start if you have complete data and are confident about the purchase price.

I generally recommend that, before a deal is struck or a bid is in place, planners represent the opportunity with a purchase price reflecting the corporate standard minus a little—just enough to show a small, positive NPV. The opportunity will still make money (earnings), and this approach allows comparison of cost, future cash flow, and production to other assets and projects—without making unrealistic promises. The acquisition price is not knowable early in the process. This approach works for portfolio analysis and provides (in effect) a zero NPV perspective on portfolio fit.

There are times, often very early in an acquisition project, before the full economics are developed, before the acquisition cost is known, and sometimes even before the fiscal regime is certain, when you must make a screening decision.

How do you determine the "opportunity cost" of a potential acquisition when little is known about the opportunity? Acquisitions are hard. You are purchasing an asset from someone who knows much more about it than you do. They're not eager to let you know about all its warts. In such cases, although your team may believe they can secure a great deal, that is rarely the outcome. Winner's Curse strikes again.

The concepts of PSV may also be used in those early screening cases, with some modifications. The screening cases do not determine the final decision, but they can aid in prioritizing and obtaining a preliminary understanding of the portfolio's suitability. (See Sparse data cases.)

The following is the text of an unpublished working paper. It is the basis of a presentation prepared for the Informs Annual Meeting in Houston, TX, in October 2017.

Calculating Opportunity Cost Using Portfolio Optimization – Framework and Implications

By Anthony Kenck, Chevron (ret.); Peter Val Kranak, Chevron (ret.); Mal Wright (dec.)

Summary

Companies often use discount rates higher than their calculated corporate weighted average cost of capital (WACC) to discount the cash flow of opportunities. The reason given is generally either to compensate for risk or to compensate for other opportunities foregone (opportunity cost). This paper aims to understand the opportunity cost aspect in a portfolio context.

Regardless of the given rationale, a higher discount rate may compensate for the opportunity cost. It is difficult to know with certainty the rate of return a company will achieve in the future on its investment program, so there is generally little basis for an accurate estimate of the "hurdle rate." Studying the corporation's investment rate retrospectively can be difficult. Trying to normalize cost and price variance is tricky, and there would also need to be compensation for projects that had early costs but never came to fruition and other costs, such as research. Therefore, hurdle rates tend to be based on heuristics or gut feeling.

Additionally, the timing of expenditure and production are important. There may be a foreseen capital expenditure bottleneck at some point in the future, but before and after that, there is none. Any project with high capital needs in its peak period could impose a high opportunity cost. Simply discounting at a higher rate does not provide temporal resolution.

Using portfolio optimization techniques, opportunity cost adjustment can be calculated directly from forward-looking data in an inventory of opportunities rather than relying on rules of thumb. The opportunity cost depends on corporate requirements and constraints and the characteristics of the existing asset base and projects. Often requirements are not precisely specified or known in advance. Management should not commit to constraints and targets until they understand tradeoffs and organizational capacities. Therefore, sensitivities around the drivers of performance need to be understood. This approach provides a more data-based, finer-tuned perspective on enterprise needs.

The expression "opportunity cost" describes a negative impact on a portfolio's net present value (NPV). In cases where a positive impact is seen, we can think of it as having a portfolio-dependent opportunity benefit. In this paper, the opportunity cost or portfolio-dependent opportunity benefit will be referred to generically as the portfolio-specific value.

Introduction

Stermole and Stermole (1987) discuss hurdle rates in section 3.7 (Minimum Rate of Return, i*). They state, "...it is easy to say that other opportunities do not exist for the use of capital but most of the time other opportunities do exist if you look for them and they fix the minimum rate of return." They then suggest that some companies use "a weighted average compound interest ROR on historical invested capital as a minimum ROR. This may not be an unreasonable approach if the future is projected to be similar to the past." They continue, "However, as it relates to discounted cash flow analysis of investments, always remember that the minimum rate of return reflects future investment opportunities thought to exist rather than past opportunities already realized."

The above paragraph describes an approach that uses a hurdle rate to assess an individual project. It would be considered a good project if the project or opportunity has a positive NPV at the hurdle rate. If its NPV is negative at the hurdle rate, it is because the value lost from not doing other projects exceeds the value of the opportunity in question. This is well aligned with the definition of opportunity cost.

Nevertheless, if a company possesses an inventory of opportunities in its database, there is no requirement to utilize past events or "future opportunities thought to exist" as a reference. They exist and are documented. More than that, optimization tools can approximate the actual opportunity cost in dollar terms.

Albers and Howell (1999) showed that a new opportunity has a "portfolio value," i.e., the change in value to a portfolio that occurs when an opportunity is brought into the portfolio optimization and kept at a constant risk exposure. Their approach is to use portfolio optimization to determine the portfolio value of the opportunity, portfolio value being the difference between the value of the optimized portfolio both with and without the opportunity. This portfolio value is distinct from its standalone value and may be higher or lower. They also noted that the value to the portfolio is dependent upon three major factors: the nature of the project, the requirements and constraints of the enterprise, and the other projects available in the portfolio.

Albers and Howell lock in portfolio requirements and constraints; the approach espoused by Rasey (2003) and Willigers & Majou (2010) makes no specific assumptions about portfolio needs. Instead, they create multiple portfolios and then use graphical means to filter them. These approaches allow the generation of multiple portfolio scenarios before a strategy meeting and allow constraints and requirements to emerge from discussion facilitated by a graphical portfolio analysis. Their papers have focused on the entire set of decisions required to achieve better overall portfolio outcomes. Rasey does not use or require mathematical programming or portfolio optimization to create the base portfolio, whereas Willigers does. This paper uses similar graphical analysis techniques, focusing on determining a value for a single opportunity.

Numerous optimization papers present efficient frontiers of value, often measured by NPV vs. risk, which is typically measured by standard deviation or semi-standard deviation. The authors of this paper focus much of their work on a different type of frontier—a Pareto frontier (Kostiuk, Valdez, Bordovsky, Mu, & Faig, 2013) of budget funds vs. NPV. Using portfolio optimization, the charts show where, for a given budget level, no additional NPV is possible and that, at a given NPV, no lower budget can be allocated. The authors of this paper have seen that decision-makers generally relate better to concrete measures, such as budget, than to more abstract statistical measures (e.g., standard deviation or discounted capital expenditure). By demonstrating how the value of the opportunity is impacted by the long-term stability of the capital budget funding levels, the focus shifts from solely valuing the opportunity to strategizing about the enterprise's investment capacity and beliefs.

Finally, the recognition that the portfolio value of an opportunity has two components—standalone value and portfolio-specific value—allows for the separation of the portfolio component, which is especially useful for opportunity screening. Construction of an acceptable cash flow model can be difficult and error-prone when there is limited information. In some cases, the fiscal regime is not even defined, making a reasonable cash flow analysis impossible. Understanding the portfolio-specific value of an opportunity can allow insights into the existing inventory and early screening of opportunities.

What is Opportunity Cost?

Opportunity cost is the cost, value, or profit forgone by choosing one option over another. For example, if there are two mutually exclusive alternatives, A and B, and if the value of A is \$800 and the value of B is \$600, selecting A might appear to be a gain of \$800, but it is a gain of only \$200 (\$800 - \$600) relative to the opportunity foregone.

From the perspective of comparing investments, some authors have suggested that when making investment decisions, the cash flow streams should be discounted using the higher of the enterprise's WACC or the rate at which the corporation would otherwise reinvest. This reinvestment rate then reflects the opportunity cost to the enterprise (Stermole & Stermole, 1987).

In common parlance, opportunity cost is negative. In the context of a portfolio, however, a given project or opportunity can add value by providing relief in filling portfolio requirements or easing constraints.

Enter Portfolio Optimization

Portfolio optimization can give us insight and another perspective.

Much has been written about assessing the portfolio fit of an opportunity. Start with a current optimized portfolio of projects and base businesses, add the new opportunity, then optimize again.

The difference between the portfolio's value with and without the new opportunity indicates how much value the opportunity adds to the portfolio. That difference can be considered the portfolio NPV or portfolio value of the opportunity. Putting an opportunity into the frame of the overall portfolio in this way can yield a portfolio value that is either higher or lower than the NPV calculated from the opportunity's standalone cash flow.

For example, suppose the NPV of a current optimized portfolio is \$1,000. A new opportunity comes in that has a standalone NPV of \$100. Many firms would value the project simply as a \$100 NPV project. The implicit assumption is that the values of the base portfolio and the project are directly additive. However, when the project goes into the portfolio mix, and the portfolio is optimized under the same requirements and constraints, the value of the portfolio increases to only \$1,050 (\$1000 + \$100) <> \$1050). What happened?

In the simplest case, unless a new opportunity (acquisition or new exploration discovery) brings its own financing capacity, human resource capability, and other necessary resources, it may stress the firm's ability to execute it along with everything else available for execution. In that simple case, something has to give. Other projects will have to be delayed, eliminated, or reduced. These changes produce a negative drag on the portfolio value because they force other NPV-positive projects and opportunities out of the initial portfolio solution. So the actual value of an opportunity to the enterprise, for a given set of organizational requirements and constraints, is the standalone value of the opportunity less (in this example) the organizational drag (opportunity cost) required to accommodate the opportunity.

This effect can be defined as follows:

$$VPfNew_{i+p,r} = VPfOld_{i,r} + [VProject_{p} + PSV_{i+p,r,p}] = \$1{,}000 + (\ \$100 + (-\$50)) = \$1{,}050$$

Where:

VPfNew is the value of the optimized portfolio **with** the opportunity;

VPfOld is the initial value of the optimized portfolio without the opportunity;

VProject is the standalone value of the opportunity;

PSV is Portfolio-Specific Value, a generic term that encompasses both opportunity cost and its opposite, portfolio-specific opportunity benefit;

i = the inventory of possible decisions and the business logic that constrains selections;

p = the project under consideration and its flexibility;

r = the portfolio requirements and objective(s).

[VProject + PSV] is the net value of the project in the portfolio context, commonly referred to as the portfolio NPV, the portfolio value, or the marginal portfolio value of the opportunity.

Using the above numbers, the new value of the portfolio with the opportunity is $1,050, rather than the $1,100 suggested by the simple addition of the portfolio and the opportunity.

Opportunity Cost Is Dependent on the Current Inventory of Asset Options and Portfolio Requirements

If the portfolio model is a simple maximization function with no requirements, such as capital, production, or reserve replacement, PSV will equal zero. In other words, the opportunity is purely value accretive because there are no constraints or requirements.

However, in the real world, there are always requirements and limitations, whether recognized or not. Using optimization, decision-makers can directly calculate a PSV that considers the firm's strategies, goals, constraints, and requirements.

The PSV is a function of the opportunity under consideration; the requirements, constraints, and objective of the optimization; and the working inventory with and without the opportunity. It can be expressed symbolically as

$$\textbf{PSV} = f\,(\,\textbf{Project}_j,\ \textbf{Portfolio Requirements}_k,\ \textbf{Inventory}_{m,\,m+j}\,)$$

In this paper, for clarity and discussion, capital expenditure has been used as a proxy for the set of inputs required to generate production and profits. In reality, limitations can also include cash flow, human resources, executive attention, and external resource limitations.

Under the Capital Asset Pricing Model (CAPM), decision-makers should try to maximize net present value (NPV) discounted at the corporation's weighted average cost of capital (WACC) (Brigham & Gapenski, 1997). However, there is an external factor involved as well. Stock analysts, who can significantly impact equity price, do not have the same view of the company as those inside. Analyst judgments are based on publicly disclosed knowledge. They have three things to go on: historical results, their imperfect projections of what a company can do with its assets, and guidance given by the company about future results.

As a result, it is wise to incorporate external expectations (such as production growth, reserve replacement, capital expenditure, earnings, and return on capital employed) into the requirements of the optimization as well. Without a portfolio perspective and a multi-objective tool, it isn't easy to know the next-best use of corporate capital. The best we can do is guess or estimate what our incremental dollars will return. With an adequate inventory and a portfolio perspective, we do not have to guess—it is in the data.

Using the PSV Framework

A new opportunity can be tested for portfolio fit, and an estimation of how much value the opportunity would add to the firm can be made (Albers & Howell III, 1999, Allan, 2001). Those papers describe an excellent methodology similar to that described above. However, there is a potential procedural problem—prior to analysis, the goals, constraints, and requirements may not be known with accuracy.

Portfolio optimization literature typically assumes that the analyst knows the organization's requirements and constraints. For example, the organization may not want to spend more than $10,000 per year in capital investments and wants to achieve a 2% growth rate over the next five years. Nothing is wrong with that goal, but such plans are often arbitrary, and sometimes there are possibilities hidden in the data that would be preferred. For example, a portfolio solution that yields higher growth for only a fraction more cost per year would be better. That type of insight emerges from analysis and is often not apparent before the fact. It is best not to commit to constraints and targets until leadership understands their tradeoffs and organizational capacities.

In practice, project analyses and decisions seldom have the luxury of the kind of time required for the full strategic investigation and management inquiry of the implications and recommended portfolio actions stemming from a single decision. Project and asset decisions often need to be made quickly and in the context of the existing strategic targets. A more typical case requires a quick turnaround and a narrowly focused answer regarding portfolio fit, with little opportunity to consult with executives on specific metrics.

Consider an acquisition decision of an upstream asset. First, the portfolio analyst should understand what goals management cares about (not necessarily the specific number, but at least a list). In this example, we will assume set targets (portfolio requirements) for capital budget levels and production. Please note that the same budget level is set across multiple years; this is not a single-year view.

Next, given the firm's goals, establish a set of baseline portfolios, without the new opportunity, at different capital expenditure levels, using NPV at the corporate WACC as the objective function. The capital expenditure levels should be over a range greater than the corporation normally considers and at a granularity that fits management's control. In a portfolio context with a robust inventory of investment options, there is no need to speculate on perceived portfolio opportunity cost. Therefore, WACC is appropriate to use as the discount rate rather than the higher hurdle rates normally applied. It is already a part of the portfolio framework.

Plot the portfolio NPV of the base portfolios versus capital expenditure levels (see Figure 1). When capital expenditure levels are high, NPV increases until it reaches a peak. After this point, the model selects everything at the fastest possible rate. As the capital expenditure levels decrease, the NPV decreases because projects are deferred or dropped to achieve the dual production and capital expenditure requirements.

Next, lock the new opportunity (Project A, on which the firm is considering a bid) into the mix and re-optimize at all the capital investment levels. Then, add the results to the plot as shown in Figure 2 (Project A In). We see how the portfolio with Project A compares to that without Project A across our range of capital budgets.

There are two pitfalls in this plot. First, if the differences between the two lines are small relative to the overall trajectory of the portfolio value, it can be tough to see any difference. Second, portfolio analysts and decision-makers sometimes want to look at the slope of the lines and treat that as a measure of efficiency—something like an NPV to investment ratio. This is misleading as the x-axis depicts the maximum annual budget rather than the total discounted investment stream that is typically used for investment efficiency measures. At the higher investment levels, the total investment is the same; the only difference is timing. Comparing NPV to discounted capital expenditure may be a more suitable method for evaluating investment efficiency.

Finally, the difference between the base optimizations and the base with Project A is calculated at each budget level. In Figure 3, the Project A line shows the difference between the two as a function of the capital budget level. This display shows how the opportunity affects the NPV of the portfolio at different capital expenditure levels. The plot shows that Project A adds value to the portfolio in the 85–100 capital expenditure range and erodes portfolio value in the 70–80 range. The portfolio value is zero at the 82.5 level, at which the standalone NPV of the opportunity is equal to its opportunity cost.

The approach of generating many portfolios beforehand and then filtering interactively has been illustrated by Rasey (2003), and Willigers and Majou (2010).

This analysis and graph show that the subject opportunity will add value to the portfolio if the enterprise can efficiently spend more than $82.5 per year.

This method can establish maximum bid amounts when the opportunity's economics do not include a bid value. The conclusion is that the bid would be dependent on the amount of capital expenditure that is available. According to Figure 3, if the anticipated capital expenditure is $90, any bid with a present value exceeding $15 would cause a decrease in the portfolio's overall value.

Divestment Analysis

This approach can also be used to analyze divestment candidates.

After running the base portfolios as above, remove the divestment candidate from the base, and optimize the portfolio across the same range of capital budget levels and with the same requirements.

Without the candidate for divestment, the new cases will likely have a different value than the base cases. The difference between the base and the divestment cases shows the value of the asset to the portfolio.

Again, this net portfolio value is the sum of the standalone asset value and the portfolio effect of the opportunity, VPfNew = VPfOld + Portfolio NPV. Remember - Portfolio NPV is the sum of the Standalone value and the Portfolio Specific Value (PSV).

The scatter plot in Figure 4 compares the standalone value of different assets (x-axis) to their average value in the portfolio. The y-axis shows the net portfolio value; the x-axis shows the standalone value. When the symbol is above the diagonal line, the net portfolio value exceeds the standalone value.

More granularity can be seen in Figure 5 by breaking out the values in the portfolios at different Capex budget levels.

As a screening tool, a firm could prioritize divestments whose standalone value exceeds the portfolio value.

Extending the Framework with Limited Data

New upstream business opportunities, especially at an early phase of assessment, have many uncertainties. Resources, development cost, acquisition cost, NPV, earnings, and sometimes even the fiscal regime can be highly uncertain.

As Figure 6 shows, the most important information is about the total hydrocarbon distribution. Moving to the right, virtually all other data is either a derivative of that or contains a fresh set of assumptions (e.g., oil price). Often, an opportunity acquisition team doesn't have reasonable estimates until after committing significant resources to assessing an opportunity. Early screening of an opportunity using the PSV approach above, along with some of the more primary information, can save time and resources while still giving good insights.

Consider a firm that has capital budgeting requirements and production growth targets. There is an implicit assumption that the barrels being pursued are economically and commercially sensible.

The firm is looking at an early business opportunity it may want to acquire. There is a question about how the opportunity will fit into the already full project queue and how it would affect the firm's ability to achieve its targets.

In the early phase, there may not be good cash flow or earnings projections. However, there is usually some idea of the production stream and capital expenditures. As long as these are metrics the firm cares about, much can be learned about portfolio fit.

First, we run the base portfolios at a range of capital expenditure levels (the same as in "Using the Framework" above). Secondly, we must lock the project into the portfolio. Without cash flow or earnings, the project is likely to be rejected. Finally, we optimize the portfolio at the same capital expenditure levels as the base.

Figure 7 shows these portfolios normalized at the relevant Capex compared to the base portfolios. This graph shows the opportunity cost imposed at the different capital expenditure levels from forcing the opportunities into the portfolio.

In Project N (a typical near-term development with high peak production and rapid decline over a twenty-year production life), there is a low portfolio cost when the capital budget is high, and a high opportunity cost when the capital budget is low. That pattern is typical. Intuitively, it would seem that if the cash flow, and therefore NPV, is set to zero, adding such a project would result only in lower portfolio value. This is not always the case.

Project L (a long-term development with flat production for many years) adds value to the portfolio at the higher budget levels despite having a zero standalone NPV. This is driven by the requirements in this particular portfolio model to deliver long-term production growth. Effectively, in high capital budget environments, Project L contributes to a longer-term production requirement, which allows the portfolio model to prioritize projects with higher returns that fill the production gap in the base case. In the lower-budget environments, Project L delays the better projects even more.

This is an example of a portfolio-specific value providing a positive portfolio-dependent opportunity benefit rather than a negative opportunity cost.

Allowing the modeled project to move in time can also provide insight. For example, it is possible that the delay of a new development opportunity can provide more portfolio value than the time-value cost of that delay. That type of insight can be helpful in negotiating agreements.

While it may be difficult to determine the actual worth of the opportunity with this method, Figure 7 illustrates the necessary conditions to increase or decrease its value beyond its isolated NPV. The y-value on the chart shows the value that the opportunity will have to overcome to deliver value to the firm at the different expenditure levels.

Setting the cash flow (therefore NPV) to zero isolates the PSV. This, in turn, provides a "must exceed" value. It is the NPV that must ultimately be realized, after bonus and other costs, for the opportunity to add value to the firm.

Concerns and Challenges with This Framework

The PSV identified through this approach is either indicative of portfolio value or represents an opportunity cost. Several factors create uncertainty in the analysis.

Factors that would cause the portfolio-specific value to appear optimistic

There is an implicit assumption that the firm optimizes its business decisions per the model. This is not always true, as any model at an enterprise level cannot capture all the intricacies of the business. This is probably the largest source of inaccuracy.

Allowing too much flexibility in the model and business rules of existing assets can also cause the calculated PSV to be higher than reality. Timing and alternative selection are often challenging to control and model. It is even worse when the assets have outside stakeholders or are non-operated.

The optimizer model used in this exercise does not incorporate a carrying cost or penalty for delayed projects. That could change the outcome as well.

Factors that would cause the portfolio-specific value to appear pessimistic

The main factor is un-modeled flexibility in the opportunity under consideration or the base data. There can be timing variation and development concept alternatives that are not captured in the model. During early phases of projects, this can be especially important.

Additionally, the model used in this analysis allows delays in one-year increments. Real projects can be delayed by months or even weeks instead of years.

Factors that can cause errors in either direction

Poor data quality due to uncertainty, incentives, or biases can cause PSV to move in either direction, depending on the nature of the error. Also, the portfolio model used does not recalculate economics on shifted projects to the new cost and price environment.

Because of the factors above, we usually consider the calculated PSV to be towards the high end, i.e., the actual PSV would be lower. Most importantly, it is imperative to remember that it is a model that can give insights when one understands how it works, since it does not provide the "answer."

Neither the base cases nor the opportunity-added cases provide an objectively correct answer. However, focusing on the differences between those cases, the errors should largely cancel out, leaving a reasonable, defensible value for the net portfolio impact.

Other issues

This paper uses only NPV as an objective function, with annual production and capital spending as the sole requirements. Other requirements (such as cash flow or probability of achieving a target) could easily have been used, but the authors limited these for clarity.

Conclusions

The PSV framework provides a valuable perspective for assessing the portfolio fit of projects and assets. By displaying the sensitivity of the portfolio fit to key variables, it changes the conversation from the binary, "Does this fit?" to a more robust open discussion about the firm's organizational capability, the robustness of its project queue, and its objectives. It can change how a firm looks at opportunity costs from an implicit backward-looking hurdle rate view to a clear, forward-looking, portfolio perspective.

Without a portfolio perspective, it isn't easy to know the next-best use of corporate capital. The best we can do is guess or estimate the return on incremental investment. With a portfolio perspective, there is no need to guess—it is contained in the data.

Using this framework can help a firm understand the value to the enterprise of building flexibility and control (especially timing) into agreements. For early-phase projects, management will have an educated perspective on whether a project will contribute to corporate needs across a range of metrics and how much the firm might be willing to pay.

Acknowledgments

The authors would like to acknowledge the contributions of Stacie Frerichs, who participated in much of the early framing of this type of analysis, Don Patton, who built Chevron's optimization tool, Stephen Rasey, who showed the way to analyze portfolios graphically, and John Howell, who has contributed immeasurably to the understanding of portfolio optimization methods.

Figure 1

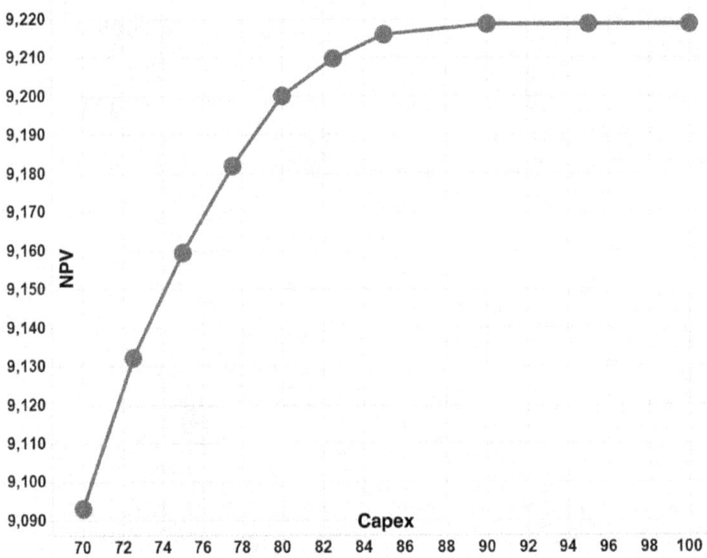

As the investment budget decreases in the base portfolio, reading from right to left, the NPV of the portfolio declines. The flattening at the higher Capex levels indicates running out of additional aggregative investment options.

▸ **Figure 2**

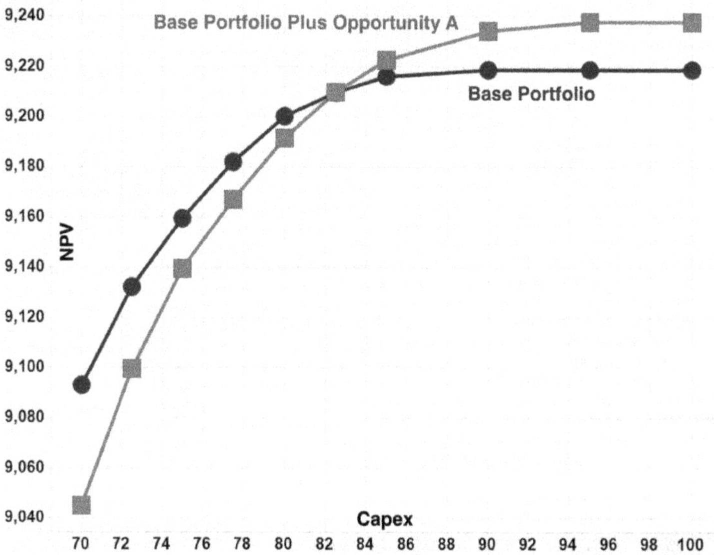

Adding a project (Proj A) to the portfolio changes the view of the portfolio. At high Capex levels, it adds its "standalone value." As Capex is reduced, it gradually adds less and less until the addition of Project A reduces the portfolio's value.

▸ **Figure 3**

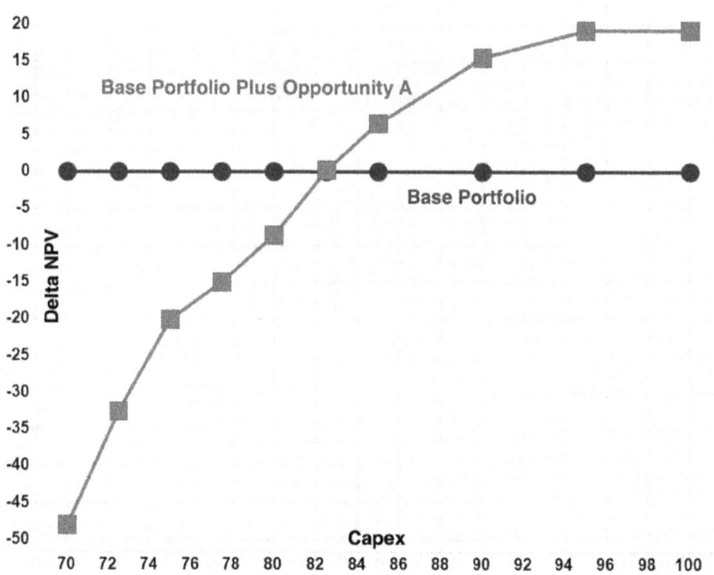

Calculating the difference between the portfolio with Opportunity A and the Base portfolio allows a better-scaled view of the project's impact.

▸ Figure 4

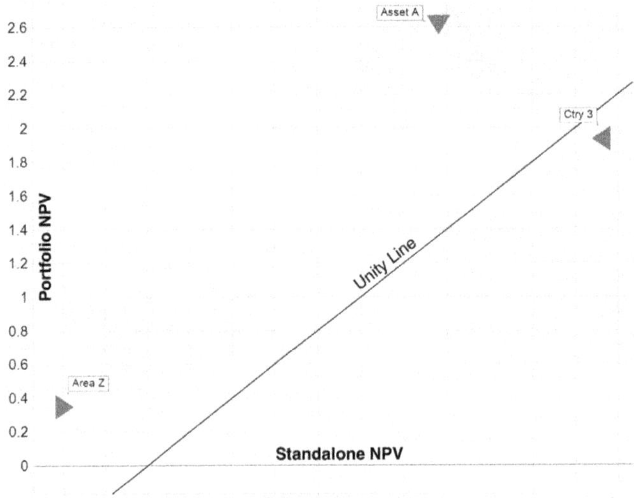

Removing an asset from the portfolio and re-optimizing reveals the asset's value to the portfolio. This view compares its standalone NPV (x-axis) with its net portfolio value (y-axis). Points below the unity line have less value as a part of the firm's portfolio than as standalone entities. Points above the line provide some utility beyond their standalone value (e.g., they may fill a critical production gap).

▸ Figure 5

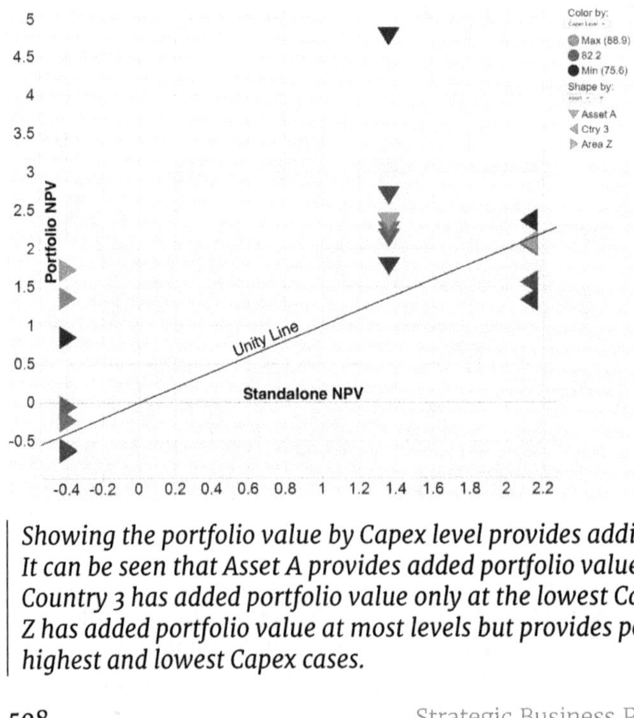

Showing the portfolio value by Capex level provides additional information. It can be seen that Asset A provides added portfolio value at all Capex levels, Country 3 has added portfolio value only at the lowest Capex levels, and Area Z has added portfolio value at most levels but provides positive NPV in the highest and lowest Capex cases.

Figure 6

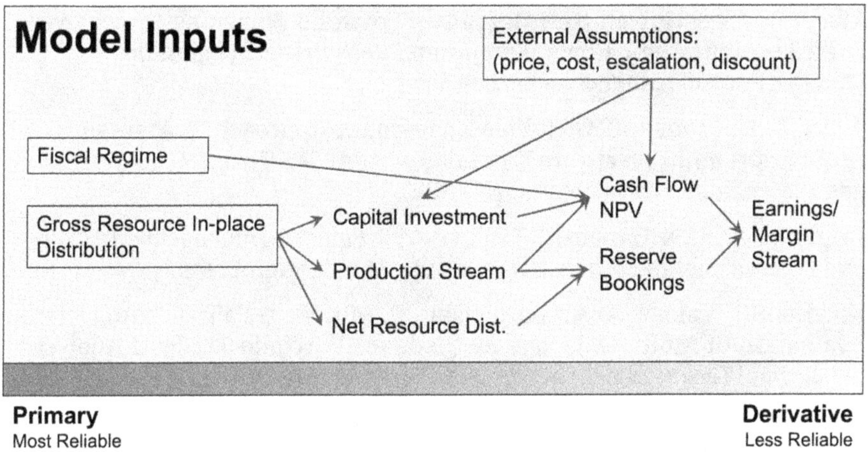

Information becomes less reliable as assumptions are added to the analysis. The best, most primary data is to the left, and it becomes increasingly less reliable to the right.

Figure 7

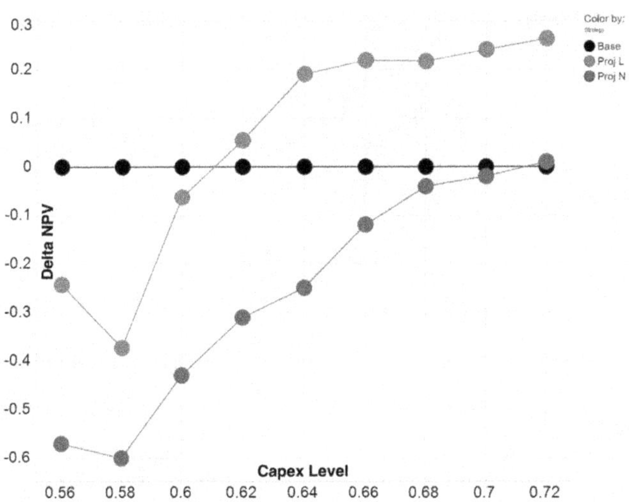

Portfolios with Projects L and N compared to the Base portfolios. Despite having an NPV of 0, Project L adds value to the portfolio because it helps achieve long-term production targets, allowing the enterprise to execute high-value projects earlier. Project N shows a more typical pattern. Its departure from zero indicates the amount of value it needs to deliver to be accretive to enterprise value.

References

Albers, J. A., & Howell III, J. I. (1999). Portfolio Balancing to Achieve Long Term Strategic Goals. *Euroforum International Symposium for Strategic Portfolio Management.* London.

Allan, P. D. (2001). A Portfolio Management Approach to Assessing Acquisition and Divestiture Candidates. *2001 SPE Technical Conference and Proceedings.* New Orleans, LA: SPE.

Brigham, E. F., & Gapenski, L. C. (1997). *Financial Management Theory and Practice, Eighth Edition.* Orlando, FL: The Dryden Press.

Kostiuk, K., Valdez, A. A., Bordovsky, J., Mu, Y., & Faig, C. (2013). Evaluation of Multi-Objective Methods for Portfolio Tradeoff Analysis. *SPE Annual Technical Conference.* New Orleans, LA: SPE.

Rasey, S. M. (2003). Spotfire Communicates Portfolio Analysis of Investment Opportunities on Efficient Frontiers of Many Measures. *Spotfire San Francisco Users Meeting.* San Francisco, CA.

Stermole, F. J., & Stermole, J. M. (1987). *Economic Evaluation and Investment Decision Methods, Sixth Edition.* Golden, CO: Investment Evaluations Corporation.

Willigers, B. J., & Majou, F. (2010). Creating Efficient Portfolios that Match Competing Corporate Strategies. *SPE Hydrocarbon Economics and Evaluation Symposium.* Dallas, TX: SPE.

APPENDIX 4

Shell Portfolio Tool

Dr. Sam Savage, of Stanford University and the Probability Management organization, illustrates a wonderful portfolio analysis from Shell.

His approach was to pre-generate a few hundred relevant combinations with a focus on risk and reward.

"In 2006, I helped Royal Dutch Shell apply MPT [Modern Portfolio Theory] to finding efficient frontiers of risky exploration projects. A small prototype model (shown below) has risk on the horizontal axis and expected return on the vertical as in Harry's [Markowitz'] original approach. It is available for download here.

[https://www.probabilitymanagement.org/s/ShellProbabilityManagement-2012.zip]

"The Shell portfolio model was assembled from smaller models of the individual exploration projects using the concept of the SIP (Stochastic Information Packet). This is a data structure that represents uncertainties as auditable arrays of Monte Carlo trials and metadata. The project SIPs were interactively aggregated into portfolios in Excel, allowing managers just two steps below the CEO to add or remove projects in real-time and see the resulting risk/return tradeoffs. The idea of SIP libraries, which had its foundations in the fields of financial engineering and insurance, has now been democratized by 501(c)(3) nonprofit ProbabilityManagement.org, of which Harry Markowitz and I were founding board members in 2013."

▸ The Shell Portfolio Tool Allows Interactive Testing of Alternatives

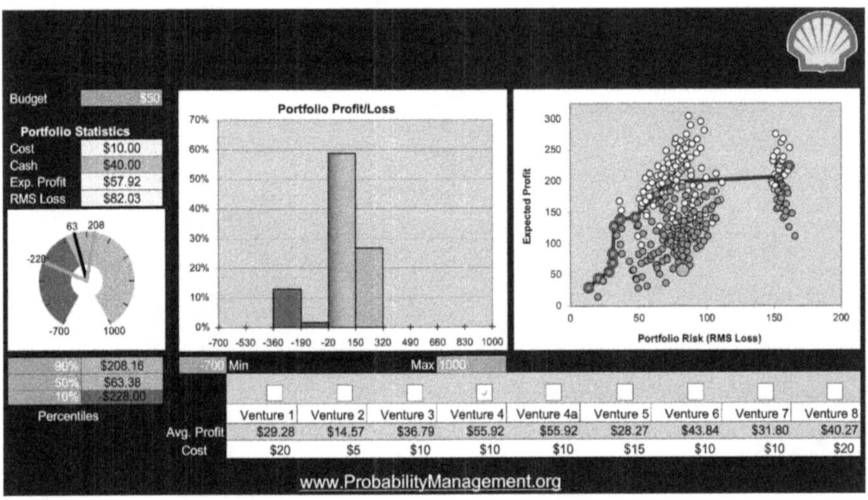

Dr. Savage worked with Royal Dutch Shell to develop an intuitive portfolio model to help executives understand how the composition of their portfolio affects its riskiness. This model sets the standard for ease of use vs. insights.

As you can see in the Excel tool, it allowed executives to interactively query and understand the impacts of changing the content of their portfolio. So rather than have analysts do a bunch of work and then present it with static PowerPoint slides, this allows for easy interactive insights by the decision-makers.

As Sam describes it, "..."interactive" simulation could similarly provide a gut feel and view out the windshield for the underlying relationships being modeled. I refer to this approach as Limbic Analytics, because the limbic system is the structure that connects the reptilian brain (the seat of the pants) with the rest of the stuff between our ears (the seat of the intellect). It allows them to connect the seat of their pants to the seat of their intellect."

This approach is an excellent example of how portfolio analysis should be done.

So why not just do it?

This approach is valuable and insightful for high-level strategic work. As detail and the number of measures of concern increase, scalability decreases. Once you go past 50 or so portfolios and four or five measures, it can be overwhelming. Simple tools become more complex, are costly to build, and take longer to develop. Simplicity has a cost.

I'm not saying it's impossible, but it gets much harder, and you need executives willing to get their hands dirty.

ACKNOWLEDGMENTS

I have been fortunate enough to work with and learn from many people who are considered experts in this field. John Howell and Steve Rasey are two of the main ones. John taught me much about framing and strategic optimization; Steve pioneered exploration portfolio visualization.

Some other influencers in portfolio include Paul Allan, Jim DuBois, Tom Keelin, Jeffrey Keisler, Sam Savage, Rich Sonnenblick, and Bart Willigers. Harry Markowitz, of course, got the whole portfolio ball rolling in the first place.

I also had the privilege of working and speaking with many smart and driven associates at Chevron and elsewhere who taught me more than they could imagine. Among them are Rob Brown, Nicolas Cooper, Ellen Coopersmith, Stacie Frerichs, Bill Haskett, Rick Highsmith, Bill Klimack, Frank Koch, George Kokolis, Peter Val Kranak, Pat Leach, Pat McIntosh, Larry Neal, Don Patton, Brian Putt, Ursula Schweighofer, Mark Wiley, Mal Wright, and Muni Zulkifli and so many others. They all contributed in meaningful ways, whether they realized it or not. We had great conversations, and I can no longer remember who came up with which ideas. Was it them or me? It doesn't matter, but probably them. Thank you all for your fellowship and friendship.

The Decision Analysis Community at Chevron and everyone who attended my portfolio training through the years have a special place in my heart. There was seldom enough time to go deeper, work with, and learn more from each other, but each one taught me something about portfolio and decision analysis.

There are people in this and related fields (Besides those cited above) whose life work has aided and abetted my thinking. Some of the important ones include Ed Capen, Bob Lewis, Peter R. Rose, Frank Stermole, and Andrew Tobias.

Also, I'd like to extend my gratitude to Chevron and Texaco, as well as my supervisors. Although they didn't always follow my guidance, they encouraged me to keep developing these ideas and concepts. There is also the Society of Decision Professionals, and the many members and leaders of decision science.

Many people reviewed this book and provided invaluable feedback before creating the final draft. Among them are Rob Brown, Nicolas Cooper, Mauricio Davidovich, Corla Davis, Tom Grossman, Bill Haskett, John Howell, Frank Koch, Peter Val Kranak, Pat Leach, Pat McIntosh, Brian Putt, Sam Savage, Daniel Schneider, Linus Schrage, Ursula Schweighofer, Rich Sonnenblick, Andrew Thrift, Eric Torkia, Mark Wiley, and Magnus Ytterstad.

I can't forget my editor and publishing coach, Bob Pimm, who made sure I didn't shoot myself in the foot in the hundreds of ways possible for a first-time author. Jaqui Lane of The Book Adviser and Rasika Um (shashika.info) were instrumental in pushing the final product over the goal in a tremendous effort. Remaining mistakes are my own. The buck stops here.

Finally, and most importantly, is my wife, Kathleen Cook, who has patiently listened to my ranting and thinking out loud for three decades. Thank you for your patience, support, and understanding.

Practically every time I think I have an original thought about portfolio or analysis, I can look at the work of the folks listed above and realize they were there before me. Truly I am blessed to have these giants' shoulders to stand on.

ABOUT THE AUTHOR

Tony Kenck formed Practical Portfolio Management LLC in 2020 after a long career with Chevron. Although he started his career as an earth scientist (Colorado School of Mines, BSc. Geophysical Engineering '79), he found himself repeatedly drawn to decision and risk analysis. He knew in his gut that those analyses could be improved and were important. He was on Texaco's Exploration Risk Committee and developed economic analyst skills to screen new opportunities more effectively.

While serving as the "spreadsheet dude" for Texaco Brazil's New Country Entry Team, he earned an MBA from the University of St. Thomas, thereby completing his journey to the dark side. He first learned about efficient frontiers in his MBA Finance class. It seemed like destiny.

When Chevron and Texaco merged in 2001, he joined the international upstream planning and strategy group. In that role, he led the development of tools and standards used at Chevron for over 20 years.

Subsequently, he became the Manager of Planning and Portfolio in Chevron's Corporate Business Development Department, providing portfolio perspectives on a wide range of multi-billion-dollar investment opportunities. He developed teaching materials and eventually trained hundreds of people in portfolio analysis and basic financial and economic decision metrics.

Since leaving Chevron, he has focused on writing ***Strategic Business Portfolio Management*** and engaged in various consulting roles.

His portfolio analysis and management experience includes corporate center, exploration, research and development, environmental remediation, acquisitions and divestitures, and carbon reduction. His passion is teaching the next generation of portfolio analysts and helping firms implement their own portfolio management practices and tools.

Tony is a Fellow of the Society of Decision Professionals (SDP) and the President of the Denver Chapter of the SDP. He and his wife, Kathleen, live in Golden, Colorado.

Tony loves to help firms discover opportunities to do portfolio work. He is available for free initial consultations and longer-term engagements and is happy to talk with anyone about portfolio management. He believes that good portfolio analysis and management is the next frontier for engineering, finance, and economics and is eager to help companies improve in that direction.

Please feel free to contact Tony through his company website, www.practicalportfoliomanagement.com

INDEX

T

U

V

W

Y

Z